THE HISTORY OF THE ASSINIBOINE AND SIOUX TRIBES OF THE
FORT PECK INDIAN RESERVATION: 1600-2012

The History of the Assiniboine and Sioux Tribes of the Fort Peck Indian Reservation: 1600 - 2012

The History of the Assiniboine and Sioux Tribes of the Fort Peck Indian Reservation: 1600–2012

~

By David Miller, Dennis Smith, Joseph McGeshick, James Shanley, *and* Caleb Shields

Published by Fort Peck Community College, Poplar, Montana

Fort Peck Community College
605 Indian Avenue
P.O. Box 398
Poplar, Montana 59255
www.fpcc.edu
406-768-6300

Library of Congress
Cataloging-in-Publication Data

The history of the Assiniboine and Sioux tribes of the Fort Peck indian reservation, Montana, 1600-2012 / by David Miller...[et. al.]. -- 2nd ed. p. cm.
Includes bibliographical references and index.

ISBN 978-0-9801292-7-4 (pbk. : alk. paper)

1. Assiniboine and Sioux Tribes of the Fort Peck Indian Reservation, Montana--History. 2. Assiniboine Indians--Montana--Fort Peck Indian Reservation--History. 3. Assiniboine Indians--Montana--Fort Peck Indian Reservation--Government relations.
4. Dakota Indians--Montana--Fort Peck Indian Reservation--History. 5. Dakota Indians--Montana--Fort Peck Indian Reservation--Government relations.
6. Fort Peck Indian Reservation (Mont.)--History. I. Miller, David Reed, 1949-
E99.A84H57 2012
978.6004'97524--dc23
2012011829

ISBN 978-0-9801292-7-4

Project management and editorial services: Suzanne G. Fox, Red Bird Publishing, Inc., Bozeman, MT
Graphic design:
Carol Beehler, Bethesda, MD

Printed by Artcraft Printers, Billings, MT
The paper used in this publication meets the minimum requirements of American National Standard for Information Sciences—Permanence of Paper for Printed Library Materials,
ANSI Z39.48-1984.

Front cover images
Top left: Fort Peck Agency Buildings, Poplar, MT (circa 1890s).
Top right: Old Main, Fort Peck Community College (1978). Original college site is on the National Register of Historic Places, Poplar, MT.
Bottom left: Medicine Bear Complex, Fort Peck Tribal Headquarters and BIA offices, Poplar, MT (2011).
Bottom right: Fort Peck Agency School Dormitory and Agency buildings, Poplar, MT (circa 1890s).
Back cover image: Greet The Dawn Building, Fort Peck Community College Administration, Business Office and Registrar. Former Fort Peck Tribal Headquarters, Poplar, MT (2011).

With the following exceptions, all images in this book are from the Fort Peck Tribal Archives and its members. All images were reproduced with the permission of the lending institutions and individuals.

In the photo credit listing, the captions for the cover images, and those for images opposite the first page of the respective chapters, the number in parentheses at the end of the abbreviated caption refers to the page on which the image appears. For the complete image and caption, please refer to that page.

Photo credits
Craig Jensen:
Tribal Centennial Parade, 1986 (423).
Department of Anthropology, National Anthropological Archives (NAA), Smithsonian Institution, Washington, DC: Assiniboine Territory in the 19th century, with modern reservations and reserves (14) and Sioux territory, early to mid-19th century (28). Montana Historical Society: The steamer *O.K.* on the Missouri River (138); Fort Peck Indian Agency Superintendent Charles B. Lohmiller's residence (138); Poplar boarding school, girls' dormitory (139); Fort Peck Indian Agency headquarters (140); Major Charles B. Lohmiller and 1911 Sioux delegation from Fort Peck Indian Reservation (140); Fort Peck Indian Agency office (141); Sioux Indian girls at Poplar Boarding School (144); Participants in Indian Fair (144, 145); the arrival of the special Great Northern Tour Train (145); Government Row (273); Fort Peck Agency (276); Poplar Post Office (276); Public School Building (277); Indian boarding school buildings (278).

National Museum of the American Indian, Smithsonian Institution: Lone Dog's Winter Count (131).
Personal Collection of Caleb Shields: Chief Andrew Red Boy Shields (282); Florence Lambert Shields (282); President Gerald Ford with Caleb Shields (419); Caleb Shields with President Bill Clinton and Carol Juneau (420); Montana Indian leaders' meeting with President Bill Clinton (424); Demonstration in Washington, DC, 1994 (429).

Chapter illustrations
Government Row, 1918 (frontispiece); Assiniboine Territory in the 19th century, with modern reservations and reserves (14); Sioux territory, early to mid-19th century (28); Lone Dog's Winter Count (131); Wich' Wanbdi' (Eagle Man), Nhoe-a-ke (Human Male War Eagle), Wica Wanbli (Man Who Packs the Eagle), Yanktonai Sioux of the Cut Head Band (131); 1904 Fort Shaw women's basketball team in their team uniforms (above) and in traditional buckskin dresses (below) (137); Lucille Bets His Medicine with a girl and young man (428); Superintendent Charles B. Lohmiller at Fort Peck Indian Agency headquarters on the day he left the reservation (275); Fort Peck Agency (276); Chiefs, spiritual men, Sundancers, and medicine men smoking and visiting before a celebration (281); 163rd Infantry Battallion (285); Chief Andrew Shields, Mr. Murphy, Murphy Oil Company, Chief Rufus Ricker, Sr., and Chief Santee Iron Ring (287); Chief Andrew Shields, Mr. Murphy, Murphy Oil Company, Chief Rufus Ricker, Sr., and Chief Santee Iron Ring, c. 1950 (287); Fort Peck Delegation to Washington, DC, 1956 (287); Demonstration in Washington, DC; Fort Peck Community College, Greet The Dawn Building (431); Tribal Buffalo Ranch Ceremony (522).

"When you develop your mind, it's as if your feet have wings so you walk with an enlightened mind, spirit, and body while you live."

—*Chief Spotted Dog*

CONTENTS

Prologue to the Second Edition

The second edition of the *History of the Assiniboine and Sioux Tribes of the Fort Peck Indian Reservation* has been expanded to include the first twelve years of the twenty-first century, 2000-2012. The book also adds new materials to existing chapters and some additional maps and pictures. The contributors to the second edition were David Miller, Joe McGeshick, and James Shanley. ❂

Prologue to the First Edition

James Shanley, Ed.D
President, Fort Peck Community College

In 1989, the Supreme Court found in *Helena Elementary School District No. 1 US v. State* that Montana's education finance system was unconstitutional. The constitution amended in 1972 contained a clause that states, "It is the goal of the people to establish a system of education which will develop the full educational potential of each person. Equality of educational opportunity is guaranteed to each person of the state." It also provides that "the state recognizes the distinct and unique cultural heritage of the American Indians and is committed in its educational goals to the preservation of their cultural integrity."

Despite the Supreme Court ruling, only stop-gap attempts were made to meet the court's demands. Another suit was filed by the Columbia Falls public schools in 2002. The state lost and appealed to the Montana Supreme Court. The Supreme Court affirmed the trial court ruling in time for the 2005 legislative session.

At the time, a record number of American Indians had been elected to the state legislature. They were Senator Gerald Pease, Crow; Senator Frank Smith, Fort Peck; Representative Carol Juneau, Blackfeet; Representative Norma Bixby, Northern Cheyenne; Representative Jonathan Windy Boy, Rocky Boy and Fort Belknap; Representative Veronica Small Eastman, Crow; Representative Joey Jayne, a Navajo living at Salish-Kootenai; and Representative Margarett Campbell, Fort Peck. Many of the legislators had worked in education and they bent diligent efforts to insure that the Indian education provisions of the constitution would be addressed in the remedy to the Supreme Court ruling. The result of their efforts was a bill titled "Indian Education for All."

In 2005, in response to the Indian legislators, Governor Brian Schweitzer submitted a Montana biennial budget to the legislature that included monies for the seven tribal colleges in Montana to write tribal histories. It was envisioned that the colleges would produce accurate tribal histories which could be the basis for the "Indian Education for All" constitutional provisions that provided curriculum about Montana tribes to all public schools.

As the legislature moved through the process (which eventually allocated the money for the tribal histories), I had real misgivings about Fort Peck

Community College taking on the task of writing a history for the Fort Peck Tribes. Much of what passed for history among Fort Peck community members were garbled accounts that had been orally passed through family and friends. And people were more than willing to argue their point of view, no matter how incomplete or inaccurate.

Still, the project became a reality. The college hired Caleb Shields, a former tribal chairman and historical figure in his own right, to serve as the coordinator of the project. A reservation-wide history committee made up of elders, educators, and knowledgeable community members was selected. Three scholars were contracted to begin work on the history with the blessings of the committee: Dr. Dennis Smith, a Fort Peck Tribal member who is a faculty member at University of Nebraska Omaha and a historian; Dr. David Miller, who had completed research on Fort Peck earlier and is an anthropology professor at First Nation University in Regina, Saskatchewan; and Dr. Joe McGeshick, an Assiniboine decedent enrolled in the Sokaogon Chippewa Tribes. Then work began.

It became evident almost from the start that rather than having a lack of historical material about the Fort Peck Tribes, there existed a huge amount of related documents. So the task expanded as the college attempted to collect as much material as possible that could eventually go to the Tribal Archives and still be organized into a coherent history.

As the writers produced page after page of tribal history, Caleb Shields set deadlines and contracted with Suzanne G. Fox of Red Bird Publishing in Bozeman, Montana, to edit the book and merge different writing styles into a smooth narrative. When the first draft was finally finished, the book was reviewed by the history book committee. The Fort Peck Tribal Executive Board then passed resolution Number 60-2007-11 in support of the history book project.

The book that follows details the survival of the groups of people that became the Fort Peck Tribes. It is a remarkable story that speaks to a resilience of human spirit and a tenacious desire to retain an ancient, honorable identity. It shows misguided federal government policy and perceptions about tribal people that are still puzzling to the people of Fort Peck. Unfortunately, the book could not weave in the fascinating tapestry of individual family histories that make up the people of the Fort Peck Tribes. This task will remain for the future. We at Fort Peck Community College hope that this book will serve as the base that insures that Fort Peck children will learn their history.

We at Fort Peck Community College would like to give thanks and recognition to the Tribal History Book Committee of which I was also a member, established to provide input and to review the progress of the history project:

Dr. James Shanley	Paul Finnicum
Dr. Margaret Campbell	Leland Spotted Bird
Dr. Robert McAnally	Victor Perry
Caleb Shields	Kenneth Shields
Robert Fourstar	Lois Red Elk
Garrett Big Leggins	George Redstone
Larry Wetsit	Wayne Boyd
Darrell Youpee	Sharon Red Thunder
Gladys Jackson	Del Wayne First
Joseph Miller	

Authors' Preface and Acknowledgments

I thank my scholarly mentor, Professor John R. Wunder of the University of Nebraska, for his years of unwavering support. Many thanks and respects to Jim Shanley for his leadership on this project and with the tribal college. It has been a privilege to work with Caleb Shields, Joe McGeshick, and Suzanne G. Fox, and an honor to work with our cultural committee. Special thanks to David Reed Miller, the real authority of our reservation history, for his friendship and extraordinary assistance to me. I am indebted to Kenny Ryan who invited me into my own culture. Thanks to my father, Thomas Carey Smith (1908—1993), who told me the stories of our reservation. This and all my future work is dedicated to my beloved twin, Deborah Kay Smith Thomas (July 23, 1950—November 3, 2007).

Dennis J. Smith
Omaha, Nebraska
November 2007

I thank Dr. James Shanley for the opportunity to be employed by Fort Peck Community College from 1985 till 1988, his support for my research on Fort Peck Reservation history, and for the opportunity to work on this project in particular.

I thank JoAllyn Archambault, Department of Anthropology, National Museum of Natural History at the Smithsonian Institution, who served as my sponsor during a one-year Junior Post-Doctoral Fellowship there from August 1988 to August 1989, where I began gathering the records for this study. I also need to thank various archivists at the National Archives in Washington, D.C., Pacific Alaska Regional Records Center, Seattle, Washington, and Rocky Mountain Regional Records Center, Denver, Colorado, for assistance from early 1983 to 2006. I thank the Office of Fellowships and Research at the Smithsonian for three short-term Visits to Collections grants, and the National Endowment for the Humanities for two Travel to Collections grants, all for trips to Washington, D.C., to work in the National Archives and the National Anthropological Archives. I also thank the

President's Fund of the University of Regina for travel support on several occasions. I also thank Acting President Blaine Holmland of Saskatchewan Indian Federated College for a semester of paid leave that I spent at the National Archives, Washington, D.C., during the winter semester 1993.

I thank Kenneth Ryan for all that he has been willing to teach me and how he allows so many of our conversations to become seminars during which I am constantly informed. I also thank Raymond J. DeMallie for his ongoing advice and friendship, and all that he has taught me. I also thank Ed and Bella Broadus, Charles Courchene, Robert Fourstar, David Moore, Kate Shanley, Caleb Shields, Dennis Smith, Lois Steele, and many others who have left us and gone to the other side.

I thank my good friends Elena Larsen and Joe Simpich for lodging on numerous stays in D.C., most of which I spent working on my Fort Peck research.

I thank my research assistants Melissa Blind and James Kennedy.

David R. Miller
Regina, Saskatchewan, Canada
November 2007

Authors' Acknowledgments for the Revised Edition

I thank Jim and Marlene Caravello for their hospitality in Helena while doing necessary research there. I thank the invaluable staff of the Montana Historical Society Research Center for their help and assistance using the important research collections in their care. I also thank Anita Scheetz and her staff at the Fort Peck Community College and Fort Peck Tribal Library. I thank the various staff members of FPCC that have helped me in various ways in both editions of this textbook.

I extend a thank you to the Austin Buckles Family, and to Johnny Bearcub, Rodney Miller, Kermit Smith, Larry Smith, June Stafne, and Larry Wetsit.

I wish also to thank Susan Elaine Gray, David McCrady, William Swagerty, and my co-authors for their advice and reflections; errors in my chapters are my responsibility for not having listened well, for not having gotten to the bottom of a matter, or just not finding information to set me straight. I offer you what I have comprehended at this point in time. I thank my daughter, Ariel, for her patience with her dad always working on something.

David R. Miller
Regina, Saskatchewan
February 2012

I would like to thank the Assiniboine and Sioux people of the Fort Peck Indian Reservation, the Fort Peck History Project Board, the Fort Peck Tribal Executive Board, Governor Schweitzer, and those many Chippewa families who live on Fort Peck and in the surrounding area. Also, many thanks to Dr. James Shanley, President of Fort Peck Community College, and Caleb Shields, former Chairman of the Fort Peck Tribes and Director of the Fort Peck History Project, who gave me opportunity to contribute to the project. My parents, Fred and Joyce McGeshick of Wolf Point, my family, Brent, McKenzie, and Dawson Welch of Bozeman, and Cole McGeshick, who have also supported me throughout the project as well as my other writing. And lastly, those past generations of Assiniboine, Sioux, and Chippewa families who survived the suffering and hardships of reservation life. May we all met happily and celebrate in the next world. Pidamiya/Migwetch.

Joseph R. McGeshick
Poplar, Montana
November 2007

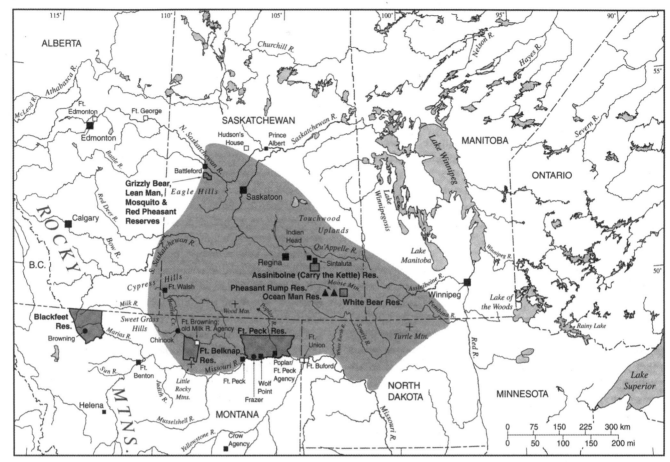

Assiniboine Territory in the 19th century, with modern reservations and reserves. Map from article "Assiniboine" by Raymond J. DeMallie and David Reed Miller. *Plains,* vol. 13, part 1 of 2. *Handbook of North American Indians,* Raymond J. DeMallie, volume editor. Washington, DC: Smithsonian Institution, 2001. Reproduced by permission.

CHAPTER 1

Fort Peck Assiniboines to 1800
Dennis J. Smith, Ph.D.

The Assiniboines of the Fort Peck Reservation are a Sioux-speaking plains people and the southernmost of a once large and diverse tribe. At the time of first European contact with French explorer-traders and Jesuit missionaries in the mid-1600s, Assiniboine homelands stretched from the woodlands of the Lake Nipigon and Rainy Lake region of present-day northwestern Ontario to the northern woodlands and parklands and tall grass prairies of Saskatchewan, and perhaps as far west as eastern Alberta.[1]

Assiniboines were first mentioned in the *Jesuit Relations* in 1640, and the first reference to Assiniboine lands appeared in the 1657-1658 *Jesuit Relations*, which placed Assiniboines one hundred miles west of Lake Nipigon. This is the same region where Daniel Greysolon Dulhut in 1678 made the first direct contact with Assiniboines. Scattered French encounters into the early 1700s consistently place these easternmost Assiniboines in the southern boreal forests in the Rainy Lakes-Lake of the Woods region of northwestern Ontario.[2]

Seventeenth-century Assiniboine homelands also extended west into the parklands and tall grass prairies of southern Saskatchewan. This was recounted by Hudson's Bay Company fur trader-explorer Henry Kelsey during his 1690-1691 trip to the interior. He departed from York Factory, the English company's first permanent trading post, established in 1670 near the mouth of the Nelson River. Kelsey went up the Saskatchewan River to the Touchwood Uplands, located in the headwaters of the upper Qu'Appelle River. Sixty years later, in 1755, another Hudson's Bay Company trader-explorer, Anthony Henday, traveled from York Factory to the Red Deer River region of southeastern Alberta, also settled by Assiniboines. It is unclear whether these westernmost Assiniboines resided in this area when Kelsey encountered parkland Assiniboines in Saskatchewan sixty years earlier.[3]

The Assiniboines who inhabited the area spanning from the Rainy Lakes-Lake of the Woods region in Ontario to eastern Alberta constituted a contiguous unit known as southern Assiniboines, also called plains Assiniboines. Except for those in the southern boreal woodlands between Rainy Lake and southern Lake Winnipeg, the majority of southern Assiniboines at this time were a tall-grass prairie and parklands cultural people.

A second extensive Assiniboine grouping was known as northern Assiniboines, or woodland Assiniboines, also occupying extensive lands bordering the southern Assiniboines. These were southern boreal forest lands in the west extending to the Athabasca River in northeastern Alberta, and extending east between the Saskatchewan River (important parklands for southern Assiniboines) and Churchill River, as far east as the Nelson River of northern Manitoba. Northern Assiniboines included a band known as "Eagle-Eyed" Assiniboines, who resided in the southern boreal forests east of Winnipeg. Southern and northern Assiniboines were consistently identified as distinct groupings since early Hudson's Bay Company writings.[4]

The easternmost southern Assiniboines, who lived in the boreal forestlands between Rainy Lake and Lake Winnipeg, were important for three significant reasons in sixteenth- and early seventeenth-century Assiniboine affairs. First, they were part of an important Assiniboine friendship and alliance, dating to at least the late seventeenth century, with the Western Cree, their Algonquian-speaking northern tribal neighbors. Like northern and southern Assiniboines, Cree homelands by the late seventeenth century spanned from northeastern Ontario to Saskatchewan. Like northern Assiniboines,

Western Crees were primarily a woodlands cultural people, inhabiting southern boreal forest lands. Significant numbers of Western Crees lived and intermarried with southern Assiniboines, however, with both tribes forming trading parties late in the seventeenth century to exchange with French traders at Lake Nipigon or with the English traders at Hudson's Bay Company's York Factory. Western Crees and southern Assiniboines also lived peacefully together in the parklands of Saskatchewan and eastern Alberta when they were encountered by Henry Kelsey in 1690-1691 and by Anthony Henday in 1754-1754.[5]

Second, these eastern woodland tribesmen were the first Assiniboines to establish trade with the French and English. As early as the 1650s, these Assiniboines were invaluable fur contributors to the Ottawa-Indian-French trade network in the western Great Lakes region. Because of French interest in expanding Assiniboine trade relations, Daniel Greysolon Dulhut in 1678 established a trading post at Lake Nipigon.

English competition with the French for the western fur market appears to have been a primary factor in encouraging Western Crees and Assiniboines to become allies. When the Hudson's Bay Company established York Factory in 1670, centered in Western Cree eastern lands, these Crees had an immediate advantage in guns and trade over other tribes, and they seem to have leveraged that quickly against Assiniboines. Already facing Chippewa (Ojibway, Anishinaabeg) enemies to the east and Dakotas to the south in northeastern Minnesota, Assiniboines as early as the 1670s opted to sue for peace. Early Hudson's Bay Company documents confirm early reconciliation and intermarriage between Assiniboines and Western Crees.[6]

By the 1680s, Western Crees and Assiniboines dominated an extensive canoe trade system along Lake Winnipeg and the Nelson River, which drains the entire interconnected watershed from

Rainy Lake, Lake of the Woods, the Winnipeg River, and Lake Winnipeg northeastward into Hudson's Bay, to York Factory. This secured for Western Crees and Assiniboines a middleman trade system between the English and French and western tribes, especially Gros Ventres and Blackfeet in the western parklands and Hidatsas and Mandans, the Missouri earth-lodge and village peoples.

With their early gun and ammunition advantage, Assiniboines and Western Crees pressed militarily against the Chipewyans in the north and the Dakotas (Sioux) to the south. This latter conflict with the Dakotas, which erupted sometime between 1670 and 1700, was the third defining feature of the easternmost southern Assiniboines at the turn of the eighteenth century. By the 1720s and early 1730s, however, the Dakotas finally secured stable French trading relations, and they then pushed aggressively against Assiniboines and Crees to their north, and the Chippewas to their north and east.[7]

By the 1730s, southern Assiniboines and their Western Cree allies evacuated the boreal forests of northwestern Ontario and southeastern Manitoba. The "Eagle-Eyed" Assiniboines, however, remained as late as the 1740s in the lands east of Lake Winnipeg.

Dakota war pressures appear to have been the primary reason for moving west. To a lesser degree, the English and French pelt trade may have been influential, as Assiniboines and Crees may have sought richer beaver lands to the west.

At that time, the French were already trying to extend their trade into southwestern Manitoba. During the 1730s, Sieur de La Verendrye, who headed western fur trade operations for the French, aggressively expanded French trading posts west of Lake Superior. He established new posts in the boundary waters area, including Rainy Lake (Fort St. Pierre, 1731), and Lake of the Woods (Fort St. Charles, 1732), and most signifi-

cantly, on the southern shore of Lake Winnipeg (Fort Maurepas, 1734).[8]

Perhaps the most important reason these southern Assiniboines and Western Crees moved west was subsistence. The predominantly conifer woodlands they inhabited were rich in smaller game such as marten, fisher, lynx, otter, mink, muskrat, and beaver, and moose was the primary big game animal. Fishing also provided crucial food, but only from spring through fall. Wild rice seems to have also been harvested, but it appears to have only supplemented hunting and fishing. The problem with living in woodlands was that winters were often desperate, if not starving, times. Lake fish retreated to deeper waters, leaving moose as the primary food resource. Western Crees informed La Verendrye in 1732 that boreal forests were "sterile country" and they wanted to no longer winter there.

Western Crees and southern Assiniboines moved west into the lower Red River watershed of southern Manitoba, south of the mouth of the Assiniboine River (at present-day Winnipeg, Manitoba). In ecological terms, this new home was markedly different from the forests they had just abandoned, for they now resided on the eastern edge of the tall grass prairies of the northern plains. Although the new grasslands and parklands supported fewer small game animals (especially beavers and muskrats) than the forests and lakes to the east, they were substantially richer in big game animals, including antelope, and mule, whitetail and red deer. The large game animal of choice, however, and the one in greatest abundance here, was the bison.[9]

Southern Assiniboines evolved a grasslands-parklands subsistence cycle. In the spring, they fished in the major rivers (the Red, Assiniboine, and Qu'Appelle), where sturgeon spawning runs were very important, as was migratory waterfowl hunting. From spring through fall, women gathered berries and fruits, and dug prairie turnips. The most significant time, however, was summer, when bison migrated south onto the prairies in large herds for rutting season. Similarly, southern Assiniboines left the parklands and descended upon the tall grass prairies for major bison hunts. Summer was the season of plenty. Deer and antelope remained in the parklands year-round and were hunted from spring through fall, but fall was also primarily bison season. Bison returned to the parklands for fall and winter shelter, but they were dispersed into smaller groupings.

Northern woodland Assiniboine subsistence patterns differed notably. Rather than summer, spring and fall were the more bountiful times. In early spring, families left their winter camps in the parklands and proceeded north for fishing and hunting waterfowl, moose, and woodland caribou along lakes and rivers. In the summer, men departed on long trading expeditions to the Hudson's Bay Company trading post at York Factory. Their families remained in the northern lakes and rivers, where they continued to fish. In late summer and early fall, Assiniboine families returned south for moose hunting and trapping in the boreal forests bordering the parklands of the Qu'Appelle and Saskatchewan Rivers. Winter camps were made in the parklands, where northern and southern Assiniboines often joined in the winter vocation of hunting bison.[10]

By the 1730s, southern Assiniboines seem to have already established trade relations far to the south in Missouri River country, primarily with Hidatsa and Mandan villages. The Mandan earth lodge villages were further downstream, located at the mouth of the Heart River (at present-day Bismarck, North Dakota). Hidatsa earth lodge villages were north, centered around the mouth of the Knife River. Southern Assiniboines and Western Crees continued in their vital middleman trade position, bringing English and French items, primarily guns, ammunition, and

metalwares, to the Hidatsas and Mandans.

La Verendrye listed the kinds of exchanged items from his 1738 trip to the Mandan villages—the first known European visit. La Verendrye departed from Fort Reine, established that year on the lower Assiniboine River, south of Lake Manitoba, and was accompanied by a large Assiniboine party. Mandans received guns, ammunition, other important metal items including knives, awls, hatchets, axes, and kettles, tobacco, and brandy. Assiniboines purchased corn and highly prized Mandan leatherworks and feather work, including painted bison robes, tanned buckskins ornamented with fur and feathers, and painted feathers.[11]

La Verendrye and his Assiniboine party traveled on foot to the Mandan villages in 1738, but by the 1750s, southern Assiniboine had started to acquire horses. Assiniboine horses were first noted by Anthony Henday in 1754-1755 in eastern Alberta, but at this time they were used only to transport goods. In 1766, William Pink reported an Assiniboine party with many horses in the Saskatchewan parklands of present-day Prince Albert, Saskatchewan, near the confluence of the North and South branches of the Saskatchewan River. Significantly, he reported that horses had become so important that Assiniboines were already abandoning canoes. The same year, Alexander Henry the Elder also noted Assiniboine horses and mentioned their use in mounted warfare. Ten years later, in 1776, Alexander Henry the Elder reported that western Assiniboines had already become known for their large horse herds.[12]

Horses reached the northern plains in surprisingly rapid fashion after southwest and southern plains tribes captured Spanish horses that escaped during the 1680 Pueblo Revolt. The horses reaching southern Assiniboines in Alberta and western Saskatchewan had come from an intertribal trade network in the

Rocky Mountains. Pueblos and Utes initiated the exchange, trading with the Shoshones and Salish. By 1740, Blackfeet and Crows had become the prominent horse traders in the region. Southern Assiniboines in Alberta and western Saskatchewan received their horses primarily from Blackfeet and Gros Ventre trade.[13]

The southern Assiniboines, primarily those in eastern Saskatchewan and southern Manitoba, acquired horses in Missouri River trade with Hidatsa and Mandan villagers. Both tribes received their horses from the Crows. The horse trade relationship was presumably rather strong between the closely related Crows and Hidatsas; the Crows were formerly part of the Hidatsa people, but had separated most likely in the late sixteenth century. Mandans acquired their first horses soon after La Verendrye visited in 1738, for in 1741 his son-in-law acquired two horses when he left the villages that year.[14]

By the 1790s, horses had been fully incorporated within southern Assiniboine lifestyles, including the new tradition of raiding tribal enemies for horses. Hudson's Bay Company traders throughout this period also noted a decline in birch canoe use, although their use does not appear to have been completely abandoned. Oddly enough, at the same time when horses had become important to southern Assiniboine life, they became increasing harder to acquire. War in the late 1770s with the Blackfeet and Gros Ventres ended that formerly ready source of horses. Eastern lower Assiniboines continued to horse trade with Mandans and Hidatsas, but the numbers remained low.

These intertribal trade complications derived in part from the opening of new Hudson's Bay Company trading posts in the interior of Saskatchewan. By the time of the French and Indian War (1754-1763), French trading operations into southern Manitoba, pioneered by La Verendrye, had been abandoned. By 1766, other

trading interests in Montreal had resurrected the former French trading operations west from the Great Lakes and were establishing trading relations into the Saskatchewan parklands. This new English trading venture developed into what in 1783 became officially known as the North West Company of Montreal. The Montreal traders threatened Hudson's Bay Company's monopoly on the interior fur trade, and forced the company to establish trading posts beyond York Factory, and into the interior parklands.

The first interior trading post was Cumberland House, established in 1774 on the lower Saskatchewan River in eastern Saskatchewan. Perhaps more significant for southern Assiniboine affairs was the 1777 founding of the Hudson's House trading post along the lower North Fork of the Saskatchewan River in central Saskatchewan. Hudson's Bay Company's new interior trading posts destroyed the middleman position of Assiniboine and Western Cree between the company and interior and Missouri River village tribes.[15]

Hudson's House was situated near the eastern margins of Gros Ventre lands between the North and South Forks of the Saskatchewan River, in east-central Alberta and west-central Saskatchewan. As late as 1772-1773, Hudson's Bay Company trader Matthew Cocking had been in this Saskatchewan River "forks" region, and commented on the peaceful trade relations between Gros Ventres and southern Assiniboines and Western Crees. The latter two tribes traded for horses and bison hides in return for English trade items for the Gros Ventres. The Gros Ventres needed guns and ammunition because they and their Blackfeet allies were warring against the horse-rich Shoshones, whom they had recently pushed from the South Saskatchewan River area, but who still managed to launch retaliatory raids.[16]

The founding of Hudson's House seemed to

have been a key factor in the outbreak of Gros Ventre and southern Assiniboine-Western Cree hostilities that erupted in the late 1770s and continued through the 1790s. Both tribal groups had a strategic interest in controlling Hudson's House's tribal trade. Assiniboines and Crees also had territorial interests, as they were trying to retain control of these western parklands, especially against penetration by the Blackfeet and particularly the horse-rich, southernmost tribe of this confederacy, the Piegans. In any case, the disruptions of peaceful relations with Gros Ventres and Blackfeet had a downside for southern Assiniboines and Western Crees, for the once-extensive horse trade between the two groups was terminated.[17]

It was during this transitional time, when southern Assiniboines had incorporated horses within the culture, trade tensions were increasing, and they were at war with the Gros Ventres and Blackfeet, that catastrophe struck Assiniboines and most upper Missouri River and Canadian parklands tribes—smallpox. An epidemic in 1781-1782 devastated tribal populations and forced radical changes in tribal relations from the Missouri River village tribes through the interior of present-day Saskatchewan. North West Company trader-explorer David Thompson stated that the epidemic commenced among the Dakotas and Chippewas in northwestern Minnesota in 1780 and that by 1781 they had carried the disease to the Missouri River Mandan and Hidatsa villages. During 1781, the pestilence ravaged Native communities in the grasslands and parklands of Saskatchewan and Alberta, taking horrendous tolls upon Assiniboines, Gros Ventres, Blackfeet, and Western Crees. Thompson estimated that these tribal populations dropped from between one-half to three-fifths of their previous populations.[18]

Hudson's Bay Company estimates of Assiniboine lodges before and after the epidemic

suggest that southern Assiniboine losses were not as severe as Thompson thought. Also, company documents suggest that Assiniboine populations rebounded rapidly. In 1776, Alexander Henry the Elder estimated that southern Assiniboine lodges numbered 300, an estimated 2,400 to 3,000 persons, calculated on an assumption of eight to ten persons per lodge. In 1809, Alexander Henry the Younger estimated Assiniboine lodges at 460, although contemporary estimates of the number of persons per lodge varied.[19]

All the profound changes affecting southern Assiniboines by the end of the 1700s resulted in one dramatic adjustment: the majority of the Assiniboines moved south. This was a significant shift, since for at least the previous century both northern and southern Assiniboines and their Western Cree allies had migrated west or northwest. Alexander Henry the Younger's detailed analysis of southern Assiniboine bands revealed the striking change: approximately two-thirds of all southern Assiniboines now resided in Qu'Appelle and Souris River parklands. They had abandoned the Red River and the entire lower Assiniboine River, southwestern Manitoba lands west of present-day Winnipeg.[20]

The remaining one-third of southern Assiniboines remained to the northwest, primarily in the parklands between the South Saskatchewan and Battle Rivers in western Saskatchewan. Significantly, Alexander Henry the Younger's 1808 band analysis included only one northern or woodlands band, the Swampy Ground band, far to the northwest, above the North Assiniboine River in north-central Alberta. Later Hudson's Bay Company reports from 1823-1824 noted one other woodlands Assiniboine tribe in northern Alberta near the McLeod River. In another major Assiniboine transformation, these northwesternmost Assiniboines had separated and developed their own tribal identity, now known as Stoneys. Oral tradition from the Bearspaw band, one of three Mountain Stoney bands now residing at the Stoney Reserve in Morley, Alberta, corroborate this separation, stating that they departed for the (Rocky) mountains to escape the diseases that were decimating the parkland Assiniboines to the east.[21]

The most striking new location for the southern Assiniboines was their extensive settlement of the entire Souris River watershed, and according to Alexander Henry the Younger, this included almost exclusively the Little Girl band, which he estimated at 200 lodges. The new Souris River location was noteworthy for two important reasons. First, the Souris River is not a parklands transition area, but rather consists of tall grass and mixed grass prairies. Second, it was significantly closer to the Hidatsa and Mandan earth-lodge villages on the Missouri River. In fact, the most southern part of the Souris River resides within the present-day United States—the "elbow" at its southern extreme is where Minot, North Dakota is now. In short, the Souris River Assiniboines were quickly transforming into a primarily northern plains tribal people.[22]

Of the changes buffeting the southern Assiniboines in the late eighteenth century, the 1781-1782 smallpox epidemic was their most important motivation for relocating to new southern lands. Assiniboines faced extraordinary hardships, having to rebuild their families, villages, and bands. One important question concerning their relocation is, why did they choose to move south? Two factors seem most important. One was bison, which may have been more numerous in the Souris and Upper Missouri watersheds than where the remaining Plains Assiniboines resided near the Qu'Appelle River. Environmental factors such as water, timber, and other subsistence needs may have also influenced this decision.

The second attraction was trade, both with Europeans and with Mandans and Hidatsas. In 1785, the North West Company established Pine Fort, its first trading post in the Assiniboine River watershed, constructed on the lower Assiniboine River a few miles below the mouth of the Souris River. Pine Fort served as the base of operations in southwestern Manitoba, but also the opening of new trade with Hidatsa and Mandan villages on the Missouri River. In 1793, the North West Company replaced Pine Fort with Fort Souris, a few miles up the Assiniboine at the mouth of the Souris River. Pine Fort was abandoned the following year. The same year, the Hudson's Bay Company belatedly established its competing trading post, Brandon House, also at the junction of the Souris and Assiniboine Rivers. Like North West's Pine Fort and Fort Souris, Brandon House served as Hudson's Bay Company's base of operations in the lower Assiniboine River area and its new trade network with the Hidatsa and Mandan villages.[23]

The nature of trade for Southern Assiniboines also changed significantly at this time. The 1781 smallpox epidemic also devastated the Mandans and Hidatsas, killing two-thirds of their estimated combined population of 11,500 persons. The Mandans fled their long-standing historic homelands at the junction of the Heart and Missouri Rivers (present-day Bismarck), and moved up the Missouri River to settle among the Hidatsa earth-lodge villages near the mouth of the Knife River. In 1785, four years after the smallpox epidemic and during the time of Mandan resettlement, the North West Company dispatched its first trading expedition from Pine Fort to the Hidatsa-Mandan villages.

The arrival of European traders to these villages transformed the nature of intertribal trade there. Until this time, Hidatsas and Mandans had received their European trade items indirectly, through tribal intermediaries, primarily southern Assiniboines and Western Crees. Now Hidatsas and Mandans were receiving their European trade items directly from the North West Company. Beginning in 1793, when Hudson's Bay Company traders arrived from the newly established Brandon House, the village tribes received modern goods from two competing companies. Not only were southern Assiniboines no longer middlemen and sources of European trade items for Hidatsas and Mandans, but the roles were reversed. Now Hidatsas and Mandans acted as middlemen, and Assiniboines had to trade with them for European trade items. Souris River Assiniboines could still trade directly with the Europeans, however, at the new trading posts at the mouth of the Souris River. Their days as intertribal middlemen ended abruptly.[24]

Trade with Hidatsas and Mandans was important for one other reason: horses, the one vital item they could not acquire from the Canadian traders. This was when western Assiniboines along the Qu'Appelle River lost their horse trade with Gros Ventres and Blackfeet. Souris River area Assiniboines appear to have continued to trade for horses at the Missouri River villages, but for unclear reasons, this horse trade—at least for Assiniboines—had always been limited.[25]

By the 1790s, southern Assiniboines found themselves in a paradoxical situation. By this time, they had truly become a horse plains people. The more western and southern Assiniboines who had received horses from Gros Ventres and Blackfeet may have possessed more horses than eastern Assiniboines, but horses had become essential to moving, hunting, and warfare. At the same time, when compared to other northern plains tribes, southern Assiniboines were relatively "horse-poor." This was an intertribal dynamic reflecting a decline in horse trade. Like other plains horse tribes, however, Assiniboines had become skilled raiders of horses, and these raids served as a key means of acquiring this invaluable resource.[26]

By 1800, southern Assiniboine cultural beliefs and practices evolved because of their long-standing plains and parklands existence. Bison were the primary staff of life, and Assiniboines continued their meticulous concentration on bison features and habits. With the arrival of horses, the most important means of hunting bison during the summer months was the surround method. This was a closely regulated system requiring as many as 100 warriors, who surrounded a herd and dispatched them primarily with bows and arrows, for early guns were difficult to load on horseback. A second method was the park or buffalo pound, another highly labor-intensive method that was the principle means of bison hunting in the days before horses. This was accomplished by building a circle of posts at the base of a bluff. Bison were drawn into the opening of the pound by bison medicine persons. Then tribesmen hiding behind piles of dirt or rocks frightened the bison in a funnel-shaped pattern, driving them off a sharp precipice at the top of the bluff. Three such Assiniboine pounds were in active use as late as the mid-nineteenth century in the vicinity of Fort Union, at the confluence of the Yellowstone and Missouri Rivers.[27]

Bison were also hunted using an approach method by individual hunters. Bison were the sole food during winters, and they were hunted in the wooded river lands into which they had dispersed seeking winter shelter. Individual Assiniboine hunters often hunted them down on snowshoes.[28]

Women were the primary gatherers of food plants, including prairie turnips, artichokes, and berries, including chokecherries, serviceberries, gooseberries, plums, and rhubarb. These were usually dried, and chokecherries were pounded with grinding stones to crush the pits.[29]

For transportation of meat after large bison hunts, and for moving people and possessions for the frequent relocation of camps, southern

Assiniboines used both horse and dog travois. Assiniboines and Western Crees were among the last northern plains tribes to extensively use dog travois. To ferry persons and goods across larger streams and rivers, Assiniboines used bull boats—round-shaped vessels made of willow frames and covered with bison hides.[30]

Assiniboine tipis are based on a three pole foundation, and required twelve or more bison hides to complete the cover. Women constructed all the items needed for daily life within the lodge, including clothing, bedding, and bison hide rugs. Women were honored for their enormous contributions within the lodge, reflected in the fact that all these items belonged to them. Women also were honored for their role in cooking and serving their families and guests, for they had property rights concerning all food items.[31]

Like many North American tribes, Assiniboine duties and responsibilities functioned within very carefully defined gender roles. Boys and young men were instructed in their primary responsibilities as hunters and warriors. Women's duties focused on child-rearing, food preparation, and making clothing and household items for daily life. The tanning and preparation of bison, deer, and elk hides for these essentials was extraordinarily labor-intensive.[32]

Like many North American tribes, the teaching and learning methods employed to prepare children for their adult responsibilities were exceptionally effective. Instruction began with maternal bonding, so that from the moment of birth, Assiniboine children learned that the world is a nurturing and secure place. Newborns and infants were placed in cradleboards so they would always be with their mothers, and the cradleboards freed the women to continue their daily work. Assiniboine mothers weaned their children around the ages of three or four years. Instruction was by example, and children

by early childhood were instructed by adults of their own gender: females by their mothers, aunts, and older sisters, and males by their fathers, uncles, and older brothers. Equally important, Assiniboine grandparents were vital teachers. Like most Native tribes, Assiniboines instructed primarily in a nurturing and positive environment, in which children were praised for successful accomplishments. For success in more important tasks, parents and grandparents honored their children and grandchildren publicly, usually including feasts and the giving of gifts. Children who misbehaved were scolded, but corporal punishment was discouraged and rarely used.[33]

Assiniboines have a bilateral kinship system, in which after marriage the husband and wife usually resided with the husband's family. Before children were born, the son-in-law had an important obligation to hunt and provide food for his wife's family. Assiniboines employed avoidance customs in which a son-in-law was forbidden to speak directly to either of his parents-in-law. Kinship terminology is of the Dakota type, in which the biological father and his brothers are termed "father," and the biological mother and her sisters are termed "mother." The parent's opposite-sex siblings (father's sisters and mother's brothers) are aunts and uncles. The children of all fathers and mothers are brothers and sisters to one another, and children of aunts and uncles are called cousins.[34]

A young Assiniboine man did not seek marriage until he had at least joined a war party, and ideally not until after having achieved a war honor. A proposal of marriage was offered by sending gifts, usually food and perhaps even horses, to the woman's family. If the offer was accepted, the woman then came to live with her husband at his village. Assiniboine men who were successful hunters, or men of proven accomplishment, could have multiple wives.

This was in part necessitated by the extensive labor required to process bison hides. A husband wishing other wives often asked permission from his wife's family to marry one of her younger sisters. Divorce was an accepted practice, and usually older children remained with the husband, and the younger ones returned with the mother to her family.[35]

Concerning self-governance, Assiniboines, like many tribes, lived in a very decentralized way in which most responsibilities and obligations resided with the individual families. Assiniboines organized into large extended family units known as bands, each headed by a chief (*hunka*), although at times other chiefs might be recognized. Chiefs were selected based on merit, which included accomplishments of bravery, success in hunting, being a good provider for his family, wisdom, and generosity. A chief had no authority to compel the action of any person, but he headed the band council.

The council was attended by accomplished hunters and warriors, and met in the Soldier's, or warrior's, lodge in the center of the camp circle. The council deliberated on matters affecting the entire band, which usually included decisions concerning major bison hunts, locations of village moves and the site of the winter camp, and issues of diplomacy with other bands, tribes, or later, with Europeans and Americans. Decisions were made by unanimous consent and decisions were carried out by warrior or Soldier's societies, which served as both a police function within band camps, and also as protection against enemies. These warriors were called *akicitas*. Crimes, including murder, were considered private matters to be resolved by the involved parties.[36]

Warfare was an important part of Assiniboine life, and included both horse raids and war party expeditions. These provided men with war honors and feats of bravery, which were important means of earning respect within the community. Horse raids were an important way to increase or maintain horse populations. War expeditions were often enlisted to seek revenge against tribal enemies.[37]

Assiniboine sacred beliefs are based upon the concept of *wakan*, applied to anything which is sacred, mysterious, and incomprehensible to man. All things in the physical world—including plants, animals, waters, rocks, and celestial bodies—are considered living beings, each possessed with spirits, and manifestations of *wakan*. Although not personified, the creator is known as *Wakan Tanga* (sacred, mysterious, incomprehensible, large, big).

Men seeking *wakan* knowledge or teachings went on solitary vision quests, in the hope that one's fasting and prayers might lead a spirit to bestow spiritual knowledge to aid the person, perhaps in hunting, war, or healing powers. Medicine men are those individuals blessed by the *wakan* and empowered with such gifts as healing, finding lost objects or persons, prophesy, and other sacred duties. Assiniboines spiritually cleanse themselves in purification (or "sweat") lodge ceremonies. Vital to Assiniboine sacred life is the Medicine Lodge, or sun dance, a collective annual ceremony usually held in June. Among many things, it is an opportunity to offer thanks for all the blessings bestowed upon the people in the past year, and to pray for continued blessings in the coming year.[38] ✵

1 Raymond J. DeMallie and David Reed Miller, "Assiniboine," in *Handbook of North American Indians*, William C. Sturtevant, ed., Vol. 13, "Plains," Part 1 (Washington: Smithsonian Institution, 2001), 572-74; Arthur J. Ray, *Indians in the Fur Trade: Their Role as Trappers, Hunters, and Middlemen in the Lands Southwest of Hudson Bay, 1660-1870* (Toronto: University of Toronto Press, 1998, 1974), 4-12, 16-23.

2 Ray, *Indians in the Fur Trade*, 4-12, 16-18.

3 Ibid., 12, 21-22; DeMallie and Miller, "Assiniboine," in *Handbook of North American Indians*, 572-73; Dale R. Russell, *Eighteenth-Century Western Cree and their Neighbors* (Hull, Quebec: Canadian Museum of Civilization, 1991), 74-76, 93-97.

4 Ray, *Indians in the Fur Trade*, 12, 16-23; DeMallie and Miller, "Assiniboine," in *Handbook of North American Indians*, 573-74; Russell, *Eighteenth-Century Western Cree and their Neighbors*, 176-84.

5 Ray, *Indians in the Fur Trade*, 6-23, DeMallie and Miller, "Assiniboine," in *Handbook of North American Indians*, 572-74; Russell, *Eighteenth-Century Western Cree and their Neighbors*, 1, 11-12, 47-53, 74-76, 93-97.

6 Ray, *Indians in the Fur Trade*, 6-13; DeMallie and Miller, "Assiniboine," in *Handbook of North American Indians*, 572-73.

7 Ray, *Indians in the Fur Trade*, 13-16; Gary Clayton Anderson, *Kinsmen of Another Kind: Dakota-White Relations in the Upper Mississippi Valley, 1650-1862* (St. Paul: Minnesota Historical Society Press, 1984, 1997), 32, 43, 47, 49-50.

8 Ray, *Indians in the Fur Trade*, 14-23, 56; DeMallie and Miller, "Assiniboine," in *Handbook of North American Indians*, 572-74; W. Raymond Wood and Thomas D. Thiessen, eds., *Early Fur Trade on the Northern Plains: Canadian Traders Among the Mandan and Hidatsa Indians, 1738-1818* (Norman: University of Oklahoma Press, 1985), 22; Russell, *Eighteenth-Century Western Cree and their Neighbors*, 50-56, 172-81.

9 Ray, *Indians in the Fur Trade*, 27-32, 35-37.

10 Ibid., 27-48.

11 Ibid., 72, 87-88; Wood and Thiessen, *Early Fur Trade on the Northern Plains*, 19-23.

12 Ray, *Indians in the Fur Trade*, 88, 156-57; DeMallie and Miller, "Assiniboine," in *Handbook of North American Indians*, 574; John C. Ewers, *The Horse in Blackfoot Culture: With Comparative Material from Other Western Tribes* (Washington: U.S. Government Printing Office, 1955), 5.

13 Ewers, *The Horse in Blackfoot Culture*, 1-5; Pekka Hamalainen, "The Rise and Fall of Plains Indian Horse Cultures," *The Journal of American History* 90: 3 (December 2003): 836-38, 845; Ray, *Indians in the Fur Trade*, 156-57.

14 Ewers, *The Horse in Blackfoot Culture*, 4-5; Ray, *Indians in the Fur Trade*, 156-59.

15 Hiram Martin Chittenden, *The American Fur Trade of the Far West*, Volume 1 (Lincoln: University of Nebraska Press, 1986), 90-93; Loretta Fowler, *Shared Symbols, Contested Meanings: Gros Ventre Culture and History, 1778-1983* (Ithaca: Cornell University Press, 1987), 42; DeMallie and Miller, "Assiniboine," in *Handbook of North American Indians*, 574.

16 Fowler, *Shared Symbols, Contested Meanings*, 41-42; John C. Ewers, *The Blackfeet: Raiders on the Northwestern Plains* (Norman: University of Oklahoma Press, 1958), 26-28.

17 Fowler, *Shared Symbols, Contested Meanings*, 42-43; DeMallie and Miller, "Assiniboine," in *Handbook of North American Indians*, 574; Hamalainen, "The Rise and Fall of Plains Indian Horse Cultures," 851.

18 David Thompson, *David Thompson's Narrative*, Richard Glove, ed. (Toronto: The Champlain Society, 1962), 235-37; Ray, *Indians in the Fur Trade*, 105-7.

19 Ray, *Indians in the Fur Trade*, 104-8.

20 Ibid., *Indians in the Fur Trade*, 94-96; DeMallie and Miller, "Assiniboine," in *Handbook of North American Indians*, 574.

21 Ray, *Indians in the Fur Trade*, 94; DeMallie and Miller, "Assiniboine," in *Handbook of North American Indians*, 574; Ian A. L. Getty and Erik Gooding, "Stoney," in *Handbook of North American Indians*, William C. Sturtevant, ed., Vol. 13, "Plains," Part 1 (Washington: Smithsonian Institution, 2001), 596.

22 Ray, *Indians in the Fur Trade*, 28, 94-96.

23 Wood and Thiessen, *Early Fur Trade on the Northern Plains*, 8-11.

24 Wood and Thiessen, *Early Fur Trade on the Northern Plains*, 3-15.

25 Ewers, *The Horse in Blackfeet Culture*, 10; Ray, *Early Fur Trade on the Northern Plains*, 156-59; DeMallie and Miller, "Assiniboine," in *Handbook of North American Indians*, 574; Hamalainen, "The Rise and Fall of Plains Indian Horse Cultures," 851-52.

26 Ray, *Indians in the Fur Trade*, 157-62; DeMallie and Miller, 574; Hamalainen, "The Rise and Fall of Plains Indian Horse Cultures," 851-52.

27 DeMallie and Miller, "Assiniboine," in *Handbook of North American Indians*, 577; Edwin Thompson Denig, *Five Indian Tribes of the Upper Missouri: Sioux, Arickaras, Assiniboines, Crees, Crows*, John C. Ewers, ed. (Norman: University of Oklahoma Press, 1961), 95-96; James Larpenteur Long, *The Assiniboines: From the Accounts of the Old Ones Told to First Boy (James Larpenteur Long)*, Michael Stephen Kennedy, ed. (Norman: University of Oklahoma Press, 1961), 63-70, 100-3, 108-9.

28 DeMallie and Miller, "Assiniboine," in *Handbook of North American Indians*, 577-78; Long, *The Assiniboines*, 106-8.

29 DeMallie and Miller, "Assiniboine," in *Handbook of North American Indians*, 578; Denig, *Five Indian Tribes of the Upper Missouri*, 68; Long, *The Assiniboines*, 81-84.

30 DeMallie and Miller, "Assiniboine," in *Handbook of North American Indians*, 577; Long, *The Assiniboines*, 20-25; Ray, *Indians in the Fur Trade*, 157-59, 161-62.

31 DeMallie and Miller, "Assiniboine," in *Handbook of North American Indians*, 575-76, 582-83; Long, *The Assiniboines*, 86-92.

32 DeMallie and Miller, "Assiniboine," in *Handbook of North American Indians*, 575, Long, *The Assiniboines*, 38-40, 86.

33 DeMallie and Miller, "Assiniboine," in *Handbook of North American Indians*, 581; Long, *The Assiniboines*, 36-41.

34 DeMallie and Miller, "Assiniboine," in *Handbook of North American Indians*, 575.

35 DeMallie and Miller, "Assiniboine," in *Handbook of North American Indians*, 582; Long, *The Assiniboines*, 27-32.

36 DeMallie and Miller, "Assiniboine," in *Handbook of North American Indians*, 586; Long, *The Assiniboines*, 17-20.

37 DeMallie and Miller, "Assiniboine," in *Handbook of North American Indians*, 579-81; Long, *The Assiniboines*, 40, 46-56; Denig, *Five Indian Tribes of the Upper Missouri*, 694-95.

38 DeMallie and Miller, "Assiniboine," in *Handbook of North American Indians*, 578-79; Long, *The Assiniboines*, 150-72.

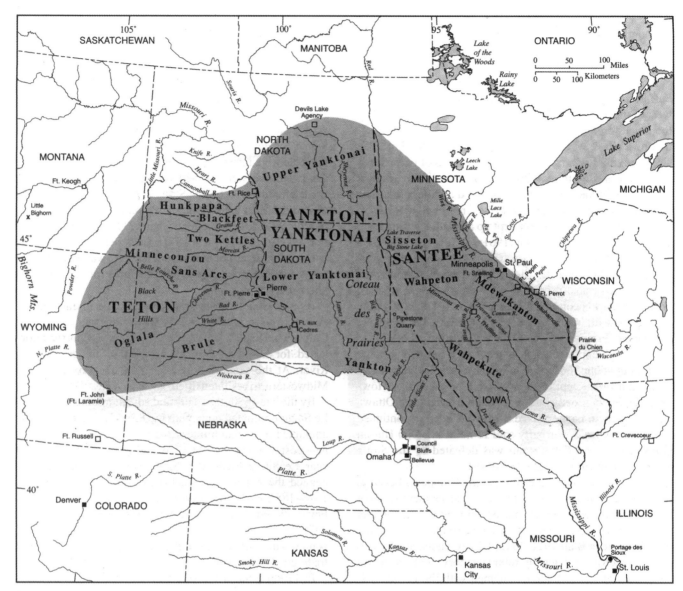

Sioux territory, early to mid-19th century. Boundaries between the divisions suggest areas of greatest use. Map from article "Sioux Until 1850" by Raymond J. DeMallie. *Plains*, vol. 13, part 2 of 2. *Handbook of North American Indians*, Raymond J. DeMallie, volume editor. Washington, DC: Smithsonian Institution, 2001. Reproduced by permission.

~

CHAPTER 2

Fort Peck Sioux to 1800

Dennis J. Smith, Ph.D.

THE Sioux residing on the Fort Peck Reservation—primarily Yanktonais, Sissetons and Wahpetons, and Hunkpapa Lakotas—come from different but closely related tribal groups within the Sioux tribe or nation. Although these tribes did not migrate into the upper Missouri River area of present-day northeastern Montana until the mid-nineteenth century, each had long-standing contact with the Missouri River area. From their historic homelands in the headwaters of the Mississippi River, in present-day north-central Minnesota, each tribe had for generations hunted the plains east of the Missouri River and traded at Hidatsa, Mandan, or Arikara earth-lodge villages.[1]

Details about Sioux historic origins and early migrations remain a little unclear. Those who became the Sioux tribe were part of the westernmost early Siouan-speaking tribal groups located west of Lake Michigan. These proto-western Siouans included those speaking a Dhegiha dialect (who later differentiated into the Omaha, Ponca, Osage, Kansa, and Quapaw tribes) and those speaking a Chiwere dialect (later becoming the Iowa, Oto, Missouri, and Winnebago tribes). These early groups—Dakotas, Dhegihas, and Chiweres—inhabited a region including present-day southern Wisconsin, southeastern Minnesota, northeastern Iowa, and northern Illinois.[2]

Early European and American accounts were limited in their understandings of early Sioux tribes and organization. Like Assiniboines, the Sioux as a distinct tribal people were first mentioned in 1640 by the French in the *Jesuit Relations*. Seventeenth- and early eighteenth-century writings did not identify individual Sioux tribes, but rather depicted them as two groups: the "Sioux of the East" and the "Sioux of the West." The geographic landmark separating the two was the upper Mississippi River in north-central Minnesota. Although not identified at the time, the Sioux of the East constituted the four easternmost Sioux tribes, which later became known as the Dakota proper, or Santee Sioux. These four tribes are the Mdewakanton, Wahpekute, Sisseton, and Wahpeton.[3]

The name "Mdewakanton" (*mde* means water or lake; *wakan* means holy, mysterious; *ton*, or *tonwa*, means village) is most commonly believed to be Mille Lacs (lake), in north-central Minnesota. Based primarily on Lakota informants during his extensive time on the Pine Ridge reservation from 1896-1914, agency physician James R. Walker noted the tribal significance associated with Mille Lacs. Lakota sources informed him of Sioux belief that Mille Lacs was the center of the world, and the pine forest woodlands extending north from it were strongly associated with the sacred concepts of a land of the pines and the direction north. Walker states that the Mdewakantons were considered the original and oldest Sioux band.[4]

The Wahpekute and Wahpeton names are also closely associated with their historic woodlands roots. The Wahpekute, or "leaf shooters" (*wahpe* means leaf; *kute*, to shoot), and Wahpeton, "leaf village" (*wahpe*, leaf; *ton,* village) both relate to woodlands life, but other details regarding these names remain obscure. The term Sisseton is based upon two identifiable terms—*sisi* and *ton*—but the original meaning of the term "*sisi*" is now lost. The two most commonly repeated interpretations—one associated with fish or fish entrails, and the other with a swampy village—do not seem useful without more corroborative details.[5]

Sioux accounts of their early historic times started to be recorded by Americans in the early nineteenth century. One important source in the mid-1820s was Mdewakanton mixed-blood Joseph Renville. He stated that the Sioux people identified themselves as the *oceti sakowi* (*oceti* means fire; *sakowi* means seven), the nation of seven (council) fires or fireplaces—referring to a governance or council tradition that may have existed among them. It is significant, however, that there are no historical accounts or references to the seven council fires in any the voluminous writings on the Sioux people since first European contact with the French in the mid-seventeenth century. This absence could reflect that the tradition occurred so long ago that it was forgotten. Another possibility, argued by preeminent Dakota/Lakota scholar Raymond J. DeMallie, is that a Sioux council of seven fires may not represent the historical past, but rather more of an ethical and folklore account defining vitally important tribal relations among the individual Sioux tribes as part of a larger tribal nation.[6]

Renville identified the seven council fire Sioux tribes as the Mdewakanton, Wahpekute, Sisseton, Wahpeton, the Iha'ktu'wa (or Ihanktonwa), Iha'ktu'wana (or Iha'ktonwana), and Ti'tu'wa (or Teton). Iha'ktu'wa, or Ihanktonwa (*iha'ke* means on the end; *tu'wa* means village), means "village on the end" and is the term used by the Yankton to identify themselves. Iha'ktu'wana, or Ihanktonwana (*iha'ke* means on the end; *tu'wa* means village; *na* is a diminutive suffix) means "little village on the end," and is the term used by the Yanktonai to identify themselves. The origins of these terms, and the reason for the diminutive form for the Yanktonai, are uncertain. The two tribal names may be explained somewhat by Walker, whose Lakota sources claimed a more historical account. In the past, the seven original tribes camped in a large circle, and the Yanktons encamped on the north side of the east entrance, and the Yanktonais on the south side of the east entrance. In this purported circle, Walker explained, the Mdewakantons camped on the west side—the place of greatest honor, directly opposite from the east entrance.[7]

The origin and meaning of the term T'itu'wa also remains unclear. This was a term used by the other Sioux tribes for the seventh original Sioux tribe, who identified themselves as Lakota. By the eighteenth century, this westernmost of the original seven Sioux tribes had expanded and differentiated into seven distinct Lakota tribes. The term T'i'tu'wa has been most commonly interpreted with such terms as "big village" or "prairie village," or "prairie dwellers," but the original meaning or meanings are not fully known. The word T'i'tu'wa has become anglicized as "Teton"—a term still commonly used to identify the Lakotas.[8]

Locations and information of the Sioux tribes during early European contact years are limited. French trader-traveler Pierre-Charles Le Sueur, who established Dakota trade relations at Lake Pepin on the Mississippi River near present Red Wing, Minnesota in the 1680s, identified twenty-two Sioux villages. These villages were placed on a 1695 map drawn by Jean-Baptiste Louis Franquelin, the first map depicting Sioux territories. The map was modified in 1699 and 1701 based on information provided by Le Sueur, and included eleven "Sioux of the East" villages in the Mille Lacs region and the nearby Crow Wing and Platt River tributaries of the Mississippi River.[9]

These eastern Sioux maintained a woodlands-centered subsistence cycle. They wintered in larger villages in the shelter of the northern woodlands, where they also hunted deer, fished, and trapped beaver. Spring through summer were perhaps the most important times of the year, when families migrated south to hunt bison in the mixed grassland-forest areas along the Mississippi River. In the summer when bison congregated in large herds, the Dakotas used a surround system to kill sometimes as many as 100 bison at a time. Bison meat was dried for year-round use. Summer villages were smaller and lodges were bison hide tipis. Small birch

canoes were the primary transportation means, but there seems to have been no dogs for overland transport, which consequently would have been primarily shouldered by women. There is evidence of only very limited corn agriculture. By fall, these Dakotas returned to the northern lakes area, where they gathered large amounts of wild rice, which was dried, and some of it stored in underground caches.[10]

Twelve villages were identified as "Sioux of the West" lands. (Franquelin identified one additional Sioux village from Le Sueur's twenty-two, included in the "Sioux of the West," but not placed on the map.) Very significantly, Franquelin's map situated one village, "Tinton," near Big Stone Lake on the upper Minnesota River, inhabited by "the nation of the prairies," a term aptly named for this location on the tall grass prairies of the northern plains.

By this time of early European (French) contact in the late seventeenth century and early eighteenth century, the tribes now known as the Yanktons, Yanktonais, and Ti'tu'wa constituted the Sioux of the West. Their defining feature was their nomadism as plains hunters, although few details about them were known. Writing in 1683, Recollect priest Louis Hennepin, who was captured by the Sioux in 1680, was informed by his captors that the western Sioux were pedestrian hunters in lands with few forests, who cooked their food over fires made from buffalo dung. Writing in 1700-1701, Le Sueur noted that the Sioux of the West were pedestrian hunters residing on the prairies between the upper Mississippi River and the Missouri River, who practiced no horticulture and had no fixed villages.[11]

The eighteenth century was a transformative period in which Sioux tribes underwent marked changes of residence and culture. By the 1730s, the eastern Sioux abandoned their ancient northern homelands in the Leech Lake and

Mille Lacs region. In part, this retreat was due to increased Chippewa attacks from the north. Chippewas were bolstered by rapidly expanding French trade operations west of Lake Superior in the 1730s, spearheaded by Sieur de la Verendrye.

Perhaps more significant was the westward shift of bison from the upper Mississippi grasslands-woodlands onto the tall grass prairies of the northern plains. Mdewakantons moved south down the east side of the Mississippi River, some traveling as far as the mouth of the Minnesota River, to where St. Paul is now situated. These Mdewakantons, who had depended on bison, were compelled to change their subsistence patterns to center upon hunting white-tailed deer. The northern woodlands that the Mdewakantons had abandoned proved to be too dangerous (due to Sioux attacks) for Chippewas to seize or control. This no-man's land, as it turns out, proved to be bountiful deer habitat, and deer populations exploded. In converting to new customs of large scale woodland deer hunts, Mdewakantons borrowed the customs of their Chippewa neighbors, who as northern woodland peoples had long depended on deer as their primary hunting resource.[12]

In moving south, Mdewakantons lost prime northern wild rice lands to the Chippewas, but they were fortunate to still have ready access to good rice wetlands from their new Mississippi River residence. These Mdewakantons remaining east of the Mississippi River were the only Dakotas (and Sioux) continuing two woodland traditions: the growing of corn and the use of birch canoes. Their new location drew them closer to French and English trade operations along the upper Mississippi River. French trade dropped dramatically during the 1740s and 1750s, however, due to wars with the English that began with King George's War in 1744, and trade all but ceasing during the French and Indian War from 1754-1763. After 1763, English traders replaced the

French, and they were influential traders because of the high quality of their trade goods. English commerce with the Dakotas increased rapidly up the Mississippi and Des Moines Rivers.[13]

For the other Dakotas, the migration shifts of the 1730s even more closely followed the contraction of bison herds west onto the tall grass prairies of Minnesota. Those Mdewakantons who refused to live without bison crossed to the west side of the Mississippi River in the region of the lower Minnesota River (present-day Shakopee area). The Wahpetons crossed the Mississippi and settled on the Minnesota River across from the Mdewakantons. Sissetons crossed to the west side and proceeded furthest up the Minnesota River to the tallgrass prairies of the Big Stone Lake and Lake Traverse areas. Late in the eighteenth century, most of the Wahpetons, probably due to declining bison hunting, moved to the Big Stone Lake and Lake Traverse areas, settling near and sometimes among the Sissetons. The Wahpekutes also crossed west of the Mississippi River, but they continued directly south, moving up the Cannon River and extending west to the Traverse de Sioux region of the Minnesota River at present-day St. Peter, Minnesota.

By the late eighteenth century, only the Mdewakantons and Wahpekutes continued to reside in wooded lands. Even so, Wahpekutes faced unique tribal conditions. Like Mdewakantons, the Wahpekutes persisted in their traditional woodlands cultural lifestyle. This contrasted with the Sissetons and Wahpetons, who as they moved further west in the upper Minnesota River area abandoned their woodlands traditions for a predominantly plains lifestyle. Wahpekutes gradually shifted even further south, inhabiting the headwaters of the Cedar, Iowa, and Des Moines Rivers of southeastern Minnesota and north-central Iowa. Like eastern Mississippi River Mdewakantons, the Wahpekutes changed their hunting priorities increasingly from bison to deer. And like the Mdewakantons, whose relations with the Chippewas increasingly deteriorated as both tribes competed over deer-hunting lands, Wahpekute conflicts with their Sac and Fox enemies intensified. The Wahpekute situation may have even been more precarious, because deer and other game populations were rapidly declining.[14]

In contrast to Mdewakantons and Wahpekutes, eighteenth-century Sissetons and Wahpetons abandoned most of their woodlands traditions for the plains lifestyles of the Yanktons, and what later came to be called the Lower Yanktonais, with whom they now so closely lived. Bison country was to the west. Sissetons and Wahpetons hunted primarily along tall grass prairies of the upper Big Sioux River, situated on the east slope of the Coteau des Prairies.

Eighteenth-century Yanktons resided in the upper Little Sioux and Floyd Rivers of north-west Iowa and the lower James River west of the Coteau des Prairies, and hunted as far west as the Missouri River. Directly north of the Yanktons were Yanktonais, who controlled the lands of eastern North Dakota west of Big Stone Lake and Lake Traverse, and the Red River of the North, which encompassed the Sheyenne and upper James Rivers.[15]

English free-trader Peter Pond in 1774 was the first to meet with the Yankton-Yanktonai. He identified this group as Yankton, but more likely they were Yanktonai. His writings about this trade encounter in the upper Minnesota River area provided the first descriptions of their lifestyles. They lived in buffalo hide tipis (fourteen feet in diameter), and, very significantly, possessed numerous dogs and horses. Men used rawhide war shields and wore hide shirts made of several layers to provide protection from arrows—both were Plains innovations. They used dried bison dung for fuel. The large number

of bison needed to provide these material items were likely harvested by the Yanktons-Yanktonais themselves, but the numerous horses in their possession were probably acquired through trade with their Lakota kinsmen.[16]

Pond was one of the few eighteenth-century observers of the Yankton-Yanktonais, and he corroborated earlier understandings that the "Sioux of the West" lived a nomadic life between the Mississippi and Missouri Rivers. Spanish fur trader-explorer Pierre Antoine Tabeau, writing during his 1802-1804 residence among the Arikaras, used the term "Yanktons of the North" in describing the Yanktonais. He was also one of the first observers to note individual Yanktonai bands, identifying the Wazikute (he called them Wasicoutais) and the Kiyuksa (Kiouxas), both Upper Yanktonai bands.[17]

West of the Yanktons and Yanktonais were the westernmost Sioux, the Lakotas, and even though they had been fully plains people during the eighteenth century, there was very little European contact with or writings about them. Although French trader-explorer Le Sueur wrote in 1700-1701 that the Sioux of the West traveled as far as the Missouri River, he provided no details except the important identification of one Ti'tu'wa (Teton, Lakota) village. LeSueur would not have known that the Lakotas by this time had expanded into four distinct tribes, and these soon would evolve into the seven Lakota tribes that now exist.

The two southernmost tribes included the Oglala ("scatter one's own") and Sicangu ("burned thighs"). These two tribes appear to have a long-established close relationship with each other, and in the early eighteenth century inhabited southwest Minnesota from the upper Blue Earth River west to the Pipestone area. Very likely their primary bison hunting lands were east of the Coteau des Prairies—the Big Sioux River area that would in a few decades be controlled by the Yanktons.

North of the Oglalas and Sicangus on the tall-grass prairies of present eastern North Dakota, just west of the Big Stone Lake-Lake Traverse and the Red River areas, were the two other early Lakota tribes. One identified itself as the Saone) *sa* means white; otherwise unknown) and Minneconjou (*mini* means water; *k'aye* means near; *wozu* means to plant, as in "plant at the water"). The Saone contained elements, most likely individual bands, that soon separated into four tribes. When established, they included the Sans Arc (a French term meaning "without bows," for *itazipa*, which means bows, and *c'ola* meaning lacking, without); Hunkpapa (*hu'kpa* means camp circle entrance; *p'a* means head), "at the entrance head"; Two Kettles (*o?ohe* means cooked (food) by boiling in a kettle; *nupa* means two, thus, "two boilings"); and Blackfeet (*siha* means foot; *sapa* means black), or Sihasapa. These are Blackfeet Lakota, not the perhaps better known Blackfeet confederacy—three affiliated Algonquian-speaking tribes in Montana and Canada.[18]

The eighteenth century was a time of extraordinary Lakota western migration to the Missouri River area. Between 1700 and 1730, Oglalas and Sicangus forced the Omahas from the Pipestone area of southwestern Minnesota, and they retreated to the Big Sioux River near present-day Sioux Falls, South Dakota. Further Oglala and Sicangu attacks forced the Omahas down the Big Sioux River to its confluence with the Missouri River at present-day Sioux City, Iowa. There they were joined by Oto and Iowa allies, but the Otoes soon crossed the Missouri River and settled in northeast Nebraska. Continued Sioux attacks (Oglala, Sicangu, and apparently also some Yanktons) forced the Omahas and Iowas across the Missouri River. For a short time, they lived up the Missouri River in the vicinity of the White River near where Chamberlain, South

Dakota, is now, but by 1750, they abandoned this entire Missouri River region of present South Dakota, relocating significantly further down the Missouri River to Omaha Creek in northeast Nebraska, where they continue to reside. The Iowas proceeded even further down the Missouri River in eastern Nebraska.[19]

At the same time to the north, in present-day eastern North Dakota, equally dramatic inter-tribal changes were being sifted out as the Saone and Minneconjou Lakotas also penetrated west. In this case, Cheyennes were the resident tribal people forced to retreat west. Around 1700 to 1730, they inhabited the Sheyenne River. This was a recent home, since they formerly had resided in the Red River and Lake Traverse regions, but they retreated west to the Sheyenne River when Saones and Minneconjous asserted control of the area. At the Sheyenne River, the earth-lodge agricultural Cheyennes faced not only continued pressure from Saones and Minneconjous, but they were also besieged on the north by Assiniboines and their Western Cree allies.

By the 1740s or early 1750s, the Cheyennes relocated all the way west to the Missouri River. By 1770, they re-established their earth-lodge villages on the east bank of the Missouri across from the mouth of the Cheyenne River, the southern boundary of the present Cheyenne River Reservation in South Dakota. The new Cheyenne villages were located north of the powerful Arikara villages along the Missouri River between the Bad and White Rivers. Probably due to the smallpox scourge that first struck the Arikaras in 1771, the Cheyennes abandoned their villages, crossed the Missouri, and proceeded up the Cheyenne River, settling in the Black Hills region by 1790.[20]

By the mid-eighteenth century, the Lakotas themselves had reached the Missouri River. By around 1760, two Oglala bands had arrived and settled on the east bank of the Missouri River, near the famous river landmark, the Big Bend, located midway between the mouths of the White and Bad Rivers. Significantly, the Big Bend area marked the south end of the extensive network of fortified Arikara villages on both sides of the Missouri. Spanish trader Jean Baptiste Truteau noted there were thirty Arikara villages with a total population he estimated at 20,000 persons, which Arikaras claimed included 4,000 warriors. Stalled from further advance, these Oglala bands appear to have established good relations with the Arikara, with some reported intermarriage, and even a brief experimentation with earth-lodge agriculture. Within a decade or so, more Oglalas and Sicangu groups arrived, precipitating Arikara hostilities. The new conflicts resulted in the oddity of some resident Oglalas allying with the Arikaras. These Oglalas soon reconciled, however, and both Oglalas and Sicangus moved to the west side of the Missouri River, crossing near the mouth of the White River. This was noteworthy because Lakotas permanently resided west of the Missouri River for the first time.[21]

Some time after 1760, a second wave of Lakotas—Saones and Minneconjous—came to the Missouri River, arriving at the Cheyenne River, above the Arikara villages. Unlike the first Oglala bands, relations between these northern Lakotas and the Arikaras were turbulent. The Arikaras were able initially to withstand the new Lakota assault, but a devastating smallpox scourge changed conditions profoundly. Between 1771 and 1781, a series of smallpox epidemics struck the Arikara villages, with individual villages increasingly collapsing. By 1796, Arikaras abandoned their remaining two villages and fled north to the Cheyenne River area. Smallpox destroyed not only an estimated three-fourths of their people, but also the Arikaras's powerful presence on the Missouri.[22]

Lakota war parties had penetrated west of the

Missouri River since they arrived in 1760, and the rapid Lakota expansion west of the Missouri River can be seen in the winter count belonging to the Oglala named American Horse. Winter counts were a means of recording history, in which the most important event of each year was recorded in art form on a bison hide. In American Horse's winter count, the year believed to represent 1775-1776 commemorates the Oglala discovery of the Black Hills.

After the collapse of the Arikara population in the 1790s, Saones and Minneconjous crossed to the west side of the Missouri River, with Sicangus progressing up the White River and the Sicangus up the Bad River, both moving west toward the Black Hills. At this point at the turn of the nineteenth century, however, some Lakotas continued to reside east of the Missouri River. Most Lakota bison hunting—spring through fall, when bison gathered in their largest numbers during their rutting season—now centered west of the Missouri. Each spring, however, as they had done for decades, Lakotas traveled east to the James River for large trade celebrations with their Dakota, Yankton, and Yanktonai tribesmen.[23]

By 1800, the Lakota world had dramatically changed. And as extraordinary as their western migration to the Missouri River had been in the eighteenth century, their transformation west of the Missouri in the nineteenth century was probably even more dramatic. The new changes were shaped by the sudden infusion of horses. Lakotas remained primarily a pedestrian people during the eighteenth century. This was true when the first Oglalas and Sicangus reached the Missouri around 1760. By the early 1700s, Arikaras had become the preeminent horse people of this part of the northern plains. Lakotas seem to have increased their horse holdings by raiding and trading with the Arikaras. When Lakotas relocated across the Missouri River in the late 1790s, they appear to have still been primarily pedestrian.[24] The low horse demographics for the Lakotas seem typical for most eighteenth-century Plains tribes living east of the Missouri River.

The horse revolution that transformed Apache and Comanche cultures in the southern plains of present-day Texas and Oklahoma in the late seventeenth and early eighteenth centuries quickly reached northern plains tribes. Acquiring sufficient horses to become a truly mounted horse people, however, was a more gradual process. The Missouri River agricultural village tribes—Arikaras, Mandans, and Hidatsas—served as the intertribal mediators of the horse exchange from the southern plains to the northern plains.

In the late seventeenth century, as Apaches and Comanches fought for dominion of the enormous southern horse trade, Shoshones established themselves as the key link in a northern-directed Rocky Mountain trade network. Shoshones purchased horses from Comanches and Utes and traded these to the north with the present-day Montana Salish (Flathead) people. The Salish, in turn, by 1740 had established an extensive horse-trading network with Blackfeet and Crows, which made all three tribes major regional brokers of horses. The Crows extended the horse trade east to the two northernmost Missouri River villages, the Hidatsas and the Mandans. The Arikaras to the south apparently acquired their first horses around 1740, from Comanches, Arapahos, and Kiowas through a trade path centered in the Black Hills. By the 1790s, when Cheyennes reached the Black Hills, they forged an alliance with the Arapahos, and from this alliance Cheyennes dominated the Arikara horse exchange.[25]

After 1800, when Lakotas converged west of the Missouri River and rapidly descended into the Black Hills, they wisely chose to forge an alliance with the Arapahos and Cheyennes. Through this partnership, Lakotas possessed horses in

numbers unthinkable only a few years before. The transformation to a fully horse-mounted culture seems to have been as rapid and dramatic as was their sudden breaching of the Arikara villages in the late 1790s. For the Lakotas, the early nineteenth century became a time of extraordinary growth, expansion, and plains cultural maturation.[26]

At the turn of the nineteenth century, Lakotas continued a long-standing spring tradition before the major bison hunts of summer commenced: They traveled east to the James River to participate in enormous trade celebrations sponsored by their Dakota, Yankton, and Yanktonai tribesmen. The journey time shortened substantially once Lakotas had more horses. The Sioux trade fairs on the James River were surprisingly large, totaling as many as 1,200 lodges. They are believed to have succeeded earlier ones convened in the Lake Traverse area, although there are yet no historical records of this.[27] These trade fairs exemplify the importance of trade both within the Sioux tribes and between them and Europeans. Equally significant, these trade dynamics depict the shades and diversities of woodland and plains cultural features among the Sioux tribes at any given time.

Throughout the eighteenth century and into the early nineteenth century, the number of horses possessed by Yanktons, Yanktonais, and the plains Sissetons and Wahpetons, was probably directly related to the number of horses that Lakotas were able to acquire. This was because horses were not only the most important Lakota trade item to Yanktons, Yanktonais, and Dakotas—in fact, Lakotas were essentially their *only* source of horses. This reflected the relative scarcity of horses on the eastern northern plains through the end of the eighteenth century. Horses did not become a significant trade resource for Arikaras, Mandans, and Hidatsas until about 1740. Remarkably, however, by 1750 horses acquired from this trade were evident across the eastern plains. At mid-century, however, horses in any significant numbers were still considered rarities.

That makes English free trader Peter Pond's observations of Yankton-Yanktonais at Lake Traverse in 1775-1776 all the more revealing, particularly his comment that they possessed many horses. This fact is all the more remarkable because Lakotas—the source of these horses—at this very time were at best a partially equestrian people.[28] It would seem that in these horse-scarce times, Sioux tribal people made it a priority to share the precious horses somewhat equitably among themselves.

The Sioux trade fairs also reveal the limitations of European trade in the eighteenth-century northern plains. For most northern plains tribes, European trade goods came indirectly, from trade with other tribes. Eighteenth-century Sioux trade items, especially guns, ammunition, knives, awls, and pots, originated primarily from Dakotas trading on the Mississippi and Minnesota Rivers. Lakotas received these at the trade fairs in exchange for horses, bison robes, bison tipi covers, and finished antelope and other leather goods which, they in turn, took west to trade for more horses from Arikaras.[29] In the early nineteenth century, when plains culture flourished for plains Sioux tribes, European and American trade increasingly entered the upper Missouri River area. The role of tribes as middlemen in a plains trade network declined sharply. With river villagers like Arikaras receiving their modern trade goods directly from Europeans, northern plains tribes increasingly acquired their horses by raiding tribal enemies.

During the eighteenth century, the Sioux world changed profoundly. The four Dakota tribes relocated south from their historic woodlands homelands in the Leech Lake and Mille Lacs regions of northern Minnesota.

Mdewakantons especially maintained their woodlands subsistence and cultural traditions. Wahpekutes, Sissetons, and Wahpetons abandoned the northern woodlands and relocated west of the Mississippi River, primarily in the Minnesota River watershed. Wahpekutes retained some woodland features, especially the conversion to a deer subsistence, but Sissetons and Wahpetons transitioned to the Yankton and Yanktonai plains lifestyle after relocating to the tallgrass prairies on the upper Minnesota River and headwaters of the Red River.

By 1800, Yanktons had moved significantly west, into the James River watershed. Yanktonais extended further north and south into both present-day North and South Dakota, and edged further west into the long-prized bison lands between the James and Missouri Rivers. Lakotas reached furthest west, inhabiting both sides of the Missouri River between the White River to the south and as far north as the newly established Arikara villages at the Cheyenne River. Many Lakotas moved swiftly up the White and Bad Rivers towards the Black Hills. The western Lakota migration would reach an important benchmark by 1830, when the last Lakotas moved to the west side of the Missouri.

Raymond J. DeMallie, the esteemed Dakota/Lakota scholar, explains that the breadth of these Sioux changes was not fully recognized by contemporary Euro-American observers. By 1800, however, seventeenth-century terms such as "Sioux of the East" and "Sioux of the West" were replaced by more precise terms, especially names of specific tribes, and even of particular tribal bands. Most important, it was not until the early nineteenth century that the categorization of Sioux tribes into divisions appeared.

This included the easternmost four tribes—the Mdewakanton, Wahpekute, Sisseton, and Wahpeton—who long identified themselves using the term "Dakota." When Lakotas,

Yanktonais, and Yanktons later resided along the Missouri River, they identified these four eastern tribal kinsmen as *isaʔat'i*, or *isayat'i* (*isa* means knife; *at'i* means to encamp at), meaning "camp at knife (quarry)," the origins of which term are obscure, and which was later anglicized as the term "Santee." Euro-Americans did not use the term "Dakota" when identifying these tribes until 1804, as duly noted first by William Clark on the famous expedition with Meriwether Lewis. It seems that Sioux and Euro-Americans alike did not appreciate the concept of an eastern Sioux division until a time when these Sioux people had geographically expanded and separated from one another.[30]

Yanktons and Yanktonais also identified themselves using the term "Dakota." Lakotas, however, coined their own term, *wic'iyela* (origin unknown, but may relate to *wic'a*, which means man; *iya* means to speak; *la* means a diminutive suffix) or the Yanktons and Yanktonais. The Dakota proper (the four eastern Sioux tribes, or Santee) did not have a collective term for Yanktons, and Yanktonais, but rather referred to them by their tribal names, Ihanktu'wa, and Ihanktu'wana, respectively. The fact that Lakotas self-identified the Yanktons and Yanktonais with one term at least suggests the concept of a middle division of the Sioux tribal people (residing in the "middle," or between Lakotas on the west, and Dakotas to the east).

Linguistic evidence, as skillfully argued by DeMallie and Douglas Parks, supports this general concept. There is a difference in the dialect between Dakotas proper (the four Santee tribes), and the Yanktons-Yanktonais. In general usage, Dakotas use the letter/sound "d" where Yanktons and Yanktonais use either "d" and "n." Lakotas (the "Tetons" or westernmost seven tribes) have always identified themselves as Lakota, dating back at least as early as their historic times in present-day Minnesota. Lakota speakers repre-

sent a third dialect difference. Where Dakotas use "d," and Yanktons and Yanktonais "d" or "n," Lakotas use "l." Since the eighteenth century, when Lakotas separated to various degrees further west from fellow Sioux tribesmen (and especially from Yanktons and Yanktonais, with whom they seem to have always been closely associated), the concept of a western or Lakota division within the Sioux people seems to have some practicality. The seminal linguistic feature that the language of the Sioux tribesmen is mutually intelligible between the three dialects supports the common ground between a tribal nation that over time has become so geographically dispersed.[31]

DeMallie and Parks explain that even though Yanktons and Yanktonais use "n" and "d" as a dialect distinction when compared to Dakotas proper and Lakotas, care should be taken not to identify Yankton and Yanktonai usage as an "n" dialect. An "n" designation properly belongs to Assiniboines and Stoneys, whose name for themselves is Nakota or Nakoda.[32] In this sense, then, an appropriate collective term for the Sioux people would be Dakota/Lakota.

The word "Sioux," however, remains the more commonly used term, even though the term originated from an Algonquian-speaking tribe, the Ottawa. The original Ottawa word was *na-towe-ssiwak* (the plural form of the word, *na-towe-ssi*). The French wrote this term as Nadouessiouak for the Ottawa singular form, *na-towe-ssi*. The French changed Nadouessiouak to plural using the French practice of adding an "x," making the word Nadouessioux. This word was abbreviated, again using standard French usage at the time, to Sioux. The Ottawa word (the singular form) *na-towe-ssi* most likely derives from an earlier, proto-Algonquian word, *na-towe-wa*, a word based on the term *a-towe* ("speak a foreign language"). There is a long-standing misunderstanding that the Ottawa word for Sioux means "snake." This most likely was based on the fact that the proto-Algonquian word *na-towe-wa* in several more recent Algonquian tribal languages means "little rattlesnake." The name Sioux never meant "snake."[33]

The Sioux presently residing at Fort Peck did not enter the area until after 1800. The majority were Upper Yanktonai Cutheads who had gradually migrated west from their historic homelands on the plains of present-day eastern North Dakota, arriving in the upper Missouri River region in the early 1860s. A large number of Sissetons and Wahpetons led by chief Standing Buffalo also came to the Fort Peck–upper Missouri River area in the late 1860s, but they were refugees from the 1862 Dakota Conflict in Minnesota. Standing Buffalo failed to secure safe surrender and returned with his band and followers to their home at Lake Traverse, Minnesota. His band proceeded west into Montana because it remained one of the last regions with plentiful bison populations. Hunkpapa Lakotas were the last distinct group added to the Fort Peck Agency. They were among the followers of Hunkpapa war chief Sitting Bull (who fled to Saskatchewan from 1877 to 1881) who were permitted to reside at the Fort Peck Agency instead of returning to their former Standing Rock Reservation.

By 1800, these tribesmen, although from diverse Sioux tribes and northern plains areas, shared a long-standing complex of plains Sioux beliefs and practices. First and foremost, they were primarily a bison-hunting people. Although still not fully a horse and equestrian people, they appear to have had enough horses to considerably ease the surround-style of hunting bison herds. Horses revolutionized transportation, and were especially significant in facilitating camp moves. Horses were capable of pulling larger travois, which meant that tipis could be made larger and women and dogs were significantly relieved of their former transportation burdens.[34]

Dakota/Lakota women did much of the butchering of bison and all of the extremely labor-intense duties of tanning and preparing bison hides. Women sewed bison tipi covers and made all the clothing, bedding, hide blankets and rugs, and storage containers. Women gathered all the plants and fruits used to enrich the family meals, which they also cooked and served. Wild onions and a variety of tubers, artichokes, and the important staple, the prairie turnip, were all collected. Wild fruits and berries constituted a vital dietary source, and included chokecherries, grapes, plums, currants, strawberries, buffalo-berries, and gooseberries. The fruits of wild roses and prickly pear cactuses were also used.[35]

In honor of their central role in the lodge—of clothing, feeding, and serving family and guests—women held complete property rights over the tipi, bedding, clothing, and food. On camp moves, the war chiefs and *akicitas* (warrior society members who served camp police and soldier functions) selected general camp locations, but women determined the location of their tipis. Women erected the tipis, and similarly disassembled, packed, and transported them.[36]

Dakota/Lakota women, especially mothers and grandmothers, were the principal caregivers for newborn children and infants. A mother used a stiff bison hide cradleboard, with her infant secured in soft, buckskin pouches, so that the infant could always accompany her during her busy day. For celebrations or other festivities, children were placed in elaborately decorated, buckskin-covered cradleboards.[37]

Mothers and grandmothers used the same nurturing ways to teach their children. Teaching and learning was predicated upon the principles of example and positive reinforcement and encouragement for completed tasks and goals. Early character formation was based upon the Dakota/Lakota Four Virtues: Bravery, Generosity, Fortitude, and Wisdom (especially the mysterious knowledge that elders acquired through living long lives).[38]

In early childhood, teaching and learning gradually shifted into gender-specific environments. Boy and girl children no longer played and learned together, but boys shifted to instruction by other men, especially their fathers and grandfathers, and girls into the domain of their mothers, grandmothers, and other women. Girls learned butchering, hide preparation, sewing, and food preparation and serving. Grandmothers were important healers, using plants and medicines for common ailments and injuries, so girls might be increasingly instructed by their grandmothers concerning these practices. Boys learned the skills they needed to become warriors, scouts, and hunters, with fathers, grandfathers, and older boys among their first teachers. Both young women and men also carefully observed and listened to other highly respected individuals who served as role models.[39]

Dakotas/Lakotas have a bilateral kinship tradition and an extended family system in which the biological father and his brothers are considered fathers, and the biological mother and her sisters are also mothers. All of the children of these fathers and mothers are considered brothers and sisters. Father's sisters are aunts, and mother's brothers are uncles, and their children are cousins. An extended family is called a *tiyospaye* (lodge group), which is the fundamental unit of the Dakota/Lakota band system. One or more *tiyospayes* resided together as a village or camp. Multiple *tiyospayes* formed a band, and each band was headed by a chief. Larger bands might have more than one chief. Chiefs were selected based upon merit, including proven acts of bravery, being good providers for their families, generosity, and wisdom.[40]

In marriage, a wife and her new husband usually resided initially with the husband's family. A man sought permission from a prospective

wife's family by having a male relative present gifts, such as horses, to her family. If the prospective wife's family accepted a young man's offer, they usually reciprocated with gifts to his family. Chiefs or other men of merit and accomplishment could have additional wives, who were usually younger sisters of the first wife. Marriage was an honored institution, but divorces were not uncommon, and were based on grounds of adultery or laziness. For women, a husband's cowardice could be grounds for divorce.[41]

Chiefs had no authority over any individuals, but were leaders when a community met in council to deliberate matters affecting everyone. The most important of such issues were related to the major bison hunts, and issues of war and peace. Councils met in a lodge known as the Tipi Iyokihe (putting together or joining many tipis into one), based on the tradition of combining more than one tipi to accommodate a large gathering.

Decisions in council were by unanimous consent only, and even when announced, the decisions were not compulsory. Central decision-making was not an ongoing governmental structure, but rather was conditional. Councils met only when matters affecting an entire community demanded such deliberations. Otherwise, Dakotas and Lakotas were expected to govern their own personal and family affairs. Luther Standing Bear explains this by noting that Lakotas were "self-governors," and the primary force "governing" behaviors were the customs. The power of the customs he describes as *wouncage* (our way of doing), which build a tribal consciousness in which the central aim was to bring ease and comfort in equal measure to everyone, for it was each person's responsibility to ensure that every person had enough to eat and was properly clothed.[42]

In times of war, as well as times of moving camp and of the major bison hunts, war chiefs controlled affairs, and in contrast to the role of civil chiefs in non-war times, directives from war chiefs were mandatory. They were enforced by *akicitas*, warrior society members selected for particular times of office. *Akicitas* were empowered to inflict corporal punishment, and if necessary, to destroy the property of wrongdoers, including tipis and horses. When the state of war ended, such as after a major bison hunt or camp moving, civil chiefs and the conditions of extraordinary individual freedom returned.[43]

Warfare was an important part of Dakota/Lakota life, and by 1800 would have included horse raids. War party expeditions and capturing horses of the enemy provided men opportunities for war honors and feats of bravery, which were one important means of earning respect within the community.[44]

Dakota/Lakota sacred beliefs are based upon the concept of *wakan*, applied to anything which is sacred, mysterious, and incomprehensible to man. Everything in the physical world—including plants, animals, waters, rocks, and celestial bodies—are considered living beings, each possessed with spirits, and manifestations of *wakan*. Although not personified, the creator is known as *Wakan Tanka* (sacred, mysterious, incomprehensible; large, big).[45]

Men seeking *wakan* knowledge or teachings went on solitary vision quests, in the hope that fasting and prayers might lead a spirit to bestow spiritual knowledge to aid the person, perhaps in hunting, war, or healing powers. Medicine men are those individuals blessed by the *wakan* and empowered with such gifts as healing, finding lost objects or persons, prophesy, and other sacred duties.[46]

Lakotas believe that a sacred being, Wohpe, also known as White Buffalo Calf Woman, brought the Lakotas their original Sacred Pipe, whose custodian is Arvol Looking Horse, the Nineteenth Keeper of the Sacred Pipe. White Buffalo Calf Woman prophesized that seven sacred rites would come to the Lakota. These seven rights include The Keeping of the Soul, *Inipi* (the rite of purification, or the "sweat lodge"), *Hanblecheya* (vision quest), *Wiwanyag Wachipi* (the sun dance), *Hunkapi* (the making of relatives), *Ishna Ta Awi Cha Lowan* (preparing a girl for womanhood), and *Tapa Wanka Yap* (the throwing of the ball).[47]

1 Raymond J. DeMallie, "Sioux Until 1850," in *Handbook of the North American Indians*, William C. Sturtevant, ed., Vol. 13, "Plains," Part 2 (Washington: Smithsonian Institution, 2001), 718-19, 725.

2 Ibid., 718.

3 Ibid., 722, 727, 729.

4 Ibid., 752; James R. Walker, *Lakota Society*, Raymond J. Walker, ed. (Lincoln: University of Nebraska Press, 1982), 10-12.

5 DeMallie, "Sioux Until 1850," 752-53; also see DeMallie's important comments about the complexities of Sioux tribal/band name origins, and the cautions with which such names should be used in Walker, *Lakota Society*, 12-13.

6 Ibid., 735, 748; Walker, *Lakota Society*, 10-12.

7 DeMallie, "Sioux Until 1850," 754, Walker, *Lakota Society*, 17.

8 DeMallie, "Sioux Until 1850," 735, 755.

9 Ibid., 720, 721-22.

10 Ibid., 720, 722-25.

11 Ibid., 720, 725.

12 Ibid., 722, 727, 729.

13 Ibid., 727.

14 Ibid., 729-30.

15 Ibid., 727-31.

16 Ibid., 731.

17 Peter Pond, *Five Fur Traders of the Northwest: Being the Narrative of Peter Pond and the Diaries of John Macdonell, Archibald N. McLeod, Hugh Faries, and Thomas Connor*, Charles M. Gates, ed. (St. Paul: Minnesota Historical Society Press, 1965), 45, 50, 52-55; Pierre-Antoine Tabeau, *Tabeau's Narrative of Loisel's Expedition to the Upper Missouri*, Annie Heloise, ed., Rose Abel Wright, translator (Norman: University of Oklahoma Press, 1939), 102-3.

18 DeMallie, "Sioux to 1850," 731, 756-60; George E. Hyde, *Red Cloud's Folk: A History of the Oglala Sioux Indians* (Norman: University of Oklahoma Press, 1937), 6-14.

19 Hyde, *Red Cloud's Folk*, 14-15.

20 Hyde, *Red Cloud's Folk*, 18; Hyde, "The Mystery of the Arikaras," *North Dakota History* 19 (1952): 41-45.

21 Hyde, "The Mystery of the Arikaras," 30-33; DeMallie, "Sioux Until 1850," 731.

22 Hyde, "The Mystery of the Arikaras," 41-45; DeMallie, "Sioux Until 1850," 731.

23 Hyde, *Red Cloud's Folk*, 21; DeMallie, "Sioux Until 1850," 727, 730.

24 Hyde, *Red Cloud's Folk*, 16-21.

25 John C. Ewers, *The Horse in Blackfeet Culture: With Comparative Material from Other Western Tribes* (Washington: U.S Government Printing Office, 1955), 5-11; Pekka Hamalainen, "The Rise and Fall of Plains Indian Horse Cultures," *The Journal of American History* 90:3 (December 2003): 835-39, 845, 853-61.

26 Hamalainen, "The Rise and Fall of Plains Indian Horse Cultures," 860-62; Richard White, "The Winning of the West: The Expansion of the Western Sioux in the Eighteenth and Nineteenth Centuries," *The Journal of American History* 65 (September 1978): 331-37.

27 DeMallie, "Sioux Until 1850," 727, 730; Hyde, *Red Cloud's Folk*, 21.

28 DeMallie, "Sioux Until 1850," 727, 731; Hyde, *Red Cloud's Folk*, 15-19.

29 DeMallie, "Sioux Until 1850," 727.

30 Ibid., 718, 722-26, 735, 750.

31 Ibid., 718, 750-755.

32 Ibid., 718.

33 Ibid., 749.

34 Patricia Albers, "Santee," in *Handbook of the North American Indians*, William C. Sturtevant, ed., Vol. 13, "Plains," Part 2 (Washington: Smithsonian Institution, 2001), 763-65, 768; DeMallie, "Sioux Until 1850," 725-27; 731-32; Edwin Thompson Denig, *Five Indian Tribes of the Upper Missouri: Sioux, Arickaras, Assiniboines, Crees, Crows*, John C. Ewers, ed., (Norman, University of Oklahoma Press, 1961), 13-14; Luther Standing Bear, *Land of the Spotted Eagle* (Lincoln: University of Nebraska Press, 1933, 1960, 1978), 53-54; James R. Walker, *Lakota Society*, Raymond J. DeMallie, ed. (Lincoln: University of Nebraska Press, 1982), 40, 74-94.

35 Albers, "Santee," 764; DeMallie, "Sioux Until 1850," 725; Denig, *Five Indian Tribes of the Upper Missouri*, 10-13; Standing Bear, *Land of the Spotted Eagle*, 57-59.

36 Albers, "Santee," 764, 767; Standing Bear, *Land of the Spotted Eagle*, 83-91, 126; Walker, *Lakota Society*, 56-57.

37 Standing Bear, *Land of the Spotted Eagle*, 1-5.

38 Albers, "Santee," 769; Standing Bear, *Land of the Spotted Eagle*, 2, 5-11, 13-21, 26, 40-41, 55-56, 66-67, 123-24, 148.

39 Albers, "Santee," 769; Standing Bear, *Land of the Spotted Eagle*, 10-11, 13-16, 26, 33-36, 39-40, 45-46, 48, 75-76, 83-90, 153-55.

40 Albers, "Santee," 766-68; DeMallie, "Sioux Until 1850," 725-26, 734-35; Walker, *Lakota Society*, 22-28, 38-39, 44-50, 57-61; Standing Bear, *Land of the Spotted Eagle*, 120, 130-133, 137-38.

41 Albers, "Santee," 766; DeMallie, "Sioux Until 1850," 726; 41-44; Standing Bear, *Land of the Spotted Eagle*, 98-106, 108-112, 116, 162-63.

42 Albers, "Santee," 767; DeMallie, "Sioux Until 1850," 726, 734-35; Walker, *Lakota Society*, 23-32, 35-39; Standing Bear, *Land of the Spotted Eagle*, 123-132, 137-40, 161.

43 Albers, "Santee," 738; DeMallie, "Sioux Until 1850," 726, 735; Walker, *Lakota Society*, 25-34; Standing Bear, *Land of the Spotted Eagle*, 36, 125, 143-47.

44 Albers, "Santee," 761-62, 767-68; Walker, *Lakota Society*, 260-81; Standing Bear, *Land of the Spotted Eagle*, 24-26, 37, 39-40, 68, 75-76, 134-36, 153-55, 169-70, 217-18.

45 Albers, "Santee," 768-69; Standing Bear, *Land of the Spotted Eagle*, 193-97; James R. Walker, *Lakota Belief and Ritual*, Raymond J. DeMallie and Elaine A. Jahner, eds. (Lincoln: University of Nebraska Press), 67-80, 153-71; Raymond J. DeMallie, "Lakota Beliefs and Ritual in the Nineteenth Century," in *Sioux Indian Religion*, Raymond J. DeMallie and Douglas R. Parks, eds. (Norman: University of Oklahoma, 1987), 27-32.

46 Albers, "Santee," 768-69; DeMallie, "Sioux Until 1850," 726, Standing Bear, *Land of the Spotted Eagle*, 203-6; Walker, *Lakota Belief and Ritual*, 83-86, 91-96, 113, 115-17, 127-37.

47 Standing Bear, *Land of the Spotted Eagle*, 49, 220-5; Black Elk, *The Sacred Pipe: Black Elk's Account of the Seven Rites of the Oglala Sioux*, Joseph Epes Brown, ed. (Norman: University of Oklahoma Press, 1953, 1989), 3-138; Walker, *Lakota Belief and Ritual*, 81-83, 87-93, 176-255; Arval Looking Horse, "The Sacred Pipe in Modern Life," in *Sioux Indian Religion*, 67-73.

~

CHAPTER 3

Convergence: Fort Peck Assiniboine and Sioux Arrive in the Fort Peck Region, 1800-1871

Dennis J. Smith, Ph.D.

B
Y 1800, southern Assiniboine populations continued to rebound from the catastrophic losses of the 1781-1782 smallpox epidemic. The southern migration into the lower Qu'Appelle and Assiniboine River areas and even further into the entire Souris River watershed continued. But devastating measles and whooping cough epidemics struck southern Assiniboines and Western Crees in 1819. The southernmost Assiniboines in the lower Qu'Appelle and Assiniboine and the Souris Rivers were hardest hit, losing an estimated 50 percent of their people. Remarkably, these populations again quickly recovered.[1]

The southern Assiniboines continued moving south to the Missouri River, with most bands migrating until around 1825. One band of sixty lodges, which later became known as the Northern People Band, migrated in 1839. Depopulation from epidemics in the 1780s affected Assiniboine kinship organization, resulting in a proliferation of smaller bands, that dispersed widely along the Missouri River. This significant southern shift accompanied a gradual contraction west. The eastern territorial boundary shifted westward, with Assiniboines abandoning the southern Souris River area and progressing west into the White Earth River region. Other Assiniboines proceeded into the Poplar River area and west to the Milk River.[2] This region between the White Earth and Milk Rivers remained the southern Assiniboine's principal lands through the agency and reservation times of the 1870s and 1880s.

In 1837-1838, a second major smallpox epidemic struck the upper Missouri River tribes, but this time southern Assiniboines—an estimated 1,000 lodges strong—did not fully recover. They contracted the disease in 1837 at Fort Union, an American Fur Company trading post established in 1829 in the center of Assiniboine lands, on the Missouri River just above the confluence of the Yellowstone River. Infected Assiniboines fled north, but they could not outrun the disease; an estimated two-thirds of southern Assiniboines died. Two decades later, the southern Assiniboine population had increased by only 100 lodges, bringing their population by the mid-1850s to 500 lodges—one-half their pre-epidemic population.[3]

Assiniboine depopulation threatened their security, for they faced many tribal enemies. This included Piegans (the easternmost of the three Blackfeet tribes) and Gros Ventres to the west, Crows to the south, and Hidatsas, Upper Yanktonais, and Lakotas to the east. In 1844, Assiniboines established peaceful relations with both the Crows and Hidatsas (two closely related tribes). This was surely an equitable arrangement for the Hidatsas, an earth-lodge village people who lost one-half their population during the 1837-1838 smallpox epidemic. Fort Union trader Edwin Denig claimed that in 1851 he brokered a second Assiniboine-Crow peace, apparently primarily with the River Crows, whose bison hunting lands in the Judith and Musselshell Rivers would have adjoined Assiniboine hunting lands south of the Missouri River. The Crow alliance benefited Assiniboines for other important reasons, for they could now acquire horses and bison meat, but the good relations appears to have lasted only until the end of the decade.[4]

In 1851, Assiniboines struck peace with their western neighbors, the Gros Ventres. This friendship served Assiniboines interests by shielding them somewhat from the Piegans, who resided west of the Gros Ventres. Like the Crows, Gros Ventres were rich in horses, and now provided a second new source for Assiniboines. But the Gros Ventre-Assiniboine alliance placed the Gros Ventres in a delicate position, for they were long-standing allies of the Piegans and other Blackfeet. In 1866, Piegan and Gros Ventre relations ignited and their alliance was ruptured. This not only

helped solidify Assiniboine relations, but it also brought Gros Ventres and River Crows into a close friendship, particularly against the Piegans. Moreover, Assiniboines and Gros Ventres could unite against the increasing threat of Hunkpapa, Sans Arc, and Blackfeet Lakota penetration into the Yellowstone River region.[5]

Of more immediate concern to early nineteenth-century Assiniboines, however, were the northernmost Sioux, the Yanktonais. Since the first known descriptions of them in 1783 by English free trader Peter Pond in the Lake Traverse area of present western Minnesota, Yanktonais seem to have increasingly solidified their control of the plains of present-day North Dakota east of the Missouri River. By the mid-nineteenth century, they controlled lands west of the Red River and Lake Traverse region in present-day western Minnesota and much of eastern North Dakota, including the Sheyenne and upper James River watershed and the South Dakota plains west of the Coteau des Prairies. With the Lakotas moving west of the Missouri River, Yanktonai lands stretched up the east bank of the Missouri River north of Medicine Knoll Creek, just south of the mouth of the Bad River at present-day Pierre, South Dakota. Yanktons controlled the east bank of the Missouri River south of Medicine Knoll Creek. Yanktonai lands extended north to the Painted Woods region, and south of the Mandan, Arikara, and Hidatsa villages near the mouth of the Knife River.[6]

In the nineteenth century, the Yanktonais separated into two groups: Lower Yanktonais and Upper Yanktonais, designations based on their locations relative to the Missouri River. The Lower Yanktonais were one large band, the Hunkpatina (hukpa means the entrance to the camp circle; t'i, to dwell; na is a diminutive term) thus "dwellers at the camp circle entrance." Upper Yanktonais constituted three bands: the Wazikute (wazi means pine; kute, to shoot at), the "pine shooters"; the Kiyuksa (to divide, break in two), the "break in two"; and the Pabaska (to cut off the head), the "cutheads." The Cutheads were the northernmost band and because of their size and perhaps significance were sometimes depicted as a separate Upper Yanktonai tribe. Cutheads extended into the White Earth River region of northwestern North Dakota, where as late as the 1850s they clashed with Lower Assiniboines who controlled this region.[7]

The origin of the Cuthead band seems to be traced to Sisseton Chief Red Thunder, who along with Sisseton chief Standing Buffalo in 1803 left a large Sisseton community on the Minnesota River near present-day Mankato and relocated to the upper Minnesota River in the Lake Traverse area. Here Red Thunder forged close relations with Upper Yanktonais (he may have had a Yanktonai wife) and he seems to have been identified both as a Sisseton and Yanktonai chief. Around 1816, in a violent confrontation with an unidentified Yanktonai, he was wounded in the head, and he departed and founded his own band, now known as the "Cutheads."[8]

Red Thunder died in 1823 and his son Wanatan (also called Waneta) assumed the Cuthead chieftainship. During Wanatan's almost twenty years of leadership, the Cutheads moved increasingly west into the Missouri River area. In part this shift was influenced by the Red River Métis' depletion of bison populations in Cuthead lands in the Pembina and Red River areas of present-day northeastern North Dakota. Red River Métis were primarily mixed-blood Chippewas, Crees, and Ottawas who had been drawn to the Pembina, lower Assiniboine, and upper Red Rivers region of southern Manitoba since the late 1770s, when the North West and Hudson's Bay Companies expanded trade into the interior parklands of Manitoba and Saskatchewan. Mixed-bloods were children of Canadian English and French men who mar-

ried Native women, and these families supplied most of the bison meat and pemmican for the interior trading posts. Large numbers of other Métis immigrated from declining Great Lakes fur trading centers in Michigan, Wisconsin, and Minnesota, especially to work in the Pembina fur trade boom from the late 1790s to 1810.

Another distinct Red River Métis community arose at Forts Garry (Upper Fort Garry and Lower Fort Garry), established in 1821 at the confluence of the Assiniboine and Red Rivers (present-day Winnipeg, Manitoba). These posts served as the Hudson's Bay Company's new headquarters when it merged that year with the North West Company. Red River Métis hunters also provided bison meat, the primary food items sustaining this community.[9]

In 1827, Wanatan bitterly complained to Santee Indian Agent Lawrence Taliaferro at the St. Peters Agency, Minnesota Territory about Métis overharvesting bison. He charged that they had already destroyed the buffalo in Canada to feed the British settlements and trading posts, and now they wanted to come into Sioux territory and destroy the buffalo. Wanatan explained that buffalo were the only thing keeping his people from starving.[10] Just before his retirement in 1839, Agent Taliaferro reminded the Indian Affairs Office about this longstanding Yanktonai complaint:

Their [Yanktonai] country is extensive and would afford ample subsistence for their population, were it not for the annual encroachments by the half-breeds and freed men from the English posts and settlements, who hunt within the limits of the Yanctonas' country and destroy an incredible number of Buffalo . . . for the Hudson bay and Red river posts. The Indians have frequently complained of this infringement of their rights at this office.[11]

By the winter of 1828-1829, Wanatan had

already wintered for the first time near the Missouri River, instead of on the eastern plains in the Lake Traverse area where formerly the camps had been situated. Although Wanatan continued close relationships with the Dakotas and Yanktonais at Lake Traverse, his trade with American fur companies shifted from the Lake Traverse region to the new posts in the upper Missouri River. These included American Fur Company trading posts at Fort Pierre on the Bad River, which was absorbed by the American Fur Company in 1827, Fort Clark, established in 1831 near the mouth of the Knife River, near a large Mandan village, and Fort Union.[12]

Under Wanatan's leadership in the 1820s and 1830s, Cuthead tribal enemies to the north included Minnesota and Pembina-Turtle Mountain Chippewas and Red River Métis, and to the northwest included Assiniboines and Western Crees. Directly west, Wanatan maintained generally amicable relations with the Arikaras, but often hostile relations with the Hidatsas and Mandans. He died in 1840 and the Cuthead chieftainship passed to Red Leaf.[13]

By the mid-1840s, rapidly decreasing bison populations caused a number of Lakotas to move north into the Little Missouri River region just west of the Arikara villages on the Knife River. These included Minniconjous, and three smaller and closely affiliated Lakotas: Hunkpapas, Sans Arcs, and Blackfeet. And like the Cutheads, these Lakotas made peace with the Arikaras, securing a rich supply of the prized resource, corn. The northern location also facilitated horse raids against Crows and Assiniboines.[14]

One key factor disrupting bison and other game hunting for Missouri River tribes was the inauguration of commercial steamboat traffic in 1830, and especially the destruction of river woodlands, from which were secured the enormous quantities of firewood to fuel the steam engines. Steamboat commerce greatly expanded the availability of trade goods at American Fur Company trading posts at Forts Pierre, Clark, and Union. Despite the increasing river traffic and trade, in the 1830s and 1840s upper Missouri River tribes such as Lakotas, Yanktonais, and Assiniboines had surprisingly little contact with whites, and that which they did was limited to fur traders.[15]

Sioux and Assiniboine contact with federal Indian agents during this period was even more limited. The Office of Indian Affairs did not establish an agency in the region until 1819, when it opened the Upper Missouri Agency, situated in the first years variously at Council Bluffs, Iowa, and Bellevue, Nebraska. In 1824, two new subagencies were established. The Sioux Subagency was established near the Big Bend (or Great Bend) of the Missouri River, a famous river landmark about midway between the White and Bad Rivers. The Mandan Subagency was established much further upstream at the Mandan villages on the Knife River and near the Fort Clark trading post, and served such tribes as Mandans, Arikaras, Hidatsas, Assiniboines, Crees, Crows, and Gros Ventres. In 1837, the Upper Missouri Agency was moved to the former subagency at the Big Bend.[16]

In 1825, the Yanktons, Yanktonais, and Lakotas signed treaties with Upper Missouri Agent Benjamin O'Fallon, who accompanied a military expedition led by General Henry Atkinson. In addition to mutual pledges of peace and friendship, these treaties specified that these Sioux acknowledged their residency within the United States, and that they recognized federal supremacy and its right to regulate all trade and intercourse with the tribes. While it is doubtful these tribes appreciated the full implications of such restrictions, these treaties did at least establish the first formal relations with the federal government. The Upper Missouri River Agency remained underfunded and ineffective in directing upper Missouri River tribal affairs.

Federal Indian affairs in the northern Plains changed dramatically after the discovery of gold in California in 1849, as unimaginable numbers of whites trekked west along the California and Oregon Trail on the Platte River. Beginning in the early 1850s, Missouri River tribal affairs became increasingly strained and violent. White land pressures forced the Yanktons in 1858 to cede the first Sioux lands along the Missouri River, an action that infuriated most Yanktonais and Lakotas. Gold strikes in Montana and Idaho in the 1860s, and the 1862 Dakota Conflict, precipitated Sioux and other tribal conflicts that simmered until the early 1880s.

The 1851 Fort Laramie Treaty was the federal government's attempt to administer northern plains tribal affairs in the crisis precipitated by the waves of Americans traveling through native lands. Tribes represented included Lakotas, Yanktons, Cheyennes, Arapahoes, Shoshones, Crows, Assiniboines, Arikaras, Mandans, and Hidatsas. These tribes agreed to permit construction of roads and military posts in their lands, in exchange for federal promises to protect them from white depredations. Each tribe identified and agreed to respect certain geographic boundaries—an unrealistic attempt by the federal government to secure intertribal peace. In addition, signatory tribes were to share in an annual $50,000 payment for fifty years, which upon ratification in 1852, the United States Senate unilaterally reduced to ten years with the possibility of another five-year extension. The total fifteen years of annuities was accepted by an amendment signed by tribal leaders in 1853.[17]

Hunkpapas came under the terms of the treaty, although they did not sign it or the 1853 amendments. The Yanktonais, for unclear reasons, were not invited to the treaty council, presumably because the treaty was intended only for tribes west of the Missouri River. That does not explain why the Yanktons, who lived on the east side of the river, were invited. Yanktonais also did not sign the 1853 amendments, yet they received treaty annuities.[18]

In 1856, General William S. Harney summoned a Sioux treaty council at Fort Pierre. He unilaterally appointed tribal head chiefs, and permitted them to designate other sub-chiefs. For the Hunkpapas, he designated Bear's Rib. For the Upper Yanktonais, he selected Black Catfish, and one of the nine chiefs Black Catfish selected was Medicine Bear. Both would become important figures at the Fort Peck Agency.

It is unclear how much significance fellow tribesmen placed in the appointment of head chiefs by General Harney. Increasing anger at the federal government's failure to keep its 1851 promises against white depredations deteriorated relations among Hunkpapas, leading to the 1862 killing of Bear's Rib by two Sans Arc warriors at Fort Pierre. General Harney's appointments did sometimes influence Indian agents, who often treated these appointees as head chiefs, especially in terms of receiving additional gifts or patronage. General Harney's influence on federal Indian policy was minimal, for Congress failed to ratify the 1856 Sioux treaty he brokered. In spite of General Harney's arrogant and authoritarian treatment of Sioux leaders at Fort Pierre, the meeting somehow did secure short-term peace between the Missouri River Sioux and the federal government.[19] Sioux-white relations worsened steadily through the late 1850s, however, due to increasing steamboat river traffic and white travel through western Sioux lands. In 1862, when the Dakota uprising exploded in southern Minnesota, Sioux hostilities to white travelers changed to war against the U.S. Army.

Missouri River Assiniboines in the 1850s were spared the intense white intrusions that traumatized Yanktons, Yanktonais, and Lakotas. Like all northern plains tribes after 1849, however,

Assiniboines could not avoid the new attention of federal Indian policymakers and the Army concerning the entire trans-Mississippi West. Except for one brief interlude in 1831, Assiniboines had limited relationships with the Indian Affairs Office.

In 1831, Secretary of War Lewis Cass ordered Indian agent John F. A. Sanford, the Mandan Subagent of the Upper Missouri Agency, to bring some upper Missouri River tribal leaders to Washington, D.C. Sanford persuaded only four tribesmen to accompany him. Two were Plains Cree, and of these the only one identified was a chief known as Eyes on Both Sides, but more commonly as Broken Arm. A third member was an unidentified Upper Yanktonai Cuthead. Last was Assiniboine Stone Band Chief, The Light (and son of Chief Iron Arrow Point).

In St. Louis, the four tribesmen met with Indian Affairs Office superintendent William Clark. Here each leader was vaccinated for smallpox, and chiefs Broken Arm and The Light posed for portraits by George Catlin. The tribal delegation met President Andrew Jackson and visited major cities including Baltimore, Philadelphia, and New York. No tribal matters were deliberated on this trip, for that was not the purpose. Secretary Cass intended to impress upper Missouri River tribes with the size and power of the United States. Anthropologist-historian John C. Ewers suggests that such tribal ventures on the upper Missouri River at this time were pushed by fur trade interests, and, most likely, by American Fur Company founder and magnate John Jacob Astor, to lure tribal business away from the Hudson's Bay Company.[20]

By 1851, the federal government had substantial interests in the upper Missouri River area, and Assiniboines were invited to the Fort Laramie treaty council. Crazy Bear, chief of the Girl's Band, and The First Who Flies, chief of the Stone Band and brother of The Light, repre-sented the Assiniboines. Inviting Assiniboines was a significant exception to the commission's authority, because Assiniboines lived north of the Missouri River and in the White Earth River area, on the east side, but the treaty commission was directed to treat only with tribes south of the Missouri River and east of the Rockies.[21]

Assiniboines agreed to a tribal boundary for Assiniboine bison hunting lands south of the Missouri River, west of the Yellowstone River to the confluence of the Musselshell and Missouri Rivers, and from that confluence southeast to the Yellowstone River near the mouth of the Powder River. Because the treaty was restricted to tribes living south of the Missouri River, Assiniboines designated a tribal boundary on lands where they did not live, but in which they often hunted. These lands south of the Missouri River and north of the Yellowstone River were bison-rich lands where Assiniboines, Gros Ventres, Piegans (one of the three Blackfeet tribes), and River Crows hunted. Of these tribes, only the River Crows could claim true residence. The Blackfeet and Gros Ventres were invited to Fort Laramie, but they did not receive word in time to attend. Like Assiniboines, they both also lived north of the Missouri River, and like Assiniboines, at the treaty council they were designated lands west of the Yellowstone River. Their lands joined the Assiniboine boundary and extended west of the Musselshell River.[22]

The 1851 Fort Laramie Treaty miserably failed to establish intertribal peace by having tribes agree to restrict themselves to designated areas. It did, however, inaugurate federal relations with northern plains tribes on a rather sweeping scale. The $50,000 annuity dispersed each of the next fifteen years was an embarrassment—"a paltry sum for so many Indians," in the words of historian Robert M. Utley—but the annual distribution of these treaty goods at least provided a regular time for meetings and conversations between tribal leaders and Upper Missouri Agency officials. For Hunkpapas and Yanktonais, these meetings were held at the Fort Pierre trading post, and for Assiniboines at the Fort Union trading post.[23]

Widespread Lakota anger at the disease and suffering caused by the flood of white travelers along the Platte River after 1849 soon soured Yanktonai relations with the federal government and white traders. This was noted by Edwin Thompson Denig, a longstanding American Fur Company trader and administrator at Fort Pierre and especially Fort Union, and an exceptionally important observer of upper Missouri River tribes. Writing in the 1855-1856 period, he did not identify which Yanktonais groups he was observing, but he said that there was widespread and increasing depredations against Indian agents and traders.[24]

The 1858 Yankton treaty ignited the already tense relations of Missouri River Sioux concerning the federal government and white emigrants. The Yanktons agreed to a massive land cession of 11,115,890 acres, nearly 23 percent of the present state of South Dakota. This cession included lands north of the Missouri River from the Big Sioux River to Medicine Knoll Creek, and east to the headwaters of Big Sioux River near the present-day town of Watertown, South Dakota. This tract included declining but still vital bison-hunting lands in the famous Coteau des Prairies and the James River watershed.

The treaty divided Yanktons, alienating the Upper Yanktons further up the Missouri River from the Lower Yanktons, headed by chiefs Struck by the Ree and Smutty Bear, who signed the treaty. The Upper Yanktons, led by Feather Necklace (also known as Feather in the Ear), Medicine Cow, Pretty Boy, and Little Swan resisted assimilation and were more determined to continue the bison-hunting lifestyle. Struck by the Ree's son abandoned his father and for a time

probably associated with these bison-hunting Upper Yanktons. At some point, he moved further up the Missouri River, eventually allying closely with Upper Yanktonai Cuthead chief Medicine Bear.[25]

The 1858 treaty infuriated the Lakotas and Yanktonais. The land cession directly affected the Yanktonais, whose primary residence and bison-hunting lands were east of the Missouri River. Sioux anger forced Upper Missouri Indian Agent Alexander H. Redfield to seek protection of forty soldiers from Fort Randall to accompany him as he distributed the 1851 Fort Laramie Treaty annuities. At Fort Pierre, Lakotas demanded that the federal government void the 1858 treaty and stop Yankton treaty payments. Further up the river, Upper Yanktonai chief Big Head sharply informed Redfield that the Yanktons had no authority to cede these lands, for they belonged to all Sioux.[26]

For Missouri River Yanktonais and Lakotas, 1862 was the tipping point in terms of hostility toward whites. The problems of white traffic along the Platte River that had plagued Lakotas since 1849 repeated themselves for the Missouri River Sioux area after the 1862 discovery of gold on western Grasshopper Creek in western Montana Territory. The surge of white travelers accelerated throughout the decade. The Grasshopper Creek gold rush created the boom town of Bannack City, but this lucrative mine field was overshadowed in 1863 by the largest gold rush in Montana history at Alder Gulch. Here arose the boom towns of Virginia City and Nevada City. In 1864, a third major gold strike was discovered in Last Chance Gulch, from which the town of Helena arose.[27]

Missouri River Yanktonais and Lakotas were angry at the federal government for all the disturbances inflicted by white overland and Missouri River steamboat travelers. In May 1862, Upper Missouri Indian Agent Samuel N. Latta arrived at Fort Pierre and met with tribal leaders of a gathering of 2,000 to 3,000 Lakotas and Yanktonais. Before distributing the seven parcels of treaty goods, he explained the "object of the annuity goods, the obligations resting upon them under the [1851 Fort] Laramie treaty." By these words, he meant tribal commitments to keep peace against other tribes and whites, and he was concerned about the lack of peace, both by continued intertribal warfare and raids and increased violence against whites.[28]

The estimated ten to twelve tribal chiefs who met privately with Agent Latta then explained their understanding of the 1851 Fort Laramie Treaty. They strongly protested that they had indeed consented to permit some right-of-way passage on the Missouri River, but *only for traders*. No white emigration was ever contemplated, either overland or by river, and they would not permit any more. They explained that white travelers brought disease and pestilence, which destroyed their people. Bison would also not return to lands where they had been pursued by white men.[29]

These "friendly" chiefs further explained how the federal government's failure to keep its 1851 Fort Laramie treaty promises, and those made in 1856 by General Harney, had forced even these friendly tribes to abandon the 1851 treaty. Recounting this encounter, Latta wrote that chiefs and principal men

Regretted to see me without a military force to protect them from that portion of their several bands who were hostile to the government, and that they were friends to the white man and desired to live on friendly relations with the government and fulfill their treaty obligations. That General Harney, at Fort Pierre, in 1856, had promised them aid; that they were greatly in the minority; that, that portion of their people opposed to the government were more hostile

than ever before; that they had, year after year, been promised the fulfillment of this pledge, but since none had come, they must now break off their friendly relations with the government and rejoin their respective bands, as they could hold out no longer; that their lives and property were threatened in case they accepted any more goods from the government; that the small amount of annuities given them did not give satisfaction . . . that they had lived up to their pledges made at Laramie in 1857 [sic], as far as it was possible under the circumstances, and still wished to do so, but must henceforth be excused unless their Great Father would aid them.[30]

The divisions had reached a boiling point among the Hunkpapas, and after Agent Latta left Fort Pierre to continue upriver, two Sans Arc warriors killed Bear's Rib inside the fort itself.[31]

In late June, 1862, Agent Latta met with Assiniboines at Fort Union and he reported that they remained peaceful with whites and tried to keep their 1851 Fort Laramie Treaty promises. Latta explained that due to increasing Sioux pressures, Assiniboines had abandoned their lands south of the Missouri River (the lands defined as theirs by the 1851 treaty) and spent part of their time hunting in Canada. He stated that they wanted to sell part of their lands (presumably these lands south of the Missouri River) and were interested in federal aid in building homes, farms, and in having their children educated. They requested a military force be stationed near Fort Union to keep back the Sioux.[32]

Although not addressed by Agent Latta, one key factor in Assiniboines' declining presence in the lands south of the Missouri was that they were probably still recovering from an 1856 smallpox epidemic that struck Crows, Assiniboines, Arikaras, Mandans, and Hidatsas.

This was the third major smallpox scourge for these tribes, although it was less severe than the 1780 and 1837 epidemics. Blackfeet Indian Agent Alfred J. Vaughn estimated in 1857 that the epidemic killed 2,000 persons, and of these, an estimated 1,200 were Assiniboines. Upper Missouri Indian Agent Alexander Redfield had accompanied Blackfeet Agent Vaughn from St. Louis, and when the Assiniboines arrived at Fort Union in mid-July, 1857, he estimated they had lost one-quarter of their total population.

He noted that thirty miles downriver, an Assiniboine camp of thirty lodges was left standing, with some deceased persons left there, totally abandoned with all material items still there. Above the Mandan and Hidatsa villages at Fort Berthold, he met with Lower Assiniboine Chief Broken Arm of the Canoe Paddler Band, and at Fort Union various groups of the Rock (Stone), Canoe, Northern, and Girls Bands came to visit him and receive their 1851 Fort Laramie Treaty annuities. He estimated total Assiniboine population at 470 lodges, which he calculated to be 3,700 persons. The imprint of the smallpox destruction still lingered. Redfield described the Assiniboines who visited him at Fort Union as looking dejected and discouraged. They were also destitute—he described them as the poorest tribesmen he had ever seen. In fact, they could council with him for only a short time, due to their lack of food.[33]

If Assiniboines complained about increasing white travel up the river and across their lands, Agent Latta failed to mention it. But he did acknowledge the problem, warning that next year he anticipated a large white emigration to the gold fields of Montana and new discoveries in Idaho. To protect whites, Latta recommended that two military posts be constructed along the Missouri River: one at the confluence of the Heart River, and one at the mouth of the Yellowstone. He estimated that one regiment

of cavalry would be enough to protect both the friendly tribes and white overland and river emigrants.[34] Latta sympathized with the need for protection of friendly tribes within his agency, but he seems to have disregarded Lakota and Yanktonai claims that the 1851 Fort Laramie Treaty prohibited white river and overland travel through tribal lands.

Just prior to meeting with Assiniboines at Fort Union, Agent Latta had returned from Fort Benton, where he had delivered Blackfeet and Gros Ventre treaty goods. The Fort Benton trading post had been established at the mouth of the Teton River in 1847 by Alexander Culbertson for the American Fur Company, and steamboats finally reached there between 1859 and 1860. Latta acknowledged that Fort Benton was an important river port, for it was the point of furthest steamboat travel up the Missouri River, and he further noted that it was 180 miles away from the Montana gold mines. Although Agent Latta was concerned primarily with the large contingent of white emigrant travelers expected in the following year, white travel to Fort Benton was already substantial in 1862, when he was there. Blackfeet Indian Agent Henry W. Reed, writing in January, 1863 from his post at Fort Benton, estimated that in 1862 at least 500 to 600 whites had passed through town on their way to the mining camps. By 1862, Fort Benton sustained a thriving steamboat business, and it expanded until peaking around 1867.[35]

The escalation of hostilities against whites in the upper Missouri River marked one turning point with the killing of Hunkpapa chief Bear's Rib. The danger to white travelers was made clear on July 25, 1862, in a written note signed by ten Hunkpapa chiefs and given to the Indian agent at Fort Berthold. The Hunkpapas warned that if the government did not stop white travelers through their country, they would do so themselves. By August 1862, Lakotas started attacking steamboats traveling up the Missouri River.[36]

These Lakota attacks soon changed to war against the U.S. Army after the Dakota uprising in southern Minnesota on August 18, 1862. After the initial attack, Little Crow's Mdewakantons and other Dakota (Santee) warriors fought a series of battles against Colonel Henry Hastings Sibley, and then wintered near Devil's Lake. In 1863, Hunkpapas, other Lakotas, and eventually Yanktonais, were slowly drawn into military conflicts, as two different Army forces entered the plains of present-day North Dakota from two different directions in a campaign to defeat what remained of Little Crow's combatants. In the spring of 1863, Colonel Sibley moved west from Minnesota, with plans to converge with General Alfred Sully, who was dispatched up the Missouri River and approached from the west.[37]

In July, 1863, on the Missouri Coteau at a place called Big Mound, east of present-day Bismarck, a variety of Sioux came together as each group was hunting bison. From the northeast had come Northern Sisseton chief Standing Buffalo, a non-combatant of the Dakota Conflict, and from the west came a party of Hunkpapa and Blackfeet Lakotas with Wahpekute leader Inkpaduta of 1857 Spirit Lake Massacre infamy. They had crossed to the east side of the Missouri River. These disparate Sioux groups joined a party of Little Crow's leaders, including White Lodge, Sleepy Eyes, and Shakpe. On July 24, Colonel Sibley arrived and was negotiating Standing Buffalo's surrender when violence erupted. After the battle, Standing Buffalo's people departed, but the Hunkpapas, Blackfeet Lakotas, and Inkpaduta engaged Sibley on July 26 at Dead Buffalo Lake and on July 27 at Stony Lake.[38]

On September 3, 1863, General Sully engaged a large camp of Inkpaduta's Wahpekutes and other Dakotas, Upper Yanktonais, Cutheads, Hunkpapas, and Blackfeet Lakotas in the battle of Whitestone Hill, located on the Missouri Coteau about seventy miles south of Big Mound. The Sioux were forced to abandon their camp, and General Sully burned an estimated 400,000 to 500,000 pounds of dried bison meat and 300 tipi lodges.[39]

During the spring of 1864, scouts and sources for Generals Sibley and Sully reported a large, unified body of Yanktonais and Lakotas determined to stop all white travel up the Missouri River and across Sioux lands. On April 30, 1864, General Sibley reported to General Sully of scouting reports from the James River confirming that a large group of Dakotas, Yanktonais, and Lakotas were concentrated on the west side of the Missouri River near the mouth of the Heart River (present-day Bismarck), and not only were prepared to stop all white travelers, but would also contest any Army penetration into their lands.[40]

On July 28, 1864, General Sully engaged this camp at a site in the Little Missouri River known as Killdeer Mountain. The extensive Sioux camp included Inkpaduta's Wahpekutes and other Dakotas, Yanktonais (Cuthead chief Medicine Bear), and Hunkpapas (including Sitting Bull and Four Horns), Sans Arc, Blackfeet, and Minniconjou Lakotas. Sully used his artillery with lethal effect, and the Sioux were forced again to abandon their village, which Sully burned to the ground.[41]

In October 1864, one of General Sully's companies brought him a small party of Sioux tribesmen, including two Lower Yanktonai chiefs: Two Bears and Little Soldier. Sully recognized them as chiefs who had long been friendly to whites, but who had fought against him at Killdeer Mountain. They explained that they did not want to fight the whites, but they and a great many others were prevented from leaving by camp soldiers (*akicitas*) who would have cut up their lodges and seized all their property and horses had they tried to do so. Sully admitted that he had heard this story from many sources about friendly tribesmen, that they were permitted to leave, "but only as beggars."[42]

Two Bears and Little Soldier further explained to Sully that the previous winter they had gone to the commander of the military post at Fort Pierre for assistance, but were refused. They could not live around military garrisons begging for food. They had to choose between starving on the prairies in the game-depleted lands near the army posts with their families or staying alive among their Sioux tribesmen who were hostile to the Army and the whites.[43] Yanktonai leaders like Two Bears and Little Soldier were living testimonials to what peaceful Sioux leaders had explained to Agent Samuel Latta at Fort Pierre in the spring of 1862. The federal government had failed to protect them, the treaty annuities were inadequate to live upon, and they had no choice but to leave the agencies to survive on the bison.

In 1865, General Sully received reports about Upper Yanktonai internal divisions concerning war and peace. Colonel Charles A.R. Dimon, commander at Fort Rice, established by General Sully on the west bank of the Missouri River, ten miles north of the mouth of the Cannonball River, reported on November 26, 1864, that Black Catfish and most of his band were interested in peace, but that Medicine Bear was strongly arguing against it. On January 24, 1865, Colonel Dimon supported a recent communication from the commanding officer of troops posted at the Fort Berthold trading post that Medicine Bear and Upper Yankton chief Struck by the Ree (the son) were concentrating anti-white Sioux forces in the Fort Berthold region. Other witnesses reported that Struck by the Ree boasted that he would never shake hands with whites, and that Medicine Bear supported killing all the Americans they could.[44]

Six months later, writing from Fort Berthold in August, 1865, General Sully wrote about a marked turn of events. He stated that at what many Sioux believed was a risk of being hanged by General Sully, Medicine Bear had come to agree to peace. The two leaders had a long, private talk. Sully admitted that Medicine Bear had been most bitter in his enmity toward whites, and that he had in fact led opposing Sioux forces in each of Sully's battles with the Sioux in 1863 and 1864. Medicine Bear stated that the greater part of the Sioux people wanted peace, but they feared General Sully, and their hearts felt bad toward him because the prairies had not yet dried from the blood he had spilled. Medicine Bear stated that the Yanktonais had suffered the most in these battles; at Killdeer Mountain in 1864, Medicine Bear stated he commanded 100 hand-picked warriors, and thirty were killed or died after the battle. Medicine Bear promised that after General Sully left Fort Berthold, he would find the rest of his camp which he said were somewhere near the Canadian border, and bring them in to surrender. General Sully pressed Medicine Bear to tell him exactly where this camp was located, but Medicine Bear said he did not know. He assuredly knew, but he was worried that Sully would seek their surrender himself.[45]

Two weeks later, General Sully sent for Medicine Bear and informed him that he had taken Medicine Bear's advice (which, by Sully's previous account, Medicine Bear had not given him) and that he would not go after the remainder of Medicine Bear's people. Sully reported that Medicine Bear seemed very pleased to hear this, and said he would bring them in. Medicine Bear's surrender was surely part of a significant pattern throughout 1865, for Sully then stated his confidence that by the fall and winter of 1865 most of the Sioux would come in and sue for peace.[46]

Sully's next remarks bore a certain amount of truth, but in terms of prophesy, they would prove wrong. The idea that these Indians had a few years ago, that united they were more than a match for all the whites in our country, has been taken out of them. They will never try a combination again to resist our troops, for they frankly admit it is useless for them to fight us, for we are better mounted and armed. . . . By keeping up the present garrisons, letting the Indians know they will be well treated if they behave themselves, and that the Government has no idea of taking from them their land, I think there will be no more serious troubles.

Sadly, there would later be a Great Sioux War, and the government would take tribal lands. But in 1865, General Sully was quite correct when he stated that "In fact, I think it better to compromise than make war any longer for the present."[47] That is generally what happened for upper Missouri tribes beginning in 1865: a series of treaties in hopes of establishing lasting peace with the Sioux.

In response to the conflicts and wars in the upper Missouri region, particularly since 1862, in 1865 a treaty commission was established. Headed by Dakota Territorial Governor Newton Edmunds and General Samuel R. Curtis, the commission also included Henry H. Sibley and Indian Affairs Office northern superintendent Edward B. Taylor. The commission met at Fort Sully from October 10 through October 28, 1865, and negotiated nine treaties: one with each of the seven Lakota tribes, one with the Lower Yanktonais, and one with the Upper Yanktonais. The key provision in each was the Sioux promise to withdraw from all present and future white travel routes. Records of the commission proceedings, however, indicate that all these Sioux tribes objected to both these overland routes and continued steamboat traffic up the Missouri

River, primarily because of the impact on bison hunting. All the Sioux signed the treaties not to permit travel through their lands, but *to repudiate these clauses*. Once the treaties were ratified by Congress in 1866, however, the clauses that permitted travel through Sioux lands became the equivalent of federal law. In addition to these serious shortcomings, these treaties did not guarantee peace because the preeminent non-treaty Lakota leaders, such as Red Cloud (Oglala), Spotted Tail (Sicangu), Sitting Bull and Four Horns (Hunkpapa) either did not attend, or those who did refused to sign.[48]

Three Upper Yanktonai chiefs signed the 1865 Upper Yanktonai Treaty: Big Head, Curley-Headed Goose, and Black Catfish. In 1869, Big Head (the son; his famous father had died) and Lower Yanktonai chief Two Bears, who had been unilaterally appointed "head" Lower Yanktonai chief by General Harney in 1856, moved to the newly created Grand River Agency in what later became the Standing Rock Reservation. It is not clear where Curley-Headed Goose settled. Black Catfish, appointed "head" Upper Yanktonai chief by General Harney in 1856, ultimately settled at Fort Peck.[49]

Upper Yanktonai chiefs Medicine Bear and Thunder Bull did not sign the 1865 Upper Yanktonai Treaty, but did sign the 1868 Fort Laramie Treaty. They did not, however, feel bound by it, for that treaty focused on Sioux tribes residing west (or south, for tribes residing west of Fort Berthold) of the Missouri River, and Cutheads identified themselves as living north (east) of the river. As early as the 1820s, they had progressively moved west toward the Missouri River as most of what bison remained also migrated west.[50]

In the summer of 1866, the treaty commissioners who negotiated the 1865 Sioux treaties at Fort Sully came further up the Missouri River and brokered treaties at Fort Berthold with the Arikaras, Mandans, and Hidatsas, and then at Fort Union with Crows, Gros Ventres, and Assiniboines. The commissioners especially wanted to secure an overland road west of the Missouri River to the gold mine fields of Montana and Idaho Territories. This would have connected an already established overland commercial link between St. Paul, Fort Wadsworth (a military post on the Coteau des Prairies in present-day South Dakota that was later named Fort Sisseton), and Fort Berthold Agency.

The commissioners planned two overland routes originating from the Fort Union area at the confluence of the Yellowstone and Missouri Rivers. One would follow the north side of the Yellowstone River and reach the mining boon town of Virginia City. The second route along the north side of the Missouri River would extend to Fort Benton, from which an overland route to the western Montana gold fields already existed. The commissioners secured rights-of-way permission through tribal lands from Arikaras, Mandans, Hidatsas (whom they called Gros Ventres), Assiniboines, and Crows. Although unspecified in their report, the Assiniboine right-of-way would surely have been across the southern region along the Yellowstone River as guaranteed them in the 1851 Fort Laramie Treaty. In addition, the Arikaras, Mandans, and Hidatsas agreed to sell a forty-mile long by twenty-five mile wide strip along the Missouri River near Fort Berthold, which was rich in timber and coal.

Assiniboines, Crows, and Gros Ventres (not the Hidatsas, for the treaty commissioners also referred to them as Gros Ventres) agreed to sell two 100-mile by twenty-mile-wide strips, one each along the Yellowstone and Missouri Rivers, and both commencing near the confluence of the two rivers. The land upon which Fort Union was situated was also ceded—although not specified, this would surely have been agreed upon by Assiniboines. These three tribes also ceded ten-mile-square parcels of land at unspecified places needed to accompany overland transportation. In exchange for all these concessions, each family of signatory tribes would be paid from twenty to forty dollars. All the tribal commitments were for naught, however, for the U.S. Senate failed to ratify any of these treaties, even though it ratified in 1866 all nine Sioux treaties negotiated in 1865 by the same treaty commission.[51]

Increasing Blackfeet-white conflicts in western Montana Territory in the mid-1860s, triggered by the gold rush settlement and the flood of white emigrants, forced the federal government to send a treaty commissioner to address tribal issues throughout the territory. Interior Secretary Orville H. Browning appointed for these purposes Special Indian Agent William J. Cullen. Although authorized to address tribal matters throughout the territory, Cullen was interested primarily in three northern territorial tribal groups: the Blackfeet (a "confederacy" consisting of the Blackfoot, Blood, and Piegan tribes), Gros Ventres, and River Crows. Between July 1 and 4, 1868, at the Blackfeet Agency at Fort Benton, Cullen negotiated land cessions almost identical to those negotiated by Blackfeet Indian Agent Gad E. Upson in an unratified treaty of 1865. Like the 1865 treaty, Special Agent Cullen's 1868 treaty also failed to be ratified by the U.S. Senate.[52]

Special Agent Cullen then left Fort Benton and proceeded down the Missouri River to the Fort Hawley trading post, situated twelve miles above the confluence of the Musselshell River, where he met with the Gros Ventres and River Crows. Cullen's priority was very likely the Gros Ventres. The Blackfeet and Gros Ventres were longstanding friends and close allies dating back to the eighteenth century. Their friendship, especially the Piegan-Gros Ventre one, unraveled in the early 1860s, and ended violently in 1866. That year a Gros Ventre-River Crow war party killed an esteemed Piegan chief, Many Horses, and the

Piegans launched a furious reprisal, killing over 300 Gros Ventres and River Crows—a brutal death count by northern plains war standards.

This dissolution complicated Indian policy affairs, for the Indian Affairs Office had treated with the Blackfeet and Gros Ventres as full parties in the important 1855 Blackfeet Treaty, negotiated by Washington Territorial Governor Isaac Stevens. The treaty established a Blackfeet Agency at Fort Benton. Now as bitter enemies, the Gros Ventres wanted their own agency away from the Piegans, and in particular, they wanted it situated in their bison-rich lands along the Milk River. Although not mentioned by the Northwestern Treaty Commission in their 1866 report, commission chairman Dakota Territorial Governor Newton Edmunds noted in a letter to the Interior Secretary in 1866 that the Gros Ventres requested a new agency on the Milk River, just above its confluence with the Missouri River. Although he had not visited the site, Edmunds strongly supported establishing an agency there.[53]

On July 13, 1868, the Gros Ventres signed a treaty, and on July 15, the River Crows signed a similar one; in each, the tribes relinquished all existing claims to tribal lands in exchange for new reservations. The Gros Ventres agreed to a reservation of yet undermined size somewhere within the boundaries of the Blackfeet Reservation. Special Agent Cullen stated that the new reservation would "probably" be located on the Milk River, at a site he preferred that was not frequented nor soon to be settled by whites. The River Crows agreed to a reservation, also at a yet undetermined location near or adjoining the new Gros Ventre Reservation. In addition, each tribe would be paid $25,000 annually for twenty years, amounting to $ 500,000 for each tribe.[54]

Neither of these two treaties were ratified by the U.S. Senate. Local Montana settlers and their territorial representatives objected that the treaties were too generous, which is rather revealing,

considering the fact that these undetermined reservations were to be placed on lands undesirable for white travel and settlement. Ironically, federal officials favored not ratifying the treaty that they themselves just negotiated. They did so because it meant denying the River Crows their own reservation and forcing them to join the Mountain Crows at no federal expense.

Earlier that same year, the Mountain Crows signed a new treaty at Fort Laramie, ceding over thirty million acres in return for a new reservation boundaried on the north by the Yellowstone River, a treaty that disenfranchised their fellow River Crows, whose residence was primarily north of the Yellowstone River. The Mountain Crows believed, however, that the River Crows would soon be granted their own reservation north of the Yellowstone. In 1869, the Indian Affairs Commissioner (most likely Nathaniel J. Taylor) agreed it would be best if Agent Cullen's 1868 River Crow treaty went unratified, for the River Crows could "doubtless be induced"—which clearly meant forced—to resettle upon the Mountain Crow's reservation. The new Indian Affairs superintendent for Montana Territory, General Alfred Sully, agreed. Having used Crow scouts in his wars against the Sioux, he believed he would have no difficulty persuading the River Crows to rejoin their Mountain Crow kinsmen. The River Crows were embittered at the loss of their own reservation, but federal officials were correct. By the late 1870s, due to smallpox, increasing Sioux and Piegan attacks, and declining bison herds, the River Crows were starved into relocating to the Crow reservation.[55]

After successfully negotiating the Gros Ventre and River Crow treaties, Special Agent Cullen found himself in a predicament. To get consent, and without any prior authorization, he had promised that the new Gros Ventre-River Crow agency would be built that fall. In a July 25, 1868 letter, he explained this to Indian Commissioner

Taylor. Taylor was able to use Cullen's plan to use the Gros Ventre share of their 1855 Blackfeet treaty annual appropriations to persuade the Interior Department to pay the remaining costs. On August 20, 1868, Agent Cullen contracted for construction of the new agency, which was named the Milk River Agency and completed in October, 1868. It was located at the "Great Bend" of the Milk River, about 90 miles upstream from the Missouri River, near the present-day town of Dodson, Montana. The agency was built near the Fort Browning trading post, owned by the Durfee, Peck & Company.[56]

Special Agent Cullen appointed Alonzo S. Reed as Acting Agent at Milk River, and Reed assumed duties on October 1, 1868. On July 27, 1869, General Alfred Sully commenced his position as Indian Affairs Office Montana Superintendent. In September, he recommended to Indian Commissioner Ely S. Parker (a former aide-de-camp for General Ulysses S. Grant, a Seneca tribal person, and the first Native American Indian Affairs Commissioner) that the Assiniboines be admitted to the Milk River Agency, for reasons of economy to the Indian Affairs Office. He also feared for their long-term survival and welfare, placing them in the same category as the Fort Berthold Arikaras, Mandans, and Hidatsas, all of whom he believed were endangered by Sioux encroachment. Sully also believed that Assiniboines would be afforded better service at the agency, for he worried that alienation might force the peaceful Assiniboines to join in Yanktonai and Lakota attacks against whites. Sully recommended that attaching Assiniboines to the Milk River Agency be contingent upon removing the River Crows to the new Crow Reservation. In the fall of 1869, the Indian Affairs Office affirmed Sully's recommendation, and the Assiniboines were formally assigned to the Milk River Agency, and the River Crows to the Mountain Crow Agency.[57]

In 1869, Assiniboines were for the first time part of a permanent Indian agency. The Gros Ventres with whom they shared it had been part of a permanent agency since the 1855 Blackfeet treaty, which established a Blackfeet-Gros Ventre Agency at Fort Benton. The Milk River Agency can clearly be seen as simply a second agency on the Blackfeet Reservation, for the eastern boundary of the reservation, as defined in the 1855 Blackfeet Treaty, was further east, at the mouth of the Milk River.

The Assiniboine reservation status was a little more complicated. Assiniboines were not parties to the Blackfeet-Gros Ventre Treaty of 1855, but Article 4 of the treaty established a common hunting ground for Blackfeet, Gros Ventres, and Assiniboines on the eastern end of the reservation. This area extended from the eastern reservation border at the Milk River confluence with the Missouri River west to Round Butte, a geographical landmark on the south bank of the Missouri River, approximately forty miles to the west. The hunting zone extended from the Missouri River to the Canadian international line, which were also the reservation boundaries. That meant that the lands east of the Milk River mouth to the Dakota Territorial line were technically not reservation lands, even though Assiniboines had long resided and hunted there. The Indian Affairs Office seems to have treated these lands as Indian lands. This issue was resolved in 1873 by federal executive order, when the Blackfeet Reservation eastern boundary was extended east to the Dakota Territory line.[58]

Intertribal relations at the new agency were particularly complicated. The Algonquian-speaking Gros Ventres had close relations with the Siouan-speaking River Crows. This would have been problematic for Gros Ventres as Blackfeet allies, since the Blackfeet and Crows were always intractable enemies. The intimate Gros Ventre-River Crow friendship following the end of the Blackfeet-Gros Ventre alliance in 1866 was also one of mutual defense, for now both tribes were Blackfeet enemies.

Gros Ventres had also longstanding close relations and intermarriage with the so-called "Upper Assiniboines," that is, those Assiniboines further upstream on the Missouri River. These westernmost Assiniboines maintained strong historic roots to the Milk River region, and were led by chiefs Long Hair and Whirlwind. During the first winter at the Milk River Agency, Agent Reed noted that a large number of Assiniboines wintered there. He did not identify them, but they were surely Upper Assiniboines.[59]

"Lower Assiniboines" resided historically more downstream on the Missouri River, generally between the Milk River and as far east as the White Earth River in present-day North Dakota. Lower Assiniboines were primarily Canoe Paddler Band members, led by such chiefs as Red Stone and Broken Arm. In contrast to their Upper Assiniboine brethren, Lower Assiniboines had generally more strained Gros Ventre relations. Assiniboines at the time of the agency founding in 1868 also had unfriendly relations with the River Crows. It is unclear if the Upper Assiniboines, because of their alliance with Gros Ventres, had more friendly River Crow relations. Lower Assiniboines and River Crows clearly had hostile relations when the agency was founded.[60]

The most remarkable transformation of intertribal relations, however, was that between Lower Assiniboines and Upper Yanktonai Cutheads. This can be seen in an observation made by the 1866 peace commissioners when they met Red Stone's band, for they noted that these Assiniboines were camped together with Medicine Bear's Cutheads. These two tribal groups frequently camped and hunted together. One Yanktonai band of thirty lodges led by Little Thigh was intermarried and resided with Lower Assiniboines, although these tribesmen still con-

sidered themselves Yanktonais.[61]

The new alliance and friendship, which reportedly included intermarriage between the two tribes, was exceptional because Upper Yanktonais and Assiniboines had warred against each other since the late eighteenth century, when both resided in the lower Red River region of present-day Minnesota, North Dakota, and Manitoba. The alliance was also very recent. Writing in the years 1855-1856, Edwin T. Denig, American Fur Trade Company trader and important observer of upper Missouri River tribes, wrote that at this time the Cutheads had been making peace overtures to the Assiniboines. He noted, however, that Assiniboines were especially cautious because they had been treacherously betrayed twenty years before. In 1836, Denig recounted, twenty-four Assiniboine men and warriors accepted a Yanktonai offer of tobacco and went to their camp for a council. But during the council they were ambushed, and only one Assiniboine escaped. For such reasons, Assiniboines were too distrustful to council together, and war between the two tribes continued.[62]

Denig's description is intriguing because he states that the Upper Yanktonai Cutheads initiated peace offers to the Lower Assiniboines. Most accounts around this period would indicate that the Cutheads were a larger tribe/band. Red Stone's camp in 1866 and 1869 was estimated at 200 lodges, while Medicine Bear's camp in 1866 was an estimated 300 lodges. When Medicine Bear appeared on the Milk River in 1871, however, that grouping was 500 lodges, but it also included other Cuthead chiefs, and to some degree would reflect their lodges.[63] The logic of tribal alliance decisions based on tribal size would lean toward Assiniboines initiating the rapprochement.

In any case, Lower Assiniboine friendship with the Cutheads strongly affected relations with the Gros Ventres at the new agency, for Gros Ventres and Sioux were unequivocal enemies. In 1869, for example, the Lower Assiniboines resided near the mouth of the Milk River and apart from the Gros Ventres, and came to the agency only for supplies, and to camp for wintertime. An 1869 smallpox epidemic then complicated tribal affairs even more.[64]

In September 1869 smallpox struck the agency, apparently first infecting Assiniboines, then Gros Ventres, and next a nearby camp of Métis. The River Crows were camped twenty-five miles away, and Agent Reed acted quickly, warning them to flee immediately to the Musselshell River area to avoid infection. They in fact evaded the disease that year, only to be infected there the following year. Agent Reed stated that 741 Gros Ventres died from the epidemic, and gave no other details. Oddly enough, then, smallpox had in effect done the Indian Affairs Office's bidding, for it was the instrument by which River Crows were forced to reluctantly leave the agency. Except for twenty-two lodges that remained with the Gros Ventres, the rest of the Agency River Crows relocated in 1869 to the Judith River basin, 100 miles away.[65]

Milk River Special Agent Reed reported that later in the summer of 1869, the Upper Assiniboines married over 100 of their women to the smallpox-decimated Gros Ventres. Saskatchewan Assiniboine oral tradition provides a sacred explanation for how this happened. When Gros Ventres and Sisseton-Wahpetons were at war with one another, some Assiniboines attacked a Gros Ventre camp and captured a medicine bundle, inside which was a pipe. The pipe spirit told an Assiniboine warrior that the pipe should be returned, warning that otherwise, the weather would turn cold and the bison would not come. The spirit also told a Gros Ventre chief that the pipe wanted to come home and if not, his people would be struck by disease. Each of these prophesized disturbances occurred, including the smallpox epidemic, which struck

the Gros Ventres hardest of all. Assiniboine and Gros Ventre leaders then reconciled and the pipe was returned.[66]

The next year, 1870, would be an equally turbulent year for the new agency. On October 22, 1870, Interior Secretary Jacob D. Cox removed Indian Agent Alonzo Reed from office, apparently on grounds of malfeasance. Investigation of Reed's misconduct began by Jasper A. Viall, the new Indian Affairs Office Montana Superintendent, almost immediately after Reed's removal. The inquiry was expanded in November, 1870, by Deputy U.S. Marshall, and Interim Indian Agent, C.S. Clark. Reed's financial misconduct included open trafficking of alcohol, stealing agency property, especially cattle, falsifying sales receipts, and selling agency blankets and other material items to agency natives for furs. Investigation also revealed diverse schemes in which agency resources, such as hay and horses, were funneled into a competing trading post operated at the agency, and for which Reed worked in obvious conflict of interest and in defiance of operating with a federal license. Chiefs Red Stone and Little Bull made the shocking accusation in 1871 that Agent Reed had killed an Assiniboine, but they provided no details. Although not a criminal matter, Agent Reed's neglect and dereliction of duty were also clear grounds for dismissal, for the agency at the time of U.S. Marshall Clark's arrival was in shocking disrepair.[67]

The most important transformative issue of the 1870s, however, and one that defined the agency forever, was the large numbers of Sioux who arrived, and the suddenness with which they did so. This was foreshadowed in September, 1869, when 1,000 Upper Yanktonais arrived at the Fort Buford military post (founded in 1866 at the confluence of the Yellowstone and Missouri Rivers) and demanded a reservation of their own. Key tribal leaders included Upper

Yanktonai Cutheads Medicine Bear, Thunder Bull, and His Road to Travel; Upper Yanktonais Shoots the Tiger, Afraid of Bear, Catches the Enemy, and Heart; and one band of Sissetons led by Brave Bear and Your Relation on the Earth.[68]

One week later, a *Takini* band of Upper Yanktonais led by Calumet Man, Afraid of Bull, Long Fox, Eagle Dog, and Standing Bellow, came to the post and made the same demand. Post commander Lieutenant Colonel Henry A. Morrow received both groups and wrote their demands on petitions which he forwarded to his superiors, until a treaty might be prepared for them. Morrow encouraged the Yanktonais to winter near the fort, and promised to help feed them. There was little game around the fort and in October he informed his superiors that unless he was permitted to issue food to these tribesmen, they would starve over the winter. In November, he received authority to do so, at least until the Indian Affairs Office decided on some course of action. That winter, 200 lodges of Red Stone's Lower Assiniboines camped with this large number of Yanktonais. In another sign of the rapid infusion of Sioux to the area, a large group of Hunkpapa and other Lakotas wintered further up the Missouri River, from which they warred against the Crows.[69]

Not coincidentally, it seems, in 1870 Agent Reed reported that the Milk River Agency and the Fort Browning trading post were attacked five times by Sioux war parties. The agencies were attacked, but no whites were ever harmed. The primary purpose of these raids was to capture horses, especially Gros Ventre horses, but agency and traders' horses were also stolen. Reed identified the perpetrators as Yanktons (probably Struck by the Ree's Upper Yanktons), Yanktonais, Cutheads, and Santees (probably from Standing Buffalo's Sissetons and Wahpetons).[70]

On April 30, 1871, Northern Sisseton chief Standing Buffalo and 260 lodges of primarily Sissetons and Wahpetons (an estimated 2,500 persons) camped on the Milk River twenty miles downstream from the Milk River Agency. Nearby were Upper Yankton chief Struck by the Ree (the son) and his camp of 140 lodges. Twenty miles further down the Milk River was an enormous Upper Yanktonai Cuthead camp of 500 lodges, headed by Chiefs Medicine Bear, Black Eyes, Black All Over, and Chasing Bear.

A large Lower Assiniboine camp situated one-half mile below the agency learned that some Sisseton-Wahpeton warriors were planning to attack the agency. These Assiniboines informed Indian Agent Andrew J. Simmons, who had assumed authority over the agency on January 17, 1871. Simmons dispatched a non-Indian trader and Sioux translator named George Boyd with tobacco and gifts, and with instructions to request the tribal leaders to "shake hands" and make peace with Simmons. Standing Buffalo consented to do so, but reconsidering that it might be a trap, he countered instead with an offer for the agent to council at Standing Buffalo's camp. Standing Buffalo promised safe travel, and Simmons agreed.[71]

The following day Simmons, Boyd, another unidentified translator, and Lower Assiniboine chiefs Red Stone and Little Bull drove a wagon full of food and gifts to Standing Buffalo's camp. After providing an agency-sponsored meal, the dignitaries proceeded to a council in the camp's warrior lodge. For Simmons, this was a meeting first and foremost about Sioux peace with the federal government whites, and the first thing he did was to extend this peace offer. Significantly, Standing Buffalo agreed that he wanted peace with the Great Father and the whites.

Equally significant, Standing Buffalo then explained to Simmons that the Milk River area was the last refuge for bison and because of the bison, he and his people had come to stay. Standing Buffalo eloquently stated that because of the bison, now he and his band were a rich people. He also explained that game no longer existed in the prairies of Dakota Territory where he had recently been. He did not explain his band's trials and tribulations since the 1862 Dakota conflict.

Standing Buffalo's Sissetons and Wahpetons lived a traditional bison-based life in the Lake Traverse area, and were respectful and responsible members of the Dakota agency. Standing Buffalo repudiated Little Crow's uprising, but he and his band were in a compromised position because without their chief's consent, a large number of his warriors had joined in Little Crow's hostilities. Standing Buffalo wanted to return to Lake Traverse, but only under conditions that neither he nor his band be punished or forcibly removed to Dakota Territory.[72]

By around 1866 or 1867, Standing Buffalo realized that he could never safely return. He also chose not to return because there were no game there. In 1867, however, he was not a rich man. His band was camped near the Souris River, and they were destitute and starving. They were encountered by Lower Assiniboine Broken Arm's Canoe Paddler Band, who fed and cared for them. This story was recounted in 1939 by an eighty-nine year old Assiniboine named Red Feather, who witnessed this as a little boy. When Standing Buffalo explained four years later to Agent Simmons that he was a rich man, he spoke with the experience of the mercurial conditions plains tribesmen often faced.[73]

Standing Buffalo seems clearly to have known that the bison days were at least in decline, for he proceeded next to bluntly tell Agent Simmons that his commitment to peace was based on one condition: that the federal government guarantee to feed his people. And on this point Standing Buffalo was explicit—he insisted on the flour, coffee, sugar, tobacco, ammunition, blankets, and all items which the Lower Assiniboines

received as agency Indians. Simmons agreed, but he reciprocated with terms equally explicit. He explained that Standing Buffalo was now in the homeland of the Gros Ventres and Assiniboines, and peace at this agency meant not only peace with whites, but peace with agency tribesmen. Simmons would have known that all Sioux were enemies with the Gros Ventres, and he probably knew this was true with the Upper Assiniboines. Simmons' terms were strict indeed, but Standing Buffalo agreed.

With a clear trust now established between these two leaders, Simmons then challenged Standing Buffalo to come to the agency to council again. Standing Buffalo agreed, and he went one step further, moving his camp ten miles closer. The next day in equally dramatic fashion, Agent Simmons and Standing Buffalo repeated and reconfirmed the conditions of peace so pointedly addressed the day before.[74]

Agent Simmons had extended a peace offer to Upper Yankton Chief Struck by the Ree, the son of the principal Yankton chief of the same name who signed the 1858 Yankton Treaty and from that time resided on the new Yankton Reservation. The son accepted Agent Simmons' offer and met him at the agency the day after Simmons had met with Standing Buffalo. Stuck by the Ree was very insistent on promises of ammunition for hunting, and although Agent Simmons was more suspicious of Struck by the Ree's behavior and mannerisms, it appears that the Yankton chief agreed to terms of peace with whites and agency Gros Ventres and Assiniboines.[75]

It does not appear that Medicine Bear and the other Cuthead chiefs made peace agreements with Agent Simmons. If they did so, such writings are not evident in Simmons' correspondence. Medicine Bear did, however, profoundly disrupt the peace and harmony that Standing Buffalo had just established.

In early June 1871, Medicine Bear invited Standing Buffalo to lead a raid against the agency Gros Ventres and Upper Assiniboines. Standing Buffalo declined, stating that he had made a promise to Milk River Agent Simmons to live peacefully with these two tribes. At this point, the verbal exchange deteriorated. Some Cutheads and even some of Standing Buffalo's own warriors derided their chief, saying he was not a chief at all if he listened to whites and refused to lead his own people's war parties. Tragedy then struck, when these critics accused Standing Buffalo of cowardice. Standing Buffalo became enraged and promised that not only would he lead the war party, he would die in the process.

Standing Buffalo returned to his camp, gave all his possessions away, and advised his son Little Standing Buffalo and his brother who was not identified to keep their peace promise with Agent Simmons. On June 5, 1871, Standing Buffalo led a large war party against a camp of Gros Ventres and Upper Assiniboines on the west slope of the Bear Paw Mountains. When faced with superior numbers of Gros Ventres and Assiniboines, Standing Buffalo charged with only his coup stick, and was slain.[76]

Standing Buffalo's death irreparably destroyed the unity of his band. They blamed Medicine Bear for their leader's death. The camp drove out their tribesmen who favored continued raids against the agency Gros Ventres and Assiniboines. These exiled Sissetons and Wahpetons then joined Medicine Bear's Cutheads. Approximately half of Standing Buffalo's band left the Milk River Agency, led by Little Standing Buffalo, and relocated permanently to Canada. Standing Buffalo's nephew, Sipto (Beads), returned to the Devil's Lake Agency in Dakota Territory. Those remaining at the agency were led by Standing Buffalo's brother.[77]

Agent Simmons tirelessly and effectively mediated the new tensions between Sissetons-Wahpetons and the Cutheads, and the delicate matter of relations that already existed among Gros Ventres, Upper Assiniboines, and Lower Assiniboines. By August, 1871, Agent Simmons was able to report that 4,850 Assiniboines and 6,800 Sioux (2,500 Sissetons and Wahpetons and 4,300 Upper Yanktons, Yanktonais, and Upper Yanktonai Cutheads) were now within the agency's jurisdiction. He did not cite the number of agency Gros Ventres.[78]

By 1871, three years after its founding, the Milk River Agency had reconstituted itself in unimagined ways. An agency established for Gros Ventres and River Crows now served Gros Ventres, Assiniboines, and Dakotas, Yanktons, and Yanktonais. As the bison had migrated west over the past century, so had Assiniboines and Sioux. Assiniboines had long historic roots to the Missouri and Milk Rivers area, and in the short period from 1869 to 1871, an extraordinary number of Sioux settled in the region. These changes would result in the dissolution of the Milk River Agency by 1872 and the creation of two new agencies. The course of the one to be known as Fort Peck would be defined by Lower Assiniboines and Sioux. ✪

1 Arthur J. Ray, *Indians in the Fur Trade: Their Role as Trappers, Hunters, and Middlemen in the Lands Southwest of Hudson Bay*, 1660-1870 (Toronto: University of Toronto Press, 1998, 1974), 104, 106-9, 111.

2 Raymond J. DeMallie and David Reed Miller, "Assiniboine," in *Handbook of North American Indians*, William C. Sturtevant, ed.,Vol. 13, *Plains*, Part 2 (Washington, D.C.: Smithsonian Institution Press, 2001), 575; Edwin Thompson Denig, "Indian Tribes of the Upper Missouri," J.N.B. Hewitt, ed., in 46th *Annual Report of the Bureau of Ethnology* [for] 1928-1929 (Washington, D.C.: U.S. Government Printing Office [hereinafter cited as GPO], 1930), 394, 403; Edwin Thompson Denig, *Five Indian Tribes of the Upper Missouri: Sioux, Arickaras, Assiniboines, Crees, Crows*, John C. Ewers, ed., (Norman: University of Oklahoma Press, 1961), 63-64, 68.

3 Denig, *Five Indian Tribes*, 72.

4 Denig, *Five Indian Tribes*, 89-90, Stanley A. Ahler, Thomas D. Thiessen, and Michael K. Trimble, *People of the Willows: The Prehistory and Early History Of the Hidatsa Indians* (Grand Forks: University of North Dakota Press, 1991), 59-60; Alfred W. Bowers, *Hidatsa Social and Ceremonial Organization*, Bureau of American Ethnology Bulletin 194 (Washington, D.C.: GPO, 1963; reprint, Lincoln: University of Nebraska Press, 1992), 24-25.

5 Denig, *Five Indian Tribes*, 91-93, 144; Loretta Fowler, *Shared Symbols, Contested Meanings: Gros Ventre Culture and History*, 1778-1984 (Ithaca, N.Y.: Cornell University Press, 1987), 49; Frederick E. Hoxie, *Parading Through History: The Making of the Crow Nation in America*, 1805-1935 (Cambridge: Cambridge University Press, 1995), 92-93.

6 Raymond J. DeMallie, "Yankton and Yanktonai," in *Handbook of North American Indians, Plains*, 777.

7 Ibid.; Raymond J. DeMallie, "Sioux Until 1850," in *Handbook of the North American Indians, Plains*, 740-43, 754-55; Denig, *Five Indian Tribes*, 34-35.

8 Mark Diedrich, *Famous Chiefs of the Eastern Sioux* (Minneapolis: Coyote Books, 1987), 29.

9 Jacqueline C. Peterson, "Gathering at the River: The Métis Peopling of the Northern Plains," in *The Fur Trade in North Dakota*, Virginia L. Heidenreich, ed. (Bismarck: State Historical Society of North Dakota, 1990), 47-54; Gregory S. Camp, "The Chippewa Fur Trade in the Red River Valley of the North, 1790-1830," in *The Fur Trade in North Dakota*, 33-37; John E. Foster, "The Plains Métis," in *Native Peoples: The Canadian Experience*, R. Bruce Morrison and C. Roderick Wilson, eds. (Toronto: McClelland and Stewart, 1986), 379-85; John E. Foster, "Wintering: The Outsider Adult Male and the Ethnogenesis of the Western Plains Métis," *Prairie Forum* 19 (1994): 1-11; Stanley N. Murray, "The Turtle Mountain Chippewa, 1882-1905," *North Dakota History* 51 (1984): 15-19.

10 Diedrich, *Famous Chiefs of the Eastern Sioux*, 34-35.

11 Harry H. Anderson, "Before the Indian Claims Commission," Docket No. 74, Sioux Nation, et al. v. United States of America, n.d., 19.

12 Denig, *Five Indian Tribes*, 29-32; Diedrich, *Famous Chiefs of the Eastern Sioux*, 33-36.

13 Denig, *Five Indian Tribes*, 30-35; Diedrich, *Famous Chiefs of the Eastern Sioux*, 33-37.

14 Denig, *Five Indian Tribes*, 24-25, 27.

15 DeMallie, "Sioux Until 1850," 734; David J. Wishart, *The Fur Trade of the American West*, 1807-1840: *A Geographic Synthesis* (Lincoln: University of Nebraska Press, 1979), 56-61, 66, 86-87.

16 DeMallie, "Sioux Until 1850," 734; Ray H. Mattison, "The Indian Frontier on the Upper Missouri to 1865, *Nebraska History* 39 (September 1958): 245, 247, 249; Edward E. Hill, *The Office of Indian Affairs, 1824-1880: Historical Sketches* (New York: Clearwater Publishing Company, 1974), 184-85.

17 Francis Paul Prucha, *The Great Father: The United States Government and the American Indians*, abridged edition, (Lincoln: University of Nebraska Press, 1984), 115-17; Jeffrey Ostler, *The Plains Sioux and U.S. Colonialism from Lewis and Clark to Wounded Knee* (Cambridge: Cambridge University Press, 2004), 35-38.

18 DeMallie, "Yankton and Yanktonai," 777, 780.

19 DeMallie, "Yankton and Yanktonai," 780-81; Robert M. Utley, *The Lance and the Shield: The Life and Times of Sitting Bull* (New York: Ballantine Books, 1993), 45-49.

20 John C. Ewers, "When the Light Shone in Washington," *Montana: The Magazine of Western History* 6 (Autumn 1956): 3-6; Denig, *Five Indian Tribes*, 86-87, 113-14.

21 Denig, *Five Indian Tribes*, 83-86; Charles J. Kappler, ed., *Indian Affairs. Laws and Treaties*, vol. 2 (Washington, D.C.: Government Printing Office, 1904), 594.

22 Kappler, 594-94; John C. Ewers, *The Blackfeet: Raiders on the Northwestern Plains* (Norman: University of Oklahoma Press, 1958, 1976), 206-7.

23 Harry Anderson, "The Controversial Sioux Amendment to the Fort Laramie Treaty of 1851," *Nebraska History* 37 (September 1956): 201-2, 210, 219-20; Raymond J. DeMallie, "The Sioux in Dakota and Montana Territories: Cultural and Historical Background of the Ogden B. Read Collection, in *Vestiges of a Proud Nation: The Ogden B. Read Northern Plains Indian Collection*, Glenn E. Markoe, ed. (Burlington: Robert Hull Fleming Museum, University of Vermont), 23; Utley, 43.

24 Denig, *Five Indian Tribes*, 36.

25 Beth R. Ritter, "Dispossession to Diminishment: The Yankton Sioux Reservation, 1858-1998" (Ph.D. diss., University of Nebraska-Lincoln, 1999), 49-51, 64; Alan R. Woolworth, *Ethnohistorical Report on the Yankton Sioux* (New York: Garland Publishing, 1974), 166, 168-69, originally published as "Ethnohistorical Report on the Indian Occupancy of Royce Area No. 410," Docket 332-A, *Yankton Sioux v. United States*, 1974.

26 Alexander H. Redfield to Charles E. Mix, Commissioner of Indian Affairs [hereinafter cited as CIA] September 1, 1858, *Annual Report to the Secretary of Interior for the Year* 1858 [hereinafter cited as *Annual Report*] (Washington, D.C.: Government Printing Office, 1858), 436-38.

27 Michael P. Malone and Richard B. Roeder, *Montana: A History of Two Centuries* (Seattle: University of Washington Press, 1976), 51-52.

28 Samuel N. Latta to William P. Dole, Commissioner of Indian Affairs, August 27, 1862, *Annual Report*, 1862, 336.

29 Latta, *Annual Report*, 338, 340.

30 Latta, *Annual Report*, 336.

31 Latta, *Annual Report*, 337; Utley, 44, 46, 48-49.

32 Latta, *Annual Report*, 339.

33 Alfred J. Vaughn to Alfred Cumming, [Central] Superintendent Indian Affairs, August 20, 1857, *Annual Report*, 1857, 408; Alexander H. Redfield to Colonel John Haverty, Superintendent of Indian Affairs (St. Louis), *Annual Report*, 1857, 416, 418.

34 Refield to Haverty, *Annual Report*, 339-40.

35 Latta, *Annual Report*, 339; Malone and Roeder, *Montana: A History of Two Centuries*, 46, 56-57; Don C. Miller and Stan B. Cohen, *Military and Trading Posts of Montana* (Missoula: Pictorial Histories Publishing Company, 1978), 12-13; William E. Lass, *A History of Steamboating on the Upper Missouri River* (Lincoln: University of Nebraska Press, 1962), 5-19, 44-46, 51-54, 63, 130-32;

36 Utley, *The Lance and the Shield*, 49-51.

37 Robert M. Utley, *Frontiersmen in Blue: The United States Army and the Indian, 1848-1865* (New York: The Macmillan Company, 1967), 264-71.

38 Utley, *Frontiersmen in Blue*, 272-73; Mark Diedrich, *The Odyssey of Chief Standing Buffalo and the Northern Sisseton Sioux* (Minneapolis: Coyote Books, 1988), 50-53; Brigadier General Henry H. Sibley to Major J.F. Meline, Assistant Adjutant General, Department of the Northwest, August 7, 1863, in *War of the Rebellion: Official Records of the Union and Confederate Armies*, series 1, vol. 22, pt. 1, 352-59.

39 Utley, *Frontiersmen in Blue*, 273-74; Diedrich, *Famous Chiefs of the Eastern Sioux*, 54; Brigadier General Alfred Sully to Meline, Acting Assistant Adjutant General, Department of the Northwest, September 11, 1863, *War of the Rebellion*, series 1, vol. 22, pt. 1, 555-61.

40 Major General John Pope to Major General H. W. Halleck, March 20, 1864, *War of the Rebellion*, ser. 1, vol. 34, pt. 2, 677-678; Sibley to Sully, April 30, 1864, *War of the Rebellion*, ser. 1, vol. 34, pt. 3, 368-69.

41 Sully to the Assistant Adjutant General, Department of the Northwest, July 31, 1864, *War of the Rebellion*, ser. 1, vol. 41, pt. 1, 141-44; Utley, *The Lance and the Shield*, 54-58.

42 Sully to the Assistant Adjutant General of the Northwest, October, 7, 1865, *War of the Rebellion*, ser. 1, vol. 41, pt. 3, 698-99.

43 Ibid., 698.

44 Sully to the Assistant Adjutant General of the Northwest, January 6, 1865, *War of the Rebellion*, ser. 1, vol. 48, pt. 1, 438; Colonel Charles A. R. Dimon to Lieutenant Colonel Edward P. Ten Broeck, Acting Assistant Adjutant General, District of Iowa, January 24, 1865, *War of the Rebellion*, ser. 1, vol. 48, pt. 1, 636-37;

45 Sully to the Assistant Adjutant General, Department of the Missouri, August 13, 1865, *War of the Rebellion*, ser. 1, vol. 48, pt. 1, 1182.

46 Sully to the Assistant Adjutant General, Department of the Missouri, August 26, 1865, *War of the Rebellion*, ser. 1, vol. 48, pt. 1, 1215-16.

47 Ibid., 1216.

48 DeMallie, "Yankton and Yanktonai," 781; George E. Hyde, *Red Cloud's Folk: A History of the Oglala Sioux Indians* (Norman: University of Oklahoma Press, 1937, 1976), 134-39; Utley, *The Lance and the Shield*, 70-71.

49 DeMallie, "Yankton and Yanktonai," 781-82, 785.

50 DeMallie, "Sioux in Dakota and Montana Territories," 29.

51 "Report of the Northwestern Treaty Commission to the Sioux of the Upper Missouri," August 25, 1866, in *Annual Report*, 1866, 171-73.

52 Ewers, *The Blackfeet*, 236-45; Secretary of Interior Orville H. Browning to Commissioner of Indian Affairs Nathaniel G. Taylor, March 26, 1868, National Archives and Records Administration, Record Group 75, Records of the Bureau of Indian Affairs, M234, Letters Received Commissioner of Indian Affairs [hereafter cited as LRCIA], Roll 492 (1872), frames 1159-60; William J. Cullen to Acting Indian Affairs Commissioner Charles E. Mix, July 5, 1868, LRCIA, Roll 488, frames 958-60.

53 Ewers, *The Blackfeet*, 242-44; Newton Edmunds, Dakota Territorial Governor, to James Harlan, Secretary of Interior, September 22, 1866, *Annual Report*, 1866, 179.

54 William J. Cullen to Acting Indian Affairs Commissioner Charles E. Mix, July 15, 1868, LRCIA, Roll 488, frames 978-80.

55 Hoxie, *Parading Through History*, 90-95, 98-101, 104-6.

56 Cullen to Taylor, July 25, 1868, LRCIA, Roll 488, frames 967-68; Acting Indian Affairs Commissioner to W. T. Otto, Acting Secretary of Interior, September 8, 1868, Roll 488, frames 970-76; Cullen to Taylor, October 22, 1868, LRCIA, Roll 488, frames 1075-77; DeMallie, "Sioux in Dakota and Montana Territories," 28.

57 Agent A. S. Reed to Montana Superintendent, Sully, August 12, 1869, *Annual Report*, 1869, 740-41; Sully to Indian Commissioner Ely S. Parker, September 23, 1869, *Annual Report*, 1869, 731, 734-35; DeMallie, "Sioux in Dakota and Montana Territories," 28.

58 Charles J. Kappler, ed., *Indian Affairs. Laws and Treaties*, vol. 2 (Washington, D.C.: GPO, 1904), 736-40, 855-56.

59 Hoxie, *Parading Through History*, 42; DeMallie, "Sioux in Dakota and Montana Territories," 28; DeMallie and Miller, "Assiniboine," 583; Reed to Sully, August 12, 1869, 741-42.

60 DeMallie, "Sioux in Dakota and Montana Territories," 28; DeMallie and Miller, "Assiniboine," 583; Reed to Sully, August 12, 1869, 741-42; Hoxie, *Parading Through History*, 94, 110.

61 DeMallie, "Sioux in Dakota and Montana Territories," 28-29.

62 Denig, *Five Indian Tribes*, 34-35.

63 DeMallie, "Sioux in Dakota and Montana Territories," 29.

64 Reed to Sully, August 31, 1870, *Annual Report*, 1870, 664-65.

65 Ibid., 664.

66 David Reed Miller, "Montana Assiniboine Identity: A Cultural Account of an American Indian Ethnicity," (Ph. D. diss., Indiana University, 1987), 106-7.

67 Acting Secretary of Interior Jacob D. Cox to Parker, October 22, 1870, LRCIA, Roll 490, frame 170; Montana Superintendent Jasper A. Viall to Parker, *Annual Report*, 1870, 827-28; Interim Agent C. S. Clark to Superintendent Viall, December 1, 1870, LRCIA, Roll 490, frames 872-74.

68 Brevet Brigadier General Henry A. Morrow to Brevet Brigadier General Greene, Assistant Adjutant General, Department of Dakota, September 9, Letters Sent, Fort Buford, RG 393, National Archives and Research Service [hereafter cited as NARS]; DeMallie, "Sioux in Dakota and Montana Territories," 28.

69 Morrow to Greene, September 14, 1869, Letters Sent, Fort Buford, NARS; DeMallie, "Sioux in Dakota and Montana Territories," 28-29.

70 Reed to Sully, August 31, 1870, *Annual Report*, 1870, 664-65; Sully to Parker, April 27, 1870, LRCIA, Roll 490, frames 436-38.

71 Special Agent Andrew J. Simmons to Jasper A. Viall, Montana Superintendent, May 12, 1871, LRCIA, Roll 491, frames 635-38.

72 Ibid., 638-42; Gary Clayton Anderson, *Little Crow: Spokesman for the Sioux* (St. Paul: Minnesota Historical Society Press, 1986),120, 135-45, 155, 172-74; Diedrich, 42-75.

73 James Larpenteur Long, *Land of Nakoda: The Story of the Assiniboine Indians* (Helena: State Publishing Company, 1942; reprint, *The Assiniboines: From the Accounts Of the Old Ones Told to First Boy (James Larpenteur Long)* (Norman: University of Oklahoma Press, 1961), 180-82.

74 Simmons to Viall, 641-45.

75 Ibid., 644-51.

76 Simmons to Viall, June 20, 1871, LRCIA, Roll 491, frames 806-8.

77 Ibid., 808.

78 Simmons to Viall, August 31, 1871, LRCIA, *Annual Report*, 1871, 846.

~

CHAPTER 4

The Sioux Transform the Milk River Agency, 1871-1877
Dennis J. Smith, Ph.D.

Milk River Indian Agent Andrew J. Simmons' peace agreements with Standing Buffalo, Struck by the Ree (the son), and Medicine Bear in late April and early May 1871 marked a significant new direction in Sioux relations with the Indian Affairs Office. Simmons honored their request for admission to the agency based on their promise to treat peacefully with the agency Gros Ventres and Assiniboines. Simmons fully understood the enormity of the situation with this substantial body of Sioux who had so recently arrived in eastern Montana Territory. In his extensive May 12, 1871 letter to his superior, Montana Indian Affairs Superintendent Jasper A. Viall, Simmons explained that these Sioux could not be compelled to return to the Grand River Agency, established in 1869 and renamed the Standing Rock Agency in 1875.[1] They had moved into the area because of bison, and they would stay as long as bison remained.

Simmons also appreciated that to secure these Sioux to the agency and keep them at peace with whites, the Indian Affairs Office would have to expend enormous sums to feed and clothe them. Simmons was confident of Standing Buffalo's commitment to peace, having met with him three times himself, and knowing of extended conversations between Standing Buffalo and Assiniboine Chief Red Stone. But Simmons doubted that Struck by the Ree's Yanktons and diverse Sioux tribal followers would remain peaceful, even if fully provided with food and clothing. "They appear to be made up of renegades from various bands composing a camp of about the worst Indians I ever saw."[2]

Superintendent Viall received Simmons' letter on May 18, 1871. From his office in Helena, Viall telegraphed a brief message to Indian Commissioner Ely S. Parker explaining that Standing Buffalo and Struck by the Ree demanded the same food and annuities provided the agency tribesmen as the terms of peace. Viall requested both permission to provide these and guidance on how much he could distribute. On May 20, Viall received Commissioner Parker's authorization to feed these Sioux "to a limited extent." Viall then authorized Simmons to distribute the Sioux food and provisions from supplies reserved for agency Assiniboines and Gros Ventres. He instructed Simmons to be economical, and that items provided the Sioux were "merely to relieve their actual wants."[3]

On May 20, 1871, the day Commissioner Parker approved limited provisions, Viall forwarded to Commissioner Simmons' May 12 letter, which fully explained his meetings and peace agreements with Standing Buffalo and Struck by the Ree. Viall in very business-like fashion endorsed Simmons' peace initiative, explaining that many of these Sioux had engaged in depredations against whites and had generally been hostile. Viall further agreed that if these Sioux kept their promises of peace, they should be admitted to the agency under the same provisions and treatment as the Gros Ventres and Assiniboines.[4]

Viall's May 20 letter and Simmons' letter enclosure were important, for they constituted the first details for Commissioner Parker about Simmons' Sioux peace diplomacy. But it was not until the following day that Viall recognized the momentous significance of the Sioux rapprochement. On May 21, 1871, Viall again wrote to Commissioner Parker, but now he confided a new unease about the Sioux presence, noting that they were "such a strong body." His real concern was the precarious nature of the new peace. He repeated Standing Buffalo's and Struck by the Ree's assertions that they came to the Milk River because of the buffalo, and they adamantly proclaimed they would not return to their former lands. Viall then explained his fears: If the Sioux were not fed by the Interior Department, "there will surely be trouble."

His immediate concern was with the Gros Ventres, who were "natural enemies" of the Sioux, but his ultimate fear was that the Sioux "if turned loose . . . will not only clear that country [the Milk River region] of friendly Indians, but make it very unsafe for many of the frontier settlers." To ensure that these Sioux would receive annuities on an equal footing with the Milk River Gros Ventres and Assiniboines, Viall recommended the government negotiate with them.[5]

For the second time in two years, federal officials were recommending treaties and agency status for the Sioux converging on the Missouri River plains in Montana Territory. In September 1869, two large parties mostly comprised of Upper Yanktonais had approached Fort Buford commander Lieutenant Colonel Henry A. Morrow, demanding reservation status. He recorded their request and recommended that a treaty be negotiated with them. Like Montana Superintendent Viall, Morrow forcefully asserted the wisdom of feeding and providing for these Sioux to secure their peace, and he appreciated the consequences of not doing so. Morrow explained that large numbers of disaffected and destitute Yanktonai warriors would be joining the ranks of non-treaty Hunkpapas like Sitting Bull, Black Moon, and Four Horns, "who are the Scourge of this Country for hundreds of Miles in All directions."[6]

The Indian Affairs Office failed to negotiate with the Montana Dakotas, Yanktonais, and Yanktons. Milk River Agent Simmons worried mightily about feeding the dramatically increased number of Natives who were now his responsibility. By mid-July, 1871, Montana Superintendent Viall had shipped almost $16,000 worth of food and provisions to replace Assiniboine and Gros Ventre annuities distributed to the Sioux. On August, 1, 1871, however, Acting Indian Commissioner H.R. Clum, who was filling in after Commissioner Parker's resignation, informed Viall that the Milk River Agency appropriations would remain unchanged at $40,000. Simmons was infuriated. He explained that he was now responsible for 4,850 agency Upper and Lower Assiniboines and Gros Ventres, and 6,800 Sioux—2,500 Dakotas led by Standing Buffalo's brother, and 4,300 Yanktons and Yanktonais.[7]

It appears that Acting Commissioner Clum was unaware of important communications between the Interior and War Departments since May 1871, when the Sioux demanded agency status. By mid-June, 1871, Secretary of War William W. Belknap had received correspondence and enclosures concerning the Milk River Agency peace agreement from Secretary of Interior Columbus Delano. On July, 18, 1871, Major W.H. Lewis from the U.S. Army Department of Dakota in St. Paul determined that any attempt to forcibly remove the Santees, Yanktons, and Yanktonais from the Milk River area would result in war. He further predicted that other Sioux bands would be drawn into the conflict. Lewis arrived at these conclusions from a recent visit to Fort Benton, on information provided by Agent Simmons. Major Lewis recommended continuing the policies already in motion: feeding the Sioux and trying to keep the peace. If this failed, the Army would have to drive the Sioux out of the country.[8]

Major General Winfield S. Hancock, Commander of the Department of Dakota in St. Paul, believed that even with a feeding program there was going to be trouble, making it necessary to settle "the Indian question" with force. But his department did not have sufficient cavalry or other troops in Montana, or throughout the upper Missouri River and Yellowstone River areas, to complete the job. He recommended deferring war until at least after the Northern Pacific Railroad had advanced further. Delay offered the opportunity to "give the Indians wiser views" and allow settlement of affairs without war. In the meantime, however, he strongly recommended additional troop and cavalry deployments at Fort Buford.[9]

Lieutenant General Philip H. Sheridan, Commander of the Division of the Missouri in Chicago, concurred with Hancock, recommending the build-up commence in the spring of 1872. This included moving at least four cavalry and three infantry companies to Fort Buford, which for the past three to four years had been "practically in a state of siege." Last, General William Tecumseh Sherman, Commander of the Army, agreed, and on August 7, 1871 forwarded his recommendation to Belknap. "The Army is in no condition to meet the requirements of a war with the Sioux in the inaccessible region about the Milk River. All our measures in that quarter are 'defensive,' and necessarily very weak."[10]

The rapid and formidable migration of Sioux into eastern Montana Territory in the late 1860s and early 1870s profoundly affected resident tribes, federal Indian policy, and Army officials. The Santees, Yanktons, and Upper Yanktonais initated the drama when in May 1871 they declared they would reside in the Milk River area and demanded admission to the Milk River Agency in exchange for peace with whites, Gros Ventres, and Upper Assiniboines. They were large and powerful, some 6,800 in number, and had been "bad" and "hostile" Sioux who had fought against the U.S. Army and attacked whites, both overland and steamboat travelers. Yet they were not the Sioux in Montana Territory with whom federal officials were most concerned. They were preoccupied with the Lakotas.

After Spotted Tail and Red Cloud led their Sicangu and Oglala Lakotas, respectively, to reservation life by signing the 1868 Fort Laramie Treaty, Sitting Bull and the Hunkpapas rose to leadership of non-agency and non-treaty Lakotas. Hunkpapas were pre-eminent in conflicts with whites and the Army in the upper Missouri region. They led the resistance to white overland and river traffic up the Missouri River after two Sans Arc Lakotas killed Hunkpapa chief Bear's Rib at Fort Pierre in June 1862.

After the Dakota uprising in August 1862, Hunkpapas hunting bison on the plains east of the Missouri River clashed with Brigadier General Henry Hastings Sibley in July 1863 in the battles of Dead Buffalo Lake and Stony Lake. In September 1863, they and Upper Yanktonais suffered a humiliating defeat by General Alfred Sully at Whitestone Hill, and again in July 1864, at Killdeer Mountain.[11]

New upper Missouri River military posts established by General Sully became important Hunkpapa targets. Notable was Fort Rice, constructed in 1865 on the Missouri River's west bank ten miles up from the Cannonball River which presently serves as the northern boundary of the Standing Rock Reservation. Fort Buford, constructed in 1866 at the confluence of the Yellowstone River and two miles downstream from the abandoned Fort Union trading post, provoked Hunkpapa fury because it was on lands they had recently controlled. Sitting Bull attacked wood and haying parties repeatedly.[12]

Hunkpapas and their close Lakota allies, the Sans Arcs and Blackfeet (Sioux), did not participate in the 1866-1868 engagements led by Red Cloud's Oglalas and other Lakota, Cheyenne, and Northern Arapaho allies in the Powder River area to close the Bozeman Trail and Forts Reno, Kearny, and C.F. Smith. After the Army closed the Bozeman Trail and abandoned Forts Kearny and C.F. Smith in August 1868, Red Cloud eventually went to Fort Laramie in November and signed the famous treaty.[13]

The 1867-1868 treaty commissioners sent Jesuit missionary Pierre-Jean de Smet to meet with the non-treaty Hunkpapas, and in June 1868, he visited their camp south of the Yellowstone River near the mouth of the Powder River. Sitting Bull told de Smet that the Lakotas should sell no land, woodcutting along the Missouri River for steamboats needed to stop, and the Army must abandon Forts Rice and Buford. Civil chiefs Four Horns and Black Moon and Sitting Bull, the head war chief, refused to accompany de Smet to Fort Rice to meet with three treaty commissioners waiting there. Instead they dispatched a delegation of lesser chiefs, headed by war chief Gall.

Gall and the others met with the commissioners, and although the treaty was read to them, it seemed clear that Gall and the Hunkpapa leaders had no real understanding of the contents. When given the opportunities to address the commissioners, Gall unequivocally asserted Hunkpapa terms for peace similar to those told earlier to Father de Smet: the Army had to abandon its posts on the upper Missouri and prohibit any further steamboat travel. These conditions openly conflicted with the treaty, yet for unclear reasons Gall and the others signed it. Gall was not authorized to sign for the primary chiefs, and he did not appear to be signing on their behalf. The non-agency Hunkpapas had clearly stated their objections to the 1868 treaty, both to De Smet and to the treaty commissioners at Fort Rice, and the signing by Gall and the other lesser chiefs in no way signified their acceptance of the treaty.[14]

Sitting Bull continued to raid Fort Buford until September 1870, when he led his last war party there. By this time, these northern Hunkpapas had changed to a defensive military posture toward whites and the government: they would take up arms only if attacked or if their bison lands were threatened. This transformation reflected the western shift of permanent residence away from Fort Buford. By 1870, they lived almost exclusively in the lower Yellowstone and Missouri River prairies of eastern Montana Territory, far from white settlements.

Hunkpapas and their Sans Arc and Blackfeet Lakota allies had quickly pushed the Crows out of the Powder River watershed, and were aggressively moving west toward the Bighorn River area. Lakotas established primary control of the bison-rich lands between the Yellowstone and Missouri Rivers as far west as the Musselshell River. In the summer, they hunted primarily south of the Yellowstone with non-agency Oglala, Sicangu, and Minneconjou kinsmen and Cheyennes. Hunkpapa winter camps now increasingly centered south of the Missouri River in the lower Big Dry and Red Water Creeks, directly across from the mouths of the Milk and Poplar Rivers.[15]

Sitting Bull's Hunkpapas were in this region in May 1871, when Standing Buffalo met with Milk River Agent Simmons. Lieutenant William Quinton had just arrived from Fort Shaw, a military post built on the Sun River in 1867, just west of present-day Great Falls, with Milk River Agency annuity provisions. According to Quinton, Standing Buffalo declared that his Dakotas and Struck by the Ree's Yanktons were merely "the advance guards of the Sioux Nation, which are expected to settle in Montana . . . they are all coming." Standing Buffalo explained that Sitting Bull and 800 Hunkpapa lodges were just across the river, and "moving in this direction."

Even more extraordinarily, Standing Buffalo correctly explained that many Lakotas joining Sitting Bull were disenchanted Oglalas from the Red Cloud Agency. He explained that Red Cloud had just visited the Great Father in Washington, and that "Red Cloud saw too much. The Indians say that these things cannot be: that the white people must have put bad Medicine over Red Cloud's eyes to make him see everything and anything that they pleased."[16]

In fact, Red Cloud had demanded and was permitted a June 1870 trip to Washington, D.C. to address a number of injustices concerning the 1868 Fort Laramie Treaty. Most important was Red Cloud's demand that his agency be established on the North Platte River near Fort Laramie. This placed the Indian Affairs Office and Interior Department in a ticklish position, for these were lands in present-day southeastern Wyoming far removed from the Great Sioux Reservation. Standing Buffalo was correct: Red Cloud achieved nothing from his trip, and his standing among his Oglala tribesmen deteriorated, as did their condition, while federal officials stalled on the agency location.[17]

Montana Superintendent Jasper A. Viall understood the strategic issues related to Sitting Bull's Hunkpapas. On August 21, 1871, he advised the Indian Affairs Commissioner Parker that Sitting Bull's Hunkpapas controlled the Yellowstone River lands where the Northern Pacific Railroad route was planned, and that to the best of his knowledge they planned to stop survey parties and railroad construction. Viall explained that Milk River Agent Simmons' peace plan for the Dakotas, Yanktons, and Upper Yanktonais was working well and would continue to do so with sustained food and provisions.

Viall asked for authority to meet Sitting Bull and offer the same conditions of food and provisions in exchange for peace. In addition, Viall suggested a new reservation for them, recommending lands between the 105th and 108th degrees west longitude and between the Missouri River and the international boundary. This region was immediately east of the Milk River Agency and extended east to approximately the confluence of the Poplar River. He strongly recommended the location for its richness in bison and remoteness from white settlement.[18]

On September 6, 1871, Secretary of Interior Columbus Delano granted Superintendent Viall's request, but Viall declined when the War Department refused to provide an Army detail to escort him to Sitting Bull's camp in the Yellowstone River area. Agent Simmons agreed to replace Viall, who instructed Simmons that the key objectives were to determine the Hunkpapa disposition for peace and their willingness to send a treaty delegation to Washington. Simmons invited the Lakotas to meet him at the nearby Fort Peck trading post, established in 1866 by the Durfee & Peck Company on the north bank of the Missouri River about three miles upstream from the mouth of the Milk River. Fort Peck was directly across the Missouri River from the mouth of Big Dry Creek, a Hunkpapa wintering area. In fact, earlier that fall the Hunkpapas had finally accepted the Fort Peck trader's repeated offers to open trading relations. Sitting Bull had even visited the post in early September.[19]

Sitting Bull informed Agent Simmons that he desired to attend, but could not due to a recent camp dispute. Agent Simmons sent an unnamed Assiniboine chief to invite the Hunkpapas to Fort Peck. While this Assiniboine was smoking with Hunkpapa leaders, someone in camp stole his horse. Sitting Bull was aghast and immediately offered to give him a horse, but the Assiniboine man, surely infuriated, refused and walked the entire fifty miles back to Fort Peck. The camp chiefs and *akicitas* (soldiers) sought out the perpetrator, and in what apparently was a turbulent affair, the *akicitas* feared for Sitting Bull's security and refused to let him leave.[20]

Chief Black Moon was the ranking Hunkpapa leader, accompanied by Chiefs Iron Dog, Song Dog, Little Wound, Sitting Eagle, and Bear's Rib, who met with Agent Simmons in fifteen lengthy meetings over a twenty-one-day period. Simmons explained that he served as a mes-

senger for the Great White Father, who wanted peace. All the tribes around the Lakotas now in Montana Territory, including the Milk River Agency Santees and Yanktonais, had made peace with the whites and were contented. Game was fast disappearing, and if the Hunkpapas continued their warfare, they would also disappear and perish with the buffalo. Simmons did not have the authority to negotiate a treaty, he explained, but he urged the Hunkpapas to send a delegation of chiefs to negotiate one with the Great White Father. Simmons would accompany them and ensure their safe travel.[21]

Black Moon declared that he too strongly favored peace, and that Sitting Bull agreed with him and would stand by him. Most of the headmen and those whom Simmons labeled "men of sense" wanted peace. Black Moon explained what the president must do to secure Lakota peace. He must stop the Northern Pacific Railroad, for it was going into their country and would destroy their game. The white soldiers and other whites must be kept out of Hunkpapa country. The Lakotas would not make peace with the soldiers, so Fort Buford must be abandoned, as must the Fort Hawley trading post near the junction of the Musselshell and Missouri Rivers. In essence, Black Moon was saying that whites had to be removed from Fort Buford on the east to the trading post on the western side. Black Moon demanded that Simmons tell these things to the President. Concerning a tribal delegation to Washington, the Hunkpapas would "smoke" over the proposition when he returned to his camp.[22]

During these meetings, one Hunkpapa declared that he would make war upon the railroad "to the last." Simmons countered that the railroad would be built, and that the Hunkpapas "might as well undertake to stop the Missouri River from flowing down stream as to stop the railroad." Simmons explained that the railroad was a good thing, which would bring presents and provisions to the Indians from the President.

Simmons repeatedly emphasized the foolishness of warring against the railroad. He argued that the Sioux had already attempted and failed to stop one railroad, referring to the Union Pacific, built through the Platte River valley, and the same would be true of this railroad. The Great Father was strong and powerful and his white children were as numerous as the trees in the mountains. However, "The Great Father's heart was good," and concerning the Lakotas, "he took pity upon them because they were weak and inferior."

Simmons said Lakota warriors should be brave men who thought of their women and children and chose not to subject them to the sacrifice of war and starvation. He warned that Lakotas could no longer wage war against white soldiers like they had in the past in the lower country further down the Missouri River. In the present world of disappearing game, now when the soldiers raided a camp, they would keep the Indians moving for thirty days; they would starve to death and die like wolves.[23]

Black Moon denied, however, that the Hunkpapas had all made up their minds about fighting the railroad. In fact, Black Moon told an extraordinary story about the lengths to which the Hunkpapas desired peace. Apparently during the negotiations with Agent Simmons, the Lakotas prohibited the departure of any more war parties, presumably against whites.

Very recently the chiefs and *akicitas* in Sitting Bull's camp had forcibly intervened to stop the departure of a war party. Black Moon stated that Sitting Bull's camp now mourned, because the *akicitas* ended up killing eight men and twenty horses, and cutting up a number of lodges. Black Moon was determined that this extraordinary measure be fully reported, and he asked Simmons if the person writing down the council

conversations did so to take it to the Great Father. Simmons assured Black Moon that this was the case. Simmons at first did not believe Black Moon's story, but he then confessed that many different sources corroborated the account in such reliable ways that he was fully persuaded of the chief's truthfulness.[24]

As negotiations neared completion, Black Moon forcefully advocated that were peace established, the federal government must guarantee to feed his people. He explained that Hunkpapas did not want the white man's civilization, for they knew the experience at the lower agencies where their children were tied up and whipped. The Lakotas simply "wanted something to eat." This would especially be the case, Black Moon continued, if the Lakotas permitted the railroad to pass and the new white settlements destroyed the game. Other Hunkpapas then testified about their often destitute conditions.

It was at this point, on November 15, 1871, that runners arrived from the Hunkpapa camp. Lakota scouts had spotted two parties of soldiers in the Yellowstone River. Black Moon confronted Agent Simmons and wanted to know if the soldiers were coming to attack his people. Simmons explained that the troops were supporting engineers surveying the proposed railroad route, and intended no harm, if not attacked. Simmons then challenged Black Moon's recent pledge of peace. Black Moon and his party deliberated and then sent Black Moon's son as a messenger to their camp advising them to avoid the soldiers and to avoid war with the whites.[25]

Black Moon and the Hunkpapas kept their word and the small surveying party proceeded without harm. As promised, Agent Simmons' letter to his superiors fully recognized this concession. In his overall assessment, Simmons exaggerated, saying that many of the chiefs and leading men fully understood the consequences of being surrounded and overpowered by whites should such things as the Northern Pacific Railroad proceed. He also categorically overstated that "They have a wholesome fear of the power of the Government and its military which will prove the most influential motive in inducing them to accept peace."

Agent Simmons assessed the prospects for peace more realistically and guardedly. That a portion of the Teton Sioux were willing and anxious to make peace was certain. And if the steps already taken (his peace agreement with Black Moon, presumably) were promptly followed, the whole Hunkpapa tribe might be reconciled. He believed that some depredations were likely, but prospects for a thorough peace with "this powerful and aggressive band" seemed uncertain and "improbable." Their recent peaceful gesture, however, justified similar peaceful gestures from the government, and he was certain much could be accomplished. He especially recommended "prompt and substantial aid" to Black Moon's peace party to help ensure the present peace.[26]

Providing for the Hunkpapas and their Lakota allies would be expensive, for Simmons estimated there were 1,400 lodges near the Fort Peck trading post. Estimating eight persons per lodge, Simmons calculated the Lakota population at 11,200 persons. On December 23, 1871, Montana Indian Affairs Superintendent Viall fully endorsed Simmons' negotiations and urgently appealed that Black Moon's 200 lodges be given the promised food and provisions.[27]

The status of the food and provisions available to the Milk River Agency Assiniboines, Gros Ventres, and Sioux (Santees, Yanktons, Yanktonais, and Hunkpapa Lakotas) during the 1871-1872 winter is very confusing. On January 3, 1872, Agent Simmons sent an urgent letter to Montana Superintendent Viall stating that funds for the fiscal year were now exhausted, but he had not received additional subsistence provisions for the large number of Santees and

Yanktonais attached to his agency during the summer of 1871. He explained that all supplies would be exhausted by the end of January, and the situation was compounded because this was one of the severest winters in years and winter bison harvests were low. He requested emergency authority to purchase 300,000 pounds of pemmican and dried buffalo meat.[28]

In Agent Simmons' annual report to the Indian Commissioner, written in September 1871, he told how agency tribesmen were forced to eat their horses and dogs. Only the timely relief from the Indian Affairs Office prevented great suffering and starvation. Simmons did not indicate when this relief arrived. In his 1872 annual report to the Secretary of Interior, however, Indian Commissioner Francis A. Walker reported that "For the Sioux at the Milk River agency [sic] an extraordinary appropriation of $150,000 was made the last year, to provide them with subsistence." This funding was truly extraordinary for the agency, which usually received annual appropriations for Assiniboines and Gros Ventres of $30,000 and $35,000, respectively.[29]

Both the nature and date of this appropriation are unclear. Surely this supplemental appropriation was needed to provide for the 6,800 Santees, Yanktons, and Yanktonais whom the Indian Affairs Office had agreed to feed and provision virtually overnight, in return for peace. The amount—$150,000—was remarkable, for the Indian Affairs Office had instructed Agent Simmons to feed the Sioux only to a limited extent, and Montana Indian Superintendent Viall directed distribution only to relieve actual needs. Simmons fed, clothed, and provided for 4,850 Assiniboines and Gros Ventres—however marginally—on $65,000.[30]

Most likely, this large sum included supplemental monies for what would be large numbers of the estimated 11,200 Hunkpapa Lakotas resulting from Black Moon's peace agreement of

November, 1871.[31] Perhaps the $150,000 appropriation cited by Commissioner Walker represented a cumulative figure, one addressing the new demands concerning Santees, Yanktons, and Yanktonais, and a much later Lakota supplement. Whatever the case, it appears that appropriations came late in the 1871-1872 winter, causing Sioux suffering and disappointment.

Equally unclear is whether this special appropriation was intended in part or even exclusively for the Hunkpapa Lakotas, with whom Agent Simmons had brokered a peace agreement of sorts in November 1871. In his 1872 annual report, Simmons stated that "After considerable delay, which came near frustrating the whole design [the peace agreement in exchange for food and provisions], I received instructions to furnish them with subsistence."[32]

During the 1871-1872 winter, Hunkpapa war chiefs Gall and Red Horn returned to the Grand River Agency, but 700 lodges of Black Moon's and Sitting Bull's followers camped near the Fort Peck trading post. They received only periodic rations. By the end of winter, the Hunkpapas appeared frustrated, for on April 16, 1872, Agent Simmons telegraphed Superintendent Viall that they wanted to know "if the government was going to do anything for them." They demanded food, blankets, and clothing, or they would break their November 1871 peace agreement. Simmons demanded immediate authority to feed them to prevent their going to war. The special Sioux appropriations must have arrived by June, for on the 9th Simmons reported to Indian Commissioner Walker that the Tetons arrived at the Fort Peck trading post almost daily for provisions, and Sitting Bull's camp was expected soon. The agency was not fully stocked, however, for Simmons asked for more blankets and clothing.[33]

The federal government continued to be preoccupied with the Montana Sioux. In May 1872, Indian Commissioner Francis A. Walker secured an even more extraordinary Congressional appropriation of $500,000. There was no ambiguity about these monies, which were directed at the Lakotas. Commissioner Walker took office in November, 1871, months after Army Generals Winfield S. Hancock, Commander of the Department of Dakota, Philip H. Sheridan, Commander of the Division of the Missouri, William T. Sherman, Commanding General, and Secretary of War William W. Belknap all recommended that the Department of Interior feed the Montana Sioux to give the Army time to expand its capabilities to militarily defeat them.[34] General Sherman called it a "defensive" military policy based on the Army's weakness in that part of the frontier. Commissioner Walker called it a "temporizing" policy, and was unapologetic about its intentions and consequences. The problem with Walker's defense of conquest was that he equated Lakota resistance with evil.

Concerning the federal government's policies with "semi-hostile" tribes, Walker challenged critics who claimed that it was "merely temporizing with an evil." He stated that if an evil was increasing, then temporizing was cowardly and mischievous. If an evil was not increasing, yet did not appear to be self-destructing from its own vices, then it must be met without hesitation.[35] Walker saw resisting tribes and tribal cultures such as the Lakotas as already in decline.

Walker believed temporizing reflected the highest statesmanship "When an evil is in it nature self-limited, and tends to expire by the very conditions of its existence." Tribes could not overcome American modernization, for "the whole progress of the physical, social, and industrial order by steady degrees circumscribes its field, reduces it dimensions, and saps its strength." Walker conceded that tribes opposed white expansion because it destroyed their subsistence and even their lives, yet the resistance was still evil. "Such an evil is that which the

United States Government at present encounters in the resistance, more or less suppressed, of the Indian tribes of this continent to the progress of railroads and settlements."

Walker believed that this cultural clash was unique in all recorded history for one reason: "never was an evil so gigantic environed, invaded, devoured by forces so tremendous, so appalling in the celerity and the certainty of their advance."[36] Taken literally, this statement admitted to American conquest of Indian tribes. More likely, Walker meant it figuratively.

In his June 13, 1872 letter to Indian Commissioner Walker announcing the $500,000 appropriation, Secretary of Interior Delano also explained he had appointed Assistant Interior Secretary Benjamin R. Cowen to a delegation to meet with the Hunkpapas and bring them to Washington, D.C., to negotiate a treaty. In his November 1872 annual report, Walker explained the purpose of Cowen's treaty commission.

Summarizing the special Indian commissions for the year, Walker's account of the Cowen commission focused on the Northern Pacific Railroad, stating Cowen provided new and important information on the "numbers and temper of the Indians who confront the Northern Pacific Railroad in its progress beyond the Missouri River." Similarly, when discussing the Northern Pacific Railroad in the general category of Indians and railroads, Walker explained that the Cowen commission "visited this section of the country during the past summer *for the especial purpose of removing the objections of the Indians to the progress of the road* [the Northern Pacific Railroad]" [emphasis added].[37]

The treaty commission headed by Assistant Secretary Cowen included N.J. Turney and John W. Wham, recently relieved as agent at the Red Cloud Agency. They reached the Fort Peck trading post on July 26, 1872. At some point they were joined by two other parties that Cowens

telegraphed on his way to Montana Territory. The one coming from the Red Cloud Agency was led by its new agent, Dr. J.W. Daniels, and a number of Lakota leaders, the most distinguished of which were Red Dog, High Wolf, and Wolf's Ears. Grand River Agent J.C. O'Connor could not attend but sent an unspecified delegation of seven Lakota leaders. Inviting these agency Lakotas was unusual, but it was likely thought that agency Lakotas might help persuade Sitting Bull and Black Moon to sign a treaty. Red Dog and High Wolf had some experience, having recently traveled with Red Cloud to Washington.[38]

As a Hunkpapa treaty commission, Cowen's entire mission was a serious failure. Most significantly, Hunkpapa chiefs failed to meet the commissioners. Sitting Bull sent his brother-in-law His Horse Looking, who served primarily to bring the message that Sitting Bull would come to the Fort Peck trading post in the winter to talk peace. The commission was resigned to meeting with what Sioux tribesmen happened to be in the Fort Peck area at the time. Medicine Bear was there with a few lodges when the commission arrived and in three days, 453 lodges had assembled, but all were Upper Yanktonais except for sixty-nine Hunkpapas.

The tribal leaders met in council on August 21 and 22, and the chiefs were most interested in the impending railroad construction. Despite their persistence, the commissioners refused to discuss it, stating the Sioux needed to take this up with the Great Father in Washington. The Sioux leaders vigorously demanded more guns and ammunition for bison hunting, but the federal officials flatly refused. The chiefs voiced a third concern about the location of an agency, apparently demanding an agency at the site of the Fort Peck trading post, a proposition the commission strongly recommended to Secretary Delano. For unspecified reasons, the Sioux chiefs unanimously and vigorously opposed sending a delegation to Washington.[39]

Joined by Milk River Agent Andrew J. Simmons, the delegation left the Fort Peck trading post for Washington on August 30, 1872. The composition of the delegation had changed. The two Lakota delegations invited to facilitate negotiations had departed before the August 21 and 22 councils, with Commissioner Cowen referring to apparent tensions between them and the Montana Hunkpapas. The Lakotas from Grand River in particular were dismissed because "their presence did not seem to conduce to the object we had in view."

In spite of widespread opposition to a delegation, Hunkpapas who went included Bloody Mouth, Bulrushes (or Bull Rushes), Lost Medicine, and Black Horn. At the suggestion of Interior Secretary Delano, a number of Milk River Agency Yanktonai chiefs and warriors joined the Washington delegation, including Medicine Bear, Afraid of the Bear, Black Eye, Black Catfish, Skin of the Heart, Eagle Packer, Red Thunder, Long Fox, and Gray Crane Walking. Milk River Agency Santees did not attend the council or go to Washington.[40]

When the delegation arrived at the Grand River Agency, commission chair Cowen added agent J.C. O'Connor, who had been unable to attend the meetings at Fort Peck. Accompanying him were Hunkpapa chiefs Bear's Rib, Running Antelope, and Thunder Hawk, and Blackfeet Lakotas The Grass, Sitting Crow, and Iron Scare. Upper Yanktonai chiefs included Big Head, Black Eye (not the same Black Eye, also an Upper Yanktonai who joined the delegation from Montana), and Big Razee. Lower Yanktonai chiefs were Two Bears, Red Bear, and Bull's Ghost.[41]

The delegation returned to the Fort Peck trading post on November 20, 1872. Assistant Secretary Cowen failed to achieve his commission's primary objective. They never met with the key Hunkpapa chiefs, Sitting Bull, Black Moon, and Four Horns, and no treaty was negotiated in Washington. In fact, neither Cowen, Indian Commissioner Walker, nor Milk River Agent Simmons mention any tribal deliberations there.[42]

The Cowen Commission proved monumentally important, however, in securing agency status for Montana Sioux, particularly to Milk River Agency Santees, Yanktons, and Yanktonais. The Indian Affairs Office treated them as agency tribesmen after their May 1871 peace agreements with Agent Simmons, though they had signed no treaties. Based in part on discussions at Fort Peck with these Sioux and the Hunkpapas, the commissioners in their report to Secretary of Interior Delano strongly recommended that the Milk River Agency be relocated to the Fort Peck trading post site. Very significantly, the commission recommended the new agency include the Tetons (Lakotas), based primarily on their belief that satisfied agency Lakotas would be less likely to join Sitting Bull and the non-agency Lakotas.

On December 11, 1872, Interior Secretary Columbus Delano accepted the commission's and Indian Commissioner Walker's recommendations, and authorized relocating the Milk River Agency to the Fort Peck site. This was an extraordinary decision for Lakotas, who now had the unprecedented right to an agency outside the Great Sioux Reservation established by the 1868 Fort Laramie Treaty.[43] The same would be true for those Upper and Lower Yanktonais from the Grand River Agency who had abandoned their agency status for the bison-hunting lifestyle in Montana. Those Upper Yanktons who remained permanently at the Milk River Agency similarly benefited, but they would have to abandon their agency on the Yankton Reservation.

The Cowen Commission recommended that a new agency at Fort Peck should incorporate Assiniboines and Sioux. The commissioners were aware that some Milk River Agency tribesmen resettled away from the agency when their enemies—Santees, Yanktons, and Yanktonais—had joined the agency the previous summer. Not sharing Agent Simmons' confidence in the peace commitments he demanded of the Sioux, the Gros Ventres and Upper Assiniboines moved forty-five miles up the Milk River. Accompanying them were River Crows who had not relocated to Crow Agency. These tribal groups settled near the Fort Belknap trading post, established that year by the Durfee & Peck Company. At this location, the Durfee & Peck Company opened that year a new trading post named Fort Belknap.

The Gros Ventres, Upper Assiniboines, and River Crows refused to even come to the Milk River Agency for annuities, compelling Simmons to transport their supplies overland. Simmons also had little choice but to use the Fort Belknap trading post as a subagency, precisely what he had to do the following year with the Fort Peck trading post to feed Hunkpapa and other Lakotas, beginning during the 1871-1872 winter.

The Cowen Commission recommended that Fort Belknap continue as a Milk River subagency, but only for the Gros Ventres and River Crows. Delano's December 11, 1872 letter authorizing the Milk River Agency to relocate to the Fort Peck site was written in broad terms, however, directing "consolidation of the tribes or band of Indians at the former agency." The Upper Assiniboines would not relocate to Fort Peck, and Simmons' permitting them to remain at Fort Belknap did not violate Delano's order.[44]

In the spring of 1872, Simmons had taken decisive action at the Fort Peck trading post to meet the demands the Lakotas. During the 1871-1872 winter, he had no choice but to use the trading post for storage and distribution of Lakota food and provisions. On June 19, 1872, and without authorization, he contracted for the immediate construction of a warehouse and

houses for an interpreter and agent, all enclosed by a stockade and attached to the Fort Peck trading post. He explained the urgency of affairs and asked Montana Superintendent Viall for approval. Viall approved the emergency construction and authorization was finalized by the Cowen Commission during their summer visit. On November 20, 1872, Simmons paid $4,850 for the construction.[45]

In the summer of 1872, Lakota affairs not only dominated Simmons' duties, but Lakota actions related to the Northern Pacific Railroad continued to preoccupy Army and Indian Affairs leaders. Hunkpapa chiefs Sitting Bull and Black Moon failed to meet with the Cowen Commission because they were launching a massive attack upon the Crows. By midsummer 1872, a diverse group of Lakotas, including Hunkpapas, Sicangus, Oglalas, and Sans Arcs, and Cheyennes encompassing an estimated 2,000 lodges gathered on the Powder River. After celebrating a Sun Dance, the approximately 1,000 warriors advanced west up the Yellowstone River near the Bighorn River, when scouts reported soldiers marching east.

This was a large force of 500 soldiers proceeding under the command of Major Eugene M. Baker from Fort Ellis, near present-day Bozeman, with a railroad engineering party of twenty, determined to expand the preliminary survey they had done the year before. Baker was ordered to meet Colonel David S. Stanley with 600 soldiers at the mouth of the Powder River. Stanley proceeded west from Fort Rice through the rugged Little Missouri River region with his own surveying party.[46]

On August 13 and 14, 1872, Lakotas skirmished with Major Baker's company at his camp along the Yellowstone River near the mouth of Arrow Creek. Lakotas charged the camp's defensive perimeter with extraordinary acts of bravery, including a daring ride by Crazy Horse along the perimeter. Sitting Bull, however, performed the greatest act of bravery that day, walking out within soldier firing range and smoking his sacred pipe. As a military engagement, this was a marginal affair, with only one soldier and two Natives killed, but the hostilities so terrified the engineers that they refused to go on down the Yellowstone River to the mouth of the Powder River to unite with General Stanley. Baker turned his troops northwest, where the surveyors studied Musselshell River lands and quickly returned to Fort Ellis.[47]

On August 16, 1872, Hunkpapa war chief Gall and a small Hunkpapa party attacked Colonel Stanley's forces on O'Fallon Creek, chased them up the creek to its mouth at the Yellowstone River, and westward to the confluence of the Powder River near present-day Terry, Montana. Unlike the encounter with Major Baker's command, the engineers with Stanley continued their work up to the Powder River. Sitting Bull and more warriors joined Gall and they harassed Stanley's party all the way to Fort Rice.

In both the Arrow and O'Fallon Creek conflicts, traditional Lakota war methods were no match for the superior rifle firepower of the Army. While posing little military threat, these two skirmishes marked the first armed resistance to the Northern Pacific Railroad, which hardened the positions of the Army, the Indian Affairs Office, and other officials who believed Lakota capitulation to the railroad was inevitable.[48]

When Simmons returned on November 20, 1872 from Washington, almost all the Hunkpapas were camped on the north bank of the Missouri River near the Fort Peck subagency. Black Moon, Long Dog, and 200 lodges waited across the river, as did Sitting Bull and his fourteen lodges fifty miles away at the head of Red Water Creek in the region where Circle, Montana is now. The great majority of Hunkpapas wintered near Fort Peck to receive blankets, clothing, and food.

Black Moon and Sitting Bull defiantly resisted these annuities, but this was a bad winter—no bison were reported in the Yellowstone or nearby Missouri River area. Simmons reported that lower agency Lakotas came to Fort Peck almost daily from the Yellowstone River area and were "about half starved."[49]

That winter Simmons fed and clothed 6,000 Lakotas, but he was not afraid to use food and clothing distribution to his advantage. Only those Lakotas who camped at the main camp on the north side of the Missouri River at Fort Peck received annuities. Simmons hoped that Lakotas receiving annuities would see the advantages of peace and agency life. Lakota suffering had limits, and for Simmons, "The best thing that has happened since my return [from Washington on November 20]" was when the inhabitants of more than 200 lodges "threw off" Black Moon, Sitting Bull, and others as their chiefs. They crossed to the main camp, declaring they would never go to the other side of the river again. They declared Bloody Mouth, one of the Hunkpapa chiefs who went to Washington, as their chief. Even Black Moon and his remaining twenty lodges could not hold out during that winter, and his lodges eventually joined the main camp.[50]

Simmons believed that Oglalas, Cheyennes, and Arapahos from the lower agencies would be the primary threat the next year to the Northern Pacific Railroad. Lower agency tribesmen, at least the ones Simmons talked to, believed that the railroad would cut them off from game to the northwest. The railroad would have been equally threatening to Montana Lakotas, but Simmons was very optimistic about the power of annuities to commit Lakotas to agency life. His enthusiasm was especially buoyed after the tribal delegation went to Washington.[51]

In the spring of 1873, Simmons prepared to implement Delano's December 11, 1872 directive and move the Milk River Agency to the

Missouri River and the Fort Peck subagency site, which had served as the Lakota annuity distribution center since the winter of 1871-1872. The tribal fault lines of the agency remained unchanged. Most important, Gros Ventres and Upper Assiniboines and, surprisingly, still large numbers of River Crows remained unwavering in their opinion that all the Sioux at the agency were a threat. These three tribal allies continued to reside as far northwest of the Milk River Agency as possible. Upper Assiniboines preferred hunting in the upper Milk River as far north as the Cypress Hills (present-day southwestern Saskatchewan and southeastern Alberta), where they associated with other Southern Canadian Assiniboines. Gros Ventres and River Crows tended to hunt west near the Little Rocky and Bear Paw Mountains, and often in long-standing River Crow country south of the Missouri River in the lower Judith River Basin.[52]

In June 1873, U.S. Army Captain M.J. Sanno from Fort Shaw investigated tribal attacks against the Fort Belknap Gros Ventres, Upper Assiniboines, and River Crows. He noted that Gros Ventres, who "have a good reputation (for Indians)," and River Crows were supplied with breech-loading rifles, but the Upper Assiniboines were not. Sanno reported that, "The Sioux have war parties out constantly" against these three tribes. He visited a recent battle site from April, 1873 near the Bear Paw Mountains, where 200 well-armed and entrenched Gros Ventres repulsed an attack by 500 Sioux and Lower Assiniboines. Sanno did not identify the Sioux, but if they were with Lower Assiniboines, they were likely Fort Peck Agency Sioux. Sanno further stated there was

a common rumour [sic] among frontiersmen that the Sioux will soon leave their agency at Fort Peck and try and dispossess the Assiniboines and Gros Ventres of their hunting grounds, and there is reason in this as the Sioux now have few buffalo while these others have them in abundance.[53]

However anecdotal, the frontiersmen's accounts confirmed that the Milk River region was quickly becoming one of the last premier bison grounds in eastern Montana Territory. This would attract both agency and non-agency tribesmen.

Captain Sanno added one other insight about the Milk River Agency. When reconstructing the April 1873 battle near the Bear Paws, he noted that "No account of this fight has appeared although the Indian authorities knew all about it."[54] However true this assertion may have been, it does appear that Simmons was dismissing or failing to hold accountable the attacks upon the Fort Belknap subagency tribes by fellow agency Sioux and Lower Assiniboines. This seems consistent with the lack of attention paid by agency officials to the Gros Ventres, Upper Assiniboines, and River Crows.

Simmons had just visited the three subagency tribes to take a tribal census. In May, 1873, he reported that the Upper Assiniboine population totaled 2,605 persons, which included 1,110 North band, 1,070 Stone (or Rock) band, and 425 Dogtail band members. Gros Ventres totaled 1,321 and the River Crows 1,162 persons, with the Fort Belknap subagency constituting a total of 5,090.[55]

Simmons properly recommended the appropriate new course for the Fort Belknap subagency. "Being at war with the Sioux their removal and consolidation with the Sioux is impracticable." "It is absolutely necessary to maintain Fort Belknap as a sub, or independent agency. I would recommend the latter." Simmons explained that detachment from the Milk River Agency offered transportation advantages, because Fort Benton was situated ninety-five miles from Fort Belknap, compared to 165 miles from Fort Peck.[56]

Montana Indian Superintendent James Wright on June 16, 1873 fully endorsed establishing Fort Belknap as a separate agency, which Delano authorized on August 5, 1873. Tribal composition at the new agency remained complicated. As early as April 3, 1873, Wright had received support from the Indian Affairs Office to remove the River Crows to Crow Agency, but this had not been accomplished, perpetuating the same ineffective policy since 1869, when Montana Superintendent Alfred Sully received the authority to remove the River Crows.[57] The River Crows refused to return because of the excellent bison hunting, and there was no way to force them.

Wright defended the removal policy, arguing that River Crow security was threatened by the consolidation of their Sioux enemies at the new Fort Peck site. He contended that the Crows would be safer from the Sioux once the Mountain and River Crows were consolidated, but Acting Secretary of Interior Benjamin R. Cowen was more ambiguous, writing that the new agency was for the Gros Ventres "and other Indians to be served at Fort Belknap, Montana." No one remarked that this included the Upper Assiniboines. Removing the River Crows fell to William H. Fanton, appointed on August 13, 1873, as Indian agent for the new Fort Belknap Agency.[58]

Less complicated was the transfer of Lower Assiniboines and Sioux from the original Milk River Agency to the new Fort Peck location, where they joined the new agency Lakotas. Simmons visited them during his agency-wide trip in May, 1873. The two tribal groups consented to relocate. For the Canoe Paddler band of Lower Assiniboines, Simmons reported 648 persons under Red Stones' band, 416 under Broken Arm, 480 with Bobtail Bear, 272 with Little Bull,

and 400 followers of Red Snow. Concerning the Sioux, Simmons listed Long Sioux's band of mixed Assiniboines and Sioux as 208 members. The primarily Sissetons and Wahpetons of Standing Buffalo's brother totaled 1,236 persons, and Struck by the Ree's (the son) Yanktons numbered 1,300. Lower Assiniboines totaled 2,216 persons, and Sioux 2,744, for a grand total of 4,600 tribesmen.[59]

Simmons did not report until June 15, 1873, on Lakotas remaining near the new main agency at Fort Peck, which he numbered at 765 lodges. The agent stated that some Hunkpapas were in the process of crossing the Missouri for the Yellowstone River country, but he intervened. Clearly concerned they would join Sitting Bull, if only for the summer or fall, Simmons secured the assistance of Lower Assiniboines in persuading the Hunkpapas to redirect their summer hunt directly west, in the vicinity of upper Beaver Creek. Beaver Creek is a southern tributary of the Milk River, and the area to which Simmons directed them adjoined the Little Rocky Mountains, where he suggested they could also secure fine lodge poles for their tipis.[60]

In his June letter, Simmons informed Cowen about the probable summer and fall locations of this large Hunkpapa camp, "in case any commissioners are coming to visit them." Simmons was referring to a small and half-hearted commission authorized by Delano in March 1873, to again secure agreement from northern, non-agency Lakotas for passage through their lands of the Northern Pacific Railroad. Compared to the substantial but failed attempt to accomplish the same thing the previous summer, this small commission was a complete failure. Headed by John P. Williamson and Dr. J.W. Daniels (the agent at the Red Cloud Agency who had briefly joined Cowen's commission in Montana), the commissioners never even left the Red Cloud Agency. They held one council attended by one

Hunkpapa chief, Red Thunder. In their short report, the commissioners naively assured the Interior Secretary that there would be no resistance to Northern Pacific Railroad activity, asserting that the Indians lacked ammunition and the subsistence and spirit for such warfare.[61]

Lakotas dispelled that notion in August 1873, when Colonel David S. Stanley returned to the Yellowstone River valley. In contrast to his 1872 deployment, this time he marshaled a much more formidable expedition of 1,500 soldiers, including ten troops of the Seventh Cavalry commanded by Lieutenant Colonel George A. Custer, to protect the 400 civilians and engineers. On August 4, 1873, Custer clashed with Sitting Bull's camp of Hunkpapas and Minniconjous near the mouth of the Tongue River (present-day Miles City). Reinforced by other Minniconjous, Oglalas, Sans Arcs, and Cheyennes, the warriors struck Custer again on August 11 near the mouth of the Bighorn River. These were heated engagements with intense firepower on both sides, reflected in Stanley's effective use of cannon fire to end hostilities against Custer's cavalry.[62]

Like the previous summer, the railroad engineering party accompanying Colonel Stanley continued their work without incident as far as the lower Musselshell River, but unlike 1872, they faced no more tribal attacks. This was the last Lakota and Cheyenne resistance to Northern Pacific Railroad activities. The Panic of 1873 bankrupted the railroad and delayed extension across the Missouri River from present-day Bismarck until 1879. With Colonel Stanley's departure, Lakotas and Cheyennes directed their energies to massive engagements against the Crows. Lakota war parties occasionally raided stock and settlers as far as the Gallatin Canyon, but like resistance against the Army in the Yellowstone River valley the past two summers, these conflicts were insignificant in terms of casualties. They did, however, powerfully rein-force public and government perceptions about the intractability of Sitting Bull and the non-agency Lakotas and Cheyennes. After the summer of 1873, Indian Affairs officials abandoned notions of negotiating peace with Sitting Bull.[63]

On August 28, 1873, the Department of Interior appointed William W. Alderson, a Bozeman resident, as the new Milk River Indian agent. On October 22, 1873, Alderson arrived at Fort Peck and officially relieved Special Agent Andrew J. Simmons of duty.[64] In his two years, Simmons had ably managed the early Milk River Agency through the extraordinary changes of the Sioux transformation. Agent Alderson in his two-and-a-half-year tenure would navigate through other major changes.

Alderson's first order of business was to feed and clothe the agency tribesmen through the 1873-1874 winter. In the fall, he provided provisions for 250 Hunkpapa lodges, but they left the agency in January for their winter hunt and only half had returned by summer. Alderson feared that many of these agency Hunkpapas had joined Sitting Bull, so he declared that hereafter Hunkpapas who received annuities would be under strict orders not to leave the reservation.

He reported that the agency provided subsistence to an "extraordinary number" of Indians that winter, including many from agencies at Fort Berthold, Grand River, and Fort Totten, who came to Fort Peck on visits and hunting trips. Alderson explained the difficulties of securing accurate census figures for those being provided for at the agency, but in his 1874 annual report (submitted in September, 1874), he claimed 7,307 persons. He contended these were very accurate counts, which included 1,998 Assiniboines, 1,065 Santees, 2,266 Upper Yanktonais, 460 Lower Yanktonais, 1,420 Hunkpapas, and ninety-eight mixed-bloods.[65]

It appears that the liberal, "temporizing" appropriations of 1872 were already a luxury of the past by the 1873-1874 winter. In mid-January 1874, Alderson reported to Indian Commissioner Smith that dried buffalo meat and pemmican stores were exhausted and that due to an ordering mix-up during the transition with Simmons, the agency had not ordered adequate beef, leaving them with only 250 head of cattle for the entire winter.

He requested permission to make an emergency purchase of 50,000 to 60,000 pounds of dried bison meat and pemmican. Finally, on March 19, 1874, Interior Secretary Delano authorized the purchase, with strict orders not to exceed the annual appropriation. On April 10, 1874, Alderson purchased 22,640 pounds of dried buffalo meat and 34,750 pounds of pemmican for $7,582, from Nelson Story, a prominent cattleman in the Gallatin Valley.[66]

Inadequate appropriations, urgent pleas for emergency funds, and the destitution and suffering of agency tribesmen comprised a shameful legacy of this agency almost every year through at least 1888. Rapidly shrinking bison populations, agent incompetence, neglect, and malfeasance only aggravated the Natives' marginal condition.

Agent Alderson's first winter of 1873-1874, while typical of the precarious nature of the Milk River Agency, also marked a watershed for the Lower Assiniboines. Admission of the Sioux over the previous two years had precipitated dramatic changes for the Gros Ventres and Upper Assiniboines, and now they disturbed relations with their friends and allies, the Lower Assiniboines. On February 4, 1874, Fort Belknap Agent William H. Fanton informed Indian Commissioner Smith that Lower Assiniboine Chief Red Stone wanted the Milk River Agency Assiniboines to join the Fort Belknap Upper Assiniboines. This was not Red Stone's preferred alternative, for he wanted to establish an all-Assiniboine agency at the mouth of Poplar

Creek and the Missouri River, where they could begin farming. Fanton seems to have informed Red Stone that this was not possible because Commissioner Smith himself had already opposed such measures.[67]

Fanton strongly endorsed Red Stone's proposal to relocate to Fort Belknap. Consolidation would improve tribal conditions at the Milk River Agency, because, according to Fanton, there was "an ill feeling" of "old standing" between Red Stone's band and the Yanktons (which likely meant or at least included Upper Yanktonais), and this was recently worsened by the killing of an Assiniboine by a Yankton.

Fanton argued that consolidation benefited Fort Belknap, for he believed that Upper Yanktonai chief Long Hair was "indeed anxious" for a reunification of Assiniboines. The Gros Ventres were a small tribe with many horses, and Fanton believed this would accelerate a recent trend of increasing Lower Assiniboine horse acquisition. Consolidation increased the Gros Ventres' ability not only to defend themselves against enemy horse raids, but also improved the overall defense and security of the Fort Belknap tribes. Fanton mentioned the fly in the ointment of this proposal, which was that the Gros Ventres still distrusted the Lower Assiniboines, not only because the latter had raided against them, but especially because of their friendship with all the Sioux.[68] Gros Ventre opposition was likely the reason Red Stone's suggestion went no further.

Having failed both to create a new Assiniboine agency at Poplar River and to relocate to Fort Belknap, Red Stone proceeded to a third alternative, which was to remain within the Milk River Agency, now moved to Fort Peck, and establish a lower Assiniboine subagency at the confluences of either Wolf Creek (present-day Wolf Point) or Poplar River. This would further burden the administration of an agency already rocked by incorporating the Sioux. To secure Indian

Affairs Office approval, Red Stone seems to have fully appreciated the attraction of his bold and extraordinary offer to take up agriculture.

Red Stone could have begun farming at any time. Simmons stated that he had discussed the possibility for two years both with the Assiniboines and the Standing Buffalo Santees. Had the Lower Assiniboines moved to Fort Belknap, Fanton would have supported farming, but at this time he was trying to persuade Indian Commissioner Smith to allow his agency Indians to become ranchers.[69] Fanton was ahead of his time in seeing the advantages of raising cattle over dry land farming in this part of the Northern Plains.

Equally important, there was no urgency by early 1874 to take up agriculture, for there still remained abundant bison herds. Lower Assiniboines had not experienced the extraordinary loss of game which Standing Buffalo's Santees, and Yanktons, Upper Yanktonais, and Lakotas had seen firsthand on the plains east of the Missouri River. As fellow bison cultural people, however, Red Stone and the Assiniboines would likely have empathized with the Lakotas who were going to war to stop the Northern Pacific Railroad. Assiniboines had themselves seen the disruptions to bison herds by increasing white presence, including steamboat traffic, wood cutters, and white trespassers on their way to the western Montana and Idaho gold mines.

Writing to Commissioner Smith on February 14, 1874, Alderson asked to purchase twenty oxen, plows, harrows, and seed for the Lower Assiniboines who wanted to farm at either Wolf Creek or Poplar River, with Alderson to determine the location. He had not yet visited either site but stated he was reliably informed that both tributaries had regular flows, productive soils, and plentiful timber and grasslands for haying.

Alderson did explain that a number of Santees and Yanktonais were also interested in agricul-

ture, but he gave no details. Later that year in his annual report, he expanded by noting that Upper and Lower Yanktonai and Lakota leaders, especially those who went to Washington, D.C., in 1872, expressed strong agricultural interests. Alderson described Red Stone as the pre-eminent advocate, and the first agency experiment would be with Assiniboines only.[70]

In a follow-up letter on March 30, Alderson candidly explained the importance of agriculture at the agency. Because of inadequate appropriations and a decline in bison populations, agency Natives needed to grow grains and vegetables simply to survive. He explained that if his request was too expensive, he hoped it would at least be partially funded so that the Assiniboines could begin farming in the spring. Bureaucratic problems ruined that. The large purchase required competitive bids, which Alderson tended to personally in Bozeman. He awarded the contract on May 28, but for unexplained reasons the Indian Affairs Office did not approve the bid until July 20, and the oxen and farm equipment did not reach Fort Peck until September. Assiniboines had no opportunity to farm in 1874.[71]

In his annual report to the Indian Commissioner in September 1874, Alderson relayed a major grievance from all agency members about harsh restrictions on purchasing guns and ammunition on certain agencies such as Milk River. Alderson explained the Indians at his agency needed guns and ammunition for one thing only: to hunt bison. He forcefully explained that agency appropriations were inadequate to feed and clothe them, so the Indian Affairs Office must either increase annuity appropriations or loosen gun and ammunition restrictions so people could feed themselves.

Alderson defended the responsible conduct of the agency tribesmen in light of what he claimed was incorrect information the Indian Affairs Office might have received. He conceded that guns and ammunition could be obtained illegally from the Canadian Métis traders, illegal trade at off-reservation trading posts, and illicit trade among other Indians, but Alderson insisted this trafficking was negligible at Milk River.

Additionally, he defended the agency trading post, which he contended scrupulously complied with the restrictions. Alderson explained that unlike many agencies with no gun or ammunition trade and purchase restrictions, at Milk River Indians could not trade or purchase to upgrade either their guns or ammunition to fixed cartridges. The agency Natives were restricted to loose ammunition, and even that was in categorically insufficient quantities.

Alderson's ultimate proof was the destitute nature and quantity of guns and ammunition at the agency. Tribesmen were poorly armed, and the few owning breech-loading guns did not have ammunition. Alderson stated that the Assiniboines and Santees were furious at the double-standard. The Great Father was treating other agency Indians better, and he said he wanted the Indians to live, but did not allow them enough ammunition to kill game.[72]

By August, 1874, Alderson finally traveled east from Fort Peck as far as Wolf Creek, and he believed that Wolf Creek was the most desirable agricultural land he had seen. Contrary to what he had been told, however, Wolf Creek was not free-flowing from spring through fall. Heavy rains prevented him from investigating the Poplar River, which many reported was a superior overall location.[73]

By early spring of 1875, Red Stone and what appears to be a majority of Lower Assiniboines relocated to Wolf Creek. Using the work oxen and agricultural supplies that arrived in the fall of 1874, agency staff helped break fifty acres, but Assiniboines planted their first crops of wheat, corn, peas, potatoes, turnips, squash, and other vegetables. They also weeded, hoed, harvested,

built fences and a large root cellar, and cut and stacked ninety tons of hay.[74]

On June 30, 1875, Alderson contracted for immediate construction at Wolf Creek of a warehouse and a double log house to lodge agency employees. The agent boldly initiated this construction without authorization from Commissioner Smith. Alderson's predicament was perhaps surprising because he and Smith had been corresponding throughout the winter about the new Assiniboine agricultural site and important changes it triggered. Most important was whether the new site should be a subagency or transformed into the new agency. Either demanded decisions about the status of the main agency at Fort Peck. Lacking the budget for construction, Alderson in February 1875 requested authority to build at least some buildings with existing Indian Affairs Office monies or through special congressional appropriations.[75]

Having received neither by June 30, Alderson took matters in his own hands. That same day, he sent a letter to Commissioner Smith requesting approval of his contract requisition, explaining he could not spare the delay that advertising for bids would entail. Bureaucratic delays had foiled his agricultural initiative the previous year, and he was determined that such red tape would not undermine the important new Assiniboine undertaking. The warehouse was essential, for in it would be stored the food annuities, clothing, and blankets Assiniboines needed to survive the 1875-1876 winter.[76]

The Assiniboine settlement at Wolf Creek served as a subagency and Fort Peck remained as the main agency, which by 1875 had changed its name from the Milk River Agency to the Fort Peck Agency. Alderson had strongly advised Commissioner Smith that the agency at Fort Peck should not be removed or abandoned unless it was replaced by a new agency of equal standing, because it was vitally important that the Indian Affairs Office continue to provide the absolute necessities for "these wild Indians" if acculturation was going to succeed.

It is unclear why Alderson selected the Wolf Creek location over Poplar River, since it appears that he had still not personally visited Poplar River. In his annual report in October 1875, Alderson claims credit for the Assiniboine decision to separate from the main agency at Fort Peck. "I induced a majority of the Canoe Indians to separate themselves from the wilder tribes of this agency, and locate at Wolf Creek."

Fort Belknap Agent William Fanton's correspondence to Indian Commissioner Smith a year earlier in February 1874 indicated the contrary: due to tensions with the agency Sioux, Chief Red Stone was already determined to separate, either to a new, all-Assiniboine agency at Wolf Creek or Poplar River, or to Fort Belknap, where they would unite with the Upper Assiniboines.

Alderson's explanation is significant because his correspondence fails to discuss any complaints or concerns presented by Red Stone and Assiniboines against the agency Sioux. It is possible that Red Stone chose not to discuss the topic with the agent. Perhaps more significantly, Alderson's phrase about separating the Assiniboines from the "wilder tribes of the agency" reflects less about the true nature of Assiniboine and Sioux relations than *his* concerns and perceptions about them. And like many Indian agents and Indian policymakers, Alderson was most concerned with "civilizing" and acculturating the agency Natives.

From an assimilation point of view, the emphasis Alderson placed on the success of the Assiniboine agricultural experiment at Wolf Creek was perfectly understandable. He was directing an extraordinary acculturation opportunity to incorporate agriculture among a people who had long followed the bison, and he fully appreciated that squandering this would further

derail an already failing acculturation process among the agency Assiniboines and Sioux. Some of Alderson's unease derived from the fact that he was a realist who understood that dry land farming in the Northern Plains was highly speculative and precarious for both whites and Indians. Alderson explained to Commissioner Smith in 1874 that difficulties included a short growing season marked by early and late frosts, and the threats of drought, hail storms, and grasshoppers. He also knew that Indian Affairs Office agricultural experiments regularly failed, noting that "many similar ones have been made with other Indians and failed."[77]

To Alderson, however, the real threat to Assiniboine assimilation was the Yanktonais. He strongly believed that in 1875 when Assiniboines had successfully launched their farming experiment at Wolf Creek, the Yanktonais must remain at the main agency at Fort Peck. Alderson shuddered at the prospect that the entire Fork Peck Agency might relocate to Wolf Creek.

Should Fort Peck be abandoned and our efforts be devoted exclusively to Wolf Creek, we should be powerless to prevent the Yanctonnais and other wild Indians of the Agency from visiting the Agency at Wolf Creek in such numbers and frequency as to utterly demoralize those who are better disposed, and thus render futile all our efforts for their civilization.[78]

Alderson seems to have suddenly realized that the hope of assimilating the entire agency depended on the Wolf Creek Assiniboines. His fears were based on the cultural perceptions of the Fort Peck Agency Assiniboines and Sioux he had formed during his two years among them.

Alderson's views typified the negative depictions of Natives and tribal cultures almost universally shared by nineteenth-century whites, both those working among Native tribes (especially Indian agents and administrators, Army soldiers and leaders, and missionaries), and the many so-called "friends" of Indians who knew little about tribal cultures, yet were zealots about forced acculturation. Writing in 1874, Alderson described all Indians as "barbarous nations," but he perceived gradations of cultural civilization among the Fort Peck tribes, however misguided and ethnocentric these assumptions were.[79]

Alderson placed Assiniboines and the Santees in the first of three "distinct classes or grades of Indians as respects their progress toward civilization. . . . These Indians, owing, perhaps, to their weakness as compared to other branches of the great Sioux Nation" and their long association with whites are

docile, friendly, and peaceable. They also appear to comprehend their situation and inevitable destiny to a much greater degree than any other uncivilized Indians living on or near the Upper Missouri; and were it not for the buffalo and other game, an irresistible attraction to the Indian. . . .the Assinaboine and Santee Sioux would be ready at once to adopt habits of industry and conform to the modes of civilized life.

In 1875, after the Assiniboines had planted their first crops at Wolf Creek, the agent commented that Assiniboines "are almost the only wild Indians I have yet seen who manifest any marked degree of gratitude for favor."[80]

Alderson placed the Upper and Lower Yanktonais in a second class. In 1874, he remarked that until very recently they had "entertained a haughty disdain for the power and authority of the government." But in his ten months working with them, Alderson believed they were more cooperative. He was especially impressed because a number of leaders who had traveled to Washington in 1872 expressed strong interests in agriculture. One year later, Alderson tendered harsh criticisms against them.

These Sioux Indians are, however, yet far from taking upon themselves the duties and responsibilities of industrial pursuits or civilized life; they are in many respects children understanding, yet with almost unlimited confidence in their own judgment and strong faith in their barbarous customs and habits of life.

And in Alderson's view, the most important hindrance to Yanktonai and Lakota acculturation was their persistence as a bison-hunting people. The agent disliked

The almost irresistible attraction of buffalo and other game. . . . It should not be considered strange that the infatuating yet comparatively indolent and desultory life of the chase, which attracts and almost uncivilizes so many white men on the frontier, should prove almost an insuperable a barrier to the civilization and christianizing of those who feel that it is their only hereditary occupation.[81]

Alderson placed the Hunkpapas in the third class. From his perspective, they were "extremely difficult to manage, perhaps as much so as any Indians in the country. They are wild, demonstrative, and ungrateful for favors." They had many Hunkpapa relatives among the non-agency Lakotas in the Yellowstone and Powder River regions, and like them, they claimed ownership of the lands through which the Northern Pacific Railroad was projected to pass. They refused to relinquish that claim without compensation, and for all these reasons, many of the agency Hunkpapas came and went from the agency as they pleased. Alderson believed that agency Hunkpapas who went to the Yellowstone River country simply to visit and hunt were "restrained and overawed by Sitting Bull, his associate chiefs, and his formidable soldier lodge, so that they cannot return to the agency when they wish." Alderson seems to have placed the Hunkpapas with the Yanktonais—both childlike, unapologetic about their "barbarous customs," and hindered in white acculturation primarily because of their bison-following lifestyle.[82]

Besides launching the first tribal farming, Agent Alderson pioneered two other innovations in 1875. He opened the first tribal schools, which were federal day schools. In February 1875, he hired a teacher at Fort Peck, but she quit after six weeks and Alderson closed the school. Beginning in July 1875, Alderson hired two full-time teachers for new day schools at Fort Peck and at Wolf Creek. In November, 1875, he expanded the Wolf Creek school by constructing three new log buildings, which like all Fort Peck agency log homes and structures were sod-roofed.[83]

Peter O. Matthews was the new teacher working at Wolf Creek. He had taught at the Crow Agency, and most recently at Fort Hall Agency in Idaho Territory. Matthews was a Native person of unidentified tribal affiliation living in California at age ten or eleven. He was brought to Jefferson, Ohio, by a Mr. Matthews, who raised him and sent him to school. He completed two years of high school there and in 1874 was confirmed as a Methodist Episcopal minister. He also served three years in the Union Army during the Civil War. Mathews remained employed for a number of years in various capacities at the Fort Peck Agency.[84]

In June 1875, Alderson established a tribal police force, the last of the major innovations that year. Composed primarily of Yanktonais, its function included keeping order in the tribal camps, prohibiting and prosecuting all trafficking of alcohol in the camps, and preventing war or horse raiding parties from leaving the agency. Alderson touted success of these goals this year, claiming that no raiding parties departed after creation of this force. This appears to have been a pioneering venture, for the Indian Affairs Office did not circulate general authoriza-tion and appropriations for tribal police programs until 1878.[85]

After what appears to have been a successful year, with Wolf Creek Assiniboines possessing at least some food reserves from their first planting harvest, and with an apparently uneventful fall, the agency seemed ready for the coming 1875-1876 winter. But the agency Natives were going to suffer terribly. On February 26, 1876, Alderson sent an urgent letter to new Indian Commissioner John Q. Smith, who had replaced Edward P. Smith in December 1875. Alderson explained that agency food provisions were nearly exhausted, and he feared great suffering if emergency provisions were not provided before the usual spring delivery of goods up the Missouri River. Conditions would likely only worsen at Fort Peck in thirty days, when 3,000 Sioux would return from their winter bison hunt.

Although he did not say the Wolf Creek Natives were already hungry, he also declared that the first boats arriving in the spring needed to bring potatoes, corn, and seeds for planting. He failed to mention that the Wolf Creek Assiniboines had stored an estimated 400 squashes, and for spring seeding they had stored thirty to forty bushels of wheat, five of beans, and 325 bushels of potatoes. Most likely, the Assiniboines had already eaten them.[86]

Aside from the real concerns of impending hardships, Alderson's letter is both confusing and disturbing when he explains the way he manipulated tribal annuities that year. In his letter, Alderson said that the 1,000 to 1,200 Wolf Creek Assiniboines had subsisted "so far, without the aid of any portion of the appropriation made for the Assinaboines for the year ending June 30th 1876." Remarkably, he then openly stated that they were using Sioux annuities from the main agency at Fort Peck, and even more remarkably, he explained that he was rewarding them for taking up agriculture. As he explained preserving the Assiniboine provisions:

This, of course, has taken no inconsiderable portion of the supplies furnished for the "Sioux at Fort Peck", but as these Assinaboines preferred remaining here to going to Ft. Belknap Agency, and as they were the only Indians that we could possibly induce to locate and labor, I thought it best to aid and encourage them to the extent of my ability.[87]

This is revealing on several counts. The reference to Fort Belknap reveals for the first time that Alderson even knew about Assiniboine Chief Red Stone's discussion in February 1874 with Fort Belknap Agent William Fenton about tensions with the Sioux and his inquiry about reuniting with the Upper Assiniboines there. Alderson says that the Wolf Creek Assiniboines had not used any Assiniboine annuities, but the way he wrote this suggested that Wolf Creek Assiniboines could use all the agency Assiniboine provisions. He failed to mention that there were 2,000 Fort Peck Agency Assiniboines, which means that 800 to 1,000 remained with the Sioux at the main Fort Peck Agency.[88] If he diverted annuities from the Sioux because they did not take up agriculture, why would Alderson not do the same for Fort Peck Assiniboines?

Equally problematic, Alderson had no right to divert Sioux food, clothing, and provisions to the Wolf Creek Assiniboines, but he seemed to be confessing these details to receive absolution from the Indian Commissioner. The Indian Affairs Office and Indian policy makers, after all, regularly used food as blackmail. Throughout the nineteenth century, one of the first punishments for tribal resistance to federal policies—however coercive and repugnant—was to withhold treaty annuities. These coercive measures were usually related to resistance to forced acculturation.

On April 18, 1876, the new Fort Peck Indian Agent, Thomas J. Mitchell, from Illinois, arrived

at the Wolf Creek subagency. Alderson had tendered his resignation to Indian Commissioner John Q. Smith on January 1, 1876. Mitchell witnessed Assiniboine destitution because all annuity provisions were exhausted. Three days later on April 21, Mitchell arrived at the main agency at Fort Peck, forty-five miles up the Missouri River. Agency annuities were also exhausted there, and the tribesmen were furious because they were starving while agency trader P.A. Langley refused to provide for them from his warehouse full of flour, sugar, and dried buffalo meat. Mitchell immediately purchased $1,600 worth of food, which of course raises the question why Alderson had not already done so.[89]

Mitchell officially relieved Alderson of duty on April 22 and took possession of all federal property at the agency. Heavy rains through early May prevented the Assiniboines and Sioux from going bison hunting. Mitchell was incapacitated with a bout of what he called rheumatism, and tribal leaders came regularly to his bedside complaining that their children were starving. Mitchell sent two agency staff members and interpreter Joseph Lambert to visit the tribal camps and confirm these complaints, which these officials fully corroborated.

Around May 27, 1876, Mitchell called a council and informed the tribal leaders (apparently only from the main agency at Fort Peck) that trader Langley had no more food and that they must embark on a bison hunt or starve. These were desperate conditions, for starving tribesmen refused to go because their families had no clothing, and they would hunt only if Mitchell gave them clothing. Mitchell agreed and purchased 245 blankets and a few hundred yards of cloth from Langley. Why had Mitchell not done that already?

On May 31, the agency tribesmen from Fort Peck headed up the Milk River, but after only eight miles were forced to stop due to heavy rains that made the streams and trails impassible. Because they had no food, Mitchell was forced to make another emergency food purchase. Why had he not done this earlier, and if Langley's trading post had no food, from whom did he purchase it? Mitchell provided no details.[90]

When Mitchell arrived in April 1876, he also had been directed by Indian Commissioner Smith to close Fort Belknap Agency for the sake of economy and to transfer the Gros Ventres and Upper Assiniboines to the Fort Peck Agency. Mitchell relieved Fort Belknap Agent William Fanton of his duties on July 1, 1876, and commenced the complicated matters of persuading the two tribes to relocate and to move the agency property to Fort Peck. Mitchell met with various groups of Upper Assiniboines who agreed to settle with the Wolf Creek Lower Assiniboines after the summer bison hunts, but it appears that they remained in the Fort Belknap area.[91]

Not surprisingly, the Gros Ventres, who remained bitter Sioux enemies, categorically refused to relocate. They told Mitchell that they were weak and the Sioux were strong and ancient enemies who would eventually take their annuities and provisions. When Fort Peck Sioux heard that the Gros Ventres might be receiving annuities at Fort Peck, they bluntly asked Mitchell to simply hand the Gros Ventre annuities directly to them, for exactly as the Gros Ventres had predicted, the Sioux stated they would be seizing these goods at the first opportunity anyway. Mitchell forcefully countered that any Sioux doing so would forfeit their own annuities.

In his new predicament, Mitchell proposed to Commissioner Smith that Fort Belknap remain open as simply a "feeding post"—essentially a subagency of the Fort Peck Reservation. He also agreed to meet with the Gros Ventres about abandoning Fort Belknap and relocating to a location of their choice on the Missouri River at what they considered a safe distance from the agency Sioux. The primary advantage to the Indian Affairs Office and the tribesmen would be the greatly more convenient transportation of goods up the river. The Gros Ventres refused, electing to remain at Fort Belknap even if it meant forfeiting all their annuities.[92]

This was classic thoughtless and cavalier Indian policy. In 1871, the Gros Ventres separated from the early Milk River Agency that had been established for them because they feared the Sioux. It seems inconceivable that they would change their minds, but they were never even consulted before the decision was made. Fort Belknap was ordered abandoned and Mitchell was actively transporting all "movable property" to Fort Peck. In the summer and fall of 1876, the status of the Gros Ventre and Upper Assiniboine remained unclear. And the Fort Peck Agency, which could not even feed and clothe its own Indians the previous winter, would be even further stretched. Mitchell did not say so, but presumably he had no choice in the fall of 1876 but to transport at least the Gros Ventre annuities and provisions to Fort Belknap, which the next Fort Peck Agency would do the next fall.[93]

In the summer of 1876, Mitchell expanded agriculture at Wolf Creek. There continued to be two distinct plots, one an agency farm worked primarily by agency staff with the assistance of some Assiniboines. The existing plot from the previous year was thirty acres, and Mitchell broke a total of 200 acres, and increased the total acreage in crops to seventy acres.

Assiniboines also had their own distinct plot from the previous year. The tribal organization of the Assiniboine farm was truly extraordinary. Mitchell met in council sometime that spring with the chiefs and they informed him that each chief wanted to farm his own individual parcels so that each could teach his respective band by example. Mitchell agreed and directed that a few acres be set aside for each chief.

The first crops were planted in June, but effects of the starving 1875-1876 winter lingered. Agent Mitchell reported that Assiniboines planted seven acres of turnips, which grew quickly, but Assiniboines were digging and eating them as soon as they were large enough to eat. This was in spite of the fact that the large Assiniboine bison hunting camps regularly sent dried bison meat back to those who remained at Wolf Creek.[94]

Mitchell reported a successful 1876 harvest. Eight acres of oats, which ran an estimated forty bushels per acre, and the same acreage of wheat had to be cut as hay because the agency lacked a reaper. These grains were very likely from the agency farm. There were also eight acres of corn, which likely was also at the agency farm, but it is probable Assiniboines also grew corn on their plots. Potatoes were the largest crop, with twenty-five acres planted, along with other vegetables including peas, beans, pumpkins, squash, radishes, beets, turnips, and onions. Mitchell credited Assiniboine chiefs Red Stone, Long Fox, Little Bull, White Shell, Broken Arm, Walking Porcupine, and Wolf-skin Necklace for their key contributions.[95]

Already preoccupied with recovery from a starving winter, expanding agriculture at Wolf Creek, and trying to administer Fort Belknap affairs, Mitchell was greatly hampered in his first year of service by open warfare between the U.S. Army and the non-agency Lakotas, Cheyennes, and Northern Arapahos. The decision for war had first been broached at an important meeting at the White House on November 3, 1875, where President Ulysses S. Grant, Secretary of War William W. Belknap, Secretary of Interior Zachariah Chandler, Indian Commissioner Edward P. Smith, and Army generals Philip Sheridan, Commander of the Division of the Missouri, which was responsible for the trans-Mississippi West, and George S. Crook, com-

mander of the Department of the Platte, all met to discuss the situation.

The key issues were how to force the Sioux to sell the Black Hills, for a treaty commission headed by Senator William B. Allison had failed in September 1875 to secure the purchase. The other issue was military—forcing non-agency Indians residing in lands designated in the 1868 Fort Laramie Treaty as "unceded Indian territory" to return to their agencies. These were vaguely defined lands in Article 16 of the treaty east of the summits of the Big Horn Mountains. These lands included the Powder River watershed, and non-agency Lakotas and Cheyennes interpreted them as including parts of the Yellowstone River region. The treaty declared that these lands were prohibited from white settlement and trespassing.[96]

Acting on a directive from Interior Secretary Chandler, on December 6, 1875 Indian Commissioner Smith sent a circular to all Sioux Indian agents to notify all non-agency Natives in the unceded territory to return to their respective agencies by January 31, 1876, or they would be declared "hostile" and would be dealt with by the War Department. Having now made the Indian Affairs Office publicly responsible for the impending Army action, Commissioner Smith resigned, and was replaced by John Q. Smith. Fort Peck Indian Agent Alderson did not even receive his letter until January 21, 1876. His Indian sources informed him that the main camp of Lakotas was camped near the mouth of the Powder River. Alderson was unable to secure any reliable whites to carry the message, so he promised to attempt to get some friendly Indians to do so.[97]

The annihilation of Lieutenant Colonel George A. Custer at the Little Bighorn on June 25, 1876 shocked many, and Agent Mitchell noted that Assiniboine chiefs Red Stone, Long Fox, and others expressed their sorrow to him over the battle. Mitchell believed they were sincere and that their sympathies were both with the whites and against the "hostile Indians." He did not believe any Fort Peck Assiniboines were at the fight, which of course would have been almost unthinkable, but that was not the case for a handful of agency Hunkpapas.[98]

Agent Mitchell stated that on May 21, 1876, one month prior to the Little Bighorn battle, he sent an agency Indian named Medicine Cloud—who was surely Hunkpapa—to Sitting Bull's camp to invite him to come to the Fort Peck Agency. Mitchell did not explain the purpose of such a visit, and it appears to have been unauthorized. Seven young agency Hunkpapas then went to Sitting Bull's camp without Mitchell's knowledge. Two returned to the agency on July 28, stating they came directly from Sitting Bull's camp, which at this time was at Killdeer Mountain, the site of the important 1864 battle with General Alfred Sully, in the Little Missouri River region of present-day northwestern North Dakota.

These two young Hunkpapas said that Sitting Bull's *akicitas* refused to let Medicine Cloud return until they held a council on the message to send to Agent Mitchell. They stated that one of their party was killed at the Little Bighorn, but they denied they were at the battle, for they escaped from camp. Four of this original party were caught in the escape attempt.

One of the two Hunkpapas who made it to Fort Peck brought with him a gray Army horse with a brand of the Seventh Cavalry. He vehemently denied that he captured it in the battle, stating that he traded it to a Standing Rock Indian for a horse and a gun. Mitchell did not believe him, but the young Hunkpapa "became very sensitive and insisted that he was telling the truth, that he had but one time to die and if he had been in the fight he would admit it, if he should be killed the next moment for it." Mitchell

let the young man keep the horse, fearing that confiscating it would discourage other tribesmen from returning other captured or stolen government property.[99]

Custer's defeat, and the failure to defeat the non-agency Lakotas, Cheyennes, and others humiliated and infuriated Army leaders, triggering dramatic changes in Indian policy. On July 26, 1876, the Interior Department succumbed to three years of pressure from General Philip Sheridan, commander of the Division of the Missouri, and agreed to transfer control of Sioux agencies to the War Department. Acting upon strict orders from Sheridan, on October 18, 1876, General Alfred H. Terry, commander of the Department of Dakota, relayed orders concerning the Fort Peck Agency to Fort Buford commander Colonel William B. Hazen.

Sheridan elected not to have Hazen seize control of the agency, but he detailed the harsh new rules and instructed Hazen not to tolerate even the slightest infraction. Most important were General Sheridan's terms of unconditional surrender for non-agency Natives: the confiscation of all their guns and horses. These were shocking terms to plains Natives because both were essential for bison hunting and feeding their families, not to mention the humiliating loss of the wealth and honor both prized items represented in tribal cultures. The terms of unconditional surrender now applied to agency tribesmen caught off the reservation, and their guns and horses would be seized.[100]

Trying to restrict the trade of any material items to the non-agency Lakotas, Terry also ordered that annuities must be given to each agency Indian in person. He instructed commander Hazen to "exercise absolute control" over the agent and the agency traders, yet he could not unnecessarily interfere or remove them. Restrictions increased quickly. On October 25, 1876, Terry notified Hazen that the Fort Peck

Agent could no longer permit agency tribesmen to communicate with non-agency Indians. Should the agent violate this order, Hazen was instructed to suspend him, place a military officer in charge of the agency, and immediately report such action to the Interior and War Departments. Mitchell protested not being able to communicate with Sitting Bull's followers, but he acquiesced.[101] As it turns out, the order was unenforceable.

On October 26, one earlier restriction was made more specific, that agency tribesmen could not give or trade ammunition, food, or clothing to non-agency Indians. Violators would be defined as "hostile," and their guns and horses would be taken. Three days later on October 29, Hazen dispatched a letter to Mitchell with the most extraordinary new restriction: the agency could distribute only food to agency Indians until all the non-agency Indians surrendered. On November 11, 1876, Mitchell informed Indian Commissioner John Q. Smith that he had received all the War Department instructions and had "obeyed them to the letter." Agent Mitchell appears to have been scrupulous in this.[102]

The Fort Peck Agency centered prominently in affairs with the Army and the non-agency Lakotas from summer through early winter of 1876. Primarily these encounters related to the Hunkpapas who passed through the area hunting bison and on their escape to Canada. Sitting Bull came on different occasions, always evading the pursuit of General Nelson Miles, but also seeking guns and ammunition, especially from Métis traders from Canada.

On September 6, 1876, Hunkpapa chief Long Dog, with twenty-three lodges, and Wahpekute leader Inkpaduta and his party of five lodges crossed the Missouri River at Wolf Creek. Like all the combatants eluding the Army after the Little Bighorn, these Lakotas did not seek conflict with whites or cause trouble. They wanted to meet with Mitchell, and to reach the Wolf Creek subagency, the agency farmer named Hughes explained that the entire party had to walk through the agency farm, and did not so much as disturb one ear of corn. This was remarkable because they were destitute and hungry.

They remained peacefully in the area and five days later, on September 11, they met Mitchell at Porcupine Creek near present-day Frazer. Mitchell had traveled east from the main agency at Fort Peck. The warriors explained that in their flight from the Army, they had abandoned their lodges and other key possessions, and they were off to Canada to build new lodges and prepare for winter.[103]

The following week, Mitchell reported that Sitting Bull had sent messengers to the Fort Peck "Yankton" (probably meaning, or at least including, the Yanktonais) and Assiniboine camps seeking friendship so he might visit their camps. Sitting Bull was most likely seeking trade, and he promised a gift of 100 horses for those who welcomed him. Both agency camps categorically rejected his offer, saying that he was the enemy of their friends, the whites, and that they wanted nothing to do with him.[104]

On September 23, 1876, Little Buck Elk, a chief of Sitting Bull's soldiers' band, arrived at Fort Peck from Sitting Bull's camp, at this point now near the mouth of the Powder River. Sitting Bull sent him to inquire about trading for ammunition, which does not seem to have been even remotely possible. Mitchell bluntly rejected the request but countered that if Sitting Bull surrendered at the agency, he would be well treated.

Little Buck Elk had fought at the Little Bighorn and he gave Mitchell some rich first-hand information, stating that the tribesmen were "as thick as bees," so many in fact that some could not participate in the fight. He stated that contrary to what some said, Custer's soldiers fought bravely. Had General Terry not arrived, however, Little Buck Elk believed Major Marcus Reno's and Captain Frederick Benteen's companies would also have been eliminated on the second day. He also stated that tribal losses were high, with more than 100 warriors killed. Little Buck Elk further noted that lots of warriors now wore the watches and carried money from the fallen soldiers. Mitchell informed Indian Commissioner Smith that he could likely recover some of these personal items if relatives of these killed soldiers could provide some descriptions of them. Last, Little Buck Elk said they did not want to fight the soldiers, but these Indians united to drive the whites out of the Black Hills. They had been offered tobacco if they would return to their agencies, but he said Sitting Bull objected to doing so.[105]

In pursuit of bison on October 10, 1876, Sitting Bull's large camp of Hunkpapas, including chiefs Black Moon and Four Horns and closely allied bands of Minniconjous and Sans Arcs, crossed the Yellowstone River, apparently near the confluences of O'Fallon Creek from the south and Cedar Creek from the north, both near present-day Terry, Montana. On October 11 and 15, they clashed with some of General Miles' soldiers who were guarding a supply wagon train.

On the 15th, Sitting Bull met wagon train commander Lieutenant Colonel Elwell S. Otis. Sitting Bull explained that his people were hungry and low on ammunition, and were tired of war and wanted peace. Otis had no sympathy for their lack of ammunition, noting that the Sioux had wasted enough of it shooting at his wagon train. He stated he did not have the resources to accept Sitting Bull's unconditional surrender, if the chief elected to do so. Otis did give Sitting Bull's camp 150 pounds of hard bread and two sides of bacon, and the commander then continued south for the Yellowstone River.[106]

Sitting Bull's camp moved north up Cedar Creek, where they camped after overtaking a large bison herd. General Nelson Miles then joined Lieutenant Colonel Elwell and then marched up Cedar Creek to Sitting Bull's camp. On October 20, 1876, Sitting Bull and Miles met under a white flag and engaged in an afternoon-long, stormy session in which Miles wanted Sitting Bull to surrender. He in turn demanded that Miles leave the Yellowstone River area and that the Army abandon Fort Keogh, which Miles had built at the mouth of the Tongue River only a few months earlier, and Fort Buford.

On the next morning, a second meeting disintegrated into anger, and both leaders returned to their respective sides. Hostilities then erupted. In this battle, known as Cedar Creek, the Lakotas moved east and then the alliance separated. Sitting Bull and thirty lodges turned north toward the Missouri River. Miles followed the larger body of Minniconjous and Sans Arcs, and at the Yellowstone River they surrendered. This group included Sitting Bull's Minniconjou nephew White Bull, an extraordinary warrior, who had counted five coups at the Rosebud battle and another seven at the Little Bighorn. Losing him was personally devastating to Sitting Bull and exemplified the splintering of Sitting Bull's Lakota following.[107]

Two days later, on October 23, 1876, Sitting Bull's thirty lodges, which included chiefs Four Horns and Black Moon, were camped on Big Dry Creek, twenty-five miles directly south of the main agency at Fort Peck. That evening, four messengers from the camp visited Mitchell at Fort Peck. They explained that the Hunkpapas had come peacefully and intended no harm, but their ammunition reserves were low, without which they could not live. In a letter written to Indian Commissioner Smith that day, Mitchell said the next morning he would send a messenger to Sitting Bull's camp explaining there would be no ammunition available at the agency.

Mitchell reported in his letter of the 23rd that

Sitting Bull, Four Horns, and Black Moon, along with Iron Dog, were among the 100 Hunkpapa lodges that were crossing the Missouri River near the mouth of Porcupine Creek, which flows into the Milk River just a few miles from the Milk River confluence with the Missouri River, near present-day Nashua, Montana, twenty-five miles east of Fort Peck. As Mitchell more accurately reported on November 11, there were actually around 119 Hunkpapa lodges on the Missouri River, but these were led by Long Dog, Iron Dog, Crow, and Little Knife, of whom all but Iron Dog were Sitting Bull followers. This large Hunkpapa gathering remained camped, presumably still near Porcupine Creek twenty-five miles east of the Fort Peck Agency.[108]

On October 31, most of this large Hunkpapa camp, including women and children, came to the agency at Fort Peck, inquiring about the government's surrender conditions, telling Mitchell that Sitting Bull and his camp awaited the outcome of these negotiations. They explained that they were destitute of food and ammunition. Mitchell said that they must forfeit their guns and all stolen federal property, including Army horses, but he did not require that they also forfeit their own horses, for he did not receive the Indian Commissioner's instructions on the terms of unconditional surrender until a few days later. The Hunkpapas reluctantly agreed, but because it was late in the day, Mitchell gave them food for an evening meal and breakfast and directed that they surrender in the morning. The agent was confident of the allegiance of the agency Indians, for he noted that the Yanktons (a term he may have used for the larger number of Yanktonais) and Assiniboines refused to allow the Hunkpapas to visit their tipis.

Later that evening, however, a runner came to the Hunkpapa camp warning them that at Wolf Point a steamboat full of soldiers was coming up the Missouri River. This was Fort Buford commander William B. Hazen and 140 men, who were transporting thirty days of rations and forage to Fort Peck for the imminent arrival of General Miles. Hazen arrived the next day, November 1, but Mitchell had no Indians to receive, for they had all scattered. Hazen unloaded the provisions, assigned Lieutenant R.H. Day and thirty men to guard them, and returned to Fort Buford.[109]

Miles, having secured matters with the surrendered Minniconjous and Sans Arcs, left Fort Keogh on November 6 to hunt down Sitting Bull. In a forced march through brutal winter conditions, he arrived at the Fort Peck Agency ten days later. Sitting Bull's camp on the Big Dry had swelled to 100 lodges, due to the recent flight of Hunkpapas from Fort Peck, but General Miles miscalculated their location and they escaped. In early December, Sitting Bull crossed the Missouri River and traded for large quantities of ammunition, presumably with Métis traders.[110]

On December 6, Upper Yanktonai Cuthead chiefs Medicine Bear and Black Tiger traveled all the way to the Wolf Creek subagency to inform Mitchell that they had just met with Sitting Bull. He had recently crossed to the north side of the Missouri River and was camped along the river bottom above the Milk River crossing, which would have been rather close to the Fort Peck Agency. Sitting Bull's camp was truly pitiful, having only three tipis and ninety-two shelter tents, which he claimed represented 250 families.

Sitting Bull inquired about the number of soldiers stationed at Fort Peck, and the Cuthead chiefs told him there were a mere thirty soldiers there. Sitting Bull replied that he cared nothing about the soldiers. In fact, he said, showing his sense of humor, "they were friends, that they had given him ammunition and he had returned it to them through the muzzles of his warriors' guns." Sitting Bull was anxious to meet with Mitchell, surely about the opportunity to trade. The chief said he was off to Canada to trade for ammunition with the Métis, but he was not making war with the whites, nor did he want to harm them in any way, for it was the Army making war on him. Medicine Bear and Black Tiger mistrusted him and believed he meant mischief, which is why they immediately contacted Mitchell.[111]

On December 7, 1876, Sitting Bull's camp on the Missouri River near the Milk River was attacked rather ineffectively by Lieutenant Frank D. Baldwin and his three companies, recently sent to Fort Peck by Miles. Sitting Bull's camp retreated to the south side of the Missouri and Baldwin, thinking that Sitting Bull had 600 warriors and was luring him into a trap with Custer-like consequences, called off the pursuit. After the Baldwin skirmish, the military officers at Fort Peck (presumably Day) warned Mitchell that it was extremely dangerous for him to travel alone to the main agency at Fort Peck, and they offered him a military escort. Mitchell refused, stating that fifty Assiniboines had already volunteered to secure his travel.[112]

With a mule train loaded with fifty boxes of ammunition from the Métis, Sitting Bull turned south for the Powder River to join with Crazy Horse. But on December 17, a determined Baldwin caught up with him at the headwaters of Red Water Creek, not far from the site of Sitting Bull's October battle at Cedar Creek with Miles. Sitting Bull was forced to flee the camp, a staggering loss because Baldwin burned all their lodges, clothing, and tons of dried bison meat.

Sitting Bull escaped with all his ammunition and united with Crazy Horse's Oglalas, and various allied Minniconjous, Sans Arcs, and Cheyennes. The tribesmen were bitterly divided over whether to surrender or continue to fight. By February 1877, when the need for bison necessitated breaking into smaller groups, the Oglalas and Cheyennes headed to the Little Bighorn and most of the Minniconjous and Sans Arcs also

scattered east. Black Moon's Hunkpapas had long since departed, and in December 1876, his fifty-two lodges crossed into Canada, where they joined 3,000 Lakotas at Wood Mountain. Sitting Bull's Hunkpapas and some Minniconjous and Sans Arcs in February 1877 also headed north, and by early March had made it to Red Water Creek. By this time in March, Hunkpapa principal civil Chief Four Horns and his fifty-seven lodges crossed into Canada. In mid-March, Sitting Bull crossed the Missouri River above the Fort Peck Agency and remained along the river bottom. Sometime during the first week of May 1877, Sitting Bull crossed into Canada.[113]

The presence of non-agency Lakotas and Cheyennes had complicated the lives of the Milk River Agency and later the renamed Fort Peck Agency tribesmen, especially since Northern Pacific Railroad surveyors had entered the Yellowstone River region in 1871. The new pressures derived especially from Indian policy and Army officials anticipating military conquest of these non-agency Indians once and for all. These concerns rose with tribal resistance to the survey parties in 1872 and 1873, and mushroomed with the embarrassing military failures in the Rosebud and Little Bighorn battles in June 1876.

For friendly agency Indians in Dakota and Montana Territories, one of the most infuriating developments was the harsh restriction on the trade of guns and ammunition. Inferior numbers and quality of guns was degrading enough, but the disturbingly chronic ammunition shortage was literally a matter of life and death. For Milk River/Fort Peck Agency Indians whose lack of annuities alone marked them for hunger and deprivation, the scarcity of guns and ammunition made their lives grim indeed.

As Fort Peck Agent William Alderson had frankly stated in his 1874 annual report to the Indian commissioner, Fort Peck Indians could trade only with the agency trading posts, which could sell only ammunition for muzzle-loading guns: gunpowder, lead balls, and percussion caps. Agency Natives could not even trade their old muzzle-loading guns for better ones, and the few tribesmen with modern breech-loading guns could not purchase metal cartridges. Alderson defended his agency Indians' exasperation at being penalized for scrupulously following these policies. They refused to trade with unregulated trading posts or with the Métis traders who illegally crossed into Montana Territory and traded with the non-agency Lakotas. Alderson even upbraided the Indian Affairs Office because the agency was so underfunded that it must either greatly expand annuities, or liberalize the guns and ammunition restrictions.[114]

Fort Peck Agency Assiniboine and Sioux ammunition reserves seem to have been adequate for summer and fall bison hunting in 1876, but beginning during the 1876-1877 winter through much of 1877, Mitchell and his successor began vigorously demanding permission to dole out more ammunition. During 1876, however, tribes across Montana Territory suffered dramatically from ammunition shortages. Territorial Governor Benjamin F. Potts advocated forcefully for changing the ammunition policy at Montana agencies. In an October 10, 1876 letter to Indian Commissioner John Q. Smith, he explained that the "Northern Indians" (the agency Blackfeet, Gros Ventres, River Crows, Assiniboines, and Sioux) were "much annoyed" because they had no ammunition for hunting in a country "alive with Buffalo."

He insisted that it was simply justice that friendly Indians be granted limited ammunition for hunting, and he also suggested that the Army supervise this at the agency trading posts. Like Alderson, Governor Potts credited agency tribesmen for diligently prohibiting their young men from trading horses or ammunition with the non-agency Lakotas and their allies. There

was not time for delay, for he noted that the Blackfeet Agency, with winter imminent, had not even received its annuities, and the Indians had no food.[115]

In response, on October 25, 1876, the Commander of the Army outlined the position which the War Department followed. Sherman appreciated the complexity of the issue, noting that this was a question with which "men differ widely and honestly." He advocated for the complaints of the soldiers that one department of government (the Interior Department and the Indian Affairs Office) aided their enemies. Sherman stated that even friendly Indians if provided breech-loading guns and metal cartridges would eventually trade these to the non-agency Natives.

Sherman offered a practical compromise— that the Indian Affairs Office permit trading of only muzzle-loading guns and ammunition, which he contended were effective hunting rifles. In addition, he suggested that modern breech-loading guns and metal cartridges be banned altogether. These would become contraband items, and the Army would confiscate them from any Indians possessing them. This policy had the advantage of being easily enforced, protecting the soldiers, and denying traders what Sherman stated were exorbitant profits in this illicit market.[116] These then became the new gun and ammunition policies.

As Fort Peck Assiniboines and Sioux prepared for the coming winter of 1876-1877, things seemed to be in pretty good shape. The tribes had rebounded from the marked hunger and deprivation which they had faced when Mitchell arrived for duty in April 1876. Bison were plentiful that summer and both the Sioux at the main Fort Peck agency and the Wolf Creek Assiniboine hunts went well. Assiniboines returned in late July "laden with meat," having killed 370 bison. The Wolf Creek harvest went well and Mitchell claimed 250 tons of hay were also cut there.[117]

But matters worsened through the winter. Mitchell reported on November 18 that blankets, which he noted were the articles most needed, had not been shipped from Bismarck. He predicted "great suffering" if they did not arrive. To help feed his agency tribesmen, on December 6, 1876, Mitchell wrote Colonel William B. Hazen, commander at Fort Buford, asking permission for Fort Peck Indians to trade for small amounts of ammunition.

Hazen explained that he believed the government had finally started to control "the ammunition question," and his ambiguous response was that "so far as I feel myself, I would not give it." Hazen's alternative proposal was not reassuring. He explained to Mitchell that the Fort Berthold Arikaras and Mandans were now *making arrows* for bison hunting, and the colonel believed all friendly Indians could do so if they wished. He forwarded the request Dakota Department Commander, Brigadier General Alfred H. Terry, but it is not clear what the response was.[118]

On January 2, 1877, Mitchell issued the last of the pemmican and most of the bacon, but he warned the Indian commissioner that four times the annuities purchased were going to be needed to feed the agency tribesmen through the end of the fiscal year in June 1877. He then stated that "The Indians on this reservation are *in a state of helplessness*; they are *without ammunition* and the means of procuring game to subsist upon" [emphasis added]. Mitchell requested permission to immediately purchase pemmican and dried meat on the open market, and for agency Indians to be allowed to trade there for small quantities of muzzle-loader gunpowder and balls. Mitchell warned that tribal conditions would be deplorable if Congress failed to make special appropriations before their adjournment.[119]

Hazen may not have approved, for on January 29, 1877, Mitchell requested to Indian Commissioner Smith to permit agency Assiniboines and Yanktonais to trade for gunpowder, balls, and percussion caps. By this time, whether friendly Indians across northern Montana Territory could trade for these items was a matter of great confusion, for Mitchell stated that he was simply asking for ammunition trading authority *already permitted* for the Upper Assiniboines, Gros Ventres, and River Crows who traded at Fort Belknap.[120]

The trading status at the Blackfeet Agency was equally unclear. On December 2, 1876, Fort Shaw commander Colonel John Gibbon wrote General Terry concerning the desperate need of the Piegans at the Blackfeet Agency for ammunition. The agency winter supplies had still not arrived. Aggravated at the worsening situation, he complained that "the government is not only starving them but refusing them the means of subsisting themselves. *Even a Christian will fight before he will starve*," and he urgently recommended authority for such trade under military supervision [emphasis added]. Both Terry and Lieutenant General Philip Sheridan, commander of the Division of the Missouri, approved Gibbon's request.[121]

Anxious to acquire better muzzle-loading rifles, in January 1877, Upper Yanktonai Cuthead Chief Medicine Bear made an unusual offer to Mitchell. He said that the Yanktonais were willing to part with their prized breech-loading rifles in exchange for higher quality muzzle-loaders of about the same caliber as the most esteemed breech-loading rifle, the Winchester.[122]

Gun and ammunition shortages even forced agency Indians to refuse service as Army scouts, which according to Mitchell "very much exasperated" the military. Mitchell strongly encouraged participation because of the extra pay, but his agency tribesmen explained it was not due to unfriendly feelings toward the government. They feared that such service would anger the non-agency Lakotas and they would retaliate, killing their people and stealing horses at every opportunity. Without guns or ammunition, the Fort Peck Indians would be unable to defend themselves. Mitchell agreed with them.[123]

It appears that Fort Peck Agency conditions remained grim during the 1876-1877 winter. On December 28, Lieutenant R.H. Day negotiated the surrender of forty-nine Hunkpapas and Blackfeet Lakotas, which included fourteen men, thirteen women, and twenty-two children. Day was now stationed at the Fort Peck Agency, following his temporary detachment there in November 1876 to protect the rations and feed delivered from Fort Buford for General Miles. These Lakotas were utterly destitute, but he could not issue them clothing and blankets from the agency, because the supplies there were so limited. Day ordered the Leighton trading post to issue poison so the Lakotas could poison wolves and use the wolf hides, which they could then trade for clothing.[124]

On February 23, 1877, Indian Commissioner Smith authorized Mitchell to issue powder, lead, and percussion caps to Fort Peck Assiniboines. In March and April, Mitchell signed individual slips to the agency traders, specifying the amounts to be traded to each Indian recipient. In April 1877, the Interior and War Departments tried to resolve the confusion over who had final authority to grant gun and ammunition trading privileges for agency Indians. On April 14, 1877, Secretary of War George McCrary recommended to Interior Secretary Carl Schurz the analysis and proposal Sheridan had submitted.

Sheridan's comments rang true on many issues. He believed that the Indian Affairs Office policies on these matters were fine, but the problem rested with Indian agents who could not and would not enforce them. They lacked the physical force, "and the moral influence which comes from it," to accomplish it.[125] Underfunded

agencies like Fort Peck were classic cases, lacking both the resources to feed and clothe their tribesmen and adequate personnel to effectively manage them. Concerning the unwillingness to enforce gun and ammunition regulations, Mitchell seems to have conscientiously and effectively managed what little of these precious materials were traded at Fort Peck and the Wolf Creek subagency. After Mitchell left office in June 1877, his complete dereliction of responsibility concerning the Fort Belknap Assiniboines, Gros Ventres, and River Crows became known. This was exactly the kind of Indian agent incompetence that infuriated Sheridan and Sherman.

General Sheridan's recommendation was as concise as it seemed reasonable: place all responsibility in the hands of each of the Army's department commanders. Each was responsible for all citizens in the respective regions, and it seemed likely that they would be as knowledgeable as anyone concerning Indian affairs in their own jurisdictions. Sheridan concluded with a remarkably insightful analysis.

I think, myself, there has always been a great deal of nonsense talked about selling ammunition to Indians. If the Indian cannot buy it he can make it. The Indians save every shell they fire, and pick up every one white men or soldiers throw away, and refill them as perfectly as is done by machinery, using a cut down percussion cap for the fulmination.[126]

This description appropriately credits the innovative and persistent Native peoples, but Sheridan is describing non-agency Indians, for only they had significant numbers of breech-loaders and metal cartridges. Fort Peck Agency Assiniboines and Sioux did not.

On March 29, 1877, Agent Thomas J. Mitchell was suspended and replaced by Wellington Bird, a resident of Mount Pleasant, Iowa. But Bird did not arrive to the agency until June, and he would administer the last major change to the Fort Peck Agency: the relocation of the main agency at Fort Peck to the mouth of the Poplar River. In his short tenure, Mitchell had consistently argued for abandoning the Fort Peck site, voicing the same complaints his predecessor William Alderson had made since 1874.[127]

The most important criticism by both agents was that the poor alkaline soils were unfit for agriculture. This problem was unforeseen when the main Milk River Agency was established because the Durfee & Peck Company trading post was already there. Durfee & Peck selected the site to attract trade with the Lakotas moving into the region, and the Indian Affairs Office relocated there from the Milk River for the same reason, to better accommodate the extraordinary numbers of Hunkpapas and other Lakotas being encouraged to join the agency.

The unsuitability had become increasingly significant since 1874, when Agent Alderson tried to initiate the first tribal farming. His other primary concern at that time was that the agency was too close to the Missouri River, where the eroding river banks were rapidly becoming a threat to agency structures. When established in 1873, the subagency and attached trading post were 200 yards from the river, but by July 1876, the river had moved to only forty yards away.[128]

A third issue was structural—the sod-roofed, log structures were not only literally rotten, but also were infested with rats. The agency facilities were hastily built in 1873 from cottonwood logs cut on site, which had not been properly cured. As the green logs dried, all the buildings warped and leaking through the roofs became catastrophic. Since the annuity food supplies for all the agency Assiniboines and Sioux were stored in these dilapidated buildings, they were constantly in danger of rotting and rat infestation.

Mitchell complained vigorously about the need to abandon the main agency from his earliest days there. In January 1877, Fort Buford commander Colonel Hazen supported the agent's case, writing bluntly that "Fort Peck is in ruins" and "The vicinity has not one feature in its favor." Both Mitchell and Hazen recommended that the main agency relocate sixty-five miles east to the mouth of the Poplar River.[129]

It is hard to imagine working in such deplorable conditions, but the Indian Affairs Office was not stirred to action. This changed dramatically in March 1877, when an extraordinarily devastating flood inundated what was already a rather marginal agency. During the annual spring melting of the Missouri River, an ice jam one mile downstream from the main agency at Fort Peck on the morning of March 23, 1877 unleashed a furious flood twenty feet high that rocked the agency at two o'clock in the morning. Agency employees fled their homes, which were swamped with water as high as their necks. The recently reinforced south stockade wall probably spared the agency from losing even a single person.[130]

Oddly enough, Sitting Bull and his followers were settled in winter camp along the Missouri River bottomlands above the Fort Peck Agency, and the flood devastated them. Equally remarkable, their lives were also spared. They were already destitute, and the flood destroyed most of what property they owned.[131]

After receiving Mitchell's shocking March 27, 1877 report of the profound damage, the Indian Affairs Office and military officials moved quickly to establish a new agency. The outstanding issue was selecting a new site. Ordinarily, these decisions were made almost exclusively by the Indian Affairs Office and the Interior Department, but because Fort Peck as a Sioux agency had been placed under military control in the fall of 1876, it was probably not surprising that the Army would make the selection.

Sheridan selected a close advisor, his military

secretary Lieutenant Colonel James W. Forsyth, to make a thorough investigation. Sheridan's May 5, 1877 instructions to Forsyth were comprehensive, and included both military and Indian Affairs Office management considerations. To General Sheridan's credit, however, the most important consideration was the potential for agency tribal agriculture.[132]

Forsyth departed from Chicago on May 10, 1877, and arrived at the Fort Peck Agency on May 26. He was supposed to meet with newly appointed agent Wellington Bird and study matters together, but Bird was delayed in Bismarck by steamboat transportation complications. Due to heavy May rains, Colonel Forsyth could not travel overland as he had planned, and the only visual inspections he could make of possible sites was from the steamboat that carried him from Fort Peck to Fort Buford. Supported by extensive interviews with agency and military officials, and other knowledgeable persons, Forsyth recommended unequivocally the Poplar River site.[133]

Bird arrived at the Fort Peck Agency on June 14, 1877, and due to unexplained delays of Mitchell, Bird did not formally receive authority over the agency and relieve Mitchell until June 23. Compared to most Fort Peck Indian agents, he was unusually prepared for service. Just prior to his Montana arrival, he had already met with Indian Commissioner Smith in Washington, D.C., and with Sheridan in Chicago. In spite of these rare opportunities, Bird was unprepared for the shocking conditions at Fort Peck. The stench of rotting food and the number of rats present right after the flood seemed to have diminished by June, but Bird reported thousands of pounds of bacon were ruined. Persistent rains aggravated conditions such that Bird feared an outbreak of malaria—quite an extraordinary concern in semi-arid northern Montana Territory.[134]

Even Bird admitted that deteriorating log structures and the flood damage were under-

standable, but he was apoplectic about the absolute neglect and disrepair of the main agency at Fort Peck. Exasperated at the lazy attitude of the staff there, he shared with Indian Commissioner Smith this story:

I said to some one—what have the employees and agent been doing—when some one replied "Oh they have been eating and sleeping and signing vouchers and pay rolls"—not far from [the] truth.[135]

Since there was no Sioux farm to help manage, and the Assiniboines and Sioux associated with the main agency were gone most of time bison hunting, there in fact was little work to do. Bird's anger was triggered by negligence.

The Wolf Creek subagency suffered the same disregard, the one place where at least in theory there actually was serious work to do. Bird was angered that only forty acres had been plowed, and only half of that was planted due to the lack of seed. As in the spring of 1876 when Mitchell had arrived, none of the large quantities of seed potatoes and turnips stored from the first successful 1875 harvest survived the 1875-1876 winter. Especially galling to Bird was that though there were no seed potatoes, he found potatoes readily available on the tables of the employees.[136]

Bird understood the urgency of establishing a new agency before winter arrived. By June 25, 1876, he had already planned the agency, estimated costs, and forwarded them to Indian Commissioner Smith. Bird had not received word on Forsyth's recommendation, but he had personally fully explored the entire area, and this was the location he selected.[137]

On June 25, 1876, the day Bird sent his draft construction plans and costs to Smith, he sent another letter fully explaining what he believed were significant resources at both Poplar River and Wolf Creek, and he argued that overall, Poplar River was the superior site. In another letter to Commissioner Smith written four days later, he reversed himself and now highly recommended Wolf Creek. Bird had not changed his ideas about the key natural advantages of either, for he still believed both had thousands of acres of excellent farmland and grazing/pasture land. But he now rejected the two agency organization (that is, one main agency and a separate subagency) which had been established when the Santees, Yanktons, and Yanktonais were admitted in 1871. At that point, the Gros Ventres, Upper Assiniboines, and River Crows had left the main Milk River agency for the Fort Belknap trading post area. After the Hunkpapas and other Lakotas were invited to the relocated main agency at Fort Peck, by 1875, most of the Lower Assiniboines had separated to Wolf Creek.

From a natural resources and administrative point of view, Bird's new perspective was innovative and commendable. Most importantly, Wolf Creek was centrally located, with rich potential agriculture and pasture lands west to Porcupine Creek and east to the Poplar River site. Another major advantage was that it eliminated the extraordinary troubles of fording rivers. Crossing the Milk River was always problematic, especially when the main agency moved to the Missouri River a few miles west of the entrance of the Milk River. This became even more troublesome in 1875 with the new Wolf Creek settlement. Bird planned to significantly use the Poplar River area, but it seems his imagined primary use was on the west side, avoiding the fording complications.

Another innovation in his Wolf Creek design was introducing extensive tribal cattle herds. Up to this time, grasslands and pasture lands had been used only for the small number of agency work animals: oxen, horses, and mules. Using the rich grasslands to introduce wide-scale tribal ranching was an idea far ahead of its time. Bird saw the economic advantages of both farming and ranching as acculturation tools.[138]

The newly found allure of Wolf Creek was clearly connected to radically new information related to Assiniboine and Sioux relations. Bird explained that everywhere he went, the prevailing view was that Assiniboines and Sioux wanted a separate subagency and could not live together in harmony. Bird explained that in an extended conversation on June 28 with agency interpreter Alexander Culbertson, he was told that Assiniboine Chief Red Stone and Upper Yanktonai Cuthead Chief Medicine Bear were on the best of friendship terms, and that at least a majority of Yanktonais would be pleased to live together with the Assiniboines.

Bird was persuaded by this because "Culbertson knows more about the real feelings of these Indians than any other white man in the Country for he has lived among them for forty years." Although at this time little evidence contradicted Culbertson's view, indicators suggest the two tribes at this point insisted on separation, which seems to be why Red Stone's Assiniboines moved in 1875 from Fort Peck to Wolf Creek. More recently, when Forsyth made his investigation for a site in May, Assiniboines told him they did not want the Yanktonais to relocate to Poplar River, which would have halved their separation from forty-five miles to twenty-two miles. The Yanktonais, on the other hand, told him they preferred that the agency remain at Fort Peck or relocate to the Milk River.[139]

In any case, Bird remained committed to the Wolf Creek site. When Smith informed him in a June 26 letter that he had selected Poplar River based on Forsyth's recommendation, Bird immediately protested. When Forsyth received Bird's rebuttal case for Wolf Creek, he refused to even dignify the critique, but instead simply forwarded his final report to Sheridan.[140]

Bird's protests against the Poplar River selection may have been fainthearted, for within days he was in Bismarck with new Poplar River construction bid proposals. These plans still required that the main part of the new buildings be constructed from cottonwood logs, but all would have shingled roofs. He believed it was too late to complete all construction by that fall, so his bid proposals called for completion of additions at Wolf Creek by November 1, 1877, and completion of the new Poplar River Agency no later than March 1, 1878. Bird telegraphed these proposals to Smith on July 18.[141]

These were significant deadlines, for that same day Bird also telegraphed the commissioner that with the banks of the Missouri River at Fort Peck "crumbling," he was immediately moving all remaining goods to Wolf Creek and diverting all new supplies there. The agent was essentially closing Fort Peck. Because his plans did not anticipate completion at Poplar River until March, the estimated 5,000 Sioux and Assiniboines based at Fort Peck would have to winter at Wolf Creek, where food and provisions would have to be provided for all agency Indians.[142]

Smith telegraphed him the next day with the surprising news that he had already advertised bids in Yankton, Dakota Territory, which were due by August 1, 1877. Bird was mystified that construction bids would be considered from such a distance, but in fact, Smith had taken the matter very seriously.

Citing Bird's telegram about the riverbank and relocation of provisions, on July 20 the commissioner wrote Schurz seeking immediate action. Ignoring the August 1 deadline of his own construction bids in Yankton, Smith insisted that the contract be awarded to the company of C.K. Peck, with the rather stiff recommendation that construction be completed by October 1.[143]

C.K. Peck in fact proceeded ahead of this already rushed deadline. Despite a number of contract delays during August, by September 11, the Indian Affairs superintendent in Yankton, J. H. Hammond, was able to report that all the construction workers, materials, and other supplies had reached Poplar River on August 31. The contractor expected to complete work by September 25, but Hammond figured it would be the end of the month.[144]

At some point, the contract completion date was pushed to October 10, but this deadline must have been met, for by October 18 Bird had transported by boat all the property from Fort Peck and assumed charge of the new agency. He also must have been pleasantly surprised that the new buildings were all pine, including a two-story agent's house.[145]

On November 14, 1877, when Bird granted final payment on the contract ($14,994), he informed Smith for the first time that the Poplar River Agency was one and one-third miles inland from the Missouri River landing. He explained that this was needed to avoid another catastrophic flood.[146]

It was not until July 1877, one month after Agent Thomas J. Mitchell had been relieved on duty, that his neglect of the Gros Ventres and Upper Assiniboines at Fort Belknap became fully known. When Mitchell assumed control of the Fort Peck Agency in April 1876, Smith had already directed him to close the Fort Belknap Agency and combine these two tribes into the Fort Peck Agency. Because of continued hostilities with the Fort Peck Sioux, the Upper Assiniboines and Gros Ventres refused to move to Fort Peck or Wolf Creek. Agent Mitchell's compromise proposal to these Belknap tribes— that a new subagency be established for them on the Missouri River, located an acceptable distance away from the Sioux at Fort Peck—never materialized. The Upper Assiniboines, Gros Ventres, and a number of River Crows remained on the upper Milk River at Fort Belknap. Mitchell stated that he placed interpreter Alexander Culbertson in charge of affairs at Fort Belknap, which by default was now a subagency of Fort Peck.

Presumably Culbertson's primary responsibility would have been securing and providing annuity provisions to these tribes. This should have included incorporation of existing provisions under the care of the former agent William Fanton, whom Mitchell had relieved in July 1877.[147] Details on Mitchell's management of Fort Belknap are sketchy, perhaps because there seems to have been no work accomplished there.

It was left for Major Guido Ilges, commander of the small infantry detachment at Fort Benton, to uncover the chaos at Fort Belknap. Due to reports of Gros Ventre threats against neighboring whites, including the killing of a man named Frank Robinson, on July 18, 1877, Ilges met with ten Gros Ventre principal men at the mouth of the Marias River, a few miles east of Fort Benton. They vigorously defended their unwavering friendship with whites, but since the government had taken away their agency and trading post, they had nowhere to trade and no agent to look after them. They were ordered to the Fort Peck Agency, but refused, "for the Sioux are our deadly enemies and will steal our horses and kill us." In addition, in the winter of 1875-1876, they had no buffalo, and now were very poor. Without government help, "our women and children will starve to death, and our young men will be obliged to steal and help themselves."

Aggravating matters, 600 lodges of hostile Sioux were threatening them. The Gros Ventres numbered only 110 lodges, and they were willing to fight the Sioux, but they were prohibited from buying ammunition, and they had no way to defend themselves. They stated they were resigned to roaming the country like fugitives.

Ilges was especially concerned about word he received concerning the Gros Ventre head soldier (war chief), Big Beaver. He reportedly said he was tired of being misused by the government, and that hereafter he was going to help himself, "like the [non-agency] Sioux," and make the whites cry. Big Beaver had reportedly met with Sitting

Bull messengers. Ilges reported that these truly friendly Indians were being driven into the arms of the hostiles. He explained that Big Beaver controlled 250 well armed and very brave warriors who would be dangerous enemies.[148]

Alarmed, Ilges on July 23, 1877 returned to the mouth of the Marias and met with Gros Ventre principal chief White Eagle and about twenty other warriors. White Eagle corroborated what the other Gros Ventre leaders had told Ilges. He explained that his people were starving, and because the non-agency Lakotas were following and threatening them, they had to move camp almost daily. They had no place to trade, no ammunition, and no bison robes to trade even if they had had a trading place.

White Eagle reported the shocking news that the Gros Ventres and Upper Assiniboines had received *no* food or annuity goods (blankets and clothing, primarily) from the Fort Belknap Agency *in three years*! Ilges stated that he fully believed White Eagle. This was clearly an indictment of Agent Mitchell, whose service began in April 1876. Even Ilges commented that at this time Fort Belknap belonged under the control of the Fort Peck Agency. The negligence of the previous two years rested with former Fort Belknap Agent William H. Fanton.[149]

Gros Ventre war chief Big Beaver refused to meet with Ilges. Just after the major left his meeting with White Eagle, an unidentified Gros Ventre man informed him that Big Beaver had joined Sitting Bull's non-agency Lakotas and they were preparing for raids in the area. Ilges turned back and confronted White Eagle with this news. White Eagle said he knew nothing about this, which led to a confrontation with the Gros Ventre man who had brought this message to Ilges. The Gros Ventre man then confessed that in fact Big Beaver had smoked the pipe with Sitting Bull's messengers, and that Big Beaver promised to bring warriors and join in raids against the whites. Few warriors joined Big Beaver, however, because most remained unwavering in their friendship with whites.

Ilges promised White Eagle that he had already informed his superiors about their destitute condition after their first meeting, and he promised to do so again after his meeting. The Army responded quickly. In an August 16, 1877 letter to Bird, Ilges explained that he was directed to provide emergency rations to the Fort Belknap Indians, enough at least to relieve their "actual distress." Ilges also asked Bird if the Fort Peck Agency possessed any Fort Belknap provisions, and if so, he requested Bird to seek authority to distribute it immediately.[150]

Bird did not write Indian Commissioner Smith until August 22, but he pointedly explained the urgency of getting food and provisions to the Gros Ventres and Upper Assiniboines. In his letter, Bird explained that these tribes had earlier refused to relocate to the Fort Peck Agency because of their "old enmity" with the Yanktonais. He incorrectly stated, however, that the Gros Ventres "have never come to, or been under the control of this agency." Fort Belknap had been a Fort Peck subagency since Mitchell's arrival in the spring of 1876.[151]

The Interior Department acted responsibly, but unfortunately, they also proceeded slowly. It was not until October 25, 1877 that Interior Secretary Carl Schurz authorized Smith to permit the Fort Peck Agency to contract without bid for transportation services for 66,000 pounds of unspecified supplies from the Poplar River Agency to Fort Belknap. In addition, the following day Schurz authorized immediate purchase on the open market of 250 sacks of flour and 16,000 pounds of pemmican, not to exceed a cost of $294.[152]

Tragically for the Gros Ventres and Upper Assinibiones, the pettiness of Generals Sherman and Sheridan denied delivery of these vital supplies early in the winter of 1877-1878. Schurz's first letter of October 25 indicated that the transportation of goods to Fort Belknap needed an Army escort, and Schurz explained he had already requested this from the War Department. Two days later, on October 27, 1877, Sherman received the Interior Department's request. Sherman wrote to Sheridan, deliberating his course. Sherman was displeased that the request for escort was made so late in the year, for he feared the escort would freeze to death proceeding to and from the Milk River. Apparently, Indian Commissioner Hayt had asked for a military escort from Fort Benton, for Sherman responded that the garrison there was too small for even such a mission. He left the decision to Sheridan, but not before asking why the Gros Ventres couldn't go down to Fort Benton, draw their rations, and return to Fort Belknap.[153]

Sherman acted small-mindedly. His comment about his soldiers freezing to death seems frankly petty. It is quite apparent that Hayt's request to Interior Secretary Schurz detailed that the military escort should come from Fort Benton. Hayt was surely operating on information provided from Ilges, who commanded the Fort Benton military post. As Interior Secretary Hayt's October 25 letter specified, however, the goods to be transported were already at the Fort Peck Agency at Poplar River. It was also from the Poplar River Agency that Bird would be expected to purchase flour and pemmican on the open market. Why in the world would a military escort travel empty-handed the 318 miles to Poplar River, when Fort Buford, only sixty miles east, was the logical choice? Sherman missed the main point too, for he limited his analysis to the size of the Fort Benton command.[154]

Sheridan replied to Sherman on November 1, 1877. He also was preoccupied with the late nature of the escort request, but unlike Sherman, he placed responsibility on the fact that "scheming contractors always manage to delay Indian supplies until winter, when the price for transportation is two or three times as much as in summer." That contractors fleeced the federal government in this way was widely known, but Sheridan offered no evidence that this was the reason for the delay in this request.

Very significantly, Sheridan told Sherman that in response to Fort Shaw commander Colonel John Gibbon's revelations about the lack of annuity supplies to the Fort Belknap tribes, Secretary of War George McCrary had directed rations be provided them. Ilges' August 16, 1877 letter to Fort Peck Agent Bird indicates that these were limited distributions addressing only their "actual distress."

Sheridan suggested the important possibility of a Fort Buford escort, but then dropped that topic. After detailing that a round-trip from Fort Benton with stops at Poplar River and Fort Belknap totaled nearly 700 miles, he summarily agreed with Sherman that the transportation be scrapped altogether. As he stated it, he recommended that "the Gros Ventres be notified that their supplies are at Poplar River, that the directions to Col. Gibbon to feed them will be withdrawn, and that they be invited to go there for them, or do without them." On November 13, 1877, the Secretary of War completed the injustice by approving Sheridan's recommendation.[155]

There is no indication that the Upper Assiniboines and Gros Ventres came to Poplar River that winter to pick up their provisions. Unsupported in their accusations of delayed requests, and with misplaced anger at white profiteers, Sherman and Sheridan then made destitute in the middle of winter the Gros Ventres and Assiniboines, the only victims in this travesty.

Things went equally poorly for Bird when on October 1, 1877, he asked Indian Commissioner Hayt to permit agency Indians to purchase small quantities of ammunition for hunting. On

November 14, 1877, Secretary of War McCrary, upon the recommendation of General Sherman, approved the request, but on November 22, Department of the Dakota commander General Alfred Terry strongly objected. He focused on the Fort Peck Yanktonais and claimed both that they were in open communication with Sitting Bull's followers, and that they traveled freely to Canada and had become fully armed with breech-loading rifles and metal cartridges. Terry insisted Yanktonais would use gunpowder, lead, and percussion caps to reload their shells, so that what appeared to be a safe policy for muzzle-loaders for hunting purposes was in fact the opposite, and increased the danger to U.S. soldiers. Sheridan endorsed Terry's challenge, and on November 30, 1877, the Secretary of War reversed the permission he had granted on the 14th.[156]

On December 10, 1877, Bird was invited to an extraordinary meeting of Yanktonai leaders at the Poplar River agency. Some Yanktonais and other agency Sioux had expressed interest in farming as far back as 1874, but for unclear reasons had yet to do so. Things were now different, for the new agency at Poplar River had been selected primarily for that purpose. This meeting demonstrated that the Yanktonais were ready. Yanktonais themselves organized the meeting and they invited Bird for one reason: to write down what they said and send their words directly to the Great Father. Principal Upper Yanktonai Cuthead chief Medicine Bear led the meeting. Attending were all the Yanktonai chiefs and leaders who had accompanied Assistant Interior Secretary Benjamin to Washington, D.C., in 1872: Medicine Bear, Afraid of the Bear, Black Catfish, Black Eye, Pack the Eagle, Long Fox, Skin the Heart, and Red Thunder. Also in attendance were other Yanktonai leaders: White Crane, Man that Bets his Medicine, Red Lodge, Man that Waves his Hatchet, Spotted Eagle, and Bloody Mouth, who may have been the Hunkpapa chief of the same name.

Medicine Bear explained that the Yanktonais had kept every promise made to the Great Father in 1872. They had remained on the reservation, lived peacefully, and given no aid to the non-agency Indians. In addition, they were not permitted ammunition, at the same time that the non-agency Indians procured all they needed. But the Great Father had made several promises to them in return for the terms given to the Yanktonais, and he had not fulfilled any of them. The Great Father promised that when these Sioux agreed to reside at the agency, they would be provided plowed land and all the material items needed to live as farmers: wagons, harnesses, plows, and other farming materials.

The Yanktonais now asked that the Great Father comply with his part of the commitments made. They demanded all the promised items in time for them to complete farming in the spring of 1878. They wanted light, narrow track wagons with harnesses, not the large and heavy ones given the Assiniboines, and they demanded plows, agricultural equipment, and sufficient and diverse seeds. Bird highly emphasized another demand for good American horses and mares to improve and expand their existing stock.

The Sioux insisted on major improvements to their annuity provisions. They needed more blankets, sheeting, and red and blue cloth, for existing supplies did not even furnish half the people. They rejected shoes, awls, awl handles, and sack coats, and wanted these replaced with larger frying pans without handles, dutch ovens, small axes (not hatchets), brass and copper kettles, and iron tea kettles. They demanded more pants, vests, and different hats and shirts of new colors, and much more heavy duck (canvas) for tents, until houses were built for them. Concerning food, they desired more flour (but they preferred hard bread), rice, corn, and hominy, coffee, and tea.

And perhaps most important to Bird, they wanted comfortable homes with roofs and floors, not rough log houses without floors and filled with bedbugs and other vermin, like those occupied by Assiniboines. They claimed that at Fort Peck nothing was done to provide homes for them. They had moved to Poplar River at the command of the Great Father and they asked him to start helping them now, with the coming spring.[157]

1 Milk River Agent Andrew J. Simmons to Montana Indian Affairs Office Superintendent Jasper A. Viall, May 12, 1871, National Archives and Records Administration [hereafter cited as NARA], Record Group 75, Records of the Bureau of Indian Affairs, M234, Letters Received Commissioner of Indian Affairs [hereafterhereinafter cited as LRCIA], Roll 491 (1871), frames 650-52.

2 Ibid., frame 650.

3 Viall to Parker, May 18, 1871, NARA, RG 75, M234, LRCIA, Roll 491 (1871), frame 603; Viall to Parker, May 21, 1871, NARA, RG 75, M234, LRCIA, Roll 491 (1871), frames 657-59.

4 Viall to Parker, May 20, 1871, NARA, RG 75, M234, LRCIA, Roll 491 (1871), frames 632-33.

5 Viall to Parker, May 21, 1871, NARA, RG 75, M234, LRCIA, Roll 491 (1871), frames 657-59.

6 Brevet Brigadier General Henry A. Morrow to Brevet Brigadier General Greene, Assistant Adjutant General, Department of Dakota, September 9, Letters Sent, Fort Buford, RG 393, National Archives and Research Service [hereafter cited as NARA]; Morrow to Greene, September 14, 1869, Letters Sent, Fort Buford, NARS.

7 Viall to Parker, July 17, 1871, NARA, RG 75, M234, LRCIA, Roll 491 (1871), frames 804-5; Simmons to Viall, September 20, 1871, NARA, RG 75, M234, LRCIA, Roll 491 (1871), frames 938-40; Raymond J. DeMallie, "The Sioux in Dakota and Montana Territories: Cultural and Historical Background of the Ogden B. Read Collection, in *Vestiges of a Proud Nation: The Ogden B. Read Northern Plains Indian Collection*, Glenn E. Markoe, ed. (Burlington: Robert Hull Fleming Museum, University of Vermont), 31.

8 Secretary of War William W. Belknap, to the Secretary of Interior [Columbus Delano], August 10, 1871, and Major W. H. Lewis, July 18, 1871, *Annual Report to the Secretary of Interior for the Year 1871* [hereafter cited as *Annual Report*] (Washington, D.C.: Government Printing Office, 1871), 849.

9 Major General Winfield S. Hancock, Department of Dakota, July 28, 1871, *Annual Report* (1871), 849-50.

10 Lieutenant General Philip H. Sheridan, Division of the Missouri, August 3, 1871, and General William Tecumseh Sherman, Commander of the Army,

August 7, 1871, *Annual Report* (1871), 850.

11 James C. Olson, *Red Cloud and the Sioux Problem* (Lincoln: University of Nebraska Press, 1965), 68-84; Robert M. Utley, *The Lance and the Shield: The Life and Times of Sitting Bull* (New York: Ballantine Books, 1993), 48-59; Robert M. Utley, *Frontiersmen in Blue: The United States Army and the Indian, 1848-1865* (New York: Macmillan Company, 1967), 271-79.

12 Utley, *The Lance and the Shield*, 62, 67-73, 75, 78, 90-1.

13 Robert M. Utley, *Frontier Regulars: The United States Army and the Indian, 1866-1891* (Lincoln: University of Nebraska Press, 1973), 95, 98-107, 121-25, 132, 134-36; Olson, *Red Cloud and the Sioux Problem*, 70-82.

14 Utley, *The Lance and the Shield*, 76-84.

15 Utley, *The Lance and the Shield*, 84, 90-2.

16 Lieutenant William Quinton to Lieutenant M. C. Danbourne, Post Adjutant, Fort Shaw, May 19, 1871, NARA, RG 75, M234, LRCIA, Roll 491 (1871), frames 1114-15.

17 Olson, *Red Cloud and the Sioux Problem*, 79-86, 88-89, 92-95, 100-110, 114-31,

18 Viall to Parker, August 21, 1871, NARA, RG 75, M234, LRCIA, Roll 491 (1871), frames 871-75.

19 Viall to Indian Commissioner Francis A. Walker, December 23, 1871, NARA, RG 75, M234, LRCIA, Roll 492 (1872), frames 637-40.

20 Simmons to Viall, December 5, 1871, NARA, RG 75, M234, LRCIA, Roll 492 (1872), frames 646-47; Simmons to Viall, September 1, 1872, Annual Report (1872), 661.

21 Simmons to Viall, December, 5, 1871, frames 642-43, 647-48.

22 Ibid., frames 648-49.

23 Ibid., frames 650-53.

24 Ibid., frames 645, 553-54.

25 Ibid., frames 655-59.

26 Ibid., frames 658-61.

27 Ibid., 659; Viall to Walker, December 23, 1871, frames 638-40.

28 Simmons to Viall, January 3, 1871, NARA, RG 75, M234, LRCIA, Roll 492 (1872), frames 763-64.

29 Simmons to Viall, September 1, 1871, *Annual Report* (1872), 660-61; Walker to Secretary of Interior Columbus Delano, November 1, 1871, Annual Report (1872), 436-37.

30 DeMallie, "The Sioux in Dakota and Montana Territories," 31.

31 Simmons to Viall, December 5, 1871, frame 659.

32 Simmons to Viall, September 1, 1872, *Annual Report* (1872), 661.

33 Utley, The Lance and the Shield, 95; Simmons to Viall, April 15, 1872, NARA, RG 75, M234, LRCIA, Roll 493 (1872), frame 15; Simmons to Walker, June 9, 1872, NARA, RG 75, M234, LRCIA, Roll 492 (1872), frame 565.

34 Delano to Walker, June 13, 1872, NARA, RG 75, M234, LRCIA, Roll 492 (1872), frame 385; Major General Winfield S. Hancock, July 28, 1871, Lieutenant General Philip H. Sheridan, Division of the Missouri, August 3, 1871, and General William Tecumseh Sherman, Commander of the Army, August 7, 1871, *Annual Report* (1871), 849-850..

35 Walker to Delano, November 1, 1871, *Annual Report* (1872), 396.

36 Ibid.

37 Delano to Walker, June 13, 1872, frames 385-86; Walker to Delano, *Annual Report* (1872), 484, 463-64.

38 "Report of Hon. B. Benjamin R. Cowen, Assistant Secretary of Interior, Hon. N. J. Turney, and Mr. J. John W. Wham, commissioners to visit the Teton Sioux at and near Fort Peck, Montana," Secretary of Interior Columbus Delano, October 15, 1872, *Annual Report* (1872), 840; Olson, 132, 143.

39 "Cowen et. al to Secretary Delano, Annual Report," (1872), 840-43.

40 Ibid., 843-44; Simmons to Viall, September 1, 1872, *Annual Report* (1872), 661-62; DeMallie, "The Sioux in Dakota and Montana Territories," 32.

41 "Report of Hon. B.R. Cowen, Assistant et al to Secretary of Interior, of his observations as one of the commissioners above mentioned," Delano, *Annual Report* (1872), 844; Commissioner Walker to Secretary Delano, *Annual Report* (1872), 486; DeMallie, "The Sioux in Dakota and Montana Territories," 32, 34.

42 Simmons to N. J. Turney, December 15, 1872, NARA, RG 75, M234, LRCIA, Roll 495 (1873), frame 753.

43 Delano to Walker, December 11, 1871, NARA, RG 75, M234, LRCIA, Roll 492 (1872), frames 461-62; DeMallie, "The Sioux in Dakota and Montana Territories," 34-35.

44 "Cowen et al to Secretary Delano, Annual Report of Commissioners,"(1872), 842-43; Simmons to Montana Indian Superintendent James Wright, May 5, 1873, NARA, RG 75, M234, LRCIA, Roll 495 (1873), frames 816-17; Simmons to Indian Commissioner Edward P. Smith, September 30, 1873, NARA, RG 75, M234, LRCIA, Roll 496 (1873), frames 101-2; Delano to Walker, December 11, 1872, frames 461-62.

45 Simmons to Viall, June 19, 1871, NARA, RG 75, M234, LRCIA, Roll 493 (1872), frames 246-47; "Report of commissioners," 843; "Report of Cowen," 846; Agent Simmons, November 20, 1872, NARA, RG 75, M234, LRCIA, Roll 495 (1873), frame 738.

46 Utley, *The Lance and the Shield*, 106-7, 111.

47 Ibid., 107-10.

48 Ibid., 110-12.

49 Simmons to Cowen, December 8, 1872, NARA, RG 75, M234, LRCIA, Roll 495 (1873), frames 760-61, 765-66; Simmons to Turney, December 15, 1872, NARA, RG 75, M234, LRCIA, Roll 495 (1873), frames 753, 756-57.

50 Simmons to Cowen, December 8, 1872, frames 761-62; Simmons to Turney, December 15, 1872, frames 755-56.

51 Simmons to Cowen, December 8, 1872, frames 765-66; Simmons to Turney, December 15, 1872, frames 756-58.

52 These tribal locations remain essentially the same from a December, 1871 rich map enclosed by Agent Simmons. See: Simmons to Viall, December 5, 1871, NARA, RG 75, M234, LRCIA, Roll 492 (1872), frame 663.

53 Captain M. J. Sanno, Fort Shaw, to Adjutant General E. D. Townsend, War Department, Washington, D.C., June 23, 1873, NARA, RG 75, M234, LRCIA, Roll 497 (1873), frames 330-40.

54 Ibid., frame 340.

55 Simmons to Montana Superintendent James Wright, May 5, 1873, NARA, RG 75, M234, LRCIA, Roll 495 (1873), frame 817.

56 Ibid., 817-18.

57 Wright to Smith, June 26, 1873, NARA, RG 75, M234, LRCIA, Roll 497 (1873), frames 252-54; Wright to Smith, April 15, 1873, NARA, RG 75, M234, LRCIA, Roll 496 (1873), frames 548-49; Montana Superintendent Alfred Sully to Parker, September 23, 1869, *Annual Report*, 1869, 731, 734; Sully to Parker, September 20, 1870, *Annual Report*, 1870, 656.

58 Wright to Smith, June 26, 1873, frames 252-54; Wright to Smith, April 15, 1873, frames 548-49; Acting Secretary of Interior Benjamin R. Cowen to the Acting Indian Commissioner, August 5, 1873, NARA, RG 75, M234, LRCIA, Roll 495 (1873), frame 213; Assistant Interior Secretary Benjamin R. Cowen to the Indian Commissioner, August 13, 1873, NARA, RG 75, M234, LRCIA, Roll 495 (1873), frame 239.

59 Simmons to Wright, May 5, 1873, frames 816-17.

60 Simmons to Cowen, June 15, 1873, NARA, RG 75, M234, LRCIA, Roll 495 (1873), frames 838-39.

61 Ibid., frame, 839; Smith to Delano, November 1, 1873, *Annual Report* (1873), 373-74, 385, 387; "Report of J.P. Williamson and J. W. Daniels, Special Commissioners to Investigate the Condition of the Indians along the North Pacific Railroad with Reference to their Probable Opposition to its Construction, *Annual Report* (1873), 534-35, Olson, 143, 145, 157-58.

62 Utley, *Frontier Regulars*, 242-43; Utley, *The Lance and the Shield*, 111-14.

63 Utley, *Frontier Regulars*, 243; Utley, *The Lance and the Shield*, 114-21.

64 O.A. Pearson, Acting Chief Clerk, Department of Interior, to Smith, August 28, 1873, NARA, RG 75, M234, LRCIA, Roll 495 (1873), frame 247; Milk River Agent William W. Alderson to Smith, October 22, 1873, NARA, RG 75, M234, LRCIA, Roll 494 (1873), frame 74.

65 Alderson to Smith, September 1, 1874, *Annual Report* (1874), 574-75.

66 Alderson to Smith, January 15, 1874, NARA, RG 75, M234, LRCIA, Roll 498 (1874), frames 55-56; Delano to Smith, March 19, 1874, NARA, RG 75, M234, LRCIA, Roll 499 (1874), frame 7; Michael P. Malone and Richard B. Roeder, *Montana: A History of Two Centuries* (Seattle: University of Washington Press, 1976), 111, 114.

67 Fort Belknap Agent William H. Fanton to Smith, February 5, 1874, NARA, RG 75, M234, LRCIA, Roll 498 (1874), frame 925.

68 Ibid., frames 925-26.

69 Simmons to Smith, June 9, 1873, NARA, RG 75, M234, LRCIA, Roll 497 1873, frame 315; Fanton to Smith, February 5, 1874, frame 926.

70 Alderson to Smith, February 14, 1874, NARA, RG 75, M234, LRCIA, Roll 498 (1874), frames 65-66; Alderson to Smith, September 1, 1874, *Annual Report* (1874), 575.

71 Alderson to Smith, March 30, 1874, NARA, RG 75, M234, LRCIA, Roll 498 (1874), frame 92; Alderson to Smith, July 20, 1874, NARA, RG 75, M234, LRCIA, Roll 498 (1874), frames 193-94; Alderson to Smith, September 1, 1874, *Annual Report* (1874), 574.

72 Alderson to Smith, September 1, 1874, *Annual Report* (1874), 576.

73 Alderson to Smith, February 23, 1875, NARA, RG 75, M234, LRCIA, Roll 501 (1875), frames 59-61.

74 Alderson to Smith, October 20, 1875, *Annual Report* (1875), 811.

75 Alderson to Smith, June 30, 1875, NARA, RG 75, M234, LRCIA, Roll 501 (1875), frames 165-66; Alderson to Smith, February 23, 1875, frames 59-63.

76 Alderson to Smith, June 30, 1875, frames 165-66; Alderson to Smith, October 20, 1875, *Annual Report* (1875), 811.

77 Alderson to Smith, *Annual Report* (1874), 574.

78 Alderson to Smith, August 7, 1875, NARA, RG 75, M234, LRCIA, Roll 501 (1875), frame 199.

79 Ibid., 577; for modern summaries of nineteenth century Native American assimilation see: Francis Paul Prucha, *The Great Father: The United States Government and the American Indian*, abridged ed. (Lincoln: University of Nebraska Press, 1984; 1986), 152-60, 198-206, 217-21; and Frederick E. Hoxie, *A Final Promise: The Campaign to Assimilate the Indians*, 1880-1920 (Cambridge: Cambridge University Press, 1984), 1-39.

80 Alderson to Smith, Annual Report (1874), 574, 577; Alderson to Smith, *Annual Report* (1875), 811.

81 Alderson to Smith, *Annual Report* (1874), 575; Alderson to Smith, Annual Report (1875), 810.

82 Ibid.

83 Alderson to Smith, Annual Report (1875), 811; Agent Thomas J. Mitchell to Smith, April 26, 1876, NARA, RG 75, M234, LRCIA, Roll 505 (1876), frames 246-47.

84 Undersigned citizens of Jefferson, Ashtabula County, Ohio to the Commissioner of the Bureau of Indian Service, July 30, 1873, NARA,

RG 75, M234, LRCIA, Roll 508 (1877), frames 142-43; Undersigned citizens of Jefferson, Ashtabula County, Ohio to Dr. James Wright, Indian Agent, Crow Agency, October 29, 1873, NARA, RG 75, M234, LRCIA, Roll 508 (1877), frames 145-46; C.A. Hibbard, Principal Jefferson High School (Jefferson, Ohio), June 14, 1873, NARA, RG 75, M234, LRCIA, Roll 508 (1877), frame 135; J. S. Cumming, Monmouth District Conference, Methodist Episcopal Church, Illinois, August 12, 1874, NARA, RG 75, M234, LRCIA, Roll 508 (1877), frame 148; Peter O. Matthews to Zachariah Chandler, Secretary of Interior, January 13, 1877, NARA, RG 75, M234, LRCIA, Roll 508 (1877), frames 158-61.

85 Alderson to Smith, *Annual Report* (1875), 810; William T. Hagan, *Indian Police and Judges: Experiments in Acculturation and Control* (New Haven: Yale University Press, 1966; Nebraska University Press, 1980), 42, 69-70, 79-81, 85-86, 91-103, 154-57, 162-68.

86 Alderson to Commissioner J.Q. Smith, February 26, 1876, NARA, RG 75, M234, LRCIA, Roll 504 (1876), frames 60, 63; Alderson to Commissioner Edward P. Smith, *Annual Report* (1875), 811.

87 Ibid., 60-61.

88 Ibid.; Alderson to Edward P. Smith, *Annual Report* (1875), 811.

89 Mitchell to J.Q. Smith, April, 19, 1876, NARA, RG 75, M234, LRCIA, Roll 505 (1876), frames 271-72; Alderson to J.Q. Smith, January 1, 1876, NARA, RG 75, M234, LRCIA, Roll 504(1876), frame 23.

90 Mitchell to J.Q. Smith, April 19, 1876, frames 271-72; Mitchell to J.Q. Smith, May 30, 1876, NARA, RG 75, M234, LRCIA, Roll 505 (1876), frames 306-8.

91 Mitchell to Commissioner John Q. Smith, April 19, 1876, frames 271-72; Mitchell to Smith, July 5, 1876, NARA, RG 75, M234, LRCIA, Roll 505 (1876), frames 378-81; Loretta Fowler, *Shared Symbols, Contested Meanings: Gros Ventre Culture and History, 1778-1984* (Ithaca: Cornell University Press, 1987), 200.

92 Mitchell to Smith, July 5, 1876, frames 378-81; Mitchell to Smith, September 26, 1876, *Annual Report* (1876), 497.

93 Mitchell to Smith, *Annual Report* (1876), 497; Agent Wellington Bird to J.Q. Smith, September 15, 1877, NARA, RG 75, M234, LRCIA, Roll 507 (1877), frames 456-57.

94 Mitchell to Smith, *Annual Report* (1876), 495.

95 Ibid.

96 Utley, *Frontier Regulars*, 245-47; Utley, *The Lance and the Shield*, 82-84, 91-92, 125-27; Charles J. Kappler, ed., *Indian Affairs. Laws and Treaties*, vol. 2 (Washington: Government Printing Office, 1904), 1002-3.

97 Utley, *Frontier Regulars*, 247-48; Alderson to John Q. Smith, January 21, 1876, NARA, RG 75, M234, LRCIA, Roll 504 (1876), frames 37-38.

98 Mitchell to Smith, July 19, 1879, Roll 505, frame 372; Mitchell to Smith, July 29, 1876, Roll 505, frame 431.

99 Ibid., 432-33; Utley, *The Lance and the Shield*, 165-66.

100 Utley, *Frontier Regulars*, 267-68; Utley, *The Lance and the Shield*, 167-68; General Alfred H. Terry to Colonel William B. Hazen, October 18, 1876, Roll 505 (1876), frame 619.

101 Ibid.; Terry to Hazen, October 25, 1876, Roll 505 (1876), frame 620; Mitchell to Commissioner J.Q. Smith, November 11, 1876, frame 618.

102 Hazen to Mitchell, October 26, 1876, frame 622; Hazen to Mitchell, October 29, 1876, frames 624-25.

103 Mitchell to Smith, September 15, 1876, frames 520-21.

104 Mitchell to Smith, September 18, 1876, frames 533-34.

105 Mitchell to Smith, September 25, 1876, frames 636-40.

106 Utley, *The Lance and the Shield*, 168-70; Pam Rietsch, webmaster, 1895 *U.S. Atlas, Montana 1895 County Maps*, available from http://www.livgenmi.com/1895/MT/County/.

107 Utley, *The Lance and the Shield*, 141, 170-73; Gregory F. Michno, *Lakota Noon: The Indian Narrative of Custer's Defeat* (Missoula: Mountain Press Publishing, 1997), 195, 205-7, 217, 234.

108 Mitchell to Smith, October 23, 1876, frames 629-30; Mitchell to Smith, November 11, 1876, frame 598; Utley, *The Lance and the Shield*, 176; Mitchell's successor, Agent Wellington Bird, provided a very useful mileage map of key Fort Peck agency sites at the end of the following letter: Bird to Smith, June 29, 1877, Roll 507 (1877), frame 319.

109 Mitchell to Smith, November 11, 1876, Roll 505 (1876), frames 598-601; Utley, *The Lance and the Shield*, 176.

110 Utley, *The Lance and the Shield*, 175-77.

111 Mitchell to Smith, December 9, 1876, frames 693-95.

112 Ibid., frames 695-96; Utley, *The Lance and the Shield*, 177-78.

113 Utley, *The Lance and the Shield*, 177-82.

114 Alderson to Smith, October 20, 1875, *Annual Report* (1875), 811.

115 Governor Benjamin F. Potts to Smith, October 6, 1876, frames 771-74.

116 Secretary of War J. Donald Cameron to Secretary of Interior Zachariah Chandler, October 31, 1876, frame 1249; Endorsement, Commander General William Tecumseh Sherman, October 25, 1876, frames 1250-52.

117 Mitchell, *Annual Report* (1876), 494-96; Mitchell to Smith, July 29, 1876, frame 431; Mitchell to Smith, September 17, 1876, frame 513.

118 Colonel William B. Hazen, Fort Buford Commander, December 10, 1876, Roll 508 (1876), frame 125.

119 Mitchell to Smith, January 2, 1877, Roll 508 (1877), frames 122-23.

120 Mitchell to Smith, January 29, 1877, frame 209.

121 Colonel John Gibbon, Commander of Fort Shaw, to Major G.D. Ruggles, Assistant Adjutant General, Department of the Dakota, December 2, 1877; endorsement, Brigadier General Alfred H. Terry, Department of Dakota, December 18, 1877; endorsement, Assistant Adjutant General R. C. Drum, Division of the Missouri, December 21, 1877.

122 Mitchell to Smith, January 26, 1877, Roll 508 (1877), frame 204.

123 Mitchell to Smith, January 29, 1877, frame 209.

124 Lieutenant R.H. Day, Fort Peck Commander, to the Post Adjutant, Ford Buford, January 29, 1877, frames 722-24.

125 Secretary of War George McCrary to Secretary of Interior Carl Schurz, April 14, 1877, frames 787-88; Lieutenant General Philip Sheridan, Commander of the Division of the Missouri, to General William Tecumseh Sherman, Commander of the Army, April 7, 1877, frames 789-90.

126 Sheridan to Sherman, April 7, 1877, frames 789-90.

127 Schurz to Smith, March 29, 1877, Roll 507 (1877), frame 788.

128 Agent William W. Alderson to Indian Commissioner Edward P. Smith, September 1, 1874, *Annual Report* (1874), 574, 576; Mitchell to Smith, June 6, 1876, Roll 505 (1876), frames 321-24; Mitchell to Smith, July 29, 1876, Roll

505 (1876), frame 424; J.K. Beidler to Smith, July 13, 1876, frames 425-26.

129 Mitchell to Smith, June 6, 1876, 321-24; endorsement, Colonel William B. Hazen, Commander Fort Buford, January 8, 1877, Roll 508 (1877), frame 183.

130 Mitchell to Smith, March 27, 1877, Roll 507 (1877), frames 58-61.

131 Utley, *The Lance and the Shield*, 181-82.

132 Sheridan to Lieutenant James W. Forsyth, Military Secretary, May 5, 1877, Roll 508 (1877), frames 812-13.

133 Forsyth to Sheridan, June 11, 1877, frames 829-33.

134 Wellington Bird to Smith, May 4, 1877, Roll 506 (1877, frame 118; Bird to Smith, May 12, 1877, frame 117; Bird to Smith, June 23, 1877, Roll 507 (1877), frames 199-204; Bird to Smith, July 7, 1877, frames 290-2; Bird to Smith, July 14, 1877, frames 261-62

135 Bird to Smith, July 14, 1877, frames 261-63.

136 Bird to Smith, June 23, 1877, frame 205.

137 Bird to Smith, June 25, 1877, frames 228-34.

138 Bird to Smith, June 29, 1877, frames 312-16.

139 Ibid., frames 312-13; Forsyth to Sheridan, June 11, 1877, frame 833.

140 Bird to Smith, July 14, 1877, frames 266-67; Forsyth to Smith, August 3, 1877, frames 310-11.

141 Bird to Smith, July 18, 1877, frames 285-88.

142 Smith to Smith, July 18, 1877, frame 248.

143 Smith to Schurz, July 20, 1877, frames 795-96.

144 J. H. Hammond, Superintendent, Dakota Superintendency, to Smith, August 30, 1877, frame 17; Hammond to Smith, September 11, 1877, frame 15.

145 Bird to Smith, September 19, 1877, frame 478; Bird to Smith, *Annual Report* (1878), 585-86.

146 Bird to Smith, November 11, 1877, frames 574-76.

147 Mitchell to Smith, April, 19, 1876, Roll 505 (1876), frames 271-72; Mitchell to Smith, May 30, 1876, frames 306-8; Mitchell to Smith, June 1, 1876, frames 291-94; Mitchell to Smith, July 5, 1876, frames 378-81.

148 Major Guido Ilges, Commander, Fort Benton Post, to the Acting Adjutant General, Fort Shaw, July 19, 1877, Roll 508 (1877), frames 873-77.

149 Ilges to the Acting Adjutant General, Fort Shaw, July 24, 1877, frames 861-62;

150 Ilges to Bird, August 16, 1877, Roll 507 (1877), frames 409-10.

151 Bird to Smith, August 22, 1877, Roll 507, frames 407-8.

152 Schurz to Indian Commissioner Ezra A. Hayt, October 25, 1877, frame 814; Schurz to Hayt, October 26, 1877, frame 816.

153 Schurz to Hayt, October 25, 1877, frame 814; E.D. Townsend, Adjutant General, by command of General William Tecumseh Sherman, Commander of the Army, to General Philip Sheridan, Division of the Missouri, October 27, 1877, Roll 508 (1877), frame 988.

154 Sherman to Sheridan, frame 988; Schurz to Hayt, October 24, 1877, Roll 507 (1877), frame 814; Sheridan to Sherman, November 1, 1877, frame 990.

155 Sheridan to Sherman, November 1, 1877, Roll 508 (1877), frames 989-90; McCrary to Secretary of Interior Schurz, November 13, 1877, frames 986-87.

156 McCrary to Schurz, November 14, 1877, frames 983-84; Lt. General Alfred H. Terry, Department of the Dakota, to the Assistant Adjutant General, Division of the Missouri, November 22, 1877, frames 1008-9; endorsement, Sheridan, November 24, 1877, frame 1010; McCrary to Schurz, November 30, 1877, frames 1003-6.

157 Agent Bird to Commissioner Hayt, December 12, 1877, Roll 507 (1877), frame 620; Agent Bird to Commissioner Hayt, December 12, 1877, frames 621-24.

CHAPTER 5

The Starving Years, 1878-1888

Dennis J. Smith, Ph.D.

Nᴇᴡ Fort Peck Indian Agent Wellington Bird had weathered the extraordinarily demanding conditions gripping the agency in June 1877, when he assumed control from the negligent administration of Thomas J. Mitchell. The agency then at Fort Peck had suffered profoundly from the catastrophic March flood, and the new agent faced the daunting task of establishing and moving the main agency to a new site. With unusual speed, Indian Commissioner John Q. Smith accomplished the construction of the new agency at Poplar River by mid-October 1877, before winter arrived.

The real test of Agent Bird's early administration was whether he could prevent the hunger and deprivation which the Assiniboines and Sioux at the chronically underfunded agency faced almost every winter. When it came to preparing adequately for winter provisions and food, Bird proved as inadequate as most agents before and after him. In late March 1878, he told Indian Commissioner Ezra A. Hayt that within the week the agency would completely exhaust most of its food: flour, bacon, pemmican, sugar, coffee, beans, and hominy. He explained that he could stretch the beef supply to end of the fiscal year (June 30, 1878) if he could limit distributions to once every three or four weeks. It appears that Fort Peck annuities were distributed weekly, but even if they were given out every other week, Bird was going to be decreasing beef distributions at the very time all the other foods disappeared. He stated that steps needed to be taken immediately to prevent the impending shortages.[1]

In early April 1878, Bird, who was at his home in Mount Pleasant, Iowa, was informed that the agency Indians had just returned from their winter hunt, and he again informed Indian Commissioner Hayt that the agency had only limited quantities of beef remaining. On May 13, 1878, Bird did not report that agency Natives were starving, but he did "have a lot of hungry

Indians clamoring for food," and he permitted both the Wolf Creek Assiniboines and Poplar River Sioux to immediately leave the agency to hunt bison. Fort Peck Assiniboines and Sioux were probably starving at this point, for Bird told Hayt that in the month or so that it would take for goods to arrive up the Missouri River, "In the meantime shall the Indians be left starving?" On May 31, 1878, Interior Secretary Carl Schurz approved the purchase of an additional fifteen percent of the existing contract (an additional 135,000 pounds).[2]

The 1877-1878 winter was the first Sitting Bull's followers and allied tribesmen spent in Canada, and Bird remained vigilant concerning relations of the agency Indians. He was most concerned with the Yanktonais. Like his predecessor Mitchell, Bird was acutely aware that General Alfred Terry, Commander of the U.S. Army's Dakota Division, would seize control of the agency for any violation of trade and cooperation with Sitting Bull's Indians.

Bird reported that the agency Natives were staunchly allied with the federal government, informing Hayt on January 14, 1878 that he found only one incident of agency Indians trading with Sitting Bull's Lakotas. Bird stated that this infraction was immediately reported by different tribal members, affirming their allegiance.[3]

Fort Benton military post Army scouts (presumably Native persons) under the command of Captain Constant Williams witnessed Yanktonai militant resistance to Sitting Bull's followers firsthand. Williams dispatched them to the Milk River area to determine the location and status of Sitting Bull's followers. They returned around the first week of February 1878, after being hospitably welcomed in the winter camp of Yanktonai chiefs Long Fox and Black Tiger. Black Catfish's 130 lodges and Medicine Bear's camp of similar size were also nearby. The scouts were in Long Fox's and Black Tiger's camp when one of

Sitting Bull's Hunkpapa hunting parties entered camp. The Yanktonais killed five of their horses, whipped the men, confiscated all their meat, and threw them out of camp. The Yanktonais berated them, saying that since they had "thrown off" the American government, they should no longer cross into this country, or Yanktonais would give them more of the same.[4]

Long Fox also confided to the chief scout that Fort Berthold tribes (Arikaras, Mandans, and Hidatsas) had sent tobacco to the Fort Peck Assiniboines and Yanktonais to go to war in the spring of 1878, with the government's permission, against Sitting Bull's followers. Long Fox said that they met in council and accepted the offer. Very significantly, he explained how this exceptional stance against fellow Sioux was strongly influenced by the destitute conditions at their agency. He said that Sitting Bull's followers made the federal government suspicious of Fort Peck tribal allegiance, and they were in turn deprived of things they needed. Long Fox complained that his people already "do not get enough provisions at the agency." Williams stated that these were surely the reasons why recently the Yanktonais had stopped some Métis trading carts.[5]

The scouts further stated that the Lakotas and Cheyennes were better armed with guns and ammunition than any tribes they had ever seen. Cheyenne warriors typically wore two or three full belts of ammunition and even had arm bracelets with fixed cartridges. The Cheyennes explained that although Cypress Hills traders drove hard bargains for trade items such as bison hides, horses, pemmican, or sacks of flour, the Indians could acquire all the guns and ammunition they desired. Due to such things as the harsh trading terms, they would return to their reservations, and were willing to surrender their horses, but not their guns. The scouts reported that all Sitting Bull's followers stated they wanted no trouble with any whites, but they were fully prepared to engage the U.S. Army if ever attacked.[6]

Sitting Bull's followers were clearly well armed to defend themselves from U.S. Army attacks, but their primary vulnerability was food, for they depended completely on bison for survival. They drifted across the international line into the upper Milk River region in the winter of 1878-1879 following bison, as did Fort Belknap and Fort Peck Assiniboines, Gros Ventres, and Sioux, who hunted predominately in the lower Milk River region, nearer their respective agencies. In early April 1878, diverse parties of Sitting Bull followers came to the main Fort Peck Agency at Poplar River reporting that many of their women and children were starving, and eating their horses to survive. Gilbert A. Skinner, the agency clerk and acting agent, reported that the warriors who visited the agency were fully armed with Springfield carbines and wearing three full ammunition belts, each holding an estimated fifty cartridges.[7]

In contrast, Fort Peck Yanktonais possessed little ammunition, a shortage noted by Williams' scouts in their February 1878 visits to Yanktonai winter camps. Fort Peck Agency interpreter Alexander Culbertson in August 1878 reported that when he visited Yanktonai camps, the Indians bitterly complained about the ammunition shortage. He explained that nearly every ammunition belt was empty, and he even saw Yanktonais hunting bison *with bows and arrows*! The ammunition shortage was particularly grating, Culbertson noted, because Fort Belknap Assiniboines and Gros Ventres were fully supplied with ammunition, a consequence of the poor enforcement of ammunition restrictions of the T.C. Power trading post there.[8]

Bird reported to Hayt on January 21, 1878, that eighty-five Red River Métis carts had just arrived at the agency, indicative, he said, of the non-agency Indians and Canadian Métis settled throughout the northern Milk River area of the reservation. The Métis traded heavily in bison robes at Fort Belknap, bringing back to the reservation illicit ammunition and alcohol. Bird asked that the commissioner remove these Indians who were disserving the interests of the Fort Peck tribesmen. In March 1878, Lieutenant General Philip Sheridan, Commander of the Missouri, authorized General Alfred Terry, Commander of the Dakota Division, to remove them, but the Métis fled to Canada first.[9]

On October 3, 1878, Bird again complained to Hayt that the Métis had returned, with 300 families taking up residence in the Milk River area. He again leveled heavy blame on the illicit trade at the Fort Belknap trading post, stating that the trader had assisted the Métis in constructing fifty log cabins. The Métis were trading for unlimited ammunition supplies, which infuriated the Fort Peck Indians, for the Métis were killing all the bison. Bird again requested aid in removing them. In October 1878, Sheridan ordered General John Gibbon, Commander of the Montana Division at Fort Shaw, to do so. Gibbon ordered Major Guido Ilges, Commander of the Fort Benton post, to remove them.[10] The results of Major Ilges' assignment are unclear.

In the fall of 1878, as agency bands returned to the agency, Bird reported that he perceived a new recklessness, insubordination, and even hostility among some Yanktonais. He attributed this primarily to their association with Sitting Bull's followers during the bison hunting season. He was correct in describing their complaints about agency failures to feed and provide them as unusually vehement and persistent. And as his second winter at the agency approached, food and provisions were again inadequate.[11]

November seemed unacceptably late to be complaining to the Indian commissioner about the inadequate food annuities. On November 1, 1878, Bird claimed that the 700,000 pounds of beef contracted for the year should actually be doubled. Once tribal bison reserves ended, he explained, the distribution of full rations would exhaust the beef supplies in seven weeks. On November 16, he noted that the remaining 107,000 pounds of flour would be expended in six weeks. On November 23, Bird reported that agency beef and flour would be gone by January 1, 1879, and food supplies would have to be shipped to the agency by wagon from Bismarck.[12]

One crisis from this mismanagement arose in March 1879. The agency Indians again had no choice but to leave the agency for winter bison hunting, but 300 old people and children who were unable to follow their tribesmen to winter camps due to deep snow were forced to eat their horses. With no food to offer them, Bird telegraphed Hayt for permission to purchase flour from Fort Buford. Two days later, the commissioner authorized Bird by telegram to purchase 800 sacks of flour on the open market, not to exceed $2,550.[13] Bird reported no further similar incidents of imminent starvation through the rest of the winter.

Bird's inability to control his agency persisted into the summer of 1879. On June 6, he stated in a letter to General Nelson Miles at Fort Keogh that he believed that Yanktonai chiefs Black Catfish, Black Tiger, and others were strongly implicated in a series of horse raids earlier in the spring. More importantly, these two chiefs and their soldiers (*akicitas*) were obstructing Yanktonai farmers at Poplar River led by such Yanktonai chiefs as Medicine Bear, Afraid of the Bear, and Turning Bear. Bird believed that Black Catfish and Black Tiger must be disarmed, and perhaps removed from the agency. Bird also mentioned that many small bands of Sitting Bull's followers came to the agency asking for rations, but when informed about the terms of unconditional surrender—the confiscation of all their horses and guns—refused to do so. Bird claimed that these bands were disturbing to the

Fort Peck Indians, and he wished they could be driven off the reservation.[14]

On June 11, 1879, Bird sent a letter to Colonel Daniel Huston, commander at Fort Buford, again focusing on the alleged roles of Black Catfish and Black Tiger in horse raids, and said that he wanted them taken from the agency. On June 15, Bird sent another, more panicked letter to Huston, urgently requesting a company of soldiers to control the insubordinate Yanktonais under Chiefs Black Catfish and Black Tiger. Bird then made the unsupported assertion that the agency was now threatened by attack by Sitting Bull's tribesmen. In response to the supposed emergency, Lieutenant Colonel Huston immediately sent a company under the command of Captain Thomas Britton.[15]

On June 28, 1879, Britton submitted his report from the Fort Peck Agency about the tempest in a teacup that purportedly had happened. Britton found the primary issue at the Fort Peck Agency was the complete lack of food for the agency Indians. In fact, Britton found that, "The Indians seem to be very peacefully inclined, *notwithstanding there is not an ounce of anything in the storehouse to issue them*" [emphasis added]. Bird explained that the agency had received less than one half its food annuities the past winter, that flour provisions due two months ago remained in Bismarck, and beef supplies from Fort Benton were equally late.[16]

Shortly after his arrival, Black Catfish and Stab Plenty came to the agency to meet with Captain Britton. When confronted with the fact that Black Catfish had refused to have his band register for ration tickets, the chief replied that "there was no use to be ticketed; *his people could not eat tickets* and that was all his father [Agent Bird] had to give him. If they would give them something to eat, he would be glad to be counted" [emphasis added].

Britton advised Black Catfish to take all the

tickets he could get, so that when annuities came, he might receive more rations. That evening Black Catfish visited Britton again, but this time he was in great humor. He had just met with Bird and requested that his entire band be registered for ration tickets, which Bird accomplished the next day. Britton remarked that after having his band ticketed: "the heretofore insubordinate chief was the most zealous of all of them to have a truthful count made." Britton concluded his report with a perfect summary of the entire debacle at Fort Peck: "Should *any difficulty* hereafter arise at this agency, it *will solely be caused on account of hunger,* for they seem to be exceedingly well disposed *considering the manner they have been neglected* by the powers that be"[17] [emphasis added].

Conditions for Fort Peck Agency Assiniboines and Sioux changed little that summer, nor did the constant turnover of Indian agents. Agent Wellington Bird submitted his resignation to Interior Secretary Carl Schurz on April 4, 1879, and it was accepted on April 7. His replacement, Nathan S. Porter, also nominated by the Methodist Episcopal Church, took charge of the agency on July 17, 1879.[18]

As Bird had been when he relieved Mitchell at the old Fort Peck Agency, Porter was shocked by conditions at his new assignment. Porter said there was nothing in the storehouses but some flour and salt, and he was informed that the agency Indians had had nothing to eat from January to March. Like Bird before him, Porter explained that the agency was appropriated about one-half of what was needed. Porter was surprised that the Lakotas and other Sioux at the Spotted Tail and lower agencies received full annuities and provisions. He reported that the Fort Peck Indians could not understand "why *this starving policy* has been adopted in regard to them"[19] [emphasis added].

Porter faced hard times on his arrival, as his predecessor had. The degree to which his difficulties were the result of Bird's mismanagement is unclear. In November 1878, agency interpreter Joseph Culbertson, the mixed-blood son of long-standing agency interpreter Alexander Culbertson, gave a sworn testimony to Fort Benton post commander Guido Ilges about Bird's wholesale malfeasance.

Culbertson claimed to have personally frequently witnessed Bird trade annuity blankets for bison hides, which he in turn traded for other items. In fact, Culbertson had served as translator for an exchange with an agency Indian named Good Hawk, who received a number of annuity blankets for ten or more bison hides. Culbertson claimed to also have served as translator in an exchange between one of Sitting Bull's followers, who received fifty rounds of ammunition for a fancy (presumably painted) bison robe. Culbertson said he had witnessed Bird's son trade Indian annuity sugar, coffee, and scarlet cloth to an agency Indian named Palecote in return for bison hides.

Culbertson further alleged that Bird had sold several tons of agency hay to local non-Indians for cash and bison hides. Culbertson said he had received a pair of agency blankets from Wolf Point subagency superintendent Thomas Henderson in return for a pair of moccasins Sitting Bull had given him. Culbertson also witnessed Henderson give a Wolf Point Assiniboine, Jack Mitchell, an agency horse in payment for an altercation in which Henderson knocked Mitchell down and beat him. Culbertson further stated that he and another agency employee (apparently a part-time employee named Sweeny) regularly purchased alcohol from agency clerk Gilbert Skinner. Culbertson said that Bird threatened to fire him and run him off the reservation if he spoke to anyone about these abuses. Major Ilges stated to his superiors that he forwarded Joseph Culbertson's sworn affidavit to them out of the interests of public service because Fort Peck Agency tribal dissatisfaction with Bird was so great.[20]

Not surprisingly, Bird bitterly repudiated Culbertson's allegations, accusing Major Ilges of using "a poor ignorant, drunken half breed boy to fabricate charges against an Indian Agent." Culbertson's father, agency interpreter Alexander, also defended Bird's honesty and integrity. Interior Department Inspector John McNeil, who investigated the agency in June 1880 during another disastrous starving year, was much more critical of Bird.

Inspector McNeil pinned significant responsibility for Porter's turbulent first year of service upon the widespread failures Bird left for him. McNeil was mystified at the incredibly shabby construction and lack of proper accommodations of the three buildings built in 1877, when the Poplar River Agency was established under Bird's administration. McNeil said that for the $18,000 paid for this construction, the work was scandalous, bordering on fraudulent.

McNeil was stunned that Bird left no requisition records for his entire two-year service, strongly suggesting fraudulent management. Bird did explain to Hayt upon Porter's arrival the sad fact that there was essentially no space at the agency. When Porter arrived with a large number of his relatives, there was literally no place for Bird to finish the numerous reports he had not yet completed. He explained to Hayt that he was taking all the records to his home in Mount Pleasant, Iowa, where he would complete them and send them to Washington.[21] This action was highly irregular at best, but appears consistent with Bird's administration.

Porter's first order of business was trying to secure adequate food annuities for the coming winter. In late August 1879, he reported that he had no copy of the flour contract for the fiscal year ending in June, 1880, so he did not

know how much he should be expecting, but he strongly urged Hayt to have at least 3,000 sacks delivered soon, before the Missouri River was too low. The crisis of delayed annuity shipments would soon preoccupy Porter, but unlike his predecessor, Porter was vigorously asserting annuity matters before winter had already arrived. Another indicator of the desperate food situation was that when Porter inquired about the four yokes of work oxen needed for planting, he was informed that the Indians had butchered them.[22]

Porter also supported Assiniboine and Sioux farms. The Yanktonai farm at the main agency at Poplar River was located at the junction of the Missouri and Poplar Rivers in a 400-acre area bounded by the two rivers and on the other two sides by a cottonwood fence. Of the 130 acres in cultivation, eighty-two were divided into ninety-three parcels, each farmed by one individual family. Six miles east of Poplar River at a site apparently known as Deer Tail, in a seventy-acre plot of broken land they cultivated thirty acres, also divided into thirty individual parcels.

Assiniboines at Wolf Creek operated two distinct types of farms. The largest was a 100-acre plot, divided into 100 individual parcels. In addition, Assiniboines planted individual farms at what appeared to be scattered family log home sites, in all totaling an estimated fifteen acres. Both tribes planted two crops, one of which was "Ree" [Arikara] corn, a small-kernelled variety with small yields, but which matured early. The other was potatoes, which regularly yielded exceptionally abundant harvests. The agency contracted to break the land, and the Sioux women did almost all the cultivation. (Porter did not elaborate concerning Assiniboines.) For unexplained reasons, the Sioux crops went in late and the harvest looked minimal; Assiniboines planted early and by the time Porter wrote his annual report in mid-August, 1879, the prospective harvest looked good. The agency employees cultivated their own farm, presumably at Poplar River, of fifty-six acres. It was more diversely planted with turnips, beans, and peas. Porter focused on the agency farm turnips, which he said went immediately to feed agency Indians.[23]

By mid-July, nearly all the agency Assiniboines and Sioux but 400 who remained to tend the crops were bison hunting south of the Missouri River. The Yanktonais hunted forty miles south of the river, and small parties returning to their hunting camp with meat to the agency camp brought portions of flour. They were angry, however, because of their lack of ammunition for hunting, so that they had resorted to shooting the bison with bows and arrows, and completed the kill by stoning the animal. They complained that inadequate food annuities compelled them to secure most of their subsistence by hunting, but the federal government refused to provide them sufficient ammunition to do the job.[24]

Many Fort Peck Natives chose to hunt south of the Missouri River to avoid Sitting Bull's followers, and many Yanktonais were doing so under the strict recommendation of General Nelson Miles, commander of Fort Keogh, located near the mouth of the Tongue River. Miles visited the Fort Peck Agency on July 10 and called a meeting with Yanktonai headmen Black Catfish, Pack the Eagle, Red Door, Bad Bear, Four Horns, and Four Crows. He strictly warned them to not camp near Sitting Bull's followers and under no conditions were they to allow the non-agency Lakotas into their camps, to which the Yanktonais fully consented.[25]

Miles was at Fort Peck on June 5, 1879 with orders from General Alfred Terry to expel Sitting Bull's followers to Canada, by armed force if necessary. Terry was responding primarily to the complaints of Indian agents, particularly Bird, about Sitting Bull's followers and Canadian Métis trespassing on Fort Peck and Fort Belknap Agency lands. On July 17, 1879, Miles' advance

companies of nearly 700 troops engaged a large Hunkpapa hunting party and camp on Beaver Creek, a southern tributary of the Milk River. Accompanying Miles' forces were 143 Crow, Cheyenne, and Assiniboine scouts/auxiliaries. Agent Porter, however, reported that 200 Assiniboines and Yanktonai chief Black Catfish were with General Miles. Sitting Bull was in this hunting camp, as was one preeminent Crow warrior named Magpie, and in the middle of the conflict, he challenged Sitting Bull to personal combat. Sitting Bull accepted, the two rushed each other on horses, and after Magpie's gun misfired, Sitting Bull shot and killed him. The battle was small but fierce, and the Hunkpapas quickly retreated across the international line.[26]

The problem of trespassing non-agency Indians and Métis continued from virtually the moment Miles' troops returned to Fort Keogh. The Métis occupation was complicated, because some were American-born mixed-bloods who had certain rights in this country. In his July 1879 engagement and removal of Sitting Bull's tribesmen, Miles also confiscated the carts of Canadian Métis. Apparently unable to distinguish Canadian from American Métis, Miles arrested both.[27]

Some were sent to Fort Buford, and one American Métis named Alexander Gordi, and approximately twenty-five families of relatives and followers were released by Commander Huston. Gordi was angry because his forced march and confinement at Fort Buford had exhausted his food resources and worn out his horses. Not only was he destitute when released, but he also was frightened that confinement had kept him from securing enough bison to survive the winter. Gordi believed, perhaps rightly, that the federal government owed him something, but Fort Peck Agent Porter, also perhaps properly, refused his request for agency annuities.

Gordi was anxious not to be unjustly arrested

again, and he carried with him a letter written by Fort Buford Captain Thomas Britton stating that Gordi and the twenty-five Métis families with him considered themselves American citizens. Britton advised that as long as these people did not violate any laws, they were entitled to kind consideration. With Porter's assistance, Gordi then met in council with agency Assiniboines and Sioux, who permitted his party to winter on their lands. They honored Gordi's request to return to the Milk River country, but he promised to stay away from Yanktonai and Assiniboine hunting areas.[28]

For Porter, the return of large numbers of Métis to reservation land was unacceptable. On October 13, 1879, he telegraphed Hayt that the Army needed to remove them. Porter then telegraphed Colonel Thomas H. Ruger, Montana District Commander, on November 3, explaining that Hayt had authorized Porter to seek military assistance to remove the Métis. He explained that a large number of Métis were presently established in the "Big Bend" region of the Milk River. Porter addressed his telegram to Fort Assiniboine, the nearest military post to this location.[29]

The U.S. Army established Fort Assiniboine in May 1879 as part of its strategy against Sitting Bull and his non-agency tribal allies. The post was situated on the upper Milk River, but far removed from the concentration of non-agency Indians and Métis in the Big Bend area, 125 miles away. On November 6, 1879, General Terry ordered Lieutenant Colonel H.M. Black, the Fort Assiniboine commander, to remove all Canadian Métis. American Métis not related to the tribes at the Fort Belknap and Fort Peck Agencies were also to be removed from the reservation.[30]

This placed Black in a difficult position, for his scouts reported to him that the Milk River region this side of the international line now contained more Indians than they had ever seen before. Very significantly, these included not only Sitting Bull's 730 lodges (an estimated 4,000 persons), and Canadian and American Métis, but also Canadian tribes, including Blackfeet, Bloods, Piegans, and Crees. As Black proceeded into the Big Bend area, many Indians and Métis he encountered informed him that all these Native people had come to the region because of the loss of bison in Canada. He learned that most of these Indians were starving, and were forced to eat their dogs.[31]

Black's primary Métis informant on conditions in the Big Bend region was an American mixed-blood named Charles Treschi, who was born and raised at Turtle Mountain. Treschi explained that most of the Métis in this Milk River area were American mixed-bloods who were as destitute as he was. They were living on the Canadian side but had crossed to the U.S. side due to starvation. He begged Black not to force him and these Métis to return immediately to Canada in the dead of winter. Other Indians had stolen most of his horses, and the only place with wood for fuel and shelter was Wood Mountain, eighty miles away, and his family would die trying to transport their carts through the deep snows. He pledged to return as soon as conditions permitted, proceeding up the shelter of the Milk River where his debilitated horses could feed on the grasses.

Black included a full testimonial from Treschi in the commander's report to his superiors. In his report, Colonel Black questioned the propriety of forcibly removing these Métis (technically American-born, but whose recent habitation was in Canada) while not removing the Canadian Indians, who were also driven upon American reservation lands by their desperate need for bison. Black requested clarification of his orders, seeking authority to use discretion in permitting the Métis to voluntarily return when winter receded, and such authority was granted.[32]

Black's decision not to interfere with these destitute, bison-hungry Indians became, as it turns out, the Army's final position on the matter. William Tecumseh Sherman, Commander of the Army, fully appreciated that bison were the primary issue for non-agency Indians and mixed-blood Métis in the Milk River country. In a January 3, 1880 endorsement forwarded to his military commanders, he said:

Until we are prepared to occupy that remote country, I see no good reason why Indians and half-breeds may not earn a bare existence by killing the Buffalo, which do not care for National boundary lines. Also, half-breeds have a right to emigrate to our soil, if they commit no crime and do not actually molest our subjects. Surely in that vast uninhabited Region, the few Indians along the Upper Missouri can find enough land to cultivate, if so disposed—or room to hunt if they will not work—without precipitating our little garrisons into a fight with 4,000 hostiles.

This was exceedingly practical advice, but its implications were enormous.

From the military perspective, Sherman's most important position concerned Sitting Bull, whose followers were now permitted to hunt on reservation lands as long as they were peaceful with whites. Sherman's policy was perfectly reasonable, for up until this point, Sitting Bull and his followers had not attacked any white settlers in this truly remote region. This was also consistent with the Army's obligation to protect American citizens, for none of the tribal trespassers endangered them.

But in terms of federal Indian policy, Sherman had sharply reversed the Army's actions concerning the trespassing on reservation lands by non-agency Indians, which included the Métis. For Agent Porter and the Fort Peck Assiniboines and Sioux, this was the *only* issue, for these tribal

intruders were destroying the agency Indians' bison hunting. Only six months earlier, General Terry had commanded Miles to remove all the Indian trespassers, by military force if necessary. Sitting Bull had been peaceful toward whites at this time also; when Miles' advance companies attacked them on July 17, 1879, the Hunkpapas were butchering bison.[33]

The complaints of Fort Peck Assiniboine and Sioux were about the destruction of their bison by fellow Indian people, an increasingly poignant story as these Natives crowded together to hunt the rapidly disappearing bison. At this same time during the summer and fall of 1879, Fort Peck tribesmen for the first time witnessed the wholesale slaughter of bison by white hide hunters. In late October 1879, General Philip Sheridan reported that these white commercial hunters had killed thousands of bison along the Red Water and Big Dry Creeks, one of Sitting Bull's most prized winter camping areas, on the south side of the Missouri River. The year 1879 was a watershed and tragic year, for it marked the advance of white hide hunters into the Montana Territory's upper Missouri River region. Within four years—by 1883—they had virtually exterminated the bison.[34]

Assiniboine eyewitness accounts of the white hide hunters' destruction during these terrible years were recounted in 1929 as the tribe prepared its J-31 docket with the U.S. Court of Claims. Many Assiniboines witnessed shootings, and even talked to the hide hunters. Assiniboine chief The Man saw hunters using six-barreled guns with telescopes, killing bison from very long distances. Henry Archdale, Sr., also was present when in 1881 three hunters killed an entire herd of 150 bison. An Assiniboine named Looking saw the killing of groups as large as 100 bison.

Images of piles of bison hides, which resembled haystacks, fill these accounts. Martin Mitchell—who was born around 1869 and said

Assiniboine country had been thick with buffalo since he was three—saw white buffalo hunters all over the country. He encountered the stacks of bison hides throughout the Missouri River country, and saw the steamboats, some with three decks, loaded high with bales of hides. Mitchell also recalled that in 1882 on an Assiniboine tribal hunt near present-day Glasgow, they found no bison, but instead stacks of bison hides. Infuriated, some were going to throw them all in the Missouri River, but Chief Red Stone stopped them, saying he had always promised friendship. Red Stone did say he wanted to stop the white hide hunters, but the Assiniboines proceeded to cut up and destroy all the bison hides stacked before them.[35]

Heavy snows beginning in November 1879 and lasting through March 1880 created a crisis for agency and non-agency Indians and Métis alike. The bison moved completely south of the Missouri River, and Fort Peck Agency Indians had no winter bison hunt, which had always sustained them through the inadequate agency provisions.[36] Since his July 1879 arrival, Porter had argued firmly with Hayt for increased annuities, stating that the level funded for his predecessor Bird met only half the needs of agency Natives.

No additional provisions were provided, however, and although Porter did not report any breakdowns in the delivery of contracted goods, he was resigned to distributing incomplete portions throughout the winter. On February 17, 1880, he reported that his weekly distributions of three and one-half pounds of flour and fifteen of beef (presumably per family) lasted only four days, and the Indians went hungry for the next three days. Porter did not present this as a new condition, and most likely he had had little choice but to issue only partial rations since November. Porter explained that this hardship was in part due to the fact that there was no winter bison hunt, and he added that the prospects for initi-

ating one were unlikely, for the bison at this date were seventy-five miles south, and moving further in that direction. Porter requested authority to make an emergency purchase of $3,000 worth of beef or pemmican on the open market, but permission was not granted. Someone in the commissioner's office did note at the bottom of Porter's letter that 120,000 pounds of flour were to be sent on the first boat up the river. That would end up being a late boat.[37]

Porter also explained to Hayt that in addition to feeding the 5,476 agency Natives, 398 Hunkpapas had surrendered to the agency. Like the Fort Peck Agency Indians, they faced their own subsistence shortages, for by June 1879, Canada had reversed its tolerant policies to Sitting Bull's exiled followers and refused to provide any more provisions for them. They were totally dependent on bison during the winter of 1879-1880, and the Milk River bison herd had migrated seventy-five miles south of the Missouri River. Sitting Bull's Hunkpapas and assorted Lakota, Cheyenne, and other tribal followers were quickly starved into surrendering. Hunkpapa war chief White Gut's forty lodges, totaling 284 persons, surrendered to the Fort Peck Agency on February 6, 1880. One hundred more surrendered by the time Porter wrote Commissioner Hayt on February 17.[38]

On that day, Hunkpapa war chief Gall came to Fort Buford and met with post commander Colonel William B. Hazen and Agent Porter. One month previously, Gall had surrendered his horses to Porter, who placed him on the tribal rolls and issued him a ration ticket. It is unclear if Gall stayed at the agency over the next month, but now Gall wanted to know the disposition concerning the surrender of his own lodges. Gall explained that except for the conditions of unconditional surrender—the confiscation of all horses and guns—they would surrender to the agency immediately. Seeing that the Fort Peck

Agency Indians were already starving, however, Gall explained that he could not surrender. To do so would be to face certain starvation.[39]

This was remarkable for two reasons. Surrendering to the U.S. Army would have secured Gall full Army rations, but some Lakotas like Gall would rather risk starvation than trust the Army. Equally significant, the conditions for Assiniboines and Sioux at the Fort Peck Agency were so destitute that even starving Indians refused to live there. In explaining the Gall encounter to Hayt, Porter admitted that Gall's argument about facing starvation at the agency without horses or guns was "to a certain extent true." Even more telling, Porter explained that he could not accept surrender of any Sitting Bull followers as prisoners of war, as the Indian Affairs Office preferred. To that, Porter would have had to offer *full Army rations*, and he did not have the food to do so.[40]

Conditions worsened at the agency, for by mid-March, 1880, another 220 Lakotas had surrendered, and by mid-April an additional 580 had come in. These surrendering Indians were shockingly destitute, and half-starving. So were their horses, most of which died shortly after arriving. On April 14, 1880, Porter explained the status of new surrenders and requested of the new Indian Commissioner, Roland E. Trowbridge, that additional provisions be sent immediately, for Porter had "but a little flour and meat to give them." He pleaded for at least some additional flour and meat. On May 2, 1880, Porter telegraphed Commissioner Trowbridge, now explaining that the Indians *had nothing to eat* and he asked immediate authority to purchase $600 worth of food until the spring order of flour arrived. Incredibly, Trowbridge did not authorize the request.[41]

Trowbridge's unconscionable refusal to honor Porter's urgent requests continued. Porter telegraphed Trowbridge on May 3 and May 14, 1880,

both times stating that he had agency tribesmen trying to plant crops, but they had nothing to eat, and he requested permission to purchase flour on the open market at a price of $6 per hundred pounds, yet the commissioner still refused to even reply. On May 18, Trowbridge was notified by telegram from Yankton, Dakota Territory, that a ship had departed with 600 sacks of flour to the Fort Peck Agency, which was expected to arrive by May 31.[42]

On May 20, 1880, Porter both telegraphed and sent a letter to Trowbridge that he had yet to receive an answer from his two earlier telegraph requests. Porter told Trowbridge that he had already received Porter's supply report submitted on May 1, showing that the agency had issued its last flour. Still incredulous, Porter then stated:

If the Department [the Indian Affairs Office] can not understand the situation of thing [sic] here, or doubt the reports, the only way they can understand it will be to send a coms. [commissioner] or some Dept. Officer to examine for I can not run this without some help from the Department.

Still, Trowbridge refused to answer.[43]

Porter was unrelenting, and on May 31, 1880, he wrote again to Trowbridge, repeating that he had still not received an answer by telegraph or letter on his request to make an emergency food purchase. Porter explained several times that the agency Indians were starving. These included statements such as they were "suffering terribly for want of the necessities of life," and that "It has been found impossible to get any labor performed by starving Indians."[44]

On June 3, 1880, Porter finally received a letter from Trowbridge accusing him of being deceived by the surrendering Lakotas. Trowbridge believed that these Indians were not surrendering all their horses and guns as required. Porter replied that was "impossible," for he had personally witnessed and dictated terms, counting both persons and property, and "I took the best they had." And he explained that this was not much, for they were in fact starving, and he had seen the trail from the Big Bend of the Milk River to the agency, littered with death mounds and scaffolds and the skeletons of horses, mules, and ponies killed either for food or having perished from starvation.[45]

The flour shipment did not arrive to the Fort Peck Agency until June 5, 1880, and Interior Department Inspector John McNeil was there to witness it. He had arrived on June 3. In his June 17, 1880 report to the commissioner, McNeil got right to the point. His second sentence was, "The first question that confronted me was one of starvation."

And he proceeded immediately to explain that Porter had 1,350 of Sitting Bull's Hunkpapas to feed, in addition to 6,000 agency Assiniboines and Sioux. McNeil explained that all food provisions had in fact been issued, even including the seed corn. He noted that the Indians had eaten their horses, which he further noted "were only skin and bone," and were living on wild turnips, flag root, and whatever small game they could find. He commented that the elder Indians and the children "look pinched and cadaverous"—they literally looked dead! McNeil then stated that one person had in fact starved to death. Things were grim even for agency staff, for McNeil stated that when the thirty tons of food (60,000 pounds, one-half of the fiscal year flour contract) arrived, "with it came relief to the starving Indians and almost starving whites."[46]

McNeil reported that the furnishings and supplies of this remote agency were so inadequate and the "embarrassments" surrounding Porter so great, that "it would be harsh and unjust to criticize this agent as one would an agent better supplied." In fact, McNeil stated that "Agent Porter with less means is laboring under greater embarrassments then I have yet seen any other agent."

Seeing what he believed to be the scandalously shabby construction of the agency buildings constructed in 1877, and finding essentially no records left by Agent Wellington Bird, Inspector McNeil blamed Bird for a great deal of Agent Porter's hardships.[47] He should have also included Indian Commissioner Trowbridge.

In May, the bison came north and the agency tribes had successful hunting through June and July, but were unable to store more than ten days worth of meat. The Yanktonais cultivated 155 acres at Poplar River and the Assiniboines 155 acres at Wolf Creek, which Porter divided into 530 individually farmed parcels. Heavy July rains salvaged crops that otherwise would have been lost, but the potato crop was limited because the hungry Indians dug up and ate the potatoes as soon as they were formed. Because of this, Porter was forced to post guards over these planted fields. The crops were primarily potatoes and corn again; vegetables could not be planted because the seed shipment did not arrive until July, too late for planting.[48]

In the fall of 1879, Porter closed the small agency day school at Poplar River and continued the equally humble day school in Wolf Point, which was poorly attended. Hayt honored Porter's analysis at the time that a boarding school was the only way education could be successful. In October 1879, Hayt requested that Porter submit plans for a new boarding school, which Porter did in January 1880. In July 1880, Porter got permission to construct the boarding school at the main agency at Poplar River, but it does not appear that construction commenced until the following year. The Presbyterian Church was granted permission to build the first parochial day school on the agency, which was erected at Poplar Creek, and Reverend G.W. Wood took up his service in July 1880. The

Methodist Episcopal Church was granted primary missionary authority over the reservations in Montana Territory, but failed to introduce any services, despite prodding in 1879 by Indian Commissioner Ezra Hayt.[49]

Porter reported that the 1880 agency Sioux numbered 5,829 persons, which included 1,116 who surrendered from Sitting Bull's followers. Assiniboines numbered 1,450, for a total agency tribal population of 7,259. Porter also reported that on his arrival in 1879, there were only two log homes in which agency tribesmen lived. During 1880, thirty-two new, sod-covered, primarily dirt-floored log homes were built by the Indians themselves. The agency carpenter placed doors and windows.[50]

In the summer of 1880, Porter worked aggressively to avoid the chronic annuity shipping delays for which the agency Indians suffered. On July 30, 1880, he recommended that Trowbridge assist him in pressuring contractors to ship directly to Bismarck instead of Yankton, greatly reducing the distance and time of steamboat transportation, with all its risks and complications. He cited the recent vegetable seed shipment from Detroit, Michigan: had it been directed first to Bismarck, the agency might have been able to plant vegetables this year.[51]

The shipping breakdowns which Porter feared were not long in arising. On August 20, 1880, a federal inspector named Pollack telegraphed Interior Secretary Carl Schurz from Fort Buford, complaining that Indian freight was lying there and in Miles City while military and private freight proceeded up the Missouri River. Clearly in response to Porter's July 30 letter to Trowbridge, the powerful Montana contractor, T.C. Power, on August 29 telegraphed the Indian Affairs Office and responded to each of Inspector Pollack's allegations, explaining that there were no unnecessary delays. He explained that Fort Peck steamboat shipments were sent as soon as suf-

ficient goods were ready, and he pledged that the Fort Peck flour would be delivered before winter.[52]

Even more remarkably, on September 10 Power reported on the progress of the Fort Peck shipments, explaining that a steamboat had just departed, and that the balance of Fort Peck goods had been ordered and directed for rail shipment to Bismarck. He promised to "stir [his] agents up" to make sure that the contracted flour reached Bismarck by September 20. In further good service seldom experienced at Fort Peck, on October 10, T.C. Power telegraphed the Indian Affairs Office again, advising them of the status of the Fort Peck and Crow and Fort Belknap Agency shipments. Remarkably, Power noted that he was personally supervising all these shipments.[53]

The flour shipment saga did not stop there. On November 9, 1880, T.C. Power's contractors delivered 2,750 sacks of flour to Fort Peck, but presumably because of low water on the Missouri River, they had to leave 1,250 sacks at Fort Buford. Four days later, Porter telegraphed Trowbridge that this flour had been exposed to the elements and destroyed by rain, horses, and cattle. Remarkably, the same day Power telegraphed the Indian Affairs Office and said that the flour was being handled responsibly and would be delivered to Fort Peck, even if he had to freight it overland. The flour was still not shipped by November 29, and Power telegraphed the Indian Affairs Office that the remaining flour would be shipped as soon as final arrangements could be made. Power promised that "nothing will be left undone."[54]

Porter's management of affairs in the summer of 1880 was also complicated by agency tensions related to what remained of Sitting Bull's followers. On August 12, 1880, Porter dispatched a letter to General Miles at Fort Keogh, asking for troops to help secure the agency. A number of Yanktonais were returning from a summer hunt accompanied by a large number of Sitting

Bull's non-agency Indians. Porter feared that both groups were eating all the potatoes and corn from the Indian farms, and his small party of tribal police was unable to control them.

On September 22, 1880, General Terry ordered two companies from Fort Custer, established in 1877 near the confluence of the Little Bighorn and Bighorn Rivers, to the Fort Peck Agency. On October 1, Captain Ogden B. Read, commanding the two companies, was ordered to establish the new post, which generally became known as Camp Poplar. In late November, larger numbers of Sitting Bull's followers sifted into the lower Milk River lands, and on December 11, 1880, Terry dispatched five additional companies under the command of Major Guido Ilges from Fort Keogh to reinforce Captain Read.[55]

Compared to the starving winter of 1879-1880, the agency tribes endured well through the 1880-1881 winter. The agency was still feeding and provisioning over 1,100 Sitting Bull followers, but the key to salvation was successful fall and winter hunting. The summer hunts, apparently south of the Missouri River, proved fairly successful, but most importantly, the early winter bison hunt which lasted into early January 1881 was highly successful, providing abundant meat and numerous bison hides for trading. In addition, an early break-up of ice on the Missouri River in February flooded the valley with up to fifteen feet of water, stranding large numbers of antelope and deer. Porter estimated that 7,000 were killed in February and March. Good fortune continued in the large summer bison hunts in July and August; an estimated 4,500 bison were harvested in a region thirty to 100 miles southwest of the agency. The agent's persistence in closely monitoring the delivery of annuity provisions also paid off, for Porter noted that supplies were sufficient throughout the year.[56]

During the 1880-1881 winter, most of Sitting Bull's followers were forced into surrendering and the major tensions related to their presence were resolved. A crisis had arisen over the encampment at the mouth of the Milk River of many Hunkpapa under the leadership of war chief Gall and renowned warrior and minor chief Crow King. On December 31, 1880, negotiations with Major Ilges at Fort Buford concerning surrender broke down.

On January 2, 1881, Ilges and 300 soldiers marched on the Hunkpapa camp on the Missouri River bottomlands. This barely registered as a skirmish. Ilges shelled the camp, and only a few shots were exchanged, but the large forced surrender Ilges desired was achieved. Over a thousand Hunkpapas surrendered and at the end of a cruel sixty-mile forced march in the dead of winter, they were impounded at Fort Buford. Sitting Bull's few remaining followers no longer posed a threat, and they suffered through the winter. With the entire camp starving, in April 1881 one of the last holdouts, Low Dog, took his twenty lodges, including most of the remaining warriors, and surrendered at Fort Buford. On May 26, 1881, those 1,126 tribal prisoners were shipped by steamboat to the Fort Yates military post at the Standing Rock Agency. On June 13, they were joined by an additional 1,641 tribesmen who surrendered at Fort Keogh. On July 19, 1881, Sitting Bull and his destitute party of 187 persons proceeded to Fort Buford and surrendered to post commander Major David H. Brotherton. Ten days later, on July 29, they were also shipped by steamer to Fort Yates.[57]

In May and June 1881, Porter transferred several small parties of Yanktonais totaling 386 persons and a small number of Hunkpapas to the Standing Rock Agency. These Yanktonais were among the large number of "northern" Sioux who migrated into the Fort Peck region in the early 1870s, and were formally placed on the Fort Peck Agency rolls in 1871. The reasons for their apparent voluntary return are unclear, but the new Standing Rock Indian Agent, James McLaughlin, stated they wanted to settle among their relatives and take up agriculture.[58]

By the end of summer 1881, Agent Nathan Porter's second year of service at the Fort Peck Agency had been rather successful. For a remote agency chronically plagued with marginal funding and frequent turnover of typically inexperienced and ineffective Indian agents, success was best measured by having a year without major deprivation and suffering. By this low standard, agency Assiniboines and Sioux had survived admirably.

The year 1881 was in many ways a tipping point year for the agency and the lives of Assiniboines and Sioux. A short-term problem, the four traumatic years between 1877 and 1881 of Sitting Bull's non-agency tribesmen, had ended, as did the extraordinary meddling of the U.S. Army in agency affairs. The most important change, however, related to the natural world.

In spite of the highly successful bison hunting in the 1880-1881 winter and 1881 summer, the most disturbing indicator of impending catastrophe was the greater distances bison hunters now had to go on their major bison hunts, up to at least 100 miles south of the Missouri River. The Milk River bison herd was disappearing, and with it went the ancient nomadic lifestyle of the Plains Sioux and Assiniboines. Once the process of establishing permanent homes commenced, with it would come the scorched earth assault on tribal communal beliefs and practices by the dominant white society, and particularly federal Indian policy officials, missionaries, and white citizens from all orbits of society: local and community, territorial and state, and national.

In 1881, the agency landscape was already changing. Porter noted that seventy Native families now lived in log homes, more than double the thirty-two log homes constructed in 1880, which in turn was a dramatic increase from

the two log homes on his arrival in July 1879. Porter did not say where the seventy homes were situated, but most likely they were in one of ten tribal farming communities, which included the main agency, Poplar River; Wolf Point, twenty-two miles west of Poplar River; Deer Tails, seven miles east of Poplar River; Alkali Creek, six miles east of Poplar River; Frenchman's Point, eighteen miles east of Poplar River; Box Elder, four miles west of Poplar River; Two Chimneys, twenty-five miles east of Poplar River; Grangerville, two miles west of Wolf Point; Little Wolf Creek, two miles east of Wolf Point; and Spread Eagle, ten miles east of Wolf Point.[59]

Very significantly, when listing these ten farming communities in his 1881 annual report to the Indian commissioner, Porter said: "By this you will see *my object is to scatter the Indians as much as possible.*" He stated this was to avoid tribal strife, which itself is a vague objective. It seems without question that his primary objective was to destroy tribal communalism, and if that was the case, the purposeful scattering of individual family home sites had the same intent.

Porter was assaulting what all Fort Peck Indians to date had hoped to protect: the Assiniboine and Sioux tribal camps. Since the establishment of the Milk River Agency in 1869, all the tribesmen attached to it did not live directly at the agency buildings, but in discreet tipi villages situated to maintain geographic separation from the agency complexes. The intent of these camps was open and unapologetic: to preserve ancient Sioux and Assiniboine cultural beliefs and practices which both peoples loved. These were the same places of communal and cultural life which Indian agents, and Indian policy, Army, and missionary officials loathed as primitive and barbaric.

In terms of tribal camp locations, these were in fact situated in the vicinity of the agency and subagency complexes during the winter, for they were essentially ancient winter camps sheltered in wooded areas. From early spring through late fall, the tribal camps followed the bison. Up to around 1881, Assiniboines and Sioux were at best only marginally agency Indians. Although the agency documents are essentially silent concerning the tribal camps, it seems quite apparent that these two cultural worlds by mutual consent kept to themselves as much as possible. This explains the almost complete lack of cultural assimilation by Fort Peck Assiniboines and Sioux from the agency's origin in 1869 to around 1881, when things began to change much more rapidly.

Fort Peck agents' preoccupation with establishing log homes for their tribesmen was an open and frankly stated assault on tribal nomadism. Agents like Nathan Porter understood that education and cultural assimilation could not be instituted as long as Assiniboines and Sioux were away most of the time hunting bison. The agency day schools at Wolf Point and Poplar River were utter failures for many reasons, but lack of student attendance was the principal one.

The Yanktonais farmed a total of 400 acres in 1881, and the Assiniboines at Wolf Point, 175 acres, all of which Porter divided into 950 individually farmed parcels. The crops were again primarily corn and potatoes, but now included more squash, pumpkins, and melons, all of which harvest was apparently adequate except for the thirty acres of turnips, which failed.[60]

And in the context of permanent tribal residence, the opening of the agency boarding school at Poplar River in August 1881 was both a symbolic and tangible example of the enormous cultural changes converging at the time. Methodist Episcopal Church reverend Samuel E. Snider, from Solon, Iowa, was appointed the first superintendent. The Methodist Episcopal Church at first resisted but finally consented to a contract to administer the school. The school

consisted of a one and one-half story building with separate male and female dormitory rooms within it. Early inspectors were concerned that it was too small, with a student capacity of only fifty students, when room for 300 would have been more appropriate.[61]

Conditions worsened in the winter of 1881-1882 due to lack of bison. The problems were two-fold. White hide hunters now controlled all the hunting lands south of the Missouri River, and they had killed most of the bison. In early January 1882, Captain Ogden Read sent a small detachment to inventory the Big Dry Creek region, formerly rich bison lands directly south of the original Fort Peck trading post, and they found only scattered small bison groups.

The white hide hunters had driven what remained of the Milk River bison herd north of the Missouri River and into the Milk River country west of the Fort Peck agencies, but the problem was that large numbers of mixed-blood Métis and Canadian Crees had reestablished themselves there, and they were actually enjoying good bison harvests. Worse, they were very careful to prevent the bison from migrating east of the Milk River area, where the agency Assiniboines and Sioux could hunt them. These Métis trafficked illicitly in alcohol and ammunition on both sides of the Missouri River. During the 1881-1882 winter and early summer, the only bison meat Fort Peck Assiniboines and Sioux were able to secure was from the carcasses left behind by the commercial hunters.[62]

Porter reported that by June 1882, the agency provisions "would not reach for all," and the tribes were forced to depart to hunt bison. It is unclear if there was tribal hunger and deprivation during the 1881-1882 winter and early spring of 1882, but it was highly significant that when Porter met with tribal leaders concerning the need to hunt bison, he stated that they went very reluctantly. He did not elaborate, but most likely they were destitute to some degree, and must have believed that the prospects of successful hunting were grim. That seems to have been what happened. Most of the agency Natives remained away hunting bison until August 1882 and left again for more fall bison hunting, but there was no game. Drought-like conditions seemed to have set in and there were no bison as far as the Milk River area.[63]

Tribal farming also expanded in 1882, but unfortunately the crops yielded a poor harvest, though Porter provided no details about that. The acreage cultivated by the scattered Sioux communities totaled 520 acres and was composed of 791 individual farm parcels. Assiniboines cultivated a total of 215 acres farmed by 320 families (which presumably meant 320 individual family-farmed parcels).[64]

Although Porter provided few details, conditions for agency Assiniboines and Sioux by the fall of 1882 must have been marginal due to poor harvests and bison hunts. To compound the already frightening subsistence conditions, Indian Commissioner Hiram Price had notified Porter in April 1882 that the agency appropriations for the 1883 fiscal year had been slashed 25 percent, from the present $100,000 to $75,000. In his September 1, 1882, annual report, Porter explained that these hardships "make a very gloomy outlook for my Indians this winter. They must abandon their homes and take to the prairie, or starve."[65]

It is unclear what conditions were like for the agency Assiniboines and Sioux during the 1882-1883 winter. Samuel E. Snider, the Indian agent who replaced Porter in July 1883, wrote on August 10, 1883, in his annual report that game had practically disappeared. Price endorsed agency Indians' complaints during the winter of 1881-1882 about the large scale Métis and Cree killing of Milk River bison. On May, 2, 1882, Price informed Porter that Secretary of Interior Henry

M. Teller had formally requested that Secretary of War Robert Todd Lincoln order the Army to remove these tribal trespassers. Unfortunately, Sherman refused. In his January 3, 1883 endorsement, Sherman contended that it would cause too much suffering for the soldiers to launch a removal campaign in the middle of winter.

For some reason, Sherman focused primarily on issues related to the non-Indian hide hunters. Captain Read's January, 1882 report had explained that Métis and Crees were the primary bison hunters in the Milk River region and that the hide hunters were all south of the Missouri River. Perhaps the white hide hunters had infiltrated the bison lands across the Missouri River, but it seems unlikely that the Métis and Crees would have retreated back to Canada.

Sherman explained that the Army had recently failed to stop the bison destruction by "these Arabs of the Prairie" (non-Indian hide hunters) south of the Northern Pacific Railroad, and he did not have the troops to do so in the Upper Missouri River region. He believed that whites had the same legal right to hunt bison as did Native Americans, even though he agreed that they were trespassing on reservation lands. Sherman further noted that in the judgment of most military men, the bison were already doomed, and the sooner they were gone, the sooner Indians would begin ranching and farming. Secretary of War Lincoln accepted Sherman's recommendation. The Army would not remove any trespassers in the winter months of 1883.[66]

As the new Fort Peck Indian Agent in July 1883, Samuel E. Snider faced the same horrible conditions Porter had confronted in the summer of 1882. The bison had essentially disappeared, and compared to what had been a dismal harvest in 1882, a severe drought had destroyed the entire 1,000 acres the agency Assiniboines and Sioux had planted. Worse, Snider admitted in his annual report, filed on August 10, 1883 that "With no crop, no game, *and as yet no supplies, the wolf of hunger is in every lodge*" [emphasis added]. Snider provided no explanations about the lack of agency supplies, nor are there any details in Porter's 1883 writings. Nor did Snider explain his cryptic note about widespread tribal hunger, but obviously agency tribesmen were destitute even before the 1883-1884 winter began.[67]

Interior Department Inspector C. H. Howard examined the entire Fort Peck Agency in late October, 1883, and he at least corroborated the need for additional food annuities. He filed two reports, one dated October 24, 1884, on the main agency at Poplar River, and one dated October 25, 1884, on the Wolf Point subagency. In the short introduction to his October 24 Poplar River Agency report, Howard told Interior Secretary Henry M. Teller that there were two pressing issues at the agency. First was the need to remove the military post, Camp Poplar, discussed in an October 15, 1884 letter to Secretary Teller. Second, due to crop failures and lack of buffalo meat, the agency needed an additional supply of food "to prevent starvation and trouble," a topic he explained in an October 17, 1884 letter to Teller. Howard did not address the lack of supplies which Snider reported on August 10, so perhaps some food supplies had arrived. In either case, Inspector Howard clearly was stating that without more food, starvation was an imminent possibility at the agency.[68]

It seems quite apparent that Howard understood that the shortage of food was worse at Wolf Point. He never even mentioned lack of food in his October 24 report of the main agency at Poplar River, which was very extensive. In his equally comprehensive October 25 report on the Wolf Point subagency, however, "Food Supply" is the first category he presented. This is a two-paragraph category, and in the first he confirmed the disappearance of the bison, saying that in the

250 miles he traveled on the reservation to make this report, he did not see a single one.

He began the second paragraph with this sentence: "Some additional supply of food is necessary or there will be starvation." He concluded by warning Teller that the degree of need for supplemental food supplies should not be calculated in the more common condition in which an agency had some game to supplement the government's provisions.[69] It seems pretty clear that at Wolf Creek, the wolf of hunger was truly in most lodges.

Agency Natives were apparently not starving when Inspector Howard visited in late October 1883, but they were by January 1884. Captain Ogden Read, Commander at Camp Poplar, explained in a January 14, 1884 letter to his superiors, that he had heard repeated accounts that the Assiniboines at Wolf Point were not only suffering for want of food, "as all the Indians at this agency have been all winter," but that they were actually dying from starvation.

On January 11, he confronted Agent Snider about these numerous accounts, and he demanded that Snider accompany him to fully investigate the matter. Snider agreed, and the next day the two traveled to Wolf Point. On that evening, Snider, Read, the subagency superintendent, and two interpreters visited every family in the immediate vicinity of the subagency. One family had just butchered a horse, but in all the remaining homes visited, "not one of them had a single mouthful of anything to eat." These Assiniboines said they had not eaten in three to four days, and that the weekly rations lasted only one or two days. The subagency superintendent who was accompanying these visits and was the person who distributed the annuities confirmed the truthfulness of these testimonials.[70]

The following day, Read and the superintendent visited the Assiniboine camp located further away from the subagency, and the accounts in

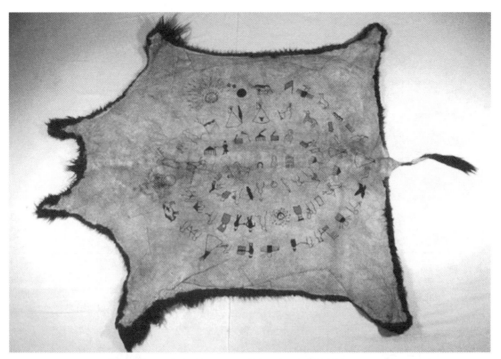

Lone Dog (Yanktonai), *Winter Count*, dating from 1800. Painted on buffalo hide.

Wich' Wanbdi' (Eagle Man), Nhoe-a-ke (Human Male War Eagle), Wica Wanbli (Man Who Packs the Eagle), Yanktonai Sioux of the Cut Head Band, 1872.

Chief Reddog, Chief He Wets It, Chief the Man, 1880s–1890s.

Last buffalo herd on Fort Peck Indian Reservation, 1870–1880.

The History of the Assiniboine and Sioux Tribes of the Fort Peck Indian Reservation: 1600 - 2012

Chief Medicine Bear (Mato Wakan)

Chief Redstone (Hoonga Ea Sha), 1833–1896

Medicine Bear was the leading Chief of the Pabaksa (Cut Head) Band of the Upper Yanktonai Tribe, who together with the Hunkpati Lower Yanktonai made up the Ihanktowanna Nation. They were considered a separate nation from the Ihanktowanna Nation because the tribe was so large. Together they were considered one campfire of the Seven Council Fires of the Great Sioux Nation, a loose confederation of bands and tribes or nations within a nation.

In 1853–54 during a fight against the Crow, Medicine Bear was shot through the body, but managed to kill the one who shot him as well as his companion. His wound was very severe and by 1865 it had not fully healed.

By the 1880s, Medicine Bear had seen that he needed to better the conditions on the reservation. He was asked by the agent where he wanted his permanent camp to be. Mato Wakan told the agent that he wanted to live by the river, so if there was no game his people would always be able to fish. This site is now the community of Fort Kipp. Mato Wakan was the principal Sioux signator of the 1886–1887 treaty, which led to the establishment of the Fort Peck Reservation in 1888.

Descendants of Medicine Bear who live on the Fort Peck Reservation are the First, Four Bear, Perry, and White Eagle families and their relatives.

Chief Redstone's life spanned the creation of the great north reservation, the creation of the Fort Peck Reservation, the coming of the railroad, and Montana Statehood. In 1866, he was named Chief of the Wadopana (Canoe Paddler Band of Assiniboine), and in that same year was a signator of the treaty that kept the Northern Pacific Railroad out of this area, protecting it as prime buffalo hunting grounds. He led his people during a time of many wars, witnessed the fur trading at Fort Union, saw the buffalo disappear, and accepted life on the reservation.

Chief Redstone selected the Wolf Point area as the home of the Wadopana. His burial site is known only to his Assiniboine people. He was the chief Assiniboine signator of the 1886–1887 treaty that led to the establishment of the Fort Peck Reservation in 1888.

Missionaries or Indian agents talking with Indian leaders, 1880s.

Maggie Iron Cloud Red Elk, 1880s. This photograph was most likely made in a photographer's studio.

Gall, mid-1880s. Also known as Walks-in-Red-Clothing and the Man-Who-Goes-in-the-Middle, Gall was a member of the Hunkpapa Sioux tribe, as was Sitting Bull. He took part in the Battle of the Little Big Horn. He traveled extensively in the Fort Peck Reservation area.

Assiniboine and Sioux children sent to Carlisle Indian School, Pennsylvania, April 1890.

Old Man Duck and White Man at the
Wolf Point Stampede, early 1900s.

Chief He Wets It,
1900s.

The History of the Assiniboine and Sioux Tribes of the Fort Peck Indian Reservation: 1600 - 2012

Top image: Fort Shaw Indian School women's basketball team, World Champions at the Louisiana Purchase Exposition, 1904. Here they are dressed in their basketball uniforms. Top row, from left to right: Nettie Wirth, Catherine Snell, Minnie Burton, Sarah Mitchell. Bottom row: Genie Butch, Belle Johnson, Emma Sansaver. Bottom image: Fort Shaw Indian School women's basketball team dressed in traditional buckskin dresses. From left to right: Emma Sansaver, Nettie Wirth, Catherine Snell, Belle Roberts, Minnie Burton, Sarah Mitchell, Rose LaRose, Genie Butch.

The steamer O.K. on the Missouri River at Williston, North Dakota, 1905.

Fort Peck Indian Agency Superintendent Charles B. Lohimiller's residence, Poplar, Montana, 1905–1917.

The History of the Assiniboine and Sioux Tribes of the Fort Peck Indian Reservation: 1600 - 2012

Minnie Smith and Tahca Site (Deer Tail), Riverside, May 1907. Tahca Site was one of the leaders at Riverside who spoke out against the Allottment Act. The government promised that the Sioux people would be given rations and money for ten years after the act was enacted. Tahca Site asked, "But what about after the ten years?"

Poplar boarding school, girls' domitory, 1910s.

Fort Peck Indian Agency head-
quarters, flagstaff, and cannon,
Poplar, Montana, 1910s.
Photograph published by
H. Cosier.

Major Charles B. Lohmiller,
Superintendent of Fort Peck
Agency, was accompanied by
five Sioux leaders to Washington,
D.C., in 1911, to meet with offi-
cials of the Taft Administration.
With Lohmiller, from left to right:
Chief Iron Whip, Chief Spotted
Eagle, Chief Horses Ghost, Chief
Grow Twice Kill Twice.

Fort Peck Indian Agency office, Poplar, Montana, 1911.

Fort Peck Indian girls, October 14, 1911. From left to right: Ella Red Boy, Elise Kills Thunder, Lizzie Keiser, Minnie Red Boy, Mary Turning Pipe, Mary Eagleman Youngman, Nellie Bruguier Clark.

Poplar dormitory, 1912.

Eddie Bear's Fort Peck Indian home, Poplar, Montana, 1912.

Government Row, Poplar Montana, looking south, 1912.

Issue Day for Assiniboines, Wolf Point, Montana, 1912.

Sioux Indian Girls at Poplar Boarding School, 1912.

Participants in the festivities at the Indian Fair held to celebrate the arrival of Olidden Tours and the special Great Northern train, Poplar, Montana, July 17, 1913.

Participants in the Indian Fair, Poplar, Montana, July 17, 1913.

The arrival of the special Great Northern Tour Train at Poplar, Montana, July 17, 1913.

Tipi of Chief Feather Ear-Ring, Fort Peck Indian Reservation, Poplar, Montana, 1914. Picture postcard produced by G.W. Staton.

Chief Big Horn's tipi, Fort Peck Indian Reservation, Poplar, Montana, 1914. Picture postcard produced by G.W. Staton.

Annie Good Left and Thelma Red Eagle, November 5, 1915.

these homes was exactly the same—there was not a mouthful of food in any of their homes. Read commented that only a short time ago this same camp was full of dogs, but Read saw only one. Assiniboines informed him that they had eaten them all, and Read heard accounts of a total of fifteen horses butchered for food, or sold for prices from two to five dollars each.

The superintendent confirmed that every week each person received about one and one-half pounds of flour, and that beef was issued only once every three weeks, and was typically consumed in one day. Captain Read said the portions of the other food items distributed (surely such things as sugar and coffee) were so small that it was scarcely worth mentioning. Read also learned that at the subagency and the main agency, forty-five gallons of soup were prepared daily, and typically about one quart was available to those who presented themselves. The superintendent told Read that the soup was all that kept many of them alive.

Captain Read did not find a well authenticated account of someone starving to death, in the typical definition of that term, but he and Snider heard that many old people and children died from causes resulting from the lack of food. Read stated that "these Indians are in the most deplorable condition of any people I have ever seen," but he believed that Snider was doing everything he could for them with the means at his command. Read then explained that Snider was under strict orders from his department (it is unclear whether Read meant the Interior Department, or the Indian Affairs Office) to make his limited supplies last until April 30. Read repeated the April 30 date, later in the letter.[71] This means that Snider refused to provide any additional food supplies, even though there is widespread evidence that the existing supplies were already at starvation levels.

This poses a number of sobering questions, perhaps most important of which is, did Indian Commissioner Price, and perhaps even Interior Secretary Teller, in fact know that Assiniboines were starving to death? If they did, they bear substantial accountability to this tragedy. If they were not properly informed, then Snider bears special responsibility. An extraordinary account by Chief Red Stone in June 1884, demonstrates that Snider did not want people to know about the starvation at Wolf Point.

On June 19, 1884, Colonel J.M.G. Whistler, Commander of Fort Buford, wrote his superiors that a few days previously Assiniboine chief Red Stone had come to the post and demanded that Colonel Whistler write down Red Stone's words and communicate them to higher authorities. Red Stone said he had sought permission to leave the agency and visit Fort Buford, but Agent Snider refused under the threat that he would put Red Stone in irons if he disobeyed. Red Stone said that 118 of his Assiniboines had died from starvation during the past winter, primarily old persons and children. He further stated that when his people were suffering, their agent (either Snider or the subagent superintendent) refused to let them sell their horses to purchase food, nor allow them to kill them for food. Colonel Whistler added that the day previously, another Assiniboine named Big Belly had visited him and told him the same thing.[72]

It seems that Snider deliberately attempted to muzzle the story of Assiniboine starvation. In sworn depositions in 1929 for the Assiniboine case in the U.S. Court of Claims, Assiniboines introduced one other feature of Snider's management during the 1883-1884 starving winter. Several Assiniboines testified that during this deprivation period whenever Wolf Creek Assiniboines attempted to go to Poplar Creek, Snider had ordered the tribal police to drive them back. These included Bear Cub (Red Stone's grandson), Martin Mitchell, Blue Cloud,

Cloud, and Mrs. Belle Medicine Walk.

According to these testimonies, Assiniboines had different reasons for wanting to go to the agency at Poplar River. Bear Cub stated that Assiniboines went to meet with Snider, to appeal to him about their destitute condition. Bear Cub even remembered the name of one particular tribal policeman. Bear Cub said that Assiniboines did not know Snider's name, but they knew that he was responsible for their starving, and they then called him "Crazy White Man." Martin Mitchell said that the soldiers used to feed them, and that Assiniboines were going to get food from them. It appears that Mitchell was talking about Camp Poplar. Cloud said that Assiniboines went to Poplar River because they had more rations than Wolf Point, and they demanded a fairer share.[73]

It is unclear what Snider's rationale was for ordering the tribal police to drive back the Assiniboines. In that desperate situation, there was at least some logic in preserving the rations level at Poplar River. If Assiniboines were in fact seeking food at Camp Poplar, Snider might have wanted to keep Assiniboines from spreading the story of their starvation.

The other notable agency activity in 1884 was construction of irrigation ditches at both Poplar River and Wolf Point. Agent Porter initiated the idea of irrigation in March 1883. Porter's original plan was too expensive and was returned to him to trim down. The idea of irrigation was strongly endorsed by Inspector Howard during his October 1883 visit, and by Snider in August 1883.

The large project consisted of constructing a dam and ditch at both the main agency at Poplar River and the subagency at Wolf Point. Snider commenced work on the two ditches in April 1884, using exclusively tribal labor. The Indian Affairs Office required at this time that all able-bodied Indian men must do some agency work to receive rations. Snider boasted in his 1884 annual report that Indian men were quick to contribute manual labor once they learned the lesson that "if they wanted anything to eat they must work and earn it like white men."[74] It is ironic in the extreme that after the horrific winter that had just passed, Snider had no reservations about using food as blackmail.

The Poplar River Dam was located seven miles north of the agency, and was well constructed of rock and willow, but the east river bank was not properly secured, and the right side of the dam failed, making the entire dam ineffective. The ditch was on the east side of the river and was two and one-half miles long. A flume was needed to divert water from the dam to the ditch, but it was never constructed. It is unclear how far up Wolf Creek the dam was. The ditch associated with it was three miles long. It does not appear that any irrigation was in fact implemented.

The project was inspected by U.S. Army Lieutenant James R. Wilson in February 1886. Had the riverbank been properly secured, he believed the dam would still be operational. He recommended that the dam be repaired. He was highly impressed with the Poplar River ditch engineering done by the agency carpenter. He believed that a new dam could be constructed at Wolf Creek.[75]

It appears that the Fort Peck tribesmen lacked adequate food even in the summer of 1884. On July 14, 1884, Snider telegraphed Commissioner Price that the agency must have flour within ten days. On August 25, 1884, Snider reported to Camp Poplar that forty-one Indians, some armed, had broken into the agency corral and taken beef and entrails. The intruders refused to surrender their guns and the tribal police were not powerful enough to seize them. Snider requested military assistance to restore order, and General Terry complied. Twenty soldiers mobilized and by evening matters were resolved, and ten Indians surrendered their weapons.[76]

But Snider's troubles were not over. About this same time, Department of Interior Inspector M.R. Barr arrived for an agency review. In his September 1, 1884 report to Interior Secretary Henry M. Teller, Inspector Barr charged Snider with fraudulent transactions with the agency trader, George Fairchild. Snider bitterly protested the allegations, but Teller insisted that he resign. On October 16, 1884, Snider tendered his resignation, effective October 31. Concerned about possible agent and trader improprieties, on November 12, 1884 Indian Commissioner Hiram Price sent George R. Milburn particularly to examine Fairchild's records. Special Indian Agent Milburn submitted his findings on December 11, 1884, and he reversed Inspector Barr's findings, and exonerated Snider on all charges. However, even though Snider asked to be reinstated, the new agent, Burton Parker had already been appointed in mid-October.[77]

Burton Parker resided in Monroe City, Michigan, and appears to have been some sort of elected or appointed official in the state of Michigan House of Representatives. He informed Indian Commissioner Hiram Price on November 17, 1884 that he was just leaving for the agency at Fort Peck, but for unclear reasons did not assume duties until January 23, 1885. He served less than one year and his administration was plagued by nepotism, irregularities, neglect, and malfeasance. He was given notice of his suspension in October 1885, but continued to serve through the end of the year.[78]

He was charged primarily with committing a number of dubious employee voucher transactions. Special Indian Agent Charles H. Dickson was sent to Fort Peck in April 1886, and he completed an exhaustive study of the agency books and administration. He stated that Parker's general management of the agency was unacceptably loose and unprofessional, and most seriously, that some of his voucher transactions were both irregular and fraudulent. He explained he could not prove Parker was profiting personally from these actions. Dickson charged these irregularities placed a "cloud" of suspicion concerning all his agency transactions.[79]

Details on tribal farming for the year are sketchy, but Inspector Hinz Ward, who reviewed the agency in April 1885, reported that a large crop of potatoes was planted. Ward believed that the entire agency showed signs of neglect. He particularly criticized the operation of the industrial boarding school at Poplar River, describing the dormitories as filthy and recommending the entire staff be replaced. The school continued to be contracted with the Methodist Episcopal Church, but Ward recommended that the Indian Affairs Office take it over.[80]

Inspector M.A. Thomas reviewed the Fort Peck Agency in October 1885, and in contrast to Inspector Ward, believed that the Poplar River boarding school was doing a good job. He found the agency buildings to be in generally good condition. During his visit, a new and larger boarding school building was being constructed by a Bismarck contractor named Healy Brothers. Thomas believed the workmanship was shoddy and that the rough lumber being used was of inferior quality. He recommended to Indian Commissioner Price that after completion the building be carefully inspected.

Price directed Special Indian Agent William Parsons to inspect the new school building. Parsons arrived at the Fort Peck Agency on November 29, 1885, and his analysis was markedly different than Thomas'. Parsons found that the building construction was of excellent quality and completely to the standards of the contract. He also believed that the materials used were high quality, and the roofing material was even of better quality than specified in the contract.[81]

Parsons returned to the Fort Peck Agency in early December, at which time he learned of the shocking condition of the agency Indians. Parsons reported that on December 9, 1885, he met with a large party of Yanktonai chiefs who were furious at the treatment they were receiving. The tribal party was headed by principal chief Red Thunder, and included Chiefs Black Catfish, Black Tiger, Long Fox, Grey Swan, Lost His Medicine, Medicine Bear (the son), and around twenty-five other headmen.

Their primary grievance was the shocking lack of food annuities they received. They explained that a lodge of three or four persons received one week's rations consisting of one piece of beef no larger than a man's hand, a hatful of flour, a little rice, and nothing else. Parsons immediately confronted Parker about the truthfulness of this, and discovered that the complaints were completely true. Parsons then inquired about the opportunities the tribesmen had to work and supplement their food annuities, and he found that there was no work at the agency, even though the Indians were very interested in work.

In exploring the conditions of the agency Indians, Parsons then realized they were in every way completely destitute. They had no clothing, no wagons or teams, and no money. Worse, he discovered that the chronic hunger and lack of clothing had led to widespread sickness. He concluded that they were "miserably poor" and that if immediate measures were not taken, they would both starve and freeze to death. He wrote an urgent letter to Indian Commissioner Price recommending that food annuity amounts be tripled, and that clothing, wagons, and other provisions be made at once.[82]

Henry R. West succeeded Parker as Fort Peck Agent and assumed his duties on January 1, 1886. Unfortunately he was also a poor choice. He became embroiled in an acrimonious feud with agency physician V.S. Benson over the appointment of agency staff positions. As it turns out, Dr. Benson was so derelict in his duties that he refused to even travel to the Wolf Point sub-agency. West demanded his resignation, and Benson refused. Agency affairs were so chaotic and disruptive that another special Indian agent, Frank Armstrong, was sent to the agency in May 1886 to resolve the matter.

Like Special Agent Parsons, Armstrong was shocked at the neglect and conditions throughout the whole agency. Armstrong found, once again, that the quantity of food rations were unacceptably low, and he increased the weekly flour amount to three and one-half pounds per person from Agent West's two and one-half and tripled the beef portion to three-quarters of a pound. Armstrong cited the destitute conditions of the agency Indians and the neglect across the agency as grounds for the removal of both Agent West and Dr. Benson.[83]

Armstrong remained at the agency until July 1, 1886, when he was replaced by Special Agent Henry Heth, who served as an interim officer until a permanent replacement could be appointed sometime around October 1886. It was unfortunate but perfectly consistent with the disorder at the Fort Peck Agency that when the newly appointed agent, Samuel Gilson, arrived for duty on October 1, 1886, he resigned and returned to his home in Erie, Pennsylvania that same day. He angrily protested that Indian Commissioner J. D. C. Atkins had promised him authority to appoint new key staff positions, and when he found that agents Armstrong and Heth had already done some of that, he refused to stay another minute.[84]

With Samuel Gilson's sudden resignation, Heth was compelled to administer the Fort Peck Agency until another agent was appointed. The new agent was D.O. Cowen, who took over on November 6, 1886. Finally the agency had a permanent Indian agent who was truly competent.

Cowen focused first on the low enrollment at the new Poplar River boarding school. When three council meetings with tribal leaders failed to increase enrollments, Cowen announced a series of strict punishments for parents not sending their children. Parents withholding students for five days would have their children forcibly taken to the school by tribal police. Parents hiding their children would lose food rations, and those resisting the tribal police would be jailed. Tribesmen told Cowen that previous agents had made similar threats that had not been enforced. Cowen must have acted upon these threats, for student enrollment jumped to fifty students and increased steadily until 200 students were attending by June and July 1887.[85]

Agent Cowen had been in office less than two months when a major treaty commission arrived. The Northwest Indian Commission had just completed a treaty negotiation with the Fort Berthold Reservation on December 16, 1886, and arrived at the Poplar River Agency on December 23, 1886. The commissioners had instructions to try and persuade all the Fort Peck Sioux to relocate to the Great Sioux Reservation. The Fort Peck Sioux seem to have immediately rejected this and the commissioners proceeded to negotiating land cession and payment matters. The commission met in council with Sioux leaders on December 27 and 28, emphasizing that this treaty would help end the marked tribal poverty. Sioux leaders agreed, explaining that ensuring the economic security to provide for their families was their primary goal. The tribal leaders agreed to payment terms of $165,000 for ten years, and then signed the agreement.[86]

The commissioners proceeded then to the Wolf Point subagency, and met in council with the Assiniboines, but proceedings for these meetings were not recorded due to the severity of the weather and the lack of a proper meeting facility. The Sioux councils were held at the boarding school at Poplar River, and there was in fact no comparably sized building at Wolf Point.

Assiniboines agreed to the same terms agreed upon by the Sioux, and Assiniboine leaders signed the agreement on December 31, 1886.[87]

Cowen was also agent at the time of another extraordinary event: construction of a railroad across the reservation. This was St. Paul, Minnesota railroad magnate James J. Hill's St. Paul, Minneapolis, and Manitoba Railroad (known as the Manitoba Railroad, and later as the Great Northern Railway). The railroad had reached Devil's Lake, Dakota Territory in 1883, and in 1886 had extended to present Minot, but stalled there for lack of a federal right-of-way easement across the Fort Berthold and the Blackfeet Reservations, within which resided the Fort Peck Agency. President Grover Cleveland signed a congressional right-of-way law on February 15, 1887, and Hill launched a furious construction operation which reached Helena, Montana Territory, by the end of 1887.[88] Fort Peck Reservation annuity provisions would no longer have to suffer the seasonal disruptions of Missouri River steamboat travel.

On May 1, 1888, President Cleveland signed a statute recognizing the two 1886 agreements (prior to 1871 such tribal documents were called treaties) signed by the Fort Peck Agency Sioux and Assiniboines. Included in the new statute were agreements negotiated by the Northwest Treaty Commission with the Gros Ventres and Upper Assiniboines at Fort Belknap Agency and the Blackfeet tribes at the same agency. Collectively these northern Montana tribes ceded to the federal government 17,500,000 acres, more than three-fifths of the former Blackfeet Reservation, which stretched from the North Dakota boundary to the Rocky Mountains. The statute established three new reservations: Blackfeet, Fort Belknap, and Fort Peck.[89]

The Fort Peck Assiniboines and Sioux had paid dearly because of inadequate congressional appropriations, especially through the 1880s. The

$165,000 ten-year annual payment provided at least some financial security to these tribal people, and the new reservation was now stable enough to truly begin the difficult task of trying to meet the promises made by the treaty commissioners of improved lives for everyone. ✸

1 Fort Peck Agent Wellington Bird to Indian Commissioner Ezra A. Hayt, March 28, 1878, National Archives and Records Administration [hereinafter cited as NARA], Record Group 75, Records of the Bureau of Indian Affairs, M234, Letters Received Commissioner of Indian Affairs [hereinafter cited as LRCIA], Roll 509 (1878), frames 241-41.

2 Bird to Hayt, April 8, 1878, NARA, LRCIA, frames 251-53; Bird to Hayt, May 13, 1878, frames 272-74; Interior Secretary Carl Schurz to Hayt, May 31, 1878, Roll 510, frames 590-91.

3 Bird to Hayt, January 14, 1878, Roll 509, frames 149-50;

4 Captain Simon Snyder, to Captain Constant Williams, Fort Belknap, February 16, 1878, Roll 512, frames 84-85; Williams to the Acting Adjutant General, District of Montana, Fort Shaw, February 23, 1978, frames 86-87.

5 Williams to the Acting Adjutant General, February 23, frame 87.

6 Ibid., 87-90.

7 Gilbert A. Skinner, Acting Fort Peck Agent, to Lieutenant F.D. Baldwin, Fort Peck Agency, April 2, 1878, frames 171-72.

8 Ibid., Roll 509, frames 401-2; Bird to Hayt, January, 1, 1878, frame 160.

9 Bird to Hayt, January 21, 1878, frames 165-65; General Alfred Terry, Division of the Dakota, to Lieutenant Colonel Brooke, April 1, 1878, Roll 512, frame 122; Endorsement, Lieutenant General Philip H. Sheridan, Division of the Missouri, November 13, 1878, frame 402.

10 Bird to Hayt, October 3, 1878, Roll 509, frames 488-89;endorsement, Lt. General Sheridan, November 13, 1878, frame 402.

11 Bird to Hayt, November 16, 1878, frames 578-79.

12 Bird to Hayt, November 1, 1878, frame 534; Bird to Hayt, November 16, 1878, frame 581; Bird to Hayt, November 23, 1878, frames 593-94.

13 Bird to Hayt, March 9, 1879, Roll 513, frame 269; Schurz to Hayt, March 11, 1879, frames 718-19.

14 Bird to Brevet Major General Miles, Fort Keogh, June 6, 1879, Roll 515, frames 780-81.

15 Bird to Lieutenant Colonel Daniel Huston, Fort Buford, June 11, 1879, frames 732-33; Bird to Huston, June 15, 1879, frame 744; Huston to the

Assistant Adjutant General, Division of the Dakota, June 19, 1879, frame 743.

16 Captain Thomas Britton to Adjutant, Fort Buford, June 29, 1879, frames 802-3.

17 Ibid., frames 803-5.

18 Schurz to Bird, April 7, 1879, Roll 513, frame 745.

19 Agent Nathan S. Porter to Miles, July 19, 1879, Roll 514, frames 887-88.

20 Major Guido Ilges, Commander, Fort Benton Post, to the Assistant Adjutant General, Department of the Dakota, November 25, 1878, Roll 515, frames 521-24.

21 Bird to Hayt, April 7, 1879, Roll 513, frames 309-10; Alexander Culbertson, Fort Peck Agency, April 2, 1879, frame 312; Report of John McNeil, June 12, 1880, Reports of Inspection of the Field Jurisdictions of the Office of Indian Affairs, 1873-1900 (hereinafter cited as Reports of Inspection), NARA, Roll 15, Fort Peck Agency, 1885-1900.

22 Porter to Hayt, August 28, 1879, Roll 514, frame 957; Porter to Hayt, August 27, 1879, frame 514.

23 Porter to Hayt, August 12, 1879, Annual Report to the Secretary of Interior for the Year 1879 [hereinafter cited as Annual Report] (Washington, D.C.: Government Printing Office, 1879), 849, 202.

24 Porter to Hayt, July 18, 1879, frame 902; Porter to Hayt, Annual Report (1879), 203.

25 Porter to Hayt, July 18, 1879, frame 902; Miles, Fort Keogh, to "the agt. of the Yanktonais," July 10, 1879, frame 890.

26 Adjutant General E.D. Townsend to the Adjutant General, Washington, D.C., July 1, 1879, Roll 514, frame 740; Miles to Adjutant General Ruggles, Division of the Dakota, July 22, 1879, frames 811-12; Porter to Hayt, July 18, 1879, Roll 514, frame 902; Robert M. Utley, The Lance and the Shield: The Life and Times of Sitting Bull (New York: Ballantine Books, 1993), 206-9.

27 Sheridan to Townsend, Washington, D.C., August 5, 1879, Roll 515, frame 820.

28 Porter to Hayt, September 8, 1879, Roll 514, frames 987-89, 991.

29 Lieutenant Colonel H. M. Black, Commander, Fort Assiniboine, to the Assistant Adjutant General, Department of the Dakota, January 28, 1880, Roll 518, frames 58-62; Porter to Hayt, December 1, 1879, Roll 514, frames 1107-9.

30 Utley, The Lance and the Shield, 204; Brigadier General Alfred Terry, Department of the Dakota, to Colonel Ruger, District of Montana, November 6, 1879, Roll 518, frame 67.

31 Black to the Assistant Adjutant General, January 28, 1879, frames 60-62.

32 Ibid., frames 58-64; Black to Captain Carroll H. Potter, Assistant Adjutant General, District of Montana, November 26, 1879, Roll 518, frames 76-77; Black to the Assistant Adjutant General, Department of Dakota, December 27, 1879, frames 78-79; Potter to Black, December 5, 1880, frames 80-81.

33 Utley, 208.

34 Sheridan to Townsend, October 31, 1879, Roll 515, frames 896-97.

35 The Assinniboine Indian Tribe, plaintiff, v. the United States, defendant, Court of Claims of the United States, No. J-31 (Washington: Government Printing Office, 1931), pp. 47-48, 50-54, 58, 78, 108-11, 117-18.

36 Porter to Hayt, Annual Report (1880), 234.

37 Porter to Hayt, February 17, 1880, Roll 517, frames 284-86.

38 Ibid.; Utley, The Lance and the Shield, 213-18.

39 Porter to Hayt, February 17, 1880, frames 300-2.

40 Ibid., frames 301-2.

41 Porter to Indian Commissioner Roland E. Trowbridge, April 14, 1880, Roll 514, frames 854-56; Porter to Trowbridge, May 2, 1880, Roll 517, frame 353.

42 Porter to Trowbridge, May 17, 1880, frames 365-66; J. C. McVay, Yankton, Dakota Territory, to Trowbridge, May 18, 1880, frame 67.

43 Porter to Trowbridge, May 20, 1880, frame 372; Porter to Trowbridge, May 20, 1880, frames 374-75.

44 Porter to Trowbridge, May 31, 1880, frames 385-87.

45 Porter to Trowbridge, June 3, 1880, frames 391-93.

46 Report of Inspection, Fort Peck Agency, John McNeil to Secretary of Interior Carl Schurz, June 17, 1880, NARA, Record Group 75, Records of the Bureau of Indian Affairs, M1070, Reports of Inspection of the Field Jurisdictions of the Office of Indian Affairs, 1873-1900 [hereinafter cited as Inspection Reports], Roll 15, Fort Peck Agency, 1885-1900, report pp. 1-3.

47 Ibid., report pp. 3-8.

48 Porter to Trowbridge, August 12, 1880, *Annual Report* (1880), 234.

49 Ibid., 234-35; Porter to Hayt, January 30, 1880, Roll 517, frames 217-29.

50 *Annual Report* (1880), 233-34.

51 Porter to Trowbridge, July 30, 1880, frames 439-40.

52 T.C. Power to E. M. Marble, Acting Indian Commissioner, August 29, 1880, frames 455-56.

53 Power to Marble, September 10, 1880, frame 461; Power to Marble, October 9, 1880, frames 485-86.

54 Roll 516, frame 135; Porter to Trowbridge, November 13, 1880, Roll 517, frame 515; Power to Marble, November 13, 1880, frame 517; Power to Marble, November 29, 1880, frame 534.

55 Raymond J. DeMallie, "The Sioux in Dakota and Montana Territories: Cultural and Historical Background of the Ogden B. Read Collection," in *Vestiges of a Proud Nation: The Ogden B. Read Northern Plains Indian Collection,* Glenn E. Markoe, ed. (Burlington: Robert Hull Fleming Museum, University of Vermont), 47-50.

56 Porter to Trowbridge, August 27, 1881, *Annual Report* (1881), 176, 180.

57 Utley, *The Lance and the Shield*, 216-33; DeMallie, "The Sioux in Dakota and Montana Territories," 50-54.

58 Standing Rock Agent James McLaughlin to Indian Commissioner Hiram Price, August 15, 1883, *Annual Report* (1883), 105-6.

59 Porter, *Annual Report* (1881), 179-80; Porter, *Annual Report* (1880), 234.

60 Porter, *Annual Report* (1881), 179-80.

61 Porter, *Annual Report* (1881), 179-80; Porter to Price, September 1, 1882, *Annual Report* (1882), 169, 171.

62 Porter, *Annual Report* (1882), 170; Captain Ogden Read, Commander, Camp Poplar, to the Assistant Adjutant General, Department of the Dakota, January 14, 1882, NARA, Letters Received Commissioner of Indian Affairs [hereinafter cited as LR, (Letters Received)], Box 63, file # 3202.

63 Porter, *Annual Report* (1882), 170.

64 Ibid., 169-70.

65 Price to Porter, April 11, 1882, NARA, Rocky Mountain Region [hereinafter cited as RMR] (Denver, Colorado), LR, Box 10, letter 6183-'82d; Porter, Annual Report (1882), 171.

66 Price to Porter, May 2, 1882, LR, Box 10, letter 7530/7584; Robert Todd Lincoln, Secretary of War, to Henry M. Teller, Secretary of Interior, January 5, 1883, LR, Box 118, letter # 452; endorsement, William Tecumseh Sherman, General of the Army, January 3, 1883, LR, Box 118, letter # 452.

67 Samuel E. Snider to Price, *Annual Report* (1883), 161.

68 "Inspection of Fort Peck Agency," Department of Interior Inspector C.H. Howard, October 24, 1884, Reports of Inspection, report page 1; "Inspection of Wolf Point Subagency—Fort Peck Agency," Inspector C.H. Howard, October 25, 1884, Reports of Inspection, report pp. 1-2.

69 "Inspection of Wolf Point Subagency," report pp. 1-2.

70 Read to the Assistant Adjutant General, Department of Dakota, January 14, 1884, LR, Box 174, letter # 2342.

71 Ibid.

72 Colonel J.M.G. Whistler, Commander, Fort Buford, to the Adjutant General, Department of Dakota, June 19, 1884, LR, Box 197, letter # 13089.

73 "Court of Claims of the United States," No. J-31, pp.42-43, 45-46, 48, 66, 69, 155.

74 Price to Porter, March 2, 1883, RMR, LR, Box 10, letter # 3448; Snider, *Annual Report* (1883), 161-62; Snider, *Annual Report* (1884), 160-61.

75 Snider, *Annual Report* (1884), 160-61; Lieutenant James E. Wilson to the Assistant Adjutant General, Department of Dakota, February 2, 1886, RMR, Miscellaneous Letters Received, Box 21.

76 Snider to Price, July 14, 1884, LR, Box 189, letter # 13408; Snider to Camp Poplar Commanding Officer, and Brigadier General Alfred H. Terry to Commanding Officer, Camp Poplar, and Camp Poplar Commander Hartz to the Assistant Adjutant General, Department of Dakota, all August 25, 1884, LR, Box 206, letter # 17360.

77 "Inspection of Fort Peck Agency, Snider Agent," Department of Interior Inspector M.R. Barr, September 1, 1884, Reports of Inspection, report pages 16-23; Special Indian Agent George R. Milburn to Commissioner Price, December 12, 1884, LR, Box 219, letter # 24107; Secretary of Interior Teller to Commissioner Price, October 13, 1884, LR, Box 211, letter # 19710.

78 Burton Parker to Price, November 11, 1884, LR, Box 215, letter # 22127; Special Indian Agent Charles H. Dickson to Price, April 10, 1886, LR, Box 302, letter # 10485.

79 Dickson to Price, April 10, 1886.

80 "Report of Inspector Ward on the Fort Peck Agency," Department of Interior Inspector Hinz Ward, April 8, 1885, Reports of Inspection, synopsis pp. 1-3.

81 Special Indian Agent William Parsons to Price, November 30, 1885, LR, Box 277, letter # 29598.

82 Parsons to Price, December 11, 1885, LR, Box 279, letter # 31119.

83 "Report of Inspector Armstrong on the Fort Peck Agency," Department of Interior Inspector Frank C. Armstrong, May 20, 1886, Reports of Inspection; Special Indian Agent Armstrong to Indian Commissioner L. Q. C. Lamar, May 20, 1886, enclosed in "Report of Inspector Armstrong.

84 Special Indian Agent Henry Heth to Indian Commissioner John D. C. Atkins, July 1, 1886, LR, Box 319, letter # 17701; Heth to Atkins, October 14, 1886, LR. Box 349, letter # 28546.

85 Agent D.O. Cowen to Atkins, August 21, 1887, *Annual Report* (1887), 225-27.

86 "Message from the President of the United States, Transmitting a Communication from the Secretary of Interior, with Accompanying Papers, Relating to the Reduction of Indian Reservations," *House Executive Document* 63 (1888), 12-13; Charles Kappler, ed., *Indian Affairs. Laws and Treaties* (Washington: Government Printing Office, 1904), 264-65.

87 Kappler, *Indian Affairs*, 262-65.

88 Dennis J. Smith, "Procuring a Right-of-Way: James J. Hill and Indian Reservations, 1886-1888," manuscript, University of Montana, 1-40.

89 Kappler, *Indian Affairs*, 262-65.

CHAPTER 6

~

Stability on the New Fort Peck Reservation, 1889-1905

Dennis J. Smith, Ph.D.

In some ways, life for Fort Peck Assiniboines and Sioux changed after May 1, 1888, when President Grover Cleveland signed the federal statute that included the treaty agreements negotiated in December 1886, and January 1887, with Fort Peck, Fort Belknap, and Blackfeet Agency tribes. Strictly speaking, after 1871 treaties were technically called "agreements," simply because Congress changed the treaty ratification process. The United States Senate no longer ratified Indian treaties, but continued to do so for treaties negotiated with foreign governments. After 1871, negotiated treaties were not ratified by the U.S. Senate but instead were enclosed in congressional bills, which if passed by Congress and signed by the president, became essentially ratified.[1]

The 1888 act, as agreed upon in 1886 by the Fort Peck Assiniboines and Sioux, established the present Fort Peck Reservation with an eastern boundary at Big Muddy Creek and a western boundary at the mouth of the Milk River, proceeding north up Porcupine Creek. The Missouri River marked the southern boundary and the reservation extended north forty miles. The 17,500,000 acres ceded by the Fort Peck, Fort Belknap, and Blackfeet tribes now belonged to the federal government and were open for white settlement. Another significant transition occurred one year later, when on November 8, 1889, the state of Montana was admitted as the forty-first state in the Union.[2]

Perhaps the most important contribution of the 1888 agreement was the annual $165,000 payment for ten years. Considering the chronic lack of agency appropriations, and the ineptitude and frequent turnover of Indian agents that had plagued the Fort Peck Agency since its establishment in 1869, the early years of the new reservation proved to be a stable, formative period. The annual treaty payments greatly expanded access to material items, including log homes, wagons, horse teams, and agricultural and stock-raising equipment.[3]

In 1889, agency tribesmen built 160 log homes, adding to the total of 480 tribal log residences already existing. Department of Interior Inspector William Jenkin reported in July 1889, however, that many Fort Peck Indians continued to live in tipis and in tribal camps. In 1891, tribal residences increased to 592 log homes, all built by the Indians themselves. By 1892, Fort Peck Agent C.R.A. Scobey reported that all agency Indians lived in log homes. These were crucial for winter protection, but since they were often infested with bed bugs, most tribal families spent the warmer seasons in tipis pitched alongside their log homes.[4]

The log homes were often close to one another, and most of these residences included small, heavily fenced gardens. These were planted primarily in root vegetables, especially corn (Arikara or "Ree," sometimes called "squaw" corn) and potatoes, but other garden vegetables were common. Beginning in 1889, large numbers of wagons were issued to families, along with increasing numbers of agricultural implements such as small plows and haying machines and reapers. In the early 1890s, tribesmen increasingly wore Euro-American clothes.[5]

In terms of health, the annual treaty payments enabled dramatic improvements for agency Indians. This monumentally important trend was succinctly explained by Agent Scobey in his 1891 annual report. He said that tribal health was excellent and had been steadily improving over each of the past four years, and he attributed this directly to the annual treaty payments. The Fort Peck tribes were no longer vulnerable to the unpredictability of congressional appropriation bills. Scobey said that now Fort Peck tribesmen were assured food and clothing.[6]

The 1888 treaty agreement had also noticeably improved material conditions for Fort Peck Assiniboines and Sioux, and significantly, it marked at long last the end of ineffective and incompetent Indian agents. D.O. Cowen arrived in November 1886, one month before the Northwest Treaty Commission visited and negotiated the treaty agreement. Agent Cowen was an able administrator who retired from the Indian Service and was replaced by C.R.A. Scobey on July 1, 1889.[7]

Scobey was a thirty-three-year-old former stock grower born in New Jersey and believed to have had significant business experience. Although not previously an Indian agent, Scobey proved to be a capable manager for an agency typically mired in petty distractions. Beyond overseeing everyday matters, Agent Scobey was most concerned with charting long-term economic enterprises that would provide jobs and self-sufficiency to the agency Indians.[8]

Scobey, various Department of Interior inspectors, and Scobey's successor, Captain W.A. Sprole, all agreed that the future of the Fort Peck Reservation depended on agriculture and stock raising, but they varied widely on particulars. Scobey believed that dry-land agriculture was not sustainable, which at the time was perfectly understandable because the region had been in a drought cycle since the late 1880s. Scobey served from 1889 through 1893, and reservation crops failed completely during each of these years.[9]

Scobey did not advocate strongly for irrigation until 1891, at which time he argued that an extensive irrigation system was necessary not only for agriculture, but also for stock raising, to provide hay crops. Because the Indian Affairs Office did not repair the failed irrigation systems initiated by Agent Samuel E. Snider in 1884, nor launch new ones, Agent Scobey was resigned to pursue other options.

Scobey focused on horses as the most important tribal livestock. He perceptively appreciated the primary advantage—horses could be wintered without hay. He claimed the Fort Peck region was extraordinary horse country because of its quality grazing lands, and in addition, Assiniboines and Sioux had quickly demonstrated they were excellent horse stockmen. In 1889, agency tribesmen owned 560 horses. The following year, Scobey purchased ninety-six brood mares and three stallions, and another fine stallion transferred from the Fort Berthold Reservation. By 1891, he estimated that Fort Peck Indians owned 1,160 horses. In 1892, Scobey issued eight more stallions, including two Clydesdales, and a large number of mares. In 1893, Scobey was replaced by Agent W.A. Sprole, who saw little future in horse raising, and Scobey's enterprise quickly declined.[10]

Scobey also appreciated that despite regular drought cycles, agency Indians should diversify into cattle raising. He stated in 1892 that cattle had not been issued to individual tribesmen since 1884, but Scobey issued increasing numbers of cows. By 1889, agency Indians owned a total of 461 cattle, including oxen, and by 1891, total cattle had increased to 596.

That year Scobey stated that it was time to again issue cattle to the tribesmen, but he believed a new policy was in order. Up to this time, it appears that agency cattle issued to individual tribal members were selected from a tribal herd run primarily by agency Indians. Scobey proposed that in the future the agency should issue cattle directly to individual tribesmen, but only to those who appeared best suited to care for them. Scobey stated that he wanted to initiate this new approach on a limited basis in 1892, but it is unclear if he in fact did so.[11]

One experiment in agency livestock was sheep, which appears to have been primarily initiated among the Assiniboines at Wolf Point. There were 300 agency sheep listed in 1889,

but the main leader on this livestock initiative was an unidentified mixed-blood (probably Assiniboine), who started with his own herd of 100 sheep, which stimulated interest among other tribal members. By 1894, Assiniboines owned 700 sheep, including 386 ewes, eight bucks, and 306 lambs. That year they sheared 2,846 pounds of wool which was shipped to Minneapolis for market.[12]

The only full-time agency employment for tribal members was as tribal police. In 1889, the police force totaled twenty-two persons, but Cowen was disappointed with the quality of those hired, stating that more industrious Indians were unwilling to work for the low salary of $8 per month, and one horse apiece. Cowen complained that his police would have been better led by a suitable white man.[13]

Scobey was much more pleased in his report of 1890. The tribal police force was reduced to nineteen persons, including twelve privates and one captain at Poplar River and five privates and one captain at Wolf Point. He believed they were able employees who followed orders, but confessed they were ineffective law officers because of their unwillingness to place themselves in danger. Sprole believed, however, that tribal police provided a valuable agency service because they were an invaluable source of information on the everyday activities of tribesmen across the reservation.[14]

In 1891, Scobey established a second feature of Fort Peck Agency criminal justice, the Court of Indian Offenses. These were minor tribal courts established under guidelines from Secretary of Interior Henry M. Teller in 1883. Teller created these to serve two functions. First, they were assimilationist instruments to help enforce new prohibitions that he announced the same year. These included banning traditional Native ceremonies such as the sun dance and scalp dances, and measures to intervene against traditional medicine men who resisted acculturation programs. Teller also banned cultural practices such as polygamy.

Second, these courts served the important function of adjudicating misdemeanor reservation crimes, including theft and property destruction, intoxication and alcohol trafficking, and minor assault. Court of Indian Offenses judges were appointed by Indian agents. The congressional statutory basis upon which Secretary Teller authorized the new courts was vague indeed, and the banning of religious practices was dubious at best. All of these religious "offenses" and criminal offenses were incorporated as a code and incorporated in volume 25 of the Code of Federal Regulations (C.F.R.).[15]

In 1892, one year after establishing the Court of Indian Offenses, Scobey changed the tribal judge selection process. As Indian agent, he was empowered to select the tribal judges, but instead he divided the reservation into three districts and had each judge elected by popular ballot of the tribal members themselves. He stated that all the electioneering tactics seen in white election campaigns were just as evident in these, but he still expressed full confidence in the importance of these courts. Agent reports at least through the early 1890s indicate that the Fort Peck Court of Indian Offenses dealt primarily with petty misdemeanor crimes. If the courts and tribal police actively interfered with traditional customs and ceremonies, these were not indicated.[16]

Tribal part-time agency employment continued to be a fundamental source of economic activity across the reservation. In 1889, agency Indians sawed 45,000 feet of the cottonwood used to construct all the agency buildings and tribal homes. In 1890, this lumbering increased to 75,000 feet. In 1889, tribal members cut 1,600 cords of firewood, 600 for the agency and boarding school, and the remainder being sold to steamboat companies. In 1990, agency Indians

cut and hauled 2,000 cords of wood. In addition, during 1889 Indians used their own teams to freight 300,000 pounds of goods for the government and traders, and in 1890 this increased to 500,000 pounds.[17]

In 1890, Fort Peck tribesmen labored on a large scale, one-time economic operation. That year they gathered and sold about 125 railroad carloads of buffalo bones. The northern plains were littered with bison skeletal remains and especially during the drought years of the 1880s, white homesteaders and Native Americans had gathered enormous quantities. During this decade, thousands of tons were sold each year, and railroad companies shipped an estimated 5,000 railroad carloads each year. The bones were sold to sugar refineries and large fertilizer and carbon products companies, particularly in such places as Detroit, Michigan, and East St. Louis, Illinois, which made bone ash (a fertilizer) and bone black (a pigment). It took 100 skeletons to amass one ton of bones, which were worth from $4 to $12. Scobey estimated that Fort Peck Indians earned $10,000 during the year through this enterprise.[18]

In terms of general agency matters, Agent Scobey explained in 1891 the improvements he instituted to prevent the closure of the Wolf Point subagency, which some Indian Affairs Office officials had recommended. He admitted that when he assumed duties on July 1, 1889, the subagency was in terrible condition. At that time, the Agency Farmer was the only white employee.

Especially unfortunate, Scobey believed, was the hiring of an Indian boy as blacksmith and wheelwright—because of his lack of skill, most Assiniboine wagons and agricultural machinery remained in complete disrepair. The agent explained that it was not possible for Assiniboines to bring these items twenty-two miles to the main agency at Poplar River for proper repair. In addition, the subagency buildings, all log structures with sod roofs, were unsafe and ready to collapse. Scobey hired a more competent man, J.K. Chase, to direct the subagency, and also hired a qualified blacksmith-wheelwright. All the old buildings were torn down and replaced.[19]

The last important agency institution requiring Scobey's attention was the Poplar River boarding school. The original school was a log building complex constructed in 1882, with surprisingly small classroom and dormitory capacities. A large, two-story frame building was completed in October 1885. At some point, a one-story addition was constructed, and the building then housed one classroom, an office, girls' reading and sitting rooms, sewing room, girls' hospital and dormitory, and employee rooms. Another two-story frame building with a basement was completed in late 1889, providing an additional 12,000 square feet of space. It included a new dining room, kitchen, one classroom, two recitation rooms, boys' reading and sitting rooms, boys' dormitory, and some employee rooms. The two school buildings could accommodate an estimated 175 students. Other school buildings included older log buildings, such as a laundry, tank-house, stables, and sheds.[20]

The boarding school employed variously from ten to thirteen persons, including the superintendent, the matron (usually the superintendent's wife), one principal teacher and two assistant teachers, one industrial teacher, a seamstress, laundress, cook, and night watchman. Of these, the superintendent, matron, and all the teachers were white, the seamstress was often white, and the laundress, cook, and night watchman positions were almost universally held by tribal persons. In addition, the boarding school employed three Native girls called student assistants, hired as assistant matron, seamstress, and laundress. These student assistants appear to have been only part-time students and they worked for minimal

pay. In 1889, these three assistants were identified as mixed-blood girls who were former students of the boarding school. Because all boarding school students were very young, these student assistant girls were likely still young.[21]

By 1891, the Fort Peck Boarding School was ten years old and well established, and its operation quite typical of other federal on-reservation boarding schools. It was a large on-reservation boarding school and was especially overcrowded until the second two-story frame building was added in late 1889. Agent Sprole reported that attendance in 1888 had peaked at 216 students, but this most likely was the number of students enrolled. That year Sprole capped attendance at 165 students.

The 165 student limitation was no longer necessary after the second new building was constructed in 1889. Student enrollment averaged around 200 students from 1889 to 1891, including 199 in 1889, 241 in 1890, and 197 in 1891. A better indicator of school conditions was the average rate of school attendance, which for the 1889 to 1891 period was 131, 151, and 132, respectively. Girls consistently outnumbered boys, usually by around one-third. In 1891, for example, enrolled girls numbered ninety-three and boys sixty-five. The most important demographic, however, was the young age of the students. Almost all attended what were called the primary grades (divided into years one through four). Only a handful made it to the first year of the advanced grade. In 1891, for example, eighty-nine of the ninety-three enrolled girl students were in the primary grades, and sixty of the sixty-five boys were in the primary grades.[22]

One reason for the high enrollment was that attendance was compulsory, and Scobey reported in 1890 that compulsory attendance "has been enforced to the letter." Neither Scobey nor boarding school superintendent J.D. Baker explained the enforcement measures taken against students or parents, which would have been carried out by tribal police. That some kind of harsh punishments were imposed was best seen in 1895. Boarding school superintendent J.H. Welch reported that there were a few runaways at the beginning of the year, but they were promptly returned to school. Significantly, he added that "*the punishment was such as to make runaways very unpopular*"[23] [emphasis added]. Welch did not elaborate. At best, this likely included some form of public humiliation, and in the worst case likely involved corporal punishment.

School officials complained that one peculiar problem disrupted enrollment each fall. This time of year many tribal families were away hunting and gathering berries and did not return to the agency until compelled to do so by winter weather.[24] Although this clearly frustrated school and agency officials, it does not appear they had any means of effectively prohibiting these fall practices, nor does it appear that they punished these families and schoolchildren.

The Fort Peck Boarding School, like all on-reservation boarding schools at the turn of the nineteenth century, was modeled on the organization and instruction pioneered by Lieutenant Richard Henry Pratt in the federal government's first off-reservation boarding school at Carlisle, Pennsylvania, founded in 1879. Pratt's goal was complete cultural assimilation, and he established Carlisle Indian School precisely to take Native children away from their reservations. Pratt created this new experiment because federal day and on-reservation boarding schools universally failed to assimilate children. These schools proved unable to overcome the cultural persistence of tribal families and communities.

Pratt's academic curriculum emphasized English language instruction, but also included rudimentary arithmetic, science, history, and the arts. Pratt instituted what became known as the "half-day" plan, in which Native students spent half the day in academic studies, and the remainder engaged in hands-on learning of the skills and vocations known as "manual" or "industrial" education. Boys learned primarily agriculture and stock raising, and such skills as blacksmithing and harness repair. Girls learned etiquette, cooking, cleaning, sewing, and poultry care. Like similar manual training schools for African Americans such as the Hampton Normal and Industrial Institute established in Hampton, Virginia, in 1868, such vocational training was based on the notion of African-American and Native American intellectual inferiority.[25]

Lieutenant Pratt's notoriety and accomplishments at Carlisle Indian School prompted the Indian Affairs Office to establish a number of off-reservation schools across the trans-Mississippi West. The first appeared in Chemewa (Salem), Oregon the next year, 1880. In 1884, new schools were created in Chilocco, Oklahoma; Genoa, Nebraska; Albuquerque, New Mexico; and Lawrence, Kansas. Montana established its first off-reservation boarding school at Fort Shaw in 1892. By 1902, a total of twenty-five off-reservation boarding schools were in operation.[26]

As Fort Peck Boarding School superintendent Baker noted in 1891, "We conform almost entirely to the [Indian Affairs Office] course of study for Indian schools." This was curriculum and administration directed by the federal Superintendent for Indian Schools, a position established by Congress in 1885. Located in the Indian Affairs Office, the superintendent was toothless, for he had no power to appoint nor fire any of the large number of federal educators, including boarding school superintendents, teachers, and staff. Hiring and firing authority rested with the Indian Affairs commissioner and to a limited degree also with Indian agents.[27]

Like on- and off-reservation boarding schools across the country, the "half-day" system of manual or industrial training at the Fort Peck

Boarding School was more than mere hands-on instruction. It provided student labor and services essential to the survival of these schools, a predicament caused by the lack of adequate congressional funding. In most cases, boarding schools needed to raise their own crops, vegetable gardens, dairy cows, cattle, and poultry simply to feed themselves.

Fort Peck boarding school students were well fed because the agency was not dependent on congressional appropriations after 1888.[28] As was true prior to the 1888 treaty agreement, Fort Peck Agency boarding school students were fed as part of regular agency rations. This was not good in the early years of the boarding school from 1882-1888, which included the 1883-1884 starving winter, when the entire agency was often on the brink of starvation.

In the 1890s, Fort Peck boarding school boys worked primarily on the school farms. The main farm was one mile away and was planted primarily in corn and root crops such as potatoes and turnips. Near the Poplar River, very close to the school, was a small vegetable plot of around eight acres, which since 1891 was irrigated with a small pump Scobey had purchased. In these early years, there was no running water at the agency or boarding school, and all water had to be brought in barrels by the young male students from the Poplar and Missouri Rivers. Around 1889, one well was drilled near the agency but the water proved too alkaline, and the well soon failed due to sand infiltration. All the school buildings were heated by cast iron stoves, and the boys cut and delivered all the firewood. In addition, they provided most of the labor for construction and other everyday school projects.[29]

Boarding school girls were too young to work in the school laundry, and because of the scarcity of "large girls" (that is, older girls), most of the washing and laundry duties had to be done by older boys. Older girl students (whose ages

remain unclear) were rare because most were sent to off-reservation boarding schools. The girls primarily worked in sewing. At Fort Peck, girls sewed all their own school clothes, and were responsible for mending all the boys' clothing. This meant that the boys' clothing was purchased for them, but not for girls. These young girl students and the three Indian student assistants (and especially the assistant seamstress) appear to have been grossly overworked. Superintendent Baker alluded to this in 1891, stating: "It is necessary to keep several girls almost constantly employed in repairing boys' and girls' clothing and sewing on buttons."[30]

That Fort Peck students were overworked seems likely, but there are no indications that this crossed the line into labor exploitation. In the early twentieth century, however, on- and off-reservation schools grossly exploited Native students under the so-called "half-day" plan. The 1928 Meriam Report, which extensively examined off- and on-reservation boarding schools across the nation, confirmed a shocking level of child labor exploitation, in which undernourished, young Native children worked in conditions in open violation of state child labor laws.[31]

A last facet of the Fort Peck Boarding School life was Christianization. Although a federal school, the school incorporated some religious instruction and service into the educational program. Church services were held each Sunday in the school, and some services and prayer meetings were held during schoolday evenings. Four nights a week were dedicated to Christian singing and study, and students were required to pray each evening before bed. Superintendent Baker reported that in January, 1891, twenty-seven students were baptized. These Sunday school and other religious activities, and religious services themselves, were directed by the Presbyterian Church. This was the only church operating at the agency, and it had established mission churches both at Poplar River and Wolf Point.[32]

In November 1891, disaster struck. On the evening of November 23, fire destroyed both two-story school buildings, which housed both dormitories and all the major school facilities. The fire began in the attic of one building, and apparently quickly spread to the other building, located immediately next to it. Superintendent Baker suspected a defective flume. In his annual report in 1895, Agent Henry W. Sprole, who had taken over the agency in July 1893, said he suspected all Fort Peck boarding school building fires were deliberate acts of arson by students. Arson was in fact a common form of student resistance at federal on- and off-reservation boarding schools.[33]

One structure remaining after the fire was the original 1882 boarding school building, a one-and-one-half-story log structure abandoned for the last two years. Within two weeks, it had been rehabilitated enough to serve as the new school. What were essentially attics served as the new dormitories, and miscellaneous school buildings (all marginal log buildings serving such purposes as a laundry and livestock sheds) were similarly adapted. Student enrollment dropped substantially, but leveled at eighty students. On June 28 1892, Scobey opened bids for building four new brick school buildings, but the Indian Affairs Office rejected them as too expensive.[34]

In his annual report in August 1892, Scobey worried about what to do with the other students. Approximately 120 students were now unable to attend school. The only solution was to send them to off-reservation boarding schools. In 1890, forty-three students (older students in the "advanced" grade or grades) were transferred to Carlisle Indian School and other off-reservation boarding schools. In 1891, another thirty went to Carlisle and other schools. Scobey especially worried about parental consent, for according to him, parents up to this time willingly consented to send their children off the reservation. He

believed this was a reasonable proportion, but he feared that to greatly expand this number would require compulsory orders from the Indian Commissioner and the delicate matter of tribal police enforcing the directive.[35]

Scobey's fears were soon tested, for later in the fall of 1892, the old log building which had been adapted into the main school building was lost by fire. Now there were no school facilities and Scobey closed classes for the remainder of the year. A total of ninety-five students were sent to two off-reservation boarding schools: Carlisle Indian School and Fort Shaw, Montana, which had opened that year. It is unclear if additional coercion was needed to achieve this large number.[36]

On July 2, 1893, Agent Henry W. Sprole relieved Agent Scobey as Fort Peck Indian agent. Captain Sprole was a member of the Eighth Cavalry, was a forty-five-year-old native of New York state, a graduate of the West Point Academy, and had been detailed for unclear reasons from the War Department to the Indian Affairs Office since 1893. Sprole had no choice but to keep the boarding school closed for the rest of 1893.[37]

In November, 1893, fire destroyed the warehouse at the Wolf Point subagency. Details of the fire were not given, but most Assiniboine annuity provisions and supplies were destroyed. Sprole reported that only the prompt action of the Indian Affairs Office prevented Assiniboine suffering from this tragedy at the onset of winter.[38]

School remained closed for all of 1893, but in January 1894, the military post at Camp Poplar was closed and all its property was transferred to the Fort Peck Agency. The military buildings included thirty-six temporary log structures, most of which apparently were barracks, constructed by cottonwood logs secured vertically into the ground. Now ten years old, most of these buildings were rotting where the logs joined the ground. Nevertheless, agency and school staff adapted them sufficiently to school uses, and on

March 21, 1894, the boarding school reopened.

Student enrollment jumped as high as 132 students but the school closed at the end of June for lack of teachers. When the school closed after the second fire, the superintendent and entire teaching staff left. By January 1894, when Camp Poplar closed, the superintendent position had not been filled and the new principal teacher, J.H. Welch, became the acting superintendent.

Welch was a forty-four-year-old native of Illinois who had been a teacher in the Indian Affairs Office for six or seven years, He had just arrived at Fort Peck from the Lemhi Agency, Idaho, on January 7, 1894, three days before Camp Poplar closed. He was not only the acting superintendent, he was also the only teacher. Agent Sprole wisely closed the school for the summer, appreciating the impossible task of educating over 130 young students with only one teacher during the heat of the summer.[39]

In June 1894, Sprole and Department of Interior Inspector C.C. Duncan both made strong appeals for the need of new school buildings, and like Agent Scobey in 1892, they recommended brick construction. The Indian Affairs Office rejected the 1892 bids for brick buildings as too expensive, but this time Sprole and Duncan made an innovative request: that the bricks and construction all be done at the agency.

In a separate letter, Agent Sprole emphasized two advantages of this proposal. First, the prospective new buildings would be considerably safer from fire. They would be more fire resistant, for he wanted the brick buildings to have metal roofs. In addition, any fire would be less likely to spread because the prospective buildings would be simple profile, one-story buildings. More important, instead of large multipurpose buildings, the proposed ones would be smaller, individual buildings, including individual girls' and boys' dormitories and separate kitchen and dining room buildings.

Second, Sprole strongly advised about the wisdom of fire prevention. He explained that the agency and Indians were fortunate indeed that not a single student life was lost in the catastrophic November 1891 fire, which destroyed the two main school buildings. If even one student died, Sprole predicted that the agency might as well close the boarding school, for he believed Fort Peck tribal families would refuse to send their children.[40]

Concerning the unique proposal of making the bricks on-site and building the school with agency Indian labor, Duncan emphasized the economic benefits. Duncan believed that constructing the new school buildings would take two years, and agency Indians would do all the work. This included burning and making the bricks at a site near the school, and cutting and supplying all the firewood for this process. He argued that this rewarded more industrious Indians, who would be paid for their services, and the money would remain in the reservation economy.

Duncan admitted that this proposal would be more expensive than if the project were bid to off-reservation companies. Duncan could have argued that the two years of employment would actually save the Indian Affairs Office money when factoring in the cost of feeding and clothing the number of Indians and their families who otherwise would have gone unemployed. Duncan did, however, insightfully argue that this proposed project would be paid for by the Fort Peck Indians themselves, because the funding would come from the treaty payments. The Indian Affairs Office would not have to draw from its own general funds nor have to seek a special congressional appropriation.[41]

Unfortunately, the Indian Affairs Office refused to fund new school buildings. The only building soon constructed was a boys' dormitory, completed in the fall of 1895, because of another fire that destroyed whatever dilapidated former Army log structure served as the boys' facility. Details on the new dormitory construction are lacking, but it was clearly not identified as brick, and most likely was frame construction.

Two new brick dormitories were eventually built in 1899, but inexplicably the Indian Affairs Office refused to construct even the most rudimentary new classroom building until after 1905. This was in spite of repeated demands of Agents Sprole and Scobey, the school superintendents, and almost every Department of Interior inspector who examined the boarding school.[42]

There was one exceptional case of violence related to boarding school attendance during the 1890s that Sprole reported in his 1895 annual report. Sometime in the winter of 1894-1895, four boys ran away from the boarding school. The parents of three immediately returned them. One boy who was not identified was closely related to a tribal group of unclear origins known as the Tobacco Eater band, which was living on allotted lands off the reservation.

The boy's uncle, named Red Eagle, challenged Agent Sprole, saying that if the agent wanted the boy, the tribal police would have to come and kill Red Eagle first. Undeterred, Agent Sprole sent six men to bring in Red Eagle and the student, by force if necessary. The party included three tribal policemen and three white men: Mr. Renz and Frank Cusker were agency employees, and Frank Eder was a "squawman" (a non-Indian married to an Indian). Sprole ordered the six men to use force only if necessary.

When the agency party arrived at Red Eagle's allotted land, they informed Red Eagle that he and his nephew were going to be taken to the agency. Red Eagle refused and then grabbed Renz, as did another Tobacco Eater woman. When Red Eagle attempted to stab Renz with a knife, Renz called on the others to shoot Red Eagle. They fired and Red Eagle was killed.

Sprole reported that Red Eagle and his group of five men and three women were armed with Winchester repeating rifles, yet the outgunned tribal police party managed to retreat safely to the agency. Sprole reported that the case was taken to federal court and the agency party was fully exonerated.[43]

In the 1890s, two Indian policy officials associated with the Fort Peck Agency, Agent Henry W. Sprole and Department of Interior Inspector William J. McConnell, made instructive comments (however unfortunate) concerning the educational and assimilation experiences of Fort Peck students returning from off-reservation boarding schools, and especially from Carlisle Indian School. Both observers spoke highly of the educational benefits of these schools, but the most perplexing part of their comments related to reservation poverty and tribal cultures.

Agent Henry W. Sprole wrote in mid-September 1893, in his first annual report to the Indian Commissioner. At this point, he had been at the Fort Peck Agency only two and one-half months. Sprole was angered at the perceived degradation of these returning educated women. He believed it was "the refinement of cruelty" to educate Fort Peck girls at "an Eastern institute" (this was Carlisle Indian School, for it was the only federal off-reservation boarding school east of the Mississippi River) for three or four years and then return them to the reservation.

He conceded that they had no choice but to return to their families, but he was horrified when they did so. To Sprole, this led directly to prostitution. As he perceived it, "There is nothing left for them but to lead the life of the other women, and with people of as lax notions in regard to female virtue there is nothing but prostitution in the end." Sprole then added that "If they had never left the reservation they would never have felt their degradation so much." Instead of returning to their families, he proposed they should "be brought to the reservation in charge of a competent person; let them be kept out of the camp . . . unless employment can be found for them at the agency, which will remove them from the evil tendencies of the camp completely."[44]

That there were misguided tribal young men and women in reservation camps or tribal communities was probably true, just as there appears to have been a level of prostitution. In the early 1880s, for example, Fort Peck Agent Samuel Snider complained bitterly about Native prostitution and other corrosive influences, which he attributed primarily to the negative influence of the Camp Poplar military post. Ultimately, however, Sprole's accusations were misguided and based on his sense of cultural superiority. Education at federal or other schools did not necessarily equate with loss of self or cultural identity for students returning to their families. His presumption that such education triggered a sense of degradation and shame of one's tribal culture was completely unsupported.[45]

Like many assimilationists in the nineteenth century (and later), Sprole hated tribal cultures, but he was ignorant, if not terrified, of tribal cultural beliefs and practices. Sprole's solution to the problem was typical: total cultural assimilation. He concluded his 1893 diatribe with this: "There is so much sentiment in the East about the Indian it appears to me that those people will be willing to take these girls, adopt them, and complete the training of them . . . instead of at the end of their scholastic term sending them back to the reservation to go to the dogs."[46]

Agent Sprole wrote even more racist depictions four years later in his last annual report in early September 1897. He began sarcastically that Fort Peck students returning from non-reservation boarding schools "can play baseball pretty well" but demonstrated little interest in work, manual labor, or earning a living.

His comments on the return of women from off-reservation boarding schools degenerated quickly into racism.

Their whole life is made abortive and the money spent on their education wasted, by allowing them to return. . . . In many instances the practical result of returning them to the reservation is to furnish a better class of prostitutes for the same; yes, and made prostitutes by the so-called educated young Indian men, not camp Indians, though they naturally drift to becoming their wives. For the Indian youth who returns to his reserve imbued with the idea of the higher education for the Indian, unless he gets some easy, clean billet, as a rule, won't work, and acquires nothing.[47]

Although extreme, if not bordering on disturbed, Sprole's theme is similar to his 1893 remarks.

Agent Sprole's racist and derogatory depiction of returning Fort Peck students was echoed one month earlier, on August 4, 1897, by Department of Interior Inspector William J. McConnell. In his report on the Fort Peck boarding school, he introduced the same topic by stating that "A careful study of the question of educating our western Indians will I think impress the un-biased mind with the fallacy of sending the young people, boys or girls to Carlisle, or other eastern schools."

Like Sprole, McConnell believed that when educated Indians returned to their reservations, they were now "unable to take up their former life, discontent and often desperation takes possession of them, and in almost every instance the young men become dissipated, and the girls courtesans [prostitutes with a courtly, wealthy, or upper-class clientele]."[48]

Inspector McConnell's next remarks are rare, openly stated defenses of racism and cultural superiority, even by standards of the 1890s.

The rising generation on the western reservations, should be educated among the people with whom they must make their future home [that is, whites]. Generations must come and go before the Indian can be elevated to the plane which the Anglo-Saxon, has been so long in obtaining. When by transplanting these young people from among their barbarous associates to the civilized and refining influences of a modern college, you bring them up to years of manhood and woman hood [sic] and then return them to the teepees of their tribe, you have done them irreparable injury having wrecked their future lives.

There is happiness in progression but the human heart having once felt that happiness is made more than proportionately unhappy by retrogression.

Our aim therefore in my judgment should be not to push the education of the Indian beyond his or her ability to maintain the position we have given them.[49]

McConnell's ethnocentrism and racism need little explanation. More germane are his shocking depictions of Fort Peck students who returned from Carlisle Indian School. Although McConnell identifies these students by name, here are some of the most reckless descriptions of various female students: "A regulation dirty squaw, married to a half-breed; Debauched by an educated Indian from Carlisle, and married to an Indian in the camp; A prostitute; A prostitute, ran off with a camp Indian; Was no use at agency, finally given a position as tailor at Devil's Lake."

Concerning returning boy students, comments included, "In the Guard-house for debauching another man's wife; Worthless, will not work when the chance is offered; Just returned from Carlisle, character not developed; Worthless, was employed as disciplinarian

at the school, discharged for meeting girls clandestinely."[50]

McConnell's remarks are significant because of his complete ignorance of Fort Peck Agency camp and family life. McConnell was in no position to speak with any authority concerning any of these students. He did not live on the reservation and his examination of the agency and boarding school at best lasted one to two weeks. That Agent Sprole was a primary informant concerning these students seems rather likely.

The real danger of Agent Sprole's and Inspector McConnell's accounts is that they offered little insight into the complexities of acculturation change and cultural persistence of these students. Equally important, these white observers failed to appreciate the complexities of cultural change and persistence within each of these student's families. Such complexities were invisible to assimilationists like Sprole and McConnell because it seems they refused, or were incapable, to learn more about the Native people they spent so much time serving.

Sprole, like his predecessor C.R.A. Scobey, believed that Fort Peck tribesmen could never become economically self-sufficient unless they had irrigation for agriculture and haying. This was impressed upon them forcefully during the drought years of the late 1880s and their service during the 1890s. Lacking funding for irrigation projects, in 1894 Sprole took matters into his own hands. That year and continuing into 1895, he constructed a new irrigation ditch, opening new farming and haying lands for the boarding school and the agency. Sprole began with the old irrigation ditch constructed in 1884 by Agent Samuel E. Snider, located seven to eight miles north of the main agency, and running an estimated seven miles east from the Poplar River. Agent Sprole's new ditch proceeded south about seven or eight miles to just north of the boarding school and main agency.[51]

From 1895 through 1897, both the school farm and the agency farm and haying operations proved moderately successful. In 1897, under the administration of Agent Sprole, a new and vigorous request for a major irrigation project was again demanded from the Interior Department. In this case, however, the request originated not from Sprole, but from Department of Interior Inspector William J. McConnell.

Oddly enough, on August 4, 1897, the same day he filed his disturbing report on Fort Peck students returning from Carlisle Indian School, McConnell also submitted his agency report, focused primarily on his irrigation proposal. Details are unclear, but it seems highly likely that McConnell worked closely with Sprole in preparing his report, since the centerpiece of McConnell's proposal was an engineering feasibility report prepared for Sprole in January 1895.

In his 1894 report, Inspector McConnell asserted (correctly, it seems) that the economic self-sufficiency of the Fort Peck tribes depended on both agriculture and stock raising, and he argued that both of these were viable only with dependable irrigation. He explained there were two irrigation options. One was a spring runoff reservoir system for the Poplar River, which he discounted as unreliable. He failed to mention that it also completely ignored at least consideration of an equivalent proposal for the Assiniboines at Wolf Creek. McConnell boldly asserted that the most viable option (and of course, the most expensive one) was an extensive irrigation system drawing from a much more reliable water source, the Missouri River.[52]

McConnell enclosed the feasibility study prepared by Charles McIntyre, a civil engineer who also identified himself as an irrigation engineer. McIntyre proposed an irrigation canal system beginning near the mouth of the Milk River and Porcupine Creek on the western boundary of the reservation and proceeding east on the north side of the Missouri River, generally near the path of the Great Northern Railway, all the way to the main agency at Poplar River. He proposed extending the irrigation canal to the east end of the reservation at Big Muddy Creek. McIntyre estimated that the total cost of this irrigation canal complex would be $119,410.25.[53]

Secretary of Interior Cornelius N. Bliss referred McConnell's report to Commissioner of Indian Affairs William A. Jones for his recommendation. Sadly, in his September 30, 1897 response, Commissioner Jones equivocated, and asserted no position, although he implied that he preferred the Poplar River reservoir approach, which of course would have cost virtually nothing to construct. In contrast to Commissioner Jones, the Interior Department seems to have taken McConnell's proposal seriously, and they asked him again for his opinion.

Perhaps not surprisingly, Inspector McConnell remained staunchly supportive of the proposal. In his December 1, 1897 response, he argued bluntly for the importance of the long-term economic self-sufficiency of the Fort Peck tribes. He stated that the real question was whether the Interior Department wants to "*maintain a boarding house on this reservation* and continue to maintain these Indians in idleness, or whether it is the desire of Congress to place them in a position where they may become self-supporting"[54] [emphasis added].

In response, on December 8, 1897, Assistant Indian Commissioner A.G. Tourver recommended that Interior Secretary Bliss request a special congressional appropriation of $140,000 for the Fort Peck—Missouri River irrigation canal project. The figure was based on civil engineer McIntyre's estimate of $119,000 plus dollars, and an additional $20,000 he calculated necessary for constructing lateral irrigation extensions.[55] Congress failed to appropriate the funds, but at least Agent Sprole, the Indian Affairs

Office, and Interior Department for the first time had fully endorsed such a major project.

Sprole did not remain at the Fort Peck Agency long enough to follow the status of the agency irrigation proposal, for he was dogged by accusations of drunkenness and financial irregularities. These charges were made primarily by three local Montana elected representatives: R.X. Lewis, state representative of Valley County; J.C. Auld, state senator of Dawson County; and William Lindsay, state representative of Dawson Country.

Investigation of these allegations was also part of Inspector William J. McConnell's duties at Fort Peck. McConnell took extensive testimonies of the accusers, Agent Sprole, and others, and in his August 4, 1897, report to Interior Secretary William A. Jones concluded that these accusations were unsubstantiated, and Captain Sprole should remain the Fort Peck Agent.

McConnell concluded that the accusations were based primarily on economic interests lost to the accusers when, based upon Sprole's recommendation, the Camp Poplar military post was closed in January 1894. According to McConnell, the claimants also had substantial financial interests in the two trading posts at the agency—one was the sutler closely associated with the military post and the other with the main agency. Sprole then invited competing trading posts to the agency. Sprole also accused the claimants of having strong financial interests with Sprole's predecessor, Agent C.R.A. Scobey. McConnell concluded that removing Sprole would be disastrous to the agency and the reservation Indians, especially if former agent Scobey or any parties associated with the claimants returned.[56]

Inspector McConnell did not examine Sprole's alleged irregular financial transactions, however, an investigation that was added to the duties of Department of Interior Inspector J. George Wright and his inspection of the Fort Peck Agency and boarding school in January and

February 1898. On January 27, 1898, Inspector Wright informed Secretary of Interior Jones that Sprole had requested an immediate resignation.

Even at this incomplete point in Inspector Wright's exhaustive examination of vouchers and agency financial records, he had uncovered three years of gross irregularities in payrolls and transactions related to the selling of cowhides. Most of the payroll records concerned the temporary employment of large numbers of agency tribesmen, and records for services rendered were often absent or incomplete. Wright also discovered that Sprole offered credits to agency Indians for hides sold at the agency, but Wright discovered no malfeasance whatsoever concerning Sprole or the agency Indians, for the inspector concluded that these transactions appeared to always benefit these Indians.[57]

In his February 17, 1898 final report to Interior Secretary William A. Jones, Inspector Wright concluded that "In the management of affairs at this agency there has been no system or business methods applied to any department or with Indians. That Capt. Sprole is honest there is no question but that he is entirely unfitted to conduct an Indian agency is equally true."[58]

Captain Sprole was quite straightforward in defending his integrity. He stated in sworn testimony that he provided Inspector Wright on February 1, 1898 that "I want to make this statement that if I become tangled up in these accounts it has been the fault of the head and not of the heart; that I have done the best I could for these people since I have been here; that *I was a miserable pauper when I came here and am one now*"[59] [emphasis added].

Surely to former agent Henry W. Sprole's great dismay, former agent C.R.A. Scobey was reappointed as Fort Peck Agent. He reassumed duties on April 22, 1898. Scobey's primary concern was establishing long-term economic self-sufficiency for the Fort Peck Assiniboines and

Sioux. This was particularly pressing because the next year, 1899, the last annual payment of the ten year-treaty payments of $165,000 would be expended.[60]

Agent Scobey explained his goal in an 1899 letter to Merrill E. Gates, Secretary of the Board of Indian Commissioners. Scobey explained that this very year, the last of the $1.65 million treaty payments would be expended. Scobey believed that livestock had proven to be the only viable economic enterprise on the reservation. He explained that agriculture had proven only marginally successful, and that only a large irrigation project could make agriculture successful.

Scobey believed that the agency Indians should immediately negotiate another treaty and sell the majority of the reservation, that is, sell what he claimed were their "useless and surplus lands." These were the northern reservation lands, located away from the Missouri River lands, where almost all the agency Assiniboines and Sioux resided. Scobey believed that the large capital gained in a treaty sale should be carefully secured for the exclusive use of the tribes.

He also stated that these prospective funds should be expended to rebuild and operate the boarding school, and to greatly expand livestock distribution among the tribesmen. The feasibility of substantial irrigation needed to be studied, and the large funds for such a project needed to be secured, though he did not specify whether from the possible land cession funds or special congressional appropriations. Rations should be slashed in half, and then the remaining reservation lands should be allotted. After all this was accomplished, and Fort Peck Indians had presumably achieved economic self-sufficiency, Scobey recommended that the Fort Peck Reservation be abolished.[61]

By 1902, Agent Scobey was still arguing that the northern part of the reservation should be ceded to the federal government, but now he actively pursued a new alternative resource for agency Indians: grazing leases to non-Indians for these northern reservation lands. On July 3, 1902, he convened a large general council to seek tribal deliberation and possible approval of this initiative. Tribal members must have concurred, for an extensive system of grazing permits was established, which by 1903 had generated $12,000.[62]

Also in 1902, Scobey inaugurated his plan to decrease rations, dramatically revising the rations system, especially as related to agency men. All agency Indians were examined by the agency physician, and all those determined physically fit for work were thereafter denied annuity provisions and rations. Scobey believed that the rations and annuities system had long been an enormous disincentive to work and employment. Now, however, he was faced with aggressively securing adequate employment for these Natives. What Scobey found were primarily temporary jobs, including employment with the agency, the Great Northern Railway, and local ranchers and farmers. He reported that even some tribal women secured work in the homes of "respectable [that is, white] families."[63]

The last important change in the management of tribal affairs near the end of Agent Scobey's second administration was in fact a transformation in his own thinking. During both his terms of service as Fort Peck agent (1889 to 1893, and 1898 to 1905), Scobey consistently asserted that dry-land farming was not viable on the Fort Peck Reservation, and sustainable agriculture could be achieved only with irrigation. By 1903, he reversed his view. The climate had not changed, and the drought cycle still persisted, but Scobey credited his new optimism with the success and expansion of neighboring white neighbor farmers. As he said, "This country is being taken possession of by the 'man with the hoe.'" Scobey attributed what he believed was increased agricultural production on the reservation to the labor of Fort Peck Indians, due in part to his slashing of rations and annuities. He felt that he had to some degree succeeded in teaching them that they needed to feed themselves.[64]

Agent C.R.A. Scobey concluded his service as Fort Peck Agent in 1905. Since establishment of the Fort Peck Reservation on May 1, 1888, administration of the Fort Peck Agency had been stewarded by two men: Agents Scobey and Sprole. Although Sprole was terminated for his poor bookkeeping and payroll practices, he had still proven to be competent and capable. Scobey proved equally so. Considering the exceptionally turbulent and unstable agency management prior to 1888, the early formative years of the new reservation proved to be at least stable and productive for Fort Peck Assiniboines and Sioux. ✪

1 Charles Kappler, ed., *Indian Affairs. Laws and Treaties* (Washington, D.C.: Government Printing Office, 1904), 264-65; Francis Paul Prucha, *The Great Father: The United States Government and the American Indians*, abridged ed. (Lincoln: University of Nebraska Press, 1984, 1985), 165-66.

2 Kappler, *Indian Affairs. Laws and Treaties*, 264; Michael P. Malone and Richard B. Roeder, *Montana: A History of Two Centuries* (Seattle: University of Washington Press, 1976), 150.

3 Kappler, *Indian Affairs. Laws and Treaties*, 262.

4 Indian Agent D.O. Cowen to Indian Commissioner Thomas J. Morgan, September 2, 1889, *Annual Report to the Secretary of Interior for the Year 1879* [hereafter cited as *Annual Report*] (Washington, D.C.: Government Printing Office, 1889), 233; "Inspection of Fort Peck Agency," Department of Interior Inspector William W. Jenkin, July 22, 1889, Reports of Inspection, General Remarks, 1; Agent C.R.A. Scobey to Morgan, August 3, 1891, *Annual Report* (1891), 282; Scobey to Morgan, August 15, 1892, *Annual Report* (1892), 298.

5 Scobey, *Annual Report* (1891), 282; Scobey, *Annual Report* (1892), 298.

6 Scobey, *Annual Report* (1891), 283.

7 Cowen, *Annual Report* (1889), 234.

8 Jenkin, "Inspection of Fort Peck Agency," report on employees.

9 Cowen, *Annual Report* (1889), 233-34; Scobey to Morgan, August 12, 1890, *Annual Report* (1890), 131; Scobey, *Annual Report* (1891), 282; Scobey, *Annual Report* (1892), 298.

10 Cowen, *Annual Report* (1889), 234; Scobey, *Annual Report* (1890), 131; Scobey, *Annual Report* (1891), 282; Scobey, *Annual Report* (1892), 298.

11 Cowen, *Annual Report* (1889), 234; Scobey, *Annual Report* (1891), 282; Scobey, *Annual Report* (1892), 298.

12 Cowen, *Annual Report* (1889), 234; "Inspection of Fort Peck Agency," Department of Interior Inspector Benjamin H. Miller, October 30, 1891, Reports of Inspection, report p. 3; Agent Henry W. Sprole to Commissioner Daniel M. Browning, September 15, 1894, *Annual Report* (1894), 184.

13 Cowen, *Annual Report* (1889), 233.

14 Scobey, *Annual Report* (1890), 132.

15 Prucha, *The Great Father*, 218-19; William C. Canby, Jr, *American Indian Law in a Nutshell*, 3rd ed. (St. Paul: West Group, 1998), 19, 63.

16 Scobey, *Annual Report* (1892), 299.

17 Cowen, *Annual Report* (1889), 234; Scobey, *Annual Report* (1890), 133.

18 Ibid., 133; Andrew J. Isenberg, *The Destruction of the Bison* (New York: Cambridge University Press, 2000), 159-60.

19 Scobey, *Annual Report* (1891), 283.

20 Cowen, *Annual Report* (1889), 233; Scobey, *Annual Report* (1890), 131-32.

21 Scobey, *Annual Report* (1890), 131-32; Superintendent J.D. Baker, "Report of Superintendent of the Assiniboine Boarding School," in *Annual Report* (1891), 284-85; "Inspection of Fort Peck Agency Boarding School," Inspector Miller, December 9, 1889, Reports of Inspection, report p. 5.

22 Cowen, *Annual Report* (1889), 233; Superintendent Baker, *Annual Report* (1891), 284.

23 Scobey, *Annual Report* (1890), 132; Superintendent J.H. Welch, "Report of Superintendent of Poplar River School," in Sprole to Indian Commissioner Daniel M. Browning, August 28, 1895, *Annual Report* (1895), 196.

24 Baker, *Annual Report* (1891), 284.

25 See David Wallace Adams, *Education for Extinction: American Indians and the Boarding School Experience, 1875-1928* (Lawrence: University of Kansas Press, 1995), 21-22, 28-55, 149-50.

26 Ibid, 55-59.

27 Baker, *Annual Report* (1891), 284; Adams, *Education for Extinction*, 68-70.

28 Adams, *Education for Extinction*, 114-17; Kappler, *Indian Affairs. Laws and Treaties*, 262.

29 Miller, December 9, 1889, report pp. 2-3; Baker, *Annual Report* (1891), 284-85.

30 Baker, *Annual Report* (1891), 284-85.

31 Adams, *Education for Extinction*, 149-53; Lewis Meriam, *The Problem of Indian Administration: Report of a Survey made at the request of Honorable Hubert Work Secretary of the Interior, and submitted to him, February 21, 1982* (Baltimore: John Hopkins Press, 1928).

32 Baker, *Annual Report* (1891), 285; Scobey, *Annual Report* (1891), 283.

33 Sprole to Browning, August 28, 1895, *Annual Report* (1895), 195; Adams, 229-31.

34 Baker, "Report of Superintendent of the Fort Peck Boarding School," in *Annual Report* (1892), 300; Scobey, *Annual Report* (1892), 298.

35 Ibid., 298-99.

36 Ibid.; Sprole to Browning, September 15, 1893, *Annual Report* (1893), 191.

37 Sprole, *Annual Report* (1893), 190-91; "Inspection of Fort Peck Agency," Duncan, 1; "Inspection of the Fort Peck Indian Agency," Department of Interior Inspector John Lane, May 2, 1896, 1.

38 Sprole, *Annual Report* (1894), 184.

39 Ibid.; J.H. Welch, Principal Teacher and Acting Superintendent, "Report of Superintendent of Poplar River School, September 15, 1894, in *Annual Report* (1894), 186; "Inspection of Poplar Creek Boarding School," Duncan, June 27, 1894, 1, 3.

40 Duncan, "Inspection of the Fort Peck Agency2-3; Sprole to Duncan, June 23, 1894, in "Inspection of the Fort Peck Agency."

41 Duncan, "Inspection of Poplar Creek Boarding School," 1.

42 Sprole to Browning, August 28, 1895, *Annual Report* (1895), 195; Welch, "Report of Superintendent of Poplar River School," September 3, 1895, in *Annual Report* (1895), 196; Scobey to Commissioner William A. Jones, August 4, 1899, *Annual Report* (1899), 225.

43 Sprole to Browning, September 5, 1896, *Annual Report* (1896), 193.

44 Scobey, *Annual Report* (1893), 191.

45 For examples of Agent Snider's moralist campaign about Fort Peck women and Indians, and Camp Poplar see Agent Samuel E. Snider to Indian Commissioner Hiram Price, August 10, 1883, *Annual Report* (1883), 162; and Agent Snider to Commissioner Hiram Price, September 7, 1883, National Archives and Records Administration, Record Group 75, Records of the Bureau of Indian Affairs, Letters Received Commissioner of Indian Affairs, Box 155, letter # 17264.

46 Scobey, *Annual Report* (1893), 191.

47 Sprole to Commissioner Jones, September 7, 1897, *Annual Report* (1897), 174.

48 "Inspection of Poplar River Indian Industrial Boarding School," Department of Interior Inspector William J. McConnell, August 4, 1897, 3.

49 Ibid., 3-4.

50 Ibid., 4-5.

51 Sprole, *Annual Report* (1894), 183; Sprole, *Annual Report* (1895), 194-95.

52 "Inspection of the Fort Peck Reservation," McConnell, 6-7.

53 Charles McIntyre to Sprole, January, 1895, in "Inspection of the Fort Peck Reservation" report, August 4, 1897, 1-3.

54 McConnell to Secretary of Interior Bliss, December 1, 1897, in "Inspection of the Fort Peck Reservation."

55 Acting Indian Commissioner A.G. Tourver to Secretary of Interior Cornelius N. Bliss, December 8, 1897, in "Inspection of the Fort Peck Reservation,"August 4, 1897.

56 McConnell to Secretary Jones, August 4, 1897, in "Report of Inspector William J. McConnell to investigate charges against Captain Sprole and Mr. F. A. Hunter," August 4, 1897.

57 Inspector J. George Wright to Jones, January 27, 1898, in "Report on Affairs at Fort Peck Agency, Montana," February 17, 1898.

58 "Report on Affairs at Fort Peck Agency, Montana,"11.

59 "Testimony of Capt. H. W. Sprole Actg. U.S. Indian Agent, relative to certain matters on the Fort Peck Agency," February 1, 1898, in "Report on Affairs at Fort Peck Agency, Montana," 5.

60 Scobey to Commissioner Jones, August 31, 1898, *Annual Report* (1898), 196; Kappler, 262.

61 Scobey to Merrill E. Gates, Secretary of the Board of Indian Commissioners, November 24, 1899, in Scobey to Commissioner Jones, August 4, 1899, *Annual Report* (1899), 258-59.

62 Scobey to Commissioner Francis E. Leupp, July 1, 1902, *Annual Report* (1902), 234; Scobey to Commissioner Leupp, August 12, 1904, *Annual Report* (1904), 233.

63 Scobey, *Annual Report* (1902), 234.

64 Scobey to Leupp, August 20, 1903, *Annual Report* (1903), 197-98.

CHAPTER 7

~

The Turtle Mountain Chippewa Indians at Fort Peck
Joseph R. McGeshick, Ph.D.

THE Fort Peck Indian Reservation is not only home to Assiniboine (Nakona) and Sioux (Dakota and Lakota) peoples, but also to a number of Chippewa. These Indians originally resided in the Great Lakes culture area and began moving into present-day northeastern Montana a few decades before the turn of the twentieth century. They began filing for land around Fort Peck in 1906.[1] "Chippewa," "Ojibway/Ojibwa," and "Anishinabe" are terms that refer to a large group of Algonquian-speaking Indians whose habitations eventually extended from the western Great Lakes to nearly the Rocky Mountains. These people shared a common linguistic tradition, but pressure from Euro-American and other Native peoples forced some of them out of the Great Lakes area and onto the northern plains.[2]

Leaving seasonal resources of wild rice, venison, and fish for an ostensibly endless supply of buffalo seemed a reasonable answer to the problems of contact and the imperial stretching of American and British Canada. By the mid-1700s, groups of Great Lakes Chippewa began their dispersal west into the waning woodlands of Minnesota and southern Manitoba and the seemingly endless plains of grass and herds of buffalo of North Dakota and southern Saskatchewan. Just about the time when Americans fought their war for independence from Great Britian, western Great Lakes Chippewa were already being lured by the call of the northern plains.

As the nineteenth century progressed, groups moved further west and north, eventually allying themselves with the Crees of the southern Canadian plains, another Algonquian-speaking tribe.[3] Soon lakes and rivers gave way to a sea of prairie and individual bands of Chippewa quickly accommodated the challenges of a buffalo-hunting/horse-riding culture. Most of the

Chippewa, along with their Cree and Métis neighbors, remained north of what was to become the U.S.-Canada border. Although the boundary functioned as a political reality after 1819, the Plains Chippewa, along with most other tribes, ignored it and freely pursued their seasonal way of life on both sides of the forty-ninth parallel. The tribal groups who remained south of the U.S.-Canada border located in two main population centers and dispersal points—the Red River settlements, highly connected to the Métis, and the Turtle Mountains in what is now north-central North Dakota.

After carving out a place for themselves among tribes such as the Assiniboine, Gros Ventre, and Cree, most Plains Chippewa, who eventually fell under American jurisdiction and whose prodigy now lives among Fort Peck Sioux and Assiniboine, settled in present-day northern North Dakota near the Turtle Mountains. It was also during this time that Plains Chippewa families constructed extremely close ties with the Métis in the Red River Valley and later in southern Saskatchewan.[4] The Chippewa who settled further west and north on the southern Canadian plains cooperated with Métis and Cree on seasonal buffalo hunts near the Saskatchewan and Assiniboine Rivers. Many Chippewa families who now live on Fort Peck Indian Reservation trace their roots to those two areas.

The Métis Rebellion of 1869-1870 created small waves of exiled families who eventually ended up in scattered communities in north-central North Dakota, the Milk River, and Spring Creek (Lewistown) areas of Montana and southern Saskatchewan. In 1885, with the Métis again serving as the impetus and the Cree playing a major role, some Chippewa found themselves in a provincial struggle for political and economic power in southern Saskatchewan.[5] Although both Métis Rebellions remain historically important for many Fort Peck Chippewa, the vast majority

of their past historically falls with the Turtle Mountain Chippewa in North Dakota.

Chippewa residing on the northern plains in the last half of the nineteenth century found themselves in a unique state of flux. Initially pressured by both Indian and white peoples, and by economics, large bands of Chippewa claimed a sizeable portion of North Dakota. By the end of the Métis-Cree wars in southern Saskatchewan, American federal authorities forced their jurisdiction upon those Chippewa who became Canadian exiles south of the border. While the American government claimed and dominated the political and economic realms of the Indian-white relationship, the public constructed cultural images of the Chippewa and other tribes. What developed was a homogenous view of Indians. To the settler, rancher, land speculator, and even reservation official, all Indians, either Chippewa, Assiniboine ,or Sioux, were the same. This assumption became the basis for government assimilation policies and practices.[6]

The Chippewa who moved from the Great Lakes culture area to the plains began another series of accommodations. The change in material culture reflected an accelerated transformation common on the buffalo frontier after 1860. White and Indian hide hunters fell into a specialized slaying of what seemed an endless resource. For the Chippewa, as well as other plains tribes, buffalo hide hunting equated into a much-desired Euro-American material culture.[7] Metal pots and pans, knives, guns, alcohol, processed food and blankets, thread, and needles—all of these helped transform plains Indian life. For whites, hide hunting developed into a systematic slaughter driven by economic necessities.

Although the change in Plains Chippewa material culture is most evident, their cultural changes were even more unique. In a matter of four generations, they accommodated buffalo meat, wild turnips, and buffalo berries, Sun

Dances, and all of the other empowerments of the plains. A people who once practiced the Midewiwin Ceremony, a ritual passing of knowledge and healing, and subsisted on wild rice, maple sugar, fish, and venison were now mounted buffalo hunters.[8] Chippewa families, bands, and tribes sought refuge in each other in reaction to these changes.

Politically, by the time the Chippewa settled near the Turtle Mountains of north-central North Dakota, their treaty experiences started an uncertain journey. Turtle Mountain Chippewa treaty negotiations actually began in 1851, when some of the bands negotiated alongside the Pembina Chippewa and Red Lake Chippewa with the then-governor of Minnesota Territory, Alexander Ramsey.[9] Those meetings failed to produce any lasting agreements that directly benefited the Turtle Mountain Chippewa. Talks resumed in 1863 for similar purposes. The land that was of most importance to the Chippewa of the Turtle Mountain area was a 100-mile-wide strip on the west side of the Red River. After 1863, these Chippewa began their struggle for recognition as title-holders of over 3,000 square miles of land and as separate negotiators in future treaties and agreements.[10] This era was also a time when assimilation and traditionalism divided not only the Chippewa, but also every other American Indian tribe. The use of terms like "mixed-bloods" and "full-bloods" grew to be political and economic realities. American treaty negotiators used these divisions to their advantage as they wrestled away title to millions of acres. Attempts to get the tribe and government to agree about who was eligible for what land ran up a chain of unsuccessful negotiations that created irreparable divisions among the Chippewa. That disjointing, directly caused by a union of government-public land interests, remained the driving force that led to Turtle Mountain Chippewa families settling on or near the Fort Peck Indian Reservation.[11]

In January 1878, Fort Peck Indian agent Wellington Bird reported that the northern part of the reservation was full of Indians who did not have rights to any of what would be eventually designated as the Fort Peck Indian Reservation. These included Chippewa from Dakota Territory and Métis from Canada, as well as some of Sitting Bull's followers. Most Fort Peck Indian did not want these groups on their land, since they were killing the few buffalo left in lower Milk River region and the Métis and their Chippewa allies carried on an illicit trade in ammunition and whiskey.[12]

By 1882, dissension caused by land title, tribal enrollment, and an overall decline in their traditional way of life, not only for the Turtle Mountain Chippewa, but for all plains Indians, pressured President Chester A. Arthur to set aside a twenty-four-by-thirty-two-mile reservation in north-central North Dakota.[13] One of the major underpinnings to this situation, however, was the question of about a million acres surrounding the small reservation, to which the tribe still claimed title. Three factors forced Arthur's action and caused lasting divisions among these people. First, buffalo numbers were falling drastically and the government's desire to make a sedentary agricultural society out of seasonal buffalo hunters pushed federal assimilation policies that became directly tied to land title. Second, railroads needed either clear title to land or trouble-free rights-of-way to their direct routes to the Pacific and for their branch lines. Finally, settlers needed cheap land for homesteading that was backed by legislative power for underlying land speculation purposes.[14]

During the last quarter of the nineteenth century, the political and economic struggles for many Plains Chippewa communities and families appeared all too dismal. Gone were the days of adventurous and festive seasonal migrations, accompanied by cheerful reunions. The future held confusion, confinement, and later starvation. Consequently, in a mere two years, the government, urged on by land-hungry homesteaders and speculators, reduced the original 1882 twenty-two township tract to two townships.[15] The next twenty years proved disastrous. Not only was the loss of land alarming, but the loss of people proved even more wrenching.

American lust for land and the resulting imposition of English land tenure was the moving force that led to the economic demise and cultural collapse of the Turtle Mountain Chippewa. What emerged was an identifiable Plains Chippewa way of life that did not completely disappear, though change and accommodation to Euro-American pressures and pleasures contributed to their cultural fragmenting. It also led to the forced relocation of dozens of Turtle Mountain Chippewa extended families to the Fort Peck Indian Reservation.[16] The reservation system, with its mechanisms of allotment, land title, and trust responsibility, caused deep social discord among the Turtle Mountain Chippewa from the late 1880s through the first decade of the twentieth century. The Assiniboine and Sioux at Fort Peck struggled with those same mechanisms. Fortunately, the people at Fort Peck retained over two million acres of land for their reservation.[17] But the allotment and its malevolent twin, white homesteading, assaulted Fort Peck land title in similar ways.

The divisions over land issues and pro-assimilation mechanisms resulted in one of the most infamous treaty negations in American history. All through the 1880s, Chiefs Little Shell and Rocky Boy, along with a few other small bands of Chippewa, seasonally led buffalo hunts west of the Turtle Mountains. They traveled as far as the Milk River in Montana and the Assiniboine River in southern Saskatchewan. As early as 1882, Chief Thomas Little Shell returned from the southern Canadian plains to the Turtle Mountains pro-

testing Euro-American encroachment and lack of government and tribal concern for Chippewa land title.[18]

After the 1884 land reduction, government officials, missionaries, and private business interests tore at the Chippewa people and their land. Propelled by concepts of blood quantum and competence, a breakdown in social accommodation occurred. Progressives and traditionalists remained even more divided after that time. On top of that conflict were the ravages of reservation life. Confinement and starvation characterized the reservation period for the Chippewa and other tribes. The winter of 1887-88 was especially severe—more than 150 men, women, and children died of starvation.[19] By 1892, Little Shell and other leaders such as Rocky Boy grew tired of government double-dealing and intertribal bickering. Since short food supplies remained a constant threat, Little Shell and his followers left for the plains of Montana and southern Saskatchewan.[20] They returned to a situation that set in motion a series of events that led to the final exile of this and other Chippewa peoples.

Food shortages and problems with land gripped all Indians, Turtle Mountain Chippewa included, living in northeastern Montana. Some of the land problems were settled when the government negotiated the Sweet Grass Hills Treaty of 1886, which Congress ratified in 1888, but food shortages remained a primary problem. In the early winter of 1893, the food storehouse at the sub-agency at Wolf Point burned to the ground, leaving many Assiniboine and Sioux to find subsistence by their own means. During the same period, a number of "half-breeds" and other Indians showed up at the agency seeking food and ammunition. Part of this group included a band of Turtle Mountain Chippewa. Agent Sprole allocated them some food and demanded they leave the boundaries of the reservation. He noted that trespassing stock owned by non-

Indians was a growing problem and he recommended fencing the reservation. Sprole's concern for these destitute groups provoked a negative response from the Jndians at Fort Peck that led to accusations against him and his clerk. Some of the accusations, made by Montana Senator J. C. Auld and Representative William Lindsay of Dawson County, included objections to allowing Turtle Mountain Chippewa to live and draw food rations and other goods from Fort Peck supplies.[21] Many different groups of Indians drifted the areas north and south of the Canadian border and the lower Milk River region looking for the last remnants of the once-vast buffalo herds or friendly tribes who retained land and food rations from the federal government. Santee Sioux exiles, Métis from Canada, and Turtle Mountain Chippewa wandered on and off the Fort Peck Reservation.

Little Shell's and Rocky Boy's and other bands of Turtle Mountain Chippewa hunted buffalo in Montana and southern Saskatchewan during the last few years of the 1880s. When they and other bands of Chippewa returned in the early 1890s, pro-assimilation leaders negotiated a land cession of approximately nine million acres for $1 million, known as the infamous "Ten-Cent Treaty." The government picked thirty-two full-bloods to determine who was legally accepted as a Turtle Mountain Chippewa, an act that left hundreds of families disenfranchised.[22] Little Shell and Rocky Boy left again, never to return, leaving Congress to ratify the agreement in April of 1904. That left the Turtle Mountain Chippewa with two townships in northern North Dakota.

The 1904 agreement also called for the allotment of reservation land. With nearly 3,000 enrolled members and nearly 2,000 more waiting for permission to take up allotment wherever land was available, there was hardly enough to meet the 160-acre average allotment.[23] Scores of Turtle Mountain Chippewa families were left with no allotments after the two townships were surveyed and divided. Consequently, by 1930 the government secured over 2,000 allotments under the 1904 agreement in Montana on public domain lands. Most of those lands came under the jurisdiction of the Fort Peck Agency. A small Chippewa community also grew up near Trenton, southwest of Williston, North Dakota. The government also granted allotments for Chippewa families in North and South Dakota near the Fort Totten, Fort Berthold, and Cheyenne River Reservations. Chippewa allotments also came into existence near the Montana reservations of Fort Belknap and Rocky Boy.[24]

The Turtle Mountain Chippewa families who ended up at or near Fort Peck filed for their allotments at the Glasgow Land Office after 1905. Chippewa families filed over 3,000 allotments totaling over 400,000 acres. These eclipsed those around other areas of Montana and in the Dakotas.[25] In the Dakotas, Turtle Mountain Chippewa took the eight allotments near the Cheyenne River Reservation near Phillip, South Dakota, three allotments near the Fort Totten Reservation in North Dakota, ten allotments near the Fort Berthold Reservation in the vicinity of Garrison, North Dakota, seventeen allotments near Stanley, North Dakota, two allotments in Burke County, and approximately sixty allotments in the immediate locality of the designated Turtle Mountain Reservation in north-central North Dakota.[26]

There came to be so many Turtle Mountain Chippewa allotments near the Fort Peck Reservation that government officials suggested that an additional field clerk for Fort Peck be headquartered at Bainville, Montana, to administer the 561 Turtle Mountain Chippewa allotments in extreme eastern North Dakota and those near the Montana settlements of Bainville, Medicine Lake, and Froid. Forty allotments south of the Missouri River across from Wolf Point and

Frazier also existed. The agency clerk at Fort Peck would handle those lands.[27]

Turtle Mountain Chippewa allotments also existed west of the Fort Peck Indian Reservation: 350 in Blaine and Phillips Counties near the Fort Belknap Reservation and sixteen south of the reservation; 114 west of Rocky Boy's Reservation; and seven allotments in southeastern Montana in Carter County. Those proved the most problematic to administer. The agent observed that reaching those lands required over 1,000 miles of travel, an almost impossible task at that time.[28]

The majority of those allotments were filed on, but few Turtle Mountain Chippewa actually lived on their lands. Most were leased to local farmers and ranchers while the Indians either moved back to the Turtle Mountain Reservation in North Dakota or settled in or near the small reservation towns. Some families also settled in or near the various non-reservation towns, accommodating Euro-American culture.

Indian education, both by missionaries and agent teachers, served as the great cultural pulverizing force that changed the minds and bodies of Indian children. By the early 1920s, boarding schools taught Assiniboine and Sioux children the basics for them to succeed in Euro-American-dominated society. A number of Turtle Mountain Chippewa children also attended those classes. For many Turtle Mountain Chippewa families who applied for allotments near the Fort Peck Reservation and who also received rations there from time to time, educational instruction at the Fort Peck boarding school was foreseeable. Since the mainstream tax structure for schools depended on local property taxes and since reservation land remained in trust status, public education was not an option for Indian children, whether Assiniboine, Sioux, or Turtle Mountain Chippewa.[29]

The spring of 1922 proved difficult for Indian children at the Fort Peck boarding school. In May

of that year, thirty-five girls ran away from the school due to the actions of the head matron, a Chippewa who proved to be narrow-minded and hot-tempered. She acted extremely strictly and also referred to the girls as "devils" and "tramps." By 1924, the total enrollment at the school was twenty-seven, about half of whom were either Turtle Mountain Chippewa or some other tribal affiliation other than the Fort Peck tribes. However, most children of school age attended the mission schools on the reservation.[30] For the ten years before 1930, Turtle Mountain paid the tuition for "a good many children" in the scattered communities that had members living on or near their allotments. Superintendent C.H. Ashbury reported that the present arrangement depended mostly on correspondence due to the distances between the Turtle Mountain Reservation and the Turtle Mountain Chippewa allotments and their communities.[31]

Disputes between Assiniboine/Sioux Indians on Fort Peck and Turtle Mountain Chippewa, who drifted onto the reservation and settled in the communities that grew up along the Missouri River and the Great Northern Railway, remained an unsettling problem for government officials and Fort Peck tribal leaders. Conflicts arose not only between Turtle Mountain Chippewa and members of the Fort Peck tribes, but also between mixed-bloods and full-bloods. They reached a new level by 1929, when a few tribal leaders even appealed to Senator Burton K. Wheeler that mixed-bloods were usurping the authority of the Fort Peck General Council. Adding to the already problematic issues of land, reservation officials and tribal leaders also complained about lands on the outskirts of Wolf Point. They protested that Canadian Cree and Turtle Mountain Chippewa squatters illegally occupied small tracts of tribal land and the city was using Indian lands for a dump, a rodeo, and an airport.[32]

The Great Depression found Fort Peck in a state that had not changed since the first days of allotment. Although starvation no longer loomed, a number of problems still posed difficulties for the Assiniobine and Sioux. In 1933, a general council was held to deal with Indian complaints. Indian Agent C.L. Walker addressed seven issues: the construction of a cross-reservation highway; land speculation adjacent to towns; housing for Indian elders; reservoir construction in grazing areas; construction of a bridge across the Poplar River; enlargement of hospital facilities; and the arranging for a more satisfactory handling of the Turtle Mountain Chippewa.[33]

Another problem that Indian agents found a constant menace was bootlegging. Since the early 1800s up until 1951, alcohol was prohibited in Indian country. Fur traders often used whiskey, rum, and brandy to lubricate the fur trade and gain an underhanded economic advantage over Indians. Indians and alcohol took on a stigma that still lingers.[34] The Métis, along with their Turtle Mountain Chippewa allies, had long provided alcohol to Indians. The Prohibition era was nothing new to the tribes at Fort Peck and keeping bootleggers off reservation lands had always been a concern. On one occasion in 1921, two Chippewa Indians near Culbertson, who were known professional bootleggers, obtained 300 pints of whiskey destined for Wolf Point. The early 1920s brought even more problems with alcohol, since the summer of 1920 saw an immense influx of Euro-American homesteaders, railroad men, and land speculators.[35]

Land problems waned after the late 1930s. By that time, a Fort Peck Reservation land field agent, with assistance of a clerk and clerk-typist, managed land matters on the reservation. Farming and grazing leases, as well as any mineral leases, were administered at Poplar, the agency headquarters. The land field agent also oversaw the 500-plus allotments of the Turtle

Mountain Indians in the vicinity of the reservation. In addition to leases, the agent took responsibility for probate records, land sales and exchanges, wills, and keeping land ownership records current.[36] After 1932, the Turtle Mountain Chippewa allotments in the surrounding area of the Fort Peck Indian Reservation came completely under their administration. Those allotments amounted to individual 160-acre tracts. In the early 1930s, the Commissioner of Indian Affairs' Washington, D.C., office authorized Superintendent C.H. Asbury to identify the total Turtle Mountain Chippewa allotments that were filed from 1906 to 1920. After a seventeen-day, ten-quarts-of-oil and five-tire journey, Asbury quantified approximately 1,133 allotments.[37]

The most plaguing problems for the Turtle Mountain Chippewa residing on or near the Fort Peck Agency were poverty and discrimination. When talk about them taking up allotments on the Fort Peck Reservation surfaced, Indians at Fort Peck adamantly rejected the idea. The Chippewa also suffered discrimination from whites, many of whom had already homesteaded much of the public domain in northeastern Montana.[38] Most, if not all, of the Euro-Americans living on or near the Fort Peck Indian Reservation, like the rest of the country, believed in homogenized tribal identity. They saw no real differences between the Assiniboine and Sioux Indians at Fort Peck and the exiled Turtle Mountain Chippewa living among them and near white communities.[39] Most of these North Dakota exiles suffered some of the same social ailments as their relatives living near Great Falls and other Montana towns. Poor self-esteem and poverty created debilitating problems for all of these Chippewa.[40]

World War II and the 1950s ushered in minute changes for not only the Assiniboine and Sioux, but also for the exiled Turtle Mountain Chippewa living in northeastern Montana.

Many enlisted and fought in both theaters. After they returned to Fort Peck and the surrounding area, new opportunities opened up in terms of employment and other services that they qualified for as returning veterans. Along with improved economic conditions came an overall improvement in social conditions. Better housing and health care followed better economic conditions. Turtle Mountain Chippewa were not eligible for subsidized tribal housing and remained tenants of almost exclusively white landlords. As for health care, even though they were not eligible for tribal health services, tribal health officials often overlooked eligibility requirements in sincere efforts to provide much-needed care to them. The Indian Health Service, which came under the Department of HEW after the 1950s, instituted more stringent requisites as budgets diminished and populations increased.[41] By the 1970s, federal allocations diminished, and the Indian Health Service no longer permitted non-enrolled Assinbioine and Sioux to use their facilities and doctors. State health offices took over the administration of Turtle Mountain families, but most found innovative and alternative methods of health care, sometimes existing with none at all.

The last quarter century of the 1900s ushered in new realty opportunities for tribal allottees. Increased interest in tribal minerals, especially in oil and coal, caused more activity in mineral leasing. The vast coal reserves in eastern Montana had always been a semi-silent motivating rationale for numerous energy companies' interests in leasing individual landholder's minerals.[42] When oil was discovered on the Fort Peck Reservation in the 1950s, Assiniboine, Sioux and Turtle Mountain Chippewa landowners saw an increase in mineral leasing. Allotments on and off Fort Peck rested on the vast Williston Basin oil field. A few Fort Peck landholders sold their minerals to competing energy companies

and enjoyed slightly more economic opportunities. According to the John Glenn Report of 1982, however, "services to Turtle Mountain allottees has always been less than adequate . . . [and they have] been treated like an illegitimate child with puritanical relatives."[43]

Numerous realty problems have existed since the Montana tribal agencies were charged with the management of Turtle Mountain public domain lands in the 1930s. As far as minerals are concerned, past policies regarding mineral retention by Turtle Mountain allottees near Fort Peck meant a mass departure of land out of trust, especially with oil leases. From the time an oil lease was negotiated and signed to the time the owner or heirs received any money took from one to two years. Turtle Mountain allottees have always harbored feelings that their lands, which are located adjacent to producing oil wells, produced only minimal, if any, benefits to their owners or heirs. Royalties also remained problematic. From the 1970s through the 1980s, a 16 2/3 percent royalty rate appeared to have been detrimental to the development of Indian lands, and the great distance of those lands from North Dakota along with inadequate staff complicated its administration.[44]

As of 2006, the total acreage of Turtle Mountain Chippewa that Fort Peck administers is 23,395 acres. Of that, 6,364 acres are in Roosevelt County, 1,310 acres in McCone County, 1,680 acres in Daniels County, and 9,943 acres in Sheridan County, with the remaining in Valley County.[45] Although the Bureau of Indian Affairs at Fort Peck handles most of the leasing, including minerals, the Bureau of Land Management also has a hand in other areas.

The families who ended up at or near the Fort Peck Indian Reservation stood out, not only culturally, but also politically and economically. Families with names like Azure, Gourmeau, Grandbois, Trottier, and others settled on the eastern side of the reservation near Poplar, the agency headquarters and unofficially the Sioux side of the reservation. Others with names such as Poitra, Dejarlais, Boyer, Brunelle, Hayes, and Beauchman carved out homes in and around Wolf Point, where a sub-agency was also located in the early years of the reservation, and which was also unofficially the Assiniboine side of the reservation. Most of these families and others retained allotments either through the 1906 Chippewa land filings or by marrying into the Assiniboine and Sioux tribes. The children of those unions inherited land from all three tribes. What resulted is a unique landholding/tribal affiliation state of affairs resulting in individual Turtle Mountain Chippewa, enrolled in North Dakota, holding undivided interest in trust land near the Fort Peck Indian Reservation. But there also exist many Chippewa, enrolled and not, who can trace their ancestry to the Turtle Mountain Reservation, who retained no land interests off their North Dakota reservation. There also remains a recognizable acreage of Turtle Mountain Chippewa trust land east and south of Fort Peck. Small farming communities like Froid, Bainville, and Medicine Lake also are home to a few Chippewa families with names like LaCounte and Poitra.

Since relocating, cultural, political, and economic hurdles challenged Turtle Mountain Chippewa living at and near Fort Peck. Although federally recognized as Indians with special relationships with the federal government, Chippewa at Fort Peck live in near-political limbo. Since they are not enrolled members of the Fort Peck tribes, their only means of participating in the tribal political process is to return to the Turtle Mountain Reservation in North Dakota. Most tribal services at Fort Peck are denied them due to their Chippewa enrollment status. They can, however, fully participate in state and local politics. Surprisingly, some have succeeded in doing so in places like Bainville and other small northeastern Montana communities. Consequently, they remain a somewhat silent but identifiable group of Turtle Mountain Chippewa, living with the challenges of the twenty-first century. ✺

1 Glasgow Land Office Allotment Roll, 1906, Turtle Mountain Chippewa Allotments. Record Group 75, National Archives, Washington, D.C.

2 Sister Carolissa Levi, *Chippewa Indians of Yesterday and Today* (New York: Pagent Press, 1956), 11-13.

3 Laura Peers, *The Ojibway of Western Canada: 1780-1870* (Winnepeg, Manitoba: The University of Manitoba Press, 1994), 51-59.

4 Fred J. Shore, "The Canadians and the Metis: The Recreation of Manitoba, 1858-72" (Ph.D. dissertation, University of Mantoba, Winnepeg, 1991), 72-73.

5 William, J. Bryan, *Montana Indians: Yesterday and Today* (Helena, Montana: American and World Geographic Publishing, 1996), 94-95.

6 Joseph. R. McGeshick, "Meatless Pemmican: Indian Tribes, Identity and PanIndianism in 20th Century Culture," in *Visions of An Enduring People: A Reader In Native American Studies*, Walter C. Fleming and John G. Watts, eds. (Dubuque, Iowa: Kendal/Hunt Publishing, Co., 2000), 67-86.

7 Peers, *The Ojibway of Western Canada*, 56-59.

8 Levi, *Chippewa Indians of Yesterday and Today*, 15-20.

9 Patrick Goumeau, *History of the Turtle Mountain Band of Chippewa Indians* (Belcourt, North Dakota: Turtle Mountain Band of Chippewa Indians, 1980), 45-48.

10 Ibid.

11 Richard J. LaFramboise, Fiduciary Trust Officer, U.S. Department of the Interior, Office of the Special Trustee for American Indians, Turtle Mountain Agency, Belcourt, North Dakota. Interview with author, December 5, 2006.

12 Douglas D. Martin, *Historical Report on the Fort Peck Indian Reservation, Part I: An Administrative and Social History*, Defense Exhibit No. FP-I, Fort Peck Indians v. United States, Court of Claims, Docket 184, p.53.

13 Goumeau, *History of the Turtle Mountain Band of Chippewa Indians*, 88-95.

14 Ibid.

15 Bryan, *Montana Indians*, 94-95.

16 LaFromboise interview.

17 Bryan, *Montana Indians*, 86-84.

18 Ibid., 69-70.

19 Gourneau, *History of the Turtle Mountain Band of Chippewa Indians*, 89-90.

20 Bryan, *Montana Indians*, 69-70.

21 Martin, *Historical Report on the Fort Peck Indian Reservation, Part I*, 89, 93.

22 Bryan, *Montana Indians*, 94-95.

23 Richard J. LaFramboise, Fiduciary Trust Officer, U.S. Department of the Interior, Office of the Special Trustee for American Indians, Turtle Mountain Agency, Belcourt, North Dakota., interview with author, December 11, 2006.

24 C. H. Ashbury, "Report to the Commissioner of Indian Affairs, Washington, D.C.," Turtle Mountain Agency, Belcourt, North Dakota, April 4, 1932, 5-6.

25 Paul Finnicum, Turtle Mountain Land Specialist, Bureau of Indian Affairs, Fort Peck Agency, Poplar, Montana, interview with author, October 14, 2006.

26 Ashbury, "Report to the Commissioner of Indian Affairs," 3-4.

27 Ibid., p. 5.

28 Ibid., pp. 5-6.

29 Bryan, *Montana Indians*, 87-88.

30 Martin, *Historical Report on the Fort Peck Indian Reservation, Part I*, 139-140.

31 Ashbury, "Report to the Commissioner of Indian Affairs," 7.

32 Martin, *Historical Report on the Fort Peck Indian Reservation, Part I*, 176.

33 Ibid., 187-188.

34 McGeshick, "Meatless Pemmican," 78-79.

35 Martin, *Historical Report on the Fort Peck Indian Reservation, Part I*, 136.

36 Ibid., p. 221.

37 LaFramboise interview.

38 Ibid.

39 McGeshick, "Meatless Pemmican," 70-75.

40 Bryan, *Montana Indians*, 47-48.

41 Indian Health Service, Vern E. Gibbs Health Center, Poplar, Montana, Records Management.

42 Martin, *Historical Report on the Fort Peck Indian Reservation, Part I*, 222.

43 John Glenn, "Final Summary Report: Identify All Potential Statute Of Limitations Cases On 567 Turtle Mountain Public Domain Allotments All Located In Montana," Bureau of Indian Affairs, Billings Area Office," June 11, 1982, 1.

44 Ibid.,1-2.

45 Anita Bauer, Rights Protection, Bureau of Indian Affairs, Fort Peck Agency, Poplar, Montana, interview with author, November 16, 2006.

~

CHAPTER 8

The First Allotments, Changes in Land Tenure, and the Lohmiller Administration, 1905-1917

David R. Miller, Ph.D.

Descriptions about the conditions facing the residents of the Fort Peck Reservation between 1905 and 1917 are often few and far between in the official records of the Indian Office and its agency in Poplar. Still, it is possible to glean many insights about the changes confronting the people there. Teddy Roosevelt was beginning his second term as President of the United States, and Francis E. Leupp was appointed the Commissioner of Indian Affairs (CIA) in 1905. A former employee of the Indian Rights Association and frequent visitor to reservations, Leupp had a certain credibility. He implemented newly legislated civil service reforms within the Indian Service, balanced day schools with the established boarding schools, utilized effective and efficient administration of government regulations, and severed the trust relationship for many.[1]

The Indian Service no longer called the top reservation agency official "Agent," using instead the title "Superintendent of the School and Agency," if there were an agency boarding school. On January 13, 1905, Charles B. Lohmiller, the former clerk at the agency, was named the first superintendent of the Fort Peck School and Agency.[2] President Roosevelt adamantly supported U.S. Civil Service reform that ended political patronage in appointments of Indian Service employees. Lohmiller served as superintendent for twelve years.[3]

His experience as clerk made Lohmiller an ideal appointee, but he was also aware that many mid-level supervisory positions needed to be filled. The overhaul of the civil service meant that the staff, consisting of twelve whites and twenty-five Indians, was being evaluated, with six already identified as dispensable.[4] A persistent lack of adequate clerical help dogged Lohmiller's administration from start to finish, becoming particularly troublesome after allotment was implemented.

During Lohmiller's tenure, the reservation was more fully surveyed, and the lands were appraised and allotted so that the surplus lands could be opened to settlers. Surplus lands were brought under the jurisdiction of the General Land Office (GLO), and disposal of these lands brought in non-Indian homesteaders. With this came the establishment of towns within the reservation that were outside federal jurisdiction.

While there had been earlier attempts to develop irrigation throughout the West, this era marked the first systematic effort to develop irrigation within the reservation, which created employment, delivered some water, and left many very frustrated. The national objective of making Indians self-sufficienct was implemented with initiatives that addressed major health problems, delivered education more effectively, and established Indian families or individuals upon lands of their own. In this period, the population of the tribes finally began to recover.[5]

The implications of the emerging cash economy, and the ways people generated cash, became the fact of economic life for the Fort Peck tribal membership. Labor patterns and endeavors upon which people labored also became important. The capabilities and circumstances in which surpluses could be created and marketed were often limited.

The annual report to the Commissioner of Indian Affairs, dated July 1, 1905, stated that the population of resident Indians was 1,116 Yankton adults (553 men and 563 women) with 278 school-age children, and 573 Assiniboine adults (270 men and 303 women) with 137 school-age children, for a total of 2,104.[5] In the next eleven years, the population minimally increased to 1,336 Yankton (684 males and 652 females) and 777 Assiniboine (385 males and 392 females) for a total population of 2,113 persons.[6]

The administrative jurisdiction of the agency in the lives of the Indian residents of Fort Peck

Reservation remained thorough, complete, and paramount. Leupp, for instance, insisted that the mixed-blood Indian trader Dan Mitchell be appointed a judge on the Court of Indian Offenses, even though regulations discouraged such an appointment. When Lohmiller pointed out the obvious conflict of interest, Leupp countered that it was important to understand trade had changed, making the intent of the regulation necessary. Mitchell had impressed the commissioner when they met, especially "the way he seeks for opportunities to be active and turn a dollar" and underscored his impression that "if more of his race had the same ambition, we should soon reduce the 'problem' to a minimum." The commissioner recommended Mitchell be allowed to try the two occupations "to see how well they work together," and if cause arose, then Lohmiller could ask for his resignation.[7]

The ways in which people lived on the land were also changing. Camping bands of the tribes had scattered along the Missouri, often where tributaries entered the north side of the river. Members of these bands then had spread out in immediate proximity. In 1900, U.S. Indian Inspector McConnell noted that camp life had disappeared, although the pattern of a contiguous rural neighborhood prevailed with individuals and groups more dispersed. Families could not make any decisions about beginning to farm, but rather, gave their attention to gardens. Their log cabins were arranged in clusters, which tended to be less than ten miles from the Missouri, giving the impression that the residents were concentrated along the southern boundary of the reservation. McConnell observed that they could not irrigate, and the only crop appeared to be hay. Farmers were being hired to live and work out along the river-oriented districts, but little farming was actually being done in 1900.[8]

The final annuities from the 1888 agreement to the contemporary reservation boundaries had been paid out on July 1, 1900.[9] Soon afterward, rations were limited to the disabled and elderly.[10] Many residents struggled because the cash economy was already well established. Under these circumstances, the idea of leasing lands on behalf of the tribes, which for the most part lived close to the Missouri, appeared to be obvious.

The first system was a permit grazing system which charged a per-head rate for a set period. The holder of the permit was expected to fence the area grazed. During the last months of the Scobey administration, eighteen grazing permits for cattle had been submitted, the earliest dated August 2, 1904 and the latest one January 23, 1905, and were awaiting final approval from the OIA in Washington, D.C. U.S. Special Inspector Chubbuck was detailed to Fort Peck to examine and report on the applications. Chubbuck reported on October 25, 1904 that "in his opinion, the permit system is not as advantageous to the Indians as the leasing system would be." He said he did not know of any other reservation where the leasing system could be adopted "with so little inconvenience and so much advantage to the people as on the Fort Peck reservation." An estimated 1.5 million acres were available for leasing, and if the leases required the lessees to build and maintain fences on their lease areas, more revenue could be generated with little administrative cost or responsibility.

Consequently, all grazing permit applications were returned but one, the application by J.M. Boardman to graze 8,400 head of cattle for one year beginning December 1, 1904, which was treated as a lease application. Chubbuck also suggested that the portion of the reservation available for lease should be divided into grazing districts, and each district should have an identified reliable source of water. The idea of moving to a leasing system was to be presented to "the council speaking for the tribe."[11]

Lohmiller had suggested that the leases not be restricted to cattle, and was attempting to secure lessees with up to 500,000 sheep. Leupp responded that the Indian Office, based on experience elsewhere in the "northwestern country," would not allow sheep because they were much more destructive to the range than cattle, and without "very careful supervision" could entirely destroy the grass.[12] In the same communication, Leupp suggested that the leasing system not commence until May 1, 1906 to allow the inauguration of a "regular leasing system" with all other permits entered into in 1906 expiring by May 1, 1906. The Indian Office simply needed "the consent of the tribe at a general council."[13]

Throughout this period, the role of the agency boarding school changed as day schools opened, and later with the rise of the public schools. The ways in which students were characterized became critical and the criterion for placing particular students in specific schools was also revealing. The role of returning students who had been sent away from the reservation to Indian Service boarding schools became interesting, and clearly later influenced political participation and leadership.

Having been asked to give a "careful study of the reservation," Lohmiller made a number of recommendations to the Indian Office on March 4. He thought it was practicable to see the reservation boarding school reduce its enrollment to "80 or 100 pupils," if three day schools could be built—"one to be located at Riverside, Montana, 12 miles east of Poplar, one at Oswego 32 miles west of Poplar, and the third near Milk River, Montana, 47 miles west of Poplar." The superintendent reported that the population within two miles of these locations could provide at least thirty children for each of the schools making winter travel reasonable. Responding to a detailed report about the boarding school and its physical plant, which consisted of the abandoned buildings of the military post of Camp

Poplar, the commissioner recommended a single building for classrooms. Two new dormitories had recently been constructed, and Leupp asked if one might be converted into classrooms. With eighty students, the remaining dorm might suffice, though a dining room, kitchen, and bakery would have to be built.[14]

U.S. Indian Inspector Arthur M. Tinker was sent to the Fort Peck Reservation in April 1905 to investigate the general conditions, and reported that he found everything peaceful and that the Indians were making progress toward civilization. Rations were being issued, finances were in order, and licensed traders sold their goods for fair prices. That said, he identified two problems. The first was that cattle belonging to non-Indians with grazing permits had broken through fences and consumed much of the Indians' hay. There was also a problem of Indian cattle "drifting away" with permittees' herds. Losing stock made Indians poorer than they had been before grazing permits were issued.

The second problem was the overall state of the agency buildings.[15] Leupp wrote Lohmiller about the 1905 inspection report, detailing how many log buildings should be taken down and making recommendations about whether the building materials should be retained.[16] Earlier in April, Leupp had peppered Lohmiller with detailed questions about the proposed day schools.[17] Clearly, Leupp was inclined to micromanagement.

Efforts were continually made to build irrigation ditches, especially one extending from Poplar Creek (River). Lohmiller asked to hire a seasonal replacement civil engineer, and with the funds in hand, he requested authorities to proceed with the work.[18] The Indian Office did not respond until September 1905, so the summer passed with no work accomplished. When finally they did reply, they asked for a full report first.[19] The office responded to the superintendent's report, dated September 25, 1905, but further action was delayed again, since irrigation projects required separate appropriations.[20]

The Indian Office was implementing more policies or programs that would not require appropriation, but rather would be revenue generating or reimbursable. Lohmiller was directed on April 11, 1905 to issue 297 heifers to "progressive and deserving Indians," and the livestock was purchased from the proceeds of the grazing permits in the 1904 season. He requested on May 3, 1905 to purchase 600 yearling heifers and twenty bulls "from the proceeds of the grazing tax." This stock was "given," so that "progressiveness, industry, and thrift may be rewarded," but many strings were attached about the care for the animals, and no animals could be slaughtered without the superintendent's permission.[21] Hides from animals butchered for rations were sold to defray the cost of the herders during the fiscal year. Only after this amount had been fully offset could excess hides be issued to deserving Indians.[22] This was the same principle as getting the permittees or lessees to construct fences where their animals grazed. When such an arrangement concluded, the fences "reverted to the Indians and became their absolute property at the end of the term."[23] The office finally realized it would have to spend something on infrastructure, that the two "Indian pastures" would need to be fenced, but again, this could be offset "from the proceeds of grazing."[24]

The annual report Lohmiller submitted, dated August 4, 1906, emphasized improvements across the reservation. The worst of the decrepit log buildings were demolished, and others were remodeled and painted. Indian labor was used to improve roads and repair bridges. One hundred thousand acres had been fenced.[25] The water systems at Poplar and Wolf Point were gradually upgraded and rebuilt.[26]

The schools also got some attention. The

favorable reputation of the Fort Peck Agency Boarding School had been established by the Scobey administration. Even after the establishment of public schools in Poplar and Wolf Point for children ineligible for the Indian schools, however, many Indian children across the larger reservation were still not being served. Consequently, the next step was to build day schools, which were less expensive to operate, would keep children at home where they could help their parents, and in some cases, would serve children not healthy enough to be sent away. The expense of operating the Fort Peck Agency Boarding School in 1905 was $30,164.96, while the day school at Blair with one-sixth the enrollment cost slightly less than $1,500.[27] The three new day schools were constructed during 1906 at Riverside, Oswego, and Milk River. Half-breed children were often sent to the county public schools. A Presbyterian mission school in Wolf Point operated as a boarding school for part of its students and a day school for others.[28]

A business committee or council was organized about this time, composed of officers chosen in a General Council. In its regular meetings, the agenda addressed mostly enrollment and adoption issues, and the approval of leases. By October 1909, an elected Business Committee was deciding on the disposition of "Indian Monies, Proceeds of Labor" (IMPL).[29]

Recent historians of Montana history have characterized the period of 1900-1915 as "The Homestead Boom." Once dry-farming methods were proposed, seeds developed for arid climates, and irrigation systems used successfully in a variety of climates and terrains, the rush for land was on.[30] Besides the land holdings of the major regional railroads, the next that could satisfy increasing demand were reservation lands.

As early as 1901, population in Montana seemed to be declining. This was partly because of the generous terms offered for individuals and families to homestead in Canada, where very little capital was needed initially. Reversing this outward migration would require federally sponsored irrigation projects and the opening of Indian reservation surplus lands to non-Indians. Politicians suggested that Montana's large reservations be allotted, knowing that surplus lands could then be offered to another generation of homesteaders willing to pay the appraised price. Republican Congressman Joseph Dixon and Senator Thomas H. Carter began orchestrating efforts to legislate allotment and the subsequent release of the surplus lands. Dixon wrote to Leupp on December 30, 1905, reporting that he was about to introduce a bill for allotment of Fort Peck. Dixon felt the decision for allotment could not be left to the Indians.[31]

Residents of the Fort Peck Reservation were engaged in many enterprises in their efforts to accrue cash. The office purchased firewood and hay from Indians for the boarding school, and spent $10,500 for 300,000 pounds of beef and $400 for firewood for the agency. The office also authorized Lohmiller on July 12, 1906 to expend $8,000 at the rate of $1.25 per day for each man, and $2.50 for a man and his team, to repair roads, bridges, and fences, to plow fireguards, and to make general improvements. Others hauled freight to and from the agency and sub-agencies. The 1904-05 rates were calculated in defined distances between locations in so many cents per hundredweight, and in the summer of 1906, rates were set in the same manner for the new day schools.[32] Labor costs for wranglers and herders for annual roundup of cattle belonging to Indians were also authorized.[33]

The "soup house system" offered meals to compensate for the limited rations issued to anyone able-bodied, including those who were irregularly employed. These individuals, estimated to be 800 persons in March 1906, worked on the reservation infrastructure.[34] Staff jobs at the agency and boarding school paid very low annual salaries, and often these individuals were provided meals at a mess hall or dining room. Women worked as seamstresses, laundry workers, cleaners, and cooks. Men worked as mechanics, herders, and laborers. Police and judicial work was also minimally compensated.[35]

Administratively, the Indian Office was becoming more overbearing, for the most part at the insistence of Congress. The tenor of Indian policy was that Indians were expected to become self-supporting, independent individuals who must be separated from the tribal estate, by force of law or regulation if necessary. Once severed from the tyranny of the group, one aspect of the "Indian problem" was presumably addressed. The security of the allotments became a further concern, however; the Indian Office and the department held that allottees should dispose of their allotments at the earliest possible opportunity, while the allottees wondered whether allotments were at all inviolable.

All these concerns had been evident since the passage of the General Allotment Act in 1887. The passage of the Burke Act in 1906, allowing for abbreviation of the original twenty-five years of trust status for allotments in certain circumstances, was the most obvious change since 1887.[36] The General Allotment Act provided the structural scheme for the allotment procedure, but further legislation was required for allotment on a specific reservation. Often the secondary legislation was proposed and passed in Congress by men of many interests. The idealized goals of civilization and assimilation for Indians "were often a poor match for individual ambition, partisan politics, and the desire to make money."[37]

The prevailing attitude was exacerbated by the demand for Montana reservations to be opened to non-Indian settlement. The Flathead Reservation was subject to allotment legislation in 1904, but the reservation was not opened

to white settlement until 1910.[38] Consequently, local ferment was rising for allotment of Fort Peck and the other reservations in Montana. The efforts for platting townsites on the reservation in December 1903 were influenced by a petition with 220 Indian names. The motivation was to accommodate the many whites who already were residents, but also to deal with the prospect of alcohol trafficking. Another petition of 190 signatures of Fort Peck Indians was sent to the CIA stating that much of their reservation was suitable for farming and stock raising, and then requesting the allotment of a minimum of 160 acres for Indian members. The request also proposed that surplus lands be leased for a five-year period and dated December 2, 1905. If approved, it could be cancelled as soon as allotment was authorized. The final request was that a delegation be allowed to come to Washington.[39]

U.S. Senator William A. Clark (Democrat-Montana) sponsored and introduced bills to open the Fort Peck and Blackfeet Reservations for allotment, which were supported by other members of the Montana congressional delegation.[40] This actually followed the pattern set at the Flathead Reservation.[41] During the fiscal year 1905-06, the General Land Office (GLO) issued contracts to survey the Fort Peck Reservation, which was reported in the GLO annual report for the year ended June 30, 1906.[42]

Diseases and health problems were persistent issues for the agency administration. Before allotment was enacted, Lohmiller in his annual report for 1906, dated August 4, 1906, described the state of health as "fair," with only a small diphtheria epidemic at the boarding school. Tuberculosis was the prevailing disease.[43] By August 1906, however, an epidemic of whooping cough began and was still raging in October, and the effects upon school attendance were evident.[44] Lohmiller organized the select leasing of portions of the range on the reservation, concentrating on securing lessees with large herds, and consequently bringing in large payments from the "grazing tax."[45] Lohmiller stated that "much advancement . . . has been shown during the past year and these Indians are quite well prepared for allotment" in that "a large number of the able-bodied Indians do irregular work, all have some stock, and a few have quite a number." He went on to report that:

All are encouraged as much as possible to increase the size of their herds, and care is taken that each Indian prepares the necessary feed to winter his stock. Almost all the Indians have small gardens, which they cultivate well, the farmers making regular rounds of inspection to see that crops, etc., are attended to at the proper time. Considerable improvement has been made to roads, bridges, fences and build-ings. Three Indian pastures were fenced this year, containing, approximately, 100,000 acres of good grazing land, the Indians furnishing the posts and performing the necessary labor gratis to build the fence.[46]

Lohmiller noted that the Indian population wore "civilized dress," and "more than one-third speak, and over two-thirds understand, more or less, the English language."[47]

Lohmiller praised the police force, which he felt should be given a raise, for "controlling the liquor traffic, watching for tresspassers [sic], and reporting crime." The Court of Indian Offenses convened every ration day and deter-mined guilt or innocence in the cases before it. The problems with liquor traffic were on the far east end of the reservation, stemming from saloon owners in Culbertson, and consequently, police accompanied any Indians who wanted to go trade there. The seven licensed traders on the reservation were operating according to regulations.[48]

The winter of 1906-1907 was severe, and

Lohmiller asked for authority to issue hay to Indians "who may require it for feeding their cattle during the present winter." The Indian Office granted the authority in situations where it was absolutely necessary, but was quick to cite the regulation that Indian labor or reimburse-ment was expected from the recipients. Assistant CIA Larrabee explained the purpose of this regulation in detail, also revealing the prevailing philosophy underpinning the Indian policy of the day:

The purpose of the law and regulation, as you doubtless appreciate, is to root out . . . the notion . . . that the chief function of Government was the distribution of gratuities. The pauper-izing influence of this idea has been insidious but far reaching, and will continue to do its damage wherever the greatest interest is not taken in making the Indians understand that they must give an honest quid pro quo for everything they receive from the Government's hands.[49]

Attempts to make a living from agriculture were discouraging for both Indians and non-Indians. There had been several good years,[50] and the war in Europe inflated prices for both grain and beef for a time, but the period of decent farming conditions ended in 1917, effectively squashing the hope that farming would make the Fort Peck tribes self-sufficient.

In August 1907, U.S. Indian Inspector James McLaughlin, experienced in dealing with the Sioux, was sent to Fort Peck at the specific request of Congressman Dixon to obtain "the views of the Indians of the Fort Peck Reservation as to allotments in severalty and the disposal of their surplus lands under the homestead laws." His letter of instruction discussed the history of the Fort Peck tribes, and said that annuities were "detrimental to the welfare of Indians, as [rations] foster idleness and lack of self-dependence, and are one of the greatest drawbacks to the progress of the Indians toward civilization." He was instructed to explain that there would be no provisions for rations in the legislation to open the reservation, but rather, everyone must be expected to "gain a livelihood." The sale of surplus lands was meant to provide the means "to promote the welfare of the Indians and start them on the road to civilization and self-support."

The Indians were also to be informed that the department intended to allot forty acres of irrigable land with 280 acres of grazing land, or "the allottee might be permitted to elect to receive 320 acres of grazing land." There was also the question of who should be given preference for the irrigation allotments. McLaughlin was to instruct the Fort Peck Indians that the cost of reclaiming the irrigable lands would be "reimbursable from the proceeds of the sale of the lands." Prior appropriation of waters would follow the conditions included in the Blackfeet allotment legislation in the Act of March 1, 1907. The surplus lands would be classified as agricultural lands, first and second classes, irrigable, semi-arid, and arid. The agricultural lands were to be disposed of under the homestead laws, and the irrigable lands under the Reclamation Act, with the semi-arid lands covered by the Desert Land Act and arid lands to be sold at public auction or by sealed bids. The price was not to be less than the appraised value, which generally was $1.25 per acre. Sections 16 and 36 of these lands would be reserved for the use of public schools. He was to report that legislation would also be sought to address the matter of town sites, the proceeds of which sales were to be credited to the tribes' trust fund if Congress consented. In council, McLaughlin was to state that Congress could legislate the opening of Indian lands without the consent of the Indians, but the department desired "to talk the matter over [with] them . . .

to obtain their views as to just how the opening might be made and that it will doubtless be to their advantage to express such reasonable desires as would be most important to them as a tribe."[51] The department was missing at least one significant point—there were two tribes.

Inspector McLaughlin reported on September 24, 1907 that the General Council meeting with the Fort Peck Indians was held on September 13 and 14, where they agreed "to allotments in severalty and disposal of their surplus lands." Apparently, the first demand by the Fort Peck people was to have 640 acres each, but on the second day, "they submitted a proposition to accept 320 acres for each person over 18 years of age and 160 acres for all under 18 years." McLaughlin countered with the proposition that there be a 320-acre allotment made to each member "of the respective tribes belong on the reservation, that is, to each man, woman, and child, legally belonging thereon. . . ." This was what had been legislated for the Blackfeet Reservation allotment.[52]

McLaughlin then discussed the issue of the bottomlands bordering along the Missouri River, and their potential as irrigable lands. The previous July, officials from the Bureau of Reclamation had expressed "doubt as to the feasibility of irrigating any of the reservation lands from the Missouri River." With the construction of an irrigation system uncertain, stock raising was the only major livelihood left. Consequently, the allocation of 320 acres per allotment to each member, "old or young, as provided in the agreement, is no greater than the families will actually need for grazing purposes in that semi-arid section of country." The promise of forty acres of irrigable lands meant "that the feasibility of an irrigation system be determined before allotment of the reservation lands is commenced."[53]

McLaughlin, based on discussions with the council, recommended issuing timber allotments, although he realized that the timber supply on the reservation was finite, mostly consisting of big stands of cottonwood in the areas closest to the Missouri and some of its tributaries. He recommended timber tracts be given to heads of families and adults over eighteen years, and that these be over and above the 320-acre allotments to these individuals.[54]

Basil Bear Fighter, described by the inspector as "a very intelligent Yanktonai Indian," asked for legislation to "prevent liquor from coming upon the lands after they are opened and towns started on the reservation." McLaughlin said he would include this request in his formal report.[55]

In conclusion, McLaughlin said that "the agreement [was] reasonable in its provisions" including being just to the Indians, and recommended its approval and ratification. He noted that there were 470 male adult Indians over eighteen currently on the rolls of the reservation, and that 379 signed the agreement, and this being four-fifths of the male adults, with the others not present, the agreement was unanimously accepted.[56] The agreement had to be transformed into authorizing legislation enacted specifically to implement the allotment on Fort Peck Reservation, which was finally accomplished in May 1908.[57]

Much needed to be done to prepare for and implement the allotment process. Meanwhile, the weather over the next decade was variable and periodically problematic. The years 1909-1910 were dry and the Indian farmers tried a variety of crops—hay, alfalfa, flax, corn, wheat, oats, and potatoes. Although the years 1911-1915 were wetter, the improved crops were attributed to new drought-resistant seeds available after 1913.[58] The business committee voted at the October 1909 meeting to take $10,000 from their IMPL account to spend on agricultural implements, seed, and building a fairgrounds.[59]

Power plows were used at Fort Peck Agency beginning in 1910, when a gas-powered plow was purchased. The following year, a steam-engine plow was delivered. Agency employees operated the equipment, plowing the fields and gardens at the cost to individual farmers of $2.50 per acre. It was reported that in 1911, 1,002 acres were plowed, in 1912, 1,669 acres, and in 1914, 4,591 acres were broken.[60]

The preliminary allotting "work" began in September 1909, with "a number of the Indians having already made their selections."[61] The Indian Office, in consultation with Lohmiller, decided that there was enough ambiguity in the reservation roll that a field officer should be detailed to prepare an accurate roll. Lohmiller said it would be less difficult, however, if he did it. Instead in January 1908, while the bill authorizing an allotment at Fort Peck Reservation was still before Congress, Special Agent Thomas Downs was sent to prepare an accurate roll. His terms of reference were the Act of 1888, creating the modern reservation boundaries, and the bill pending congressional approval, which stipulated that allotments were to be made "(1) to all persons rightfully enrolled with the tribe, and (2) to all unenrolled persons rightfully belonging on the reservation and affiliated with the Indians thereof."[62] Based on the Flathead and Blackfeet allotment acts, Downs was instructed "that to be allotted those unenrolled individuals would have to be shown to have been affiliated or be descendents of those affiliated with the Fort Peck tribes by 1888."[63] Downs used the most recent census in making a new roll.[64] If Indians at Fort Peck were also enrolled at other agencies, duplicate enrollments were investigated and decided in favor of one agency or the other. In all claims of blood or by means of adoption, such persons were to present formal applications accompanied by affidavits in support of their cases. Acceptable evidence for those claiming to be relatives was a family history with details of its affiliations.

Particular attention was paid to whether individuals and their families were residing upon the Fort Peck Reservation and drawing rations at the agency from 1886 to May 1888, and subsequently, whether they were present when the Executive Agreement of December 28, 1886 was ratified. Adoptees were required to formally explain how they came to be admitted to "tribal membership," including their degree of Indian blood, as much detail about their families as they could provide, tribal affiliation, and a brief history of the "tribal benefits" they had received to date.[65]

Downs then had the authority to call a "full and representative council," present the applications and supporting evidence to public scrutiny, and seek "an expression of the tribal will." The council was to express the reasons for their vote about the applicant, with the voting numbers for and against enrollment indicated.[66]

Anticipating that much money was about to materialize as the lands of the Fort Peck Reservation became commodified, some Indian leaders grew uneasy because they were not sure much of the material gain would accrue to their constituencies. On March 12, 1908, Isaac Blount, of Wolf Point, wrote the CIA, requesting permission for a delegation of Assiniboines to travel to Washington, D.C., to consult with the Indian Office about a Senate bill that would only allot twenty acres of irrigable land and 280 acres of grazing land, since this fell short of the agreement between the people at Fort Peck and Inspector McLaughlin.[67] In a letter dated the next day, Lohmiller wrote to the CIA transmitting Isaac Blount's request, but asked that it be disapproved because he felt such a trip was an unnecessary extravagence.[68] But James Garfield, chairman of the Assiniboine, sent two telegrams to Washington, D.C., asking for permission to send a delegation. Lohmiller, angry about being disobeyed, asked the CIA in a letter on March 18, 1908, if he could punish Garfield, to make an

example of him.[69] A telegram to Lohmiller from Larrabee on March 17, 1908, said that the superintendent was to tell Garfield that "Congress [was] very busy; [any] extended hearing impracticable. If must come Office insists you see that they have private funds for coming, going home and while here." Lohmiller, in his letter of March 23, 1908, reported that he had ordered J.D. Flynn, Farmer in Charge, Wolf Point Sub-Agency, to tell Garfield his telegram had been received, but that this was not a good time to travel to Washington. Lohmiller said that he had received on March 21 another telegram from Larrabee, instructing him that he was "to immediately follow telegraphic instructions of March 17th."

Lohmiller stated again that he was not opposed to the delegation, other than it was wasteful of the "scant supply of funds belonging to the Assiniboin [sic] Indians—even if it was foolishly donated by them, to two or three glib talkers who comprise this delegation." Consequently, Lohmiller explained that he had sent a telegram to Farmer Flynn on March 21: "Notify Garfield that delegation can go to Washington, delegation to report to me for instructions before leaving." Lohmiller ended by saying that the delegation had not yet reported to him.[70] Lohmiller wrote to the office on March 26, 1908, that the Garfield delegation had "dwindled down to one person, Walter Clark, an Assiniboin [sic], on account of lack of funds, and has left this p.m. for Washington, D.C." Assuring the office that they had money for their expenses, Lohmiller indicated that Dan Mitchell, the Agency Interpreter, was accompanying Clark.[71]

Garfield wrote the SI on March 29, 1908 that the Assiniboines had elected himself and Dan Mitchell as delegates to Washington, and then indicated that "Walter Clark not delegate went with the fund sent by Agent investigate cause help us that may see you with our last request." There was no answer in the file to this unclear communication. In a telegram dated March 30, 1908, Garfield wired the SI: "Help and fix so four may come at once, answer quick." In another telegram dated April 3, 1908, Garfield inquired, "Why no answer to my message of March 29 and 30, we are waiting please answer quick."[72] Larrabee informed Garfield in a telegram on April 6, 1908, that the bill had passed in Congress giving each Indian at Fort Peck 320 acres and declared, "Therefore useless expense for you to come to Washington." There was no information about the outcome of the delegation in the office file.[73] This marked the beginning of delegations to Washington by Fort Peck tribal leaders.

The act of May 8, 1906, had set forth responsibilities on the subject of heirship, and consequently, Downs distributed materials to the agency "to systematize the compilation of family histories." Once the cards were completed, the information was transcribed in ledger books and forwarded to the Indian Office.[74]

With this preliminary phase completed, the allotment process was started. The 1907 agreement was enacted into law on May 30, 1908. This enabling legislation put the allotment of the lands at Fort Peck under the previous mandate of the General Allotment Act.[75] The act provided for the allotment and survey of the reservation, and for sale and disposal of all surplus lands. The survey of the southern tier of the reservation lands was done by the GLO, and completed by the end of the summer of 1908. The Reclamation Service and the Geological Survey, both also agencies of the Department of the Interior, assessed water and mineral resources. Based upon specific recommendations, the SI was authorized to construct irrigation projects and to identify and reserve irrigable lands for new construction. Coal lands were also identified and locations recorded for new reclamation projects. Upon the completion of the official survey, every Indian eligible to receive allot-

ments was to be given, if possible, forty acres of irrigable land and 320 acres of grazing land. Allottees were numbered and recorded. Timber allotments of from two and one-half to twenty acres were granted to heads of families and single adults over the age of eighteen. An appropriation provided $200,000 for building irrigation works, but stipulated that this and any additional funds appropriated for this same purpose were to be reimbursed from proceeds of land sales. This was not meant to charge the Indian allottees with the cost of the construction of irrigation works, but rather, "operation and maintenance costs were to be pro-rated and shared by Indian allottees and any non-Indian purchasers of tribal land within irrigable areas."[76]

The enabling allotment act set aside certain lands for agency, school, and religious purposes, and lands were set aside to the Great Northern Railway for water reservoirs, dams, and right of ways for pipelines. These latter lands, not in excess of forty acres in any one location, were not to exceed one plot for each ten miles of the main rail line across the reservation. The railroad was required to pay the reasonable value, not less than $2.50 per acre, and was expected to cover damage sustained by tribal members as a result of securing these lands. With the initial allotment completed, an appraisal commission was constituted to value all lands not allotted or reserved. The commissioners were to complete their work in nine months, classifying land as agricultural, grazing, arid, and mineral lands. All except mineral lands were to be appraised.[77]

Ever enterprising, Lohmiller remained convinced that leases could be profitable until allotment was fully implemented. In a General Council called on March 23, 1910, with 175 persons in attendance, a proposal was made to lease a large area "lying idle," dividing it into two grazing districts.[78] Lohmiller was authorized to proceed with the understanding that the leasing could not exceed three years. Commissioner Valentine, on April 4, 1910, summarized the information that had been supplied by Lohmiller in a letter dated June 22, 1909, and in doing so, described the agricultural situation on Fort Peck:

. . . District 1 contains 547,200 acres, less a Government Beef Pasture of 31,622 acres and an Indian pasture of 11,520 acres; that 600 Indians owning approximately 1,000 horses, and 2,000 head of cattle live in the district, and the capacity of the district is 18,240 head of cattle, 182,400 sheep, or 15,000 horses.

District No. 2 contains 437,760 acres, less two Indian pastures aggregating 84,700 acres. Five hundred Indians owning approximately 1,500 horses, and 2,000 head of cattle live in the district. The capacity of the district is given at 14,592 head of cattle, 145, 920 sheep, or 12,000 horses.[79]

Meanwhile, Lohmiller recommended to the SI a list of potential town sites. There were seven locations in addition to Poplar, all along the southern perimeter of the reservation: to the east of Poplar, Brockton and Blair; to the west, Macon, Wolf Point, Oswego, Frazer, and Milk River. While the Indian Office favored early sale of the town sites, GLO paperwork and checks for accuracy took a while. The 1908 enabling act stipulated that the sale of lands within the platted town sites required individuals already living there to make permanent improvements. They could preempt up to five town site lots. Traders took advantage of these provisions, especially at Poplar and Wolf Point. In Poplar, as the town lots went on sale, the whole business district was already on patented land.[80] At this stage, churches were urged to seek patents on church building lots, including for cemeteries and missionary schools, just as the Great Northern Railway was urged by the Indian Office to seek patents to any additional lands for their operations.[81]

With the appraisal of the surplus lands completed, these lands were transferred to the jurisdiction of the GLO, to be disposed of under the Homestead, Desert Land, Mineral, and Town Site laws of the United States, which included the exclusion of sections 16 and 36 in every township or replacement lands reserved for "common school purposes" for the State of Montana. These state school lands were reimbursed by the U.S. Treasury to the tribes' trust fund at the rate of $1.25 per acre. Once a presidential proclamation officially opened the lands, settlers were expected to pay the fully appraised value as their entry fee, in no case less than $1.25 per acre. Entrymen and/or women were to pay one-fifth of the value of the acreage at entry, and the remainder in four equal annual payments. After five years, undisposed lands were to be sold at public auction, but not for less than $1.25 per acre. Lands unsold after ten years were to be sold at auction to the highest bidder for cash with no required minimum bid, but no person or company was allowed to purchase more than 640 acres.[82]

Congress was not making this allotment a gratuity by authorizing the allotment, but rather, the costs of the survey and appraisal of the Fort Peck lands were initially advanced and later deducted from proceeds of land sales. Up to $100,000 was provided for the lands granted to the State of Montana, and another $100,000 for the expense of the survey, allotment, classification, and appraisal of the surplus lands. The remainder of sale funds were then credited to the Fort Peck tribes in the United States Treasury, and funds were to draw a rate of return of 4 percent per annum. The act also indicated the SI could draw upon the principal and interest periodically for the benefit of tribal members in their "education and civilization," the construction and maintenance of the irrigation works, and payments including "suitable per capita cash payments."[83]

The underlying premise—that there was a high demand for the lands—did not necessarily prove true, however. The appraisal was based on an estimated 487,000 acres of agricultural land available and appraised at between $5 and $7 per acre. Grazing land was estimated at 737,000 acres with an appraisal value of between $2.50 and $3.50 per acre. The surplus lands, authorized by legislation in 1908, amounted to 1,343,408 acres worth $5,150,409 by 1913. The proclamation from President Wilson, dated July 25, 1913, opened these lands to homesteaders. There was at first only a trickle of settlers, but in three years time, over 1,200 homesteaders were living on the reservation, and the consensus was that most of the good land was gone.[84]

On April 17, 1909, Lohmiller wrote the CIA that the Assiniboine Indians were still adamant about sending a delegation to meet with the commissioner about matters concerning the Fort Laramie Treaty of 1851. Lohmiller had met with the Assiniboines on April 17 and they presented a series of questions which Lohmiller restated in his letter. Part of the concern was the ratification question and the sources of funds for rations prior to 1886, and their claim to land belonging to them as ascribed by the treaty. The Assiniboines went on to ask how the Yankton band of Sioux came to live on "our reservation," how they were subsisted, and how they came to share in the benefits of "this reservation." Consequently, Henry Archdale, Isaac Blount, and Growing Four Times were authorized to travel to Washington, D.C., to interview the commissioner. The council declared that they wanted the superintendent to accompany them. Lohmiller recommended that the cost of travel and expenses be taken from the fund, "Indian Money, Proceeds of Labor, Fort Peck." The question of whether anything was due to them interested the Indians most. Lohmiller provided context for the proposed meeting:

It has been explained to them, not only by the writer, but by various agents and inspectors, that the above agreement [Fort Laramie Treat of 1851] was never ratified but still the impression lingers that they have been misinformed that the government has violated its obligations and that there is money due them and they wait, to determine to their satisfaction, a final decision by the Honourable Commissioner to them in person as nothing else in the past or in the future will give them satisfaction.[85]

The Indian Office wrote to Lohmiller on June 2, 1909, taking each of the questions and providing detailed answers. The letter explained how the Senate changed the duration for annuities from fifty to ten years, and how appropriations had been made for this term. It also stated that the records of the office documented that the annual gratuity for the Assiniboine included $30,000 per year during the years 1868 to 1876, and from 1877 to 1888 annual gratuity appropriations were made ranging from $15,000 to $100,000. The final question of how the Sioux were placed on the reservation was not answered, other than to state that the Yankton Sioux were also parties to the Fort Laramie Treaty.[86]

The matter of delegations was put aside until Lohmiller again raised it in a letter to the CIA on March 4, 1910, having been told that his name was on a list of superintendents authorized to visit Washington the coming spring. He proposed that he bring a delegation of Assiniboine Indians, if they covered their own expenses, and then that he also bring a delegation of Yankton Indians who had requested to see the CIA. Based on Article 4 of the agreement made with Inspector McLaughlin, promises were made for benefits from the proceeds of the sale of surplus lands, and the Indians were anxious to begin receiving these benefits. The Indians were also interested in receiving per capita payments from the accrued grazing monies. They also sought to have their children who had been born since the closing of the allotment roll receive allotments. Lohmiller declared that he had tried to explain all of these matters, but the Indians were concerned about issues such as the rising costs of constructing and maintaining irrigation projects and how these were to be charged against the benefits from the surplus land entry fees. Lohmiller closed with, "Inasmuch as this delegation is going to defray their own expenses in going to, and returning from Washington, as well as while there, I would respectfully recommend that they be allotted to go when I receive instructions to come to Washington."[87]

On March 25, 1910, Lohmiller wired the CIA asking if the Assiniboine delegation could visit Washington, that they were competent to travel alone, and if they could come right away, they would be back in time for farming. CIA Valentine responded that the delegation might come to Washington if the "sufficient money placed in your hands to cover transportation here and return." In a letter to the CIA, Lohmiller wrote that the delegates were Isaac Blount, Henry Archdale, and Growing Four Times.[88]

Arriving in Washington, the Assiniboine delegation sent a memo to the Indian Office that outlined the questions about the Fort Laramie Treaty of 1851. They also requested that the office pay their hotel expenses.[89] The CIA replied in writing, on April 8, 1910, to the delegation's statements of April 4. It was unclear whether a meeting with the CIA ever occurred. The amounts of annuities were again summarized. On the matter of land title, the CIA cited a treaty made with the Assiniboines at Fort Union, Montana (actually North Dakota), on July 18, 1866, also unratified, but he declared that the Assiniboines "by their acceptance of a home on the reserve set apart for the Blackfeet and other Indians, 15 April 1874, did practically relinquish

their rights in and to the land in question." The annuities accepted by the Assiniboines from 1868 until 1888 contributed to this acceptance. The matter of the Yankton Sioux was explained as their being parties to the Fort Laramie Treaty who were entitled to benefits, but the CIA stopped short of defining other issues of entitlement. The CIA expressed his determination that the Assiniboine Indians had been dealt with "justly, and even liberally," and that there was no claim against the U.S. on account of stipulations in these unratified treaties. Finally, the CIA reminded the delegation that the superintendent had informed them that "if the delegation visited Washington, it must pay its own expenses."[90]

On June 21, 1910, a business committee was elected by a reservation-wide General Council that met on March 23-24, and the names were submitted to the Indian Office for approval. Lohmiller sought the advice of this group and felt it legitimized his authority in some circumstances.[91] For example, as situations of heirship began arising, the establishment of Individual Indian Money (IIM) accounts also became necessary. There was some guidance offered—for example, the Circular 279, Second Supplement, dated April 29, 1909, provided guidelines to superintendents in administering Individual Indian Moneys, especially cautioning the regulation of such accounts so that no individual was allowed to squander these resources. Only in dire necessity and exceptional circumstances could resources be spent as a monthly allowance.[92] Moreover, Lohmiller was faced deciding which bank could hold the reservation's IIM accounts.[93]

Agricultural issues took center stage in Lohmiller's annual report for the fiscal year 1910, dated July 30, 1910. The superintendent reported that about half of the male adult Indians were cultivating approximately 3,000 acres, with the person who was working the most tilling 200 acres. The acreage represented a 50 percent increase over the previous growing season, with the anticipation that this same degree of increase would occur in 1911. Lohmiller made a critical observation: "The difficulties of getting these [Fort Peck] Indians to farm is the expense of starting farming, uncertainty of crops, and the fact that they must wait a long time for their returns." Moreover, he reported that probably as many as 75 percent of male Indians on Fort Peck were raising animals. While "every effort" was being made to increase the size of the herds, the overall stock raising was contributing "as much to the support of these Indians as their own efforts at farming." Stock raising was something which most understood and "which those who are not able-bodied can engage in."[94]

Lohmiller explained that some 200 Indians were working for the Reclamation Service on the reservation, and reported that "several live off the reservation in adjoining as well as distant towns, and make their own living, seldom calling for any assistance." He further described the work force: "About 50 are employed permanently at the Agency and schools of this reservation, while an average of 75 or 80 work at irregular labor for [the] agency." He observed that no industrial training was needed beyond information about farming and stock raising.[95] He commented, however, that students who had returned from boarding schools away from the reservation did their work "in a more intelligent manner than that of the average Indian, however, many of them are inclined to seek employment requiring very little physical effort."[96]

Lohmiller reported that as of July 1910, a good number of tribal members had made their allotment selections, several allotting agents were working in the spring and summer, and a number of these allots had begun building houses and other outbuildings on their lands. Some were plowing, and others were farming on their allotment lands already. Lohmiller recom-

mended that Indians be supplied with "sufficient wire to fence their allotments" and that they be allowed to cut fence posts from their timber allotments. He recommended that the wire be purchased and distributed "instead of any payments of cash annuities."[97]

Lohmiller, in his report for the year 1911, reported his approach to the cultural activities of the tribes:

The old Indians occasionally indulge in their folk dances, but these occur at intervals of several months, and last but an evening, and they never dance without first securing the required permission; they have committees to preserve order and the dances are usually an occasion to visit with each other. With the control that exists over dancing on this reservation, I do not believe it has any injurious effects on the morals or advancement of these Indians. It would be my policy to allow the old people to dance once in the while, and as they die off, the custom will also die.[98]

The general state of health was reported as being in "good condition." Lohmiller indicated his awareness that "general sanitary conditions around the Indian homes are not good, as it is very difficult to have them observe the laws of health." He hoped that many would soon be moving to their allotments and building new houses, in which improved sanitary conditions could be maintained. The two agency physicians had tried to instruct patients about public health, but Lohmiller attributed the slowness of strides to "the natural aversion of the old Indians to medicines [with which they were unfamiliar], to live under proper health conditions is a difficulty, and there seems to be no way to overcome it."[99]

The boarding school and the four day schools were following the same State of Montana Course of Study as the public schools in Poplar and Wolf Point. The "industrial training" for boys at the boarding school included farming, gardening, and stock raising, and for girls, cooking, sweeping, laundry work, sewing, and similar tasks. Demonstration gardens at the boarding school and the day schools were maintained, and all produce was used for the pupils.[100] This emphasis mirrored the larger demonstration farms put in by the Agency Farmers, and while the season was dry, there had been a fair return on some of the operations. Lohmiller reported that there was considerable interest by the Indian farmers in the demonstration farms.

Flax was the main crop, which was often planted in ground recently broken from native prairie, and was "hardy, standing considerable frost and a good deal of drought." The season's flax crop was expected to average six to eight bushels an acre, with a price of over $2 a bushel, and Lohmiller was expecting it would be highly profitable. But weather remained challenging; hot, dry winds and lack of rain were causing many crop failures. Of particular concern was the ground recently broken because it could not be "worked deep enough for a year or two to secure sufficient moisture to insure a fair crop without rain." Since he reported a good and convenient market for all grains, with elevators "reasonably convenient," Lohmiller was trying to save seed for next year, noting "the plan being to have seed gathered and saved from the best fields, properly marked with the owner's name and stored in the Government Warehouse."[101]

Clearly, many Fort Peck people were adapting to an agricultural economy, but there were also detractors. Lohmiller discussed the portion of the population "opposed to farming." Obviously, he hoped that the success of others provided encouragement to "backward Indians." In contrast, Lohmiller noted that "considerable machinery is owned by Indians, and they have purchased a good deal of the agency [equipment belonging to the agency] during the past

year, at actual cost." Progress on irrigation works was reported; the unit on Porcupine Creek, located on the far west end of the reservation, was finished and expected to irrigate about 1,240 acres, and while two ditches in the Poplar River unit were still under construction, the area to be irrigated would be greater than that of the Porcupine unit.[102]

Many Indians were building homes on their allotments, as well as fencing them. Herds of cattle and horses were improving in quality. Lohmiller reported that Indians had to acquire a permit from the agency office before they could sell, trade, or slaughter any livestock, that all transactions were recorded carefully, and that permits were given only in a few cases, so the total livestock numbers showed only a slight increase. Very few losses were reported for the previous winter, and "each Indian's premises is examined to see that he has sufficient forage to winter all of his stock, and he must provide first this before he is permitted to sell hay to others." The grazing permits required the non-Indian stockmen in the grazing districts to keep their livestock separate from Indian stock. The first agricultural fair was held with good exhibits, and Lohmiller felt it would be an incentive.[103] In the 1910 fiscal year, a per capita payment of $9.80 was made to all enrolled Indians from the accumulated grazing funds, which Lohmiller described as being used "in a very sensible manner, usually for the purchase of food and clothing."[104]

Lohmiller expected the "allotment work" to be completed by September 30, 1911. He noted that there were twenty-one IIM accounts, from which seven or eight received a monthly payment of support, and others were permitted to have machinery, horses, and other things purchased on their behalf.[105]

In late 1910, Sisseton and Wahpeton Sioux at Fort Peck requested Lohmiller to seek permission for a delegation of two to travel to

Washington. The superintendent sent the request on November 14, 1910, requesting to be in Washington when delegations from the Devil's Lake and Sisseton Agencies were there. The CIA responded on December 2 that these Indians could handle their concerns by correspondence.[106]

At the end of December 1911, Lohmiller wrote to the CIA to seek authority for a Yankton delegation to come to Washington. On January 9, Senator Joseph Dixon wrote to the CIA saying that considering that the Fort Peck Reservation was to be appraised and opened during the coming year, it might be appropriate to invite Major Lohmiller "to come down to Washington for two or three weeks visit and instructions." On January 11, the recommendations were made in the Indian Office that Lohmiller visit the city with a delegation of Indians representing the Yankton from Fort Peck, expenses for Lohmiller charged to the "Indian moneys, Proceeds of Labor, Fort Peck Indians, and the delegates to pay their own expenses; Senator Dixon to be notified." The delegation of Yankton Indians from the Fort Peck Agency was authorized on January 13, 1912, to come immediately at their own expense. The delegation consisted of Charles Thompson, Rufus Ricker and Crazy Bull, and in a communication dated December 29, 1911, they outlined eight issues that they hoped to discuss. Superintendent Lohmiller was given permission to accompany the delegation.[107]

On January 22 and 24, the delegation and Superintendent Lohmiller met with Assistant CIA F.H. Abbott and Dr. Goins of the Indian Office. On January 31, 1912, the Assistant CIA wrote to delegates in Washington, addressing each of their concerns. In a series of letters over the next months, the Indian Office attempted to discuss and resolve the unfinished business from the January visit of the delegation.[108]

In his annual report for 1912, Lohmiller suggested a reimbursable loan of $1 million to allow Indians to improve their homes and home sites. The agency physicians had personally canvassed each home on the reservation, and recorded the conditions including the state of the home, details about the personal health of each person, and recommendations to improve sanitation.[109] The superintendent also recommended that a specialist in trachoma be brought to examine affected tribal members, so that suggestions for prevention and a cure could be implemented. Lohmiller noted: "Special foods for the infants and the sick should be allowed, for the mortality is very high among the children of the Indians."[110]

Lohmiller was increasingly repetitious from previous annual reports in many of his statements, including those about the progress of the pupils and the operating of the schools. He touted the "wonderful improvement" in the extension of farming operations on the reservation.[111] The three Agency Farmers devoted much of their time to instruction of Indian farmers "along the lines of the latest scientific methods known." Lohmiller explained that the combination of weather, rainfall, and little damage by pests or diseases, had made the crops plentiful. He went so far as to say that the "past three years of farming experience by these Indians has been of great educational value to them, as to all residents of this part of the country." The Agency Farmers were arranging to set aside seed for the next growing season, and would not need to purchase any. However, he also explained that the price was not "very high" due to the large crop in the Northwest. All Indians were encouraged to make all their improvements on their own allotments, and "almost without an exception the farming work is done on their own land." Lohmiller indicated,

Much of this land has been broken for the Indians, seeds furnished the past three seasons, and much machinery lent them to assist them in getting a nice start. Many of them have purchased their own machinery, and they will be in a position to do better work from now on. . . . Almost all of the able-bodied Indians have been farming or improving their allotments. The splendid crops this year will be of valuable assistance in convincing the backward ones from farming is a profitable industry.[112]

He also suggested that the need for much more machinery and work horses persisted, which was part of the purpose for requesting the reimbursable fund in June 1912. While considerable barbed wire had been issued to "deserving Indians" to enclose their farmlands on their allotments, the superintendent explained that roads were being created along many of the section lines. Because the county was building a system of public roads on the reservation and selective bridges over reservation streams as needed, much more wire was needed.[113]

Most allotments by 1912 had the improvements of a house, stable, corral, pasture, and sometimes a well, and the farmland was fenced and enclosed. While the allotment schedule had not yet been approved, the allotment system was accepted by the agency and tribal members as *fait accompli*. None of the allotments were leased "for the reason that patents have not yet been approved or issued." Lohmiller observed:

It is a far better plan to have the allottee farm all his land he possibly can, and where necessary to lease, he should be required to farm at least as much as he leases out. Such leases should be made only for the purposes of improving the allotment, as cash payments are generally injurious to a beginner in farming.

Superintendent Lohmiller's discussion in this annual report about livestock pursuits re-emphasized the importance of the mixed economy between farming and stock raising and revealed the Indian Office's goal for this particular economic adaptation and vocation. Lohmiller commented that non-Indian grazing permittees on the reservation had generated $20,000 more than in past years, with no visible damage to the range, but he anticipated that once the surplus lands were opened to settlers, there would be no room for allottees, unless parts of the reservation were not filed on and taken up.

Lohmiller wrote the CIA on January 13, 1913, saying, "I would like very much to make a per capita payment to these people during the intense cold weather, providing there is enough money to do so." The Indian Office ordered Lohmiller to "prepare a statement of all outstanding liabilities" to date and forward it to the office without delay. Lohmiller responded with a report, dated February 5, 1913. These delays prompted Sioux and Assiniboine delegates to request permission on February 12, 1913 to send a delegation to discuss the establishment of a reimbursable fund from "the future sale of their surplus lands."

On March 1, 1913, the Indian Office rejected the request for the delegation, saying that there were limited resources for such activity, and besides, it questioned the necessity of another visit considering that the delegation in January 1912 had brought up similar topics. A delegation composed of Charles Thompson and P.H. Hayne was in Washington for a hearing with the Indian Office on April 7, 1913. They presented eleven points for which they sought answers. Many of these issues concerning dispersal of trust funds and questions about allotments had been brought up before, which suggests that either the answers were not satisfactory to the delegations, or the questions were never answered at all.[114] Abbott wrote the delegates a detailed response addressing each point, dated April 12, 1913.[115]

The tally of the allotments by June 1913 totalled 715, 806.57 acres of grazing, agricultural, and timber lands, and the allotment schedules were approved. Subsequently, the trust patents on these lands began to be issued. Another facet of the allotment process was also beginning. From the start of the allotment process at Fort Peck in the fall of 1908, people had died and others were born, causing problems with allotments already made and raising the issue of granting allotments for offspring not listed on the allotment rolls. An administrative decision was made that upon the death of an allottee, his/her allotment would be held in trust for the benefit of the heirs until the end of the trust period, though this was often unrealistic, depending on the ages and resources of the descendents.

The 1902 act allowed land belonging to deceased allottees to be sold. By 1906, with the passage of the Burke Act, Congress authorized the SI to determine heirs of the deceased who had not received fee patents and issue fee patents or payment for the sale of the land to the heirs.[116] In 1910, however, Congress passed other legislation to establish a framework for heirship policies and practices that remained in place till 1934. The act of June 15, 1910, authorized the SI to determine the legal heirs of any Indian who died before receiving a fee patent or making a will, but at this point, the competency of heirs became an issue. If more than one of the heirs was incompetent, the SI could have the lands sold, even against the wishes of the heirs; if there was a benefit from partitioning the allotment, the SI could issue fee patents for the shares of the competent heirs.[117]

Regulations formulated in 1910 gave the SI the power to prepare an inventory and list the claims against it for a deceased restricted Indian. Consequently, notice of a probate hearing was posted twenty-five days or more in advance of the arrival of an authorized federal probate examiner. Prior to the hearing, the examiner inspected the agency records to prepare a list

of the heirs and notified them of the hearing. Moreover, "two disinterested witnesses with a direct knowledge of the decedent's family history" were called to appear. Once the hearing was held, the examiner sent a report of the hearing to the Indian Office, where the report was then reviewed by the Indian Office and the Office of the Interior Department Solicitor, before approval or revision, and implementation. Almost immediately, this procedure proved far too time-consuming because of the backlog of cases developing.

By 1913, nationally, 40,000 heirship cases were awaiting the determination of the heirs. This land was estimated to be worth about $60 million. In the Indian Office, 1,500 cases were awaiting final action and the CIA was pleading to Congress for more money to bring this process current.[118] By June 1913, 214 Fort Peck allottees had died. Only after trust patents were issued could the process of apportioning the original allotments among any legitimate heirs commence.[119] Consequently, policy directives in December 1913 determined what information superintendents had to submit about these Indians, so the Interior Department could determine competency to force patents.[120]

President Woodrow Wilson on July 25, 1913 proclaimed the Fort Peck surplus lands open to public entry. Within the boundaries of the Fort Peck Reservation, "1,225,849 acres of non-mineral, unallotted, unreserved lands not designated for irrigation were available to applicants willing to pay the appraised values ranging from $2.50 to $7.00 per acre." The proclamation stipulated that anyone interested was to submit an application at GLO locations in either Glasgow, Havre, Great Falls, or Miles City between September 1 and 20, 1913. Names were drawn at random and the successful applicants were notified, with "selection and entry . . . to begin on May 1, 1914, and prospective settlers were given ten days to complete their entries. On June 30, 1914 all land subject to entry but not entered or filed upon were [then to be] opened to general settlement."[121]

In the annual report for 1913, dated August 27, 1913, Lohmiller reported that the reservation had become divided in two within the geographic areas of Valley and Sheridan Counties. There was continued discrimination against full bloods, "owing to the ravages of tuberculosis and trachoma, where there were objections to the intermingling of races in schools."[122]

The farming operations had made "the greatest progress." More than 194,000 bushels of grains were raised in 1912, and yields of 100 bushels an acre for oats, 40 bushels for wheat, and 25 bushels for flax, were achieved. Lohmiller emphasized the need for more machinery and horses, so tribal members could "become promptly and substantially established upon their allotments and in agricultural pursuits." He noted that some have purchased "up-to-date machinery" and realized "the importance of owning their own farming implements."[123]

There was no leasing of allotments "as patents have not been approved." Grazing permits were still issued and the revenue generated was considerable, but fewer were renewed or issued, "on account of the early opening of the reservation." Lohmiller opined that "the presence of this stock has not been detrimental to the Indians, and there has been no trouble over it." Lohmiller saw himself in solidarity with other superintendents, arguing that only through the removal of restrictions could the Indians advance and become citizens. Consequently, fee patents allowed them to sell part of their land and use the proceeds to establish farms or raise cattle on the rest of the land. Even though there were only two examples of this by the summer of 1913, the "promise" of such flexibility was obvious to those who subscribed to the assimilationist assumptions that rationalized the impact allotment had on land

tenure and economic development.[124]

A delegation to Washington, consisting of Charles Thompson, Rufus Ricker, Paul Hayne, and Chester Arthur, met with CIA Cato Sells on February 4, 1914, to discuss a series of matters. Practically all the issues discussed were similar to those brought up by other delegations, but one new issue was on the table—the citizenship of allottees. The issue of concern was that citizens and their assets became subject to taxation, and if taxes were not paid, their lands could be attached for debt and sold. Once they became citizens, the government of the United States would have no responsibility for them as wards, and would not provide them with aid.

Sells formally responded in a letter dated February 11, 1914. For the most part, his answers did not provide the delegates with much comfort. He closed by saying, "The Office has been pleased to see and to talk with you concerning the needs of your people and hopes to hear good reports of the progress you and your people are making toward self-support and civilization." Problems arose over expenses of the delegation in Washington, and arrangements had to be made to get them home.[125]

On September 29, 1914, when Lohmiller forwarded his annual report for the year ending June 30, 1914, his earlier optimism was waning. He pointed out that the lands were "mainly bench land, with here and there, typical 'bad lands' of this western country. Of its 2,094,035 acres, over one-third has been allotted, and allotments to children are still being made." But the anticipated land rush for the opened lands had not materialized. The superintendent noted that

The year just closed has not, from a farming standpoint, been very good. In some places the crops were fair, but despite an enormous (for this country) June rainfall, the crops generally have not been good. This condition has obtained both on and off the reservation, so that the Indians' efforts will compare favourably with those of their white neighbors.[126]

Lohmiller emphasized that the sanitary conditions were "constantly improving," but he noted that "until [the Indians] have sufficient funds to build comfortable frame houses, and until then, sanitary conditions cannot be all that is desired." At one point during the year, the boarding school was under quarantine because two of the employees had smallpox. He also indicated that the Agency Physicians were attempting to segregate tuberculosis patients and instructed them "in the proper care of bedding, clothing, etc." An eye specialist had visited during the year to provide "a good deal in the treatment of trachoma and other diseases of the eye." Lohmiller hoped that a specialist could visit regularly, so that the good work against these afflictions would "not allowed to go for naught."[127]

Lohmiller noted "the influence of the white settlers on and adjacent to the reservation can be noticed in the progress of the Indians who, especially the younger generation, seem to try to follow the example so set."[128] He cautioned: "It must be remembered that farming in northeastern Montana dates back only eight or ten years, and in that time many failures were registered on the account of the application of eastern methods to western conditions."

Elsewhere, Lohmiller explained the frustrations inherent in trying to make a living from the land. While the amount of land on the reservation was constantly being increased, "the prospects for the year 1914 are not good, rainfall not having come when most needed" and considering "no threshing has as yet been done, those well acquainted with conditions state that the crops generally are far from good." It appeared that the beginning of a period of drought was materializing. He observed:

The farming done by Indians, other than on their own allotments is negligible. Improvements are being erected on their lands, and more are taking up farming all the time. . . . In spite of the poor crop of 1913, and the poor prospects for 1914, the Indians who have started to farming [sic] do not seem to be discouraged, and are going ahead with their farming and improvements.[129]

Lohmiller, trapped within his familiar agenda for progress, continued to advocate that the Indians needed for "farming purposes" farm machinery and better work horses. Space was being reserved for roads to be built, and "very little difficulty has been experienced in having the Indians leave section lines open for future roads." Sheridan and Valley County authorities were putting considerable efforts to improving roads and building bridges.[144] The Reclamation Service reported that two of the Poplar River irrigation units and the one at Little Porcupine Creek were nearly completed. Lohmiller reported that a few allotments had been leased for farming purposes. While Lohmiller was a pragmatist, he was also somewhat of a realist:

It is my opinion that the leasing system can be made one of the greatest evils, if the proposition is allowed of making cash payments. It is true that the Indian needs the money, but the payment of cash only whets his appetite for cash, and as a usual thing induces him to give up working for himself, and to depend on the income from his leases for his support.[130]

The superintendent knew leases and permits had provided funds for development, but there were also challenges including the work ethic that he hoped to foster among individual Indian farmers and stockmen, the number of individual tribal members who did not farm or raise stock, and the undermining effect of new sources of cash. Farming and stock raising were recognized as enterprises not without risk, but they involved a balancing act between years of profit and years of loss. The Indian Office and Lohmiller continued to issue stock, and in fiscal year 1914, another 150 heifers and five bulls were issued to tribal members who were interested. Because the Indians of Fort Peck appeared to not be utilizing all of their range lands even though the reservation opening and allotments forced a curtailment, Lohmiller continued to take advantage of the interval between when allotments were implemented and the range was still available. For a number of years, sheep had been grazed on the reservation, and by 1914, Lohmiller described these areas as "practically the only sheep range of any size now left in Montana." In previous years, the proceeds had accrued to the tribal trust fund, but beginning in 1914, the revenue from lands allotted to individuals accrued to them.

Clearly frustrated, Lohmiller lauded the work of his Agency Farmers, and the establishment of three substations, one each at Box Elder, Wolf Point, and Frazier, with another supervisory Farmer stationed at the agency in Poplar. In addition to instruction and demonstration of agricultural methods, and maintaining the agency-owned machinery, the Agency Farmers engaged in surveillance over all in their district. While tracking the progress of individual farmers, the Agency Farmers could report individuals for incidents not acceptable to the development program. Despite the contest with the elements, Lohmiller expected his fledgling farmers and stockmen to work "consecutively" on their enterprises:

The work of the [agency] farmers is more in line of encouraging the Indians to work con-secutively [Lohmiller's emphasis]. Most of the Indians are willing to work for a few days, but it

is the consecutive work that counts, and it is to this end that farmers bend their efforts.[131]

The Fifth Annual Fort Peck Indian Fair was scheduled for October 1 to 3, 1914 at the agency. Lohmiller stated that even though the crops had not been "very good," he expected the fair to be successful, and particularly so, in that "interest has been stimulated by competition between the various farming districts (on the reservation), and a good collection of agricultural exhibits is looked for." It was unclear whether any Indian dancing was formally allowed at the fair.[132]

In his final statements, Lohmiller indicated that about half of the trust patents had been delivered to allottees. In the Indian Appropriation Act for the fiscal year 1915, however, he reported that a provision was included that would re-open the allotment rolls to include the names of children who had not received allotments, but because Lohmiller had not yet been granted his request for a second clerk, additional administrative chores and paperwork could only be anticipated. Only one patent in fee had been issued in the current year, but several were pending. The one allottee with the patent in fee was said to be serious about keeping his land. The other applicants were said to be "more progressive Indians" with "their object being the improvement of their lands," which was a "commendable proposition." Lohmiller noted that no sales of inherited land had been made. In contrast, the surplus lands and their disposition were below what had been anticipated, "there being but about 300 filings up to August 1, 1914."[133]

Lohmiller, clearly concerned that the surplus lands were not bringing in the kind of cash that he and the tribal members had been led to expect, was ready to recommend how the sale of the surplus lands might be advanced. On February 15, 1915, he responded to a request by the CIA for suggestions as to whether reappraisals of surplus lands might stimulate sales. He did not support reappraisal, but favored an extension of time, perhaps ten years instead of five, to allow homesteaders to invest in their improvements and still make their necessary payments for the lands.[134] Lohmiller had previously reported that it was cheaper to pay for a land locator to obtain land of similar or better quality off the reservation than to pay the appraised value. The Indian Office reported that by 1915, only 53,600 acres on the eastern one-third of the reservation had been taken up for homesteads, and two years later, an inspector reported a total of 3,000 tracts had been taken up on the whole reservation.[135] This was the beginning of a political struggle that continued until John Collier became CIA in 1932.

The anticipated proceeds from town sites also had not materialized. The SI had authorized the opening of ten town sites, not including other proposed town sites along branch lines, some already built and others proposed, of the Great Northern Railway on or adjacent to the reservation. Lots sold well in Poplar, Wolf Point, and Oswego, and in Frazer and Brockton there was fair interest, but in Blair, Sprole, Facon, and Milk River (Wiota), only a few lots were sold, and none had been sold to date in Chelsea. By mid-July of 1914, there were 1,006 town lots sold for a total of $81,452. John McPhaul, in charge of the town site lot sales for the GLO, and Lohmiller wrote a joint letter to their respective superiors, reporting their assessment:

It was found that those few white settlers who have come to this reservation have settled in scattered localities, and that at the present time, there are not enough of them in any one locality to justify the existence of any new towns, other than those now on the reservation and adjacent thereto. However, having in mind the future developments of the reservation, and believing that settlers will come in the future, until town-

sites become a necessity, it is believed that some of the townsites now reserved should be abolished, and only a few retained.

Assuming that towns should be ten or twelve miles apart, McPhaul and Lohmiller recommended that seven named town sites be abolished and four be retained, but not surveyed for subdivision unless conditions warranted their development.[136]

As progress was being made about implementing the full measures of allotment, other developments by the Reclamation Service were proceeding. The preliminary investigation and surveys in 1908-1909 had identified 152,000 acres as potentially irrigable within seven project areas: Big Porcupine Division (4,000 acres), Little Porcupine Division (2,000 acres), Poplar Division (28,000 acres), Little Muddy Division (16,000 acres), Missouri River Division (84,000 acres), Galpin Division (8,000 acres) and Milk River Pumping Division (8,000 acres). The total cost was estimated to be an enormous sum of $5,220,000, leaving questions about where and how such irrigation infrastructure might be funded, and whether all the proposed divisions were even viable. At this time, Congress was not disposed to fund fully any such construction, but preferred that all reclamation work should be supported by those who benefited from irrigation. This was not always possible for developments on reservations, but it was thought that if non-Indians were also to benefit from the reclamation infrastructure on a reservation, then the service receivers should also contribute.[137]

Lohmiller described the opening of the reservation in his annual report for 1915 as being no problem in terms of law and order, but he viewed the towns as places that "furnish more temptation to the Indian to loaf and spend money foolishly." The introduction of liquor was a minor concern because whites brought in what little there was, and most whites were confined to the non-reservation allotments near Culbertson. Lohmiller's sarcasm showed when he stated that some of the whites caught with liquor were "persons carelessly leaving some in their pockets when coming on the reservation to transact business," but there was little need to be concerned, because there was a special officer in Poplar for much of the past fiscal year.[138] State, county, and on-reservation towns were cooperating to prevent the sale of liquor to Indians. Only one licensed trader was left on the reservation, but he was following all instructions about any extracts containing alcohol. Lohmiller recommended having local trials, as well as locally administered sentences, to deter trafficking, but also to make sure no one escaped punishment. Lohmiller went so far as to recommend that a local U.S. Commissioner might be authorized to try offenders in liquor cases, which would also prevent the absence of the superintendent from the reservation for cases tried elsewhere. He stressed that it was in the towns where Indians were exposed to what little gambling and liquor trafficking that did exist, blaming influences from mixed-bloods and whites.[139]

Health conditions remained only "good," with cases of trachoma, whooping cough, and tuberculosis continuing to occur. Overall sanitary conditions were improving, especially as younger residents heeded the precautions to safeguard their health. As more and more frame homes were built, keeping them clean became easier. The only reservation hospital was at the boarding school in Poplar, where students and "serious cases among the adult Indians of the reservation" were treated.[140] The doctors were making house calls besides meeting patients in the "dispensaries," although no location was indicated for the latter. They were visiting the schools regularly and indicated the schools were "as clean as the average homes of white people." Dr. C.H. Dewey,

an eye specialist, had attended to those afflicted with trachoma, and continued treatment was arranged for these patients.[141]

All reservation Indian children of school age were in school unless physically disabled, and the Montana State course of study was followed in the Indian schools. The industrial courses at the boarding school in Poplar predominated— farming, livestock raising, dairying, gardening, sewing, cooking, baking, laundering, housework, and general repair work. The old building at the boarding school burned on April 30, 1915, prompting the need for a new building. The first seven grades were taught in the boarding school and four or five grades in the day schools. The Presbyterian Mission School in Wolf Point followed a similar pattern as the boarding school in Poplar. Students were encouraged to look to the many new settlers within and adjacent to the reservation as examples of the advantages of farming. Students who had returned from other boarding schools away from the reservation and graduates from the public schools were able to gain "suitable and profitable employment" locally, but not always in their training concentrations: "common labor pays good wages and there is no prejudice against Indian labor; the girls can get plenty of housework to do, in good homes, at fair wages." Students in the reservation schools with demonstrated aptitude were transferred to the public schools. A few students were interested in seeking higher education, while the majority were satisfied to have training for "the environments of his future employment."[142]

In hindsight, the two agricultural seasons of 1913 and 1914 fell far short of the bountiful season of 1912, in yield per acre. The crop of 1915 was "a very fair one," and prices were expected to be reasonable. The combined diversification between stock raising and farming was stressed, and balanced operations were able to make some profit. The overall farming acreage was increasing, and several white husbands of tribal members were engaged in large-scale operations. The better than average crop was credited to heeding the advice of agricultural research stations and "scientific methods of farming and stock-growing." Even though the crop's amount and value were expected to be fair, it would not be a repeat of 1912. Lohmiller reflected:

It is surprising that the Indians do not get discouraged in farming, as it is sometimes trying to the whites who have [the] advantage of many generations of activities by their ancestors while the Indian is new to civilization, yet the men seem to take hold of each year with increased determination and faith.[143]

Most of the Indians engaged in farming on the reservation were fairly well equipped, which was only possible because of the reimbursable fund. Consequently, their farm equipment was comparable to that of the homesteaders in the vicinity. It was far better for Indians to own their machinery than to borrow it, since they appeared "to take better care of it." The introduction of larger work horse stallions had contributed to better animals for farming, so the small pony stallions of the "old-time Indians" were arbitrarily castrated by the reservation employees to reduce the "serious menace to the development of good horses." The stock and machinery acquired on loans from the reimbursable fund "enabled them to increase their farming, and caused them to do better work; however, the better effects or results will be seen next season as much as the supplies were received very late and not in time to do much with the crop this year." Lohmiller talked only about the advantages of loans from the reimbursable fund, but "The loan is a good thing for the industrious Indian with the right intentions, but it also furnishes opportunities to those who show industrious prospects and intentions, to secure the use of articles for a

while and perhaps not make the first payment."[160] Crassly, the disadvantage was indebtedness and the temptations of consumerism that also created new dependencies. Without other capital, few options remained and social control smothered any individualism fostered by allotment and the receipt of fee patents.

While building roads certainly improved the lives of reservation residents, Lohmiller indicated that the Indian Office actually expected Indians to volunteer to work on roads near their homes without any compensation. But the reservation residents could not see why they should do road work free of charge when they were not the majority citizens. They saw few, if any, of their white neighbors doing such work without pay, except perhaps working a poll tax. The Indians were more interested in building irrigation systems, and harvesting the hay from the initial irrigatable areas.[144]

The rural residences upon allotments were frame buildings built by the Indians themselves. Wells were dug and outbuildings like barns, corrals, and granaries were added after lands were fenced and fields cultivated. Lohmiller reported that in 1915, very few allotments were leased for "farming purposes," since most of the Indians who were farming preferred to improve their own lands. Sheepmen were still taking annual leases in the grazing districts, mostly on the west end of the reservation. Additional stock was made available under the reimbursable plan, and all stock transactions were reported to the agency, including requests to sell or slaughter animals. Revenue from the leases no longer went to the tribes, but were paid out in per capita payments. Owing to the slow settlement on surplus lands, grazing leases seemed to have only another five or six years of viability. The four Agency Farmers were devoting all their time to the farming and livestock raising in their respective districts, but also they made issues, submitted reports, and completed paperwork related to land work. An Agency Herder at the Box Elder Sub-station handled the care of cattle for the agency and the boarding and day schools. Efforts to encourage and teach dairying were inhibited because the nearest creameries were in Culbertson and Plentywood, but, even if access to these creameries by rail were possible, other factors such as time, convenience, and distance remained obstacles.

Lohmiller described in detail the four farming districts. The Agency Farmer for the eastern district, headquartered at Box Elder, supervised the Agency Herder and the beef herd, and in bad weather, issued rations to old people in the vicinity. The next district to the east covered an area twelve to fourteen miles east and west from Poplar, with the farmer headquartered in Poplar, where he had charge of the Agency (School) Farm, which in the 1915 season was planted in alfalfa and needed little attention.

The next district was the Wolf Point Sub-Agency, headquartered in Wolf Point, extending from the edge of the Poplar district to the west end of Sheridan County, west of Wolf Point. The Agency Farmer there was kept quite busy. The far west district covered the remaining areas of the reservation encompassed by Valley County and the Porcupine Creek Irrigation Unit, and the farmer was yet to have permanent housing supplied so he was housed at the Frazer Day School. Each Agency Farmer was equipped with horses and rigs for transportation purposes, and some tools to loan to those who needed them.

The Agency Farmers were responsible for holding meetings in the winter with Indians in their districts to assess needs and make plans for the coming season, but they were in almost daily contact with the Indians in their districts to encourage them, answer questions, and provide advice. The farmers received the latest agricultural research station reports, and passed around agricultural periodicals and information to help manage risks, especially the constantly changing weather conditions. Proper maintenance of machinery was also encouraged. Planting and harvests were planned, as were marketing strategies. Most of the Indian farmers lived within six to eight miles of a railroad station and competitive grain dealers in the small reservation towns, making most marketing relatively easy. In many of these locations, stock buyers were looking for beef cattle and horses for the war effort and for sale to incoming settlers.[145]

Lohmiller, for the first time in his annual reports, described the timber on the reservation. Mostly cottonwood was available, with little use beyond firewood, since it was prone to rot. Cut lumber available from companies on the reservation included pine, fir, and larch. The scrub timber and brush, including willows, made excellent fuel. Sawable local timber was in very short supply, since wood could no longer be taken south of the Missouri River, because those lands had been settled.[146]

The original and initial allotment was declared completed under the Act of 1908, and most of the trust patents were delivered to the allottees. The provision of Congress in 1914 for re-opening the allotment rolls to give land to the children born after the former allotment work closed; the selection for this allotment was underway and was expected to continue as long as land was available. During the 1915 fiscal year, twenty-five fee patents were issued to individual tribal members. Several of these immediately disposed of some portion of their lands, to purchase further livestock and machinery, for cash to capitalize their operations further, and to make their homes more comfortable. Most of these individuals were reported to have fine prospects and plans, but once they received their fee patents, the limits of their resources were soon reached. Lohmiller recommended that fee patents be issued for only a portion, such as half, of the allotment, so that "the Indian is in a way put on probation which is a safe-guard on his conduct." As of his report, August 22, 1915, there had been only 600 filings on the surplus lands. The work of sorting out the heirs of deceased allottees was advanced by the visit of Examiner of Inheritance W.D.Goodwin, with his stenographer, in early August. The work was expected to take four to five months, with about two hundred cases pending. By June 30, 1915, seventy-three active IIM accounts were reported, twenty-six represented by deceased persons, and the remainder included many school- or pre-school-age children. Since July 1, as many more had been added, mostly for minors and deceased persons.[147]

Supervisor of Schools L.F. Michael noted in a report dated November 9, 1915 that the "two principal industries" of Indians at Fort Peck were farming and stock raising. The crops grown in the 1915 season were predominately wheat, flax, oats and barley. Michael explained that corn and potatoes were not raised because of cold springs and early fall frosts. The total number of acres cultivated on the reservation was estimated to be about 25,000. He recommended that much more could be done to make stock raising increasingly viable, mostly by supplying more breeding sires for horses and cattle. As cold weather was already setting in, Michael observed how inadequate much of the housing was. Among the old, infirm, and dependent, he said that rations were insufficient for the winter season, and should be increased with beans, hominy, and additional beef. Some were forced to survive by seeking the charity of their friends and relatives. A considerable number of men, not able to establish a farming and/or livestock operation, worked irregular labor. Michael noted that as much as $450,000 dollars had been expended to date on irrigation works on the reservation, referring to the Ketchum Commission investigation of the

previous year, but when he sought to find out exactly how much land was irrigated, he was only able to report that less than 400 acres had been irrigated in the 1915 season, much of it hay land. In cases where Indians with irrigation allotments were not taking advantage of the water actually available, efforts were then made to lease these lands to white farmers so that the construction costs could begin to be recovered. The total spending in 1915 for individual men employed full time in wage labor was approximately $8,000, and often this work was arranged so as not to interfere with work on the farms.[148]

Michael also indicated that the number of fee patents issued since July 1, 1915, was twenty-four for a portion of allotment, and nine for the entire of the allotment. The recent visit from the Competency Commission recommended thirty-five persons for fee patents. No official records were made of the disposition of these titles, but in Michael's words, "it is the general opinion that many are sold outright and others are mortgaged, and few, if any redeemed," and "no destitution from the sale of patented land have been reported to the local office."[149] While no tracts had been sold in the current year, the regulations were being strictly followed, but the demand was not great, since such a large amount of land was still available to homestead entry. Leasing was still active. Michael reported that 433 farming and grazing leases were in force, and that 400 of these grazing leases for 320-acre allotments were leased for fifteen cents an acre. The remaining farm leases were made mostly for "grain rental; others for cash and part improvements." Michael, however, felt the grazing permits for the grazing districts, which consisted of twelve in number for sheep, three for horses, and one for cattle, were undervalued. He recommended raises in the rates for horses and cattle, and that the sheep grazing permit and leasing system needed to be carefully reorganized and "the rate materially increased." He recognized that the sheepmen would not be in favor of this, but he declared, "The Indians need the money and the tribe can make good use of its portion of the income from this source."[150]

The balance in the Fort Peck Trust Fund in the U.S. Treasury, as of December 20, 1915, derived from the proceeds from the first homestead entries, totalled $97,327.46. The Indian Office, often with little or no consultation with the Fort Peck tribes, determined how these funds would be spent.[151]

A group of Yankton Sioux at Fort Peck asked through Superintendent Lohmiller that a delegation of three men be allowed to visit Washington, D.C., for the purposes of ameliorating conditions arising from the non-fulfillment of agreements and legislative mandates.[152] Lohmiller endorsed their claim to the "benefits to which they are entitled."[153]

The Indian Office wrote, on February 15, 1916, asking for an investigation of these conditions. The office cautioned Lohmiller to make sure that there was no suffering among the Indians this winter, and directed him to thoroughly investigate and "take prompt steps to relieve any destitution found to exist."[154] Lohmiller, writing on the same day he had received his instructions, asked his Agency Farmers to conduct a house-to-house canvass of the Indians, to report on the conditions of each family, to supply food where necessary, and to advise the agency of all actions taken.[155] On February 29, 1916, Lohmiller reported that few, if any, cases were identified where relief was needed. Lohmiller actually quoted the reports of his Agency Farmers in full to demonstrate the extent of his administration and his attention to details. He also included the lists of names and reports of conditions among individuals and families living in the Box Elder and Brockton districts.[156]

The Fort Peck delegates in Washington,

Charles R. Thompson, Gus M. Hedderick, and T. W. Mayle, wrote to CIA Cato Sells on March 6, 1916, requesting the appointment of a "special representative of your office to investigate conditions on our reservation." The tone of their letter and what they described was very different from the positive picture Lohmiller had consistently represented to the Indian Office:

As a whole, the Indians on this reservation today are no better off than they were ten years ago. Then, they had better homes, more horses, more cattle, more of them had gardens, raising vegetables and corn, and were better able to support themselves than they are at the present time. Today, in place of the horses and cattle are the starving camp dogs and nothing remains of the once garden spots but the trampled down wires of the fences which surrounded them. Today, the Indians on our reservation are in such destitute circumstances that it is not an uncommon thing for them to travel distances after the carcass of horses and cattle, killed by trains, died of starvation, or diseases, nor is the statement untrue that they often frequent hotels, restaurants, and other places to secure refuse from the garbage cans and other offal, to keep body and soul together.

Such are a few of the intolerable conditions as exist today among a once proud and independent people—a class of people whose property, according to the figures of your office, is worth approximately five million dollars. If like conditions are permitted to continue, as they have been in the past, what will become of these Indians ten years hence, who, today, are worth millions?[157]

The delegates blamed these conditions upon Lohmiller, "due principally to his lack of interest and encouragement." They cited his roles in building the Gateway Hotel and as a board member of the Trader's State Bank, both in

Poplar, and his ownership of many lots in the town, though despite his influence and authority, Poplar was also home to gambling joints and bootleggers.[158]

The delegation claimed that Lohmiller's mismanagement extended to the leasing of allotted and surplus lands. They contended that reports about the sentiments of Indians at Fort Peck about the reservation irrigations projects, a reference to the 1914 commission investigating irrigation projects on Montana Indian reservations of which Lohmiller was a member, was an illustration of how he misrepresented the "true sentiment" of the people on the reservation. They also accused the superintendent and many of his employees of sitting in their offices in Poplar and not traveling on the reservation to familiarize themselves with the "conditions as actually exist."

Their interest as government employees goes no further than their salary checks and their daily routine office work and, occasionally as a diversion, transmitting to your office glowing reports of the progress of the Indians, reports of bounteous crops and successful stock raising among the Indians. Such conditions exist principally on the papers they are written on. There are exceptions, it is true, but these exist in spite of rather than to any efforts on the part of the office forces.

Several of the Agency Farmers were called "twelve hundred dollar men" who were not worth two cents, and were described as rarely willing to respond to the requests of their Indian charges. The delegates also charged that the farmers were linked to Lohmiller's business ventures, suggesting conflicts of interest. The delegates charged Lohmiller with "incompetency, mismanagement, and gross neglect of duty, in his administration of the affairs of our people on this reservation." They concluded by cautioning that the delegates "not be considered as 'chronic

kickers,' but as those who desire to better the living conditions of our people and raise the administration of our affairs to the highest standard attainable."[159]

Lohmiller wrote the CIA on May 4, 1916, reporting again that clerical help at Fort Peck Agency was "inadequate" to the volume of work, which included correspondence, the next round of allotments, granting patents in fee, leasing work, tracking land sales, dealing with probate and heirship matters, overseeing the Individual Indian Money accounts, administering the reimbursable loan fund, administration of the boarding school, and handling physical property. He said that his staff had worked overtime much of the year, had foregone much of their vacation time, was working holidays, and still was unable to keep up. F. L. Michael, present to conduct an agency inspection, wrote an endorsement, saying that the superintendent's requests for additional clerical help should be granted at the earliest possible date.[160]

In this same letter, however, Lohmiller said that the office should "give no consideration to one Thomas W. Mayle" for any of the positions at the agency, though he was seeking reinstatement in the Indian Service. Lohmiller did not object to the reinstatement, but he did not want him employed at Fort Peck, saying that as a member of the tribes, Mayle "has of late been given to muckraking and criticisms of this Office," that "he was a trouble-maker," and that it had been a mistake to have him as an employee among his own people, whom he was prone to mislead.[161] Lohmiller responded on the same day, May 4, 1916, to the request by the Indian Office to make a report about "Gus Hedrick [sic]," who complained that a patent in fee had not yet been delivered to his wife. Lohmiller explained in detail his decision to cancel the patent in fee for specific reasons. Heddrick, described as a "mixed blood," was married to an "inexperienced Polish woman . . . absolutely under his sway."

[He is] an agitator by profession and a shiftless prevaricator by choice; invariably enters into a conversational conspiracy of ignorance, inquisitiveness, impertinence and intolerance; will not work and passes his time in the various stores in Poplar, relating to what he has done and what he is going to do to the undersigned. About a year ago, he received a patent in fee for his grazing land. I did think then that I could make something out of him, but I have learned since that my efforts were wasted on useless soil. All he has left from the proceeds of his patent in fee is a second hand "Case" automobile, which he uses chiefly for "joy rides."

Aware that the patent and the land were to be sold, Lohmiller felt it was better to cancel it, and stated his determination not to aid Heddrick in any way. He reported that Heddrick had been absent from Fort Peck Reservation almost continually since last February 14, when he and two others went to Washington without authorization, "publically to help the tribe [sic], personally to help themselves." The delegation returned around March 14, but were away again on two trips for much of April, with Heddrick explaining to others that he was going back to Washington to "straighten up matters with me."

Lohmiller reported that on April 20, Heddrick came to the agency office with Charles Thompson, and inquired of the lease clerk whether his wife's patent in fee had arrived. He was told that he would have to speak with the superintendent. Heddrick was reported to have replied that he had written Washington, and because he was beyond the authority of the superintendent, he transacted all of his business with the Indian Office directly. The next day, Heddrick returned with two men whom he wanted as witnesses, and entered the superintendent's office to demand his wife's patent.

Lohmiller explained that he stated he would only speak to Heddrick in private, and that otherwise he would ask the group to leave. Heddrick asked if his wife's patent had been received, and Lohmiller said that he declared that he would not say if it had or had not arrived, and three times refused to answer the question.

Lohmiller asserted that he could not too strongly recommend the cancellation of the patent in fee, because his authority was at issue, including his dislike for detractors not interested in assisting with the reservation's development.[162] Lohmiller was adamant that he should be able to assess individuals that he felt had demonstrated by their behavior that they were unfit for citizenship and should have their applications for patent in fee cancelled. Lohmiller recommended the same action in the case of David Dupree, who, with the assistance of Charles Thompson, had written to Senator T. J. Walsh, demanding an inquiry into delays.[163]

Lohmiller also addressed the encroachments of stockmen who were trespassing on areas of the reservation that were difficult to police. Having figured out who the perpetrators were, especially on Wolf and Smoke Creeks, Lohmiller was hamstrung. He urged legal action against three trespassers, all men of means, so that they might be made an example. The rules relative to excess stock on allotted versus unallotted lands were not clear, but this made enforcement difficult since the stockmen were responsible for indicating their numbers of stock, and consequently payments were made more or less on the honor system, which Lohmiller found frustrating and inaccurate.[164]

The Act of May 18, 1916 authorized the Indian Office in appropriations for "the purposes of paying the current and contingent expenses of the Bureau of Indian Affairs, for the fulfilling of treaty stipulations with various Indian tribes, and in full compensation for all offices and salaries" provided for services in the fiscal year 1917. But the allotment process and its expenses were considered a lien against the tribes and their trust accounts. Upon payment of the delinquent charges, these accounts were at the discretion of the superintendent. The appropriations for developing irrigation by the Reclamation Service were recoverable, and this legislation allowed for expenses over and above appropriation, as well as the value of expended appropriated money, for building and maintaining irrigation works that would be charged against individual allottees and be paid in installments, if their irrigable allotments received and used irrigation waters. The legislation also allowed for expenses to be paid against tribal trust funds as deemed necessary.[165] These new administrative powers were disconcerting to some of the tribal members.

L.F. Michael, Supervisor of Indian Education, was dispatched to Fort Peck Agency to investigate the charges against Lohmiller. On May 22, 1916, Michael met with a delegation representing a group of traditional Indians, calling themselves "The Committee of Twelve." The delegates were Big Foot, Circling Eagle, and Henry Shields. Big Foot, speaking for the group, said that he had authority from the superintendent to name this committee to work for the good of all the old Indians. Big Foot began:

You went around and saw how we eat and live. I would like to be informed about this reimbursable fund. I would like to know if any thing is left. We old people would like to get some of it to get food with. Have we any money that can be divided to help out the old people? I ask this because if we had such money for some of the old people, there would be money to buy coffins with and give us decent burial. A lot of settlers have come on our land, but we have not seen one cent for this; we would like to get something out of our land. We intended to talk about the grazing money. The young fellows get all the benefits in the way of improvements, but we old people get nothing out of the fund. A long time ago the chiefs did the business; so I formed the committee of the old people to work for the good of the old Indians. We are non-English speaking people and are bashful and we got nothing from this fund . . . the way it is now, half of the tribe is only benefited; I mean [the two halves being] the old and young people; I want them to share alike, to work for the benefit of all the Indians.

Big Foot expressed disdain for "these white men who have married Indian women" and the Indians who have their patents in fee for not wanting to share the tribal funds. He continued to argue that the younger people were getting the best of everything:

. . . we are old people trying to get together and do something for ourselves and our good; there are many poor people, and the blind who have a hard time; we don't want to depend on the young people for what we get; we want to get it from the Superintendent as long as he is here; we want to get our share of what is coming to the old people; the young people don't do anything for the old people; we want to get together for the old people and for their good; if there is any money to the credit of the Indians, we old people would like to get our share of this money for our use, grazing money or land sale money; we want the Agent to help us in this and not give all the help to the young people; the squaw-men and the mixed bloods should not be allowed to share in what is coming to us old people; they should take care of themselves and not depend on what is the property and belongings of the old Indians; we old people want to see some good from the sale of our reservation and get some of the money for our use to help us to live better. . . .

All of the Indians of the Fort Peck Reservation did not understand Lohmiller's agenda. Big Foot's group thought the money spent on irrigation works was wasted, and they were concerned with how much had been borrowed by individuals and on behalf of the tribes.[166] Circling Eagle had one thing to say:

We have been taught by the [Agency] Farmers to care for our stock, but we don't always do it; Indians don't put up enough hay; we need better homes and stables; lots of stock was lost last winter on this account; one of the troubles is that the Indians run to the irrigation ditches to earn a few cents and neglect their homes; they do not farm enough; the Indian would make more money by farming.

Henry Shields, worried that he was in a conflict of interest because he was an agency policeman, only asked whether he could have a "voice in the councils" because of his employment.[167] Michael asked the Indian Office to write to Big Foot and the Committee of Twelve through Lohmiller, advising them that their delegates' talk before Michael had been reported to the office.[168]

On May 27, 1916, Michael reported to Lohmiller the CIA's instructions to investigate the complaints made by Gus M. Heddrick, T.W. Mayle, and Charles Thompson about his administration. He summarized the complaints, and explained how he had taken sworn statements from witnesses at a hearing held at the agency office in Poplar. In response to the charges of neglect and lack of traveling the reservation to observe conditions, Michael suggested that Lohmiller state approximately how much time he spent traveling and meeting Indians in their homes. As to the complaints made about his political and commercial activities in the town of Poplar, the supervisor suggested that he fully state "what part, if any, you take in political

matters concerning the town of Poplar." As for the charges of failing to suppress gambling and bootlegging, Michael urged him to detail what steps he had taken against these activities, and what he knew about the complaints against Ezra Ricker, the agency interpreter, and Dan Mitchell, the policeman. In response to the statements made about allotments, leases, claims against the G.N.R.R., irrigation projects, his work on the Irrigation Commission, and the comments he reportedly made about the Indian Service and his position, again Lohmiller was urged to place his statements on the record. Michael then handed to the superintendent the original complaint and copies of the testimony, and asked for his responses in five days.[169]

In June 1916, Meritt and Lohmiller were exchanging letters about citizenship issues for Indians who had received allotments and fee patents, since thereafter they were considered citizens and thus had the right to vote. The question was, if an Indian received a fee patent for inherited land, did that individual person then automatically become a citizen as well, including eligibility for other kinds of land acquisition? In Meritt's words, "An Indian who maintained his tribal relationship and has received a patent in fee for an allotment would not be estopped [sic] thereby from taking a homestead on the public domain as a citizen of the United States should he comply with the requirements of the Federal homestead laws."[170] Not discussed were the consequences of taking a homestead, and any continuance of membership in a tribe.

Lohmiller reported to the CIA on June 29, 1916 on the amount of stock on the reservation and the status of authority for various leases and permits, in response to the agency's inspection. For counts to be confirmed, he explained that the sheep were enumerated at the shearing plant in Frazer, and in other parts of the reservation, Agency Farmers visited shearing operations. For cattle and horses, the farmers were expected to know and count these animals in their districts. All permittees had to swear affidavits as to the numbers of stock they owned, which ensured discrepancies could be identified quickly. The superintendent reported that the "grazing situation is well in hand although it is a big job," referring to farmers, policemen, and other employees often working after hours, overtime, and on Sundays and holidays.[171] The Indian Office issued new regulations for farming and grazing permits on July 1, 1916.[172]

Asked to report on the number and areas of allotments made in the field up to June 26, and not yet reported or submitted to the office, Lohmiller provided, on July 3, 1916, as accurate and up-to-date a report as he could, given the shortage of clerical help. Under the Act of August 1, 1914 (38 Stat. 593), there were potentially 335 allottees, entitled to 320 acres each of non-irrigable land. He reported that of the 335, all but twenty-four had made selections, the "clearance" of many being before the local land office; "many of the 331 had formerly made selection near allotments of their family for which trust patents have [been] issued but owning to instructions from the Department they have been compelled to select lieu lands for the reason that those formerly chosen are embraced in that territory classified as coal or mineral lands." This made proximity a problem, and trying to find lands meant many families were traveling about camping in their search. The number of homestead entries also meant that what remained for selection was limited, and sometimes families were competing for the same lands. Lohmiller described the local land office as one of the "busiest government offices in the U.S," which meant the waiting times to hear about applications were lengthy. He closed his report saying "of the 311 selections already reported, approximately 99.520 acres" were included.[173]

Having considered Michael's reports, the Indian Office made its determinations about Superintendent Lohmiller on July 10, 1916. Commissioner Cato Sells addressed a series of points. In his attention to balancing stock raising and farming, the two industries at Fort Peck were not yet going "hand in hand." To the statement that Lohmiller was not interested in the welfare of the reservation's people, it was stated that he spent too little time in "field duties," resulting in his failure to "realize and know the conditions first hand." The superintendent was chastised for his business involvements in Poplar, which had detracted from his duties and responsibilities of the agency. The involvement with the financial institution where constituent Indians secured loans and credit was improper, "reprehensible and subversive of good administration." Involvement in local politics was also inopportune. His acquisition of town property in government town sites was contrary to regulations. He had not pursued questions of trespassing adequately, nor did he push to a legitimate conclusion these matters "as a Superintendent should." The claims of Indians were not being treated as vigorously as those of white claimants. The disposition of all applications for patents in fee was not addressed "as promptly and in strict compliance with the rules and regulations governing the same." And finally, Lohmiller had not "directed an active and aggressive campaign for bettering the housing conditions of the old and dependent Indian population of the reservation."

Sells was quick to say, "These allegations affect your work very seriously as a Superintendent of this important agency," and while he did acknowledge Lohmiller's long service to Fort Peck Agency, his business associations had left the impression that his "administration of the affairs of the Indians on the reservation is not in their best interests." Although Michael had assessed the complaints of Heddrick, Thompson, and Mayle as "overdrawn" and without foundation, Lohmiller had given ammunition to these detractors by the existence of "certain conditions and practices which are not excusable." Sells concluded that "some relief must be had for this condition." The CIA then stated: "At one time you expressed a desire to retire from the Service, and if you still desire to do this, I will without any further action on this report, accept such resignation if tendered promptly."[174]

Lohmiller responded on July 17, 1916 that he disagreed with the many statements in Michael's report, and while he had no desire to remain indefinitely at Fort Peck, he wanted to complete "the unfinished work at the [Agency] Office," as there was "a great amount of special and unusual details to finish as well as the plans of the season from an agricultural standpoint; after having been associated with these people for twenty three years I need three or four months to round out the business and close my work in a manner that will be for the best interest of the Service."[175] He argued that if his separation from the service could be "disassociated" from the "two or three trouble making Indians," that any time they wanted a change in employees, they only had to complain to Washington. Anticipating that once he was separated from the service the affairs of the reservation would be "a sealed book to me," he asked to continue in his position until November 30 or October 31.[176]

To ensure that he could leave on his own terms, Lohmiller sent his letter of resignation to Senator H.L. Myers, and asked him personally to hand-deliver it to Commissioner of Indian Affairs Cato Sells. Myers' schedule forced him to have Lohmiller's letter delivered to the CIA, though the Senator endorsed Lohmiller's request to continue until November 1. He stated that Lohmiller was owed "for the good of the Department and the orderly closing up of this work." Myers wrote, "I would greatly appreciate

it if you would grant his request." The senator asked the CIA to please not make Lohmiller's resignation effective, without first giving Myers a chance to come from Capitol Hill to see him. In that case, the Senator said he would come no matter when or what the demands on his time, so that he could confer with the CIA personally. Lohmiller's letter of resignation, dated July 22, 1916, offered to leave at the pleasure of the CIA.[177]

Lohmiller submitted his last annual report on October 26, 1916. He described the lands surrounding the reservation as having been "thickly settled with white people and there are perhaps 1,200 homesteaders on the reservation and a hundred or more lessees." A little more than a third of the reservation's acreage, or 2,094,035 acres, had been initially allotted, as children were now receiving allotments.[178]

Crops were variable during the 1916 growing season.[179] The market value of the grain crops successfully harvested was increasing. Subsequently, the value of land on the Fort Peck Reservation and vicinity had "increased at least 25% this year" and there was a greater demand for agricultural leases. Grazing leases were also in demand, and Lohmiller reported that the amounts earned were the best to date. He also reported conducting four land sales, selling 26,081.01 acres, which netted $200,363.90, for an average of $7.6801 per acre. He noted that these sales caused an "immense increase" in office work at the agency, and again requested an additional clerk. This land sales record for the region was an important benchmark.[180]

The outsiders coming into the region were a "high class of agriculturalists" who would be of "benefit by way of industriousness and successful management." But this had to be contrasted with the rapidly growing "undesirable element" who were living in towns on and off the reservation, under the control of municipal, county, and state authorities except relative to liquor. Lohmiller said that "these towns furnish an incentive to many of the Indians to loaf and play pool; and the environments of such places are injurious to the young Indians, and these towns exercise bad influence generally over school children where the schools are close to a town."[181]

Asked to comment on "dancing," a term which meant all things traditional including ceremonialism, Lohmiller said that "dancing" was "almost forgotten by these Indians," and that "only once or twice a year a few of the old people gather and do a little dancing for a few hours before midnight; the order is good and it is largely a perfunctory matter as there is little interest shown in these dances." Lohmiller described the "dances" that he was allowed to view as social occasions where people "talk over old times," and he sanctioned these because the reservation police were "always on hand to insure good order." He gave a qualified comparison: "The dancing they do indulge in is far less injurious to them than is the usual white dances to the white people." He explained, "I would continue to hold a firm hand over what little dancing is done having police present and if other reservations are like this[,] the custom will die out in a few years when the older generation gets too old to engage in them." He tried to attribute the causes:

The children or returned students seldom go to these dances and then are spectators; sometimes a young fellow will show a few steps of the modern white dance; sometimes the young Indian people hold dances in the Indian dance hall where nothing but the modern dances are indulged in.[182]

A major influence in suppressing dancing was conservative Protestantism, with its stand against all social dancing, alcohol consumption, and sexual promiscuity.[183] A long-term regularization of legally sanctioned domestic relations paral-

leled the documentation of marriages and the securing of marriage licenses at the county clerk of courts offices, and if divorce was sought, it also was granted under Montana law. Compliance with these conditions and jurisdictions was complicated by the traditional practice of marriage among Assiniboines and Sioux, which were more consensual agreements between families through public acknowledgement of the relationship. Often living together was considered trial marriage; for the young, it was a time to try out relationships, and for the older adults, accommodations which might eventually be formally sanctioned at a community event. Courting was often done at social and cultural events, and the schools often made interactions possible. Lohmiller, however, did not understand this: "They [the Fort Peck reservation Indians] are not following the state law carefully in securing divorces as they are in marriages, likely due to the expense and difficulty of securing separations in this manner each time." This obsession for enforcing domestic laws led to additional surveillance: "We are ever vigilant in urging the Indians, when they find it absolutely necessary to separate, to go according to the State laws; for there is then a better method of getting and keeping records that may later be of vital importance in estates, etc." Clearly, Lohmiller and his office staff understood the implications of the allotment of lands upon disputes arising about inheritance.[184]

The issue of the Indians' morality was a concern of the Christian missionaries on the reservation. The Roman Catholic, Presbyterian, and Church of Latter Day Saints were engaging in their activities, but they refrained from any sectarian strife. The reservation residents were very interested in religion, "often times not very devout, however religion plays a strong part in improving their conditions and civilizing them." Coinciding with the joint Indian and County Fair in September 1916, a church celebration and gathering was held at the agency; it was not clear if this was denominational or non-denominational.[185]

Prohibition and its enforcement had its forerunners in the pursuit of liquor traffickers on reservations. Beginning in November 1916, the State of Montana began steps to implement statewide prohibition. Lohmiller pointed to incidents in Culbertson just off the east end of the reservation. A number of Indians living on non-reservation allotments, and "a few of the young men who received fee patents and who live where they get into the towns often have been drinking some," were the source of cases. Admitting that relatively little liquor was introduced to the reservation in 1916, Lohmiller continued to blame "irresponsible whites" in the larger towns along the southern tier of the reservation, suggesting they were smuggling liquor. The previous sites of consumption were saloons, which had a long history of supplying "individual use." Lohmiller explained: "A few of the Indians go to Culbertson, and to places south of the Missouri River, usually getting it from swampers or irresponsible loafers around saloons as the legitimate saloon will not sell liquor to any one supposed to have Indian blood." He noted that before 1888 no saloons were located on the reservation, nor had there been any there earlier. He called for the reassignment of another special officer. A coordinated effort from county and state officials to suppress alcohol use was put in place.[186]

Lohmiller reemphasized his previous proposal for a U.S. commissioner, declaring that dealing with offenders was "cumbersome and expensive as well as tedious." Transporting offenders to the nearest federal court for trial was a great inconvenience.[187] The superintendent explained that in Richland County, which bordered the reservation across the Missouri River for more than fifty miles, several blind-pigs were eluding detection of county authorities, but Lohmiller remained convinced that liquor from these sources was still making it onto the reservation.[188]

On a positive note, younger tribal members were constructing comfortable and sanitary homes, and others made repairs to existing structures. Physicians were constantly urging the upgrades, especially floors and insulated walls, and they often made rounds of the Indian houses to make further suggestions for improved sanitation. The education efforts appeared to be reaching many young people. Older persons had sold portions of their allotments, and used the proceeds to improve their conditions, especially making their homes more comfortable, and "practically every land sale has had a good share of the money used for a residence or the repair of one." Treatment for children and adults restricted to the agency school hospital was excellent, but requests to the Indian Office for medicine were not adequately met. Tuberculosis remained the primary disease problem, and the precautions to keep patients isolated and cared for were working. A few scarlet fever and polio cases developed among whites only, and through careful quarantine and care, both diseases were contained. The physicians also established several temporary tent hospitals for treating adults and "ineligible children." A "Save the Babies" campaign had been launched. Community meetings were held at several locations on the reservation where literature was distributed and advice was given, with agency teachers, farmers, physicians, and nurses in attendance. One event sponsored was a healthy baby show at the joint Reservation and County Fair, in which thirty Indian babies were among the contestants. Another important effort was a house-by-house canvass conducted to assess conditions and identify needs of individuals and families. Subsequently, Agency Farmers carried food and medical supplies with them so they could respond immediately when assistance was needed. Prenatal instruction sessions to young mothers had already contributed to saving the lives of several infants.[189]

Lohmiller described the relationships between Indian families and the schools as "very good." While prejudice was reported against full-blood children, the mixed-blood children in the public schools "get along nicely":

. . . they seem to be equal or slightly above the average white child in their progress in the public schools. The Indian child whose parents are not full bloods usually learns English at home and the home conditions are generally better due to the experience and training the parents received and for that reason they are able to compete in public schools better than full-blood children; also they are usually neater than full-blood ones.

Eager to detect progress in assimilation, Lohmiller saw the industrial training in the boarding and day schools as a practical complement to the State of Montana mandated curriculum. The Presbyterian Mission School in Wolf Point compared favorably with the Indian reservation schools.[190] Lohmiller observed that in so far as the morality of students and their parents was concerned, "they are progressing as rapidly as their white neighbors; in fact many are too prone to follow the example of their white neighbors in the way of buying automobiles, etc., when they could do without." He spoke of the splendid opportunities available to students who had returned from boarding schools away from the reservation. Market prices for livestock and grain were rising, largely because World War I was already raging in Europe. Lohmiller felt the example of the white settlers working hard on their lands both on and off the reservation might counter those "few students who were not using their education in a profitable way but were spending their time in comparative

idleness, living from the earning of others, and occupied in finding fault or trying to find fault with persons or conditions, instead of remedying matters." Because wages were good, Indian labor was in great demand. Lohmiller was fixated upon fostering a work ethic, but his philosophy of assimilation went further:

There is little objection to the intermingling of the races where the degree of Indian blood is not great; but there is prejudice in much mixing of full-blood children; this will be gradually removed as the quantity of white blood in the Indians increase and as they improve their health and home conditions.[191]

Progressive members among the tribes who subscribed to assimilation undoubtedly found the superintendent's view an inevitable consequence of modern life. Traditionalists or those somewhere in the middle were uneasy, if not threatened, since the education available to their children, with its vocational emphasis, was a far cry from their cultural values. Particularly revealing was Lohmiller's vision of education and the reservation's development:

I believe it will be nearly fifteen years before the Government schools here will no longer be required; by that time the lands will be settled up; much of that owned by the old people will have been sold and white people coming in to farm such lands will establish public schools that they should soon be in reach of the Indian children. By that time all the Indians will be clean and neat appearing as the whites and most of the children then going to school will have as parents those who have had and realize the advantage of a school training, and they will be easily able to enter and compete fairly in the public schools with the white children.[192]

Lohmiller envisioned a time when taxes would support all the schools on the reservation, but the Indians would be expected to conform to the cultural expectations of the taxpayers, who naturally would control these school boards.

Lohmiller's narrative about the labor patterns of the Indians on the Fort Peck Reservation in the fiscal year 1916 included the heading "Industries," where the farming and stock raising were described in detail. "In this way [the seasonal round] they [tribal members farming and stockraising] will be kept busy and at home most of the time and as with the whites they are happier and more apt to be out of mischief when they are busy." Lohmiller said that the tribal member farmers who had been farming for a number of seasons drew upon their practical experience and decided what crops to grow, knowing when and how to plant and harvest. Because many had also worked for "thrifty experienced white men," planting and harvesting, the tribal farmers had gained from such experiences. Natural causes, such as adverse weather, had limited the success of the 1916 growing season, and left some without crops.[193]

The high prices were "a great inducement" for many to expand their farming operations, and almost all of the farming was being done on their respective allotments. The reimbursable loan fund was "encouraging new men to begin farming," but this meant borrowing money to do so. Many tribal farmers bought good quality machinery and horses with the loans. Others received their patents in fee for part of their lands, and either by selling or leasing these purchased good equipment. Others bought livestock. Prosperity made these loans and subsequent debts look inconsequential. Practically all of those tribal members who were interested in agriculture equipped themselves with teams and farm implements. In Lohmiller's words,

. . . in their frequent visits [presumably to the Agency Office] the [tribal] farmers pointed out the advantages of farming and improving their allotments, so that almost all the able bodied are doing some farming. About the only class it is hard to get interested is a few smart fellows who have a good education but prefer to live from the efforts of others and spend their time in belittling the efforts of the Government or employees and trying to pick flaws and find fault.[194]

Irregular seasonal work was available from the Reclamation Service, which was responsible for building and maintaining water ditches and reservoirs for irrigation, but limited appropriations had slowed progress. Other tribal members were making moccasins, belts, watch fobs, and hatbands to sell. Several others were supporting themselves by making carved diamond willow canes. Still others supplied hay and forage to settlers and livery and feed barns.[195] Lohmiller reported that two-thirds of the employees at the agency boarding school, one-fourth of the day school staff, and more than half of the agency employees were Indian, mostly tribal members. In Lohmiller's assessment, "We believe that our Indians are earning the best wages of any in the country and we have more than they can do except in extreme weather."[196]

Allotment had scattered individuals and families out on the reservation's southern tier. Most leasing was of land not in use or that an owner had been unable to develop, often "by reason of his having other lands or it being far from his home place." According to Lohmiller, some tribal families held upward of 2,000 acres, and often were unable to farm all of it. Many leases involved lands belonging to older individuals or incompetent persons. For others, there was "a tendency . . . to depend somewhat on the rentals for a living."[197] With no leases to non-Indians for more than a year in duration, surplus range not used by Indians continued to be sold. Again, the price of beef the world over was rising, and normally it would have been unprofitable to use high-priced grain to feed beef cattle, but as long as the prices held stable for grain and beef, the advantage was obvious.[198] Considerable acreage continued to be leased to sheepmen. Many grazing allotments were leased for grazing cattle and horses, and other permits were also taken out for cattle and horses in areas not being used by non-Indians. This meant that all of the reservation was in use during the 1916 season, either producing grain or stock. Again indicative of the inflated prices in the world market, increased rates for grazing cattle and horses brought more revenue to the Indian owners.[199]

Lohmiller offered a detailed summary of allotment on the Fort Peck Reservation. By 1916, 70 percent of the patent in fee land issued on the Fort Peck Reservation had been sold. In Lohmiller's assessment, many of those who received fee patents were extravagant with their spending, although these same people were acknowledged to have made advancements. Some of the proceeds were squandered, especially for "things people had done without and could not do without," but "having the oppor-

tunity to purchase them and seeing their white neighbors doing the same was a temptation for them to follow suit." Land not sold at quarterly land sales through the agency did not bring as much, but the need to convert a title into cash occasionally preempted waiting for a competitive bid. In a few cases, Indians may have received articles or property as partial payment for land, and probably did not obtain their full value in the exchange, but were unwilling to heed advice to the contrary.[200]

There was no business committee required, "as we found it was no longer necessary to have them or for the best interests of the reservation to continue them."[201] More to the point, the Indian Office found that any democracy among reservation Indians required more administrative work, and it was more convenient to proceed in the best interests of the Indians without consulting them, no matter how paternalistic and undemocratic this was.[202]

Superintendent C.B. Lohmiller remained on the job into the first months of 1917, when he re-entered the U.S. Army.[203] Supervisor Michael remained in Poplar to facilitate the arrival of the new superintendent, E.D. Mossman. ✪

1 See Donald L. Parman, "Francis Ellington Leupp (1905-1909)," *The Commissioners of Indian Affairs, 1824-1977*, Robert M. Kvasnicka and Herman J. Viola, eds. (Lincoln: University of Nebraska Press, 1979), 221-232; also see discussion of Leupp's appointment and his philosophy in Frederick E. Hoxie, *A Final Promise: The Campaign to Assimilate the Indians, 1880-1920* (Lincoln: University of Nebraska Press,1984),163; and Tom Holm, *The Great Confusion in Indian Affairs: Native Americans and Whites in the Progressive Era* (Austin: University of Texas Press, 2005), 163.

2 Francis Leupp, Commissioner of Indian Affairs (hereinafter CIA), Washington, D.C., to C.B. Lohmiller, Superintendent of Fort Peck Agency (hereinafter FPA), Poplar, Montana, January 27, 1905, FPA, Letters Received (hereinafter LR) from CIA, 1904-1908, Letterbook (hereinafter LB) vol. 1, RG75, National Archives (hereinafter NA) Rocky Mountain Region-Denver.

3 Douglas D. Martin, *Historical Report on the Fort Peck Indian Reservation, Part I: An Administrative and Social History*, Docket 184, Defendant Exhibit No. FP-I, *Fort Peck Indians v. United States*, Court of Claims, Docket 184, 102.

4 Francis Leupp, CIA, Washington, D.C., to Lohmiller, Poplar, Montana, February 24, 1905, FPA, LR from CIA, LB v. 1, RG 75, NA-Denver; CIA Annual Report (hereinafter AR) 1905: 526 as cited in Martin, *Historical Report on the Fort Peck Indian Reservation, Part I*, 103; "Major Charles B. and Mary Lohmiller," *Roosevelt County's Treasured Years* (1976), 49.

5 Ibid.

6 Annual Statistical Report, Fort Peck, 1921, 15 (Reel 52), *Superintendent's Annual Narrative and Statistical Reports From Field Jurisdictions of the Bureau of Indian Affairs, 1907-1938*, National Archives Microfilm Publication M1011 (Washington, D.C.: National Archives Trust Fund Board, NARA, 1977).

7 Leupp, CIA, Washington, D.C., to Lohmiller, Poplar, Montana, February 1, 1905, FPA, LR from CIA, LB v. 1, RG 74, NA-Denver.

8 McConnell Inspection report for July 1, 1900 cited in Martin, *Historical Report on the Fort Peck Indian Reservation, Part I*, 97.

9 Ibid.

10 CIA AR 1902; Martin, *Historical Report on the Fort Peck Indian Reservation, Part I:*, 99.

11 Leupp, CIA, Washington, D.C., to Lohmiller, Poplar, Montana, 10 February 1905, FPA, LR from CIA, LB v. 1, RG 75, NA-Denver.

12 Leupp, CIA, Washington, D.C., to Lohmiller, Poplar, Montana, 27 March 1905, FPA, LR from CIA, LB v. 1, RG 75, NA-Denver.

13 Ibid.

14 Ibid.

15 Leupp, CIA, Washington, D.C., to Lohmiller, Poplar, Montana, March 11, 1905, FPA, LR from CIA, LB v. 1, RG 75, NA-Denver; Report on Fort Peck Agency and Reservation by U.S. Indian Inspector Tinker, RG 48, quoted in Martin, *Historical Report on the Fort Peck Indian Reservation, Part I*, 104.

16 Leupp, CIA, Washington, D.C., to Superintendent of Fort Peck School, Poplar, Montana, April 15, 1905, FPA, LR from CIA, LB v. 1, RG 75, NA-Denver.

17 Leupp, CIA, Washington, D.C., to Superintendent of Fort Peck School, Poplar, Montana, April 6, 1905, FPA, LR from CIA, LB v. 1, RG 75, NA-Denver.

18 Lohmiller, Poplar, Montana, to CIA, Washington, D.C., February 1, 1905, 10204-1905, Letters Received by CIA 1881-1907 (LRCIA), RG 75, NA-Washington, D.C.; Lohmiller, Poplar, Montana, to CIA, Washington, D.C., March 2, 1905, 17417-1905, LRCIA, RG 75, NA-Washington, D.C.

19 Acting CIA, Washington, D.C., to Lohmiller, Poplar, Montana, September 20, 1905, FPA, LR from CIA, LB v. 1, RG 75, NA-Denver.

20 C.F. Larrabee, Acting CIA, Washington, D.C., to Lohmiller, Poplar, Montana, October 12, 1905, FPA, LR from CIA, LB v. 2, RG 75, NA-Denver.

21 C.F. Larrabee, Acting CIA, Washington, D.C., to Lohmiller, Poplar, Montana, April 11, 1905, FPA, LR from CIA, LB v. 1, RG 75, NA-Denver; Lohmiller, Popler, Montana, to CIA, Washington, D.C., May 3, 1905, 35299-1905, LRCIA, RG 75, NA-Washington, D.C.

22 Lohmiller, Poplar, Montana, to CIA, Washington, D.C., August 10, 1905, 64485-1905, LRCIA, RG 75, NA-Washington, D.C.

23 C.F. Larrabee, Acting CIA, Washington, D.C., to Lohmiller, Poplar, Montana, 10 May 1905, FPA, LR from CIA, LB v. 1, RG 75, NA-Denver.

24 Ibid.

25 CIA AR 1906: 260; Larrabee, Acting CIA, Washington, D.C., to Lohmiller, Poplar, Montana, May 1, 1906, FPA, LR from CIA, LB v. 2, RG 75, NA-Denver; Lohmiller, Poplar, Montana, to CIA, Washington, D.C., June 16, 1905, 47624-1905, LRCIA, RG 75, NA-Washington, D.C.

26 The 1905 inspection report as cited in Martin, *Historical Report on the Fort Peck Indian Reservation, Part I*, 105.

27 CIA AR 1905: 508.

28 CIA AR 1906: 259-260.

29 Martin, *Historical Report on the Fort Peck Indian Reservation, Part I*, 109.

30 Michael P. Malone, Richard B. Roeder, and William L. Lang, *Montana: A History in Two Centuries*, rev. ed. (Seattle: University of Washington Press, 1991), 232.

31 Congressman Joseph M. Dixon, House of Representatives, Washington, D.C., to Leupp, CIA, Washington, D.C., December 30, 1905, 30-1906, LRCIA, RG 75, NA-Washington, D.C.; see discussion of the Lone Wolf decision of the U.S. Supreme Court (187 U.S. Reports, 553) in Blue Clark, *Lone Wolf v. Hitchcock: Treaty Rights and Indian Law at the End of the Nineteenth Century* (Lincoln: University of Nebraska Press, 1994).

32 Larrabee, Acting CIA, Washington, D.C., to Lohmiller, Poplar, Montana, June 15, 1905, FPA, LR from the CIA, LB v. 2, RG 75, NA-Washington, D.C.; Larrabee, Acting CIA, Washington, D.C., to Lohimller, Poplar, Montana, July 12, 1906 [see D184 Chrono file]; W. A. Jones, CIA., Washington, D.C., to Lohmiller, Poplar, Montana, August 23, 1905, FPA, LR from CIA, LB v. 2, RG 75, NA-Washington, D.C.; Larrabee, Acting CIA, Washington, D.C., to Lohmiller, Poplar, Montana, July 18, 1905, FPA, LR from CIA, LB v. 2, RG 75, NA-Washington, D.C.; Lohmiller, Poplar, Montana, to CIA, Washington, D.C., June 23, 1906, 54152-1906, LRCIA, RG 75, NA-Washington, D.C.; Lohmiller, Poplar, to CIA, Washington, D.C., June 23, 1906, 54202-1906, LRCIA, RG 75, NA-Washington, D.C.; also see Martin, *Historical Report on the Fort Peck Indian Reservation, Part I*, 108.

33 Larrabee, Acting CIA, Washington, D.C., to Lohmiller, Poplar, Montana, July 7, 1906, FPA, LR from the CIA, LB v. 2, RG 75, NA-Denver.

34 Lohmiller, Poplar, Montana, to CIA, Washington, D.C., March 10, 1906, LRCIA, RG 75, NA-Washington, D.C.; Larrabee, Acting CIA, Washington, D.C., to Lohmiller, Poplar, Montana, July 12, 1906, FPA, LR from the CIA, LB v. 2, RG 75, NA-Denver.

35 In the documentary record of the agency, there is considerable correspondence related to appointments and quarterly reports of irregular employees and of policemen. In some positions with minimal pay, there was considerable turnover and many dismissals for various causes.

36 See discussion in Janet Ann McConnell, "The Disintegration of the Indian Estate: Indian Land Policy, 1913-1929" (Ph.D. dissertation (Marquette University, Milwaukee, Wisconsin, 1980), 1-4.

37 Burton M. Smith, "The Politics of Allotment: The Flathead Indian Reservation as a Test Case," *Pacific Northwest Quarterly* 70 (July 3, 1979): 131-140, quote on page 132.

38 Ibid.

39 "Platting Lands in the Fort Peck Reservation, Mont.; Letter from the Secretary of the Interior, transmitting a Communication from the Commissioner of Indian Affairs Relating to the Platting of lands within the Fort Peck Reservation in Montana," January 4, 1904, *House of Representative Document No.* 285, 58th Congress, 2nd S., U.S. Congressional Serial Set, Washington, D.C.; Undersigned Indians of the Fort Peck Indian Reservation, Poplar, Montana, to CIA, Washington, D.C., December 30, 1905, 651-1906, LRCIA, RG 75, NA-Washington, D.C.

40 Senator W.A. Clark, U.S. Senate, Washington, D.C., to Leupp, CIA, Washington, D.C., January 25, 1906, 8230-1906, LRCIA, RG 75, NA-Washington, D.C.

41 Endorsement, receipt of letter from Congressman J.M. Dixon, April 16, 1906, 33883-1906, LRCIA, RG 75, NA-Washington, D.C.; GLO AR 1906: 16, 28, in Docket 184 (D184), Chronological (hereinafter Chrono) File, General History 1901-1910, Fort Peck Tribal Archives, Poplar, Montana.

42 Endorsement, receipt of letter from Congressman J.M. Dixon, April 16, 1906, 33883-1906, LRCIA, RG 75, NA-Washington, D.C.; GLO AR 1906: 16, 28, in Docket 184 (D184), Chronological (Chrono) File, General

History 1901-1910, Fort Peck Tribal Archives, Poplar, Montana.

43 CIA AR 1906: 260.

44 Lohmiller, Poplar, Montana, to CIA, Washington, D.C., August 29, 1906, 76552-1906, LRCIA, RG 75, NA-Washington, D.C.; J.L. Atkinson, Physician, FPA, Poplar, Montana, to CIA, Washington, D.C., October 1, 1906, 113174-1906, LRCIA, RG 75, NA-Washington, D.C.

45 Re: Boardman lease, Lohmiller, Supt. FPA, Poplar, Montana, to CIA, Washington, D.C., August 9, 1906, 69439-1906, LRCIA, RG 75, NA-Washington, D.C.; Endorsement, F.G. Niedringhaus, St. Louis, Missouri, to CIA, Washington, D.C., October 20, 1906, 92915-1906, LRCIA, RG 75, NA-Washington, D.C.; Lohmiller, Supt. FPA, Poplar, to CIA, Washington, D.C., September 1, 1906, 78566-1906, LRCIA, RG 75, NA-Washington, D.C.; affirmative decision on Niedringhaus lease, including proceedings of Business Council, Lohmiller, Supt. FPA, Poplar, Montana, to CIA, Washington, D.C., December 3, 1906, 107755-1906, LRCIA, RG 75, NA-Washington, D.C.

46 Ibid.

47 Ibid.

48 Ibid., 260-261.

49 Larrabee, Asst. CIA, Washington, D.C., to Lohmiller, Poplar, Montana, February 2, 1907, FPA, LR from CIA, 1904-1908, LB v.2, RG 75, NA-Denver.

50 Martin, *Historical Report on the Fort Peck Indian Reservation, Part I*, 109.

51 Congressman J.M. Dixon, House of Representatives-Montana, Endorsement-Bill for the Opening of Fort Peck Reservation, request for Inspector McLaughlin to be sent to secure agreement, 33883-1906, LRCIA, RG 75, NA-Washington, D.C.; G.W. Woodruff, Acting SI, Washington, D.C., to James McLaughlin, U.S. Indian Inspector, St. Paul, Minnesota, August 17, 1907, FPA, LR from CIA, LB v. 7, RG 75, NA-Denver; 34 Stats. 1035 (Act of March 1, 1907).

52 Woodruff to McLaughlin, August 17, 1907, ibid.

53 Ibid.

54 Ibid.

55 Ibid.

56 Ibid., Minutes of Council held by James McLaughlin, U.S. Indian Inspector, with the Indians of the Fort Peck Reservation, Montana, from

September 10 to 14, 1907, inclusive, relative to allotments in severalty and opening the surplus lands to settlement, CCF 79584-1907 Fort Peck 308.1, RG 75, NA-Washington, D.C.

57 The Act of 30 May 1908, 38 Stats. 1952.

58 Martin, *Historical Report on the Fort Peck Indian Reservation, Part I*, 109-110.

59 Ibid., 109.

60 Ibid., 110.

61 SANR Fort Peck 1910: 21.

62 Douglas D. Martin, *Historical Report on the Fort Peck Indian Reservation in Montana, Part II: The Allotment Program*, Docket 184, Defendant Exhibit No. FP-II, *Fort Peck Indians v. United States*, Court of Claims, Docket 184, 8.

63 Ibid.

64 Ibid., 8-9.

65 Ibid., 8-9. Martin is presumably quoting from Downs' letter of instruction.

66 Ibid.

67 Isaac Blount, Wolf Point, Montana, to CIA, Washington, D.C., March 12, 1908, CCF 18501-1908 Fort Peck .056, RG 75, NA-Washington, D.C.

68 Lohmiller, Poplar, Montana, to CIA, Washington, D.C., March 13, 1908, CCF 18501-1908 Fort Peck .056, RG 75, NA-Washington, D.C.

69 Lohmiller, Poplar, Montana, to CIA, Washington, D.C., March 18, 1908, CCF 18501-1908 Fort Peck .056, RG 75, NA-Washington, D.C.

70 Lohmiller, Poplar, Montana, to CIA, Washington, D.C., March 23, 1908, CCF 18501-1908 Fort Peck .056, RG 75, NA-Washington, D.C.

71 Lohmiller, Poplar, Montana, to CIA, Washington, D.C. March 26, 1908, CCF 18501-1908 Fort Peck .056, RG 75, NA-Washington, D.C.

72 James Garfield, Oswego, Montana, to SI, Washington, D.C., March 29, 1908, CCF 18501-1908 Fort Peck .056, RG 75, NA-Washington, D.C.; James Garfield, Chairman, Oswego, Montana, to SI, Washington, D.C., Telegram, March 30, 1908, CCF 18501-1908 Fort Peck .056, RG 75, NA-Washington, D.C.; James A.Garfield, Chairman, Oswego, Montana, to SI, Washington, D.C., April 3, 1908, CCF 18501-1908 Fort Peck .056, RG 75, NA-Washington, D.C.

73 Larrabee, Acting CIA, Washington, D.C., to James A. Garfield, Chairman, Oswego, Montana, telegram, April 6,

1908, CCF 18501-1908 Fort Peck .056, RG 75, NA-Washington, D.C.

74 Ibid., 9-10; The Act of May 8, 1906 was also known as the Burke Act (34 Stat. 182).

75 Ibid.,10.

76 The Act of May 30, 1908, 38 Stats. 1952; Martin, *Historical Report on the Fort Peck Indian Reservation in Montana, Part II*, 10.

77 Martin, *Historical Report on the Fort Peck Indian Reservation in Montana, Part I*, 113; Martin, *Historical Report on the Fort Peck Indian Reservation in Montana, Part II*, 11-12.

78 Proceedings of a council held at Fort Peck Agency, Poplar, Montana, March 22-24, 1910, FPA Correspondence (March-April 1910), RG75, NA-Denver.

79 Valentine, CIA, Washington, D.C. to Lohmiller, Poplar, Montana, April 4, 1910, FPA Correspondence (April 1910), RG 75, NA-Denver.

80 Martin, *Historical Report on the Fort Peck Indian Reservation in Montana, Part I*, 113.

81 C.F. Larrabee, Assistant CIA, Washington, D.C., to Superintendent in Charge, FPA, Poplar, Montana, October 23, 1907, FPA, LR from CIA, v. 5, RG 75, NA-Denver; Larrabee, Acting CIA, Washington, D.C., to Superintendent, FPA, Poplar, Montana, February 6, 1908, FPA, LR from CIA, v.6, RG 75, NA-Denver.

82 Martin, *Historical Report on the Fort Peck Indian Reservation in Montana, Part II*, 11-12.

83 Martin, *Historical Report on the Fort Peck Indian Reservation in Montana, Part II*, 12-13.

84 Martin, *Historical Report on the Fort Peck Indian Reservation in Montana, Part I*, 113-114; McConnell, "The Disintegration of the Indian Estate," 51-52. See also SANR, Fort Peck 1914: 38.

85 Lohmiller, Poplar, Montana, to CIA, Washington, D.C., March 23, 1909, CCF 23394-1909 Fort Peck .056, RG 75, NA-Washington, D.C.

86 R.G. Valentine, Acting CIA, Washington, D.C., to Lohmiller, Poplar, Montana, June 2, 1909, CCF 23394-1909 Fort Peck .056, RG 75, NA-Washington, D.C.

87 Lohmiller, Poplar, Montana, to CIA, Washington, D.C., March 4, 1910, CCF 23394-1909 Fort Peck .056, RG 75, NA-Washington, D.C.

88 Lohmiller, FPA, Poplar, Montana, to CIA, Washington, D.C., Telegram, March 25, 1910, CCF 23394-1909 Fort Peck .056, RG 75, NA-Washington, D.C.; R.G. Valentine, Acting CIA, Washington, D.C., to Lohmiller, Poplar, Montana, Telegram March 16, 1910, CCR 23394-1909 Fort Peck .056, RG 75, NA-Washington, D.C.; Lohmiller, Poplar, Montana, to CIA, Washington, D.C., March 29, 1910, CCF 23394-1909 Fort Peck .056, RG 75, NA-Washington, D.C.

89 Delegation of Assiniboin [sic] Indians from Fort Peck Agency, Montana, Haliday House, Washington, D.C. [presumably a memo sent to the CIA], April 4, 1910, CCF 23394-1909 Fort Peck .056, RG 75, NA-Washington, D.C.

90 R.G. Valentine, Acting CIA, Washington, D.C., to Isaac Blount, Henry Archdale, Growing Four Times, Delegates from the Assiniboine Tribe, Washington, D.C., April 8, 1910, CCF 23394-1909 Fort Peck .056, RG 75, NA-Washington, D.C.

91 Lohmiller, Poplar, Montana, to SI, Washington, D.C., June 21, 1910, FPA Correspondence (June 1910), RG 75, NA-Denver.

92 Circular No. 279, Second Supplement, R.G. Valentine, Acting CIA, Office of Indian Affairs, Department of the Interior, Washington, D.C., to Superintendents, April 29, 1909, attachment to letter C.M. Zeitack, Superintendent of Fort Totten Agency, Fort Totten, ND, to Lohmiller, Poplar, Montana, May 18, 1909, FPA, Correspondence (May 1909), RG 75, NA-Denver; n.d., "General Instructions for the Preparation of 'Individual Indian Reports,'" with attached forms, 19377-1910, FPA, Correspondence (1910), RG 75, NA-Denver.

93 R.G. Valentine, Acting CIA, Washington, D.C., to Lohmiller, Poplar, Montana, June 8, 1910, FPA, Correspondence (June 1910), RG 75, NA-Denver; also see various letters in this file from banks explaining their terms.

94 SANR Fort Peck 1910: 2-3.

95 Ibid., 3.

96 Ibid., 8.

97 Ibid., 4; 21.

98 SANR Fort Peck 1911: 2.

99 Ibid., 4.

100 Ibid., 5-6.

101 Ibid., 8; 9.

102 Ibid., 9-10.

103 Ibid., 11-14.

104 Ibid., 18.

105 Ibid., 19.

106 Lohmiller, Poplar, Montana, to CIA, Washington, DC, November 14, 1910, CCF 91498-1910 Fort Peck .056, RG 75, NA-Washington, DC; R.G. Valentine, Acting CIA, Washington, DC, to Lohmiller, Poplar, Montana, December 2, 1910, CCF 91498 Fort Peck .056, RG 75, NA-Washington, D.C.

107 Lohmiller, Poplar, Montana, to CIA, Washington, D.C., December 28, 1911, Central Classified File (CCF), 1907-1939, 313-1912-Fort Peck .056, RG 75, NA-Washington, D.C.; Senator Joseph Dixon, U.S. Senate, Washington, D.C., to CIA, Washington, D.C., January 9, 1912, CCF 313-1912 Fort Peck .056, RG 75, NA-Washington, D.C.; H.W. Shipe, Acting Chief Industries Section, Indian Office, Washington, D.C., Memo, January 11, 1912, CCF 313-1912 Fort Peck .056, RG 75, NA-Washington, D.C.; C.F. Hauke, Acting CIA, Washington, D.C., to Indian School, Poplar, Montana, Telegram, January 13, 1912, CCF 313-1912-Fort Peck .056, RG 75, NA-Washington, D.C.; Proceedings of hearing of a Delegation from Fort Peck, January 27, 1912, [29300-1912] CFF 23394-1909 Fort Peck .056, RG 75, NA-Washington, D.C.; C.F. Hauke, Second Asst. CIA, to Charles Thompson, Rufus Ricker, Crazy Bull, Delegates of the Fort Peck Tribe [sic], Washington, D.C., January 31, 1912, [29300-1912] CFF 23394-1909 Fort Peck .056, RG 75, NA-Washington, D.C.

108 See Extract from Lohmiller's letter April 15, 1912, "Fort Peck School," Chrono File-General History, Docket 184 Collection, Fort Peck Tribal Archives, Poplar, Montana.

109 SANR Fort Peck 1912: 5.

110 Ibid., 6.

111 Ibid., 9.

112 Ibid., 10-13.

113 Ibid., 13.

114 The questions were 1) whether money had ever been appropriated to buy farming implements for Fort Peck Indians; 2) when would trust patents be issued; 3) could allotments made on poor land be exchanged for better land; 4) could grazing lands be leased for a period before trust patents were issued for same lands; 5) could absent Indians be granted allotments; 6) could a prog-

ress report be made on the costs of constructing irrigation reservoirs that were being assessed against the trust funds; 7) could no more money be spent on irrigation ditch construction at this time; 8) could allotments be made to children born since the first allotment; 9) could Indians who have their allotment crossed by the right of way of the Great Northern be given other lands; 10) when were the surplus lands to be thrown open to settlement; and 11) could there be a per capita payment of "our grazing money" to enable a start of farming and taking care of "old folks better."

115 Lohmiller, Supt. FPA, Poplar, Montana, to CIA, Washington, D.C., January 13, 1913, Chrono File-General History, Docket 184 Collection, Fort Peck Tribal Archives, Poplar, Montana; C.F. Hauke, Second Asst. CIA, Washington, D.C., to Lohmiller, Supt. FPA, Poplar, Montana, January 27, 1913, Chrono File-General History, Docket 184 Collection, Fort Peck Tribal Archives, Poplar, Montana; Lohmiller, Supt. FPA, Poplar, Montana, to CIA, Washington, D.C., February 5, 1913, Chrono File-General History, Docket 184 Collection, Fort Peck Tribal Archives, Poplar, Montana; Lohmiller, Supt. FPA, Poplar, Montana, to CIA, Washington, D.C., February 12, 1913, Chrono File-General History, Docket 184 Collection, Fort Peck Tribal Archives, Poplar, Montana; Abbott, Acting CIA, Washington, D.C., to Superintendents and Other Disbursing Officers, February 20, 1913, Chrono File-General History, Docket 184 Collection, Fort Peck Tribal Archives, Poplar, Montana; C.F. Hauke, Acting CIA, Washington, D.C., to Lohmiller, Supt. FPA, Poplar, Montana, March 1, 1913, CCF 109402-1912 Fort Peck 916, copy in Docket 184 Collection, Fort Peck Tribal Archives, Poplar, Montana; Memorandum-Fort Peck, by Charles Thompson and P.H. Hayne, Washington, DC, DC,[presumably to Indian Office] April 9, 1913, CCF 44824-1913 Fort Peck .056, RG 75, NA-Washington, DC; F.H. Abbott, Acting CIA, Washington, DC, to Charles Thompson and P.H. Hayne, Fort Peck Reservation, Washington, D.C., April 12, 1913, CCF 44824-1913 Fort Peck .056, RG 75, NA-Washington, D.C.

116 Martin, *Historical Report on the Fort Peck Indian Reservation in Montana, Part I*,114; Act of May 27, 1902 (32 Stats. 245, 275); Act of May 8, 1906 (34 Stats. 182); McConnell, "The Disintegration of the Indian Estate," 92.

117 Act of June 25, 1910 (36 Stats. 855); McConnell, *The Disintegration of the Indian Estate*, 93.

118 U.S. Office of Indian Affairs, Rules and Regulations Relating to the Issuance of Patents in Fee and Certificates of Competency and the Sale of Allotted and Inherited Indians Lands, 1910, pp. 5-6; McConnell, "The Disintegration of the Indian Estate," 93-94.

119 CIA AR, 1913, 2; McConnell, The Disintegration of the Indian Estate, 94.

120 McConnell, "The Disintegration of the Indian Estate," 101-103.

121 Proclamation July 25, 1913; Martin, *Historical Report on the Fort Peck Indian Reservation in Montana, Part I*, 114-115.

122 SANR Fort Peck 1913: 8.

123 Ibid., 10.

124 Ibid., Section 9:17; McConnell, "The Disintegration of the Indian Estate," 132.

125 One issue was the request for a per capita payment, but Sells reported that there was only a balance of $9,000, so no per capita payment could be granted at that time. The third issue was the concern about the allotment of children after the allotment rolls were closed on 30 April 1912. Sells explained that the roll had to be closed to allow the appraisal commission to commence with its phase of work. The Indian Office was constrained from any authority to open the rolls; only Congress could do this.

The fourth issue was the manner in which surplus irrigable land would be disposed of. Again, Sells stressed that the Fort Peck Allotment Act outlined the terms by which land was classified, and that the office could to do nothing but implement the law. The fifth issue focused on the exchange of allotments, especially in the case of lands on the river bank of the Missouri River, where lands were created or taken by the river, and an exchange of lands was obviously needed. With the report of the superintendent, such exchanges were certainly possible. The sixth issue was that all absent Indians be enrolled and allotted. The seventh involved the need for cash payments in lieu of rations by the old and needy, but the regulations of the Indian Office prevented such payments. The final issue concerned the manner in which government aid was made to Indians. Current efforts were underway to secure Congressional authorization for

the creation of a reimbursement fund, and should the appropriation also be approved, the outcome would be up to the legislative process. Cato Sells, CIA, Washington, D.C., to Fort Peck Delegates, Washington, D.C., February 11, 1914, FPA Correspondence file "February 1914," RG 75, NA-Denver; also see communications in CCF 11493-1914 Fort Peck .056, RG 75, NA-Washington, DC.

126 SANR Fort Peck 1914: 1.

127 Ibid., 6-7.

128 Ibid., 10.

129 Ibid., 14-15.

130 Ibid., 16.

131 Ibid., 19.

132 Ibid., 20-21.

133 Ibid., 1, 23, 25.

134 Supt. C.B. Lohmiller, FPA, Poplar, Montana, to CIA, Washington, D.C., February 16, 1915, Fort Peck Reservation Letters Folder 2 "1 February 1915-7 December 1917," General Land Office Additional Papers, Indian Reserves 1907-1955, RG 49, NA-Washington, D.C.

135 Martin, *Historical Report on the Fort Peck Indian Reservation in Montana, Part I*, 115.

136 Ibid., 115-116; John McPhaul, GLO, and C.B. Lohmiller, Supt. FPA, Poplar, Montana, to Commissioner of GLO and the CIA, Washington, D.C., August 1, 1914, FPA, Correspondence (August 1914), RG 75, NA-Denver.

137 Martin, *Historical Report on the Fort Peck Indian Reservation in Montana, Part I*, 116-117; Report of Commission to Investigate Irrigation Projects on Indian Lands (Blackfeet, Flathead, and Fort Peck), December 8, 1914, House of Representatives Document No. 1215, 63rd Cong., 3rd Sess., pp. 1-13, 39-40; Lohmiller was a member of this commission, as were the superintendents from Blackfeet and Flathead Reservations and three Superintendents of Irrigation.

138 SANR Fort Peck 1915: 3-4.

139 Ibid., 5-6.

140 Ibid., 7.

141 Ibid., 8.

142 Ibid., 10-12.

143 Ibid., 13-16.

144 Ibid., 18-19.

145 Ibid., 19, 20-21, 22-24.

146 Ibid., 24.

147 Ibid., 27, 29-30.

148 L.F. Michel, Supervisor, Indian Schools, Belcourt, North Dakota, to CIA, Washington, D.C., November 13, 1915, Chrono File, General History, 1911-1915, Docket 184 Collection, Fort Peck Tribal Archives, Poplar, Montana.

149 L.F. Michael, Supervisor, Fort Peck Inspection Report, November 9, 1915, 124183-1915 Fort Peck 300, copy in Chrono File, General History, 1911-1915, Docket 184 Collection, Fort Peck Tribal Archives, Poplar, Montana; apparently, the report of the competency report was not received by the Department until the following September (1916) according to McConnell, "The Disintegration of the Indian Estate," 120.

150 Ibid.

151 E.B. Meritt, Assistant CIA, Washington, D.C., to W.C. Pollock, Assistant Attorney for Interior Department, Washington, D.C., December 20, 1915, Correspondence File, January 1916, RG 75, NA-Denver.

152 The five conditions were: (1) curtailing development of irrigation works on the reservation; (2) modifications to enhance settlement of surplus land in reference to proposals for reassessing land values on the reservation; (3) the proposal to extend irrigable and timber allotments to minors and other tribal members over and above the 1914 legislation; (4) a proposal to amend Section 2 of the original allotment opening the reservation, relative to the sale of irrigable allotments; and (5) the necessity to provide for "old and indigent noncompetents so they may have the comforts and benefits of the proceeds of their allotments, and not have the same left to [be] financially embarrassed, and, in some instances, ungrateful heirs."

153 Lohmiller, Poplar, Montana, to CIA, Washington, D.C., January 20, 1916, Correspondence File, January 1916, RG 75, NA-Denver.

154 Meritt, Assistant CIA, Washington, D.C., to Lohmiller, Poplar, Montana, February 15, 1916, Correspondence File, February 1916, RG 75, NA-Denver.

155 Lohmiller, Fort Peck Agency, Poplar, Montana., to All Farmers, Fort Peck Agency, in various locations on the reservation, February 19, 1916, Correspondence File, February 1916, RG 75, NA-Denver.

156 Lohmiller, Poplar, Montana, to CIA, Washington, D.C., February 29, 1916, Correspondence File, February 1916, RG 75, NA-Denver; F.E. Farrell, Farmer, Box Elder District, Box Elder, Montana, to Lohmiller, Poplar, Montana, February 29, 1916, Correspondence File, February 1916, RG 75, NA-Denver; F.E. Farrell, Farmer, Brockton District, Brockton, Montana, February 29, 1916, RG 75, NA-Denver.

157 Charles R. Thompson, Gus M. Hedderick, and T.W. Mayle, Washington, D.C., to Cato Sells, CIA, Washington, D.C., March 6, 1916, Chrono File, General History 1916-1920, Docket 184 Collection, Fort Peck Tribal Archives, Poplar, Montana.

158 Ibid.

159 Ibid.

160 Lohmiller, Poplar, Montana, to CIA, Washington, D.C., May 4, 1916, FPA Correspondence folder "May 1916," RG 75, NA-Denver.

161 Ibid.

162 Lohmiller, Poplar, Montana, to CIA, Washington, D.C., May 4, 1916, FPA Correspondence, Folder "May 1916," RG 75, NA-Denver.

163 Lohmiller, Poplar, Montana, to CIA, Washington, D.C., May 5, 1916, FPA Correspondence, Folder "May 1916," RG 75, NA-Denver.

164 Lohmiller, Poplar, Montana, to CIA, Washington, D.C., May 9, 1916, FPA Correspondence, Folder "May 1916," RG 75, NA-Denver; Lohmiller, Poplar, Montana, to CIA, Washington, D.C., May 16, 1916, Folder "May 1916," RG 75, NA-Denver.

165 The Act of May 18, 1916, Stat. 123, 64th Congress, 1st Session, Chapter 125; see copy in Chrono File General History 1916-1920, Docket 184 Collection, Fort Peck Tribal Archives, Poplar, Montana.

166 Memorandum, Talk of Big Food, Circling Eagle and Henry Shields, to Supervisor L.F. Michael, representing the Committee of Twelve, on May 22, 1916, Chrono File, General History, 1916-1920, Docket 184 Collection, Fort Peck Tribal Archives, Poplar, Montana.

167 Ibid.

168 Ibid.

169 L.F. Michael, Supervisor, Poplar, Montana, to C.B. Lohmiller, Superintendent Fort Peck Indian School, Poplar, Montana, May 27, 1916, Chrono File, General History, 1916-1920, Docket 184 Collection, Fort Peck Tribal Archives, Poplar, Montana.

170 E.B. Meritt, Asst. CIA, Washington, D.C., to Supt. Lohmiller, FPA, Poplar, Montana, June 16, 1916, CCF 54092-1916 Fort Peck .053, RG 75, NA-Washington, D.C.

171 C.B. Lohmiller, Supt. FPA, Poplar, Montana, to CIA, Washington, DC, June 29, 1916, FPA Correspondence, Folder "June 1916-CIA Press Copy," RG 75, NA-Denver.

172 Regulations Covering the Leasing of Allotted Lands for Farming and Grazing Purposes, July 1, 1916, FPA, Document collection, 1912-1930. RG 75, NA-Denver.

173 Lohmiller, Supt. FPA, Poplar, Montana, to CIA, Washington, DC, July 3, 1916, FPA Correspondence, Folder "July 1916-CIA Press Copy," RG 75, NA-Denver.

174 Cato Sells, CIA, Washington, DC, to C.B. Lohmiller, Poplar, Montana, July 10, 1916, Chrono File, General History, 1916-1920, Docket 184 Collection, Fort Peck Tribal Archives, Poplar, Montana.

175 C.B. Lohmiller, Superintendent FPA, Poplar, Montana, to Cato Sells, CIA, Washington, DC, July 17, 1916, Chrono File, General History, 1916-1920, Docket 184 Collection, Fort Peck Tribal Archives, Poplar, Montana.

176 Ibid.

177 Lohmiller, Supt. FPA, Poplar, Montana, to Cato Sells, CIA, Washington, DC, July 22, 1916, Chrono File, General History, 1916-1920, Docket 184 Collection, Fort Peck Tribal Archives, Poplar, Montana; Senator Henry L. Myers, U.S. Senate, Washington, DC, to CIA, Washington, DC, August 2, 1916, Chrono File, General History, 1916-1920, Docket 184 Collection, Fort Peck Tribal Archives, Poplar, Montana.

178 SANR Fort Peck 1916: 1.

179 Ibid., 2.

180 Ibid., 3.

181 Ibid., 5.

182 Ibid., 5-6.

183 See the discussion of this denominational disposition by Steven Talbot, "Spiritual Genocide: The Denial of American Indian Religious Freedom, from Conquest to 1934," Wicazo Sa Review 21 (2) (Fall 2006): 7-42. For a discussion of Protestant moralism and shifting ideas and behaviors in the twentieth centery see Ira L. Reiss, "Social Class and Premarital Sexual Permissiveness: A Re-examination," American Sociological Review 30 (5) (October 1965): 747-756.

184 SANR, Fort Peck 1916, 6.

185 Ibid., 6, 33.

186 Ibid., 6-8; Mary Murphy, "Bootlegging Mothers and Drinking Daughters: Gender and Prohibition in Butte, Montana," *American Quarterly*, 46 no. 2 (June 1994): 174-194.

187 SANR Fort Peck 1916: 9.

188 Ibid., 10.

189 Ibid.,12-15.

190 Ibid., 16-17.

191 Ibid., 19-20.

192 Ibid., 21.

193 Ibid., 22-24.

194 Ibid., 25-26.

195 Ibid., 26, 30, 32.

196 Ibid., 33-34.

197 Ibid., 27.

198 Ibid., 28-29.

199 Ibid., 33-34.

200 Ibid., 39.

201 Ibid., 36.

202 See discussion in Holm, *The Great Confusion*, 160-161, 172-179.

203 Lohmiller was commissioned a First Lieutenant in the Quartermaster's Corps, and was promoted to Major and discharged at Camp Stewart, VA, on May 21, 1919. He reentered the Indian Service, and was Superintendent for the Omaha Agency until January 1924 when he was transferred to Northern Cheyenne Agency, and retired from the Indian Service on July 1, 1931. He died in June 1932; Obituary, "Maj. Lohmiller, Veteran Superintendent of Fort Peck Reservation, Passes Away," *Great Falls Tribune.*

~

CHAPTER 9

The Mossman Administration, 1917-1921
David R. Miller, Ph.D.

Most of the allotment work was completed by 1921, but there were still a few unallotted reservations. Hundreds of Indians had been born since the original allotment rolls were closed on their reservations and were entitled to allotments. As good land became scarce in the 1920s, the government came under increasing pressure to complete the allotment work so that the surplus reservation land could be opened to settlement. In hindsight, the slow disposal of the surplus lands actually benefited the tribes at Fort Peck. In 1921, allotment work continued, but this was also underway on a select number of other reservations.[1]

Fort Peck was touted as a place where conceivably 7,000 acres of irrigable land and 30,000 acres for dry-land farming could be made productive through leases to white settlers, assuming the infrastructure was built to support development.[2] The tribal membership of the Fort Peck Reservation not only was allotted, and its surplus lands put in the jurisdiction of the General Land Office (GLO) for entry by homesteaders, but by 1917, the membership began being subjected to forced patent in fee of their lands. Once individuals were considered competent, the patents with all of their liabilities became a reality.

Much of this land passed out of the hands of tribal members due to sales and mortgages. Since the Burke Act, enacted in 1906, however, the length of trust protection for allotments had become moot. Trust patents were issued to individuals as the temporary title to their allotments, and once a patent in fee was issued, title was bestowed upon the individual Indian, which carried with it the rights of citizenship with all of its benefits including the right to vote, but also the obligation to pay property taxes.

Observing how much land was being sold, and how many citizen Indians were being left indigent, several superintendents recommended fee patents be issued for only part of an Indian's land, which amounted to putting the person on probation. This regime was meant to give the Indian a chance with a small part of his land, which seemed better than waiting until the trust period expired and removed restrictions on all the land at once. Even if he sold the portion of his allotment and wasted the proceeds, he would still have some land left and might learn a valuable lesson.[3]

Surplus lands disposal required a number of different measures. The first efforts to dispose of the Fort Peck surplus lands were the openings in 1913 and 1917. Many whites who had come and taken land gave up and left the reservation, while others were unable to raise money to keep going. The prospects for selling land in northern Montana and western North Dakota were also poor. The variable quality of the land became an issue, leading to questions about the accuracy of the original appraisals and land classifications. Settlers could not earn enough off the land to meet the taxes, much less to pay interest they owed.[4]

The impact of these developments upon the cultures of the Assiniboine and Sioux tribes were obviously dramatic. Based on what was fundamentally misunderstood about cultural practices, giveaways, and dancing, these were topics that made it into the official records. But people also practiced ceremonies privately, and this continued until the arrival of John Collier as CIA in 1932, who lifted all restrictions on cultural practices, especially religious ones.

This was part of what was called the Progressive Era. After the Great War, it was the beginning of the Roaring Twenties. The progress visited on Indians was a mixed blessing. Among many tribal members, no longer could there be passive acceptance. Questions would be asked, and answers would be sought, and self-determination would be pursued.

E.D. Mossman's first annual report was for the fiscal year 1917, and it was much more concise than Lohmiller's. Horrified that office space at the agency was inadequate, Mossman was immediately concerned with the physical plant, and although he was satisfied with the employees, he did recommend hiring an additional stockman to help collect trespass fees.[5] Anticipating that many of the Indians of this agency would soon be considered citizens and "out of the control of the Agency," old Indian dancing was "not indulged in a great deal." Nothing else was stated about ceremonialism. Mossman's disposition was epitomized in two back-to-back statements: "(a) I recommend the policy of repression and at the same time instruction to show the uselessness of these practices. (b) No limitations are placed on returned students attending the infrequent dances."[6] Mossman noted that several denominations were operating on the reservation and that the Y.M.C.A. was "quite active." He described the churches as being "under control of Indian Preachers, and as a result religious matters are at a low ebb."[7]

Mossman noted that all his Agency Farmers could make arrests in matters involving liquor or liquor trafficking. He reported that only in the most eastern district near Culbertson was there "liquor trouble," and noted that "liquors were being introduced on the reservation by white bootleggers and Indians." He clarified that "the worst cases we have are those who have been given their citizen papers." Mossman said that while the state was scheduled to go dry, the fact that national prohibition was not expected to go into effect for one more year would only help in terms of enforcement.[8]

The day schools also were becoming community centers where many meetings were held. Community education initiatives like the

Healthy Babies campaign, coupled with efforts to improve sanitation, appeared to have a positive impact, but there was no regular sanitation inspection, and many homes still had dirt floors. Mossman particularly disliked the inefficient physical plant of the boarding school in Poplar, but otherwise the educational program met with his approval. He reported fifty children at the Presbyterian Mission school in Wolf Point, and noted the Morman Church had established a boarding and day school five miles west of Wolf Point, but had "thus far done very little"; no student count was given.[9]

Mossman thought that reservation-supported education programs would be needed for at least ten to twenty years, mostly because of drought, and incomplete homestead entry, even in the towns where there were comparatively few whites. He also emphasized the need for industrial training in the Indian schools. Moreover, there were special populations to be served, particularly orphans.

If most of the Indians ended up in the public schools, the boarding school could take whites who lived far from public schools, but whose parents were unable to educate them. The superintendent had already identified three areas of emphasis. First, he planned a building program focusing on eliminating residences with dirt floors. Second, he wanted to bring "all of the various factions of the tribe [sic]" together so that "they work together." One of his ideas for doing this was to establish a tribal newspaper. Third, he vowed to suppress the liquor traffic and encourage "a greater activity among the missionaries." To perform increased enforcement against liquor, Agency Farmers at all of the substations would be deputized as Special Officers.[10]

Farming and stock raising as the primary economic possibilities were limited by climate and environment, and making a profit required considerable time, effort, and resources. The reimbursable fund was both a boon and curse. While it was a source of cash, much of it went for farm implements, home improvements, and stock, and resulting debt was also a reality. The poor growing season in 1917 was attributed to the prolonged lack of moisture. The initial outlook had been for a good crop, but when this did not materialize, efforts were put to haying, and to plowing and putting more land under cultivation. Mossman noted that many Indians on the reservation were farming under the direction of the Agency Farmers. His immediate predecessor, Michael, had "made a special effort to have every Indian farm at least have a garden." Mossman remarked that "from what little I know concerning purchase of property for these Indians, from re-imburseable [sic] funds it has been a failure here." The superintendent did not explain this cryptic observation. His next statement was "a few of the Indians have been successful with the cattle issued," seemingly implying that loans for stock had had better results.

Mossman was full of plans. He wanted to dig as many wells as possible, and to improve fencing in many places. In Mossman's words, "there is so much allotted land [belonging to] these people that as a rule they lease their grazing allotment and farm their irrigable land." He noted that it was difficult "to utilize all our cultivable lands as there are not people enough in the country to farm them." In contrast he observed that

it is impossible to keep white men away from the reservation. I will say that on account of the cupidity of the ordinary white man he gets the better of the Indian and where the two are placed side by side on equal footing the white man will sooner or later own all the property and drives the Indian away. This can be seen in the case of the squaw men, who own more personal property on this reservation than all the Indians put together.[11]

Mossman described the former students from boarding schools as needing no assistance, and stated that "they live among the whites." He characterized them as "partly of the class called Agitators and assume to be Lawyers and Grafters representing the older people," and consequently, "many are succeeding very well."[12] The superintendent reported that there was an elected Tribal Business Committee, but he declared that "they have been distinctly a hindrance." Frustrated by their agendas, he stated that the business committee, "instead of taking up the matters that were handed them for consideration they immediately began their plan of considering matters of personal importance."[13] Mossman thought this a new-found sense of self-determination, rather than a persistence that could no longer be controlled by coercion of the Indian Service.[14]

The state of the Indian lands was not positive from Mossman's perspective. While the allotment selections had been made for the first wave of Indian children since 1913, the allotment schedule had yet to be approved by the Indian Office. The surplus lands continued to be taken up by homesteaders. Another 120,000 acres of mineral land waited to be opened. Mossman gave his assessment of the issuance of patents in fee:

Issuance of patents in fee and removal of restriction have been particularly disastrous here. These people have not been allotted long enough to have their land turned loose. A few of them have done fairly well but as a rule they have been failures.

(a) Practically all of the patented land is sold, if not sold, it is mortgaged.
(b) Probably 75 per cent of the money secured is squandered.
(d) [sic] As a rule, fair prices are received.

The inherited allotted lands were being sold

as fast as the agency could dispose of them. Non-competent Indians were being allowed to sell a portion of their lands so that they could improve what remained, especially in cases in which individuals had not inherited lands. Older people were encouraged to sell their lands so that the proceeds could support "their comfort."[15] A per capita payment of $25 was received in the spring, which they used "for the purchase of food, clothing, seed and gasoline."[238] The agency was left to administer many IIM accounts from which money was "paid out to the old people as monthly payments and to the young people for improvements on their allotments."

The Sisseton-Wahpeton people, who were tribal members of Fort Peck, petitioned the CIA on February 1, 1918 to be included with the claim made by the Santee, who had been punished in the 1860s with the suspension of their treaty rights and annuities because of the Dakota conflict of 1862. Charles Thompson's was the first signature on the document.[16]

On January 30, 1918, Superintendent Mossman forwarded a list of Indians of less than half blood who were of legal age to the Indian Office, and recommended issuance of their patent in fee to their allotment lands. In the case of fifteen others, Mossman did not recommend them, and explained why in each case. J.H. Dortch, Chief Clerk, Fort Peck Agency, wrote Mossman on February 20, asking for a report of payments these individuals had made for reclamation developments and any amounts owing. A similar report would be necessary for reimbursable fund agreements. Mossman forwarded these reports to the CIA on March 21, 1918.[17]

The superintendent wrote the CIA on May 21, 1918 to transmit the proceedings of a Delegates Council meeting on May 11, 1918. Mossman discussed the various delegates chosen and their constituencies, and once everyone was seated, they moved to act on a series of petitions for membership in the tribes, which included requests for allotment lands. All the actions taken were indicated, with the rejections numbering twice the number of acceptances, and the minutes were signed by the council members.[18]

Mossman, in his second annual report dated October 4, 1918, noted that the amount of records accumulating at the agency exceeded vault space to store them. He felt his complement of employees was adequate, but requested a stockman and two line riders "to keep the surplus stock off the reservation and collect trespass fees." The superintendent declared that "old Indian dances" were not indulged in by restricted Indians because they were limited by the Agency Police and Farmers, but he stated "as soon as these Indians are turned loose they will spend their time at the dance halls." His response was to recommend the "policy of repression with instruction." He also explained that no limitations were placed on returned students attending Indian dances, because "They are in fact the ones who arrange these dances and the ones most objectionable in arranging the objectionable features to the dance."[19]

There was no evidence to indicate that any Fort Peck tribal members considered citizen Indians were drafted to serve in World War I, but a number volunteered. The superintendent reported that many had contributed and raised about $2,000 for the Red Cross. A "work or fight order" was enforced, so that many more were working than usual. However, "about thirty Indians" were serving in the armed services. None of these were draftees "as these people are not citizens and not subject to draft." The superintendent then opined, "I think it is a vital mistake that they are not drafted." He continued: "They are receiving more from the Government for less than anyone else, and they do less than anyone else." Mossman did affirm that the Indians of the reservation were "loyal" and that

he knew of no one working against their loyalty.[20]

The threat of a smallpox epidemic was contained by "excellent work" of the agency physicians and other employees, so that not one case occurred at the boarding school, and the only casualty was one elderly woman who died "indirectly from this disease." Mossman was concerned, however, about the extreme differences of quality of housing and sanitation throughout the reservation. While more than forty new homes had been constructed since his arrival, there were still far too many homes with dirt floors. Because there was no regular sanitary inspection, he wanted to organize a systematic survey by the agency physicians, who would visit every home on the reservation to facilitate planning and set priorities. To this end, he also requested one or two field matrons, one at Oswego or Wolf Point, and the other at the agency.[21]

The school report for 1918 repeated much of what was in his 1917 report. The only new information about the mission schools was that the Mormon school had only fifteen students, and fifty were attending the Presbyterian school in Wolf Point. While he said the morals of the Indians were for the most part very good, he declared:

Their progressiveness consists in their desire to spend their subsistence in any possible manner to get rid of it. They are even anxious to give it away. If allowed to do so two-thirds of them would give every particle of their property both real and personal away before tomorrow evening. I even have to limit them as to what they give to the Red Cross.[22]

Besides his house construction program and the priorities of 1917, Mossman cited a campaign to buy milk cows and chickens for every family, but he also wanted to develop a more ambitious agricultural program so that each man would raise not only a garden, but also a field of grain.

Even though it had been another dry growing season, putting up hay was still possible and very much needed. The Agency Farmers organized farmers in their districts, but Mossman observed that many of the Indian farmers were "capable of doing their own farming if they so desire." Beyond their gardens, most men on their allotments also had small fields, and some had attempted farming on a larger scale, having two or three hundred acre crops.[23]

The Agency Farmers had become master administrators, defacto sub-agents. They did most of their instruction in the homes and fields of the Indian farmers. The Farm Chapters held regular meetings throughout the year, assisted by the superintendent. The rates of wage labor were $9 per day for a man with a four-horse team, working on the irrigation projects, and Mossman noted that even at these wages, it was difficult to get enough individuals to take the jobs.[24] Mossman applauded the current business committee, which he described as better than the former one. A per capita payment of $200 was made last fall, but he paid the old people and those declared incompetent $20 per month throughout the year, and this replaced rations. He felt that many were improvident with money, especially those who were given their payment in a lump sum.

A few of them made permanent improvements. Many of them bought horses which they did not need. A large number of them supplied themselves with provisions for the winter. Had it not been for this money I do not see how we could have cared for these people during the winter.[25]

Other changes were also occurring as more non-Indians came to live in northeastern Montana. Roosevelt County was created from the southern end of Sheridan County on February 18, 1919.[26] The new county operated initially with Mondak as a county seat, but soon a political struggle developed about whether Poplar or

Wolf Point, both on-reservation towns, would be better. Another question was which location would make administrative sense.[27]

A resolution adopted by the business committee to suspend action on applications for adoptions as the basis for tribal membership was transmitted by Mossman to the CIA on March 24, 1919. The volume of petitions was increasing and the implications for allotting these additional members influenced the moratorium.[28]

Mossman called a council among the Yankton on the eastern half of the reservation, held at the Riverside Dance Hall, on August 26, 1919, to consider the homesteaders' call for reappraisal of the lands on the Fort Peck Reservation. Sixty-seven men and three women were present, and they elected Grover Cleveland as the president, and George Washington as the secretary. Gus M. Hedderick [sic] and Alvin Warrior were elected as delegates, but no provision was made to pay to send the two delegates to Washington.[29]

Hugh L. Scott, a member of the Board of Indian Commissioners, arrived on September 5, 1919 to inspect the reservation for the Department of Interior. He noted the extent of the drought, but said that there was forage on the ranges, but "not enough stock to eat it." Flax had done particularly well on the uplands, so corn and flax were the only successful crops. The unfinished irrigation projects, in his opinion, left production levels limited. He also noted that the amount of paperwork was enormous: 850 communications from the Indian Office alone, 5,850 incoming pieces of correspondence, 725 communications to the Indian Office in Washington. The total annual outgoing correspondence was 5,500 pieces. He described Mossman as having "the interests of Indians very much at heart," and that he "has the reputation of fighting for them to the limit." He was available to tribal members, "receiving them in his office in a very sympathetic and kindly manner." He was described as "occupied very much in the office," and therefore, hiring a "bonded disbursing officer" was recommended so Mossman could "give more time to the Indians and less to their property." The number of arrests and the range of crimes were considered comparable to a white community of the same size. Scott examined the hospital facilities and services, and the school facilities and programs, making suggestions for improvements or long-range plans. He suggested that the surplus horses on the reservation be purchased for the value of their hides, and the meat then issued to those in need in the winter.[30]

Mossman submitted his annual report for 1919 on November 5, 1919. Again he repeated many of his responses, many in the very same words as in his previous reports. He was still requesting a full-time stockman and line riders, even though seasonal employees had done a fairly effective job of collecting trespass fees for the Indians. Liquor offenses had declined overall, but he noted that there were some mixed-bloods around Poplar "who bring in booze from Canada."[31]

On the health front, the influenza epidemic was being handled well.[32] Again, he recommended a systematic survey and visit to each Indian home by medical professionals.[33]

Mossman pointed out that the majority of school-age children in the Indian families on the reservation lived "out of reach of the public schools and must attend boarding schools if they go to school at all." While some returned students became "agitators and assume to be lawyers and grafters representing the old people," others acquit themselves "creditably."[34]

The superintendent reported that ten more houses had been built. In his efforts to foster reconciliation among factions with a tribal newspaper, he stated that "in accordance with the Congressional action I found it necessary to discontinue the issuance of this paper." In terms of improvements to allotments, Mossman reported a sprinkling of pretentious houses on the allotments of these Indians and "if land sales are fairly successful for two or three years we will have the old log house replaced by frame houses," and "all of these houses made through the office are plastered, back plastered and made in the best manner possible for wind, comfort and stability.[35]

The stockman and line riders had assisted the Agency Farmers in collecting the largest amount of trespass fees to date. The total amount of grazing and trespass fees was expected to total more than $30,000 for the fiscal year. It was from these funds that per capita payments were made—$100 in the previous fall and another $100 in the spring. Mossman explained that these funds were put to the credit of children and "old folks."

Appropriations legislation was enacted in February 1920, authorizing allotments to unallotted children that would be made from this point in time onward from the remaining irrigable lands.[36]

Promotional literature targeting incoming settlers in 1920 described lands on Indian reservations, and demonstrated what was being portrayed as the inevitability of land being available for sale every year. These were lands "belonging to diseased or non-competent Indians, are offered for sale at public auction, the appraised price of the tract being the minimum bid accepted." "Many of these tracts are irrigated and are desirable in every way."[37] A discussion of the development plans for the Fort Peck Indian [Reclamation] Project emphasized opportunities for securing lands:

The irrigable land is withdrawn from entry at present. When the works are completed the total cost per acre will be announced and the land opened for entry by public notice from the Secretary of the Interior. A considerable number of the Indians are receiving patent in fee to their allotments and these are being disposed of, the purchaser assuming payment of the construction of the irrigation works.[38]

E.B. Meritt, Assistant CIA, wrote to the Clerk/Recorder of Roosevelt County on August 31, 1920 to explain the rights of veterans. Congress failed to legislate that all Indians were citizens subject to state laws. But a bill was passed that provided that honorably discharged veterans might be declared citizens if they made application. The Indian Office circular No. 1587 contained the provisions of the act, effective November 8, 1919, and circular No. 1618 explained how to implement this act. Meritt also stated that the provisions of the Burke Act meant that anyone having received allotments prior to May 8, 1906 became a citizen, and was entitled to all the privileges, rights, and immunities of such status.[39]

Mossman submitted both a narrative and statistical report for the fiscal year 1920, on September 18, 1920, including considerable new information. In his discussion of "Law and Order," Mossman made the contrasting statements of having no difficulty in maintaining order on the reservation, and yet, of having insufficient officers to address the stock trespassing situation. Exasperated, he explained:

Recently I tried to get an attachment on some cattle that have been on this reservation for two years and the lawyer to whom I went said that it was a purely federal matter and could not be taken up in State Court. When I wrote to the District Attorney he stated that there was no way in which the Government could attach these cattle.[40]

Mossman's limited understanding of the cultures of the Fort Peck people was revealed in discussion about dancing that ensued from their celebrations:

The Old Indian dances are indulged in just in the

degree that we allow them. If allowed to do so these Indians would do nothing but dance. The dance itself is extremely demoralizing because when they dance they insist upon giving away property. More than one-half of these Indians if allowed to would give away all of their property. The Indian dance has a direct influence against the Church influence.

(a) I think myself these dances should be discontinued entirely. The sooner these Indians are citizens, this will be one of the principal ways in which they will disperse their property. They have an imported dance from Standing Rock called the "Owl Dance." This dance is a true half breed and like most half breeds has the bad qualities of both its white and red ancestors. It is a sort of cross between an Indian dance and white dance.

(b) The returned students are crazy about the Owl Dance and both them and the children take part in the old dances. There is really no line where you can divide them.[41]

These statements are particularly revealing. Some Indians among both tribes believed and practiced traditional ways, including both their religious and secular dances and ceremonials. Generosity, a paramount value among northern plains Indians, was reason for giving away possessions and gifts to honor family members, living or deceased, and this often was done at public events where powwow dancing was performed. The social dance, the Owl Dance or Kahomani, were often done in secret in isolated places where boys, girls, men, and women danced all night, beyond the control of the superintendent, the farmers, and the agency police. Mossman could not control these activities, which he considered a threat to weaning the reservation population away from their cultures.

Mossman reported that the Roman Catholics

were "quite active on the reservation," and had established "five or six congregations." The Presbyterians had "about the same number of congregations," and the Mormons were "very active during the last year or so." Mossman declared, "The Mission work might well be pursued with greater vigor by all the churches concerned."[42] Among the Fort Peck population there were many Christians, and several of the congregations were longstanding.

Mossman described the operation of the Court of Indian Offenses:

We have two Judges, one for the Assiniboines and one for the Yanktons. The Yankton Judge has his court at Poplar and the Assiniboine has his court in Wolf Point. Their decisions are generally very fair and if anything are like more courts, too lenient to the offender.[43]

Stating that the liquor traffic among the Indians was "very well in hand," Mossman declared that the "Bootleggers haul it from Canada and Moonshiners make it on the South Side of the Missouri River."[43] In his opinion, the state authorities should leave enforcement of liquor laws on the reservation to federal authorities. Saying that the liquor service needed to be reorganized, Mossman reported:

About the only legislation we would like would be a law so that we could convict [owners of] a car or other vehicles of introduction if we secure it on the reservation with booze in it. At present the District Attorney wants us to prove that the car came on the reservation with booze in it. This of course is next to impossible.

Mossman observed that while state Prohibition had put the saloons out of business and made it more difficult for the Indians to procure booze, the benefits from national

Prohibition had not been forthcoming because state officers consumed alcohol themselves.[44] At another place in his report, he declared: "I have practically eliminated booze as an influence among the people. Every assistance possible is given the missionaries to improve them."[45]

Having ducked the flu epidemic, Mossman reported health conditions as excellent. A complete medical inspection of all residences was incomplete, since there were only two physicians to serve the entire reservation population.[46]

Coordination between the reservation and public schools was described as "excellent." The statistical report for 1920 indicated that 173 non-contract Indian students were attending public schools.[47] Sixty-two children were reported enrolled in seven different boarding schools away from the reservation.[48]

Mossman was proud that another ten homes had been built under his watch, and numerous barns erected, many wells dug, and a lot of new fencing accomplished. However, when it came to discussing the agricultural program, Mossman candidly explained, "We have not progressed much in farming because we have had four [seasons of] failures." He noted that the agency crop of alfalfa was mostly winter killed, and he observed "the Indians who farm mostly on the gumbo lands along the river had poor crops with few exceptions." Poor weather, shortage of rain, and "a plague" of grasshoppers were all noted. The hay crop was fairly good, with enough for the farmers' use and for sale. Mossman had made every effort to induce the able-bodied to live on their own lands, and so far, most of them did. Many of the farmers continued to participate in the farm chapter meetings. While most of the families had plenty of horses, nearly all purchased under the reimbursable fund were dead, and practically all were geldings. Mossman insightfully observed that the reimbursable fund was unsatisfactory, because "not enough care was exercised in what was purchased for the Indians," and they were expected to repay the loans. It was not clear from these statements if individuals just refused to pay or fell behind.

Most individuals and families had enough horses, although many horses had died the previous winter. Animals apparently had to be fed for seven months out of the year. Plenty of feed had been put up for the coming winter, and despite the setbacks, stock was increasing. Few had improved their grazing allotments, choosing instead to live on their forty-acre irrigation allotments close to the Missouri River. Mossman commented on the pattern of land use: "As a rule we rent these grazing allotments without reference to the physical condition of the lessor. . . . There is more land included in the allotments than the Indians can farm and we can lease also. Much of the land remains idle."[49] The tribal trust lands were scattered about, some in very small parcels, and fees for most of the grazing on this land were paid directly to the allottees. Mossman noted that this was the only way to "dispose of such grazing fees." He stated: "We have no way in which to know whether a piece of land is still vacant or [is entered and] homesteaded."[50]

The more experienced and educated individuals were, the better their chances of succeeding as farmers, and because of the difficult climate, diversification was recommended. According to Mossman, the Agency Farmers stood ready to help. The County Agricultural Extension Agent and the agricultural teacher of the Poplar Public School assisted with the winter meetings of the farmers' organization. Sunflowers were tested as a crop during the last growing season.[51]

Indian fairs had been held since 1909, and in 1913, the Indian Fair was combined with the County Fair. A combined fair allowed Indians and non-Indians to compete and be judged "on an equal basis," and consequently, "a very large portion of the premiums and prizes" were

secured by tribal members. The Indians owned the fairgrounds, located in American Legion Park in Poplar, on the north side of the Poplar River, and therefore they paid no admission fee. Mossman was quick to point out how much tribal members enjoyed the fair.[52]

Mossman was clearly frustrated about whether tribal members took advantage of wage labor when it was available. He noted that there were plenty of opportunities for men locally, either as farmhands or for the Great Northern Railway as section men. He commented: "These Indians need no assistance in finding work. The difficulty is to get them to work when the employment is found."[53]

Allotments were issued to children at birth. Mossman stated again that he had no disposition on the amount of surplus lands left, either entered for homesteads or left untaken. Most startling, however, was Mossman's assessment of land sales. In his estimation, 90 percent of the patented land had been sold, and 90 percent of the proceeds of these sales had been squandered. Mossman indicated he had regularized the sale of surplus lands once a year in June, and inherited lands once a month, usually on the 26th. He noted that those who sold through his office got five times "the actual benefit from their money as those getting patents in fee," and the houses and improvements upon allotments all had come from their land sale monies. The heirship work was reported as current due to a recent visit from an inheritance examiner.[54]

Mossman, in begrudging terms, noted that the nine members of the business council were fairly intelligent and reliable: "Generally I do not think much of the idea [having a business council], but these men have done very well."[55]

The management of the Individual Indian Money accounts was, Mossman stated, "the most difficult and unsatisfactory feature of our work." While the agency office was constantly striving to get the "greatest benefit possible for the Indian from his money," efforts to give individuals "the great possible amount of liberty in the use of his money" often contradicted the former impulse. "There is a continuous question before us as to whether we are placing too much restriction on his funds. As a very general rule I think we err on the side of too much privilege."[56]

U.S. Indian Inspector John W. Bale arrived to inspect Fort Peck Agency on September 22, 1920, which he reported to the CIA on October 2. He was particularly charged with investigating the conduct of Isaac Blount, the temporary Agency Farmer at the Frazer Sub-station. He confirmed Mossman's statements that drought conditions were "exceedingly discouraging" to anyone trying to make a living from agriculture on the reservation, and consequently, "the disease of discouragement [when it] seizes a white home-steader and lessee you can expect very little from the Indian." The inspector focused on the physical plant of the boarding school, its water sources and waste disposal, the curriculum, and the amount of food grown in the school's gardens and fields. Bale praised the public schools and their facilities, saying most of the southern tier was well served except for the area east of the Brockton Day School.[57]

Meritt wrote to Mossman about several paragraphs in the report. The inspector made a series of assessments about what would be needed for "profitable farming." The issue of larger scale farming was raised, but this would only be possible with tractors. Many of the lessees had these more advanced and expensive tools. Self-sufficient farming would not yield cash crops. The inspector noted that there was still a vast area of the reservation suitable for agriculture. Meritt reacted in an opposite manner in his instructions to Mossman: "You should do everything you can to counter-act the tractor idea as applied to the small farming units operated by the

average Indian." The implications were obvious. Without any effective means of capitalizing more advanced machinery purchases, the ability of Indian heads of family to bear debt loads varied. The negative impact of the use of the reimbursable fund attested to this situation. While forbidding the use of tractors on small parcels of land, Meritt commended Mossman for encouraging the Indians to farm more land each year. Meritt also asked if the same intensity of effort devoted to breeding horses might be directed to other livestock. The Assistant CIA asked Mossman to report on whether he was doing everything possible to increase the numbers both of horses and cattle.[58]

The presidential election in November of 1920 sent Republican Warren G. Harding to the White House. He appointed Albert B. Fall Secretary of the Interior and Charles H. Burke CIA.

Early in 1921, the Indian Office reported that it had received an expression of "the desire of certain Indians" at Fort Peck to have a "Tribal Council." Mossman explained that "what they mean by a Tribal Council is to call all the Indians of the reservation together to Council." Based on the information he had, he concluded,

With reference to reasons given for wanting this Council called, the Indians give two reasons. The first is that there is a petition in circulation in the Riverside district which [sic] should be considered by a tribal council.

The second reason is 'that there is a question as to the integrity of office vested in the present administration.'

Mossman explained in a letter of February 2, 1921 that the Indians from the Poplar District were requesting the council, which they expected to be held in the Poplar dancehall in the center of the reservation. But Mossman declared that there was "no necessity whatever for a tribal council at this time." He noted that the committee had "waited on me this afternoon and I told them I would not approve their request to the Commissioner for the following reasons." The first point was that no necessity existed. Secondly, to cut the costs of traveling, time, and effort, Mossman had allowed the Indians to have district councils "whenever they wished and each council can appeal to me directly or to their Business Committee or to the Commissioner." The Poplar District had held four or five council meetings in the last month. The third reason was that "already too many councils [were operating] on the reservation and the Indians are demoralizing instead of advancing and they had better get to work."

The superintendent was aware of what had been the subject of a petition in the Riverside District, and this in no way adversely affected the Poplar District population. The fifth point was the challenge to the superintendent's integrity, to which he said that tribal members were welcome to call for an investigation, but he would not be intimidated and had nothing to hide. His sixth reason was that a General Council in midwinter was simply "preposterous." Mossman suggested that "fellows who want this Council know this and expect only a few of the agitators from the outlying districts to join them when they will have a majority at the council and they can do as much mischief as they desire." Mossman's final point was:

I am opposed very generally to the holding of councils and especially to a general council for as a very general rule the better Indians stay at home rather than go to one of these councils and squabble. The man with the loudest mouth secures the widest hearing and nothing good seldom comes from these councils.

Furthermore, I consider an Indian Council a very poor civilizer. For these reasons I have

disapproved the request of these men for a General Tribal Council and also for the reason that if they feel they have anything which I cannot take up honestly with them, they can appeal directly to the Commissioner of Indian Affairs or they can ask me to call their elected Tribal Council of nine men in session at any time which I will do.

Certainly the degree to which Mossman's influence might be waning was evident.[59]

Mossman anxiously wrote to CIA Charles M. Burke, on April 29, 1921, that four tribal members had left the reservation that morning for Washington. He explained, "it is only fair to the Indian Office and to myself that the Office should know what manner of people these men are." Before engaging in detailed discussion, the superintendent stated,

These men are citizen Indians. As far as I know all of them have received everything that is coming to them in this office. I do not know why they are going to Washington except from reports as they of course have said nothing to me about going to Washington. They have been trying to secure a lawyer to go to Washington with them for the purpose of securing a change in administration here and for purpose of reinstating a former Superintendent who was once relieved here.

These men were I think all of them instrumental in the investigation which relieved [sic] the former Superintendent who they are now trying to reinstate. Charles Thompson was particularly active in this matter.

Mossman then made disparaging comments about citizenship, but suggested that the kind of work they were engaged in doing was not "responsibility," but "license." He described the four embarked for Washington as responsible for "practically all the trouble we have on this reservation." Even if they were citizens, they still attend the Indian dances seeking audiences, as "they are plausible talkers." Reportedly, "their ordinary method is to get up at the Indian dance where citizen Indians have no business to be and make inflammatory speeches against anyone in general," and "one of their most regular lines of talk is to lay stress on the idea that they are 'fighting for their people.'" Mossman noted that these were the same kind and often only kind of Indians who appeared before congressional committees. He noted that often misrepresentations were made. One was the circulation of petitions proposing to reinstate C.B. Lohmiller, by the same group that had engineered his demise. Another was alleging that with the change in the superintendent, all monies in the office to individuals' credit would be paid out immediately, which was false. Another group supported his administration and circulated a petition to that effect with about 500 names collected. The "agitators" personally attacked Mossman's private financial reputation, but as they fell short of proceeding with criminal libel charges in state courts, he was without any recourse. Mossman discussed his frustrations:

I have been trying to get the Indians to farm this spring and to do this I am getting ready to give them a payment as soon as we can secure the money, requisition for which was made several weeks ago. These men who are supposed to have gone to Washington have been travelling back and forth on the reservation all winter trying to stir up opposition and as a matter of fact in the district where they live practically no farming has been done.

While none of these men dance at Indian dances themselves, they belong to that class of men who are always on a committee to come see if they can have an Indian dance at one of the Dance Halls. These Indian dances are to my mind one of the greatest bars to progress among the Indians. I am unable to secure work from the Indians when these dances are being held.

These men belong to that class of citizens who never do any work but after spending their own properties they quarrel to secure all of their children's moneys and properties and then to live upon the credulity of the ignorant Indians. To do this they must resort to every imaginary subterfuge. They assist as lawyers in preparing applications for patent in fees. They assist as lawyers in presenting cases of Indians to the office to secure money from their accounts. They assist as lawyers in representing Indians before regular lawyers as interpreters and advisors.

They desire a council called ordinarily about once a week where they orate to the tribe on the wrongs that are being done to "my people." I have been trying for two or three weeks to get the Indians of the district in which these people live to get to work on their farms but I have secured meagre results. In the district where none of these men live I have had a report from my field clerk that all Indians are plowing and seeding and that everyone was busy.

Mossman clarified that only one of the four men presumably on the train to Washington did any farming. They had secured funds to get to Washington, under a presumption that once they arrived, the government would pay their way back. In the opinion of the superintendent, until such individuals were told to go home and work instead of being allowed to present "such stuff," "we can never have a sense of security in the field which we must have if we are to secure any amount of efficiency." With all of this information as a preface, Mossman discussed in detail the political and financial careers of Charles Thompson, Martin Mitchell, Arthur Fourstar, and James Archdale.[60]

Obviously, such a communication is revealing on a number of levels. Mossman did not want opposition to the agenda of the Indian Office, which was to promote conformity among its charges, who were expected to live productive lives by taking responsibility for supporting their families. The superintendent and the growing bureaucratic office of clerks armed with forms, procedures, and regulations were the paternalistic authority in all matters defined by their jurisdiction within the reservation.

In contrast to the official aspects of the public sphere, no matter how interfering, Indian life at Fort Peck was still in many ways independent of the superintendent and his underlings. Dances clearly were an arena where many convergences occurred. The young politicians were not without their personal histories as individuals, and drew on their educations and experiences to serve not only their own interests, but also those of their relatives and associates. Amid Mossman's cynicism, many political and cultural dynamics were revealed, showing the degrees of frustration many had with the imposed order expected by the U.S. government. In contrast, the traditional political orders were being transformed by the generations of educated youth—"the school boys and school girls"—to face the entanglements that came with allotments, reimbursable fund debts, IMM accounts, competency, and citizenship. The constraints and opportunities of a changed economic order brought hardships with few rewards.

By the time Mossman submitted his annual report on July 1, 1921, for the fiscal year 1921, his effectiveness was waning, but he presented the report to demonstrate his competence. Still misunderstanding the most basic elements of Assiniboine and Dakota cultures, Mossman stated:

The Indian dances are the bane of the lives of myself and the [Agency] farmers. Its bad features are that it takes the Indian away from his home. It is a direct cause of the give away practice among the Indians. It is inimical to the church work among the Indians.

(a) These dances should be absolutely prohibited. There is nothing good about them. There is much that is bad. However, we should give the Indian something in their stead when we stop the dances entirely. . . . The owl dance is still an evil we have not been able to successfully combat.

(b) The young people are crazy about the Owl dance which is a mixture of the white dance and the Indian dance combining the objectionable features of both.[61]

The public giveaways to honor individuals demonstrated generosity and respect, and symbolized the importance of coming to the aid of both family and tribal members in need. The urgent pressures to inculcate individualism often were viewed in terms of what was being devalued. The importance of relatives, families, friends, and supporters demonstrated essential Siouan values. Allotment and its implementation, as well as its corollary policies designed to detach individuals from the influence of the tribe, were working their damaging effects upon the people of the Fort Peck Reservation, and all of this was intentional. Non-Indians believed Indian dancing led to debauchery, drinking, and uncontrolled actions they viewed as savage and primitive. All of this was considered improvident, dilatory, and distracting from self-reliance.

Again, Mossman repeated much verbatim from previous reports. He was still just as frustrated that state authorities would not enforce certain laws, especially the state prohibition violations by non-citizen Indians. While the judges of the Indian court continued to render "fair" decisions, Mossman noted, ". . . like most courts they err if at all in favor of the accused."

He expressed his preference that this court only deal with criminal matters, and leave all civil matters to the Agency Farmers and the superintendent. Health matters remained unchanged. Cooperation between the public schools and the Indians remained "excellent."[62] Returned students were reported "if anything in worse shape than the other Indians as they have secured patents and dissipated their property."[63]

Mossman's program of development was again hindered by a poor agricultural year, although the previous winter had been considered "extremely mild." He took credit for more houses being built, although he did not indicate how many. Over 100 wells had been dug or drilled, and fencing was done with wire, again in more plentiful supply. Nearly all the Indians were living on their lands. Mossman reported that much of land remained idle after the leasing of the grazing allotments, and attempted to get as many of the tribal member farmers to farm as much of the remaining lands as he could. The effectiveness of the irrigation works "amounted to little, because there was no water storage capacity constructed for the projects, the one exception being the Little Porcupine unit, but because of its size only a limited number of acres received water."[64] Some Indians were contracted to work on the roads.[65]

Mossman closed his report with his opinion that in 90 percent of cases where patents in fee were issued, it has been a "failure" as far as "benefiting the Indian concerned." He noted that "nearly all [patents in fee] is either sold or mortgaged," and of the proceeds "nearly all is squandered." A further pattern was developing, in his observation: "During the last year patented land has had to be practically given away as there was no money with which to buy it. Generally a big store bill, a little cash[,] a little due bill on some store and a few worthless horses tell the sordid story."[66]

Mossman's administration had run its course. The Harding Administration was ready to put its stamp upon the Office of Indian Affairs. ✹

1 Similar efforts were underway on the Gila River, Umatilla, Lower Brule, Cheyenne River, Hoopa Valley, Torres-Martinez, Blackfeet, Flathead, and Salt River reservations. Janet Ann McConnell, "The Disintegration of the Indian Estate: Indian Land Policy, 1913-1929" (Ph.D. dissertation, Marquette University, Milwaukee, 1980), 203-205, chapter 6, footnote 3; CIA AR 1921: 22, 25; CIA AR 1922: 14-15; SI AR 1921: 25; SI AR 1922:48.

2 McConnell, "The Disintegration of the Indian Estate," 171-172, chapter 5, footnote 2; U.S. Department of Interior, Report on the Cultivation of the Public Domain and Indian Lands, S.Doc. 127, 65th Congress 2nd Session, 1917, serial 7329 (Washington, D.C.: Government Printing Office, 1917).

3 Statistical and Narrative Report [hereinafter cited as "SANR"], Fort Peck, 1915: 29; McDonnell, "The Disintegration of the Indian Estate," 136-137, chapter 3, footnote 68.

4 McConnell, "The Disintegration of the Indian Estate," chapter 7, footnote 39; SANR, Fort Peck, 1926, section 5 (Reel 53); SANR, Fort Hall, 1924, section 6 (Reel 49); "Report on the Chippewa, Turtle Mountain, North Dakota," September 5, 1921, p. 7, BIC, Special Reports II; SANR, Cheyenne River, 1923, p. 19 (Reel 17).

5 SANR Fort Peck 1917: 1.

6 Ibid.

7 Ibid., 2.

8 Ibid.

9 Ibid., 3, 6.

10 Ibid., 6, 7.

11 Ibid., 7, 9.

12 Ibid., 5.

13 Ibid.

14 Ibid.

15 Ibid., 10-11.

16 Charles Thompson, et. al, Poplar, Montana, to CIA, Washington, D.C., February 1, 1918, CCF 13987-1918 Fort Peck .056, RG 75, Washington, D.C.

17 E.D. Mossman, Superintendent FPA, Poplar, Montana, to CIA, Washington, D.C., 20 January 20, 1918, Fort Peck Agency [hereinafter cited as "FPA"] Correspondence-"February-March 1918," RG 75, NA-Denver; J.H. Dortch, Chief Clerk, FPA, Poplar, Montana, to Mossman, Poplar, Montana, February 20, 1918, FPA Correspondence "February-March 1918," RG 75,

NA-Denver; Superintendent FPA, Poplar, Montana, to CIA, Washington, D.C., March 21, 1918, FPA Correspondence "February-March 1918," RG 75, National Archives and Records Administration [hereinafter cited as NARA], Rocky Mountain Region—Denver.

18 Mossman, FPA, Poplar, Montana, to CIA, Washington, D.C., May 21, 1918, FPA Correspondence, "May 1918," RG 75, NA-Denver.

19 SANR Fort Peck 1918, 2-3.

20 Ibid., 3.

21 Ibid., 3-5.

22 Ibid., 5-6.

23 Ibid., 7-8.

24 Ibid., 10-11.

25 Ibid., 11-12.

26 Leota Hoye, ed., Roosevelt County's Treasured Years (Great Falls: Blue Print and Letter Company, 1976), 64.

27 Ibid., 66-69.

28 Mossman, FPA, Poplar, Montana, to CIA, Washington, D.C., March 24, 1919, CCF 39418-1919 Fort Peck .053, copy in General History, Chrono folder "1915-1920," Docket 184 Collection, Fort Peck Tribal Archives, Poplar, Montana.

29 Proceedings of Council, Riverside Dance Hall, August 26, 1919, CCF 85249-1919 Fort Peck .054, RG 75, Washington, D.C..; copy in General History, Chrono folder "1915-1920," Docket 184 Collection, Fort Peck Tribal Archives, Poplar, Montana.

30 Hugh L. Scott, BIC, Poplar, Montana, to SI, Washington, D.C., September 16, 1919, General History, Chrono folder "1915-1920," Docket 184 Collection, Fort Peck Tribal Archives, Poplar, Montana.

31 SANR Fort Peck 1919: 2-3, M1011 Superintendent's Annual Narrative and Statistical Reports from Field Jurisdictions of the Bureau of Indian Affairs, 1907-1938, RG 75, NARA Washington, DC.

32 Ibid., 3.

33 Ibid., 3-4.

34 Ibid., 4-7.

35 Ibid., 7-9.

36 The Act of August 1, 1914 (38 Stats. 593), the Fort Peck Allotment Act, the Act of May 30, 1908 (35 Stats. 558); see the Act of February 14, 1920 (41 Stats. 408).

37 Untitled, p. 24, General History, Chrono folder "1920-1925," Docket 184 Collection, Fort Peck Tribal Archives, Poplar, Montana.

38 Promotional publication, no title page given, pp. 54-55, in General History, Chrono folder "1920-1925," Docket 184 Collection, Fort Peck Tribal Archives, Poplar, Montana.

39 E.B. Meritt, Assistant CIA, Washington, D.C., to John C. Dwyer, Clerk/Recorder [Roosevelt County], Mondak, Montana, August 31, 1920, General History, Chrono folder "1920-1925," Docket 184 Collection, Fort Peck Tribal Archives, Poplar, Montana.

40 SANR Fort Peck 1920: 1.

41 Ibid., 1-2.

42 Ibid., 2.

43 Ibid.

44 Ibid. 3.

45 Ibid., 7.

46 Ibid., 4-5.

47 SANR Fort Peck, Statistical report 1920: 10.

48 Ibid., 9.

49 SANR Fort Peck Narrative Report 1920: 7-9.

50 Ibid., 11.

51 Ibid., 10.

52 Ibid.

53 Ibid., 11-12.

54 Ibid., 13.

55 Ibid., 12.

56 Ibid., 13.

57 John W. Bale, Inspector, FPA, Poplar, Montana, to Cato Sells, CIA, Washington, D.C., October 2, 1920, CCF 85491-1920 Fort Peck [decimal designation not clear on the copy], copy in General History, Chrono folder "1920-1925," Docket 184 Collection, Fort Peck Tribal Archives, Poplar, Montana.

58 Meritt, Washington, D.C., to Mossman, FPA, Poplar, Montana, October 28, 1920, General History, Chrono folder "1920-1925," Docket 184 Collection, Fort Peck Tribal Archives, Poplar, Montana.

59 Mossman, FPA, Poplar, Montana, to CIA, Washington, D.C., February 2, 1921, CCF 7165-1921 Fort Peck .054, copy in General History, Chrono folder "1920-1925," Docket 184 Collection, Fort Peck Tribal Archives, Poplar, Montana.

60 Mossman, FPA, Poplar, Montana, to
    Charles H. Burke, CIA, Washington,
    D.C., April 20, 1921, CCF 37005-1921
    Fort Peck .053, RG 75, NA-Washington,
    D.C.; also copy in General History,
    Chrono folder "1920-1925," Docket 184
    Collection, Fort Peck Tribal Archives,
    Poplar, Montana.

61 SANR Fort Peck 1921: 1.

62 Ibid., 2-3, 4, 5.

63 Ibid., 5.

64 Ibid., 6.

65 Ibid.

66 Ibid., 10.

~

CHAPTER 10

The Roaring Twenties, the Great Depression, and the Indian New Deal, 1921-1935

David R. Miller, Ph.D.

Over the next fourteen years, the peoples at Fort Peck confronted significant choices and changes. The handful of veterans from the Great War discovered the agricultural boom of the war years had passed. Prohibition had unfolded, as did universal citizenship. The Roaring Twenties did not bring prosperity for the Indians at Fort Peck Reservation, but rather foreshadowed the Great Depression. True to the metaphor, Indians were the miner's canary for the nation.

The "progressive era" that characterized the first two decades of the twentieth century ended as Wilsonian idealism was dismissed as insufficiently pragmatic. In its place, the Republican Party (Grand Old Party, or GOP) imposed an aloof and elite politic through the administrations of Presidents Harding, Coolidge, and Hoover, relegating administration of reservations to managers and clerks. Indian affairs had become an administrative problem, increasingly entangled by the technicality of laws and regulations, and a bureaucracy burgeoned to handle it. Machinations around land and its uses continued. The agenda of incorporation managed all aspects of Indian life.[1]

In the period leading to the 1932 election of Franklin Delano Roosevelt, superintendents came and went at the Fort Peck School and Agency. The specific reasons for this were connected to the fact that returned students and their contemporaries wanted to play prominent political roles. Tribal members sought greater roles in decision-making, often through involvement in the general councils and the business council.

By 1924, Indian citizenship was universal. The implications were broad and deep, especially when coupled with the wide acceptance of patents in fee, which meant eligibility for taxation.

The onset of the Great Depression was more gradual on Fort Peck than in the rest of the country, since the region already was economically depressed. The Democratic administration of FDR brought some pragmatic relief to the rural regions of the upper Midwest. The tribal members of the Fort Peck Tribes had mixed reactions to the New Deal, and specifically to the Indian New Deal offered by CIA John Collier. The Fort Peck Tribes sought their own relationship with the Indian Office and the rest of the federal government. Tensions within the population became more evident.

In Mossman's last months as superintendent, his detractors remained persistent. Samuel Conger, Chairman, and Meade Steele, Secretary, requested permission on January 31, 1921 to hold a General Tribal Council, based on a petition circulated in the Riverside District, and problems with the superintendent. Mossman disapproved, but the request was forwarded to E.B. Merritt, Assistant CIA.[2] Mossman, writing the Indian Office in a report dated February 2, 1921, described the people wanting the council as "Indians of the Poplar District, which they expect to be in the Poplar District at the Dance Hall which is at the center of the reservation." Mossman said there was no reason for a council at that time, and that he told the committee that visited him that afternoon that he had not approved their request. Besides believing the council to be unnecessary, Mossman wished to reduce excessive travelling. District councils were becoming time-consuming, with the Poplar District having already had five the previous month. The superintendent declared there had already been too many councils, because "the Indians are demoralizing instead of advancing," this was the time to "get up their wood and posts for spring work," and there were Agency Farmer organization meetings to attend in each district. Mossman welcomed any investigation of his official actions.

I consider an Indian Council a very poor civilizer. For these reasons I have disapproved the request of these men for a General Tribal Council and also for the reason that if they feel they have anything which I cannot take up honestly with them, they can appeal directly to the Commissioner of Indian Affairs or they can ask me to call their elected Tribal Council of nine men in session at any time which I will do.[3]

Merritt wrote to Meade Steele through the superintendent on February 15, 1921, to indicate that the requested authority for a General Tribal Council for the reasons set forth was not granted. The Assistant CIA suggested that he "take up with your Superintendent" a more suitable time, and welcomed any communications. This certainly signalled the office that Mossman had lost the confidence of a portion of the population at Fort Peck.[4]

Superintendent James B. Kitch's appointment as superintendent was effective on July 1, 1921. As Kitch arrived, the Indian Bureau, as the Indian Office was then called, sought an assessment of heightened political activism among tribal members. A report titled "Fort Peck Indian Agency, Montana: Unrest Among the Indians," written by Fred C. Morgan, Special Supervisor, was received by the Indian Bureau on November 7, 1921. Morgan described "a great deal of unrest among the Indians particularly the mixed bloods who, in my judgement, desire to fill all field positions with members of their own tribe, particularly themselves." This early manifestation of Indian preferential hiring included efforts to see Indians in the position of Agency Farmer in particular, since Indians already held most agency positions. James A. Garfield had been temporarily hired to fill the position of Agency Farmer in the Frazer district, but Morgan asserted that Garfield's minimal knowledge of English was a serious impediment. Morgan asserted that the appointment "of such [an] unqualified men to such responsible positions smacks in my judgement of Indian politics and can not but end disastrously."

Morgan was investigating charges made by Arthur Four Star, James Archdale, Charley Thompson, and Martin Mitchell against the Wolf Point Sub-Agency Farmer Simon B. Kirk, but reported that he found not one person willing to substantiate the charges. He said that Wolf Point had a reputation for harboring "a large number of bootleggers." Since Kirk had been "very efficient in apprehending and prosecuting bootleggers," he was "inclined to believe that some of the white people living in the vicinity of Wolf Point have influenced the Indians to request Mr. Kirk's removal." Morgan, upon questioning the complainants, was not able to ascertain specific incidents of misconduct, other than they wanted Kirk dismissed. They seemed to think that he was a relative of Mossman's, and "also for the reason that he was an Indian brought from the Sisseton country [that] they objected to his filling the position, or having any authority over them."

The individuals holding the respective Agency Farmer positions were Burton M. Roth in Poplar, and in Box Elder (west of Brockton), Alvin (incorrectly identified in the report as "Albert") Warrior. The complaints stated that these men were "inefficient and careless of the welfare of the Indians in their districts," which Morgan also found untrue. Morgan found Alvin Warrior, an educated full-blood tribal member, to be "absolutely honest and interested in his work." Morgan concluded that both men appeared loyal to Mossman, which may have been the real basis of the complaints. Consequently, Kitch was cleared of any improprieties.[5]

Prior to Morgan's departure, James Archdale, Charles Thompson, Arthur Four Star, Gus Hedderich, and others presented him further

complaints—that homesteaders were often grazing stock free of charge on the reservation, and that they objected to the introduction of sheep grazing on the reservation.[6] Income from stock raisers was being eclipsed by the rising cost of living and the demands of the cash economy. Economic independence continued to be elusive. In 1922, Kitch changed the leasing system to "an exclusive per acre system." Consequently, he was able to report for the 1921-22 fiscal year that receipts for leasing had increased 300 percent, to a total of $153,956.19. Kitch over the next two years implemented an "intensive 'industrial' [agricultural] program" to increase productivity among the farm families.[7]

At the end of October 1921, the Indian Welfare Association, with J.W. Culbertson, Jr. as president, and G.H. Conner as secretary, forwarded a petition through Kitch to the CIA. Aware that $265,597.88 had accrued in the U.S. Treasury trust accounts from sale of surplus lands, and stating that "the stringency in money and the extreme low market prices in livestock and can not sell same, the Indians are unable to obtain credit from local stores to provide food for themselves and children," the association petitioned for a per capita payment of $75 on December 1, 1921 and that another per capita payment be made in March 1922 to finance "farming purposes." One hundred and fifty-six names were on the petition.[8] Kitch faintly endorsed the petition in a letter dated November 4, 1921, saying that few collections had been made on leases or land sales, and while he was making up this shortfall, he was clearly concerned about replenishing the fund. Kitch did support a per capita payment, but in the lesser amount of $40 each.[9]

F.M. Goodwin, Assistant SI, wrote Kitch on November 18, 1921, granting the per capita payment of $40 to approximately 2,113 individuals from the "Ft. Peck Reservation 4% Fund." His instructions were specific:

The shares of competent Indians including the shares of their dependent minor children and of any other such children under their care, should be paid to such competent Indians directly in cash and the shares of incompetents, including the shares of incompetents, shares of their dependent minor children and of any other such children under their care, should be credited to the accounts of such incompetents and minors respectively in your discretion, subject to expenditure under the individual Indian money regulations.

Kitch was also instructed not to create undue hardship in collecting "past due indebtedness" from the reimbursable funds.[10]

In the first days of December 1921, Kitch requested clarification on the matter of mixed-blood children's participation in the per capita payment. The office was willing to allow a per capita payment, but was taken aback on the mixed-blood children question. The rights of specific children were to be determined based on facts of their birth, residence, and ancestry through a complicated process involving the Tribal Business Committee, the superintendent, and the Indian Office. The approximate balance for the payment was $84,520.[11]

Fort Peck's coal lands and any other restricted lands were opened for lease in legislation that was finally passed, after a number of attempts made since 1917, on September 20, 1922.[12]

Inspector F.E. Brandon, in his inspection of the Land Division at Fort Peck dated May 22, 1922, revealed that thirty leases were delinquent to the value of $36,479. Brandon was quick to point out that economic conditions were such that several farmers and stockmen were not able "to meet their obligations or engage in new business" and that this contributed to "a decline in rentals." Without a change in conditions, pragmatism was in order. Land sales were

unsuccessful owing to financial conditions and recurring drought. Among 508 new allotments, fourteen were to include 320 acres grazing and forty acres irrigable lands. Irrigable and timber allotments were being made to others who had not received them previously, because there remained enough such lands to do so.[13] Subsequently, homesteaders on reservation lands were given a legislated two-year extension for money still owed.[14]

Difficulties at the boarding school in Poplar prompted District Supervisor James H. McGregor to report to Kitch on June 10, 1922, that in May, thirty-five girls rebelled against the treatment of Mrs. Gruette, the head matron, by running away. McGregor reported a clash between two employees, Mrs. Gruette, "an uneducated woman of French descent who was one-eighth Chippewa," and Mrs. Smith, a laundress, who was also a gossip. Gruette was extremely strict with the girls, often calling them "devils" and "tramps." McGregor recommended that both women be transferred.[15] Initial complaints against the school principal, James Glasscock, were not taken seriously, though one of the women the principal had harassed was Gruette's daughter.[16]

During the summer and fall, Kitch and his five office clerks remained buried under paperwork relating to leasing and the ongoing allotment. Kitch gave considerable attention to the backlog, which meant he and his clerks only got some leave when a two-week quarantine was necessary. By December 1922, the agency office needed another typist. This problem prompted changes in the leasing system, greatly reducing the amount of paperwork.[17]

The superintendent in his annual narrative report for 1922 ending June 30 addressed perennial issues. Kitch chose to place the constant trespass of stock problems, their enforcement, and the inability to address these in courts within the discussion of "Law and Order."[18] "Dancing" did not particularly concern Kitch, and religious dancing, described as the "goose dance or other adaptations of the old Sun or Ghost dance," was prohibited. One dance in particular did worry Kitch, however: "The Kahomina or [sic] dance should be completely abolished but this is very difficult when most of the participants are citizen Indians and legally empowered to hold dances in their homes." He intended "to gradually break down this dance without attempting immediate elimination," and his instructions were to prohibit the participation of any children or returned students in "the old Indian dancing."[19]

State officials were not cooperative in dealing with minor offenses. The Court of Indian Offenses operated with a judge for the Assiniboine and a judge for the Sioux.[20]

The Presbyterian, Catholic, and Mormon denominations all had churches on the reservation. Kitch, however, complained about the practice of holding annual celebrations for which church members had to travel, taking them away from home during the very times when their attention to farming was most required.

I believe that the religion by the Indians should be the same as for the white people in that they should have a local church so that it would not be necessary for them to spend several weeks out of each year traveling to a convocation any more than white people. . . . it would be impossible for any religious denomination to take a certain number of white people engaged in farming away from the reservation during the early part of July and I can see no reason why Indians should be permitted to leave their homes at this time.[21]

Kitch commented that a large number of bootleggers had been arrested that year, many with stills on the south side of the river adjacent to Brockton, Poplar, Wolf Point, and Frazer. Contradictory state and federal laws made "the apprehension of liquor makers and dispensers almost impossible."[22] Health was reported as very good, other than a mild epidemic of chicken pox at the boarding school and isolated cases of diphtheria and smallpox countered by vaccinations and inoculations. Homes were increasingly sanitary. Inroads were being reported on trachoma and tuberculosis. Indian women were reportedly welcome to join the Civic and Federated Women's Clubs of Montana, which emphasized health matters and Indian welfare.[23]

Kitch reported that the department's failure to compensate the public schools for tuition for Indian students was undermining the otherwise "splendid" cooperation between the systems. He went on to point out that there were public schools in all of the reservation towns and that over 43 percent of the Indian children were attending them. The boarding school graduates had sixth grade educations, and available employment was only domestic or manual labor. Graduates from boarding schools off the reservation sometimes spent two years before finding jobs. Kitch commented that the "morality of these Indians on this reservation is above the average and find them taking an active part in civic development."[24]

Community education was successful in promoting Indian gardens, milk cows, and chickens. The organization of Farm Bureau Clubs was a joint venture between the County Agent and agency officials.[25]

In an aside, Kitch explained that the original assistance with farming was provided between 1912 and 1915, when the agency supplied plowing with government tractors, but then this "temporary industrial condition . . . vanished as soon as the Government aid was removed." During 1916 and 1917, when efforts were being made toward "war farming," the poor climatic conditions discouraged many Indians, but most had gardens. Kitch described his current efforts as an endeavor

to start them in an individual method of farming, that is home production, trying to bring them the necessity of producing sufficient food and forage for their home and cattle, feeling that those who are successful in this and who are industrially able to spread out will cultivate larger farm areas.[26]

With pride, Kitch noted, "We have a large number of Indians who are cultivating from twenty to one hundred acres who show an increase of 100% and many of them including one farming eighty acres who farmed nothing for the last few years." On the school farm, rapeseed was planted for feeding hogs, millet for "milch" cows, fodder corn for the silo, and Cossack alfalfa, which were all new crops on the reservation. One of the lessons taught in the community meetings was seed testing. Another outcome was the organization of four farm clubs affiliated with the County Farm Bureaus. The officers and project leaders of the clubs were Indians.[27] Kitch declared that he could see very little good coming from "reimbursable assistance" since "the Indians like whites cannot be expected to appreciate anything for which they pay nothing."[28]

Most Indians, with a few exceptions, lived on their "forties," the irrigable forty-acre allotments. Efforts were made to build root cellars and shingle roofing for log houses was provided. The first frame buildings were inferior to log cabins at retaining heat.[29]

Revenue from leasing was increasingly inadequate. Generally, the Indians had no cattle, and without any available grazing, the only option would be to run cattle on the north end of the reservation, but that would be too difficult to monitor. This precluded any serious stock raising, so Indian grazing lands were only profitable when leased. Because Indians could not

effectively use their grazing lands, others took advantage. In Kitch's words,

The presence of stock and white men on this reservation is a source of unanimous complaint. . . . It is absolutely impossible for any person or group of person to round up approximately 8000 head of [trespassing] horses in the first place and in the second place they would be violating State laws by doing so.

A new system of leases based on 15 cents per acre per year was implemented for the 1922 season to help eliminate any enforcement relative to stock trespass.[30]

Employment patterns were diverse. Several tribal members worked for the county. During farming and threshing seasons, requests for labor were posted on the agency bulletin board and spread by Agency Farmers, Stockmen, and other employees. But bad weather often prevented much employment between November and May. Besides farm and ranch work, there was a demand for labor on the county roads.[31] Kitch said money issued to Indians was being spent well.[32]

Kitch found upon taking charge "a large number of selections and a large amount of miscellaneous allotments which had not been taken care of owing to the lack of sufficient help." Allotting Agent Simington had been detailed to resolve these matters. Completion of the new work was expected by October 1, 1922. No information was available about the status of homestead lands opened to settlement on March 21, 1917, April 28, 1917, and March 14, 1918. About sales of patent in fee lands among Fort Peck Indians, Kitch estimated that most had sold their lands and "squandered the proceeds." In his assessment, "issuance of patents in fee unquestionably leads to extravagance but I believe that it puts them on an independent basis and in many cases even though their land is squandered it is an advantage." A "general financial depression," coupled with three years of drought, meant that there was "practically no sale for any land on this reservation." Heirship cases had piled up since they were last current in 1920, and the last examiner had left a large number of intricate and difficult cases unresolved. Another examiner was promised by winter, and Kitch asked that the examiner remain until the backlog was eliminated. All regulations pertaining to IIM accounts were being followed. Payouts from this money were curtailed as far as possible, and children's funds were being used in only the "most urgent case and then only for food purposes."[33]

The statistical report that accompanied the annual report for 1923 named the five largest acreages farmed by individual Indians: Maurice Big Horn, a full blood, aged thirty-five, farmed 191 acres of wheat valued at $2,500; Thomas Buckles, one-half, aged forty, farmed 107 acres of wheat valued at $1,200; Annie Helmer, one-quarter (married to a non-Indian), aged forty-seven, farmed 987 acres of wheat valued at $7,000; Charles Hall, one-half, aged thirty-six, farmed 191 acres of wheat valued at $2,000; and Mr. Catelle, one-half, aged forty-six, farmed 177 acres of wheat valued at $2,000.[34]

At the end of April 1923, Kitch asked Supervisor of Schools Carl Stevens to visit Fort Peck specifically to investigate "rumors and accusations regarding the improper conduct of Principal James L. Glasscock" with female employees of the Fort Peck Boarding School. Arriving May 17, Stevens toured the school, and then Kitch gave him written statements sufficient to begin the investigation. The evidence was overwhelming, and the scandal had been made public, so Glasscock was removed.[35]

The student population included reservation Sioux children and Turtle Mountain Chippewa children, mostly students who could not pay tuition to attend public schools. The enrollment in 1924 was 127, with just over half enrolled Fort Peck Indians. Another ninety children were reportedly attending the mission schools on the western end of the reservation, with less than forty enrolled at the off-reservation boarding schools. A total of 284 tuition students were attending the various public schools in the towns on the reservation. A small number of children in poor health were not in school.[36]

In contrast to the previous report, the relative state of health on the reservation was described as poor. In 1924, tuberculosis numbered 128 cases, and trachcoma, 286 cases. The following year, a specialist estimated that more than 10 percent of the Sioux and 25 percent of the Assiniboines had trachoma.[37] Nevertheless, fertility was gradually outstripping morbidity and by 1924, the reservation population numbered 2,215.[38]

In Wolf Point on March 27, the Superintendent of the Presbyterian Indian Mission School, Cynthia D. King, died at age seventy-one. She had come to Wolf Point in 1893 with her husband Reverend Richard King, "a full-blooded Sioux," and after his death on May 21, 1894, stayed on and established the school, which by the time of her death included a church, a dormitory, and several other buildings at the old sub-agency.[39]

The Annual Report of the Commissioner of the General Land Office for fiscal year 1923 explained the extension of time for payment of Indian lands. Attempts to enforce payment had been suspended between June 24, 1921 and March 4, 1923, pending legislation before Congress for the relief of "delinquent homesteaders," but Congress adjourned without taking action. Further representations had been made to the department that conditions had not changed in that locality, and in response to this, on March 22, 1923, "local officers were directed to advise any entryman of those lands that adverse action on his entry will be suspended for one year, provided he files in that office his corroborated affidavit setting out the reasons for his inability to make the required payments, accompanied by all the delinquent interest."[40]

Consequently, these revenues were not accruing to the trust fund of the Fort Peck tribes. In the Annual Report of the Commissioner of the GLO for 1924, the extension was addressed in several ways. Because of the continuing drought, the GLO has been "overwhelmed the past year with requests for extensions of time for payment on homestead entries of ceded Indian lands." Apparently, homesteaders had been unable to borrow money and in several cases, banks had gone under between the time checks and drafts had been drawn and the local land office had processed extensions. Relief legislation was introduced again in the Sixty-Eighth Congress, but died in the adjournment between sessions, which prompted the department on July 5, 1924 to approve instructions "directing the local officers not to report any entry of these lands for cancellation for non-payment until further advised." Thus adverse action was withheld by the GLO until Congress or the department determined policy.[41] Not until the Act of March 4, 1925, however, was any adverse action suspended. The Commissioner of the GLO, in the Annual Report for 1925, stated,

Under section 1 of the act actual settlers on the reservation are required to pay one-half of the amount, both principal and interest, due on their entries on or before November 1, 1925, and the other half on or before November 1, 1926. Under section 2 these persons who have abandoned residence on or before November 1, 1925. Regulations were issued under this act on March 24, 1925, and by May 1, 1925, action thereunder [sic] had been taken on all the entries affected, approximately 2,000.[42]

Rural lands could only be taxed when the owner possessed unencumbered title to his property, which many were systematically avoiding. The lack of revenue was limiting county services.

Whether or not the boarding school scandal was a factor, Kitch was transferred. He was succeeded in the fall of 1923 by Peter H. Moller, described as a capable and "kind and patient" administrator, and characterized by one inspector as an "ideal" superintendent.[43] During his tenure, a five-year plan modeled upon one on the Blackfeet Reservation where he had served was implemented at Fort Peck.[44] The Fort Peck Farming and Livestock Association, at a fall convention in Poplar, featured guest speakers from the Blackfeet Reservation talking about the successes achieved there. Superintendent F.C. Campbell brought exemplary Blackfeet Indian farmers Richard Sanderville and Split Ears, and all three spoke to the assembled delegates. Campbell told that the first crop to come in under the plan implemented at Blackfeet was only 1,000 bushels, which he attributed "to the propensity of his charges to spend too much time during the growing season building the Medicine Lodge." Gophers, weeds, and the scarcity of frost-free days proved challenging, but the farmers persevered to increase the yield of crops, and that year, two new flour mills were built on the reservation. But Campbell also warned that times might be coming when money would be less plentiful. To succeed at modern farming, thrift was necessary. Alvin Warrior, described as the "boss farmer" at the agency who had worked with five superintendents, translated for most of the speakers, and when it was his turn to speak, talked "in Indian" because he wished the old Indians to understand him well. A newspaper account reported that "he urged the Indians to realize the value of the plans of the association and to cooperate with Mr. Moller in his plans for their benefit."[45]

In legislation signed into law by the President on June 2, 1924, Congress granted citizenship to all non-citizen Indians within the United States, declaring that the granting of citizenship "shall not in any manner impair or otherwise effect the right of any Indian to tribal or other property."[46] Nevertheless, sorting out jurisdictions was not easy. C.F. Hauke, the chief clerk of the Indian Office, responded on April 11, 1925 to tribal member Martin Mitchell, living in Wolf Point, who had asked if Indians being made citizens meant they had to pay state taxes. Hauke replied that the legislation did not affect trust status property, which included "restricted property of Fort Peck and other Indians," but he declared, "The Indians are, however, subject to payment of any taxes required by the State of persons qualified to vote."

Many Indians, approximately three-fourths of the Indian population [of Fort Peck], were citizens of the United States before the passage of the Act, either by allotment, by leaving their tribe and adopting the habits of civilized life, or derived citizenship from their parents, who were citizens during their children's minority. Their citizenship, however, did not effect [sic] the taxable status of their property.[47]

What had been given by one jurisdiction could be taken away by another. A trend began in the 1920s that increasingly saw the Indian Office turning to the trust funds for expenses, rather than asking Congress for appropriations. At the SI's request, congressional legislation passed in June 1924 authorized spending tribal funds for construction, repair, and rental of agency buildings and related purposes.[48]

The weather in northeast Montana only periodically favored agriculture. The brief respite of increased rainfall for the years 1922 to 1925 gave farmers good crops and improved prices, which led to several to invest in tractors and related machinery. This coincided with the period when dry-farming methods were coming to the fore, although very few Fort Peck Indians could afford to use these techniques.[49]

In 1918, the Bureau of Reclamation began to charge for water delivered by its irrigation divisions. The basic fee charged was $1 per one and a half acre-feet of water, and $.75 per acre for additional water. By 1922, this formula was revised so landowners were charged a flat $1 per acre for land under the ditches, whether the water was used or not. The basic entitlement allowed users one acre-foot of water per acre, and additional water cost $1 per acre-foot. Collections between 1918 and 1922 totalled a mere $3,203.[50] The bureau began billing the construction costs of the irrigation works throughout the West. The initial charge was $.50 per acre irrigated, and by 1921, the charge was applied to all irrigable acres. But collections fell far below projections, and "the uncertainty of water supply [also] discouraged potential users." On Fort Peck, only 22,794 acres were served by irrigation works by 1922, including the new Big Muddy unit, yet only 622 acres were actually irrigated on the entire reservation during that year.[51] Little new construction was done the summer of 1922, and the next year, all construction was halted. The project supervisor reported that the Poplar and Big Muddy units were unreliable because no reservoirs had been constructed, and wooden flumes on the Big and Little Porcupine creeks already needed replacement.[52] The 1923 season saw above average rainfall and a record 2,069 acres irrigated, but the average declined in the next years as the drought returned. In these same years, portions of the system had failed and some were not rebuilt. In 1931, the management of the Fort Peck units was placed under the Fort Peck Agency. The advantage of irrigable land simply had not been realized.[53]

Retired General Hugh Scott, a member of the Board of Indian Commissioners, inspected the agency in October 1924. His descriptions of the economic and social conditions were bleak. During the past season, 212,000 acres had been leased for grazing and 16,000 acres for farming. The Sioux were farming 2,857 acres and the Assiniboines, 1,900. The allotting agent indicated that 237,000 acres still were unallotted or entered for homestead purposes. A total of 622 fee patents had been issued, but most had been sold and little was left to show for the proceeds. The superintendent was not aware of anyone who had received a fee patent that still retained his land "intact and unencumbered," and Scott reported that "some of the patentees have gone to work but many live off of the older people." Scott was troubled that there were six farming districts, but only two Agency Farmers. Since the Farmers were the "right hands of the superintendent," he should have a Farmer in each district. Scott noted that the superintendent could not be "held responsible for the results" in that "it was not reasonable to expect him to make bricks without straw." In the margin of the Indian Office's copy, an annotation was made by someone at the Indian Office, with the words "No Funds" with initials.

While Scott praised the superintendent's belief that progress was being made, he also noted that the Indians were still far from prosperity from farming or stock raising. It was still necessary for the agency to issue rations twice a month to 162 individuals.[54] Scott indicated the five-year plan for industrial agriculture was being "put into force as rapidly as possible on this reservation with good results as far as it has gone." The irrigation was worthless, Moller said, because "the ditches are often dry at the time the water is most needed for irrigating the lands."[55] Scott also reported that the numbers of cattle the Indians owned were dwindling, probably because stock was being slaughtered and eaten.[56]

Increasing concern about land matters char-

acterized the 1920s. The erosion of the Fort Peck land base provoked complaints from Indians who found the methods of sale and leasing practices problematic, but most perplexing was that homesteaders were not forced to pay what they owed. Inspections and special investigations examined these allegations, but the depth of the erosion was not investigated until the spring of 1926. Sales of the surplus lands would have been simple but for the difficult climatic conditions. During World War I and the early 1920s, when fee patents were being given without even asking, most of this land was sold at far below its full value. The multiple factors associated with agriculture on the reservation meant that the first allotments had not brought economic self-reliance and independent sustainability.[57]

Soon the entire land situation at Fort Peck came under scrutiny and assessment. Coinciding with these developments were considerations for reappraisals which some homesteaders wanted, thinking the lands they had originally chosen had been overvalued. The reappraisals of the lands fell to the Agency Farmers. James R. Holsclaw, a Farmer in the government service since 1918 who had served at Standing Rock and Rosebud Reservations, was transferred to Fort Peck Reservation and appointed Agency Farmer in the Wolf Point District. He was found by a special inspector to be an honest native of Iowa who saw a real difference between the lands of the Iowa, Standing Rock, and Rosebud Reservations, and the lands at Fort Peck. Unfortunately, very quickly, homesteaders learned that Holsclaw would give them favorable reappraisals. While no corruption or evidence of any personal gain was discovered, he was asked to resign.[58]

Other factors were revealed in the Blair inspection about the disposition of land on the Fort Peck Reservation. A short-lived boom in sales had occurred among whites in 1920, but by 1926, lands sold to others resulted in losses. Blair indicated that for the most part, the homesteaders in 1913 had been real farmers, but then some land speculators "drifted in and filed on certain pieces of land." Most of the serious homesteaders were Germans who concentrated on improving the properties. In contrast, the speculators bought unimproved lands, and most of the appeals for reappraisals came from them.[59]

The promotional volume *Montana Resources and Opportunities* described Montana as having the lowest taxes of any state except for Arizona: "Taxes in Montana on all lands have been reduced in 1925 from 16 cents per acre to 14.9 cents per acre according to the Montana State Board of Equalization."[60] The average value of all plowed lands per acre between March 1, 1916 and March 1, 1925 changed accordingly: 1916 at $29, 1920 at $36, 1924 at $21, and 1925 at $19.[61] By 1925, Montana taxed various lands thus:

	Grazing	Non-irrigated	Irrigated	All Lands
Assessed value	$4.93	$13.43	$51.30	$9.55
Tax per acre	.077	.21	.80	.149[62]

Inspector Blair discovered that with few exceptions, those who made homestead entries on these lands were delinquent, and in most instances, these homesteaders could discharge their obligations to the government "without embarrassment to themselves." As much as he could ascertain, the primary reason that the homesteaders were slow to pay was that as long as they were indebted to the government, they could not receive title to their lands and so could avoid state taxes. So as not to violate the terms of their homestead entry, these homesteaders sought extensions for their final payments.

Blair's impression of the tax situation that faced the homesteaders was different from that being promulgated by the state. Blair felt that the non-Indian farmers at Fort Peck were taxed on farming land at exceedingly high rates, but he did determine that the homesteaders had discovered

it was cheaper to pay the federal government interest on a delinquent payment than to pay state taxes. Moreover, this was hardly fair to those farmers who had paid in full for their lands and had received title, since they were carrying the entire tax burden. Not surprisingly, Blair recommended that homesteaders be refused extensions, further reappraisals, or reductions.[63]

Under the act of March 4, 1925, approximately 1,800 entrymen on Fort Peck had been required either to make complete payment by November 1, 1925, or to pay half the amount on that date and the balance one year later. While more than half complied, many did not. Consequently, on February 17, 1926 the department suspended adverse action for nonpayment "pending consideration by Congress of legislation for the relief of such homesteaders." Legislation passed by Congress on June 15, 1926 granted a further extension providing the entryman filed affidavits "satisfactorily showing . . . his inability to make the required payments, accompanied by the interest [owed]."[64] The matter had clearly become politicized, irrespective of the interests of the Fort Peck Tribes.

Another major development became influential for at least a decade. After the initial boom on land sales in 1920-1921, fifty-eight allotments had been sold, but by 1922, there were no more sales. To take advantage of this situation, in 1923 the Frye Cattle Company of Seattle, Washington, leased a large area of the reservation and soon began purchasing Indian allotments and homestead lands from settlers ready to sell out. The Frye Cattle Company in a very short time controlled several hundred thousand acres. The company's managers were careful to treat Indians fairly, however, employing a number of them, and because of its operational size, it was able to make a profit where individuals had not. In 1923, the Frye Cattle Company purchased its first three allotments, and in 1924, twenty-one, in 1925, eighty-nine, and in 1926, sixteen. In all cases, the company paid minimally the appraised value of the land, but often paid more. By the time of Samuel Blair's inspections in the spring and summer of 1926, a small number of complaints had accrued about the monopolistic presence of the Frye Cattle Company.[65]

None of these developments were lost on the tribal members of the Fort Peck Reservation. As early as November 1923, requests were being made for delegations to go to Washington to discuss land matters.[66] Another such request was made at the end of January 1924, and Washington asked questions about the motives of the representatives.[67] The business committee members refused to empower Meade Steele as a delegate, which gave the Indian Office the excuse not to entertain a delegation, even though, as Moller conveyed, Indians were becoming "dissatisfied with the homestead situation, particularly with the reference to the deferment of payments."[68]

Commissioner Burke commented on what he thought were Meade Steele's motives, suggesting that delegates to Washington needed to have specific tasks to accomplish, and not to stay "to agitate and endeavour to discredit the Service," and that he was not in favor of delegates coming for "a junketing trip and to have a good time at the expense of their tribe."[69] Meade Steele, however, was already in D.C., and wrote to Burke on the same date that he came to speak against the legislation authorizing extensions to homesteaders. He accused the CIA of working in favor of the whites. Steele also voiced his suspicions about the land grab he saw the Frye Cattle Company engaged in at Fort Peck, with what he saw as a conspiratorial "combination" with agency officials. In Steele's words, there was a particular poignancy:

Our necessities are made worse by extending the payments for our land because then there is no money to relieve our distress, and greater advantage may be taken of us. You do not seem to understand our viewpoint, or care about our welfare in these matters. You have the power to withhold our funds and prevent us securing consideration, except as you so considerately advise, by saying, "we have no objections to any member of the tribe coming at any time in his individuals [sic] capacity as long as he does so without expense to the tribe." Then when he comes, he may be ignored and discredited by your office.

It looks to me as though you and your entire office and field service are working with the white people against the Indians and making it possible for them to take all we have. To starve us out entirely.

While overseas my land was leased, used and exploited by Indian service employees. I was coerced into signing the lease in order to get the rental so that I might get back to my command within the limit of my furlough.[70]

Moller, writing Burke on February 12, 1924, said that sentiment at Fort Peck was that Steele not be considered a representative delegate and his contact with a Wolf Point faction that had been having secret meetings for some time was acknowledged. If a general council did not select a delegation, then it was not recognized as legitmate, but the superintendent declared that the "entire tribe" was in favor of a delegation and expected one to be authorized. Speaking of Steele's work, which included organizing a Chapter of Red Men on the reservation, Moller stated that such organizations distracted from what he characterized as the objective of the Indian Service: "I believe that it is only a matter of time now before we have them all organized and thinking of other things than money, land and treaties."[71]

While in Washington, Steele met with

attorneys working on Sioux claims, and this resulted in a letter from C.C. Calhoun to the CIA, dated February 18, 1924, requesting that a delegation from Fort Peck be allowed to come to Washington to discuss elements of their local claims that might be incorporated in a larger claim on behalf of the Sioux.[72] Moller responded by stating that he was calling the necessary general councils to make the selection, and that he did not have available funds at the agency to support a delegation, but rather, this would have to come from trust funds.[73]

An election was held on March 11, 1924, with Charles Thompson and George Conners chosen by the Yanktons and Meade Steele by the Assiniboines, and they were authorized to go to Washington at "tribal expense."[74] In a second letter on the same day, Moller described to Burke the individuals chosen. Thompson had a "keen knowledge of tribal matters," making him "a very satisfactory delegate," but George Conner was a "Meade Steele man," and clearly considered another agitator. Moller had been asked to accompany the delegation, but he declined, not wanting to undo his industrial work to date, and he declared that he wanted to stay out of "tribal matters, treaties, claims, etc." knowing "feelings always run high." He asked that in the future, if reports and information were needed on this subject, that an inspector could be "detailed to the reservation for that purpose." Moller noted that he was making a report on certain leases on the reservation made to the Frye Cattle Company, "which have aroused considerable feeling among the Indians," but asked in the future, if a "traveling official" might be given the task of making further reports about the role of the company in land matters. Before ending his communication, he asked if James Archdale, the candidate closely defeated by Meade Steele, might be asked to come as a delegate after all. Moller pointed out that this would mean a lot to

his constituency, that he would work well with George Thompson, and was very much in favor of the industrial program.[75] While Moller identified Archdale as an Agency Policeman, the superintendent downplayed that this was a conflict of interest, and suggested that it was no problem if the employee were authorized to be a delegate.[76]

In the midst of these developments, the thirteenth per capita payment was dispersed from the 4% Fund, which amounted to $25 per tribal member, constituting a total of $1,623,915.90 paid out since the first such payment in the fourth quarter of 1917. The pattern had been established with a second payment in 1918, and then two payments each year through 1923, and already there was an expectation that this could be a regular source of money.[77] Unfortunately, this fund was diminishing faster than interest was accruing, and individuals with political aspirations saw the funds as a source of political influence, as well as a means to travel to Washington.

Just as various Sioux claims were coming to the fore, the Assiniboines also were anxious to have their claims addressed. In a letter dated March 22, 1924, James Archdale reported to Burke that on March 6, Congressman Scott Leavitt of Montana had introduced H.R. 7686, the Assiniboine Claim bill, which would authorize the Montana Assiniboines at both Fort Peck and Fort Belknap to bring a claim before the U.S. Court of Claims, in the U.S. House of Representatives. Archdale asked that "your Department" defer any report of this bill to the House Committee on Indian Affairs until Assiniboine delegates could come to Washington to "make a proper justification for the bill." Archdale closed by saying that a delegation was soon to be in D.C.[78]

Moller was told after the delegates were selected that the office was declining to consider a delegation because there were no funds to support it. In a letter to Burke on March 31, 1924,

Moller said he thought this a "great mistake" because the "opponents of the administration" could now say "that the Indian Office does not plan to tolerate a delegation to Washington that is not friendly to the Bureau." While Moller could understand the reasons given, he was sure the Indians would not.[79] Burke responded on April 7, 1924, that a bill introduced in the Senate would provide $3,000 of the Fort Peck 4% Fund for a delegation, but if the legislation failed, no funds would be available.[80]

Meanwhile, the delegates were anxious to leave for Washington. A conflict arose over whether Charles Thompson, who had been duly elected to the delegation, or Gus Heddrick would go. The dispute was complicated by lost correspondence and confusion at the Indian Office, and questions about how the trip would be paid for. Moller reminded the CIA on May 14, 1924 that he had authorized the delegation, and since several members were already in Washington, he urged that Charles Thompson's travel be facilitated, because if this confusion was made known it would become an issue both on the reservation and among the delegates already in D.C.[81] Moller wrote James Archdale a letter of introduction to Commissioner Burke, dated May 9, 1924, stating that on March 11, the Assiniboine Council elected him, and wanted Archdale to go to Washington before the current session adjourned. Moller noted that Archdale would not stay long because he was a farmer with considerable work to accomplish for the coming season.[82]

Clearly, this delegation was not of a single mind. From all appearances, the delegation did not even travel or lodge together, but its expenses were accumulating. According to Moller, Gus Heddrick had usurped Charles Thompson's position as delegate, and Moller, who had been trying to have Heddrick's transfer of his membership to Fort Peck revoked, suggested that Heddrick had apparently succeeded in getting the transfer

issue curtailed since arriving in Washington. In Moller's opinion, the only way to respond fairly was immediately summoning Thompson to Washington as a delegate.[83]

The delegates jointly wrote the CIA on June 7, 1924, asking that legislation be put forward so that the Fort Peck Indians could have access to the $80,425.75, appropriated by the Act of May 18, 1916, to be added to both the 4% Fund and the fund itself.[84] Moller and the office finally sorted out the delegation's expenses, for a total of $1,218. Political opponents of some of the delegates questioned this because they were worried that personalities were distracting the delegates from the issues.[85]

Elections that fall included the first U.S. presidential race since citizenship was granted to all Indians. Burke sought Moller's assessment of Fort Peck tribal members' participation, including the number voting and how votes were cast. Moller responded that between 700 and 800 voters were registered with 98 percent voting. Although he had no means to obtain precise figures, he estimated that about 95 percent voted for President Coolidge. Moller indicated that there was "quite an organized movement among the Indians for President Coolidge, and their chief talking point was that you [Charles H. Burke] would be retained in office and hence their interests would be best served, mentioning particularly the Black Hills claim." Senator Walsh received a heavy Indian vote, as did Congressman Leavitt and Governor Dixon. Moller observed that "the Indians seemed to know little about party platforms, but did not care particularly about those things, but voted rather for the man than for the party." The Indians of the reservation appeared to appreciate the "right of francise" [sic], which reinforced their support for President Coolidge, who had signed the citizenship legislation.[86]

Another factor in Moller's industrial initiative

was organizing the drafting of a constitution and bylaws for a business committee to bring "order" to the struggle between factions. His attempt was more an effort to see bylaws, and thus, procedures, created for resolving matters before the Tribal Business Committee.

The annual election of Business Committee members was held on December 2, 1924, in accordance with the new constitution, which divided the reservation into five districts, east to west: Drew, Riverside, Poplar, Wolf Point, and Frazer Districts. Two individuals were elected from the Drew, Riverside, and Poplar Districts and three from the Frazer District, but no one was elected from the Wolf Point District, which refused to participate in the election, just as they had the previous year. Moller attributed this response to the "agitators" residing there, and although he would allow them to have another special election, if no one was elected, the superintendent proposed they not be represented on the Tribal Business Committee for the coming year.[87] Moller later reported that James Garfield, Sr., Pointing Iron, and Martin Mitchell were elected. In passing, he noted that although Meade Steele received the same number of votes as Martin Mitchell, Steele was not eligible because he resided in another district.[88]

Six members of the Tribal Business Committee, James Garfield, Sr., Pointing Iron, Santee Iron Ring, Rufus Ricker, Sr., William Whiteright, Sr., and Andrew Red Thunder, wrote Moller on January 26, 1925 to "protest against self-elected delegates who are now in Washington" and "against their expenses being paid from tribal funds."[89] This protest was communicated to Senator Burton K. Wheeler, who inquired of the Indian Office. Burke replied on February 14, 1925 that Moller had explained

Most of the Indians feel that the practice of Indians going to Washington on pretext of

having tribal business and then have their expenses paid out of tribal funds should be discontinued. They realize too that it is difficult for the Office to decline to pay expenses of such delegates and that as long as this is done these expeditions will continue. They also feel that in as much as most of these trips are of a more or less private nature and for purposes in which the tribe as a whole is not interested, the tribe should not be put to this expense.

The individuals "composing this delegation," Burke explained, were well aware that unauthorized delegations were not welcome.[90] Gus Heddrick wrote E.B. Merritt from Poplar on February 10, 1925, to settle his expenses from the delegation in May 1924. In a postscript, he stated, "What in the world Jim and Mede [Steele] are doing down their [sic] send them back on the first freight train leaves [sic] out of Washington. Seal [sic] them up and send them back to the good old land of Ft. Peck Reservation."[91] James Archdale was identified as the other unauthorized delegate.[92]

The Tribal Business Committee met on March 3, 1925, and opposed legislation before the current session of the 68th Congress to again extend payments on homestead entries on Fort Peck. The resolution also demanded that all delinquent amounts should draw an annual rate of interest of 5 percent per annum until paid, but if deadlines for payment were not met, all entries should be cancelled, and "the land revert to the status of other tribal lands of the Fort Peck Indian Reservation."[93] Moller, in his letter of transmittal of the minutes to the Indian Office, dated March 14, 1925, explained that the day after the meeting when the bills before Congress were enacted into law, all of this unknown to the Business Committee as it made their resolution irrelevant on the "homestead problem."[94] Congress had enacted legislation granting another extension, making the business committee resolution a moot point.

The clamor for democracy and self-determination was attractive for many progressives, especially returned students and mixed-bloods who believed in political processes. The Indians who supported Meade Steele were also adherents of the Indian Protective Association, a movement that had made inroads at the Crow and Blackfeet Reservations in the mid-1920s.[95] Two petitions dated March 23, 1925 were addressed to Moller with separate sets of signatures, one signed first by Meade Steele and fifty-one others, and the other signed first by Gus M. Heddrick and seventy-two others. The text declared that the undersigned "discovering evidences that our tribal affairs, the Tribal Business Committee is now under Indian Bureau domination, do hereby enter our protest against such domination. . . . We are now citizens of the United States and are now entitled to all privileges of such citizenships; Therefore, we do hereby declare the Tribal Business Committee dissolved and that the tribe transact its business through the regular Tribal Council."[96] Meade Steele wrote a cover letter, dated April 12, 1925:

We charge that there is a conspiracy, well organized, and subtly active, to bring the political life of the Indians more and more under the control of the few, under the domination of the Indian Bureau.

If we are to grow to the full stature of citizenship we must be free from bureaucratic interference. In the past under the so-called "wardship" the Indian was a helpless victim of arbitrary rule.

Therefore, if we are to enjoy the privileges, rights and duties of citizenship—which means the right, the authority of the people to manage and control their own affairs—we must respectfully but vigorously protest the present movement; we must be free.[97]

Moller transmitted the petitions to the CIA on April 17, 1925, declaring, "These petitions were circulated by a few of the Indians who found that they could not be dominate [sic] the business committee, and it appears that they are therefore dissatisfied and have taken this means to gain their purposes." Moller noted that Meade Steele had been secretary of the committee that had crafted the constitution under which the business committee was currently operating. He thought the sentiments in the petitions were not that of a majority "in favour of this move." However, he noted that he "certainly would interpose no objection," if this were to become the majority opinion.[98]

In the first days of November, the Indian Protective Association held a meeting in Helena and called for the removal of Charles H. Burke as CIA, charging that his administration had seriously eroded the amount of trust lands in the hands of Indian tribes and individual members. Fourteen councilmen from the seven reservations in Montana signed the resolutions. A picture was taken of those present. Joshua Wetsit, an Assiniboine from Fort Peck, was elected the group's treasurer.[99]

In the annual election of the Tribal Business Committee, held on December 1, 1925, James Garfield, Sr., Wesson Murdock, Pointing Iron, George Washington, William Whitright, Sr., Charles Thompson, Claude Reddoor, Lloyd Red Eagle, Crazy Bull #1, James Archdale, Bedford Forrest, and Arthur Four Star were selected.[100]

Moller wrote the Indian office on January 13, 1926 forwarding a set of resolutions left for him by Rufus Ricker. Moller described the resolutions as "purely and simply Indian Protective Association products." The resolutions declared that the rights of the Fort Peck Indians "under their agreements with the United States and under their congressional Acts and in the administration of their affairs" were being violated.

First, the trust funds were being held without interest, and were being "authorized to carry on the activities of the Indians Bureau." Second, funds currently "standing to the credit" of the Indians were not being paid out "as agreed." Third, foreclosing on and taking back lands homesteaders had defaulted on was "not being carried out fully by the proper authorities to the loss of the Indians." Fourth, the SI was accused of allowing "reappraisements of lands sold in trust by the United States to the loss of the Indians and without the authority of law." Fifth, the Indian Bureau had "exerted its influence to promote and retain complete control over the so-called Tribal Committee so as to leave them and retain them in a position where they could make no official protest against improper administration." Sixth, lands purchased from Indians, known as "School and Agency lands," were sold without consent of tribal members, causing a "great loss to the Indians." Seventh, mineral, oil, and gas rights on the reservation were "without consent" taken by the United States.

The resolutions were forwarded to the Montana senators and congressmen. Moller reported that he had heard that there were only nine tribal members present at the meeting: Meade Steele, Thomas Hancock, Gus M. Heddrick, George Long, William Whitright, Sr., Joshua Wetsit, Rufus Ricker, Basil Reddoor, and George Conner. Except for Whitright, who was the source of his information, Moller considered all of them long-term "opponents of the Indian Bureau and the local administration."[101]

The resolutions provoked several responses. The Education-Industries section addressed the third, fourth, and sixth points in a memo. Cancellation of entries for non-payment of principal had been suspended by the department since 1921 in the cases of entrymen who had paid the interest due on their deferred payments. In response to the third point, the Act of March 4, 1925, was described as "primarily enacted for the relief of homesteaders on the Fort Peck Reservation," extending until November 1, 1925 payment of half the amount due including principal and interest. The balance was due on November 1, 1926.

Meade Steele and Rufus Ricker escalated the debate in April 1926 when they charged Moller and a number of his employees with mismanagement. Ironically, the superintendent was also accused of allowing the Indians to have their traditional dances and giveaways, and thereby impoverishing themselves. The accusation was also made that Moller's administration had permitted land sales that were less than the true value of certain lands.[102]

While these charges could not be substantiated, Moller had, in other ways, begun to compromise his authority. A charge was made that Chief Clerk L.D. Rodgers had taken a lease and worked a piece of land that was originally an Indian allotment. Even though the land had been purchased by non-Indians, it was found that Rodgers and Moller had an interest in the lease. While the CIA's opinion was that this land was no longer Indian land, and therefore did not violate any departmental regulation, the Indian Office felt for appearance's sake that Moller and Rodgers should divest themselves of their interests in the property as soon as they could.[103]

Moller's accusers claimed that he refused to give an accounting of individual Indian monies. Moller countered that Steele and Ricker were bringing older, and often illiterate, Indians to the agency office, and interpreting the information in their accounts, and then charging them for this service. Moller, finding this despicable, was refusing to give them any information. There were no other complaints about the superintendent denying information to individual Indians.[104] They next suggested that Moller was interfering in the composition of the Tribal

Business Committee and had placed ex-convicts on the committee. An investigation indicated these allegations were false. An individual was elected to the committee who had been convicted of murder and had served his time, but he was elected because of the confidence of his constituents.[105]

The eventual investment of the Frye Cattle Company in their Fort Peck operations was extensive. The company purchased much of its land adjacent to the Missouri River, which had been designated as irrigable or timber allotments. While the irrigable tracts had been meant to be used for agriculture, many of these forty-acre parcels had not been cultivated. Consequently, the company hired Indians to clear brush, brought in a tractor-pulled plow to break the sod, and planted grass for hay. In his inspection in 1926, Inspector Blair estimated that the company had spent $21 per acre clearing land, and once the cultivation and seeding were factored, the total was approximately $50 per acre.

Even though the company was far from breaking even in 1926, Blair was clearly in favor of these developments. [106] In his inspection report dated August 31, 1926, Blair declared that the Frye Cattle Company was a great benefactor to the Fort Peck Tribes. The company had hired Indian laborers, purchased fence posts and hay from Indians, and by 1926, was paying more than $100,000 annually to the Fort Peck Indians for leases. The company also ran a commissary and allowed Indians who worked for it to use it. Prices were often 10 percent above wholesale, much lower than elsewhere in the reservation.

The company made the most of its advantages, however. Blair discovered that it was able to deduct the cost of fencing on the leases, and recommended this be changed in future leases.[107] Moller explained that because leases were so short, it was often in the second lease that any planting was accomplished, and only in the

third year could a lessee expect to realize any profit.[108] The scale of the Frye Cattle Company's operations, while key to its profitability, was also a problem for some individual Indians who complained that the company was not addressing their personal situations to their satifaction. While magnanimous, the company was faced with claims on its resources by some individuals; some complaints could not be settled.[109]

Several practices that Frye used in its interactions with tribal members were discouraged, mostly making cash advances to individuals whose land was for sale instead of making bids through the agency office.[110] In a letter dated October 4, 1926, Moller wrote the CIA explaining that Inspector Blair had examined the small number of complaints made by tribal members against the Frye Cattle Company relative to the disappearance of cattle. Understandably, the company could not just pay for animals without investigation. Moller declared that the managers of the Frye Cattle Company were fair, honest, and upright, willing to pay compensation where it was due, but could not let a situation develop that would make their business unprofitable.[111] The CIA wrote Moller, on October 13, 1926, with specific recommendations. First, all leases with the Frye Cattle Company would be for fifteen cents per acre for one season with no deductions for fencing costs. Second, a clause will be inserted into every lease that whenever any Indian allotment was advertised for sale, the leases covering said allotment shall automatically be cancelled when the sale was consummated.[112]

The first annual narrative report that survives for the Moller administration was for the fiscal year ending June 30, 1926, filed on January 31. The superintendent lamented the impossibility of keeping office work current, particularly within the land division. The volume of the work connected to land sales and leases, reflecting improvement in economic conditions, remained too much for a single clerk, and the agency work force was insufficient.

Moller saw law enforcement as problematic, with federal laws applying only to a few crimes on the reservation, and state courts unwilling to accept jurisdiction over cases where crimes were committed on trust lands. Moller described the legal solitudes as "a sort of twilight zone which none are able to distinctly pierce." Without legislation to "draw a distinct line" indicating where one jurisdiction ended and the other began, inequities were bound to continue.[113] Moller noted that some people coming before the Court of Indian Offenses asserted their rights as U.S. and Montana citizens, and therefore were not subject to the Indian court.[114] Enforcement of Prohibition under federal and state laws was only as effective as whites would tolerate, but local authorities were not willing to see a situation of no tolerance. Access to alcohol was never to be completely prevented if whites demanded it. Moller lamented an inability to enforce the old Indian liquor law in favor of the Volstead Act, which was more lenient relative to trafficking on reservations.[115]

In his discussion about old-time dancing, Moller indicated that social dances were "indulged in" for pleasure. He acknowledged that dancing had to be regulated because some individuals and families were "prone" to becoming "ever-indulgent and neglectful of their farms, homes, stock and everything that they have for these dances." Older Indians generally were interested in the dances as social and cultural events, while some younger men frequently brought liquor to these gatherings to impress and debauch young women. Moller mentioned that the Indian dance committees, which were responsible for regulating their events, worked hard to prevent disorder. Moller anticipated that once older Indians were gone, this kind of dancing was expected "gradually [to] die out."[116]

The numbers being educated were increasing and overall health conditions were improving. Public education was promoted and former day schools were available for use by the public school system. Graduates from the boarding school were "better fitted to support themselves" compared to the graduates of the public schools, because of the "vocational training" and while the "men and women graduating from the high schools as a rule are progressive and in a number of cases continue school work in colleges and universities," the returned students in the non-reservation schools were trained in trades in which they could not make a living on reservations.[117] The two mission schools, one in and the other near Wolf Point, continued operation. The Presbyterian Wolf Point Indian Training School, in the charge of Miss Faith H. Haines, taught grades one to six, and while stressing religious training, was performing work of "high character," and "filling a need in the community."[118] The year's enrollment was fifty-five students.[119] The Mormon school, located four miles east of town, never had any more than twenty students at any one time, most of them quite young. The school was not expected to open for another season due to lack of interest, and because the two employees were more committed to adult missionary work.[120]

Moller reported that morality among Indians was comparable to the whites "with whom they come in daily contact." He noted that there were fifteen church organizations, some with "affiliated organizations," addressing "the moral welfare of the Indian people." Among these, he described "native helpers" who were "always willing to admonish their parishioners." These individuals and families he contrasted to the "incorrigibles," especially returned students, the "chronic knockers." A second class of returned student he recognized as the progressive young person "who not only manifests that he wants to help himself but also wants to be of service to the community." Unfortunately, many of this group could not find local employment because of the trades they had acquired at school.[121]

Moller was unabashed in his enthusiasm to replicate the five-year development program. He emphasized that the program had yielded "marked progress" in farming and industrial activities, and that "under our program and thru [sic] our organizations" individuals and many families were "working more wholeheartedly" and were "striving in every possible way to advance their condition and place themselves on a more substantial basis." Moller suggested that the climate could be managed by "learning and adopting modern methods of farming," especially if irrigation could be better utilized. The promotion of modernity, however, also meant the promotion of mechanization. Moller pointed out that many had spent a large portion of the $100 per capita payment the previous spring for machinery, farm equipment, and livestock. One disappointment was that reimbursable funds were used unwisely, making retirement of these debts impossible.[122]

The superintendent described the home of an "average progressive Indian":

A good frame or log house; a log barn, corrals, implement shed—generally of logs, a log house over the well, a pump and wind mill, a water tank for stock, a hen house, a water closet and a root cellar.

These Indians have each a 40 acre irrigable allotment and a 320 acre grazing allotment. The 40 acre allotments are located along the Missouri River bottom mostly, and the grazing allotments out on the bench land, away from the river. There are only a very few of the Indians who have their irrigable and grazing land in one body. The result is, of course, that the Indians all have their homes on their irrigable 40's on the river bottom, where there is plenty of wood and water. These allotments are, therefore, not leased as a rule, but grazing allotments, some of them 40 or 50 miles away from their homes, are leased, for farming and grazing purposes. The leasing of these allotments therefore, does not dispossess the lessor of his home, during the term of the lease, but on the contrary, provides an income for the lessor to use in connection with his farming and livestock activities on his home place.[123]

Moller and his contemporaries were beset with their efforts to establish a work ethic that would produce self-reliance and focus among their Indian clients. Celebrations were cultural events and were considered problematic; while whites had their rodeos, stampedes, and various celebrations, with commemorations like July 4th, Indian celebrations usually lasted several days, and were clearly considered outside social control. His criticisms about the distractions of church conferences and congresses in particular, however, arose mostly because he felt they interfered with concerted husbandry. In his opinion, neglect eroded the value of property and its development.[124]

In the section on allotments in his annual narrative report for 1926, Moller noted that an accumulation of surplus lands was resulting from abandonment by settlers, and while the law stated that these lands should be sold at auction to the highest bidder, that had been deferred from year to year "owing to financial depression throughout [sic] the country and local climatic conditions which have not been favorable for good crops during the past few years."[125]

Drought returned in the spring and summer of 1926, threatening the hay crop. There were no resources in the agency budget, but a per capita payment was arranged to pay for hay for those who needed it. Moller arranged for a purchase of 430 tons of hay at $25.90 per ton, for a total of $11,138.39, from his friend C.W. Flint, without a competitive bid. The transaction was later declared improper, and the price paid was well above the going rate for hay. While Flint profited with a margin of $250 on the exchange, the report stated that there was no evidence that Moller benefited from the deal.[126]

District Superintendent Campbell, in his report in November 1926, noted that Moller's detractors were a distinct minority. He spent two days traveling with Moller as he inspected thirty homes and investigated his industrial program. He estimated that the Indians joining with the chapter and auxiliaries encompassed "about 90 per cent of the population of his reservation." Consequently, the remaining 10 percent were what the Indians called "objectors," or more frequently, the "kickers" or "agitators." Campbell declared that Moller had no more than thirty actively opposing him, and of these, five or six made this their livelihood.[127]

Ironically, the faction that had been successful in removing Lohmiller actually proposed later in 1926 that the former superintendent be reinstated. Inspector Blair observed that the troublemakers had demonstrated that they had no credibility. Blair felt that if put to a vote, Moller would be elected, because he had done so much for so many tribal members.[128]

By September 1926, the demand for an immediate distribution of all tribal trust funds was not taken seriously. Even though Blair had described the Fort Peck Indians as "poor," "poverty stricken," and obviously in great need, he suggested that any per capita payment not be given until late fall, and that a monthly payment, not a lump sum, would prevent this resource from being wasted.[129] By the end of the month, the CIA wrote to Meade Steele and Rufus Ricker that their complaints and charges had been investigated by Inspector Blair, and that these were not sustained or supported.[130]

But the superintendent was tiring of the battle. Moller, having been in poor health for some time, was diagnosed with an enlarged heart, which prompted him to begin seeking a transfer. He did not depart until the spring of 1927. Investigations of charges and complaints continued, however, and it was discovered that in his last year Moller had neglected some aspects of the agency program because of his personal affairs. In a sense, the five-year program "simply disappeared" through his neglect. The overall handling of land sales, leasing, and trespass left much to be desired. The state of the irrigation works was ignored for much of his administration. While the growing season for 1927 turned out to be fairly good, the failure of the five-year program resulted in the "small amount of Indian agricultural activity that year."[131]

Charles Eggers took charge of the reservation in early April 1927. He was a fifty-nine-year-old ordained minister and a twenty-two-year employee of the Indian Service. The staff numbered approximately fifty employees, thirty of them Indians. The employees were under the impression that Moller had taken a six-month leave and was returning, and consequently, Eggers had some difficulty with some of them during his first weeks on the job. Two actually circulated a petition seeking Moller's return.[132]

A General Council was authorized shortly after Eggers' arrival, and it was held at the American Legion Hall in Poplar on April 15 and 16, 1927. The CIA had asked whether the tribal committee had the authority to speak for the reservation population, and questioned whether a group could be elected that could assume these responsibilities. Eggers, upon opening the meeting, declared that he hoped that anyone present could feel free to discuss whatever was concerning them, and they should not be hampered and influenced by the presence of government employees. An election of officers was held, and Joshua Wetsit was elected chairman and Meade Steele, secretary. During the two-day meeting, the issues discussed and decided were:

1) the use of the Fort Peck 4% fund to drill for oil, 2) a petition to grant Indians the right to withdraw from the protection of the Indian bureau, [and] 3) protest against the presumed authority of the Indian Protective Association. By a vote of 79-2 the council dissolved the tribal business committee, and a resolutions committee was organized to formulate statements on the other issues. The council then unanimously approved (67-0) a resolution to create the "Fort Peck Assiniboine Council" and the "Fort Peck Sioux Council" to transact the affairs of each tribe. Whenever the council met together, the joint council was to be known as the "General Council of the Fort Peck Reservation, Montana."[133]

On the second day, Eggers announced his plan to increase the efficiency of the agency office, especially to address the backlog of leases. He proposed that the District Farmers be given more responsibilities for purchases, reimbursable funds, leases, and the sort, but also in the delivery of checks. By the end of fiscal year 1927, this had been demonstrated as more productive.[134] The council, after considerable discussion, resolved to inquire of the SI about whether he would approve of use of the 4% Fund to drill a test well on tribal land.[135]

The overall economic condition of the Fort Peck population was declining. Even with a relatively good crop year for 1927, tribal members had received half a million dollars from annuities and leases that year, but were making no substantial improvement. District Superintendent Campbell suggested that larger payments might be more helpful than the $50 per capita payments that had become the pattern.[136] While leasing revenues for fiscal year 1927 totalled $117,845.28, it

averaged only $51.20 per tribal member.[137]

Education remained at the forefront in priorities. Students at the Fort Peck Boarding School in Poplar were not satisfied to complete only the first six grades. In 1928, two students from the boarding school were enrolled at the Poplar Public Schools in the seventh grade. By 1929, the boarding school was teaching courses through to the eighth grade.[138] It was taking Indian students longer to advance through the grade levels, however, than their white counterparts. Sixty-two percent of full-blood children at the boarding school, according to a 1929 study, were "retarded in their progress."[139] The move to public schooling continued.[140]

A General Council was called in the fall of 1927. The council elected a twelve-member Executive Board, consisting of two delegates from each of six districts: Fort Kipp and Brockton on the east end of the reservation, Poplar and Burshia, and Wolf Point and Frazer on the west end. The members, elected to one-year terms, were Fred Buckles and Erza Ricker for Burshia District; Maurice Big Horn and George Boyd for Fort Kipp District; James Walking Eagle and Charles Parshall for Brockton District; Reverend Basil Reddoor and Andrew Red Thunder for Poplar District; Growing Four Times and George Long for Wolf Point District; and James Archdale and Henry Archdale, Jr. for Frazer District.[141] The council addressed questions of the membership's consent of tribal funds; homesteader extensions, land reappraisals, and Wolf Point airport lands; high power lines over tribal trust lands; and the basis for per capita payments. The General Council also elected eight individuals for a delegation to Washington, D.C., that would leave sometime after January 1, 1928, to work for legislation pending, which included further authorization to determine the scope of the Black Hills and Sisseton-Wahpeton Treaty claims, and the bill passed in the last Congress authorizing the

Government Row, Poplar, Montana, looking north, with Fort Peck Indian Agency headquarters building in the background, 1915. Superintendent Lohmiller's residence is at the end of the street at left. Agency offices were in the buildings in the right foreground, with other buildings housing the Indian boarding school and a public school. At the far right is the government doctor's residence at the end of the street on the right side.

Superintendent Charles B. Lohmiller at Fort Peck Indian Agency headquarters on the day he left the reservation, 1917.

Fort Peck Agency, 1918.

Poplar Post Office, 1918.

Public School Building, Poplar, Montana, 1918.

Indian men gathered in a tipi to sing, smoke, and visit, 1920s.

Left to right: Henry Archdale, Sr.,
Mr. Mollar, Superintendent, Isaac Blount,
Thomas Growing Four Times, 1920s.

Indian boarding
school buildings,
Poplar, Montana,
1920s.

The History of the Assiniboine and Sioux Tribes of the Fort Peck Indian Reservation: 1600 - 2012

Brockton School, built 1923. Students and teachers not identified.

Women at the Wolf Point Wild Horse Stampede, 1924. From left to right: Mrs. Louise Follet Garfield, Mrs. Whiteman (Pte Gi Wiya), Ada Murdock, Fourstar Matthews, Mrs. Sophie Hamilton, Mrs. Louise Fear Bear, Mrs. May Knorrr, and Mrs. Lena Follet.

Annie Hancock, 1930s.

Indian family sitting around the fire before supper, Fort Peck Indian Reservation, 1930s.

Chiefs, spiritual men, Sundancers, and medicine men smoking and visiting before a celebration, 1930s.

Poplar men's basketball team, Montana state champions, 1935–1936. From left to right: Joe Dauphine, Maurice "Scoop" Archdale, Jim O'Connor, Louis Longee, Coach Carl O. Hansen, Dib Adeline, Duncan Dupree, Eddie Bauer, Mark Denny.

Chief Andrew Red Boy Shields, 1938.

Florence Lambert Shields, 1938.

The History of the Assiniboine and Sioux Tribes of the Fort Peck Indian Reservation: 1600 - 2012

Chief Spotted Dog, 1940s.

Indians gathered at Brockton, Montana, 1940s.

Delegation sent to Washington, D.C., to meet with Franklin D, Roosevelt, 1940s. Front row, left to right: Azue Ricker (kneeling), Andrew Shields, Dave Johnson, Santee Iron Ring, Joshua Wetsit, Dolly Akers, Clara Ricker, Lucille Rick (girl), Elizabeth Lambert, girl, Rufus Ricker. Second row: Willard Sweeny, Cynthia Johnson. Third row: Basile Roddor, Mrs. Hale.

Bible School class at Mnisida Presbyterian Church, Chelsea, summer 1942. Front row, from left to right: Imogene Red Elk Gibbs, Tommy Brown, Jimmy Pipe. Second row: Hubert Brown, Delmar Brown, Myron "Buddy Pipe, Yvonne Reddoor, Jack Pipe, Jr., Min Su Pia. Third row: Billy Lambert, Kenneth Red Elk, Joanne Lambert, Unidentified boy, Marvin Eagleboy. Fourth row: Bessie Comes Last Brown, Elaine Red Elk Pipe, Helen "Maska" Lambert, Josephine "Ste" Eagle holding Zelma Eagle, Sarah Reddoor Margin, Mable Shields holding David Reddoor. Last row: Alice Gray Bear, Maggie Iron Cloud Red Elk, Sarah Brown Weeks, Herman Red Elk, Sr., Solomon Grey Bear, unidentified man, Chester Arthur, Dave Reddoor, Jack Pipe, Sr., Hubert Brown, Sr., holding two undentified children.

Company B, First Battalion, 163rd Infantry, Poplar, Montana, 1943. First row, from left to right: J. Melbourne, Jr., J. Black Dog, Jr., H. Red Elk, Jr., A. Zimmerman, H.J. Hayne, M.L. Peterson, A.B. Casper, R.H. Edeline, F.E. Proctor, A.G. Savior, W.H. McClammy, J.A. Smith. Second row: M. Longtree, D. Youngman, L. Half Red, L.E. Dupree, M. Murray, R.N. Jones, R. Brown, L.E. Longee, L. Shields, M. Brown, W.A. Hawk. Third row: R.F. SHields, F. Jones, J. Shields, H. Gelgarde, W.J. Culbertson, L. Red Dog, S. Jones, A. J. Lambert, I. Red Dog, G. Red Elk, E. Jones, J. Reddoor.

First row, from left to right: D. McClammy, C.R. Trinder, M. Lockman, C. Davis, W.J. Redfox, E.E. Booth, W.M. Davis, J.W. Dauphine, J. Red Thunder, C. Standing Bear, G. Smith, J.G. Delorme. Second row: F.R. Joshua, B. Little Head, W.C. Warren, W. Buckles, M.E. Black Dowg, A.E. Hollow, W.D. Morin, D. Left Hard Thunder, P.J. Eder, J.H. Kirn, J. Mason, Jr., A.L. Mohr, P. Kidder. Third row: E.D. Bear, W. Buck Elk, H. Buck Elk, R.D. Murray, R.L. Ogle, B. Lambert, A. Red Boy, C. Adams, A. Brown, R.M. War Club, Jr., M.D. Adams, S.Q. Red Boy, J. Cantrell, F. Bauer, Jr.

Gathering, 1943–1944. From left to right: Leroy Big Leggins, James Garfield, Nelson Chaisng Haw, Clarence Fear Bear, John Hunger (Stoney Chief), Joe Martin, Joyce Clark, Verdell Birdsbill, Earl Clark, Jr., Isabelle Wetsit, Joshua Wetsit, Iris Whitehead Anderson, Sibley Firemoon, Growing Four Times, Alan Smoker, Henry Blacktail, Pointing Iron.

Charlie and Angeline Iron Bear, 1950

The History of the Assiniboine and Sioux Tribes of the Fort Peck Indian Reservation: 1600 - 2012

From left to right, Chief Andrew Shields, Mr. Murphy, Murphy Oil Company, Chief Rufus Ricker, Sr., and Chief Santee Iron Ring, c. 1950.

Fort Peck Delegation to Washington, D.C., 1956. Front row, from left to right: Norman Hollow, James Archdale, Joseph Gary, President of NCIA, Austin Buckles. Middle row: William Smith, Leslie Four Star, Edwin Reddoor. Back row: Congressman Lee Metcalf; Senator James E. Murray; Chief Joshua Wetsit, Senator Mike Mansfield, Henry Archdale, Jr.

Tribal Adoption Ceremony for Mr. Mitchell and Mr. Larson at Poplar, Montana, March 5, 1957.

Fort Peck Indian Tribal Delegation to Washington, D.C., 1964. Seated, from left to right: Dolly Akers, Frances Linner, Edwin Reddoor, Leslie Fourstar, William Youpee. Standing: Unidentified, Carsten Beck, unidentified, Dale Balwin, Norman Hollow, unidentified, unidentified, Marvin Sonosky, unidentified.

Tribal Executive Board, 1973–1975. From left to right: Elphius Big Horn, Raymond White Tail Feather, Jim Black Dog, Leonard Boxer, Stanley Yellow Robe, unidentified BIA official, National Cow Boy Long Hair, Norman Hollow.

First raising of tribal flag, 1975. From left to right: Lonnie Reddog, Linda Azure, Marshelle Lambert, Ray K. Eder, Caleb Shields, Rita Talks Different, Darlene Buck Elk, Shirley Perry, Rodney Miller, Tribal Chairman Norman Hollow, Jack Bighorn, Jr., Roscoe White Eagle, Rurton Ryder, and Sylvia Roberts.

Some Fort Peck Tribal Executive Board members meeting with a Northern Cheyenne Tribal Council delegation at Poplar, Montana, 1977.

Fort Peck Reservation Tribal Flag, 1975.

The History of the Assiniboine and Sioux Tribes of the Fort Peck Indian Reservation: 1600 - 2012

Assiniboine claims. The council also instructed the Tribal Executive Board to prepare a constitution and bylaws for consideration.[142]

Burke, in a letter dated November 10, wrote Eggers to declare that since the meetings for purposes of selecting delegates had not been approved in advance, so neither the actions taken or the delegates chosen were approved. Eggers was asked to make a more detailed report and to supply minutes of the meetings. He was sent a copy of Circular 1652, dated January 15, 1921, and was asked to give particular attention to the last paragraph of Circular 2292, dated March 8, 1927, about the importance of adequate representation and traits expected in delegates, e.g. "honourable and trustworthy."[143]

On November 16, 1927, the General Council reconvened, meeting in the gymnasium of the boarding school in Poplar. Eggers opened the meeting by warning that tribal delegations must be selected by a strict protocol. Delegates must be chosen at an authorized meeting specifically called for that purpose. Eggers read from letters from the CIA stating that no tribal funds could pay for a delegation without previous authorization and confirmation that the delegates had been chosen at a legally authorized meeting. Eggers said that the October meetings had been too lightly attended to reflect adequate representation. He told the assembly that he was not there to dictate what they must do, but simply wanted to articulate the position of the agency and the Indian Office. The superintendent left the meeting, but asked Policeman Charles Thompson, a tribal member and former delegate to Washington, to take notes and report to him the proceedings. A discussion took place about the role being played by mixed-bloods in the political dynamics of the council and on the reservation, and especially for trying to speak and act without authority. A series of resolutions proposed the expenses and logistics for the eight-person delegation.[144]

The council then turned to the adoption of the constitution and bylaws prepared by the Tribal Executive Board. One article provided authority for the council or its executive board to call future General Council meetings, disputing the practice of the CIA and SI to pre-authorize meetings where delegates could be selected.[145]

The commissioner communicated to Eggers his refusal to accept the delegation that had been selected in the October meeting. Rather, he directed Eggers to call meetings of the Assiniboine and Sioux Councils where each could respectively select two representatives.[146] The four-person Fort Peck delegation included James Archdale and Walter Clark representing the Assiniboines, and Charles Thompson and Meade Steele representing the Sioux. Eggers appeared to grasp that Assiniboine and Yankton-Sioux interests were separate, and that the existence of two tribes, not one, was an important distinction that for the most part had been ignored by the Indian Office.

As I understand it, the Yankton-Sioux here have an interest in what is known as the Black Hills claim and the Assiniboines have an interest in extensive treaty claims in Montana. Now as far as these two claims of separate and distinct tribes are concerned, as I understand it, they are not connected. The Assiniboines are not interested in the Yankton claims, and the Yanktons are not interested in the Assiniboines' claim.[147]

The struggle between the Indian Protective Association faction and what Eggers had characterized as the other 90 percent of the population was the origin of the charge that the General Councils were not representative. Meade Steele, the main person at Fort Peck, was behind the Indian Protective Association. George Conners, tribal member, wrote to Eggers on February 7, 1928, "This associations [sic] one idea is to find fault with the Indian Bureau and everybody else connected with it and the Indians who are not of the same mind with the association that are in no way connected with the Indian Office are called the Superintendent's dogs." Conners presented recriminations against Steele, and suggested that Steele was fooling a good many people into "following his ideas about protecting the Indian." The postscript noted that A.A. Grurod, "the originator of the Indian Protective Association," was reported in the *Great Falls Tribune* for February 9 as about to be disbarred for defrauding a client.[148] Asked by the office to comment on Conners' standing, Eggers noted that Conners was in good favor with the majority of Fort Peck Indians, having the backing of his petitioners. He also stressed that Conners felt his authority to represent the Assiniboines in Washington was still in good stead. In no way would he oppose his nomination as a delegate, but Eggers could not recommend it in his official capacity.[149]

In a second letter of the same date, Eggers forwarded the minutes from the General Council that began in October and concluded finally in November. He described the work of the council and its efforts to transact a large amount of business, but also noted how the council was not representative given the large numbers of individuals who stayed away, among whom were old-time Indians. Eggers pointed out he had tried to provide advice about what would be needed for the council meetings to be accepted as legal, but felt his advice was not heeded.[150]

The Council of the Fort Peck Assiniboine Indians met in an "informal meeting" at Charles Hall's place on January 17, 1928, with fifty-eight individuals present. James Garfield, Sr., the Acting Chairman, called the meeting to order. Among the many issues discussed were the inequality of the homesteaders receiving payments because of the reappraisals of their lands, considering how many had extended the time of

when their full payments were due; the matter of certain Chippewas living east of Wolf Point, seeking to buy lands upon which they were squatting; and the matter of access of parents to their children's money that Burke had implemented, which meant that a demand be made for all leases of land belonging to minors be cancelled, that no reimbursable fund debts be forcibly collected, but rather a $100 per capita payment be made. There being business requiring councils, a motion was made requesting an Assiniboine council be held on January 24, at Charles Hall's place, and for a joint council with the Sioux to be held in Poplar on January 24, but it was defeated.[151] The Sioux council was held at Riverside Dance Hall on January 31, 1928, and the Assiniboine council met at Charles Hall's place on February 1, 1928, both meetings selected delegates to be sent to Washington, D.C.[152]

The delegation traveled to D.C. in early February and stayed for over a month. Each delegate was paid eight dollars a day, with a total of $1,800 having been authorized from the 4% Fund for their expenses. The CIA informed them on March 22 that they must return home as their per diem was being cancelled effective March 24.[153]

The manner in which the delegation had been elected was still a political issue. Eggers had described himself to the CIA as having taken the utmost care not to take an overactive role in the councils called to elect the delegates. Claude Reddoor, chair of the Sioux Council, had charged that the superintendent had interfered with the election. Eggers said that he had anticipated such charges. He described Reddoor "simply as a 'tool' of Steele, Wetsit, and Rufus Ricker," expressing his frustration with this faction:

There is no way that I can discover that this element can be satisfied. I have been patient, have taken their insults in silence, listened to their unwarranted charges of misconduct on the part of the office without becoming incensed, but this attitude on their part continues and I am entirely at a loss to know how to overcome the matter.[154]

The charges appeared to be a protest against the CIA's instructions and constraints about General Councils.

Eggers responded to the CIA about various points raised in the most recent inspection report submitted by Trowbridge. One of his explanations was particularly insightful about "Farm Activities and the Five Year Program." Eggers admitted that while there was a record of an industrial program having been instituted, in effect, there was little evidence. During the early part of the previous growing season, "the agitation was so strong and carried on so extensively on this reservation against the policy of conserving minors' funds." Eggers explained that when the policy had just come into effect, "the agitating element went up and down the reservation advising the Indians to retaliate in a measure by putting in no crops or making no effort at self-support whatever." At this point, Eggers asserted his opinion, "in other words to endeavour to get themselves in to that condition where it would be absolutely necessary for the Government to step in and render them assistance with the idea that to pay over to the parents, the minors funds." He continued, "I believe, however, that the better class of our Indians are viewing the matter differently and the Industrial Program can be revived again this coming season." He requested $10,000 in reimbursable funds to expend for sheep and milk cows, trusting that this would encourage industrial activities.[155] In a contradictory statement elsewhere in the report, however, Eggers noted that reimbursable loans had become increasingly very hard, if not impossible, to collect.[156]

On May 28, 1928, legislation was enacted to authorize the lease or sale of lands reserved for agency, schools, and other purposes on the Fort Peck Indian Reservation.[157] The SI was directed to seek specific instructions from the Fort Peck Reservation General Council for all sales of lands, and that all mineral rights on tribal lands were reserved for the Fort Peck Indians. All proceeds derived from the sale or lease of tribal lands were to be deposited in the Fort Peck 4% Fund in the U.S. Treasury.

In the next months, a number of the complaints resulted in the CIA authorizing or directing some changes at the agency and its programs. Due to the ongoing problem of illegal trespass on trust grasslands, two additional line riders were hired, and the position of Superintendent of Livestock was abolished. District Superintendent Campbell, in an inspection report, noted that some were beginning to buy tractors, demonstrating the seriousness among those wanting to make a living. Campbell reported that on April 16, 1928, a $50 per capita payment was made, bringing to a total the sum of $472,000 having been expended since February 1927 in such payments. Campbell did not see, without another extension to homesteaders, how money could accrue quickly enough to afford further per capita payments. Many family and individuals were already in economic freefall. The old and indigent were relatively all right, due to IIM accounts, with funds from inherited land sales and lease monies, and the more able-bodied were raising gardens.[158]

The resignation of the lease clerk in the spring of 1928 caused productivity in the agency office to nosedive. Turnover was becoming more frequent. By the spring of 1928, only two employees who had been employed prior to Eggers' arrival were still on board, but one of them, the financial clerk, was also resigning. A major factor may have been the increased number of inspections, which caused delays, impeded productivity, and encouraged a "spirit of insubordination among the Indians."[159]

By June, another petition was put forward seeking the removal of Superintendent Eggers. Again, Eggers was cleared of all of these allegations, but the nature of the struggle between incorporation and independence was further epitomized. While some of the charges were meant only to make trouble, others focused on Eggers' biases, including his unwillingness to allow certain land sales, and his failure to provide requested funds, to collect debts, or to solve marital problems and standoffs between families. In several ways, there were many Indians who blamed the government for everything, and the superintendent as the symbolic presence of the faraway authority in their midst bore the brunt of their displeasure. The new restrictions barring parents or relatives from access to their children's money were deeply resented, and Eggers was particularly blamed for this. Growing impatience with the local bureaucracy was increasing. Requests for money were referred to the District Farmer, who had to report to the superintendent for a decision. This particularly rankled when Indians knew what they needed better than the District Farmer. Resentment prevailed no matter the intentions of the system, and situations of non-cooperation increased.

Increasing costs of tuition for the children of untaxed Indians were quickly becoming too expensive. In 1928, the CIA directed that payments would no longer be made for any child with a blood quantum of less than one-quarter. Equally problematic, no payments were made if parents owned taxable real property, unless they held both taxable and non-taxable property, the latter the larger.[160]

The report in March 1929 on agricultural conditions at Fort Peck was mixed. The report compared a group of progressive Indians with the rest, noting that some of the former had

farming operations that were "practically on an equal basis with the better class of white farmers in the district." The rest had not displayed significant progress, and were not very interested in agricultural subsistence. Eggers believed that the farming operations should be kept to a scale that was viable, beginning small and simply. However, many people engaged in farming observed their white contemporaries buying power machinery, and naturally thought they should have similar conveniences. At the time, many white farmers on the reservation planted wheat using the dry-farming methods and had no stock, and they were on their farms only in the growing season, living in towns the rest of the year. When some Indians attempted this, because so many also had stock, they were faced with disposing of everything when they left their farms in the fall, so they were forced to start from scratch the next spring.[161]

Eggers was becoming concerned with the growing dependence on reimbursable loan funds to promote agricultural efforts. By spring 1927, the superintendent had extended loans from the minors' fund totalling $18,000 and in 1929, he had loaned additional funds for the purchase of sheep, but he saw little prospect that many could ever repay the loans. By January 1929, the outstanding debt level for the reimbursable fund totalled $35,000, and the level kept increasing. Ironically, in 1932, many of these debts were either cancelled or adjusted.[162]

The faction led by Meade Steele and Joshua Wetsit, however, protested Eggers' efforts to make reimbursable funds available, instead of pressing for another per capita payment from what they perceived as trust funds they should control. Campbell wrote in detail to the CIA on March 16, describing the way the "organized objectors to all constituted authority" had secured control of their own General Council. The former business council had been eliminated, the General Council organized in its place, and then members of the faction elected themselves officers who called meetings at their pleasure and conducted tribal business whether the superintendent approved or not.[163]

The political conflicts between the IPA proponents and others less ideologically driven about the use of the General Council continued. District Superintendent Campbell reported to the Indian Office about charges made against Eggers in March 1929. He noted that he had not observed elsewhere such "organized objectors to all constituted authority" as at Fort Peck. He identified their continual charges as a systematic protest against any superintendent or any representative of the government's policy of incorporation, assimilation, and social control.[164]

The IPA faction contended that its executive officers could call the General Council into session whenever they chose. Once a specific item was proposed, the officers would adjourn from day to day to keep the council in continuous session, so that other business could be transacted. Most of the reservation population were busy making a living and could not take days to attend the council, thus forfeiting the operations of the council to those "agitators" who made the work of the council and organizing their occupations, but who represented only a small portion of the reservation's population.[165]

Commissoner Burke wrote to Eggers on March 27, 1929 that additional reimbursable funds were indeed to be made available, but reminded Eggers that these funds could only be dispersed to restricted Indians and not to fee patent Indians, as the latter did not have any collateral that could be sold to collect debts, but that this money must be handled "in accordance with banking customs, and assist only those who may be classed as good risks." Burke continued,

Of course, in order to get the Indians to utilize

their resources and make an effort in self support, the Superintendent will in some instances, render assistance in cases which bankers would refuse, but the risks must be restricted to such an extent as is consistent with the idea of helping those who help themselves.[166]

Ironically, a similar philosophy of pragmatism and self-reliance was being dispensed by the Indian Protection Association or Self Protection Association advocates, who saw themselves as advocates for control of the tribes' assets and the purposes to which fiscal resources should be applied. The rising conflict between mixed-bloods and full-bloods reached another level in 1929. Joshua Wetsit, Rufus Ricker, and Claude Reddoor represented themselves as full-bloods and organized a group called "Better Government Organization of the Fort Peck Indian Reservation."[167] They openly criticized the superintendent for not preventing the formation of the "Council of Fort Peck Indians," organized by Charles Hall and designed to be a forum for mixed-bloods.[168] The full-blood group tried to appeal to the Montana congressional delegation that the mixed-bloods were organizing to usurp the authority of the General Council. The Indian Office and Eggers equivocated and stalled, feeling they had no business interfering with these political organizations.[169] Assistant CIA J. Henry Scattergood wrote Senator Burton K. Wheeler on October 31, declaring that between the recent rival councils, neither was representative of the Indians of the Fort Peck Reservation.[170]

In 1929 the drought that would last until 1937 began. In April, Eggers wrote the CIA, full of optimism that the coming growing season would be a success because "our Indians are showing a very commendable spirit at this time."[171] He had no way to anticipate how dry the season would be. The growing despair by the fall of 1929 was only compounded in October by the stock market crash that heralded the beginning of the Great Depression. In many ways, the economic depression was already well underway in northeastern Montana, and the deepening depression created new problems and exacerbated old ones.[172] In August 1929, Board of Indian Commissioners member H.L. Scott filed his inspection report. In his opinion, far too many Indians still lived in dirt-roofed log houses. Most of the crops had been lost, and he advised the families that had unsalable horses to slaughter them for food rather than overgraze the range further.[173]

During fiscal year 1929, the agency hired additional clerks to bring the work current.[174] Former Superintendent Moller was hired to assist with the backlog problem. Much of this staffing appeared to be accomplished by transfers.

Early in 1930, Charles Eggers' tenure ended. In April, a decision Eggers had made a year before, routing the highway northward from the Macon Bridge across the Missouri River and into Wolf Point rather than north to the cross-reservation highway, was investigated. The new highway cut a sweeping curve through twenty Indian allotments; the investigation showed that Eggers appeared to have "sold out to the Wolf Point interests," and consequently, many Indians lost confidence in him.[175]

Additional complaints were investigated. Many Indian people had objected to agency employees collecting "unauthorized indebtedness" from them. Meanwhile, merchants were complaining about "long delays" in securing payments authorized by the agency. Trowbridge determined that the agency had issued improper purchase orders drawn on Indian accounts, some of which were without funds, and also had issued orders for Indians who held patent in fee certificates and had no current accounts. Once pointed out to Eggers, he explained these as "unofficial orders," and said that he would settle all outstanding accounts with the merchants if the

Indians did not. Eggers had been fair with both his supporters and opponents. The inspector also discovered that the Frye Cattle Company had been particularly liberal with advances to Indians from which they leased lands, with the apparent purpose of ensuring the renewal of the company's leases. The inspector declared this a "bad practice," and the Frye Cattle Company manager agreed to discontinue it. In conclusion, Trowbridge recommended more stringent adherence to the Indian Office regulations about financial matters, especially in the administration of Indian monies. In an attempt to determine what caused these circumstances, Trowbridge identified what he thought was a central problem:

that the superintendent is too soft-hearted to withstand the demands or appeals for assistance, and the tendency to comply, together with his apparent wavering attitude, has been taken advantage of by some of the Indians, especially the mixed-blood Patent-in-Fee Indians, most of whom perform no work, have little if any income, and expect more than the full blood restricted Indian.[176]

However, other matters also demanded attention, some because of Eggers' actions, some attributable to other employees, others to the high turnover in agency staff, and still others to the struggle between the mixed-bloods and full-bloods.[177] One issue was the land adjoining Wolf Point that was leased as a grazing unit, but used for an airport and as a rodeo grounds for the Wolf Point Annual Stampede. Another matter was a small tract occupied under an illegal trespass agreement arranged by the agency lease clerk. Another involved lands near Wolf Point being occupied by "Canadian Cree squatters." The city of Wolf Point was also using Indian lands for the city garbage dump.[178] An ongoing dispute between the farmer James Smith and the Frye Cattle Company about the use of the

Box Elder Sub-Agency buildings and grounds resulted in the permit being revoked. Trowbridge recommended the cattle company vacate the sub-agency buildings to settle the dispute. Another matter was that coal kept in railway cars needed to be protected from theft by employees. Other circumstances relative to the coal mining on the reservation revealed that a lack of oversight had lead to abuses. Trowbridge recommended that the Superintendent of Livestock position be reinstated with duties to include the supervision of coal permittees.[179]

The entire situation with agency personnel gave rise to a number of recommendations. For more efficient administration of the agency's work, Trowbridge found too many positions were being filled by tribal members from the Fort Peck Reservation—twenty-six out of forty-nine—and in his opinion, when the ratio exceeded one-third, "the organization is bound to become weak."[180] He did not state whether he was concerned about conflicts of interest, nor did he appreciate the economic importance of these positions to the tribal members.[181]

The neglect of the old and indigent was another problem. Trowbridge attested that he thought Eggers had done what he could, but felt that in cases in which older tribal members had relatives with money, their families should support them.[182] Several matters about land sales raised questions about how to close the estates of deceased tribal members, and whether the continuous disposal of lands would leave many more Indians homeless.[183]

While Trowbridge sifted through the details of Eggers' administration, he still found the superintendent competent, an advocate for Fort Peck tribal members, and an "active and patient administrator."[184] His administration had resulted in tangible accomplishments; the acreage farmed had increased from 4,286 acres in 1927 to 25,000 acres in 1930, and revenues from

leasing had increased from $87,452 to $163,008. Mixed-bloods tended to support Eggers, while full-bloods tended to oppose him. Trowbridge hesitated to recommend a change in administrations, knowing that no individual was likely to satisfy both factions.[185]

During Eggers' administration, the Indian Office tried to be a better trustee of the reservation grazing lands, striving for more systematic use and conservation of the grasslands. In 1930, a comprehensive report on the grazing situation on the reservation was written by George Nyce, Assistant Range Supervisor. He recommended that "a systematic long-range grazing program be initiated." The main obstacle was the pattern of land-holding created by the institutionalized allotment. Nyce's profile identified 122,793 acres of tribal and reserved lands, all but about 2,000 acres classified as grazing land. Of the allotted lands totalling 1,076,286 acres, 937,600 acres were classified as grazing land. The alienated lands totalled 895,065 acres, including homesteads, fee patents, and sales. What was particularly problematic was that categories of land were intermixed, making any attempt to create large blocks impossible unless individual allottees allowed their lands to be included with the tribal lands.[186] Furthermore, 375 individuals were identified as active farmers, and only forty-five of these, mostly mixed-bloods, were indicated as stock raisers. The total amount of Indian stock included 3,100 horses, 817 cattle, 890 sheep, 300 hogs, and twenty goats. Nyce observed that "the small number of stock raisers and the relatively small size of their herds made it impractical to establish a reserved area for Indian stock."[187]

Nyce gave the leasing program at the Fort Peck Reservation a mixed review. The lease fund was receiving fifteen cents per acre, which was three and one-half cents more than the state of Montana got for leasing land. The land-holding pattern gave rise to a selective practice by some lessees, who strategically leased allotments that controlled water, and then wherever circumstances permitted allowed their stock to run on unleased surrounding lands, so that only 60 percent of the grazing lands were actually being utilized in a given season.[188] Leasing suffered from inadequate monitoring and enforcement. The acquisition of stock through reimbursable loans simply complicated matters, since keeping herds separated required the kind of surveillance not available.[189]

Nyce recommended several changes that would contribute to greater stability, including five-year terms for the leases and permits, and a requirement that holders be responsible for fencing the units. He suggested that the units be created with a minimum grazing fee per head once the carrying capacity of particular range units had been ascertained. Nyce argued that it was important that the agency track and document the number of animals being grazed on the range, since only then could regulations be successfully enforced. He suggested that acreage for horses be fixed at two horses to one cow and acreage for sheep be five sheep to one cow. Another need was for consolidation, so the lands of leaseholders could not be used to prevent checkerboarding by some lessees to control substantially more land that they had actually leased. Nyce felt that with these kinds of changes, the grazing lands could be more productive, and conservation would also improve.[190]

The viability of the leasing program was a huge concern to the tribal members, since leasing provided most of the contingency funds. In 1931, the grazing lands were blocked into units, with estimates made about carrying capacities. [191] The agency sought to implement the new regulations, but Fort Peck tribal members were increasingly divided. The holders of land on the west end, mostly Assiniboines, were in favor of the new format, but the Sioux, who held most of the east-end range, were opposed. The Fort Peck Council, being mostly Sioux, opposed the new payment per head plan, but Joshua Wetsit, the Assiniboine chair, supported it. With no concensus emerging, the CIA suggested that the superintendent implement the new scheme where there was support, and maintain the previous formula in other areas.[192]

The amounts charged for leases were contested between tribal members and the potential lessees. The interested stockmen, citing their deteriorating economic condition, pressed for a reduction from the fifteen cents per acre that tribal members expected. There certainly were individual Indians willing to agree to a lower rate, but the superintendent had been cautioned by the Indian Office to secure their acceptance in writing. Meanwhile, the states of Montana and Wyoming were reducing their rates for grazing on public lands. Approval came in 1932 for a series of one-year leases of grazing units, mostly to homesteaders, with the admonition that their stock must be kept on the leased acreage. In succeeding years, for all grazing permits issued, 60 percent of landholders had to sign powers-of-attorney before the superintendent.[193]

In view of other complaints about the Wolf Point highway decision and Eggers' cavalier approach to regulations, the CIA transferred him to a new post at Shawnee Agency. The new superintendent appointed in September 1930 was Halle D. McCullough, a person with no experience. Within months, McCullough asked that a qualified Forest Service person be sent to Fort Peck to assist with leases of grazing lands. McCullough clearly was not impressed with the two systems and the variations in between.[194]

Frustration at Fort Peck grew when so little appeared to be done to prop up the local economy. Recovery in the past had depended on per capita payments. Reimbursable loan funds had also been another source. But the Depression was deepening and the drought was not abating. This adversity put many at odds.

By late 1931, the "Assiniboine" Council stated that they felt the Sioux were receiving more relief. This counter council, dominated by mixed-bloods, opposed the manner in which the Executive Board of the General Council operated, dominated by Meade Steele and Gus Heddrick. Joshua Wetsit and Charles Hall were the leaders of the Assiniboine Council. In General Councils the majority ruled, and leadership depended upon who had the majority present at elections of board members. Voting took place in public at the meeting, displaying to all present who supported whom.

During the Eggers administration, the Tribal Business Committee had been dissolved in a General Council by a unanimous vote in the spring of 1927. To satisfy the inquiries of Congressman Scott Leavitt, however, the Indian Office relented and encouraged the reestablishment of a representative body to express opinion and consent. In an authorized General Council on October 18, 1927, Joshua Wetsit (Assiniboine) was elected chairman and Meade Steele (Yankton-Sioux) was elected secretary. This council represented both tribes, and was authorized to handle all business matters.[195] Under instructions received on March 20, 1930, Eggers had drafted a constitution and bylaws, which he based on Klamath and Blackfeet documents.[196]

Meanwhile, the change in superintendents occurred, and McCullough wrote the CIA on November 24, 1930 that in the previous three months, he had needed the action of a business committee. He also had worked on the draft constitution, and had asked select tribal members to read his draft and offer their opinions. He also clarified the district boundaries for elections and had asked that each district have election clerks. He proposed to ask whether

voters supported the idea of a council to transact business on their behalf.[197] The referendum and write-in ballot were held on December 15, 1930, over the objections of Meade Steele and Claude Reddoor.[198] McCullough wrote the CIA on December 19 to report that in a vote of 360 to 260, the proposition of a Tribal Business Committee was approved, and he listed the councilmen elected: Joshua Wetsit, Oswego; Nimrod Davis, Frazer; James Archdale, Frazer; Sam Savior, Poplar; Andrew Red Thunder, Poplar; George Washington, Poplar (Riverside); Grover Cleveland, Poplar (Riverside); Maurice Big Horn, Brockton (Drew); Lloyd Red Eagle, Brockton (Drew); Meade Steele, Wolf Point; and John Adams, Wolf Point. McCullough noted how much more efficient this form of government was compared to the "cumbersome and inefficient method of doing business" represented by the General Council.[199]

McCullough had arranged for the election on the day per capita checks were distributed, to ensure as many people as possible participated in the election. But as critics pointed out problems with the election, McCullough had to admit it was not as well conducted as he had originally thought. Moses White Horse and Meade Steele wrote McCullough on January 19, 1931, and pointed out that of 1,287 votes cast (they may have meant eligible voters), 667 voters did not vote for the representative business committee, but rather voted for committee men, and they claimed only 354 cast ballots for committee men, leaving 933 not voting for a representative. They also noted how close some of the races were. They went on to declare,

It will be plainly seen that the purpose of the election was not understood by a large majority of non-English-speaking Indians. It is unfair for the Indians to have to accept this election, and we therefore respectfully request that in order to know the true sentiment and attitude of the Indians regarding whether we should have a business committee or General Council, as the official body that another election be held to decide the matter.[200]

The Indian Bureau had ignored suggestions about business committees, and such a committee was often manipulated by the bureau to get approval for "things that the Bureau want [sic] are always injurious to the Indians and to their welfare."[201] In turn, McCullough responded that important correspondence had been mislaid, and so the issue of a constitution and bylaws needed more discussion before being submitted to the "Tribal Council" for adoption. He had not found the authorization for the General Council sent to Eggers on April 24, 1929, nor another communication, dated October 31, 1929, asking why a General Council had not been authorized. Therefore, the election had been held in a political limbo, and McCullough called himself a "bonehead" for his misunderstandings. He demonstrated that his total of votes was more complete than those of White Horse and Steele. He concluded that Claude Reddoor's observation was correct, that "you had better withhold approval until the whole matter shall have been presented to a general council next summer." McCullough closed saying,

In the meantime, I could have the committee in some day in an advisory capacity. The educational work in favour of a committee and the demonstration of the fact that a supervised election could be held in which the office did not seek to influence the vote in any way would justify the work already done.[202]

On April 24, 1931, McCullough announced a General Council for May 19 in Poplar.[203] The council began by electing officers. Meade Steele was elected Secretary, and Joshua Wetsit,

President, with Rufus Ricker as Vice-Chairman. Fifteen resolutions were brought before the council, necessitating meeting a second day. One proposed permanent trust status for Indians "as long as Indians live and Indians to be exempted from taxation."[204] Another called for Congress to enact legislation to provide that in "property for individual Indians the contract for purchase shall be executed by the Government of the United States or its representatives on reservations," and in holding such title, be held in the same status as other property held by the U.S. government, "not subject to liens or mortgages or writs of attachments for debts or any encumbrance of any nature."[205] And another asked for cancellation of "reimbursable charges" on Fort Peck irrigable lands.[206] The next morning, a motion was approved to elect a Tribal Executive Board of seventeen. McCullough, writing his report to accompany the minutes, accepted the General Council to replace the business committee, stating that the number discussing and voting on resolutions indicated "representative attendance," and that the "general attitude of the Indians was fine," in that they expressed the sentiment that this was a "good council," the "first legitimate council we have had since 1927."[207]

In this report, McCullough stressed that the context for Resolution No. 5 had been that cars and tractors bought on installment had been repossessed from tribal members who failed to make their payments. He went on to explain:

In order to get a license for his car, an Indian must not only pay his license fee, but submit a tax receipt or a statement from the County Treasurer that his car was not taxed last year. The Treasurer has refused to give any such statements. Hence, most of the Indians have had to pay taxes on their cars before they could get the 1931 license. Since the Treasurer is the only person who has first-hand information on this subject, he is the only one who could make such a statement. We have been using a Bill of Sale form No. 367G on reimbursable purchases of chattel property this spring. The use of this Bill of Sale by Indians purchasing cars, tractors, trucks, etc. would, I think, solve the difficulty indicated in Resolution No. 5.[208]

Assistant CIA J. Henry Scattergood responded to McCullough with both caution and clarification. When the title belongs to the seller under a conditional sales contract, the best course would be to discourage purchases of cars or other farm machinery "unless the Indian has enough money to make full payment therefore [sic] it would seem to be unwise for this Service to sanction purchase of an automobile for him." Scattergood then reminded McCullough that the form the superintendent was using was not meant for expenditures over $50.[209] While consumerism and distances on Fort Peck Reservation were realities the Indian Office did not want to acknowledge, the dangers of indebtedness were a concern, but little could be done in the face of an insidiously rising pauperism.

The General Council had called for another delegation to Washington, asking that $3,000 from the 4% Fund be set aside to support a delegation when Congress convened in December 1931.[210] Scattergood asked that this be put off.[211]

Events from May to December 1931 were unclear. A conference in Washington, D.C., on grazing and leasing prompted the selection of one delegate for the Assiniboine and the Sioux respectively. Joshua Wetsit was chosen to represent the Assiniboine, and Meade Steele, the Sioux. They proceeded to Washington, D.C., in December 1931 to conduct business as a delegation. This was not really acceptable to the Indian Office, and additional ratification of their continued delegation was sought and received in correspondence with McCullough and various

members of the Tribal Executive Board.[212]

By January 28, 1932, the political processes of the tribes were not working well, and Chairman of the General Council Executive Board Joshua Wetsit wrote to Acting CIA J. Henry Scattergood about Assiniboine objections to joint councils with the Sioux. He related how the Assiniboines had always been "fair and liberal." He explained that the Assiniboine had been in the region for a very long time, pre-dating the arrival of the Sioux, and historically had always been cooperative with the U.S. government. The Assiniboines, he said,

wish to have a separate council of their own in which to take all matter(s) and transact affairs at their Agency on west end of the Reservation, Wolf Point, Montana. We are handicapped we live too far away from the main agency, they out number us and are unfair minded and unreasonable. They [are] obstructing any program that we think it is of the best interest of the Indians. Our problems, our interests are the same and we have equal rights to a certain extent.[213]

On March 24, 1932, Wetsit was deposed by the other members of the General Council, who were all Sioux. He was replaced by Gus Heddrick, a controversial individual who at one point had been banned from the reservation. Although this executive committee appointed three other Assiniboines to the board, the Assiniboines felt they had been effectively excluded.

Two days earlier, the Assiniboine Council sent a resolution to McCullough and the Fort Peck Council, demanding a separate agency at Wolf Point, and by implication their own reservation. Their feelings of political disenfranchisement were embodied in the first paragraph, a direct borrowing from the American Declaration of Independence, substituting the "Assiniboine Indians" for "American Colonies." The last sentence of this paragraph read, "Such has been the patient sufferance of these Assiniboine Indians and such now is the necessity which constrains them to alter their present intertribal form of Government." The next paragraph asserted their vision of political independence:

Therefore, we the undersigned enrolled Assiniboine members of the Fort Peck Reservation, Montana do hereby declare to you to take notice that so far as physically possible our inter-tribal relationship through council or otherwise is hereby severed, insofar as our tribal and inter-tribal business shall pre-serve good friendship and friendliness toward each other. Furthermore we have found that we cannot follow the leadership of the Sioux Nation on account of the caliber [sic] of men now being installed as leaders of the Fort Peck Council and rather than to get into any political or legal entanglement we feel that we should not jeopardize our other interests on account of personalities. We desire to be free in our own councils unbiased and unprejudiced to con-sider the many problems coming before us. For these reasons we feel that the interests of the Assiniboine Indians shall best be served under this plan that it is self evident that the Indians of the country is sorely in need of constructive leadership, men of ability with absolute and unimpeachable Christian character and fur-thermore under the constitution of the United States whether in council or out of council constructive criticism from the Assiniboine of the Government will be heard and understood in Washington.[214]

Eighty names were affixed to the resolution, and the petition was forwarded to the CIA asking for intervention on their behalf. Joseph Parnell, the first signatory, wrote an accompa-nying letter expressing the desire that some new procedure should be established for handling intertribal business, but he was emphatic on the point that a General Council of both tribes was no longer acceptable.[215]

McCullough, in a letter to the CIA, dated March 31, 1932, attempted to give his perspective of the Sioux dominance of the council. During a meeting of the council the summer of 1931, the board passed a resolution appointing Charles Parshall and Gus Heddrick to a resolutions committee, and also to act as councilmen. It had become a practice of the council for councilmen to bring proxies from tribal members and then to vote these in blocks. The superintendent went on to explain,

You will note that the officers of the council are now all Sioux. The five chief officers of the Council are now all Sioux. The outstanding so called "agitators" or "Bolsheviks" of the reservation. With one or two exceptions the entire council is composed of politically minded Indians. To quote the words of a good many substantial Indians who goes "too far." I feel that the Council is going not only too far but too fast for the general run of the population to follow.

"My sympathies are rather with the Assiniboines," McCullough continued. "They are outvoted at the Council meetings and have become so discouraged that they have practi-cally ceased to attend the meetings of the general council and the executive committee."[216] He noted that provisions were in place for separate Sioux and Assiniboine councils relative to their respective land claims. McCullough stated that reservation-wide concerns were supposed to be discussed and resolved in the General Council.[217]

In June 1932, Congress passed an act that allowed expenditures up to $5,000 of tribal trust funds "for expenses of the Fort Peck Indian Tribal Council and authorized delegates of the tribe." With this authorization, the executive committee set a per diem of $3.10 per mile for travel expenses to and from council and executive meetings, and in addition, wanted to claim per diem and travel expenses for a committee of twelve to travel from the reservation to report to Congress. McCullough felt the mileage allowance was too much and since the executive committee was comprised of representatives from various regions of the reservation, he questioned why their travel could not be accomplished without additional expense. The expenses for a stenographer for the executive committee of three days per diem for typing the minutes of each meeting were also too extravagant.[218] Overreacting to this criticism, at the next General Council meeting McCullough did not even provide a meal, and over 300 people went without supper. This made a lasting negative impression on all in attendance. Clearly, the superintendent had not learned the cultural value of generosity during his two-year stay at Fort Peck, and this was not lost on the Tribal Executive Board and their constituents.[219]

As the Depression brought shortages, people sought to meet their needs. A narrative written several years later discussed the coal mining that had happened in recent years, all for local consumption. The coal was not "good commercial coal," so it was mined and sold on and off the reservation. Only a few tribal members were at all interested in the coal development.[220]

By the fall of 1932, a new list of forty-odd charges were brought against Superintendent McCullough by a faction working for his removal. G.E.E. Lindquist of the Board of Indian Commissioners conducted an investigation. Once again, factionalism was identified as the source of the various charges, most with substantiation. McCullough had clearly been hampered by his inexperienced staff, his tendency to remain more in his office rather than to travel about the reservation, and his minimal understanding of "Indian psychology." Given the intractability of

factions at Fort Peck, the commissioner recommended that McCullough be transferred and someone more experienced be appointed.[221] The recommendation was acted upon soon after by CIA Rhoads.[222]

Almost as an afterthought, the situation of forced patents was somewhat alleviated. Of 200 or so patents at Fort Peck that fell into this category, forty were cancelled by the terms of the 1927 law suspending such practices.[223]

Faced with responding to the Depression, FDR's administration reduced the size of government and appropriations for Indian agencies. The Fort Peck Agency budget faced a decrease of $16,000 from fiscal year 1932 to fiscal year 1933. This did not preclude new money for cooperative high schools at Poplar and Frazer, however, nor for agency capital projects. The balances in the Fort Peck tribal trust funds were continuously being drawn on for "capita payments, agency and support services, and delegation funds at a time when the income for the tribes was decreasing." Many tribal members believed the funds would soon be gone. By 1933, a total of 455 agricultural leases were in force with 185 grazing leases and permits issued. Sixty-seven leaseholders were delinquent, with ten cases referred to the U.S. District Attorney.[224]

Reimbursable loans had been the stopgap, but the accumulated indebtedness had grown to over $92,000, with $67,000 considered delinquent: "Loans had been made for the purchase of livestock, farm machinery, seeds, fence wire, repair and construction of homes."[225] Tribal members, seeking "decent houses," because there had not been much improvement since 1929, continued to apply for reimbursable loans.

The growing demands for relief and rations reflected the impact of the Depression. In the previous fiscal year, relief for indigent Fort Peck tribal members totalled $31,225. Recipients complained about being required to work for the funds and about the poor food issued. The effort in the winter of 1932-33 for a ration list based on calories and supported by the American Red Cross helped, but simply adding tomatoes, molasses, raisins, and carrots was insufficient.[226]

Complaints about medical services were also increasing, including "alleged neglect and inattention." School matters were in flux. "The old Poplar boarding school had been turned into a boarding home for approximately 127 boys and girls, over half of whom were orphans or were from broken homes." These children had begun attending the public school that the government was already funding. For the 100 students enrolled in the Wolf Point Public School, tuition of forty-two cents per day was charged, and about half of the students were at least one-quarter Indian. Among the other schools, there was clear educational progress.[227] The Indian Office contributed $35,000 to the Wolf Point Public Schools in 1933 to meet a tuition increase, which supplied hot lunches and funded a home economics program. The rural Wetsit School was closed and the children were bussed into Wolf Point.[228]

McCullough was replaced by C.L. Walker in December 1932. This occurred upon the eve of Franklin D. Roosevelt's inauguration, and the translation of the rhetoric of the New Deal into a tangible response to the Great Depression. Roosevelt soon appointed Harold Ickes as SI, and accepted the recommendation of Ickes that by April 1933, John Collier, the reformer, become the CIA. Walker's administration was destined to be even shorter than McCullough's. Walker's program was proposed to a Fort Peck General Council on August 10, 1933. Walker's key points for the development of the reservation and his new administration were mostly designed to respond to complaints of tribal members.[229] The council, chaired by Gus Heddrick, gave full approval to Walker's proposals. Unfortunately,

Walker's plan overlooked the extent to which the reservation economy was beginning to imperil the livelihood of tribal members.

New Deal work programs were available on the reservation by the fall of 1933, including the Civil Works Administration (CWA) and Civilian Conservation Corps (CCC). Many tribal members were again at work for actual wages. But the demand for work exceeded the number of positions sponsored by relief agencies. Various subsets and factions tried to influence who might be replaced by others on the CWA rolls. Factionalism flourished, with good men being dropped from rolls, and those with criminal records retained.[230]

While the council approved Walker's development plan, others were more impatient. Complaints by Delegate Theresa Spindler was presented to the Indian Office in Washington in February 1934. Her "Statement of Facts" pointed to great suffering and starvation, laying the blame at the superintendent's door. She claimed he was stingy with relief goods and suggested misappropriation of relief employment funds. She told of the failure to drill a proper water well at Fraser, and when salt water was found instead, it was put in a reservoir, presumably for irrigation purposes. She noted a plan for a pasture for Indian stock where no Indian stock was left, with horses sold and cattle eaten. She was also critical of the efforts to create truck trails across the reservation and fire lanes in the timber. Spindler was particularly critical of the council chairman, Gus Heddrick, comparing his $107.50 monthly salary to the $6.48 the average tribal member made. She was outraged at Walker's arbitrary "persecutions" of particular tribal members.[231]

In the Statistical and Narrative Report for 1934, Walker expressed hope that many Fort Peck tribal members would get to work on the Fort Peck Dam, a major public works project.[232] Initially, complaints were made about disparities in wages that the Walker administration allowed. Pay for unskilled labor was fifty cents per hour, but Indians received half that rate.[233] Whether this disparity existed is not clear, but the numbers working on the dam diminished as the project progressed.

Walker tried to quell the unrest, but even with the support of Chairman Gus Heddrick and the local school superintendent, his days as superintendent were clearly numbered. By midwinter, there was a clamor for the General Council to select delegates to go to Washington, to appeal for relief. Another petition was circulated by Joshua Wetsit, Theresa Spindler, Rufus Ricker, and others, seeking removal of the superintendent and a number of other agency employees. Heddrick, however, remained loyal to Walker. By spring, the Executive Committee of the council heard and discussed even more complaints. Inefficiencies in scheduling ration days caused hardships for many. By June, delays in paying out lease money created further anger. By the end of the month, Walker departed, with senior clerk H.M. Knutson acting as superintendent until another arrived in September.[234]

John G. Hunter's tenure as superintendent lasted from September 1934 to April 1939. During Hunter's tour of duty, the drought and the general economic depression affected the people of the Fort Peck Reservation badly. The unrelenting drought had impaired both farming and stock raising. Efforts to develop local markets and incentives for agriculture were undermined. The programs begun or continued under the Rhoads-Scattergood administration were being either discontinued or carefully evaluated by John Collier, the new CIA. But federal relief money was more readily available. Expertise was brought to bear upon managing rangelands, more effective ways of sustaining agriculture were introduced, and educational and health endeavors were emphasized. These initiatives translated to some degree into "opportunities for the Indian population," often in the form of jobs, and better delivery of services.[235]

The 1932 election brought the Democratic Party back to power with FDR as president. Both faced the challenge of pulling the nation out of the Great Depression. The former governor of New York had promised a "New Deal" to the American people, and once elected, appointed Harold L. Ickes as SI, which led to the appointment of John Collier as CIA. The New Deal offered to Indians was put forward in a legislative proposal called the Wheeler-Howard Act of 1934, also known as the Indian Reorganization Act (IRA). Its passage was not easily accomplished because many Republicans resisted the kinds of comprehensive changes Collier wanted to initiate. Collier openly recognized elected tribal governments, and fostered their self-determination, albeit within certain limits. The IRA provided voluntary programs to the tribes willing to accept and participate in the initiative. Most central was recognition of cultural independence, including a new freedom of religious practice. Collier, a former Indian policy reformer and advocate, brought an enlightened agenda to the fore. This demarcated the beginning of a very different Indian policy.[236]

The Johnson-O'Malley Act was enacted on April 16, 1934, enabling states to acquire funds for tuition and incidentals for restricted Indians so they could attend public schools.[237] A vote on acceptance of the IRA was scheduled for each federally recognized Indian group and reservation.[238] The vote for the Fort Peck Tribes was scheduled for December 1934.[239] Meanwhile, a General Council on June 16 discussed the latest draft of the Wheeler-Howard Bill, but the attendance was smaller than expected, with only 175 present.[240] Factions for and against the bill were present. When a vote was taken, it resulted in a tie, 59-59. Many opinions were aired, from the anticipated effect of the IRA on the treaties to the impact of new money for schooling children.[241]

The previous July, prior to Hunter's appointment, the Indian Office circulated a lengthy questionnaire to ascertain how tribal government functioned and how it might better fulfill its responsibilities. Fort Peck, relying upon the General Council model, operated with a Tribal Executive Board, which was "authorized to act on all tribal matters except adoptions and election of Washington Delegations," those resting with the General Council. By this time, the board had empowered the superintendent "to act on all tribal leases in accordance with existing rules and regulations."[242]

A delegation of six persons and two bus drivers was sent to Glasgow, Montana, as the Tribal Reception Committee on August 6, 1934, to welcome President Roosevelt and to travel to Fort Peck Dam for its dedication.[243] The visit did not appear to affect the debate about the IRA.

One critical element of the IRA was that it suspended immediately any further allotments of land to individuals. Collier already had suspended allotment until the passage of the IRA, being determined to stop the erosion of the land base of tribes. In 1930, the total number of fee patents at Fort Peck totalled 766, which included approximately 200 "forced patents." Patents had been forced on a number of mixed-bloods who had not applied for them, and on the Fort Peck Reservation, problems existed in how this policy was applied. Although there had been provisions in the 1927 Act for cancelling such patents and reinstating trust status, in practice less than fifty trust patents had been reinstated or were under consideration by 1932. The remainder of those with forced patents had already disposed of all or part of their lands.[244] The practice of continuing to allot lands to new generations of Fort Peck tribal members had given rise to a sense of a right to allotments, a sentiment that had existed

for more than twenty years by 1934, when ten further allotments had been made since the first allotment in 1913.[245]

As the December 15 vote came closer, debate about the acceptance of the IRA intensified. Supporters, many of them progressive, argued that the benefits outweighed the drawbacks, while the opponents argued that dangers lurked in the legislative scheme. The opposition was quick to point out the negative possibilities, including the loss of future allotments, threats to allotments already held, and the SI's authority to refuse allotments to certain Fort Peck children. A letter was circulated from former Superintendent Charles Eggers attacking the legislation. The non-Indians living in towns on the reservation, however, were a major source of opposition. Businessmen from Wolf Point specifically were opposed to the proposal that the federal government be able to buy back submarginal lands and return them to tribal trust status. Fearing the loss of tax revenue and a reduction of the county tax base, the opposition attacked the IRA as a threat by some politicians who wanted several northeast Montana counties consolidated into one. Partisan political competition was also a factor, with Republicans working against a Democratic program of reform. These interests were threatened by the changes in Indian policy, particularly as they applied to land.[246]

A number of individuals represented the IRA position, including several Indian leaders, agency employees, and Indian Office administrators at Fort Peck.[247] This was in keeping with Collier's efforts on the Sioux reservations and the Navaho reservation, when the degree of resistance was identified.[248]

Notwithstanding an intensive lobbying effort, the vote on December 15, 1934, rejected participation in the IRA by a two-to-one margin. Of the 1,027 eligible voters, 578 voted against it and 276 voted to accept it.

Fort Peck Vote by District on Acceptance of IRA

	YES	NO
Fort Kipp	37	64
Brockton	26	17
Riverside	12	63
Poplar	68	193
Wolf Point	28	107
Oswego	48	26
Frazer	17	68
Absentee	<u>40</u>	<u>40</u>
	276	578

(1,027 eligible voters)[249]

Reactions to the plebiscite were mixed. Hunter expressed his disappointment, blaming the Wolf Point business interests and Eggers' letter. Among tribal members, there was concern about what this would mean for future relations with the Indian Office and the U.S. government. Interest was expressed in sending a delegation to Washington to explain the vote to the Montana congressional delegation, the CIA, and SI.[250] Tribal members such as James Garfield, Sr. wrote Collier that many Indians at Fort Peck were disappointed that the measure was defeated, stating that far too many did not understand fully what was at stake and that misrepresentations had been made about the land matters.[251]

The Indian Office reacted like a preoccupied scorekeeper as reservations across the country voted. One official several months later suggested to Hunter that perhaps separate councils for the Fort Peck Tribes would allow the "Executive Committee [to become] more representative and sparking competition between the Assiniboines and Sioux." Hunter was not enamored with this suggestion because he felt he had the reservation well in hand.[252]

In a General Council in Poplar on a stormy and cold winter day on January 12, 163 persons heard a presentation about a constructive program to address their problems and develop-

ment. The plan was to build on irrigation development, without which the people would be left to appeal for relief. Hunter recognized that while the Fort Peck Tribes had developed a reputation as "being particularly difficult to work with and to do anything for," he countered that he felt they had been misrepresented:

It has been difficult to manage them, to satisfy them and to gain their cooperation because no program, offering any measure of independence has ever been inaugurated. Their only opportunity in this regard, that I am able to learn of, was their chance to accept the Indian Re-organization Act, and because of misrepresentation, and because of various adverse influences being brought to bear they turned this down, which has seemed to me their only hope.

Now that they have excluded themselves from the Indian Re-organization Act, they seem to have reached a crisis in their affairs which demands immediate and proper attention and because of this quite extreme situation, it is their belief that a delegation of four representative Indians should go to Washington, in order to present to you and your staff their many problems together with their suggestions toward the solution of such problems. After studying conditions relating to this jurisdiction I realize more and more as the days pass that these people are beset with greater problems and difficulties than any people that I have ever known, and because of this situation, together with the earnest desire on the part of the greater number of them to develop a constructive program so as to afford an opportunity for a measure of independence, I thoroughly concur in the advisability of a delegation being authorized to go to your Office. I feel this so strongly that I wish to especially urge your favorable consideration.[253]

The General Council of January 12, 1935 decided to delay the selection of delegates, working instead on the details of their development program. The council agreed that a delegation was of the greatest importance. The General Council convened on February 23, 1935, and authorized Joseph Parnell and Charles Renz as delegates.[254] The plan was presented to the Indian Office with great success, even though the two official delegates were inexperienced. George Conner, Sr., explained that in his work for the passage of IRA acceptance, the minority had been composed of many tribal members with large families, who held properties greater than the majority voting against the act. The minority were left to take a middle course by helping Hunter draw up a program that, if accepted by a General Council, could then be forwarded to the Indian Office for approval.[255] In the memorandum prepared for Hunter by John Collier, Walter V. Woehlke of the Indian Office and the four delegates explained what they were told. The need for a long-range economic plan was discussed, and this led to the matters of land consolidations to counter checkerboard areas. Solutions needed to be found to the land situations for Fort Peck Tribes to be eligible for economic development grants. Collier told the delegation that he did not have a solution since the tribes had rejected the IRA, but suggested that they might study various sections of the draft Thomas-Rogers Bill, and then suggest "a scheme for the Fort Peck [sic] might be developed along those lines." This bill was being proposed by Senator Edgar Thomas, Chair of the Senate Indian Affairs Committee and Representative Will Rogers of Oklahoma, to provide a modified version of the IRA to the tribes of Oklahoma, which did not become law until June 1936. The delegates thanked Collier and indicated that they would "study" the situation. However, Collier was bothered to hear that once the delegates arrived on Capitol Hill, they were told that since they had rejected the IRA, little

could be done for them. The delegates proceeded to state that the Indian Office could do nothing for them, which was wrong. Collier stated that this willful misrepresentation must be cleared up, before he would have any further discussion with the delegation.[256]

Perceiving the chosen delegates as Sioux only representing Sioux interests, the Assiniboine Council elected James Archdale and George Connor, Sr., in a meeting on April 23, and authorized them to travel to Washington to represent the Assiniboine interests; however, they did so without any authority granted by the Indian Bureau.[257] Hunter had also traveled to D.C. accompanying the delegation. The delegation returned from Washington with little more than a promise of cooperation. Since the tribes had rejected the IRA, development was left in the hands of the local politicians and the extent of their willingness to work with the superintendent and other federal agencies.

In the 1934 narrative section of the annual Narrative and Statistical Report, it was observed that from 1913 until 1934, the interspersal of white homesteaders among tribal members influenced them. The superintendent suggested that tribal members had become educated to a level that they were no longer content with "old ways of living" and "yet they have not learned to satisfy their modern desires and cravings by their own effort." Acknowledging this as a turning point, he continued, "This results in much dissatisfaction and constant scheming to acquire money and modern luxuries such as their white neighbours have. Naturally these desires and cravings often bring the Indians into conflict with the law and increase their suffering." Hunter continued with his recommendation:

It is certain that some plan must be put into effect soon for the consolidation of their land holdings and prevention of further alienation of their lands or they will soon be landless and at the mercy of the Government. A few have already reached this stage but it is hoped that the restriction will continue so that no more may come to this sad plight.[258]

In this same report, the superintendent is quite thorough in his assessment of social conditions, beginning with the point that there were few natural resources to be exploited. Discussing the potential for industrial development of the reservation, Hunter acknowledged climatic limitations. He noted that large quantities of coal were being mined for local consumption, but it was unsuitable for commercial use. It was being utilized by homesteaders and others living on or near the reservation. Few Indians were part of this development; while some had mines on their allotments and operated these themselves, most depended upon non-Indians to operate mines. Much of the mining was on tribal lands, and the resulting income went to the trust fund. Another resource was sand and gravel of commercial quality, and most recently this had been "cut and sold" for highway and other road construction. Depending on locations, this brought considerable income annually to individuals and to the tribes. The chief source of natural resource income, however, came from grazing permits and farm leases. Hunter criticized how many homesteaders, in their efforts to prove their claims, plowed acceptable grazing land to create poor quality farming land. The result was "that one of the finest ranges in the country has been destroyed and we have hundreds of poor farmers scattered about the reservation, who most of the time depend upon Government aid for their existence." Ideally, Hunter recommended that "this sub-marginal class of land . . . should in some way be restored to the reservation and to its status as grazing land."[259]

Hunter reported a continuum of employment available to tribal members. Besides building U.S. Highway 2 through the length of the reservation, the Indian Office spent $80,000 in 1933-1934 building the Indian Highway from one end of the reservation to the other, serving most communities and allotments closest to the Missouri River. Hunter explained, "This road program has furnished employment to practically all needy Indians during the past three months." He hoped that the program could be continued throughout the coming year.[260] Hunter described the orientation of those living and working off the reservation:

Since all of the Indians, with the exception of a very few who are self-supporting, live on the reservation, little needs to be said here regarding this phase of the situation. It is possible that as many as 500 Fort Peck allottees reside off the reservation but these are considered self-supporting and live where they do by choice because they are better enabled to provide for themselves off the reservation than they would be at home.

Heretofore it has not been possible to find employment near the reservation for the reason that farming activities outside were at a very low ebb and there was not other sources of employment. At present, plans are under way for the construction of a huge dam at the old site of Fort Peck, on the Missouri River. It is hoped that while this work lasts we will be able to secure employment for a large number of Indians of this jurisdiction.[261]

The estimated number working off the reservation in farm labor was twenty-five, but compared to all those who needed work locally, this provided negligible relief.[262]

The superintendent shifted his emphasis to the economic conditions on Fort Peck, which he characterized as "very poor." Essentially, tribal funds had been depleted with the most recent per capita payment, and with reduced lease rentals, land sales income, and income from the few engaged in large-scale farming to raise surplus cash crops, the outlook for accumulation of trust funds was bleak. In the profile he said,

The estimated family income for the year was approximately $150 per family. Outside of a few who had irregular employment in reservation towns, most of the Indians, who are able and willing to work couldn't find employment except that furnished on Government projects, such as road building and repair of irrigation ditches.[263]

While this kind of work had been "sufficient for all needs" during the past year, the future did not bode well. General rationing had begun in 1931 because of the crop failure, and continued until the summer of 1932, when gardens started producing and returns from the next crops and crop share leases were secured. The surge of temporary work meant no rations were made to able-bodied Indians. Raising enough to carry families through the winter was difficult, however, because those with plenty often shared with the less fortunate, so the overall food supply was never adequate for the average family.[264] Homes were in very poor condition. The superintendent turned judgmental:

Indians marry young without previously acquiring a home often without means of support. Immorality, divorce and wife desertion are common. Homes are often overcrowded with two or three families living together. Efforts have been made throughout the year to get parents to assume more responsibility for their children.[265]

On a more positive note, he praised the County Home Extension Agent who worked with seven home extension clubs and four 4-H clubs on the reservation. A four-point program emphasized food preparation, food preserva-

tion, home improvement, and sewing clothes. Coordinating efforts between the Agency Farmers, other Interior Department agencies and programs, and the home extension staff meant that work with the fifteen farm chapters (a number of these on the reservation), eight home extension clubs, and twelve 4-H clubs in Roosevelt County served Indians as much as non-Indians. The objective of the Home Extension Service was to assist "the Indian to make a better living for himself and family out of his land and labor." Their programs were designed to assist the immediate needs of Indian families while "laying a foundation for a long-time program of development," often through farm visits and involving families in the chapters and clubs, and promoting self-sustaining practices and sources of profitable income.[266] In the face of this optimism, what was undeniable was that harvests were lower than in previous years because of the drought and grasshoppers.

The superintendent was aware that the Fort Peck Tribes had plenty of land, but lacked the means to capitalize on it. Consequently, when rentals were fewer, tribal members would suffer financial hardship until as a group they managed to produce commodities from their land base, either by agriculture or some other means.[267]

At the midwinter fair the previous year, courses and information displays were presented. Over 2,000 people attended, with more Indian speakers on the program than ever before. Two Farm Bureau films, one emphasizing canning skills, and another, *Life at Home*, were shown in eleven sittings to 275 persons.[268]

More efforts were spent on gardening in 1934 than in any previous season, encouraged by the 1933 growing season. From a total of 424 gardens in 1932, there were 504 for the 1933 growing season. Seventy-five were of the size to support a family of five for twelve months. Many gardens were increased by 20 percent in overall size:

"There were 3,525 bushels of potatoes produced, 4,165 lbs. of onions, 37,250 squash and pumpkins, 1,250 cabbages, 3,480 lbs. of carrots, 16,555 lbs. of beets, 1,300 lbs. dry beans, and 15,550 lbs of cucumbers." But there were also setbacks, primarily that most of the dry-land gardens produced only a limited quantity of food "due to drought and insects." Thirty families raised a sufficient quantity of garden produce to "carry" them through the winter.[269] Garden contests were sponsored through the 4-H chapters, and many more root cellars were dug.

The livestock program had aimed in 1932 to have twenty families purchase milk cows during the year, which required building fifteen new stock barns and starting eight new beef herds. The goal was only partially realized as twelve families purchased sixteen milk cows and one bull; eleven new barns were built and nine others repaired. Nine families secured twenty beef cows and four bulls with private funds, taken in on lease and land sale settlements, and by trades. Livestock operations on the reservation were limited to eighty-eight families who owned 255 milk cows, sixty-five families who owned 754 beef cattle, nine families who owned 1,455 sheep, four families who owned sixteen milk goats, and thirty-four families who owned 222 pigs. Since milk and meat were lacking in the Indian diet, expansion of cattle raising in particular was a means to increase annual income of farm families. A parallel expansion in properly housing animals and growing feed for them was hindered by inadequate capital.[270] Several families were raising poultry, including turkeys.[271]

Housing remained a major problem, and because there was no regular building program, little financial assistance was available. In the 1933-1934 year, twenty-five new homes were constructed and twenty-six were improved. However, a shortfall remained on the reservation—622 resident families were identified, but there were only 523 houses. Superintendent Hunter noted:

A good many families have two houses, one in the country where they live in summer and one near town where they move in the winter to put children in school. This makes the shortage appear greater that would appear above. Also a few have two houses in the country, a frame one which they use in the summer and a log one beside it for winter use.[272]

Under the Hoover administration, there had been money for a chief of police and four "privates," but due to the "enforced economy" of the new administration, the force was reduced to a chief and two privates. The superintendent declared that this was simply inadequate, and without assigned vehicles, this situation was unacceptable. With the end of Prohibition, the legal sale of 3.2 beer resulted in some difficulties, but later the situation improved. The major concern, however, was domestic conflicts, including wife deserters, wife beaters, adulterers, and Indians who failed to support their families. A capable judge was on the bench who had the trust of tribal members; anyone brought before him knew they would receive a sentence if they deserved one. Considerable difficulty arose over the need for either "additional laws" for the reservation Indians or for a separate jurisdiction for Indians for offenses not punishable under federal statutes or before the Indian Court.[273]

In his statement of a proposed program for 1934, Hunter praised the 500 Indians living off the reservation, describing them as finding a better life, and most of them as "self-supporting," and consequently there was little incentive for them to return. Some included women married to white men, described as being "very well taken care of." These individuals were left to find their way without agency assistance. In contrast, in his discussion of "Welfare and Social

Conditions," Hunter described the health situation reservation-wide as "generally good" and the education work as well in hand. He hoped that the economic condition could be improved if more Indians became self-supporting. Hunter's program emphasized: 1) no more sales of Indian land to whites, with the only exception when needed to facilitate consolidations, 2) consolidation of present land holdings in blocks as near to the Missouri River as possible through purchase or exchange, 3) irrigation for all agricultural land held by Indians to the extent that each Indian family might have enough "irrigated agricultural land to enable him to produce all his subsistence supplies and stock feed on his own land," 4) "encouraging and educating Indians along the lines of most approved methods of farming in order that they may better understand how to produce their own living," and 5) discouraging all leases of land that could be utilized by the Indians themselves.[274]

In the years 1934 and 1935, two decisions in particular had a significant impact on the people of the Fort Peck Reservation. By late summer 1934, the authorized purchase of 100,000 acres of sub-marginal reservation lands had begun, and by fall, approximately 104,300 acres were identified for purchase at an average price of $4.99 per acre. Though the initial intention had been to purchase only lands south of and including Township 29 to consolidate lands where tribal members mostly lived, the proposed purchase was expanded to include some tracts in the northern part of the reservation to block out grazing units that then might be available to lessors.[275]

A second decision involved withdrawing from possible sale or entry all undisposed surplus lands by two departmental orders. A total of 41,400 acres was withdrawn and held until a decision was made to return these to the tribes.[276]

The years from 1921 to 1935 saw democratic self-determination increasing among Fort Peck tribal members. Furthermore, diverse opinions dominated the political scene for much of this period with factionalism evident, with some people inspired by ideas and actions off the reservation, and others by associations and dispositions within the reservation.

The lands within the reservation boundaries that remained in trust status were finally viewed as a resource that should be protected. Clearly, the diminishment of the tribes' estate in this period was profound and disturbing, but so was the experience of the Great Depression and the ways in which the drought exacerbated the circumstances. Delinquent homesteaders and their manipulation of the system meant that they shortchanged both the trust fund of the Fort Peck Tribes and county and state taxes, but this finally was solved with legislation.

Sending delegations to Washington, D.C., became as habitual as per capita payments. Tribal members used these infusions, never very large, to adjust to the cash economy. While health and education facilities and services were improving, their delivery remained problematic. Transportation was improving and the demand for automobiles was increasing.

The political shift from the Republican administrations of the 1920s to the election of Democrat FDR brought new policies and approaches. John Collier's efforts to introduce the IRA did not succeed at Fort Peck, and later had an impact upon the ways in which the Fort Peck Tribes dealt with the Indian Office, the Department of the Interior, the U.S. Congress, other federal agencies, and municipal, county, and state jurisdictions. Finally, the manner in which the Fort Peck Tribes related to the outside world profoundly influenced internal dynamics in the districts, communities, families, and among individuals. ✪

1 Stephen Cornell, *The Return of the Native* (New York: Oxford University Press, 1988); Thomas D. Hall, "Native Americans and Incorporation: Patterns and Problems," *American Indian Culture and Research Journal* 11 (2) 1987: 1-30.

2 Samuel Conger, Chairman, and Meade Steele, Secretary, to E.B. Merritt, Asstitant CIA, Washington, D.C., January 31, 1921, CCF 7165-1921 Fort Peck .054, RG 75, National Archives and Records Administration [hereinafter cited as NARA], Washington, D.C.

3 E.D. Mossman, Superintendent, Fort Peck Agency [hereinafter cited as "FPA"], Poplar, Montana, to CIA, Washington, D.C., February 2, 1921, CCF 7165-1921 Fort Peck .054, RG 75, NARA-Washington, D.C..

4 Meritt to Steele, in care of Mossman, FPA, Poplar, Montana, February 15, 1921, CCF 7165-1921 Fort Peck .054, RG 75, NARA-Washington, D.C..

5 Fred C. Morgan, Special Supervisor, "Fort Peck Indian Agency, Montana: Unrest Among the Indians," not dated, rec. November 7, 1921, 89896-1921 Fort Peck 121, copy in the Chrono folder "General History, 1920-1927," Docket 184 Collection, Fort Peck Tribal Archives, Poplar, Montana.

6 Ibid.

7 Douglas D. Martin, *Historical Report on the Fort Peck Indian Reservation, Part I: An Administrative and Social History*, Docket 184, Defendant Exhibit No. FP-I, Fort Peck Indians v. United States, Court of Claims, Docket 184, 138-139.

8 J.W. Culbertson, Jr., President, and S.H. Conner, Secretary, Indian Welfare Association, Poplar, Montana, to CIA, Washington, D.C. and attached petition, October 28, 1921, Central Classified Files-General Records, Bureau of Indian Affairs, 1907-1939, 83298-1920 Fort Peck 211, RG 75, NARA-Washington, D.C.

9 Superintendent Kitch, Poplar, Montana, to CIA, Washington, D.C., November 4, 1921, CCF 83298-1920 Fort Peck 211, RG 75, NARA-Washington, D.C.

10 F.M. Goodwin, Assistant SI, Washington, D.C., to Kitch, Poplar, Montana, November 18, 1921, CCF 83298-1920 Fort Peck 211, RG 75, NARA-Washington, D.C.

11 Kitch, Poplar, Montana, to CIA, Washington, D.C., December 2, 1921, CCF 83298-1920 Fort Peck 211, RG 75, NARA-Washington, D.C.; Burke, Washington, D.C., to Kitch, Poplar, Montana, December 21, 1921, CCF 83298-1920 Fort Peck 211, RG 75, NARA-Washington, D.C.

12 No specific approval for the extraction of oil was granted. See *Congressional Record* for November 10 to 23, 1921, debate and order of third reading of S. 2312 U.S. Senate, page 7646, Docket 184 Collection. Designation of coal lands was authorized in 1908 Fort Peck Allotment Act (Public Law No. 177, May 30, 1908, Chapter 237, 60th Congress, First Session, 558), and leasing for all unallotted lands and unrestricted lands opened to utilization including mineral activity. This was authorized in an act, September 20, 1922, Public Law No. 313, 20 September 1922, Chapter 347, 67th Congress, Second Session, 847

13 F.E. Brandon, Inspection Report, June 10, 1922, Chrono file "General History, 1920-1927," Docket 184 Collection, Fort Peck Tribal Archives, Poplar, Montana.

14 Public Law 329, September 21, 1922, 42 Statute 994.

15 Martin, *Historical Report on the Fort Peck Indian Reservation, Part I: An Administrative and Social History*, 139-140; James H. McGregor, "Fort Peck Schools, Special Report," June 10, 1922, Chrono file "General History, 1920-1927," Docket 184 Collection, Fort Peck Tribal Archives, Poplar, Montana.

16 Ibid.

17 Martin, *Historical Report on the Fort Peck Indian Reservation, Part I: An Administrative and Social History*, 139; Kitch, Poplar, Montana, to CIA, Washington, D.C., December 19, 1922, Chrono file "General History, 1920-1927," Docket 184 Collection, Fort Peck Tribal Archives, Poplar, Montana.

18 Superintendent's Narrative Report Fort Peck Reservation, M1011, *Superintendent's Annual Narrative and Statistical Reports from Field Jurisdictions of the Bureau of Indian Affairs,* 1907-1938 [hereinafter cited as SANR Fort Peck] [RG 75], NARA-Washington, D.C., 1977 [microfilm publication], 1922: 1-2.

19 Ibid., 2-3.

20 Ibid., 3.

21 Ibid.

22 Ibid., 4-5.

23 Ibid., 8-9.

24 Ibid., 9-11.

25 Ibid., 12-16.

26 Ibid., 16.

27 Ibid., 16-17.

28 Ibid., 18.

29 Ibid.

30 Ibid., 19.

31 Ibid., 22.

32 Ibid.

33 bid., 23-24.

34 SANR Fort Peck 1923-Statistical: 26.

35 Carl Stevens, Supervisor of Schools, Poplar, Montana, to CIA, Washington, D.C., May 25, 1923, Chrono file "General History, 1920-1927," Docket 184 Collection, Fort Peck Tribal Archives, Poplar, Montana.

36 Martin, *Historical Report on the Fort Peck Indian Reservation, Part I: An Administrative and Social History*, 140-141.

37 Ibid., 141.

38 Ibid.

39 Marvin J. Presser, *Wolf Point: A City of Destiny* (Billings: M Press, 1997), 46.

40 *AR-Commissioner GLO*, 1923: 22-23, Chrono file "General History, 1920-1927," Docket 184 Collection, Fort Peck Tribal Archives, Poplar, Montana.

41 *AR-Commissioner GLO* 1924: 27.

42 *AR-Commissioner GLO* 1925:23.

43 Martin, *Historical Report on the Fort Peck Indian Reservation, Part I: An Administrative and Social History*, 141.

44 Martin, *Historical Report on the Fort Peck Indian Reservation, Part I: An Administrative and Social History*, 141-142.

45 "Indian Association Has Successful Convention," *The Poplar Standard*, n.d., v. 15, n. 43, Chrono File "General History, 1920-1927," Docket 184 Collection, Fort Peck Tribal Archives, Poplar, Montana.

46 43 Stat. 253.

47 C.F. Hauke, Chief Clerk, Washington, D.C., to Martin Mitchell, Fort Peck Reservation, Wolf Point, MT, April 11, 1925, CCF 21196-1925 Fort Peck .053, copy in Chrono File, "General History, 1920-1927," Docket 184, Fort Peck Tribal Archives, Poplar, Montana.

48 SI file, "Indian Office, Tribal Funds-Legislation," 66th to 70th Congresses, portion of the file, Chrono file "General History, 1920-1927," Docket 184 Collection, Fort Peck Tribal Archives, Poplar, Montana.

49 Martin, *Historical Report on the Fort*

Peck Indian Reservation, Part I: An Administrative and Social History, 142.

50 Martin, *Historical Report on the Fort Peck Indian Reservation, Part I: An Administrative and Social History*, 142.

51 Ibid., 143.

52 Ibid.

53 Ibid.

54 Hugh L. Scott, Member, Board of Indian Commissioners, Princeton, N.J., to George Vaux, Jr., Chairman, Board of Indian Commissioners, Department of Interior, Washington, D.C., October 1, 1924, Special Reports, BIC, Vol. 5, 237-241; copy in Chrono File, "General History 1920-1927," Docket 184 Collection, Fort Peck Tribal Archives, Poplar, Montana.

55 Ibid.

56 Ibid.

57 Ibid., 144..

58 Inspector Samuel Blair, Poplar, Montana, to CIA, Washington, D.C., via Office of Chief Inspector, March 29, 1926, Chrono File "General History, 1920-1927," Docket 184 Collection, Fort Peck Tribal Archives, Poplar, Montana.

59 Ibid.

60 *Montana: Resources and Opportunities*, 279; copy in Chrono File, "General History, 1920-1927," Docket 184 Collection, Fort Peck Tribal Archives, Poplar, Montana.

61 Ibid., 278.

62 *Montana: Resources and Opportunities*, 278; ibid.

63 Blair, Poplar, Montana, to CIA, Washington, D.C., via Office of Chief Inspector, March 29, 1926, Chrono File "General History, 1920-1927," Docket 184 Collection, Fort Peck Tribal Archives, Poplar, Montana.

64 *AR-Commissioner GLO* 1926: 21.

65 Blair, Poplar, Montana, to CIA, Washington, D.C., through Inspection Division, August 31, 1926, copy in the Chrono File, "General History, 1920-1927," Docket 184 Collection, Fort Peck Tribal Archives, Poplar, Montana; Martin, *Historical Report on the Fort Peck Indian Reservation, Part I: An Administrative and Social History*, 145-146.

66 Moller, Poplar, Montana, to CIA, Washington, D.C., November 19, 1923, and Burke, to Moller, telegram, November 23, 1923, CCF 89612-1923 Fort Peck .056, RG 75, NA Washington, D.C.

67 Telegrams between the CIA and Moller, two dated January 26, 1926, and January 30, 1926 and January 31, 1926; and attached Minutes of Meeting, November 23 and 24, 1923, Steele, Secretary, and attached correspondence, Charles Eder, Member Tribal Committee, to Moller, Poplar, Montana, January 23, 1924, and Rufus Ricker, Sr., Chairman of Tribal Committee, to Moller, Poplar, Montana, January 30, 1924, CCF 89612-1923 Fort Peck .056, RG 75, NARA-Washington, D.C.

68 Moller, FPA, Poplar, Montana, to CIA, Washington, D.C., January 31, 1924, CCF 89612-1923 Fort Peck .056, RG 75, NARA-Washington, D.C.

69 Burke, Washington, D.C., to Moller, Poplar, Montana, February 8, 1924, CCF 89612-1923 Fort Peck .056, RG 75, NARA-Washington, D.C.

70 Steele, Washington, D.C., to Burke, Washington, D.C., February 8, 1924, CCF 89612-1923 Fort Peck .056, RG 75, NARA-Washington, D.C.

71 Moller, Poplar, Montana, to Burke, Washington, D.C., February 12, 1924, CCF 89612-1923 Fort Peck .056, RG 75, NARA-Washington, D.C.

72 C.C. Calhoun, The Attorneys for the Sioux Nation, Washington, D.C., to CIA, Washington, D.C., February 18, 1924, CCF 89612-1923 Fort Peck .056, RG 75, NARA-Washington, D.C.

73 Moller, Poplar, Montana, to Burke, Washington, D.C., March 3, 1924, CCF 89612-1923 Fort Peck .056, RG 75, NARA-Washington, D.C.

74 Moller, Poplar, Montana, to Burke, Washington, D.C., March 18, 1924, CCF 89612-1923 Fort Peck .056, RG 75, NARA-Washington, D.C.

75 Moller, Poplar, Montana, to Burke, Washington, D.C., March 18, 1924, CCF 89612-1923 Fort Peck .056, RG 75, NARA-Washington, D.C.

76 Ibid.

77 "Schedule of Per Capita Payments Made to the Fort Peck Indians under Act of May 30, 1908," n.d., attached to letter E.B. Meritt, Assistant CIA, Washington, D.C., to James Archdale, Fort Peck Delegation, Washington, D.C., June 3, 1924, CCF 89612-1923 Fort Peck .056, RG 75, NARA-Washington, D.C.

78 Archdale, Frazer, Montana, to Burke, Washington, D.C., March 22, 1924, CCF 89612-1923 Fort Peck .056, RG 75, NARA-Washington, D.C.

79 Moller, Poplar, Montana, to CIA, Washington, D.C., March 31, 1924, CCF 89612-1923 Fort Peck .056, RG 75, NARA-Washington, D.C.

80 Burke, Washington, D.C., to Moller, Poplar, Montana, April 7, 1924, CCF 89612-1923 Fort Peck .056, RG 75, NARA-Washington, D.C.

81 Moller, Poplar, Montana, to CIA, Washington, D.C., May 14, 1924, CCF 89612-1923 Fort Peck .056, RG 75, NARA-Washington, D.C.

82 Moller, Poplar, Montana, to Burke, Washington, D.C., May 9, 1924, CCF 89612-1923 Fort Peck .056, RG 75, NARA-Washington, D.C.

83 Moller, Poplar, Montana, to CIA, Washington, D.C., June 6, 1924, CCF 89612-1923 Fort Peck .056, RG 75, NARA-Washington, D.C.

84 Archdale, G.H. Conners, and Steele, Washington, D.C., to CIA, Washington, D.C., June 7, 1924, CCF 89612-1923 Fort Peck .056, RG 75, NARA-Washington, D.C.

85 Garfield, Wolf Point, MT, to Meritt, Washington, D.C., November 17, 1924, CCF 89612-1923 Fort Peck .056, RG 75, NARA-Washington, D.C.; Merritt, Washington, D.C., to Garfield, Wolf Point, MT, December 8, 1924, CCF 89612-1923 Fort Peck .056, RG 75, NARA-Washington, D.C.

86 Burke, Washington, D.C., to Moller, Poplar, Montana, November 8, 1924, and Moller, Poplar, Montana, to Burke, CIA, Washington, D.C., November 19, 1924, Misc. Correspondence, 1918-1924, FPA, RG 75, NA-Denver)

87 Moller, Poplar, Montana, to CIA, Washington, D.C., December 4, 1924, CCF 89612-1923 Fort Peck .056, RG 75, NARA-Washington, D.C.

88 Moller, Poplar, Montana, to CIA, Washington, D.C., February 16, 1925, CCF 89612-1923 Fort Peck .056, RG 75, NARA-Washington, D.C.

89 Garfield, Pointing Iron, Santee Iron Ring, Rufus Ricker, Sr., William Whiteright, Sr., and Andrew Red Thunder, Poplar, Montana, to Moller, Poplar, Montana, January 26, 1925, CCF 89612-1923 Fort Peck .056, RG 75, NARA-Washington, D.C.

90 Burke, Washington, D.C., to Senator Burton K. Wheeler, Washington, D.C., February 14, 1925, CCF 89612-1923 Fort Peck .056, RG 75, NARA-Washington, D.C.

91 Gus M. Hedderich, Poplar, Montana, to Meritt, Washington, D.C., February

10, 1925, CCF 89612-1923 Fort Peck .056, RG 75, NARA-Washington, D.C.

92 Moller, Poplar, Montana, to CIA, Washington, D.C., March 14, 1925, CCF 89612-1923 Fort Peck .056, RG 75, NARA-Washington, D.C.

93 William Whitright, Secretary, Minutes of a Meeting of the Business Council of the Indians of the Fort Peck Indian Reservation held at Poplar, Montana . . . 3rd Day of March, 1925 . . . ," CCF 89612-1923 Fort Peck .056, RG 75, NARA-Washington, D.C.

94 Moller, Poplar, Montana, to CIA, Washington, D.C., March 14, 1925, CCF 89612-1923 Fort Peck .056, RG 75, NARA-Washington, D.C.

95 IPA Subject File, Montana Historical Society, Helena)

96 Petitions to Moller, Poplar, Montana, March 23, 1925, CCF 89612-1923 Fort Peck .056, RG 75, NARA-Washington, D.C.

97 Steele, Wolf Point, Montana, to Moller, Superintendent, Poplar, Montana, April 12, 1925, CCF 89612-1923 Fort Peck .056, RG 75, NARA-Washington, D.C.

98 Moller, Poplar, Montana, to CIA, Washington, D.C., April 17, 1925, CCF 89612-1923 Fort Peck .056, RG 75, NARA-Washington, D.C.

99 IPA Subject File, Montana Historical Society, Helena).

100 Moller, Poplar, Montana, to CIA, Washington, D.C., December 15, 1925, CCF 89612-1923 Fort Peck .056, RG 75, NARA-Washington, D.C.

101 Moller, Poplar, Montana, to CIA, Washington, D.C.., January 13, 1926, CCF 2648-1926 Fort Peck .054, RG 75, NARA-Washington, D.C.

102 Martin, *Historical Report on the Fort Peck Indian Reservation, Part I: An Administrative and Social History*, 155..

103 Martin, *Historical Report on the Fort Peck Indian Reservation, Part I: An Administrative and Social History*, 155-156.

104 Martin, *Historical Report on the Fort Peck Indian Reservation, Part I: An Administrative and Social History*, 156..

105 Ibid.

106 Inspector Samuel Blair, Poplar, Montana, to CIA, Washington, D.C., 31 August 1926, copy in Chrono File, "General History, 1920-1927," Docket 184 Collections, Fort Peck Tribal Archives, Poplar, Montana; Historical Report on the Fort Peck Indian Reservation, Part I: An Administrative and Social History, 146.

107 Martin, *Historical Report on the Fort Peck Indian Reservation, Part I: An Administrative and Social History*, 147.

108 Ibid.

109 SANR Fort Peck 1926, Section 4: 10.

110 Burke, Washington, D.C., to Moller, Poplar, Montana, September 28, 1926, Chrono File, "General History, 1920-1927," Docket 184 Collection, Fort Peck Tribal Archives, Poplar, Montana.

111 Moller, Poplar, Montana, to CIA, Washington, D.C., October 4, 1926, Chrono File, "General History, 1920-1927," Docket 184 Collection, Fort Peck Tribal Archives, Poplar, Montana.

112 Burke, Washington, D.C., to Moller, Superintendent, FPA, Poplar, Montana, October 13, 1926, Chrono File, "General History, 1920-1927," Docket 184 Collection, Fort Peck Tribal Archives, Poplar, Montana.

113 SANR Fort Peck 1926:1.

114 Ibid., 2-3.

115 Ibid., 4-5.

116 Ibid., 2.

117 Ibid, section three, 3.

118 Ibid., 3.

119 SANR Fort Peck 1926, Statistical Report 1926: 8.

120 SANR Fort Peck 1926: 3.

121 Ibid., 4.

122 SANR Fort Peck, 1926, section 4, 3-4.

123 Ibid., 5.

124 Ibid., 9-10.

125 Ibid., Section 5 Allotments, 1..

126 Martin, *Historical Report on the Fort Peck Indian Reservation, Part I: An Administrative and Social History*, 158; F.C. Campbell, District Superintendent, Standing Rock Agency, Fort Yates, SD, to CIA, Washington, D.C., May 22, 1928, Chrono File, 1928-1932, Docket 184 Collection, Fort Peck Tribal Archives, Poplar, Montana.

127 Campbell, District Superintendent, Fort Berthold Agency, Elbowoods, ND, to CIA, Washington, D.C., November 20, 1926, Chrono File, "General History, 1920-1927," Docket 184 Collection, Fort Peck Tribal Archives, Poplar, Montana.

128 Ibid., 159.

129 Ibid.

130 Burke, Washington, D.C., to Steele and Ricker, Poplar, Montana, September 28, 1926, Chrono File, "General History, 1920-1927," Docket 184 Collection, Fort Peck Tribal Archives, Poplar, Montana.

131 Martin, *Historical Report on the Fort Peck Indian Reservation, Part I: An Administrative and Social History*, 159-161.

132 Ibid., 161.

133 Ibid., 162.

134 Ibid., 162.

135 Ibid., 162-163.

136 Ibid., 163.

137 Ibid.

138 Ibid., 163-164.

139 Ibid., 164.

140 Ibid.

141 General Council Minutes, October 24, 1927, 2, CCF 51716-1927 Fort Peck .054, RG 75, NARA-Washington, D.C.

142 Ibid.; General Council Minutes, October 25, 1927, 3-6, CCF 51716-1927 Fort Peck .054, RG 75, NARA-Washington, D.C.

143 Burke, Washington, D.C., to Superintendent Eggers, FPA, Poplar, November 10, 1927, CCF 51716-1927 Fort Peck .054, RG 75, NARA-Washington, D.C.

144 General Council Minutes, November 16, 1927, 9-10, CCF 51716-1927 Fort Peck .054, RG 75, NARA-Washington, D.C.

145 Constitution-1927, Billings Area Office Collection-Fort Peck, RG 75, NARA-Central Plains Regional Archives, Lenexa, Kansas; Minutes of General Council, 16 November, CCF 51716-1927 Fort Peck .054, RG 75, NARA-Washington, D.C.

146 Martin, *Historical Report on the Fort Peck Indian Reservation, Part I: An Administrative and Social History*, 166.

147 General Council Minutes, November 16, 1927, CCF 51716-1927 Fort Peck .054, RG 75, NARA-Washington, D.C.

148 George H. Connor, Poplar, Montana, to Eggers, Poplar, Montana, February 7, 1928, CCF 51716-1927 Fort Peck .054, RG 75, NARA-Washington, D.C.

149 Eggers, Poplar, Montana, to CIA, Washington, D.C., January 14, 1928, Chrono File, 1928-1932, Docket 184 Collection, Fort Peck Tribal Archives, Poplar, Montana.

150 Ibid.

151 Garfield, Chairman, and Connor, Secretary, Minutes of Informal Council, Fort Peck Assiniboine Indians,

Charles Hall's Place, January 17, 1928, Chrono File, 1928-1932, Docket 184 Collection, Fort Peck Tribal Archives, Poplar, Montana.

152 See minutes for each meeting, Chrono File, 1928-1932, Docket 184 Collection, Fort Peck Tribal Archives, Poplar, Montana.

153 Martin, *Historical Report on the Fort Peck Indian Reservation, Part I: An Administrative and Social History*, 167.

154 As quoted in Martin, *Historical Report on the Fort Peck Indian Reservation, Part I: An Administrative and Social History*, 167.

155 Eggers, Poplar, Montana, to CIA, Washington, D.C., February 14, 1928, Chrono File, 1928-1932, Docket 184 Collection, Fort Peck Tribal Archives, Poplar, Montana.

156 Ibid.

157 45 Stat. 774.

158 Campbell Report, n.d., CCF 57783-1927 Fort Peck 150, partial copy in Chrono File, "General History, 1920-1927," Docket 184 Collection, Fort Peck Tribal Archives, Poplar, Montana

159 Ibid., quoted in Campbell's report.

160 Martin, *Historical Report on the Fort Peck Indian Reservation, Part I: An Administrative and Social History*, 169.

161 Milton Johnson, Indian Office Director of Agriculture Report, March 1929, see Chrono File, "General History, 1928-1932," Docket 184 Collection, Fort Peck Tribal Archives, Poplar, Montana.

162 Martin, *Historical Report on the Fort Peck Indian Reservation, Part I: An Administrative and Social History*, 171; F.C. Campbell, District Superintendent, FPA, Poplar, Montana, to CIA, Washington, D.C., March 16, 1929, Chrono File, "General History, 1928-1932," Docket 184 Collection, Fort Peck Tribal Archives, Poplar, Montana.

163 Campbell, Poplar, Montana, to CIA, Washington, D.C., March 16, 1929, Chrono File, "General History, 1928-1932," Docket 184 Collection, Fort Peck Tribal Archives, Poplar, Montana.

164 Ibid.

165 Martin, *Historical Report on the Fort Peck Indian Reservation, Part I: An Administrative and Social History*, 172-173.

166 Burke, Washington, D.C., to Eggers, Poplar, Montana, March 27, 1929, Chrono File, "General History, 1928-1932," Docket 184 Collection, Fort Peck

167 Tribal Archives, Poplar, Montana.
Kirkwood Smith, Poplar, Montana, on stationery of the Better Government Organization of the Fort Peck Indian Reservation, to Charles J. Rhoads, CIA, Washington, D.C., September 18, 1929, Chrono File, "General History, 1928-1932," Docket 184 Collection, Fort Peck Tribal Archives, Poplar, Montana.

168 Charles H. Renz, Secretary, Council of Fort Peck Indians, Poplar, Montana, to CIA, Washington, D.C., October 8, 1929, with attached By-Laws, Chrono File, "General History, 1928-1932," Docket 184 Collection, Fort Peck Tribal Archives, Poplar, Montana.

169 Martin, *Historical Report on the Fort Peck Indian Reservation, Part I: An Administrative and Social History*, 173; Eggers, Poplar, Montana, to CIA, Washington, D.C., October 14, 1929, Chrono File, "General History, 1928-1932," Docket 184 Collection, Fort Peck Tribal Archives, Poplar, Montana.

170 J. Henry Scattergood, Asst. CIA, Washington, D.C., to Senator B.K. Wheeler, Washington, D.C., October 31, 1929, Chrono File, "General History, 1928-1932," Docket 184 Collection, Fort Peck Tribal Archives, Poplar, Montana.

171 Eggers, Poplar, Montana, to CIA, Washington, D.C., April 6, 1929, Chrono File, "General History, 1928-1932," Docket 184 Collection, Fort Peck Tribal Archives, Poplar, Montana.

172 Ibid.

173 H.L. Scott, Member Board of Indian Commissioners, Poplar, Montana, to Samuel A. Eliot, Chairman, Board of Indian Commissioners, Washington, D.C., endorsed for transmission to SI, Washington, D.C., August 5, 1929, Chrono File, "General History, 1928-1932," Docket 184 Collection, Fort Peck Tribal Archives, Poplar, Montana.

174 Ibid., 171-172.

175 Ibid., 174; C.R. Trowbridge, Field Representative, Denver, Colorado, to Chas. J. Rhoads, CIA, Washington, D.C., April 28, 1930, CCF 26330-1930 Fort Peck, 150, copy in Chrono File, "General History, 1928-1932," Docket 184 Collection, Fort Peck Tribal Archives, Poplar, Montana.

176 Ibid., 175; Trowbridge, May 5, 1930, to Rhoads, Washington, D.C., May 5, 1930, Inspection report, 4-6, CCF 26360-1930 Fort Peck, 150, copy in Chrono File, "General History, 1928-1932," Docket 184 Collection, Fort Peck Tribal Archives, Poplar, Montana.

177 Ibid., 176.

178 Ibid.

179 Ibid., 176-177..

180 Ibid., 177.

181 Ibid.

182 Ibid.

183 Ibid., 177-178; Trowbridge inspection, 27.

184 Martin, *Historical Report on the Fort Peck Indian Reservation, Part I: An Administrative and Social History*, 178)

185 Ibid., Trowbridge Inspection, 1-6.

186 Martin, *Historical Report on the Fort Peck Indian Reservation, Part I: An Administrative and Social History*, 179; Nyce Report, CCF 5245-1931 Fort Peck .301, 1-8, RG 75, NARA-Washington, D.C.

187 Ibid., 279, Nyce Report, 11-12, 61-62.

188 Nyce report, 50-56.

189 Nyce Report, 56-59.

190 Nyce Report, 68-69.

191 Martin, *Historical Report on the Fort Peck Indian Reservation, Part I: An Administrative and Social History*, 181.

192 Ibid.

193 Ibid., 181-182.

194 Ibid., 182..

195 Moses White Horse, Sec. I.P. Assn. Of American, Wolf Point, MT, to Rhoads, Washington, D.C., February 27, 1930, CCF 22281-1929 Fort Peck .057, RG 75, NARA-Washington, D.C.

196 Eggers, Poplar, Montana, to CIA, Washington, D.C., May 17, 1930, CCF 22281-1929 Fort Peck .057, RG 75, NARA-Washington, D.C.

197 Superintendent H.D. McCullough, Supt, FPA, Poplar, Montana, to CIA, Washington, D.C., November 24, 1930, CCF 22281-1929 Fort Peck .057, RG 75, NARA-Washington, D.C.

198 See telegrams, CCF 22281-1929 Fort Peck .057, RG 75, NARA-Washington, D.C.

199 McCullough, Poplar, Montana, to CIA, Washington, D.C., December 19, 1930, CCF 22281-1929 Fort Peck .057, RG 75, NARA-Washington, D.C.

200 Moses White Horse and Steele, Wolf Point, to McCoullough [sic], FPA, Poplar, Montana, January 19, 1931, CCF 22281-1929 Fort Peck .057, RG 75, NARA-Washington, D.C.

201 Ibid.

202 McCullough, Poplar, Montana, to CIA, Washington, D.C., January 22, 1931,

CCF 22281-1929 Fort Peck .057, RG 75, NARA-Washington, D.C.

203 McCullough to Indians of the Fort Peck Reservation, April 24, 1931, CCF 22281-1929 Fort Peck .057, RG 75, NARA-Washington, D.C.

204 Resolution No. 2, General Council Minutes, May 19, 1931, CCF 22281-1929 Fort Peck .057, RG 75, NARA-Washington, D.C..

205 Resolution No. 5, General Council Minutes, May 20, 1931, CCF 22281-1929 Fort Peck .057, RG 75, NARA-Washington, D.C..

206 Resolution No. 9, General Council Minutes, May 20, 1931, CCF 22281-1929 Fort Peck .057, RG 75, NARA-Washington, D.C.

207 McCullough, Poplar, Montana, to CIA, Washington, D.C., May 26, 1931, CCF 22281-1929 Fort Peck .057, RG 75, NARA-Washington, D.C..

208 Ibid.

209 Scattergood, Washington, D.C., to McCullough, Poplar, Montana, July 7, 1931, CCF 22281-1929 Fort Peck .057, RG 75, NARA-Washington, D.C.

210 Resolution No. 7, General Council Minutes, May 20, 1931, CCF 22281-1929 Fort Peck .057, RG 75, NARA-Washington, D.C.

211 Scattergood to McCullough, July 7, 1931, CCF 22281-1929 Fort Peck .057, RG 75, NARA-Washington, D.C.

212 See correspondence, CCF 2060-1932 Fort Peck .056, Part I, RG 75, NARA-Washington, D.C.

213 6249-1932 Fort Peck .054, January 28, 1932, RG 75, NA-Denver, Colorado.

214 6279-1932 Fort Peck .054, March 22, 1932, RG 75, National Archives-Denver, Colorado.

215 Ibid., 22 date March 1932.

216 6279-1932 Fort Peck .054, March 31, 1932, RG 75, NA-Denver, Colorado.

217 Ibid.

218 Martin, *Historical Report on the Fort Peck Indian Reservation, Part I: An Administrative and Social History*, 193-184.

219 G. E. E. Lindquist, Report on the Fort Peck Reservation, Montana, with Special Reference to Superintendent McCullough's Administration, November 7, 1932, Chrono File, General History 1928-1932, Docket 184 Collection, Fort Peck Tribal Archives, Poplar, 13-14.

220 SANR Fort Peck 1934:3.

221 G. E. E. Lindquist, Report on the Fort Peck Reservation, Montana, with Special Reference to Superintendent McCullough's Administration, November 7, 1932, Chrono File, General History 1928-1932, Docket 184 Collection, Fort Peck Tribal Archives, Poplar.

222 Rhoads, CIA, memo to file, u.d., CFF 70804-1931 Fort Peck .150, RG 75, NARA-Washington, D.C.

223 Martin, *Historical Report on the Fort Peck Indian Reservation, Part I: An Administrative and Social History*, 185.

224 Martin, *Historical Report on the Fort Peck Indian Reservation, Part I: An Administrative and Social History*, 185.

225 Quoted in Martin, *Historical Report on the Fort Peck Indian Reservation, Part I: An Administrative and Social History*, 185-186, presumably from the Linquist inspection report.

226 Martin, *Historical Report on the Fort Peck Indian Reservation, Part I: An Administrative and Social History*, 186; Lindquist report.

227 Ibid., 186-187.

228 Ibid., 187.

229 They included: 1. the construction of a highway across the reservation south of the railroad; 2. preservation of speculators in obtaining land adjacent to towns; 3. providing housing for the old and helpless Indians at or near the agency and sub-agencies; 4. the construction of reservoirs in the grazing areas to attract more lease-holders; 5. the clearing of fire lanes through the timber lands; 6. petition for the construction of a standard bridge across the Poplar River; 7. the enlargement of hospital facilities; [and] 8) arranging for a more satisfactory handling of the Turtle Mountain Chippewas Martin, Historical Report on the Fort Peck Indian Reservation, Part I: An Administrative and Social History, 187-188); Superintendent C.L.Walker, FPA, Poplar, Montana, to CIA, Washington, D.C., August 18, 1933, Chrono File, General History, 1933-1938, Docket 184 Collection, Fort Peck Tribal Archives, Poplar, Montana.

230 Martin, *Historical Report on the Fort Peck Indian Reservation, Part I: An Administrative and Social History*, 188

231 Ibid., 1988-189. Montana State Representative Dolly Cusker complained that Walker had reneged on an agreement to buy some of her cattle. Ibid., 189.

232 SANR Fort Peck 1934, 4.

233 Martin, *Historical Report on the Fort Peck Indian Reservation, Part I: An Administrative and Social History*, 189; Walker, FPA, Poplar, Montana, to CIA, Washington, D.C., January 15, 1935, Chrono File, General History, 1933-1938, Docket 184 Collection, Fort Peck Tribal Archives, Poplar, Montana..

234 Ibid., 190)

235 Martin, *Historical Report on the Fort Peck Indian Reservation, Part I: An Administrative and Social History*, 191.

236 Lawrence C. Kelly, *The Assault on Assimilation: John Collier and the Origins of Indian Policy Reform* (Albuquerque: University of New Mexico Press, 1993); Kenneth R. Philp, *John Collier's Crusade for Indian Reform, 1920-1954* (Tucson: University of Arizona Press, 1977); Francis Paul Prucha, *The Great Father: The United States Government and the American Indians*, 2 Vols. (Lincoln: University of Nebraska Press, 1984), 2: 917-1012.

237 Margaret Connell Szasz, *Education and the American Indians: The Road to Self-Determination since 1928* (Albuquerque: University of New Mexico Press, 1974), 89-105.

238 Indian Reorganization Act, June 18, 1934, 48 Stat. 984.

239 Martin, *Historical Report on the Fort Peck Indian Reservation, Part I: An Administrative and Social History*, 192.

240 C.L. Walker, Superintendent FPA, Poplar, Montana, to CIA, Washington, D.C., June 26, 1934, CCF 2060-1932 Fort Peck .056, Part I, RG 75, NARA-Washington, D.C.]

241 Minutes, General Council of Fort Peck Indians, June 16, 1934, CCF 2060-1932 Fort Peck .056, Part I, RG 75, NARA-Washington, D.C.

242 Quoted from a tribal organization document in Martin, Historical Report on the Fort Peck Indian Reservation, Part I: An Administrative and Social History, 192.

243 John G. Hunter, Superintendent FPA, Poplar, Montana, to CIA, Washington, D.C., June 25, 1935, CCF 2060-1932 Fort Peck .056, Part I, RG 75, NARA-Washington, D.C.

244 Martin, *Historical Report on the Fort Peck Indian Reservation, Part I: An Administrative and Social History*, 37.

245 Martin, *Historical Report on the Fort Peck Indian Reservation, Part I: An*

Administrative and Social History, 26.

246 Martin, *Historical Report on the Fort Peck Indian Reservation, Part I: An Administrative and Social History*, 192-193; George Washington, Chairman, Fort Peck Tribal Council, Poplar, Montana, to CIA, Washington, D.C., January 3, 1935, CCF 2060-1932 Fort Peck .056, Part I, RG 75, NARA-Washington, D.C.

247 See Collier Office file on Fort Peck re: IRA

248 Graham D. Taylor, The New Deal of American Indian Tribalism: The Administration of the Indian Reorganization Act, 1934-45 (Lincoln: University of Nebraska Press, 1980), 32-33.

249 Martin, *Historical Report on the Fort Peck Indian Reservation, Part I: An Administrative and Social History*, 193.

250 Cover letter, Hunter, FPA, Poplar, to John Collier, CIA, Washington, D.C., January 15, 1935, CCF 2060-1932 Fort Peck .056, Part I, RG 75, NARA-Washington, D.C.

251 Garfield, Wolf Point, MT, to CIA, Washington, D.C., January 11, 1935, CCF 2060-1932 Fort Peck .056, Part I,

RG 75, NARA-Washington, D.C.

252 Martin, *Historical Report on the Fort Peck Indian Reservation, Part I: An Administrative and Social History*, 194.

253 Cover letter, Hunter, Poplar, to Collier, Washington, D.C., January 15, 1935, CCF 2060-1932 Fort Peck .056, Part I, RG 75, NARA-Washington, D.C.

254 Washington, Chairman, Fort Peck Council, Poplar, Montana, to CIA, Washington, D.C., February 23, 1935, CCF 2060-1932 Fort Peck .056, Part I, RG 75, NARA-Washington, D.C.

255 George Conner, Sr., Poplar, Montana, to E.J. Armstrong, Indian Office, Washington, D.C., October 23, 1935, CCF 2060-1932 Fort Peck .056, Part I, RG 75, NARA-Washington, D.C.

256 Memo, Commr JC, Memorandum for Superintendent Hunter, March 12, 1935, CCF 2060-1932 Fort Peck .056, Part I, RG 75, NARA-Washington, D.C.; discussion of Thomas-Rodgers Bill in Taylor, *The New Deal and American Tribalism*, 35-36.

257 See discussion of this matter, Collier, Washington, D.C., to Hunter, Poplar, Montana, June 17, 1935, CCF 2060-1932 Fort Peck .056, Part I, RG 75, NARA-

Washington, D.C.

258 SANR Fort Peck 1934a: 2.

259 SANR Fort Peck 1934: 3.

260 Ibid.

261 SANR Fort Peck 1934a: 4.

262 Ibid.:12.

263 Ibid.

264 Ibid.

265 Ibid., 5.

266 SANR Fort Peck 1934a:5-6.

267 Ibid., 3-4.

268 Ibid.,11.

269 SANR Fort Peck 1934a, 9

270 SANR Fort Peck 1934a:10).

271 Ibid.

272 Ibid., 12.

273 SANR Fort Peck 1934a: 5-6.

274 SANR Fort Peck 1934 Program: 2.

275 Martin, *Historical Report on the Fort Peck Indian Reservation, Part I: An Administrative and Social History*, 194.

276 Martin, *Historical Report on the Fort Peck Indian Reservation, Part I: An Administrative and Social History*, 194-195.

CHAPTER 11

~

Self-Determination within the New Deal, the Winds of War, and the Rise of the Post New Deal, 1935-1948

David R. Miller, Ph.D.

Eternal events and forces at work far from the boundaries of the Fort Peck Reservation caused worldwide economic depression, which condition eventually gave rise to war. The poverty of reservation life shaped the experiences of generations of tribal members. The collateral development of public institutions, such as schools, hospitals, and libraries, meant that the majority of Fort Peck Indians had come to live in much the same manner as their white neighbors,[1] but this did not mean that prejudice and injustice did not continue to occur from time to time.

One important catalyst to progress among the tribes was the Indian New Deal. Even though the Fort Peck tribes had sidestepped the reforms of the IRA, they sought to negotiate their own course of relations with the Office of Indian Affairs (OIA). John Collier's independent leadership as CIA was instrumental to increasing self-determination among Indians, including Fort Peck tribal members. The evolution of the first business committees into subsequent General Councils and their elected Executive Boards meant that debate began to replace consensus-building. An escalation in programs brought increased paperwork and required additional personnel to complete it. The Bureau of Indian Affairs, with its new layer of bureaucracy, the district offices, simply epitomized this escalation. As the tribes assumed responsibilities for some programs, the need for tribal employees increased, just as the staff of the agency also increased to meet the range of demands for information and accounting. With increasing demands for technical knowledge, a political sophistication among the Tribal Executive Board began to emerge to meet the challenges. Because board members by General Councils were indirectly elected, a crisis in representation was also emerging, pitting Assiniboines against Sioux.

The rejection of the Indian Reorganization Act (IRA) was not without consequences. During the next decade and a half, tribal members' interactions with various government agencies, including the Bureau of Indian Affairs, became more flexible. The end of the Depression, the repeal of Prohibition, and the impending world war tested the mettle of tribal members.

Roosevelt's New Deal, lead by Harold Ickes (SI), John Collier (CIA), and Henry Wallace (Secretary of Agriculture), allowed for a tangible New Deal for Indians. Relief funds arrived on the reservation under the jurisdictions of the alphabet soup of federal agencies—the Works Progress Administration (WPA), Public Works Administration (PWA), Civil Works Administration (CWA), Civil Conservation Corps (CCC), Federal Emergency Relief Administration (FERA), and Indian Emergency Conservation Work (IECW). The Farm Security Administration of the Department of Agriculture (USDA) provided loans and drought relief to farm families, and the Soil Conservation Service conducted surveys and entered conservation agreements. A Technical Cooperation unit of the BIA, known as TC-BIA, was responsible for surveys of dependency patterns, range management, and soil conservation of trust lands.[2] Though much was accomplished, there were limits to relief efforts, and Indians were rarely at the front of the line.

Superintendent Hunter became preoccupied with making agricultural progress at Fort Peck, and consequently felt that further construction of irrigation infrastructure was essential. Only 2,345 acres were actually irrigated in 1934.[3] After 1935, records for irrigation units were spotty. There was no record of any irrigation on Big Muddy; irrigation on the Big Porcupine ended in 1939, when the dam washed out; by 1939, the Poplar Unit was down to only 155 acres receiving water; and the Frazer-Wolf Point Unit, benefiting

from a new pump unit that drew water from the Missouri, went from 537 acres in 1940 to 3,051 acres in 1946.[4]

Other money at Fort Peck went into construction of roads, stock dams and reservoirs, and conservation projects. Some resources from FERA and WPA went to producing arts and crafts, eventually marketed by the Indian Arts and Crafts Board. In some cases, this is how many people learned skills from previous generations.[5]

The USDA provided money to Indians engaged in stock raising to purchase what became known as "drought cattle." For every animal received, the individual had to return either a heifer or male calf to the pool.[6] This incentive influenced a gradual increase in the Indian use of grazing areas on the reservation. In 1934, 80,550 acres were utilized, by 1936, the amount had increased to 102,510 acres, and by 1938, some tribal members were "cooperative leasing and grazing small range units."[7]

Individual Indian Money accounts with balances numbered 1,003 as of December 31, 1934, and totalled $50,663.48. Two clerks at the agency maintained the accounts. There were usually two paydays a month when checks were issued to certain Indians, but those engaged in farming were often asking for more on a seasonal basis. One of the clerks was Mr. Archiquette, described as an educated Indian who was said to disburse money from the accounts with "care and discretion." Monthly checks ran in number from 700 to 1,200. By the end of the year, the total of almost 2,000 accounts had to be posted, and in some cases, overdrafts occurred. The practice initiated several years before of holding back 40 percent of any payment for emergencies was finally eliminated by the end of 1934, reducing labor and paperwork. Interest received in July 1934 was distributed in August 1934, and interest received in January and February 1935 had not, as of March

31, 1935, been distributed.[8] For many, this was their only source of capital.[9]

Funds from the IEWC and other agencies were used to improve the reservation road system. Collier responded to Hunter's request for clarification about allowing Indians with teams to do road work on the reservation, as favored by the Fort Peck Tribal Council. He noted that he was not aware of any "great amount of machinery being used on road work" on the reservation. The Indian Service agreed to employing as many Indian teams on road work "as will promote reasonable efficiency in the construction program." While the cost would need to be kept within bounds, and decided locally by the superintendent, the Road Engineer, and the District Road Engineer "in cooperation with the Indians," the CIA emphasized that the "road appropriation is not a relief fund," so a balance would have to be struck between using machinery and teams.[10]

As the Depression dragged on, able-bodied Indians kept looking for work. Hunter spent considerable effort finding out about federal relief and recovery programs. He wrote to CIA John Collier in early 1935 of his efforts to find employment for Fort Peck tribal members. There was a Washington regulation that prevented "ward Indians" from working on projects such as the Fort Peck Dam, but Hunter asked Collier's assistance in getting tribal members employed there. Consequently, by 1936, approximately 150 tribal members, mostly young men, were employed on the dam as assistant carpenters and welders, laborers in the tunnels, and waiters in the barracks and messrooms. Beginning pay rates were from $.50 to $.90 per hour. Many had never worked alongside non-Indians, and accommodations in the shantytown near the construction site were far from adequate. Many tribal members soon went back to the reservation, with "only a handful of Indians . . . remain [working] at the dam."[11]

One follow-up to the IRA rejection was anthropologist H. Scudder McKeel's visit to the reservation on behalf of the Indian Service. The question was whether tribal members at Fort Peck might reconsider accepting the IRA. In a letter to Walter V. Woehlke in the Commissioner's Office dated October 9, 1935, McKeel recommended a slow and cautious approach, as "many feel apprehensive that they [tribal members] may be tricked into the New Deal—so look on with suspicion and concern, at the various E.C.W., and other improvements being made on the reservation." Well aware of the problems of representation in the "Executive Committee," Hunter hoped that the various communities on the reservation might realize the inequities. Rather, he pointed out that the communities had "lost a good deal of their homogeneity," which was particularly the case among the Assiniboines. McKeel observed that Sioux tribal members appeared to be satisfied with the political order because they dominated it. However, the Assiniboine, who found that their interests did not always align with the Sioux, appeared to be more "advanced," and "fall more readily into white patterns." McKeel did note the high rate of intermarriage and a pattern he called cross-allotments, meaning Sioux individuals married Assiniboine and lived among them and visa versa. He discussed the matter of separate councils, but warned that to do so might upset the equanimity of the Sioux, but suggested that possibly every other meeting might be held in Wolf Point rather than all in Poplar.[12] In an Indian Office memorandum written by Fred Daiker, dated December 3, 1935, McKeel's recommendations to "organize these Indians in a more modern fashion" were discussed. Daiker stated,

It seems to me it should be made very plain to these Indians that unless they are willing and do cooperate in the matter of organization that the social and economic program must be postponed indefinitely. Of course, that might be considered as using force, etc., but I believe we are justified. In other words, let them show that they are willing to play ball and then we can send our people to help them.[13]

The last sentences implied that the problem was the use of general councils: "They certainly need organization in the worst way." This suggested the Indian Office planned to reorganize the governance of tribes even when they had not accepted the IRA.[14]

Reimbursable loan requests were increasing, requested by the Tribal Executive Committee and forwarded by Hunter, but funds from the usual sources, especially the Fort Peck Reimbursable Loan Fund, had been depleted by September 1936. A.C. Cooley, Director of Extension and Industry for the Indian Service, wrote to Ruth Bronson in the Commissioner's Office on September 15, 1936, to discuss the Fort Peck loan requests. Cooley explained that making loans did not really advance the purpose of the fund, which was to eventually relieve the need for appropriations to cover certain expenditures. Refusing to use the principal was not a reasonable response, but with decreasing appropriations, the fund had become the only source of funds for Fort Peck tribal members. "In allocating this fund, however, there are so many Indians needing it who have no tribal funds or any other source of loan funds that we feel it only fair to give such Indians preference." Loans had been approved for the most recent student requests, but this looked unlikely in the next fiscal year, because of insufficient funds in the appropriation "Industry among Indians, Education, 1937."[15] The office emphasized that there really was no more money. Relief had limits, and the office was sustaining budget cuts, especially for "Industry among Indians." The explanation was offered that some tribes had

absolutely no resources, and the small appropriation was directed to these, and groups with other resources were left to cope. All this was in the spirit of being equitable. E.J. Armstrong, writing for the CIA, closed his response thus:

At the present time we are unable to make you an allotment from Industry among Indians. If at a later date . . . you find it necessary to request assistance from this fund, it will be appreciated if you will outline your plans for its use in detail.[16]

Superintendent Hunter's honeymoon was over by 1936. He retained support among some members of the Tribal Executive Board, but many others were critical of his administration. In mid-October 1936, Indian Service Field Representative Floyd W. LaRouche visited the Fort Peck Agency, and soon after filed a three-part report titled "Fort Peck Agency in 1936." The first part was about "matters of official conduct," while the others "contain facts and comments on various administrative and economic matters" requiring attention. Charges of misconduct had been made against Hunter and Dr. A.W. Dahlstrom, the senior physician, about their consuming alcohol on duty. The allegations had been made by a discharged field nurse and another dismissed agency employee.[17]

The investigation revealed that Hunter was a competent administrator. However, "hunger and idleness [among Fort Peck Indians] were the exception rather than the rule," and with limited resources, "Hunter was both a sympathetic and skillful administrator." A departmental investigator asserted that nothing interfered with Hunter's performance, and stated, "My own opinion is that Fort Peck would drive any normal person to drink. The wonder is that Hunter does not drink more."[18]

The second part of the report, dated November 11, 1936, was subtitled "Just One Big

Happy Family." LaRouche's first sentence reinforced an impression clearly held in Washington: "Traditionally volcanic Fort Peck, relatively quiet for a period of almost two years, now shows signs of eruption." The dismissal of the field nurse had not received immediate action from Washington, during which interim sympathy for the nurse had been engendered. Discussing the disposition of Indian Service employees, LaRouche related that employees assigned to Fort Peck often give it the label "The Devil's Island of the Indian Service," suggesting its isolation, turmoil, and work loads. Hunter was commended for encouraging agency staff and tribal members to work together as "one big happy family." LaRouche observed that in many ways, this had been achieved:

In a blanket answer to such accusations, Superintendent Hunter stated that Indians are employed on a basis of proved efficiency and dependability. No other factors, he declared, are allowed to enter into consideration of an applicant for employment and it just happens that both the Kirn and Smith families contain a large number of eligible and employable males.

It is possible that Mr. Hunter has, perhaps unwittingly, bowed to the dominant political factions on the reservation. As a means of keeping peace this may have been the policy of the greatest expediency. Whether it is the best policy for the long swing is another matter. Criticisms from minority groups may indicate that such a policy is not a complete solution.[19]

Employment was a central concern for Hunter's administration and the Tribal Executive Board. At one point in 1936, Hunter was accused of spending too much time away from the reservation, but actually these trips involved traveling to locate employment possibilities for tribal members off the reservation.[20]

Grazing money long had supported per capita payments, and consequently the Tribal Executive Board continued to focus on the grazing lease program. Several different agencies were concerned with range management, and the executive committee regularly addressed questions about grazing leases. By 1935, considering the poor economic conditions, the committee agreed that the tribal lands would be leased for eight cents per acre, intending to raise the rate to fifteen cents per acre the next year. They also lumped all lands reserved for reclamation into the grazing units, but excluded all government reserves south of the Township 29. By December 1935, the sentiments about lease money and its disposition prompted a diverse debate, so decisions were left to the chapters about their respective districts. Seeking to raise the fee to between ten cents and fifteen cents per acre, the committee set a minimum fee of ten cents for the 1936 season. Hunter was authorized to issue 1937 grazing permits at eight cents per acre on allotted lands in the grazing units when a majority of the allottees agreed.[21]

The utilization and disposal of both tribal and individual Indian lands dominated the committee's agenda. Stock trespassing demanded renewed attention, so the Tribal Executive Board tried to obtain a record of the brands of all whites married into the tribe "so that trespassing stock could be more readily identified." If circumstances warranted, the committee authorized the auction of individual allotments. It also loaned tribal funds to tribal members for "improvements." Two acres of tribal land were sold to Poplar for an armory. In Brockton, the local school board delayed a land purchase because of concerns about lands withdrawn from sale until "it was determined whether or not they would revert to tribal status." When individuals were squatting on withdrawn lands, the Indian Office recommended access and use be regulated with short-term revocable permits.[22]

Compounding the situation was "home-steader delinquency." These farmers communicated to Congress the ongoing severe drought and their consequent worsening economic conditions, and once again they received a "leave of absence" for the years 1932-36 so that they might seek employment elsewhere and not be accused of abandoning their homesteads. By 1940, further legislation authorized reinstatement of "any entry of purchase, in existence [as of] December 31, 1936, on opened lands with the ceded areas" on Fort Peck and other named reservations in Montana and the Dakotas.[23] The agenda of the Tribal Executive Board was expanding to include oil and gas rights, reflecting "a growing awareness of the Fort Peck Indians in the importance of their reservation resources and the need to assure their proper and legitimate use."[24]

A narrative section of a statistical annual report discussed the extension organization on the reservation in 1936. There were sixteen active Farm Chapter organizations, four livestock associations, ten Indian women's auxiliaries, and "a host of individual leaders who have been interested in the extension program." The farm organizations boasted 227 male and 140 female members. Family and community gardens and canning kitchens were successful.[25]

Another contribution to the New Deal was the 1934 Johnson-O'Malley Act, named for the chairmen of the Senate and House Committees on Indian Affairs, and amended in 1936. This law allowed state governments to enter into contracts with the federal government to pay for equipment, facilities, and services for status Indian children whose families were not paying taxes. It authorized the Secretary of the Interior to arrange for the education, medical attention, agricultural assistance, relief of distress, and social welfare of Indians.

Federal dollars for educating Fort Peck children provided for many opportunities. Most of the school-age children were attending public schools on or off the reservation, enabled by tuition payments for all children minimally one-quarter Indian. During 1936, tuitions ranged from fifty cents per day at Wolf Point to sixty cents per day at Culbertson, Medicine Lake, Oswego, and Poplar. The 1935 appropriation had made construction loans for school buildings and related facilities. Wolf Point received $50,000, Brockton $40,000, and Poplar and Frazer each received $25,000. These school boards were reluctant recipients of these funds, which were repayable over thirty years at 3 percent interest; they would have preferred a non-repayable grant.[26]

Although Prohibition had been repealed, Indian Office provisions regulating the sale of alcohol to status Indians continued until the early 1950s. In one case, Anton Karge, a non-Indian charged with selling liquor to Indians, claimed to have been entrapped by enforcement officers, but a list of his purchases from the Montana State Liquor Control Board store in Wolf Point derailed his argument.[27]

The changes in Indian policy under the leadership of John Collier were profound and far-reaching, and the CIA was accruing a lot of opponents. His adversaries viewed him pretty much as they did all New Dealers—as communistic and anti-religious. Collier's call to stop interfering with Indian religions offended assimilationists and missionaries. His support for Indian tribal government and democratic self-determination was an affront to the rugged individualism so long encouraged. Many Indians were as suspicious of Collier's agenda as non-Indians. Congress for the most part cooperated with the administration in its Indian policy until 1937.[28]

Controversy arose when the Supreme Court declared several of Roosevelt's relief programs unconstitutional, which resulted in FDR's call for an increase in the number of federal judges and six more seats on the Supreme Court. A shift in the court in the spring of 1937 made FDR's efforts to affect changes in its composition moot, and no further decisions struck down New Deal programs. The court-packing scheme marked the beginning of a more difficult political struggle for the New Dealers,[29] and for Collier's program.

The tribal membership enrolled at Fort Peck continued to increase in the 1930s, with the percentage of mixed-bloods also increasing, and the growth among Assiniboines greater than the Sioux. The enrolled population in 1937 totaled 2,796, but only 2,395 members resided on the reservation. By this time, nearly half the on-reservation population was living in Brockton, Poplar, Wolf Point, Oswego, and Frazer, where they represented 40 percent of the population. In contrast, tribal members residing in rural areas were "substantially outnumbered by approximately 3,300 whites that were mostly of German, Russian or Scandinavian background."[30]

Ralph S. Bristol, with the Division of Extension and Industry, OIA, filed a report for his visit on June 5-6, 1937. He noted how little latitude there was going into the coming fiscal year, and that careful coordination was needed to avoid overexpenditure. ECW had employed 400 men during the winter, but could employ only 200 during the summer. The drought was severe enough that "grazing on the reservation is almost entirely ruined for the present year," prompting "the lessees . . . [either] liquidating or shipping out their stock." Crops on seeded lands had mostly blown away, except for areas directly irrigated, including the community gardens. Any new homes or home improvements and new wells were directly financed from the reimbursable funds. One hundred and seventy-five resettlement grants were made along with thirty-five regular loans. Bristol was candid: "Destitution is serious and the Indians are in bad condition for

the actual necessities of life."[31]

Later in June, Boyd Faulkner, the Agricultural Extension Agent, further delineated the extent of the drought.[32] By the last day of June 1937, Hunter reported that the 4% reimbursable fund was exhausted, having been disbursed for home repair or building, work horses purchased, and feed-crop seed loans for the farmers and livestock owners. Repayments were steady despite the "adverse" weather conditions and "frequent intervals of unemployment," but their intentions were clear. A further $6,900 in reimbursable funds were requested, and a detailed justification made, saying that while irrigable areas needed improvements, in all other dry-land areas, loans for livestock and seed were "inadvisable" where "a living is never insured."[33] Replying on August 8, 1937, E.J. Armstrong for the CIA authorized an allotment of $1,148, since appropriations were still pending. The investment in wells was praised, but warning was given that the funds were for "individuals living in irrigated districts where rehabilitation is feasible and where the returns insure repayment." Ironically, a very small percentage of those trying to live on the land were in these areas.[34]

The reimbursable accounts increasingly worried the Indian Office. New direction was given in a circular dated December 28, 1937, guiding the preparation of agreements. Purchasing was complicated by the use of purchase orders and inspection certificates, and no property was delivered to individuals until the agreements were properly executed.[35] Clearly, this process did not facilitate the "industry" it was meant to foster. In a form letter dated April 26, 1938, R.S. Bristol, Acting Director of Extension and Industry, directed the superintendents that further revision was needed in handling credit for Indians and the Revolving Credit Fund. A pending appropriation bill would permit Indians to purchase commodities, instead of selling them commodities that required property accounting. This change also meant that loans could be made from two or more sources of funding instead of a single source. This flexibility in administration of a new credit system, however, required the office to gather more personal information about the loan applicants. More paperwork did not necessarily make such a reform efficient.[36]

Boyd Faulkner wrote the annual report for the extension program for the Fort Peck Agency for the 1938 calendar year. He noted that a survey of 220 farm families indicated the average annual income was $289. Enrolled families numbered 759, with those enrolled elsewhere 35, and non-enrolled 43, for a total of 837 families residing on the reservation.[37] Contributions to infrastructure were being made by the extension program:

Community Halls and kitchens were built at Riverside, Macon, Garfield, and Wiota communities this year. The storage building at Wolf Point was repaired and made into a community canning kitchen. The Indian School kitchen in Poplar, which is modestly equipped, was used for canning purposes in the Poplar District. The large community hall at Fort Kipp was built two years ago. These buildings are used for community and chapter meetings, occasionally as work rooms, and for canning.

Mission houses have been used in some communities for canning work, but these are not satisfactory. None of the community dance-halls are suitable or proper equipped for food preservation work. New community canning kitchens are needed at Box Elder, Chelsea, and Oswego.[38]

The effects of the ongoing drought were particularly evident. While the calf crop increased, raising forage for feed was consistently a challenge. Losses of cattle, whether through sales or drought, prompted a shift to raising turkeys and chickens, staggered in such a way that there was a crop for most seasons. Crop production from

irrigated lands was still quite small—119 acres of alfalfa, 120 acres of corn, 50 acres of sugar beets, 11 acres of potatoes—and the overall quality was diminished by grasshoppers and disease. Ten families were reported to have begun irrigating, but adversity was a watchword:

Dryland crops produced very little because of cut worms, grasshoppers, rust and other diseases, and hail. Most of the harvested crop was used for feed. Native hay, however, was abundant and all livestock are assured winter feed. 182 families planted irrigated gardens. Many families planted only dryland gardens because of the abundant moisture early in the spring, but only a few good yields were obtained.[39]

Over 200 families were reported using food preservation methods, fifty of which canned over 200 quarts each, because of the four new canning kitchens. A total of 160 individuals were enrolled in food preservation training in eight communities. Many women were also involved in making clothes, handicrafts, and home furnishings.[40]

Superintendent O.C. Gray provided a concise summary of the progress in collecting reimbursable loans since April 1, 1939:

I note the total indebtedness on the June 30th report was $122,890.46. The collections on the total indebtedness were $4,606.36 or .037 percent. The total delinquent agreements amounted to $100,779.00 on which the collections were $3,986.36, or .039 per cent.[41]

Wage labor for federally funded programs contributed to economic viability, but often these opportunities caused families to relocate "temporarily from the farms."[42]

By the end of the decade, the agency and its staff reflected the policy concerns of the Collier period. At the arrival of Orin C. Gray, who succeeded Hunter as superintendent in April 1939, the staff was divided into divisions responsible for specific policies. There was a pool of office clerks and typists. An Education Field Agent was responsible for education. The agency had a Social Worker, Roads Engineer, Range Supervisor, Land Field Agent, and Agricultural Extension Agent. Other staff managed irrigation. There were physicians and nurses, including a Field Nurse. There were close connections between the Indian Service and other federal, state, and county agencies, and representatives attended each other's staff meetings when feasible.

One example was the field agreement among the Soil Conservation Service of the USDA and Fort Peck Agency of the Bureau of Indian Affairs. This agreement addressed the Frazer-Wolf Point irrigation project area, supported most recently by the new Missouri River pumping station that supplied cheap electrical power generated at the Fort Peck Dam.[43] Surplus houses and furnishings from the Fort Peck Dam were brought to the expanded irrigation area for a number of families. Wells were dug and seven families were established in the first of the new farmsteads by early 1940. The plan was to locate as many as sixty families in similar fashion. The field agreement governed cooperation among government agencies to provide surveys of the farmsteads for this small project.[44]

One important achievement of the Indian Office's expanded programs was the effort in 1939-1940 to organize the Indian farm chapters into cooperative agricultural associations and the stockmen into similar livestock associations. These constituencies were encouraged to become more productive while remaining democratic in decision-making. Membership in these associations meant a nominal membership fee and annual dues.[45]

The way the Department of Interior and its agencies acted as stewards of Indian trust lands under the New Deal was not always clearly com-municated. The drought years from 1932 to 1936 were particular hard, and subsequently bankers and mortgage companies in eastern Montana ended up with an abundance of land. The few Indians still holding their patents had also taken loans on their lands, and many lost them to mortgage companies. The financial institutions appealed to Montana's senators for "relief from the heavy real estate burden." In the effort to sustain so many through the mid-1930s, the National Industrial Recovery Act (NIRA) of 1933 was enacted. However, in 1937, all these lands were purchased under Title II of the NIRA, and by Executive Order in 1938 were transferred to the Department of Interior. The order directed the Secretary of the Interior "to administer, through the Commissioner of Indian Affairs such lands . . . for the benefit of such Indians as he may designate."[46] Part of the submarginal land acquisition project at Fort Peck Reservation included approximately 83,000 acres.[47] Land purchased under this project off the reservation was administered by the Department of Agriculture. Under Title III of the Bankhead Jones Farm Tennant Act of July 22, 1937, Section 31 allowed for the "retirement of land which are submarginal or not primarily suitable for cultivation." The "badlands" outcrops and other formations along the edge of the benchlands qualified for this designation. But not all land purchased within the Fort Peck jurisdiction was submarginal. The Frye Cattle Company went bankrupt in 1936, and because the company had purchased several thousand acres from Indian people, much of the Frye land was purchased by the submarginal land project.[48]

In 1940, Congress authorized the Tribal Executive Board to use $50,000 in tribal funds to purchase additional lands to be converted to trust lands. This same act forbade spending the funds without approval of the board, but did allow some expenditures if ten-year leases could be obtained for tribal members willing to develop parcels.[49]

A General Council that assembled and initially met on April 13, 1940, chose Louis Youngman, George Washington, Joshua Wetsit, and George Connor, Sr. as delegates to Washington. Among the proposals was one for creating a tribal retail store, especially for the aged and disabled to receive rations. Opening such a store would cost an estimated $5,000. Other items for consideration included pending legislation, Sioux and Assiniboine legal actions, allotment issues, and the need to deal with delinquent and squatting entrymen.[50] A summary of the meeting with the Fort Peck delegation, Vigeant, and Critchfield was written by Field Representative Allan G. Harper on May 14, 1940. The viability of the tribal store proposal hinged on the handling of purchase orders for relief. While this arrangement would be administratively possible, the economic viability was not so certain. In the end, the delegation was instructed to request the appointment of a committee to compare store prices and estimate the costs of such an operation. Critchfield also agreed to ask Superintendent Gray and Extension Supervisor Asbury in Billings for a thorough study of the problems with the proposal. Vigeant reported that in the coming fiscal year, money for relief was slated for reduction or elimination:

A study of relief expenditures from all sources at Fort Peck in fiscal year 1939 showed a total outlay of $382,000, or an average per capita for the entire reservation of $129.00; for the number actually received and benefited from relief (2462), the per capita was $155.00; and when the figures were calculated on a 100 per cent basis for 1421 persons, the per capita was $269.00. These figures compare with $100.00 which was the all-Montana average per person per year. The non-relief income at Fort Peck was

estimated at $280,000, or $94.63 per person. The obvious solution of this unsatisfactory situation is the vigorous pursuit of a program which would put the Fort Peck Indians on a self-support basis.[51]

Rufus Ricker, Sr., wrote to Senator James E. Murray, on May 18, 1940, to encourage him to work with the delegation currently in Washington. The question of removing O.C. Gray as superintendent was added to the agenda, however, and Ricker hoped Murray could support the delegates' opinion that they did not "want him here." Ricker opined: "[H]e is inhuman, he is not here forsake of the Indians, but he is here just to draw the monthly salary, that is all."[52] Gray wrote the CIA on June 30, 1940 that the delegation had returned, but was somewhat chagrined when they suggested they should become an ongoing liaison committee to represent the tribes in future delegations. Apparently, Gray did not know that the delegates were working to remove him. His reports indicated, however, that he was bothered by what the delegates had been saying upon their return.[53]

Based on further discussions with the delegates, John Collier wrote to Gray on June 1, 1940, about the debt situation and collection procedures for reimbursable loans, and how this was making impossible any efforts to "develop and enlarge their farming operations and become independent." The delegates noted that material progress was being wiped out by required payments for delinquent loans. The delegates requested a two-year moratorium on payment of delinquent debts, which as of December 31, 1939, totalled $100,903.78. The number of delinquencies had not decreased materially in the past two years, and "during the past year the amount becoming delinquent was as great as the reduction in delinquencies through collections." Collier continued:

During 1937, 1938, and 1939, loans amounting to $25,500 became due, while payments toward these amounted to only $19,000, adding another $6,500 to the old debts.

During this same period, 1937, 1938, and 1939, the Fort Peck Indians borrowed still an additional $30,500. Total collections for the period amounted to $33,000, only $2,500 in excess of the loans.

It is apparent, therefore, that on the whole the Indians are doing little more than to keep up with current loans and are applying very little to delinquent accounts. Judging from the comments of the delegates, the Indians do not realize this and feel that they are having to give up too large a part of their income to apply on the debts incurred years ago and which no longer have meaning to them.[54]

Collier discussed the plan for addressing collections, which needed further consideration by "the Council." Borrowers were called on to first pay on current indebtedness due on loans made since January 1, 1933; second, within their Individual Indian Money accounts, they should budget funds "necessary for the purchase of livestock, equipment, seed, and other comparable items necessary to maintain or increase production"; and finally, individual debtors should pay as much as possible, "without working an undue hardship on himself or his family, toward loans which became delinquent prior to January 1, 1933."[55] The delegation stated very clearly that anyone drawing less than $50 per month could hardly be expected "to set aside money for livestock, seed, etc., pay 10% of their income toward indebtedness, and still have enough remaining to support his family."[56] Only individuals with an aggregate annual income of $600 might be able to put 10 percent of their income toward debt repayment. Therefore, it was proposed that the agency ensure that such a deduction be made from those able to make such a payment. Repayment of existing debts would indicate whether tribal members would be eligible for future loans.[57]

Another result of the discussions with the Fort Peck delegation concerned the interests of tribal members on non-irrigated lands relative to advancing their livestock operations, primarily for feed production and storage. Collier in another letter to Gray dated June 11, 1940 noted that many of those with previous indebtedness were on non-irrigable operations. Collier reluctantly agreed to loan tribal funds, but only if the Tribal Executive Board made an effort to collect debts and established procedures to do so.[58]

The Oswego Unit of the Frazier-Wolf Point Irrigation Project advanced when members of the Oswego Agricultural Association got a loan from the "Fort Peck Reservation 4% Fund (Industrial Assistance, Reimbursable) 1929-1941." The first amount was $15,000, dated October 29, 1940, for loans to individuals for "the construction of homes and the purchase of seed, animals, machinery, tools, implements, building materials, and other equipment and supplies." An additional $8,000 was made available on November 22, 1940.[59]

Gray in his commentary letter of June 20, 1941 forwarded the minutes of the Tribal Executive Board meeting on June 12, 1941, when the tribal store was discussed in detail. Gray made a list of tasks[60] and cautioned that until they were accomplished, he and agency employees could not "advise and assist in the establishment of a retail store."[61]

The Supervisor of Extension and Industry from Billings visited October 8-11, 1941 and reported on the inspection, to which Gray commented in correspondence with the CIA, dated October 24. Extension efforts at Fort Peck Reservation were "never . . . adequate." The first tribal members were moving to the Oswego Unit. In only a few days, the mattress-making operation had produced ten mattresses. One Indian woman and five white women were involved in this cooperative county-extension project.[62]

Then came Sunday morning, December 7, 1941. The Japanese launched their surprise attack on Pearl Harbor, and one day later, FDR asked Congress to declare war on Japan. By December 11, 1941, Germany and Italy declared war on the United States, and the United States responded in kind, making it truly a world war.[63]

Prior to the reinstated draft in 1940, many boys recently out of high school or without employment or other income joined the Montana National Guard to earn $1 a day, which was considered "big money" that "went a long way."[64] In September 1940, the 163rd Infantry, Montana National Guard, were placed at Camp Murray, outside Fort Lewis, Washington, numbering approximately 1,500 men. Many of the men in M Company and more than half of the troops in B Company were tribal members from several Montana reservations. Of the eighty-eight men in B Company, all but ten were Sioux from Fort Peck, including three of the four officers. The company had been reorganized in 1922 after World War I. The members of M Company had been recruited from Fort Belknap Reservation.[65] After training in California and Washington, the 163rd was assigned to defend the Washington coast in February 1942.[66] Shortly thereafter, the regiment was mobilized to San Francisco, and without even time to write a letter, on March 19, 1942, the men boarded the British vessel RMS *Queen Elizabeth*, final destination a secret. It turned out that the major destination was near Sydney, Australia. The regiment was shipped to Melbourne, and then sixty miles inland to Seymour, an old Australian military camp dating to World War I. By July 1942, the regiment boarded trains and was taken north and west to Rockhampton on the Queensland coast.[67]

In March, General Douglas MacArthur arrived to take command of the Allied Forces

that had survived massive Japanese advances in Guam, Wake Island, the Marshalls, Hong Kong, and Burma. The general disagreed with the Australian army's strategy of defending Australia, stating that the Japanese should never set foot on the continent. This meant the fight would take place in Indonesia and other South Pacific islands.

On July 22, 1942, the Japanese invaded the north coast of New Guinea, but the 163rd remained in Australia until they were mobilized to assist the 32nd Division (Michigan and Wisconsin National Guard). Most of the 41st Division, including the 163rd Infantry, was ordered into action in New Guinea. The regiment arrived on January 1, 1943 at the airfields at Dobodura and Popondetta, the first full American division "to fly into combat in the southwest Pacific theatre."[68] It was sobering to see the remnants of the 32nd Division emerge from the jungle. The 163rd joined with the remainder of the 41st Division, which was better trained than the 32nd and ready to engage the enemy. No one knew how large the Japanese force in New Guinea was.[69]

The New Guinea jungles were constantly wet, and the Japanese used the density of the foliage to camouflage their positions, being both everywhere and nowhere at almost the same time. Early in the 163rd's engagement, during several hour-long Japaneses attacks launched at two places on the American perimeter, Company B lost its first six men. The following day, the commanding officer of Company B, Captain Robert Hamilton, ordered a counterattack. The initial patrol was sent to locate a Japanese machine gun along the road to Sanananda. The patrol was turned back, but the location of the gun was ascertained. A second patrol was lead by Sergeant Joseph Reddoor from Poplar. The pillbox was discovered, but the sergeant was hit in the hip and foot. He managed to get behind a tree, and when his patrol was unable to advance, Reddoor tossed two grenades toward the gun. Several enemy soldiers were killed, but the machine gun continued to fire. Seeing the bravery of his tribesmen, Sergeant Herman Belgarde, a Chippewa from Brockton, Montana, rescued Reddoor under enemy fire. Belgarde was also hit, but both men lived to fight another day.[70]

The Pulizer Prize winning journalist George Weller of the *Chicago Daily News* described the warfare that characterized the struggle:

This was but the opening move in a kind of cat's cradle series of attacks, back and forth, across and between the flooded Sanananda road and Killerton track which, by gradually shaving off and slicing up the Jap network of dugouts and fire lanes, eventually turned the whole 80 square miles of jungle into a kind of madhouse, where men slept in water, when demented Japs wandered alone and by dozens, and where many on both sides died alone in fern-strewn glades.[71]

Ordered to take the position once and for all, two Company B platoons advanced. Unaware that the gun in question was really one of five, the platoons worked forward from two different directions. Although the plan was to attack simultaneously, the second platoon attacked before the first platoon could get in place, and one of its men was killed. The second platoon was forced back. The first platoon began its attack, but when the day ended, eight men were dead and three wounded, and the enemy guns were still in place.[72]

The conditions of this struggle were hampered and particularly debilitating:

The men sat in their trenches enduring a heavy New Guinea rain that never seemed to end. When it wasn't raining the jungle dripped water from prior storms. Trenches filled with runoff, leaving men aggravated and miserable. Some tried to bail water with helmets. It was no use. Each hour brought new hardships.[73]

As the battle for Sanananda entered its second week, Company B was again sent after the deadly guns. This time, an attack was launched by Company C against a second Japanese position across the road. Met with heavy resistance, C Company lost eight men and thirteen were injured. B Company also was thwarted, with six men killed, one missing, and ten wounded.[74] Other elements came into play as the Japanese began using both cut-and-run patrols and tree snipers, and countersniping became a means of defense. On January 9, 1943, the Second Battalion was ordered to block the Killerton Trail, which put the Japanese forces deep in New Guinea in a box and cut off its supply lines.[75]

Companies of the 163rd continued to root out the Japanese positions, and periodically B Company was assigned particular objectives. Desperation was setting in among the Japanese, with many of them "dying of starvation, sickness, and a shortage of ammunition."[76] The victory at Sanananda came on January 19, when the Japanese stronghold was finally overrun.[77] Further down the Japanese line, other companies were engaged. On January 20, Captain Duncan Dupree of Poplar was killed along with several others when an American mortar shell fell short. Within a week, another stronghold and the heads of many tunnels were overrun.[78]

The battle-hardened 163rd returned to Australia in July 1943 for further training. Meanwhile, the Allies pursued the Japanese army along the New Guinea coast, successfully driving it from Salamaua and Lae. MacArthur ran a sting operation, pretending to prepare for an assault of Wewak, and instead concentrated on Hollandia and Aitape, further up the coast, hopping ahead and cutting supply lines to the Japanese concentrated at Wewak.

On April 22, 1944, the men of the 163rd were among 22,000 landing at Aitape to secure an airfield called Korako in the Tadji airdrome. After landing, the Allied forces realized they were thousands of yards off target. Two days after their arrival, they discovered the main escape route for the Japanese and the fight for Kamti ensued.[79] The 163rd moved ahead to support MacArthur's leapfrog strategy of taking the airfield on Wakde Island in May 1944. Heavy resistance was encountered, but the airfield was secured in two days.[80] The 163rd, attached to the 41st Division, was next sent to the island of Biak, where there were three airstrips. As island after island fell into Allied hands, their bombers were put within reach of Japanese forces in the Philippines, Borneo, and Sumatra, all of which supplied oil for the Japanese war machine.[81]

Biak was an island of high coral ridges, complete with caves, many fortified by the Japanese. However, the terrain was such that the 105mm cannons that had been so effective at Wakde were useless. The challenge was to clear the island of the Japanese, but Japanese forces had dug in with considerable supplies, including pillboxes among the caves. Ambushes increased as the Allies probed to ascertain the enemy's strength. On June 26, a surprise assault resulted in a stalemate. A three-day artillery barrage begun on July 4 to soften up the Japanese positions failed. At about this time, portable flamethrowers arrived and were used with some success, but a more decisive force was needed. On July 22, the Army Air Corps sent in eight B-24 bombers with 1,000-pound bombs on delayed fuses. The infantry followed the bombs, and the resistance was eliminated.[82]

Once Australia was safe, the campaign shifted to the Philippines. On March 1, 1945, the air assault began, and by March 10, 1945, the invasion force assembled in the waters off Zamboanga. The city was taken without much resistance, the Japanese having retreated into the hills. By the end of March, the 163rd had accomplished its objective in Zamboanga, and parts of the 186th Infantry relieved the 163rd. At this point, every original member had earned the eighty-five points needed for a discharge and a ticket home. These veterans were rotating out at a rate of 3 percent per month. The Philippines was taken one battle at a time, hopping from one island to the next. In April, the 163rd was sent to the island of Jolo. Well received in the city, they began dislodging a Japanese infantry brigade in the mountains some 800 feet above the city. Ill-equipped and supplied, the enemy faced daily air raids and artillery bombardments, and fighting was fierce. Soon after, the 163rd was listed as one of the units to invade Japan.

With the war over in Europe, the use of the atomic bomb was contemplated for Japan, since the fighting had been so dramatic on Okinawa. In the first days of August, the bombs were dropped on Hiroshima and Nagasaki, and by the time the Japanese surrendered, the Montana soldiers of the 163rd had returned home. In December 1945, the 163rd Infantry was deactivated.[83]

The war affected Indian people in a number of ways. The entire U.S. government had to reorganize to conduct the war. Many civilian agencies were moved from Washington to free office space for the War Department. In 1942, the Bureau of Indian Affairs moved its offices to the Merchandise Mart building in the heart of downtown Chicago, Illinois, where it remained for the duration.[84]

Government spending was diverted to this new priority, which inevitably meant cutbacks in domestic spending and consequently, reductions in the relief and recovery projects that had sustained many Indians. But the war brought employment opportunities for those who did not choose to serve in the armed forces. The labor demands of ever-expanding defense plants, hard at work building war materials, meant off-reservation employment with steady incomes.[85] For example, Austin Buckles moved to Akron, Ohio in the fall of 1941 to work in defense industry.[86]

The patriotism of the Fort Peck tribes has never been questioned. Within four days of the attack on Pearl Harbor, the Fort Peck Tribal Executive Board passed a resolution supporting the newly declared war, pledging men, women, and materials, and asking that the President of the United States take $10,000 from the 4% Trust Fund to purchase "Defence [sic] bonds."[87]

Collier's 1941 annual report reflected the adjustments Indian Affairs was making to accommodate the war effort. Program adjustments were inevitable: 1) reclamation projects either shelved or slowed; 2) coordination with Selective Service about employment replacements for individuals serving in the armed forces as opposed to exceptions for those working on defense industries; 3) increased industrial training in the schools and CCC programs; and 4) "the educational program would reflect intensified efforts to instil an understanding and appreciation of democracy, of better nutrition, health practices, and other matters that would make the Indians even better and more capable citizens."[88]

The rejection of the IRA meant that the Tribal Executive Board continued to function under its Constitution of 1928, and was not compelled to accept an IRA-style constitution. Operating along its previously established principles and authorities, the board hired people to do tasks whenever necessary and if resources were available. Consequently, the board had to monitor its resources. Capable of dealing with most issues, the board began operating with openness and efficiency. From all appearances, it exhibited a growing sophistication in renting tribal lands in or near the towns on the reservation as business sites. In a resolution passed in September 1941,

the board outlined the plan whereby rentals would be based on the value a business had reported to the Internal Revenue Service. If this procedure was not applicable, the amount of rent would be a minimum of $1 per month for a 50-by-150-foot lot.[89]

Most of the Fort Peck tribal membership did not favor ending the allotment system, and this had been the primary reason that they rejected the IRA. The Fort Peck membership believed that allotments should be made to newborn children. However, by 1941, Collier approved the last additional allotment schedules at Fort Peck.[90] Obsessed with how much land had passed out of trust, Collier did not understand fully how critical it was for many Indian families and individuals to be able to sell land in times of need. In a 1941 resolution, the Tribal Executive Board stated its opposition to a "withdrawal of cancelled homestead lands from disposal," reminding the bureau that stipulations in that legislation still applied to them. The board demanded that the government accept this and record the allotments pending approval at the time of the withdrawal of land. In the spirit of self-determination, this was allowed, though for the last time.[91]

Grazing leases continued to be a source of income in this period, but the amount of return fluctuated.

In 1934 the per head fee for cattle was $1.50, but the following year it jumped to nearly $3.00. In 1936 it dropped to $2.50, went up the following year, and dropped back down in 1938. From 1939 to 1942 the per-head fee remained fixed at $1.80 per head. Rates for sheep that had reached 60 cents per animal a few years earlier had dropped to 36 cents, or calculated on a per-acre basis, in the period 1939 to 1942 the return was 6 cents, well below the 15 cent per-acre charge that had been standard a decade before.[92]

The key variable was whether the land was tribal-held trust land or allotted trust land. On allotted lands, only grazing permits were issued, whereas lessees paid for using tribal lands just as if they were being penalized for trespassing. In 1941, permittees numbered 119 non-Indians and eleven tribal members. Fewer Indian cattle were being grazed on the open range because many Indians had become members of livestock associations, which allowed them cooperatively to graze their cattle on fenced range leased to the associations.[93] During the early 1940s, the U.S. Attorney left the resolution of trespass cases to the superintendent for out-of-court settlement. The superintendent demanded prosecution only if parties refused to compensate tribal members or the tribes.[94]

Throughout the war, the Indian Office tried to bring debt loads under control. However, other money was loaned to purchase lands to get "Indian clients" into irrigated farming.[95] In some cases, individuals handed over lands to the tribes to satisfy reimbursable indebtedness, and the lien of the tribes against the land was merged and extinguished without any formal action by the Department of Interior or Congress. In response, the tribes were expected to generate a waiver of existing indebtedness.

In some cases, the land passed to numerous heirs, especially when the landowner died without a will. The land became so fractionated that it was thought better to keep the parcels intact for leasing purposes, or for sale or transfer, with the heirs receiving any money generated, no matter how small. Transfers might be necessary to put parcels of land into large enough tracts to make leasing viable. These transactions had to be tracked by hand-generated records. The interests of minors could be handled this way, but with "a proper monetary consideration or equivalent value," e.g., a land parcel exchange, instead. The interests of relatives and guardians also needed to be regulated.[96]

At one point, an allocation of $50,000 from the appropriated land re-purchase fund was confused with the 4% Tribal Industrial Assistance Fund, and the mix-up was identified in a memo, dated April 1, 1942. A resolution from the Tribal Executive Board, dated February 19, 1942, asked to be eligible for an application for allotment. As of April 1, 1942, the entire balance in the Tribal Industrial Assistance Fund was $16,937.07, but Chairman George Washington wrote asking for $25,000, which had been endorsed by Superintendent Hunter. The Industrial Assistance money was set aside to assist farmers and livestock operators for another season. A.C. Cooley, Director of Extension and Industry, could not ascertain if the money for land purchases had ever been used, since the report from the Fiscal Division indicated $58,248.52 was available in the 4% Fund. Individual land repurchase funds had been targeted to encourage tribal members to relocate to the Oswego irrigation unit, with a good number of relocatees.[97]

In a communication with Gray dated September 8, 1942, H.M. Critchfield, Supervisor of Credit, noted that the move to Chicago had made many Fort Peck files inaccessible. Asking Gray to be conservative in his spending, Critchfield requested a plan for a loan program.[98] By September 11, Gray submitted a program based on a request for $6,000 to consist of "miscellaneous short-time loans" for several livestock associations, for milk cows, seed, equipment, and work horses for farmers, and finally for "operating expenses to take care of labor on pumps for community gardens, plowing and preparing seed beds, maintenance and operation of the irrigation and entire system."[99]

Superintendent O.C. Gray, who had held that position since 1939, was succeeded by Fuhrman Asbury in the spring of 1943. Asbury, formerly with the Credit Division, brought his familiarity with reimbursable loans and their collection to his new appointment.

Business savvy sometimes came by way of the school of hard knocks. The Oswego Agricultural Association in April 1943 negotiated a share-crop contract with the D.L. Piazza Potato Company. Essentially, the contract stipulated that Piazza provide the seed potatoes, a planter, a duster, and a digger, and pay half the picking expenses, warehousing, and shipping, and then market the potatoes. The tribal members contributed their labor, and were responsible for planting, cultivating, harvesting, and supplying the fields, and a series of incidental costs. Unfortunately, once the crop was harvested, local markets were ignored, and Piazza demanded that the crop be shipped east for storage. When it came time to settle accounts, Piazza claimed that his company's expenses had exceeded the price for the crop, and that the association would receive no money. When the Indian Office looked into the circumstances, the vague language of the contract did not provide grounds for any legal action. Asbury vowed that he would never allow Fort Peck Indians to become involved in any such arrangement.[100]

The Tribal Executive Board, in a resolution dated June 30, 1943, expressed its desire to have from $50,000 to $60,000 of credit funds extended in Tribal Industrial Assistance funds. However, the OIA was unable to agree.[101] In another memorandum to Extension and Industry dated July 21, 1943, Joe Jennings, Acting Director, Tribal Relations, noted that the Fort Peck Tribal "Council" was requesting an appropriation of $100,000 for "rehabilitation (including loans for education, improvements, and for land consolidation) of returned soldiers and reestablishment of returned industrial workers." The board's foresight was commended, and the resolution was to be studied.[102]

An OIA accountant and auditor, Martin Overgaard reported to the CIA in Chicago on August 7, 1943, on several fiscal irregularities involving the organized tribes and various Indian associations for the year ending June 30, 1943. The Fort Peck Tribes had no funds under their sole jurisdiction, not having accepted the IRA. He acknowledged minimal balances in the tribal rehabilitation funds. He pointed out that no accounting records were being kept by the tribal officers, and no elected treasurer was needed as there were not sufficient funds to require such oversight. Funds granted to individuals were transferred though Individual Indian Money accounts. Record-keeping by the agricultural and livestock associations was also loosely managed by the extension staff, but basic accounting records were necessary.[103] Asbury wrote the CIA on August 20, 1943, having met in Billings with district officials about a $600,000 appropriation for funds, but non-IRA tribes were excluded unless a means for participation could be devised. Asbury recommended the payments be made to individuals.[104] Woehlke responded on September 10, 1943, questioning the unspecific nature of the Tribal Executive Board resolution, especially what they meant by "rehabilitation":

The records of this Office show that there is $58,790.60 of appropriated tribal funds on deposit in the United States Treasury to the credit of the Fort Peck Indians; that the annual income for the past three fiscal years, beginning with the fiscal year 1940, has been $5,485.27, $10,135.18 and $15,812.39, respectively, making an average annual income of $10,477.62 for the three years.

Inasmuch as the entire $100,000 involved in the resolution is not available at the present time and inasmuch as the time was short to get this item into the budget justifications in connection with the 1945 Appropriation Act, we have included an item of $50,000 as tribal industrial assistance.[105]

Woehlke further wrote Asbury that the OIA was formulating regulations for loans to and by unincorporated tribes. The office was reluctant to make an exception for the Fort Peck tribes. He did acknowledge receipt of the resolution from the Tribal Executive Board requesting the administration of the "existing repayment cattle contracts" be turned over to the tribes. This appeared to be somewhat contradictory to ask that all such dealings, including cash loans, be made directly with the U.S. government. The transfer to the tribes was approved, but making loans direct from the United States from the revolving fund was not allowed.[106]

The executive board on a number of occasions opposed extensions to homesteaders for payments on their homesteads. Once the conditions of these extensions were not met, the homesteads were cancelled, and the lands reverted to surplus tribal lands, which in many cases were leased, and the rental money treated as tribal revenue. Asbury asked the CIA, on September 15, 1943, that such cancelled homestead lands be considered tribal property, and for an assurance that these lands would not be available for any further homestead entry.[107]

The wartime economy had tangible effects that were far more complex for Indians than non-Indians. Rationing stretched the shortages of the Depression out into the first years of the war. But income for the tribes and individual tribal members increased because of government programs, Indian entrepreneurial activity, and the demands to satisfy the wartime economy. By 1943, families on the reservation had an annual average income of $1,445 from agriculture, lease revenues, relief payments, dependency benefits, and miscellaneous earnings.[108]

By 1944, collecting on reimbursable fund debts made for circumstances where individuals still in possession of land could voluntarily convey these to settle the debts. Ironically, this was comparable to what happened in disposal of allotments for money in the 1920s, and lands again were surrendered for their market value.[109]

Weather in the spring of 1944 had left springs and stock dams in poor shape. Eight dams had been washed out by spring ice jams, with four completely destroyed. New concrete bases were to be constructed once the war was over, to provide more grazing areas for Indians. Roads for school buses also needed more gravel.[110]

Farm and ranch families by 1945 accounted for 46 percent of the 523 resident families. Overall agricultural production increased that year despite scarce labor, a shortage of machinery, and hail, a cold spring, and insects. Throughout the reservation, the five district community gardens were productive, and livestock associations were "active." The agricultural extension agent reported the purchase of thirteen registered Hereford bulls that year between the two established associations and a number of individual members. He also reported that two new stock associations and the three established ones were leasing over 50,000 acres of grazing land. While the majority of tribal members owned no livestock, by 1945, there were 179 herds on the reservation, and most were fairly small operations, including one individual who had one sheep.[111] Use of grazing lands increased during the war years. In some grazing units, usage was so intense that tribal funds were required to buy seed for portions of the range.[112]

The enrolled population of the Fort Peck tribes by 1945 reached 700 families, and 3,079 individual members. Families resident on the reservation totalled 510. In 1945, 2,190 individuals were of more than one-half Indian blood, and 334 were of less than one-fourth. There were fewer old-time Indians who did not speak or write English, especially evident with the pattern of attendance by children in public and non-reservation schools. As a majority of tribal members were intermingling with non-Indians and their "non-reservation neighbors," an observation was made that many Fort Peck Indians were acquiring the "ways of non-Indians."[113]

Beyond the war and the Depression, accomplishment appeared brief, but unlimited. The Bureau of Reclamation (BOR) and the U.S. Army Corp of Engineers were devising plans for flood control of the Upper Missouri basin. BOR was most interested in maintaining irrigation districts under its direct supervision. By January 1945, preliminary planning was underway on expanding the irrigation capacities at Fort Peck Reservation and integrating that with a canal planned to run between the Souris and the Missouri Rivers. Developing the Medicine Lake Game Refuge as a catch basin was also part of the plan. This had implications not only for Fort Peck trust lands, but also for a fair number of Turtle Mountain allotments. Building a reservoir on the Big Muddy required a canal to distribute water to Poplar and Wiota irrigable allotments, but the challenges of doing this were enormous. An estimated 48,000 acres of Indian trust lands, virtually all in individual allotments, were expected to be affected. While 2,400 acres of submarginal land would be submerged from Medicine Lake and southward, many of the forty-acre irrigable allotments in the Big Muddy vicinity, approximately 733 original allotments, and several tracts of tribal lands would also be affected.

A partial justification was that very few Indians in this area were operating their own lands, the drinking water was "bad," there was no wood, and what was leased was only for grazing or for hay. Finally, many allotments were in heirship status, complicating sales. To initiate such a process, congressional action would have to be secured.[114] After all this planning, this project was never undertaken.

The same document assessed development of irrigation on Fort Peck Reservation. If the Montana division of the Missouri-Souris Project proceeded on its projected 1945 schedule, local development was to wait further definition, so that maximum integration of schedules and infrastructure could be achieved. The Big Porcupine unit needed extensive reorganization and construction, as well as economic evaluation. However, the plan for completion of the Frazer-Wolf Point Project was expected to proceed as soon as the "funds, machinery, and man power" required were permitted. The big canal would deliver water to the Frazer pumping station by gravity flow, making electric pumping unnecessary. The Poplar River Reservoir, anticipated for so long, could only be justified if more land was available for irrigation, but with the big canal construction, the Poplar Reservoir was no longer needed.

The next goal was irrigation development of the Missouri River bottomlands in the eastern end of the reservation with a pumping station southwest of Brockton, near the Riverside school. The large canal would then necessitate a series of laterals, but all of this would be delineated after initial authorization had been received. The cost of water, by which the Bureau of Reclamation expected to recover part of its costs, was expected to be about $3 an acre annually, not withstanding the capacity of Indian farmers to pay this rate. It had been the responsibility of the Indian Irrigation Service to maintain and acquire Missouri River water from the on-reservation pumping stations, making adjustments to rules and regulations of the Bureau of Reclamation more cumbersome and costly. One observation offered was: "It appears that there will be more Indian-owned irrigated land than Indians of this reservation are likely to require for many years, if ever." The Flood Control Bill that was to create the Pick-Sloan Plan had already been passed by Congress in 1944. Congress did not want to replicate the bureaucracy of the Tennessee Valley Authority, and so the fate of the Missouri-Souris Project was undetermined.[115]

John Collier's resignation was accepted by FDR on January 22, 1945. FDR had begun serving his fourth term, but his health was failing, and he died on April 12, 1945, leaving Harry S. Truman, his vice-president, to succeed him.

The end of the war brought many changes in the lives of Fort Peck Indians. Victory-Europe Day was May 8, 1945, but the war in the Pacific lasted until Japan's formal surrender on September 2, 1945.[116]

With Collier's departure, the opponents of the Indian New Deal set about undoing its accomplishments. There was talk of emancipating Indians from an inequality binding them by special laws and regulations, to put Indians on an "absolutely equal footing with white citizens." This other side called for termination of the special relationship, including the treaty relationship, with Indians and the U.S. government.[117]

The potential for prosperity brightened in 1946, as livestock and hay production increased. Twenty-two families started new farm operations, but loan funds were limited, which prevented others from following suit. Agricultural success continued to be very differential. A total of 219 families were engaged in farming operations on their own lands in 1946, as compared to 320 others working on lands belonging to others. Success was also coupled with weather and crop conditions. For example, on the Oswego unit of the Frazer-Wolf Point irrigation project, a total of thirty-seven families were productive, raising "forage crops, cereal grains, sugar beets, potatoes and other vegetables" despite difficulty with the irrigation system. Net income was reportedly doubled for these farmers in the 1946 growing season to $1,133 per farm.[118]

In April 1945, Representative Henry Jackson, Chairman of the House Committee on Indian Affairs, introduced legislation to empower the Department of the Interior to purchase and consolidate the title of all the submarginal lands on Montana reservations and convey these to the tribes, and to make available IRA acquisition money for purchasing these lands for Montana tribes that had rejected the IRA. In October 1945, the Tribal Executive Board rejected congressional action to turn over to tribes all available submarginal lands on their reservations. Rather, it requested Congress "to recognize the Indian interest in these lands and to protect them before any of this land was disposed of." The resolution stopped short of favoring return of these lands to the tribes. Again, on January 10, 1946, the executive board resolved that "also was not a clear-cut endorsement of the transfer of title to the tribe [sic]."[119] Councilman Roy Track provided further context in a statement to a General Council on June 1, 1946:

Beginning in 1942 the Poplar Commercial Club, the American Legion Post, and the Board of Supervisors of Roosevelt County petitioned Congress for the disposal and sale of the Fort Peck submarginal lands. In 1945, Representative D'Ewart and Senator Wheeler introduced numerous bills directing the Secretary of the Interior to sell specified tracts to a named individual at a specified price. Usually the price was the amount which the United States paid for the particular tract. All the prices named in these bills were far below present market value. Should any of these bills be passed it is probable that the President, acting on the advice of the Budget Bureau and the Comptroller General, would veto these bills against public policy.[120]

On November 8, 1945 at an executive board meeting, Dolly Akers was elected a delegate to lobby Washington about the submarginal lands and other tribal matters. She was the wife of John Akers, a farmer and former elected member of the Montana House of Representatives. Irrespective of the questionable authority of the executive board to authorize delegates, Akers had asked for credentials, but was intent on traveling to Washington on her own resources. She had corresponded extensively with the congressional delegation and individuals in the OIA, mostly with Walter V. Woehlke, Assistant CIA. Clearly, her influence was substantial.[121]

Much of the dithering on the submarginal lands issue was linked to questions about rehabilitation opportunities for Indian veterans, especially those who had not received allotments. The proposal that submarginal lands be sold rather than returned to the tribes limited the numbers of individuals who could benefit. The annual proposed "reservation program" had been prepared by Dolly Akers, James Archdale, and George Boyd, Sr., to be presented by delegates to Chicago and Washington, and "one of the items was the acquisition of sub-marginal lands." Apparently, it came as a surprise

that the delegates found out in Chicago as well as in Washington that she [Akers] was working towards disposing certain tracts of sub-marginal lands by advocating the sale of these tracts to different people who were named in bills which were introduced by Congressman D'Ewart and Senator Wheeler.[122]

For a number of days in November and December 1945, Dolly Akers visited Washington to lobby on the submarginal lands issue. At this time, she was an elected member of the Tribal Executive Board, but it was unclear to what extent she revealed that affiliation. She apparently was urging Senator Wheeler to sell the submarginal lands, rather than transfer them to the tribes. Track's account reported:

It was proposed to Senator Wheeler that the Departmental Bill, H.R. 3061 might be amended to provide that the Fort Peck submarginal lands should, in line with the resolution of the Executive Board, be classified by Government soil experts, that the land found to be good agricultural land in class I and II might be offered for sale at prices not less than the amounts the United States paid for the tracts, that priority for the purchase of any given tract would be granted to (1) veterans who are enrolled members of the Fort Peck Tribe; (2) present Indian users of the tracts; (3) all other veterans; (4) former owners of the submarginal tracts; (5) lessees of tracts in 1945; (6) all other applicants. Each class to have 30 days in which to exercise its preferences. The proceeds of the sales of the land, it was suggested, were to be used 75% to assist in the rehabilitation of Fort Peck Indian veterans and 25% to the counties in lieu of taxes. Any tract of agricultural land remaining unsold at the end of the year would revert to the Fort Peck Tribe.[123]

For non-agricultural grazing lands, the CIA might "direct the issuance of permits to the use of these grazing lands to owners of contiguous commensurate properties for a maximum period of 10 years substantially in compliance with the applicable provisions of the Taylor Grazing Act." Indian livestock raisers would get first pick of grazing permits, and the revenues would be split 75-25 between the tribes and Roosevelt County. In December 1946, a petition from the Poplar Chamber of Commerce, the Roosevelt County Commissioners, and eleven other organizations endorsed these proposals. This was a compromise from the previous resolution of late January 1946 when the coalition proposed the outright unconditional sale of the submarginal lands with proceeds going to the Federal Treasury.[124]

A general council was called in February 1946 by the executive board, under the leadership of Chairman Carl Walking Eagle, to elect delegates to proceed to Washington. The delegates elected were Roy Track, Joseph Reddoor, and Austin Buckles. But the delegation was politically outflanked by Dolly Akers, whose position reflected the coalition of non-Indian interests because her husband wished to acquire a tract of submarginal land adjacent to their property.[125]

Consequently, a general council was called for June 1, 1946 to throw Dolly Akers off the executive board. She was present and pointed out that among the 143 persons present, Assiniboines were particularly underrepresented. She requested the Assiniboines be counted, and only thirty-eight were present. Akers "stated that 38 people is not a representative body of the Assiniboines."[126] George Thompson observed that the 1908 Allotment Act stated that a two-thirds voting population was standard, but rationalized that "there can never be two-thirds present at any meeting and if this group [the general council assembled] is considered as a quorum it should proceed with its business." The vice-chairman, Pete Eagle, stated that there had been ten days notice for the meeting and "if more Assiniboines were interested in the meeting they could have been present." No one mentioned that when meetings were held in Poplar, the Assiniboines living in the western half of the reservation were at a disadvantage. Andrew Red Thunder declared that the group was representative and that it should proceed. Chairman Carl Walking Eagle stated that he had been on the executive board for twelve years, implying that after the meeting he was resigning, "as he had other interests such as cattle to take care of."[127]

The chairman called on Roy Track, chairman of the Washington delegation, to read his charges. After his summary, he charged that Dolly Akers "did not support the [reservation] program" in Washington.[128]

Dolly Akers stood up and declared that she had gone independently to Washington, spending $500 of her own money, because "she happened to be friendly with the politicians in Washington and talked to them, which friendship she gained in her political party." She declared that the "reservation program" included statements about "the acquisition of submarginal lands," and what she was working for was not inconsistent with this agenda, suggesting Track was not informed on the issue. Akers then read a statement about the history of the submarginal lands issue, and suggested that conversion of surplus lands to homestead lands meant that "the Indians do not have any claim on the land."

Her opponents clamored that the tribes might get submarginal lands as a gift. Akers countered, quoting a letter from Congressman Wesley A. D'Ewart to Joe Frerich of Poplar. The congressman explained how he had introduced bills to authorize the sale of certain submarginal areas to Indian and white veterans within the Fort Peck Reservation, but these actions had been opposed by the Indian Office. He noted:

Recently, three members of the Fort Peck Tribe were here in Washington and appeared before the Committees of the House and Senate, asking that this land be turned over to the Fort Peck Tribe. All of this made the situation more difficult. I have had several meetings with Mr. Brophy [CIA] and his staff, asking that they set a definite policy as regards this submarginal land. At first they said the policy could not be established until the new Secretary [Interior] was appointed. The new Secretary is in and we still do not have the policy.[129]

The congressman explained that extensive hearings before the Senate Committee on Indian Affairs were planned that would define the submarginal lands policy for Fort Peck and other reservations. The various bills introduced on the subject would also be examined, and recommendations for legislation would have to await the outcome of those hearings. Zimmerman with the OIA stated "none of the veterans will get any of that submarginal land," but this meant that Congress was left with the laborious task of writing policy following the outcome of the hearings.[130]

George Thompson explained that he had tried to get the submarginal lands, but that it looked like the land was going to be sold to white veterans: "The last chance the people had on all of this land was through the Land Enterprise Program which provided for the leasing of the submarginal land at $.015 an acre and sub-lease it to our Indians." Thompson reminded those present that this program had been "passed" by the executive board on May 9, 1946, and "every Sioux Indian who was in the room objected to it, and that they had protests from the Poplar, Riverside, and Fort Kipp districts, but the Assiniboines accepted it." Thompson said he was convinced that "it was for the best interests of the tribes to accept the Program." However, the superintendent wrote Thompson expressing what the latter interpreted as disapproval of the program, and consequently Thompson "turned around." Approval was stricken from the minutes and left for a future General Council.[131]

The members of the Tribal Executive Board set out to punish Dolly Akers for her political independence. One compromise proposal was to address submarginal lands below Township 30, and not to try for lands north of this "Maginot Line." Akers' political experience was to seek compromise, but she was not willing to be condemned by the General Council without a fight. She had pointed out that at one point, an individual who was not a tribal member had been allowed to take part in the February 23 General Council when the delegation was selected. Her opponents considered her objection mean-spirited and a sign of a poor loser. She was also accused of being against the veterans, and it was

pointed out that her own brother-in-law, who was not a tribal member, was an honored veteran from the reservation. Austin Buckles pointed out that "Indian veterans fought for their country for a democratic and American way of life and when they get back home they have to fight all over again for the privileges which are being denied them." More personal charges were made, and finally Akers objected. Buckles suggested that she had not been elected as a delegate and had not supported the prevailing position, which could not be advanced without unity,

that they [the majority on the Executive Board] did not want compromise legislation on sub-marginal lands, and that when the Indian boys were inducted into the armed forces they did not compromise with them by saying you can have this and can have that when you come back. He further asked that as far back as November 10, 1937 there were charges made against Mrs. Akers when she was a relief worker, and that petitions were circulated at that time against her and sent in to Washington.[132]

Buckles then moved

that because of the opposition and for not working for the best interests of the tribes in her capacity as Executive Board member, that she be impeached and dismissed as a member of the Board and be forever barred from representing the Fort Peck Reservation in tribal affairs.[133]

The motion was seconded by Joe Reddoor.

Akers asked James Archdale to address the issue of credentials and the action taken in the executive board meeting of November 8, 1945. She explained that she had gone to Washington to seek dispositions about the submarginal lands issue, and to ascertain whether a formal delegation would be welcomed. She then stated that she had correspondence from CIA Brophy saying that she could not be charged with anything if she was not spending tribal money, and even though there was an offer to pay for the trip, she had not accepted this offer. Debate ensued about her credentials, and Archdale stated that her credentials were valid for the purposes upon which she traveled. Further discussion insinuated that Akers was not advocating that the submarginal lands be transferred to the tribes, and was at odds with much of the rest of the board. Just as the debate was running its course, Charles Hall suggested that the members of the executive board "were the ones to blame" and the problem really was the matter of issuing credentials when it did not have the right to delegate authority to Akers in the first place. He moved that the executive board was to blame and should be impeached. It was seconded, but not taken seriously, as no vote was taken. The chairman declared that the vote on the impeachment of Dolly Akers was at hand, and asked that the motion be read.[134] The vote was taken: 76 were in favor, and 28 against, so the motion passed.

Dolly Akers rose to ask if this meant that she was being expelled from the reservation, since the Solicitor's Office of the Interior Department would have to approve such an action. Austin Buckles responded that it did not remove her membership, only prevented her from being a member of the executive board and representing the Fort Peck tribes in any matter. She asked that the minutes of the meeting be sent to the Secretary of the Interior, which was seconded, but no vote was taken.[135] The political outcomes of these events were long-lasting.

Carl Walking Eagle, Chair of the Tribal Executive Board, wrote an undated report titled "Credit Activities Under Tribal Operations," submitted by Asbury with the Annual Credit Report on June 25. Walking Eagle noted that loans totalling $80,525.93 had been granted, and of this amount, $33,584.00 had been used to buy

cattle "to supplement the tribal revolving cattle program." Loans totalling $41,363.43 had been made to seventy-three individuals to support farming. The loans had been made for "productive purposes," and nearly all of the borrowers filed long-term farm plans. Twenty veterans were among those assisted. Crops looked promising. The chairman observed, "Most borrowers should have little trouble in meeting their payments. Machinery was difficult to obtain, but a number of clients were able to procure new equipment such as tractors and haying tools."[136] While this arrangement contributed to agricultural productivity, the lack of tribal funds for such operations was unsettling, especially when many tribal members "lack foresight or interest in the loaning program and do not wish to supplement tribal funds with revolving credit funds."[137]

But the administration of the loan program was not without its problems. Certain fees were not being collected, resulting in a shortfall for salaries of Extension Division employees at Fort Peck. Even after a thorough orientation on procedures and regulations, tribal clerks were having problems.[138] Certainly the executive board and superintendent supported those who wanted to capitalize farming and livestock operations, but accomplishing this was not without bureaucratic responsibilities.

On August 15, 1946, Chairman Carl Walking Eagle sent a telegram to the SI:

We Executive Board of Fort Peck Agency do hereby demand an investigation by the Department of Interior Inspector Arbitrary handling of our land funds[,] grazing[,] law and order[,] medical[,] Indian veteran rights[;] condition unbearable condition dissatisfied with condition existing here[.] Evidence[,] Affidavits[,] Proofs will be furnished the inspector on arrival.[139]

Visitors were present at the executive board

meeting on September 12, 1946 to discuss the current law and order situation, and the efforts to propose new regulations. Walter McGee, the District Special Officer, and Ben Rifle, the new Tribal Relations Officer, distributed the draft regulations. McGee introduced Rifle, a Rosebud tribal member. After answering questions about law and order, Rifle brought greetings from his reservation to the people of Fort Peck and explained that he was a veteran, and that he had accepted the job to travel to Nebraska, the Dakotas, Montana, and Wyoming to help tribal councils and the District Office seek solutions. The team was investigating the impact of having no Indian court operating in the mix of jurisdictions affecting tribal members in their entanglements with the law. Rifle then made a statement about veterans:

the veterans were taking an active part in government affairs, and that he noticed in the papers that 75% of the candidates for public office who were successful were returned veterans and stated that the State of Tennessee some rough necks were running the government and when the veterans came back they chased the sheriff and others out and took over the government to bring about a better law and order in their state. Mr. Rifle said that this was his first experience in visiting Indian reservations and he did not know to what extent young Indians men and women were working towards bringing about a better life on this reservation for themselves and their children, and said that many Indians has given up their time and many of them had given up their lives in order to bring about a better land in which to live, and the people who stayed at home and kept the home fires burning, making it easier for the Indian veterans, should all get their shoulders to the wheel to make for a better life for all.[140]

Later in his career, Ben Rifle served as a Republican congressman from the Second Congressional District, South Dakota, from the late 1950s into the 1960s.

Assistant CIA William Zimmerman, Jr. did not respond to Walking Eagle's telegram until September 22, 1946. He observed that the telegram did not include enough information "to justify sending an investigator from Washington or this office." Rather, he was referred to Mr. Fickinger, District Director in Billings, asking the executive board to submit its complaints to him, "he may be able to help you."[141] The creation of the Area Offices in 1946, initially called District Offices, was instituted without consultation, and added another layer to the bureaucratic cake.

James Archdale wrote the CIA on November 28, 1946 to clarify the situation of the balance owed for educational loans of his deceased son, Staff Sergeant Percy J. Archdale, and for Captain Duncan Dupree, also deceased. Since these loans were made with tribal money, the Tribal Executive Board hoped to see them cancelled. In Archdale's son's case, the rental money for his grazing land was not being paid to his widow because a hold was placed on his account pending a decision about the unpaid education loan. Archdale stated that if the Indian Office could not approve the cancellation, then maybe congressional legislation could grant this authority to the CIA.[142] Asbury wrote the CIA on December 11, 1946, again asking direction as to how to dispose of these education loans.[143] H.M. Critchfield for the CIA wrote James Archdale on December 31, saying there was no authority to cancel such loans, but legislation was being prepared to permit cancellation, and if secured, consideration would be given to the initial request.[144]

Population continued to grow, reaching 3,825 by 1949, of whom 1,236 were identified as full-bloods.[145] Housing on the reservation was divided between 53 percent log houses with the remainder frame construction. The diet of most was bread, potatoes, meat, and canned fruit and vegetables. While overall health was improving, diseases of infancy and childhood still afflicted tribal members, as well as pneumonia, tuberculosis, and cardiovascular problems. There were still cases of malnutrition, influenza, respiratory and gastro-intestinal problems, conjunctivitis, cancer, and dental cares.

Education became increasingly important in the lives of tribal members and their families: "By 1947 eighty-seven percent of the Fort Peck Indian children enrolled in schools were enrolled in public schools, for which education the government paid tuition. Small numbers of children attended private schools and non-reservation government schools."[146]

World War II had opened up the outside world to many tribal members. Certainly, off-reservation boarding school attendees or graduates had glimpsed the "modern" world, but the men and women who served in the armed forces carried this experience into the future. The knowledge of training, the experience of teamwork, and the situations demanding leadership shaped those veterans who came back. In many ways, the New Deal programs were running out of steam by the late 1930s, and efforts and resources for relief were also nearly exhausted. The war

in Europe had already erupted. With the attack on Pearl Harbor, FDR was justified in leading the country to war. The war effort, with all of its reconcentration of resources and people, gave purpose to economic sacrifice, which became the vehicle that finally vanquished the Depression.[147] The war galvanized tribal members, whether in the military, working in defense industries, or remaining at home, with a new resolve. While the war took the lives of a number of tribal members, most were spared and were ready to come home when it ended.

With the war over, the reorientation of people and resources resulted, nationally and locally. Many tribal members returned home, but others did not. For those who had been away, finding a way to fit into the new era was challenging, but at the same time, revitalizing families and communities became a priority. The search for opportunities to rehabilitate veterans was taken up by political leaders at Fort Peck as a natural transformation of the cultural value warriors held within Assiniboine and Sioux society. This reunion was not simple, only deliberate. The baggage of the vanquished Depression was debt, much of it held by individuals and their families. Challenges were identifiable, and resourcefulness was an important character trait with which to face the days and years ahead. ✪

1 Douglas D. Martin, *Historical Report on the* Fort Peck *Indian Reservation, Part I: An Administrative and Social History*, Docket 84, Defendant Exhibit No. FP-I, Fort Peck *Indians* v. United States, Court of Claims, Docket 184, 232.

2 Martin, *Historical Report on the Fort Peck Indian Reservation, Part I: An Administrative and Social History*, 197.

3 Martin, *Historical Report on the Fort Peck Indian Reservation, Part I: An Administrative and Social History*, 196.

4 Ibid.

5 Ibid.

6 Ibid.

7 Martin, *Historical Report on the Fort Peck Indian Reservation, Part I: An Administrative and Social History*, 198.

8 George A. Cunningham, Special Agent, Division of Investigations, Interior, Billings, Montana, to CIA, Washington, D.C., May 27, 1935, Chrono file, General History 1933-1938, Docket 184 Collection, Fort Peck Tribal Archives, Poplar, Montana.

9 Ibid.

10 John Collier, CIA, Washington, D.C., to Superintendent John G. Hunter, Fort Peck Agency [hereinafter cited as "FPA"], Poplar, Montana, July 16, 1935, CCF 24171-1935 Fort Peck .054, copy in the Chrono File, General History 1933-1938, Docket 184 Collection, Fort Peck Tribal Archives, Poplar, Montana; Martin, *Historical Report on the Fort Peck Indian Reservation, Part I: An Administrative and Social History*, 199.

11 Martin, *Historical Report on the Fort Peck Indian Reservation, Part I: An Administrative and Social History*, 198-199; LaRouche Report, Part II, "Employment at Fort Peck Dam," 18-20, Chrono File, General History 1933-1938, Docket 184 Collection, Fort Peck Tribal Archives, Poplar, Montana.

12 H. Scudder McKeel, Pine Ridge Agency, Pine Ridge, S.D., to Walter V. Woehlke, OIA, Washington, D.C., October 9, 1935, Chrono File, General History 1933-1938, Docket 184 Collection, Fort Peck Tribal Archives, Poplar, Montana.

13 Daiker, memo to Woehlke, December 3, 1935, attached to McKeel correspondence Woehlke, OIA, Washington, D.C., October 9, 1935, Chrono File, General History 1933-1938, Docket 184 Collection, Fort Peck Tribal Archives, Poplar, Montana.

14 Ibid.

15 A.C. Cooley, Director of Extension and Industry, memo to Mrs. Bronson, September 15, 1936, Chrono File, General History 1933-1938, Docket 184 Collection, Fort Peck Tribal Archives, Poplar, Montana.

16 E.J. Armstrong, OIA, Washington, D.C., to Hunter, Poplar, Montana, October 7, 1936, Chrono File, General History 1933-1938, Docket 184 Collection, Fort Peck Tribal Archives, Poplar, Montana.

17 LaRouche Report, Part I, Chrono File, General History 1933-1938, Docket 184 Collection, Fort Peck Tribal Archives, Poplar, Montana.

18 Martin, *Historical Report on the Fort Peck Indian Reservation, Part I: An Administrative and Social History*, 202-203; see LaRouche Report, Part I, Chrono File, General History 1933-1938, Docket 184 Collection, Fort Peck Tribal Archives, Poplar, Montana.

19 LaRouche Report, Part II: 12, Chrono File, General History 1933-1938, Docket 184 Collection, Fort Peck Tribal Archives, Poplar, Montana.

20 Ibid.; see discussion in LaRouche Report, Part I.

21 Martin, *Historical Report on the Fort Peck Indian Reservation, Part I: An Administrative and Social History*, 200.

22 Martin, *Historical Report on the Fort Peck Indian Reservation, Part I: An Administrative and Social History*, 200-201.

23 Ibid.

24 Martin, *Historical Report on the Fort Peck Indian Reservation, Part I: An Administrative and Social History*, 202.

25 Annual Report of Extension Workers, January 1, 1936-31 December 1936, December 21, 1936, CCF 931-1937 Fort Peck .031, RG 75, NA-Washington, D.C., also in Chrono File, General History 1933-1938, Docket 184 Collection, Fort Peck Tribal Archives, Poplar, Montana.

26 Martin, *Historical Report on the Fort Peck Indian Reservation, Part I: An Administrative and Social History*, 203.

27 See Martin, *Historical Report on the Fort Peck Indian Reservation, Part I: An Administrative and Social History*, 203-204; Anton Karge, Wolf Point, Montana, to Senator B.K. Wheeler, Washington, D.C., March 6, 1937, Chrono File, General History 1933-1938, Docket 184 Collection, Fort Peck Tribal Archives, Poplar, Montana; and Walter Magee, Special Officer, Indian

Field Service, Great Falls, Montana, to W.M. Nash, Acting Chief Special Officer, Indian Service, Denver, CO, June 3, 1937, with attached list, Chrono File, General History 1933-1938, Docket 184 Collection, Fort Peck Tribal Archives, Poplar, Montana.

28 Ken Philp, *John Collier's Crusade for Indian Reform* (Tucson: University of Arizona Press, 1977), 198.

29 See discussion in George Brown Tindall and David E. Shi, *America: A Narrative History*, 4th ed. (New York: W.W. Norton & Company, 1996), 1185-1186.

30 Martin, *Historical Report on the Fort Peck Indian Reservation, Part I: An Administrative and Social History*, 205-206..

31 Supervisor's Report, Ralph S. Bristol, June 6, 1937, Chrono File, General History 1933-1938, Docket 184 Collection, Fort Peck Tribal Archives, Poplar, Montana.

32 Boyd Faulkner, FPA, Poplar, Montana, memo to Hunter, June 22, 1937, Chrono File, General History 1933-1938, Docket 184 Collection, Fort Peck Tribal Archives, Poplar, Montana.

33 Hunter, Poplar, Montana, to OIA, Washington, D.C., June 30, 1937, Chrono File, General History 1933-1938, Docket 184 Collection, Fort Peck Tribal Archives, Poplar, Montana.

34 E.J. Armstrong, for the CIA, Washington, D.C., to Hunter, Poplar, Montana, August 6, 1937, Chrono File, General History 1933-1938, Docket 184 Collection, Fort Peck Tribal Archives, Poplar, Montana.

35 Hunter, Poplar, Montana, to CIA, Washington, D.C., December 31, 1937, Chrono File, General History 1933-1938, Docket 184 Collection, Fort Peck Tribal Archives, Poplar, Montana.

36 R.S. Bristol, Acting Director of Extension and Industry, OIA, Washington, D.C., to Hunter, Poplar, Montana, April 26, 1938, Chrono File, General History 1933-1938, Docket 184 Collection, Fort Peck Tribal Archives, Poplar, Montana.

37 AR of Extension Workers, Fort Peck Agency, January 1, 1938 to December 31, 1938, December 23, 1938, Chrono File, General History 1933-1938, Docket 184 Collection, Fort Peck Tribal Archives, Poplar, Montana.

38 Ibid., answer to "question 5," n.p.

39 Ibid., Narrative Summary, 3.

40 Ibid.

41 Superintendent O.C. Gray, FPA, Poplar, Montana, to CIA, Washington, D.C., August 3, 1939, Chrono File, General History 1939-1959, Docket 184 Collection, Fort Peck Tribal Archives, Poplar, Montana.

42 AR of Extension Workers, Fort Peck Agency, January 1, 1938 to December 31, 1938, December 23, 1938, "Narrative," 5, Chrono File, General History 1933-1938, Docket 184 Collection, Fort Peck Tribal Archives, Poplar, Montana.

43 Field agreement between Superintendent of FPA and Regional Conservator, Soil Conservation Service, Lincoln, NB, March 1940, Chrono File, General History 1939-1959, Docket 184 Collection, Fort Peck Tribal Archives, Poplar, Montana.

44 Martin, *Historical Report on the Fort Peck Indian Reservation, Part I: An Administrative and Social History*, 207; H.M. Critchfield, Acting Supervisor of Credit, Indian Service, Billings, Montana, to CIA, Washington, D.C., August 11, 1939, Chrono File, General History 1939-1959, Docket 184 Collection, Fort Peck Tribal Archives, Poplar, Montana.

45 Martin, *Historical Report on the Fort Peck Indian Reservation, Part I: An Administrative and Social History*, 207-208.

46 Executive Order No. 7868, April 15, 1938, see Dolly Akers discussion in Minutes, Tribal Executive Board, June 1, 1946, Chrono File, General History 1939-1959, Docket 184 Collection, Fort Peck Tribal Archives, Poplar, Montana, 4; Martin, Historical Report on the Fort Peck Indian Reservation, Part I: An Administrative and Social History, 208.

47 Martin, Historical Report on the Fort Peck Indian Reservation, Part I: An Administrative and Social History, 208.

48 Dolly Akers discussion about the history of the submarginal lands project in Minutes, Tribal Executive Board, June 1, 1946, Chrono File, General History 1939-1959, Docket 184 Collection, Fort Peck Tribal Archives, Poplar, Montana, 4; Martin, Historical Report on the Fort Peck Indian Reservation, Part I: An Administrative and Social History, 208.

49 Martin, *Historical Report on the Fort Peck Indian Reservation, Part I: An Administrative and Social History*, 208.

50 Subjects the delegation would investigate were: 1) a Sioux Settlement Bill to set up a Commission to negotiate outstanding claims with the Sioux Nation and their respective attorney; 2) a Sisseton-Wahpeton Bill, for a claim to descendents of the 1851 Treaty with the Sisseton-Wahpeton, currently before Congress; 3) an Assiniboine Bill, also currently before Congress, to disallow the off-sets claimed by the U.S. Government and instead, to adjust the value per acre amount, and grant the payment of the claim settlement; 4) a requested allotment of available surplus land to another group of children be allowed; 5) action needed about delinquent entrymen on lands that had been declared surplus, which they had not paid the balance of their value, but still were resident on lands after the last extension expired December 31, 1939; 6) asking to be paid the difference in the value of lands due to reappraisals of surplus homestead lands for the amount of loss in value, $112,008.00; 7) a system of rentals from agency and school reserve lands needs to be in place for non-ward older Indians living on these lands; 8) a full accounting of the reimbursable fund payments was needed; 9) the administrative burden of the Turtle Mountain off-reservation allottees needed assessment; 10) exchanges of inherited lands and allotments should be encouraged to reduce situations of complicated heirship; 11) the practice of having people assign power-of-attorney agreements when arranging block leasing units is opposed by tribal members; 12) a bill needed to authorize and demand a settlement on all delinquencies of reappraisements and homestead entries; and 13) revisions are needed in the Indian Law & Order Code to improve quality of personal and equipment needed for effective law enforcement (Minutes, April 25, 1940, CCF 2060-1932 Fort Peck .056, RG 75, NA-Washington, D.C.).

51 "Conference of Fort Peck Delegation with Messrs. Vigeant and Critchfield, 5-14-40," Chrono file, General History 1939-1959, Docket 184 Collection, Fort Peck Tribal Archives, Poplar, Montana.

52 Rufus Ricker, Sr., Poplar, Montana, to Senator James E. Murray, U.S. Senate, Washington, D.C., May 18, 1940, CCF 2060-1932 Fort Peck .056, RG 75, NA-Washington, D.C.

53 Gray, Poplar, to CIA, Washington, D.C., June 20, 1940, CCF 2060-1932 Fort Peck .056, RG 75, NA-Washington, D.C.

54 Collier, Washington, D.C., to Gray, Poplar, Montana, June 1, 1940, 1-2, Chrono file, General History 1939-1959, Docket 184 Collection, Fort Peck Tribal Archives, Poplar, Montana.

55 Ibid., 2.

56 Ibid.

57 Ibid., 3.

58 Collier, CIA, Washington, D.C., to Gray, Poplar, Montana, June 11, 1940, Chrono file, General History 1939-1959, Docket 184 Collection, Fort Peck Tribal Archives, Poplar, Montana.

59 Woehlke, Washington, D.C., to Gray, Poplar, Montana, November 22, 1940, Chrono file, General History 1939-1959, Docket 184 Collection, Fort Peck Tribal Archives, Poplar, Montana.

60 The tasks delineated were 1) lists to be filed in the Agency Office and in Washington, of good or articles to be stocked, and their quantity and estimated value; 2) the retail or local cost set out next to each item on the list; 3) a schedule of cost of freight rates from jobber warehouses, which can be obtained from the Great Northern local railway agent; 4) the proposed selling prices of these articles listed for sale; 5) the proposed wages to be paid the manager and clerks; 6) the estimated costs of heat, lights, gas, or other utilities for the facility; and 7) the cost of the building, or maintenance cost of a store building (Board Minutes, Executive Board, 12 June 1941, attached to letter, Gray, Poplar, Montana, to CIA, Washington, D.C., June 20, 1941, Chrono File, General History 1939-1959, Docket 184 Collection, Fort Peck Tribal Archives, Poplar, Montana.

61 Ibid.

62 Gray, Poplar, Montana, to CIA. Washington, D.C., October 24, 1941, Chrono File, General History 1939-1959, Docket 184 Collection, Fort Peck Tribal Archives, Poplar, Montana.

63 Tindall and Shi, *America: A Narrative History*, 1228-1233.

64 Martin J. Kidston, *From Poplar to Papua: Montana's 163rd Infantry Regiment in World War II* (Helena: Farcountry Press, 2004), v.

65 Kidston, *From Poplar to Papua*, 1-6.

66 Kidston, *From Poplar to Papua*, 16.

67 Ibid., 26-27.

68 Ibid., 33-34.

69 Ibid.

70 Ibid., 40-41.

71 Quoted in ibid., 42.

72 Ibid., 42-43.

73 Ibid., 43.

74 Ibid., 46-47.

75 Ibid., 47-49.

76 Ibid., 64.

77 Ibid., 63-64.

78 Ibid., 65-67.

79 Ibid., 85-102.

80 Ibid., 103-119.

81 Ibid., 120-121.

82 Ibid., 122-135.

83 See names of officers and enlisted men, pp. 161-184; Ibid., 163-156. Much research needs to be done on the participation of Fort Peck tribal members in the European theater of the war.

84 Martin, *Historical Report on the Fort Peck Indian Reservation, Part I: An Administrative and Social History*, 209.

85 Ibid.

86 Gray, Poplar, Montana, to CIA, Washington, D.C., December 24, 1941, commentary on special meeting of Executive Board on November 22, 1941, Chrono file, General History, 1939-1959, Docket 184 Collection, Fort Peck Tribal Archives, Poplar, Montana.

87 Ibid.; Fort Peck Tribal Resolution, December 11, 1941, Chrono file, General History, 1939-1959, Docket 184 Collection, Fort Peck Tribal Archives, Poplar, Montana.

88 Ibid., 210.

89 Ibid., 210-211.

90 Martin, *Historical Report on the Fort Peck Indian Reservation, Part I: An Administrative and Social History*, 11; Douglas D. Martin, *Historical Report on the Fort Peck Indian Reservation in Montana, Part II: The Allotment Program*, Docket 184, Defendant Exhibit No. FP-II, *Fort Peck Indians v. United States,* Court of Claims, Docket 184, 26.

91 Martin, *Historical Report on the Fort Peck Indian Reservation, Part I: An Administrative and Social History*, 211.

92 Summarized in Martin, *Historical Report on the Fort Peck Indian Reservation, Part I: An Administrative and Social History*, 212.

93 Martin, *Historical Report on the Fort Peck Indian Reservation, Part I: An Administrative and Social History*, 212.

94 Martin, *Historical Report on the Fort Peck Indian Reservation, Part I: An Administrative and Social History*, 212-213.

95 Gray, Poplar, Montana, to CIA, Washington, D.C., January 10, 1942, Chrono file, General History 1939-1959, Docket 184 Collection, Fort Peck Tribal Archives, Poplar, Montana.

96 Woehlke, Memo for the CIA, January 12, 1942, Chrono file, General History 1939-1959, Docket 184 Collection, Fort Peck Tribal Archives, Poplar, Montana.

97 A.C. Cooley, Director of Extension and Industry, OIA, Chicago, IL, Memorandum for Mr. Greenwood, April 1, 1942, Chrono file, General History 1939-1959, Docket 184 Collection, Fort Peck Tribal Archives, Poplar, Montana.

98 Critchfield, OIA, Chicago, IL, to Superintendent Orrin C. Gray, FPA, Poplar, Montana, September 8, 1942, Chrono file, General History 1939-1959, Docket 184 Collection, Fort Peck Tribal Archives, Poplar, Montana.

99 Gray, Poplar, Montana, to OIA, Chicago, IL, September 11, 1942, Chrono file, General History 1939-1959, Docket 184 Collection, Fort Peck Tribal Archives, Poplar, Montana.

100 Martin, *Historical Report on the Fort Peck Indian Reservation, Part I: An Administrative and Social History,* 213.

101 Tribal Relations, Memorandum to Extension, July 20, 1943, with attached copy of resolution of June 30, 1943, Chrono file, General History 1939-1959, Docket 184 Collection, Fort Peck Tribal Archives, Poplar, Montana.

102 Joe Jennings, Acting Director, Tribal Relations, OIA, Chicago, IL, July 21, 1943, Chrono file, General History 1939-1959, Docket 184 Collection, Fort Peck Tribal Archives, Poplar, Montana.

103 Martin Overgaard, Accountant and Auditor, Billings Office-OIA, Billings, Montana, to CIA, Chicago, IL, August 7, 1943, Chrono file, General History 1939-1959, Docket 184 Collection, Fort Peck Tribal Archives, Poplar, Montana.

104 Superintendent F.A. Asbury, FPA, Poplar, Montana, to CIA, Chicago, IL, August 20, 1943, Chrono file, General History 1939-1959, Docket 184 Collection, Fort Peck Tribal Archives, Poplar, Montana.

105 Woehlke, Chicago, IL, to Asbury, Poplar, Montana, September 10, 1943, Chrono file, General History 1939-1959, Docket 184 Collection, Fort Peck Tribal Archives, Poplar, Montana.

106 Woehlke, Chicago, IL, to Asbury, Poplar, Montana, September 11, 1943, Chrono file, General History 1939-1959, Docket 184 Collection, Fort Peck Tribal Archives, Poplar, Montana.

107 Asbury, FPA, Poplar, Montana, to CIA, Chicago, IL, September 15, 1943, Chrono file, General History 1939-1959, Docket 184 Collection, Fort Peck Tribal Archives, Poplar, Montana.

108 Martin, *Historical Report on the Fort Peck Indian Reservation, Part I: An Administrative and Social History,* 216; "First Ten Post War Years," attached to Asbury, Poplar, Montana, to CIA, Chicago, IL, January 24, 1945, Chrono file, General History 1939-1959, Docket 184 Collection, Fort Peck Tribal Archives, Poplar, Montana, 2.

109 Woehlke, Chicago, IL, to Asbury, Poplar, Montana, September 20, 1944, Chrono file, General History 1939-1959, Docket 184 Collection, Fort Peck Tribal Archives, Poplar, Montana.

110 Minutes, Executive Board, November 9, 1944, Chrono File, General History 1939-1959, Docket 184 Collection, Fort Peck Tribal Archives, Poplar, Montana.

111 Martin, *Historical Report on the Fort Peck Indian Reservation, Part I: An Administrative and Social History,* 214.

112 Ibid.

113 Ibid., 214, 216; Asbury, Poplar, Montana, to CIA, Chicago, IL, January 24, 1945, and attached "Program, Fort Peck Agency, First Ten Post War Years," Chrono File, General History 1939-1959, Docket 184 Collection, Fort Peck Tribal Archives, Poplar, Montana.

114 Ibid.

115 Ibid.

116 Tindall and David E. Shi, *America: A Narrative History*, 4th. ed., 1275-1281.

117 See Francis Paul Prucha, *The Great Father: The United States Government and the American Indians*, abr. ed. (Lincoln: University of Nebraska Press, 1986), 340.

118 Martin, *Historical Report on the Fort Peck Indian Reservation, Part I: An Administrative and Social History,* 224.

119 Roy Track statement, Minutes June 1, 1946, Chrono File, General History 1939-1959, Docket 184 Collection, Fort Peck Tribal Archives, Poplar, Montana.

120 Ibid.

121 See copy of letter quoted in Minutes, Fort Peck Executive Board, June 1, 1946, Chrono File, General History 1939-1959, Docket 184 Collection, Fort Peck Tribal Archives, Poplar, Montana.

122 Ibid.

123 Ibid.

124 Ibid.

125 Ibid.

126 Ibid.

127 Ibid.

128 Ibid.

129 Congressman D'Ewart letter, quoted verbatim in Minutes, General Council, June 1, 1946, 4-5, Chrono File, General History 1939-1959, Docket 184 Collection, Fort Peck Tribal Archives, Poplar, Montana.

130 Ibid.

131 Minutes, General Council, June 1, 1946, 5-6, Chrono File, General History 1939-1959, Docket 184 Collection, Fort Peck Tribal Archives, Poplar, Montana.

132 Ibid., 14.

133 Ibid.

134 Ibid., 18.

135 Ibid.

136 Walking Eagle Report, attached to correspondence, Shirley N. McKinsey, Credit Agent, OIA, Billings, Montana, to Asbury, Poplar, Montana, July 1, 1946, Chrono File, General History 1939-1959, Docket 184 Collection, Fort Peck Tribal Archives, Poplar, Montana.

137 Ibid.

138 Shirley N. McKensey, Credit Officer, OIA, Billings, Montana, to CIA, Chicago, IL, September 7, 1946, Chrono File, General History 1939-1959, Docket 184 Collection, Fort Peck Tribal Archives, Poplar, Montana.

139 Walking Eagle Telegram to CIA, August 15, 1946, CCF 35939 1946 Fort Peck .150, RG 75, NA-Washington, D.C.

140 Minutes, Executive Board Meeting, September 12, 1946, attached to correspondence, Asbury, Poplar, Montana, to CIA, Chicago, IL, October 4, 1946 Chrono File, General History 1939-1959, Docket 184 Collection, Fort Peck Tribal Archives, Poplar, Montana.

141 William Zimmerman, Jr., Assistant CIA, Chicago, IL, to Walking Eagle, Poplar, Montana, September 22, 1946, Chrono File, General History 1939-1959, Docket 184 Collection, Fort Peck Tribal Archives, Poplar, Montana.

142 James Archdale, Poplar, Montana, to CIA, Chicago, IL, November 28, 1946, Chrono File, General History 1939-1959, Docket 184 Collection, Fort Peck Tribal Archives, Poplar, Montana.

143 Asbury, Poplar, Montana, to CIA, Chicago, IL, December 11, 1946, Chrono File, General History 1939-1959, Docket 184 Collection, Fort Peck Tribal Archives, Poplar, Montana.

144 Critchfield for the CIA, Chicago, to James Archdale, Poplar, Montana, December 31, 1946, Chrono File, General History 1939-1959, Docket 184 Collection, Fort Peck Tribal Archives, Poplar, Montana.

145 Martin, *Historical Report on the Fort Peck Indian Reservation, Part I: An Administrative and Social History,*, 232.

146 Martin, *Historical Report on the Fort Peck Indian Reservation, Part I: An Administrative and Social History,*, 233.

147 Stephen E. Ambrose, *Rise to Globalism: American Foreign Policy since 1938* (Baltimore, Maryland: Penguin, 1971), 11-46.

CHAPTER 12

~

The Shift in Indian Policy under Truman Leading to the Republican Ascendancy and the Oil Boom, 1948-1952

David R. Miller, Ph.D.

THE era from the Truman Fair-Dealers to the Eisenhower Terminationists spanned a period of growth and prosperity fostered by the post-World War II economic recovery. While some regions of the Fort Peck Reservation prospered, it was not until oil was discovered on the reservation that individuals fortunate enough to possess mineral lease lands where drilling was successful began to benefit. For the larger portion of the tribal membership, however, economic options remained limited.

Increasingly, tribal members became involved in local, state, and national partisan politics, and consequently, the Fort Peck public sphere was influenced from outside the reservation. In response to pressures for individuals to stand on their own without the supports that had characterized the New Deal, many mixed-bloods became Republicans and accepted the goals of acculturation and assimilation. Among the Assiniboine, longstanding animosity for the starvation of 1883-1884 under Democratic President Grover Cleveland influenced many at that time to accept the political party of Abraham Lincoln, the Great Emancipator. This trend persisted in more contemporary political choices.

What was most disconcerting, however, was the new movement that suggested government should withdraw entirely from Indian life. At first glance, it was a plan to rid Indians of the Indian Office. Trusteeship had provided many tangible opportunities for tribal members. Since the Indian Bureau held tight control over the tribes' assets, this became an obstacle to tribal leaders who wanted to secure substantial gains for their constituents. At first, efforts were made to seek "home rule," but soon this was seen as an excuse for the government to include Fort Peck on the list of tribes from which trusteeship would be withdrawn. The Fort Peck tribes had to fight to remain off the graduated lists.

Particularly in the early 1950s, McCarthyism gave rise to a surreptitiousness that pervaded government and American society. Abandonment of principles was justified to save the nation from itself, and resulted in political leaders becoming pragmatic, even unprincipled, for the sake of personal agendas. Prosperity brought perils, such as new threats to autonomy and self-determination, but there was also the lure that the tribes' assets could yield the improved livelihood that so many needed. The challenges were exciting, but also crucial. As many tribal members relocated to cities to secure education, training, and employment, the drain of talented people had an immediate impact. But though these individuals became far-flung, they were not disinterested in the development of tribal affairs on Fort Peck.

Economically, new oil leases had become, for select individuals and for the tribes, the equivalent of what the grazing leases or per capita money and homestead fees had been. It would be hard to call the Fort Peck tribes affluent in this era, since pockets of real poverty persisted across the reservation, but tribal farm families were the mainstay of the earning power among tribal members. As northeastern Montana was changing, so were conditions and opportunities for the Fort Peck tribes and their members.

The Indian New Deal fostered several key principles based in cultural relativity and pluralism. Harold Ickes and John Collier had made these principles central to their political philosophy and reforms by reversing the earlier programs of assimilation that had dominated Indian policy from the late nineteenth century. But the actual successes of their efforts could only be judged situation by situation. With Collier's departure in 1945 and Ickes' in 1946, however, the Truman administration capitulated to detractors of the Indian New Deal. Once again, the Indian "problem" seemed to be getting Indians to assimilate "once and for all, and thus to end the responsibility of the federal government for Indian affairs."[1]

Francis Paul Prucha, historian of Indian policy, characterized the rhetoric of the new age:

There was talk of *freeing* or *emancipating* the Indians from a status that bound them by special laws and regulations and placing them instead on an absolutely equal footing with white citizens. The other side of the coin was *withdrawal* or *termination* of federal responsibility and federal programs for Indian groups and Indian individuals. At one time the Bureau of Indian Affairs preferred the word *readjustment*, in an attempt to avoid words that had developed emotional overtones. But overall, it was *termination* that best described the movement, and the word came to be used not only of the government's responsibilities towards the Indians but of the Indians themselves. It became common, thus, to speak of terminated Indians and tribes [Prucha's emphasis].[2]

The role of government in the lives of its Indian citizens had been influenced by treaties, and later, by executive orders or agreements, case law, and various administrative arrangements, and therefore federal trusteeship was in place. Conservatives and libertarians interpreted freedom and emancipation differently than Collier had, however, and instead made this the mandate for the removal of discriminatory legislation no matter its original protective context. The years immediately following Collier's departure saw the transition to a new policy of federal withdrawal from Indian affairs.[3]

One example that translated into partisan political positions was the creation of the Indian Claims Commission (ICC). Collier had long advocated the creation of such an entity to address the many injustices done to Indian tribes in their dispossession from their lands.

Tribes had been limited to congressional action for approval to bring suits into the U.S. Court of Claims, the Department of Interior and OIA had discouraged Indians from hiring lawyers, and whomever they hired had to be approved by the department. Collier and Ickes envisioned a commission and not a court, where claims could be heard and settlements could be negotiated. Numerous bills had been introduced and several sets of hearings held between 1935 and 1945 about creating such a commission. But there was a strong opposition, mostly from western congressmen and senators who were adamant that land title could not be restored and wanted Indians to simply be paid cash for their land. But this arrangement was viewed as "a raid upon the Treasury" intended to benefit Indians and their lawyers.[4] The obvious contribution of Indian men and women in the armed forces during World War II made settling claims a worthy goal.

The Indian Claims Commission Act was approved on August 13, 1946. It provided for three commissioners to hear claims against the United States, the defendant in these actions, and the plaintiffs, "any Indian tribe, band, or other identifiable group of Indians residing within the territorial limits of the United States or Alaska."[5] While there was no statute of limitations in effect, the U.S. was allowed to use all other defenses, and in determinations of relief, was allowed to use offsets, including all money expended or property given for the benefit of the claimant group in the entire history of their relations. Similar to what happened to the Assiniboines in the United States Court of Claims in the 1930s, settlements for many groups were not substantial, or were non-existent, after offsets were subtracted. Lawyers' fees were limited to 10 percent of an awarded claim. A five-year window was delineated for filing claims. For many groups, this meant finding a lawyer, preparing the claim, and then submitting it to the commission before the deadline of August 12, 1951. Based upon the Royce maps, maps made on treaties, and subsequent actions, 176 tribes or bands were notified, and most filed claims, so that 370 petitions were entered.[6]

The great majority of cases were land cases, which involved three stages: determining the claimant's title to the land (either Indian title based on continuous, exclusive occupation or recognized title based on some treaty or law), determining the value of the land and the amount of liability of the United States, and then determining gratuitous offsets to be subtracted from the government's liability. A second class of cases comprised cases concerned the fiduciary culpability on the part of the federal government in the management of Indian funds.[7]

The first commissioners were conservatives and lawyers, and even though the intention had not been to make the proceedings adversarial, the commissioners turned the commission into a court. The only remedy offered was monetary settlements, but this did not mean that groups seeking return of lost lands were satisfied, which dissatisfaction eventually fueled political activism in the 1960s and 1970s.[8]

The ICC was expected to complete its work in ten years, but the cases moved very slowly. The era of the ICC gave rise to original research and new scholarship about the specific Indians who were presenting the history of their dealings with the United States and its colonial predecessors.[9] As the ICC process stretched into the 1950s, so did the long-term assault upon Indian sovereignty in Congress, which was not resisted by the Truman and Eisenhower administrations.[10]

The prosperity emanating from the war began to fuel inflation, and wage and price controls were attempted. This set off more partisan wrangling. The Democratic promise of full employment was proving impossible, and the Republican-dominated Congress set its sights on restricting organized labor. Truman was faced with serious erosion among traditional supporters for the Democratic party. In September 1946, Truman dismissed Henry Wallace as Secretary of Agriculture over a foreign policy disagreement, which angered left-wing Democrats. In the 1946 congressional elections, the Republicans won majorities in both houses of Congress for the first time since 1928.[11]

The formal beginning of termination can be traced to the testimony of acting CIA William Zimmerman, Jr., on February 8, 1947, before the U.S. Senate Committee on Civil Service. He stated that decreasing numbers of Indians needed the expensive services that the BIA provided, and he presented three lists of tribes:

The first group, he said, could be denied federal services immediately; the second could function with minimal federal supervision within ten years; the third would need more than ten years to prepare for withdrawal of bureau support. The categories had been determined according to the degree of acculturation of the tribe, the economic condition of the tribe, its willingness to dispense with federal aid, and the willingness and ability of the state in which a tribe lived to assume the responsibilities dropped by the federal government. In addition to the lists and criteria, Zimmerman presented three specimen bills, for the Klamath, Osage, and Menominee tribes, groups that he thought would be suitable for beginning the withdrawal process.[12]

Zimmerman later said his intentions were for planning, but claimed that his testimony was "repeatedly misquoted and misinterpreted."[13] Notwithstanding his disclaimers, the Interior Department and the Bureau of Indian Affairs purported to favor a much more moderate form of termination. However, the BIA set to the task of planning for "the withdrawal of federal responsibility for the Indians."[14]

In 1947, Truman had appointed a Commission on Organization of the Executive Branch of Government, chaired by former President Hoover, to make recommendations for a new era of efficiency in government. By 1948, the commission had established a special task force on Indian Affairs, which reported that "assimilation must be the dominant goal of the public policy."[15] It argued that the historic Indian way of life was gone, and traditional tribal organization had been replaced for at least a generation. Only a handful of reservation populations, meaning full-bloods, could be considered real Indians, but that did not even total .03 percent. The report argued that assimilation could not be prevented; rather, the questions were, what kind of assimilation would it be, and how fast could it be accomplished? The commission endorsed the report, stating its recommendations should become "the keystone of the organization and of the activities of the Federal Government in the field of Indian Affairs."[16] The commission

recommended complete integration of the Indians into the mass of the population as taxpaying citizens, and until that could occur it wanted the social programs for Indians to be transferred to state governments, thus diminishing the activities of the Bureau of Indian Affairs. Tribal governments, it thought, should be regarded as a stage in the transition of federal tutelage to full participation in state and local government.[17]

Truman's campaign for election in 1948 became very close in the end, and consequently he shed as much of the New Dealer image as he could to appeal to constituencies that no longer were stable Democratic strongholds. Much of the West had started to oppose Truman during his first administration, so caving in to conservatives on Indian policy was politically and regionally pragmatic. Consequently, Truman's Indian policy after the 1948 national election focused on preparing tribes for termination. Conservatives were already alleging that communists were infiltrating government agencies and programs, beginning a period of red-baiting that led to the McCarthyism of the early 1950s.

Ironically, ICC awards began being viewed by conservatives as a payout that would prepare tribes for eventual termination. The Assiniboine claim was declared *Res Judica*, and was not allowed another hearing; legislation in 1980 brought about a settlement in 1984. The Sioux claims were diverse, but the most attention was directed to the Black Hills claim. The Fort Peck Reservation Indians were the subject of an accounting claim, Docket 184, which was returned to the U.S. Court of Claims after 1978, and finally settled out of court. The Black Hills claim still remains unsettled, even though a final judgment was rendered in 1979. Most of the Sioux groups continue to hold out for return of the lands. The claims process for the Fort Peck Tribes did not bring any immediate gain, leaving many tribal members skeptical.

More troubling was the inclusion of the Indians of the Fort Peck Reservation on the second list of Zimmerman's 1947 testimony.[18] For the groups that appeared on these lists, the future was uncertain. Dillon S. Myer, former head of the War Relocation Authority from 1942 to 1946, was appointed CIA on May 5, 1950. Myer programmatically set to work on the termination agenda. He reportedly made a "standing" offer to Indian tribes "to work constructively with any tribe which wished to assume either full control or a greater degree of control over its own affairs."[19] Indians who had supported the New Deal, many who had worked in the Indian Service, and non-Indian New Dealers belonged to the Association on American Indian Affairs, which lobbied hard against the new direction and new policies.

The association was particular adamant about "drawing a sharp distinction between wardship and trusteeship."

Wardship [Prucha's emphasis] is defined as restriction on personal freedom of action, a remnant of paternalism; trusteeship, on the other hand, did not touch the person of the Indian or his personal freedom as a citizen, but was a necessary means of protecting Indian property. It set up a trustee-beneficiary relation in which the trustee was the servant of the trust beneficiary. The critics of termination were adamant in demanding the continued protection of Indian property by the trusteeship provision—which the termination bills almost universally sought to end.[20]

Myer refused to accept the distinction, stating that "the only way to end the paternalism of wardship or guardianship was to eliminate the trusteeship."[21] Part of the movement toward termination was a reorganization of the BIA. In September 1949, the SI created eleven area offices, including one serving reservations in Montana and Wyoming, located in Billings.[22] Another part was the reduction of Washington division directors to staff officers, concentrating administrative authority in the hands of the CIA, and granting considerable authority to area directors, who played key roles in termination. This made the BIA less flexible and eliminated the last of Collier's influence among the division heads and reservation superintendents.[23]

Many Indians across the United States were not willing to wait for fair treatment or to endure further the paternalism that accompanied programs and services of the BIA. Many individuals and a number of tribes joined the National Congress of American Indians (NCAI), founded in 1944. Fort Peck was an early supporter of NCAI, and many tribal members actively supported its agenda, which primarily promoted

Indian self-determination.

By 1950, educational levels were improving on Fort Peck. Among the adult reservation population, there were thirty college graduates, 300 high school graduates, and 700 who had completed grade school. One estimate indicated that only 3,030 adults were unable to read and write in English, and only fifty individual adults were not English speakers. Only 1.5 percent of children between the ages of six and eighteen were reported not attending school.[24]

The economic history of the Fort Peck tribes had been characterized by choices made by individual families. The use of land remained a steady source of income. By 1950, tribal members were using approximately 202,000 acres of trust lands, mostly for grazing. The amount of livestock was relatively steady: 3,984 beef cattle, 143 dairy cattle, 535 sheep, sixty-five hogs, and 3,017 horses. Several thousand acres were farmed, mostly in wheat, oats, barley, and forage.[25] In comparison, non-Indians used 985,924 acres of reservation land, including 37,000 acres under lease by several companies searching for oil. Timber resources were not commercially viable. Fish and game returns for 1949 totalled $26,380.[26]

Tribal members who earned wages both on and off the reservation totalled 966, with 566 off the reservation and 400 on the reservation. Mainly they worked as farm machine operators, office workers, or skilled laborers, and the rest were unskilled workers. The average family income for a Fort Peck tribal member in 1950 was $2,100.[27]

Capitalization was again a problem in the post-war era. The Fort Peck tribes continued to loan substantial amounts of money to individuals and groups from its modest resources. By 1949, loans totalled over $235,000, and the balance in IIM accounts totalled nearly $466,000. Hardly self-sufficient, the members of the Fort Peck tribes were utilizing their "ingenuity, hard

work and ability" to take advantage of government programs.

This was also when counties attempted to tax Indians, encouraged by the new rhetoric of equality. However, this was the issue that prompted the tribes to hire lawyers to advise them on tax liability. The need to act on land claims and increasing technicalities of legislation, regulations, and statutory obligations furthered the importance of the tribes retaining lawyers.

On May 10, 1949, Arnold H. Olsen, Attorney General for the State of Montana, addressed a legal opinion to the County Attorney of Big Horn County in Hardin about taxing automobiles purchased by Indians with funds from the leasing of trust patented lands, declaring these funds distinct from restricted funds issued to non-competent Indians. In this case, Olsen contended that individual Crow Indians had "the burden of establishing" any exemption, and that the county assessor "must tax all automobiles and can only exempt property from taxation upon receipt of conclusive proof of non-taxability." The assessor needed a certificate signed by an official of the Crow Reservation defining "the restricted nature of the funds used to purchase the property for which an exemption" was claimed.[28] That this opinion applied to all reservations in Montana was taken for granted.

A General Council meeting was called for on September 17, 1949, with David Buckles, Chairman, presiding, to obtain a status report on the claims situation and discuss hiring a tribal attorney. James Archdale was first to speak, saying that many of the younger children born since 1941 did not have allotments, and the ICC deadlines for submission were only twenty-three months away. Sioux members present did not see the urgency, since attorney Ralph Case was working on the Black Hills and related claims for them. Archdale and the Assiniboines pressed ahead, declaring that a tribal attorney was needed to go before the ICC. Representatives from the districts were nominated and a committee of four members was elected to choose an attorney. The council also affirmed the retention of the 1927 Constitution and Bylaws as the basis of government.[29] On September 24, Archdale and other delegates from Fort Peck attended the annual meeting of the NCAI in Rapid City, South Dakota, and met with James E. Curry, the attorney for the NCAI. Curry was already securing contracts from tribes and he agreed to represent Fort Peck. Curry had sample contracts sent to Archdale on September 30, one for work at the rate of $100 per month, with a ninety-day notice on change of fee clause, and another for a retainer fee of $3,500 a year, with a two-year review of the fees and work done.[30]

Archdale wrote Curry on October 31, 1949 that Curry had the contract as tribal attorney, and would be asked to come to Poplar to work out the final terms.[31] On November 2, 1949, Superintendent E.J. Diehl wrote Curry that the Tribal Executive Board, in a meeting held on October 29, had voted to hire him to represent him in their claims. The superintendent formally invited Curry to visit. The firm of John G. Brown and William A. Brown Law Offices, Helena, would represent the tribes in local matters.[32] Curry wrote Archdale on November 4, 1949, that he had already investigated the particular claims matters that the selection committee had discussed with him in Rapid City, and he was ready to provide advice once his contract was finalized.[33]

But approval of James Curry's contract soon became protracted. William Zimmerman, Jr., Assistant CIA, wrote Diehl on November 15, 1949, asking him to remind the Assiniboines at Fort Peck that they had an approved attorney contract with the Washington law firm of Davies, Richberg, Beebe, Busick, and Richardson for seven years from May 5, 1949. While this could be terminated by the CIA with the consent of the tribe if cause

could be provided, Zimmerman asserted that he did not see a reason to select a new attorney for claims. He also noted that for "unorganized tribes," meaning tribes who did not accept the IRA, procedures were outlined in Section Nos. 15.7 to 15.25, *Code of Federal Regulations* (CFR) 25, for the execution of attorney contracts. Zimmerman sent Curry a copy of the letter.[34]

Diehl telegraphed Curry on December 5, 1949 that the executive board was concerned with claims "arising from laws enacted for reservation exclusive of either Assiniboine or Sioux Tribes treaty Claims." The last line of the telegram stated: "What is your reaction?"[35] The next day, Curry telegraphed Diehl that he would accept the terms of employment contained in the correspondence between them dated November 2, 1949.[36] Curry, in a letter to Diehl dated the same day, stated that he was looking for an opportunity to go to Poplar, but asked if he could get temporary approval that would make him eligible for a reimbursement of his travel expenses. Curry noted that when he discussed his representation with the selection committee at the NCAI, he communicated that the contracts would need to be executed for him to be compensated for his travels to Fort Peck. He was most concerned, however, that his discussions with the selection committee were for a representation not only for claims, but also for all other matters. Curry noted that from his perspective, he would prefer a general services contract to a claims contract.[37]

On December 10, 1949, oil and gas leases were offered for sale by sealed bid on both tribal and allotted lands, including those of Turtle Mountain allottees, in the West Poplar and East Poplar Prospect.[38] On that same day, the bid of C.H. Murphy, Jr., El Dorado, Arkansas, for the lease of 21,257.12 acres in East Poplar Prospect was accepted by the Tribal Executive Board, as was the joint bid of Carter Oil Company and the Phillips Petroleum Company for 16,253.56 acres in the West Poplar Prospect.[39]

After receiving a letter dated December 29, 1949, from Diehl urging Curry to come on his own expense if he was truly interested in the work, Curry conferred with I.S. Wiessbrodt about claims possibilities and urged him to prepare a memorandum on the subject.[40] The day after Christmas, Curry wrote to Archdale that he would come to Poplar when he had to visit Fort Berthold. He explained that Weissbrodt was continuing to study claims opportunities.[41] Weissbrodt wrote Curry a memorandum dated February 1, 1950, providing his preliminary investigation, the first indication that a historic investigation of the spending of appropriated and tribal funds was underway.[42]

Diehl wrote the commissioner on February 13, 1950 to recommend Curry as attorney for claims of the Fort Peck Indians independent of the Assiniboine and the Sioux Black Hills claims. He reported that an executive board meeting had been held on February 11, 1950 expressly for the purpose of considering Curry's contract.[43] In the midst of the Curry matter, Howard Trinder, Vice-Chair of the Executive Board and active member of the American Indians of Montana, wrote Curry about taxation of personal property and his protest of taxes for his automobile that had been purchased with restricted money. Curry instructed Francis L. Horn of his practice to research the personal property matter so Curry could discuss it when he visited in early February.[44]

Department of Interior Solicitor Ted Haas wrote Trinder on January 26, 1950 that a certificate of non-taxability must be presented to the County Assessor. "Even if the taxing process has been completed and taxes levied, the Board of County Commissioners, on evidence presented that personal property is restricted, must remove it from the tax rolls."[45] Francis L. Horn in her initial memorandum "Taxability of Personal Property on Indian Reservations" discussed the doctrine of "federal instrumentality," which had been challenged by the state of Montana in the legal opinion about taxability of Crow cars. Issue property or purchase property by Indians was considered non-taxable for the same reason, but removing property from trust property made mobility a factor, which was obviously the case with a car used off the reservation.[46] Curry persuaded Congressman Mike Mansfield to write the Commissioner of Internal Revenue, whose response, dated January 25, 1950, discussed questions about income tax and whether there were any exemptions in the way that homestead allotments had escaped tax liability.[47]

Initially, Diehl was willing to sign the necessary affidavits, as it appeared that Assistant CIA Zimmerman and Solicitor Haas had no objections. Then suddenly Diehl refused to sign any more, and directed the Roosevelt County Court House not to accept any affidavits of non-taxability. Diehl had promised Buckles and Trinder to provide the affidavits during Curry's visit in Poplar. What had not been anticipated was the disposition of Regional Director Fickinger, who took the position that Indians should be paying such taxes:

I . . . note your comments to the effect that you had supposed that the Indian Service officials would support the Indians in their attempt to avoid paying taxes on their automobiles. I assure you that we stand ready to go right down the line in defense of the Indians on matters that involve legal rights. In this particular instance I do not see that we are doing the Indians any favour by trying to help them to avoid what appears to us to be a just obligation. Furthermore, it seems to me that the Attorneys for the Tribes would be doing a much greater service to the Indians by assisting them to an understanding of some of their obligations.

Certainly the Indians can not be indefinitely both "fish and fowl" at the same time and the sooner they accept certain responsibilities as citizens the sooner they can expect to be accepted as full fledged citizens.[48]

Fickinger sent Curry copies of correspondence sent to all superintendents in Region 2, dated June 2, 1949, and a letter to J.W. Wellington, superintendent at Fort Belknap, dated January 24, 1950, about the office's position on tax liability of personal property, particularly automobiles.[49] Fickinger explained in a letter dated February 21, 1950 to Zimmerman that Fort Peck was the only place in Montana where there was any resistance to the tax on automobiles. After refusing to sign additional affidavits, Diehl proceeded to Billings for clarification. Fickinger said it was at this point that he had looked into the matter. Upon seeing a copy of the affidavit, Fickinger called Zimmerman, saying that he "was unwilling for Superintendent Diehl to sign such a certificate and that I was unwilling to say to Mr. Diehl that I had no objections if he wanted to sign them." When Trinder objected to Diehl not signing the affidavits, Fickinger told him "it would be totally unfair to all the rest of the Indians [in Montana] who had gone ahead and paid their taxes"[50] Diehl explained in a lengthy letter to Curry, dated March 6, 1950, that he had to clear any action with his area director; he copied the letter to Buckles and Trinder.[51] Curry responded that he had not heard Diehl's statement about the area director, and both had ended up embarrassed. As far as Curry was concerned the matter was over, unless "my clients" wanted to pursue it.[52] The argument with Fickinger would be the first of many. Clearly, this incident contributed to how long it took to get Curry's contract approved.

On March 7, 1950, Frances L. Horn wrote Buckles that there was no word on the approval of the tribal attorney contract. Curry had thought delivering the contract to Zimmerman personally would speed up the approval, but the contracts had been sent to the Land Office of the BIA, and were still there.[53]

Curry arranged with John Bayuk, an attorney in Wolf Point, to work for him on local matters, and Bayuk began regular correspondence and made occasional phone calls, mostly to report details or provide context.[54]

Curry wrote Buckles on March 24, 1950 about Truman's appointment of Dillon S. Myer as CIA. Curry saw no reason to object, offering his opinion that Nichols was a ditherer, but he hoped that Myer, as a veteran bureaucrat "will serve the interests of the Indians."[55]

A General Council was planned for April 1 to "draw up" a reservation plan that could be taken to the districts for discussion. In a special meeting in Poplar on March 23, 1950, followed by a General Council on March 18, there was a brief discussion between Lee Martin and Santee Iron Ring, the latter trying to kill the idea of a reservation program in favor of per capita payments. The board tried to discuss the implications this would have for "different departments in the Agency Office which are operating on Tribal money." Former Tribal Chairman Carl Walking Eagle said that he was not in favor of killing a reservation plan approved in the General Council of March 18. Charles Track opined that until the reactions of the area office were known, the board should not transact any business.[56]

Previously, the executive board refused to use tribal money for some renovations at the Frazer Community Hall, because it was presumably government property. William Knorr, in a meeting of the executive board on April 13, 1950, moved to transfer title of all community halls to the tribes, which carried in a vote of eight for and one opposed.[57]

Oscar Chapman, SI, wrote the Speaker of

the House of Representatives on April 21, 1950, introducing a bill "Authorizing the restoration to tribal ownership of certain lands upon the Fort Peck Indian Reservation, Montana, and for other purposes." These 41,450 acres had previously been withdrawn by departmental orders of September 19, 1934 and November 5, 1935, pending legislation. This did not include lands in reclamation projects. With the SI's endorsement, the legislation was introduced.[58]

Fickinger's stance on the auto tax matter infuriated many executive board members, and consequently the board supported the NCAI position against creating the area offices. The executive board passed Resolution 10-50, dated April 10, 1950, contending that the Fort Peck tribes, an "unincorporated tribal group," had not been consulted.[59] On May 18, 1950, David Buckles wrote Senator Carl Hayden about the Fort Peck tribes' support for the bill abolishing the area offices, but the bill had been defeated. Buckles asked that when the bill came to the Senate Appropriations Committee, it be supported there. Buckles asked why money was being spent on area offices when hospitals, doctors, nurses, police forces, and schools all needed additional funding. Area directors did not know more about conditions in Indian reservations: "The officers from the area offices spend a few hours on the reservations on hurry trips and profess to know of our problems." Area offices did nothing to decentralize the work of the Washington office of the BIA; what actually occurred was that power to make many decisions was taken from the agency. "The area offices are great stalling place [sic] on all Indian matters because they represent one more set of offices that had to pass on each problem before it is decided."[60]

In a statement dated May 10, 1950, Fort Peck Sioux delegates Edwin Red Door and Rufus Ricker outlined their position on Indian liquor laws, area offices, and land acquisition legislation.

Already in Washington to consult on the Black Hills claim, Red Door and Ricker supported the repeal of "discriminary laws" denying Indians liquor after all that had done by veterans, the White amendment abolishing the funds for area offices, and Congressman D'Ewart's bill that would provide government guaranteed loans for farming.[61]

In a letter dated May 13, 1950, Curry informed Buckles that Zimmerman had been replaced by Rex Lee as Assistant CIA. Curry hoped this would mean action on his yet unapproved contracts.[62] Buckles informed Curry in a letter dated May 18 that Reddoor and Ricker were in Washington only on Sioux claims business: "They are not official delegates on Fort Peck Tribal matters. I realize the situation as it is, but without Fort Peck General Council actions I am completely powerless."[63] Curry responded to Buckles on May 20, 1950 that the Fort Peck Sioux delegates had left for home, but that they had done a very good job representing tribal interests, even if they were not authorized to speak on behalf of the "entire tribe." Curry asked if another delegation that could speak for everyone might be sent "to talk over with members of Congress and administrative officers various important matters of interest to the tribe." What Curry was not saying was that he was actively getting others of his client tribes to do much the same. He ended by offering to provide a list of subjects for such a delegation to address.[64]

Meanwhile, the executive board had convened in Poplar on May 11, 1950, to draw up "a Reservation Program." The main concern appeared to be how each district could be ensured its fair share. The Fort Kipp District Council wanted to draw up its own plan. The Poplar and Riverside districts had no representatives present. Kirkwood Smith declared that the Poplar district could be put on the record as opposing any program, but Charles Track,

Joshua Wetsit, and William Smith, representing respectively the Wolf Point, Oswego, and Frazer districts, reported their districts were completely in favor of a "long range Reservation Program." The suggested date for the next meeting was June 8, 1950, and the agenda was set to be the "final showdown" for proposing the reservation program.[65]

Curry discovered the tribes had applied for a reimbursable loan program, but had made "patent errors" in the application. He asked to see the application, so that he could help with another application.[66] On the same day, Curry wrote John Bayuk that he understood that the last General Council asked to "kill the program," and instead of using their tribal funds for credit purposes, they wanted a per capita distribution. Not sure whether there would be another chance to submit an application for a loan program, Curry said he was most interested in finding out "information of importance to us in learning the economic status of the tribe," since justifications for such programs could then be made.[67]

A special meeting of the executive board was held on May 31, 1950 with an official from Phillips Petroleum Company, Denver, Colorado, to examine the agreement for operating the West Poplar unit area. There being no discussion, the vote was called, and the agreement was unanimously accepted.[68]

Dillon Myer, CIA, wrote Sioux delegates Reddoor and Ricker on June 7, 1950 to comment further on discussions held during their visit. Five certificates had been executed on exemption from personal property tax on automobiles before the area director decided not to sign any more, but most car owners apparently paid the tax on their vehicles and procured their license tags. On the issue of requesting a per capita payment from proceeds from oil leases, this income was mandated for distribution by a vote of the General Council. Myer stated that for such a distribution to be authorized, however, a "full and complete report from the Superintendent and the recommendation of the Area Director" were required:

We should know as to the plans and program for the reservation, whether the needs of the people are such as to require distribution of this money, the amount and source of all other tribal income, and the budget for the next fiscal year covering the activities of the Tribal Council including relief, council expenses, law and order, loan program, land acquisition, etc. We want to be satisfied that need exists and that payment of this or any part of the money would be to the benefit of the individual members in a program for their rehabilitation.[69]

The Wolf Point District representative made the only report to the executive board meeting held on June 8 about what they wanted in a reservation development plan. The weather was bad, so many representatives were not present. After some discussion, Knorr moved that the reservation program be tabled and that copies of the one program submitted be distributed for study.[70] There was also discussion about whether another delegation should be sent to Washington, and it was decided not to do so at that time.[71]

At the same time that Curry was representing Fort Peck, he was also the lawyer for the NCAI, and was lining up a number of tribes as clients. The manner in which he was proceeding clearly concerned the BIA and the Secretary of Interior.[72] Curry aggressively sought to bring pressure whenever he felt the interests of his clients were being infringed, but the department and BIA pushed back. In many ways, Curry was targeted because of his style, but also because he offered legal representation that was informed, coordinated, and integrated with the interests of the tribes. No longer were lawyers circumscribed to dealing with claims matters; they became advocates and lobbyists for their tribal clients.

Bayuk wrote Curry on June 6, 1950 that he had been told by the acting superintendent at the agency in Poplar that the CIA had instructed the area office not to give Curry any official correspondence.[73] This was further complicated because Curry's contracts for representing Fort Peck in reservation-specific claims and as tribal attorney still had not been approved. Curry had written Myer on June 8, 1950, hoping he was not being subjected to discrimination. The contracts for Fort Peck, two in number; Colville, two in number; Angoon, and Kake, were awaiting approval, several for six months already. He acknowledged that he had received a letter dated June 5 asking for the status of his contracts, and that he was preparing a report.[74] He was more candid in a letter to Bayuk on June 11, 1950:

No doubt there are people in the Indian Office who would like to prevent approval of my attorney contract with Fort Peck. It is a lot easier on the Administration if they are left free to do what they think is right or wrong in all cases. This is not always easy for them to do if the Indians are in a position to put an effective argument. An example of the embarrassment that the Indians can cause, if they have a lawyer, is the recent dispute about tax exemption of automobiles. This matter is not yet settled, by any means, and will not be until the Indians tell me to back down.

During the delay in approval of my contract, it is possible that pressure will be brought on the Indians to change their minds about hiring me. They may be urged to hire, instead, some lawyer whom it is easier for Indian Office officials to dominate. But I am still confident that the Indians will not give way. I am sure, that, in the near future, the contract will be approved.[75]

He noted that he had just received some

official correspondence from the CIA, and so was skeptical about the acting superintendent's statement.[76]

Alvin Warrior, Secretary of the Tribal Executive Board, prepared a summary of the activities of the board and General Councils between January 1 and June 30, 1950. The board created four committees for "work projects." The Committee for Relief and Welfare was comprised of Jacob Big Horn, Henry Archdale, and Charles Track. Austin Buckles, Carl Walking Eagle, and Fred Buckles made up the Committee for Land Matters. The Committee for Loans and Repayment Cattle had George Boyd, Norman Hollow, and William Knorr as members. And the Committee for Education had Leslie Four Stars [sic—the family now spells its name "Fourstars"] and Edwin Reddoor as members.[77]

The Agency Relief Department (BIA) and the Relief Committee of the Tribes coordinated efforts to assist the neediest tribal members. Federal funds totalling $10,642.98 were distributed to 250 households. However, in February, only $548 were available in federal funds, but other sources of relief were $450 of buffalo meat purchased from tribal funds plus $145.92 in delivery costs; $250 in aid from the Wolf Point chapter of the Red Cross; and 17,500 pounds of federal relief potatoes and army surplus shoes, which were delivered and distributed. By March, $6,081 in federal funds relieved 274 families, with an additional three families being granted tribal purchase orders totalling $123.64; 855 pounds of dried eggs were also distributed. For April, 200 households were supported by stipends in federal funds, and fifty households were supported by stipends in tribal funds. The tribes also distributed 187 boxes of apples and ten barrels of dry milk. In May, federal funds for relief amounted to $7,800.[78]

Warrior also summarized the oil leases. In the West Poplar Unit area, the Carter Oil Company and Phillips Petroleum Company entered into agreement with the Fort Peck Tribal Executive Board. From this lease area, seventy-seven individual allottees had received lease payments. "The total Tribal land in this area is 3,983.29 acres or 16.6180% of the total acreage in this area. Individual Indian allotments comprise a total of 12,268.10 acres or 51.1815% of the total acreage in this area."[79] The oil companies paid a total of $55,417.24. The East Poplar Prospect area circumscribed 2,937.87 acres of tribal lands. The C.H. Murphy and Company paid $3,672.40 rent and a bonus amounting to $34,843.14 for these, making for a total of $38,515.54 in tribal income. Within this area, a total of 222 individual allotments, comprising 20,538.66 acres, were paid for leases. The rent and bonuses derived from this acreage amounted to $269,261.64.[80]

Warrior also listed the resolutions passed in the six-month period. Besides approval of James Curry's contracts, resolutions from the list included one giving preference in hiring to allotted Indian men over non-allottees, a resolution asking for the state Tuberculosis Association to hold X-ray clinics on the reservation, and a resolution "reducing the rental on submarginal lands to $1.00 per acre for farming and $.15 per acre for grazing. This reduction applying to Indians only." The General Council of March 18 had voted down the proposed reservation development program. The General Council of April 1 had voted to organize the reservation program by districts, allowing the six districts to decide their programs of development.[81]

CIA Myer's Order No. 556, dated August 8, 1950, titled "The Conduct of Tribal Government," detailed "The Responsibility of the Indian Service," "Responsibility of Tribal Governments" (a. "To Inform the People," b. "To Understand Their Authority," and c. "To Manage Finances"), and "Procedure." This document particularly revealed the extent to which the "Fair Dealers"

of the Truman administration wanted Indians to participate in the demise of their own sovereignty. Regular annual reports, including financial records, were expected by various levels of the BIA. One change was the declaration that minutes were not a record of actions alone, but had to be in the form of ordinances and resolutions, and the previous practice of minutes being endorsed by the superintendent or some other functionary was no longer necessary. The bulk of the document addressed procedures for ordinances and resolutions, especially those requiring secretarial review as distinguished from those requiring approval. The importance of tribal constitutional and bylaw processes was emphasized, which had already been addressed by groups who had accepted the IRA. Fort Peck's preference to have a direct relationship with the CIA and the BIA was already being undermined by the area office.[82]

Finally, Curry learned that the CIA had not approved his two contracts with the Fort Peck tribes, along with five for other tribes. Curry was notified of this by letter on September 6,[83] just after he returned from the National Congress of American Indians annual convention in Bellingham, Washington. Curry speculated to Buckles that the refusal was because he would not be a "yes-man" for the BIA. "I advise you to stand firm and insist on the approval of these contracts," he said. Since other contracts were also rejected, Curry noted,

By doing this, they deprive me of fees that they know I need in order to meet my current business expenses. Obviously, they are trying to run me into bankruptcy so that I will have to go out of business, so the Indians will not have proper representation and so that they can "put over on them" whatever they want.[84]

Curry intended to appeal each of the refused contracts to the Secretary of the Interior.[85]

Buckles wrote Curry for the executive board on September 15, 1950, saying he was sorry that the department had rejected Curry's contracts, and that the tribes were faced with finding another attorney. The board was worried about losing time by standing by Curry in this controversy.[86] But Curry was not ready to give up. He turned to Harold Ickes, the former SI, whom he asked to represent him. In a long appeal brief, Curry catalogued the history of his legal representation. Curry sent the draft and a list of exhibits to Ickes on October 16, 1950, and asked him to comment.[87] On September 26, 1950, Curry wrote to SI Oscar Chapman, appealing the decision of the CIA: "Mr. Ickes handling the appeal, appearing as my attorney before the Secretary of the Interior."[88]

Curry was also appealing all his other rejected contracts. One of Myer's objections was that Curry had too many other clients, twenty-six as general counsel and thirty-one for prosecution of claims. Curry countered that

He [Curry] has only 19 straight claims contracts (not 31) of which six are with the various segments of the Apache Nation and seven more are with the various segments of the Paiute Nation, and six are with separate tribes. Furthermore, the Commissioner fails to mention that Curry has associated with him in the handling of these claims a group of at least a dozen other lawyers.

Curry also has 25 general representation or combination contracts. Thirteen of these, more than half, are in Alaska, with the various segments of the Tlingit and Haida Tribe. The principal job Curry has to do in this connection is to defeat the attempts, such as the Department has made in the past, to grab the land of the Indians and to turn it over to the pulp interests and the fishery monopolies. The principal problem of all these towns are [sic] similar.

This makes a total of 44 contracts, not 57 as the Commissioner says.[89]

Curry's vision of legal representation involved coordinated efforts, with specialist lawyers handling special legal representation. The fact that the Fort Peck Reservation claims were different from tribal Assiniboine or Sioux claims was lost on Myer and his officials, who were especially unwilling to consider claims arising from reservations inhabited by more than one tribe. The final brief for a hearing before the SI was filed on November 27, 1950.[90]

What at first appeared to be acceptance of the contracts turned out to be just spoiling for a fight. Just as Curry had suggested weeks before, another delegation was chosen that included Knorr, Edwin Reddoor, Dolly Akers, and Santee Ironring, which arrived in Washington on January 2, 1951. Over the next twelve days, the delegates met with congressmen and senators and many officials to secure approval of Curry's contract, whom the delegates insisted they wanted for the Fort Peck tribes' attorney. The SI had begun hearings on January 3 on the Department of Interior's attorney contract regulations for Indian Affairs specifically, which the delegates attended. Outside the hearings, the delegates worked out with Curry the statements they were to make. On January 4, they attended the hearing. Knorr, the new tribal chairman, explained that at a General Council meeting on September 17, 1949, a motion was made to hire James E. Curry to prosecute reservation claims and serve as general counsel, which Curry had done for two years and three months while waiting approval of his contract. The previous March, Curry had been approved to handle the claims matter only. Knorr explained that an oil boom was occurring on the reservation, and this was no time for the tribes to be without legal advice:

We were told by Indian Bureau officials that we could get legal advice from their lawyers.

But when we asked for it we never can get any definite answers. If we had our own lawyer, we could ask him legal questions and if he didn't answer them we could fire him and get another one. But [the difference is] the Indian Bureau lawyers are paid by Uncle Sam and we can't fire them.

Knorr suggested that it was a sign of intelligence and sophistication to know when a lawyer was needed, and to know when a legal arrangement was fair. The chairman stated that the purpose of the delegation, which was present at considerable expense, was to press for approval of the attorney contract without further delay. The chairman was not to be stopped in his criticism of the "self-determination" of the Fair Dealers. He pointed out that Montana Indians had long used the ballot box, and he put the Montana congressional delegation on warning that several were in office thanks to the obligations they owed Montana Indians, but that it was time to collect on those obligations: "If they expect the Indians to vote for them like white people do then they ought to treat the Indians like they do white people." The chairman went on to suggest that if he did not get their advocacy this time, these individuals would hear from Indians in the next election. He spoke to a series of key objections the CIA had made to the Curry–Fort Peck contract, dispelling each. The tribes wanted control of the personal property of its members and were frustrated by the problems of the "supervised sale by the government."

We are the kind of people now that know enough to get a lawyer and know enough to tell him how to act in our interest. I don't think that the government should stand in the way of our doing that. It has stood in our way now for two years and three months and we don't want this situation to continue any longer. We intend to stay here until this contract of ours is approved or until someone tells us a good reason why it should not be approved.[91]

On the point of political and legal sophistication, Knorr noted that in the membership of the delegation was a person who, at age twenty-eight, had become the first Indian elected to the Montana legislature, suggesting she knew her way around politically. When Akers' turn came, she represented the tribes, but also was an Indian who was long a member of the Republican Party:

These rules violate and disregard the principles of self-determination. There can be no real solution of the so-called Indian problem unless the Interior Department embraces the principle of self-determination of Indian people by actual practice. As, for instance, Indian people should be allowed to learn by trial and error. The time has arrived when this well intentioned paternalism on the part of the Indian Bureau must be abandoned. The Indian people must be allowed to participate in all planning for their own good, to learn democracy, freedom and responsibility by practicing them. The archaic protective rules and laws merely tend to hamper the Indian people from attaining their final goal of self-sufficiency, which is the goal of Congress for the Interior Department to foster. The Interior Department is supposed to be the administrative arm of Congress and in trying to promote these rules on attorney contracts I charge the Interior Department with disregarding the intent Congress had for eventual assimilation of all American Indians into the general citizenry.

We, the Fort Peck Indians, are outside the Reorganization Act, having voted ourselves outside of that Act, and the power for the Commissioner to act for us regarding the attorney contracts, if it exists, must be in some statute of 1872. Most certainly, Indian people of 1952 have progressed past any old statute of 1872. Non-Indians feel the need of new laws in their respective States every two or four years, and it is not unusual for laws to be repealed after a two- or four-year period of use. Why should Indian people be forced to live under a law made some 80 years ago. That is the year in which the Indian Commissioner referred to Indians as wild beasts. This 1872 statute refers to Indians who are not citizens. The Congress did make all Indians citizens in 1924. Therefore, it would seem impossible for the present Commissioner to have unlimited authority over all Indian tribes as stated in an opinion by the Solicitor of the Interior Department.[92]

Santee Iron Ring made a brief statement in support of Knorr's statement, and Edwin Reddoor did not speak.[93]

Unfortunately, former SI Harold L. Ickes was ill and had been hospitalized before Christmas in the Georgetown University Hospital.[94] Ickes sent his regrets to Chapman on January 4, noting that he was greatly disturbed about his inability to be present, as "The issues to be discussed involve the whole future of Indian self-government." He declared, "As one of those who, under the New Deal, sat in at the birth of this great program, I want to do all I can to keep it from being murdered in its youth." Ickes declared that if Chapman did not desist from issuing the new regulations, he would take the matter to the President of the United States, which was the next step in administrative law. While the "Indian side" needed to be heard by the secretary personally, Ickes declared that he wanted to be heard as well, "to lay the proper groundwork for a personal appeal to the President if that should become necessary." Optimistically, he asked that he be given another opportunity "to have a personal public hearing before the Secretary as soon as my doctors release me."

He also asked that decisions on the contracts so long in abeyance should be made immedi-

ately: "Some of the legal affairs of the tribes have been thrown into chaos by this long delay, including the work on their claims against the United States." He asserted that this constituted a "tyrannical deprivation of the right to private counsel, to which Indians are entitled the same as white people." In his place, he appointed Gardner Jackson to represent him and Curry.[95] Statements were also made by representatives of the American Bar Association, the Indian Rights Association, the Association on American Indian Affairs, and the National Congress of American Indians. "The witnesses universally condemned the action of the Commissioner of Indian Affairs in interfering with the right of Indians to choose their own attorneys on their own terms."[96]

On Saturday, January 5, the delegation went to the office of the SI for a brief council. The secretary had planned to take the delegation to see President Truman, but this was not possible because Winston Churchill was visiting. On Monday, January 7, further meetings were held with Assistant SI Dale Doty and his staff about the attorney contract. Later that morning, a meeting was held with Assistant CIA Rex Lee to discuss income taxes, investigation of a series of matters at the agency, and the need for a special team to handle the extra business created by the oil boom at Fort Peck. Later in the day, more meetings were held with Doty and his staff. On the morning of January 8, a conference was held with the Montana congressional delegation, with more meetings in the afternoon with Doty and his staff. The delegation spent the evening with Curry preparing for the congressional hearing beginning the next day.[97]

On January 9, 1951, Curry's office issued a press release, saying that Chapman had approved the tribes' general counsel contract with him. The press release noted that the contract was approved on the second business day after the secretary's hearing. The delegation was said to be grateful that the SI had allowed a "very fair hearing" and "for having eliminated this interference with their basic rights." Senator James Murray and Congressman Wesley D'Ewart were praised for their help.[98]

On the morning of January 9, the delegation attended a hearing before the Indian Subcommittee of the House Committee on Interior and Insular Affairs. In this venue, the delegation complained about delays they experienced about land matters. There was also an exchange about "home rule." Knorr described the progressiveness of the tribes, asserting that the population of Fort Peck was ready to support itself, and seemed only to be hampered by the rules and regulations governing the reservation. He stated that these rules had been developed for IRA tribes, and Fort Peck, a non-IRA reservation, should be able to operate without the department's supervision. Knorr said that the sooner he was considered "a full-fledged American citizen, given all the rights to which I would be entitled," the better Indians would be able to make their way. Asked if the rest of the population felt the same way, Knorr hedged, saying the population would have to be polled, but Akers noted that if authority could be delegated to the agency level, much tribal business could be completed. She also stated, "I think the time has come when we are going to have to stand on our own feet and be citizens just like everybody else." Lee, responding for the bureau, noted that there was always willingness to work on ways to present programs to Congress that best met the needs of tribes, but some responsibilities in relation to trust land and supervision of resources could only be changed if the BIA was relieved of those responsibilities by law. Lee said that the BIA was not prepared "to recommend that we go out of business on Fort Peck." If the Indians wanted to handle their own affairs, then a definite program needed to be worked out, so competent members

could pursue their interests, and the incompetent could be protected. The rest of the day was spent in conference with Senator Murray and other members of Congress.[99]

On Thursday morning, January 10, 1951, the delegation met with Myer and his staff for an "extended discussion" about royalty sales. Myer stated,

If your Council feels that Indians generally are competent to handle their business, if you would like to have the restrictions removed for the sale of all or half or any part of your allotment, then I am willing to go to the Secretary tomorrow and recommend that we go to Congress to ask that they remove all the restrictions without any question.

Now secondly, if you don't want the restrictions removed but some part of them removed, we are willing to sit down with your Tribal Council and your tribal group and spend a good deal of time in the next weeks together to try to consider all the problems which you have to face with respect to your welfare and all the other things . . . and the other services being provided to see whether or not we can work out a program as to the responsibilities you want to accept and as to the responsibilities you want to relieve us from and see whether or not, after doing so, after we have thought the whole thing through, if we can agree, and see if we can go about having legislative restrictions removed so that you are free to handle your business yourself.

My thought is this, that if the Tribe has business that they want to carry on and would like to assume more responsibility for, I am willing to have our folks sit down with the Tribe as we are now doing with the Navajos and see if we can work out an agreement where some of my responsibilities without legislative restrictions removed can be transferred to the Tribe under an agreement whereby we have a pretty thorough-going understanding as to who is going to carry on the operation and how and gain some experience in carrying it on. . . .

I am unwilling to do that unless we do have pretty thorough-going safe-guards as to the administration and the way of handling it, if I am going to give up my responsibility, you see, to somebody without legislative approval.

If a majority of Indians feel that way, we are all ready to go tomorrow and ask that your responsibilities be removed, and in doing that we are ready to sit down with you and work it out so that we could see how it should be done so that it will not work any hardship on the class of people you are talking about.

There will have to be some kind of provision made. You still will have your tribal organizations and tribal funds I am sure. . . .

You still would be in a position to handle your business, to carry on your welfare work with tribal funds if you wish, that would not restrict that as far as I can see if we can work out a proper program. . . .

What I am trying to have is for us to try to go to work out a constructive pattern for getting rid of that trusteeship on some basis, a tribal basis or some other basis so as to eliminate the kind of irk that you people feel now, and I am willing to be. I am not trying to force the issue, I am simply trying to clarify the issue in a way so that you can understand it.[100]

Curry then asked Myer, "Could you give us assurances that you will sit down and discuss a transfer to the Tribe of a greater degree of control over its own affairs, without taking a whole-hog-or-none attitude?" Meyer responded,

Sure, Jim. I have said to you time and time again, and I say it again to *this* group, that I want it done in an atmosphere of constructively trying to work out something in the tribal

interest, and in an atmosphere of trying to examine all of the problems involved, rather than being pressured to simply relinquish my responsibilities with no safeguards. Now that is what it comes down to. We discussed that in connection with Standing Rock.[101]

The interference of the area offices was also protested. Santee Iron Ring stated, "The people from Fort Peck want to know if they can go direct to Washington. We want your help for Fort Peck direct from Washington."[102] Lee indicated the CIA's willingness to work out with tribal representatives "a way of giving up Indian Bureau authority." D'Ewart disagreed, saying that it was not a question of giving up authority, but rather of sorting out authorities, and allowing the local superintendent to act in local matters. That afternoon, further discussions were held with Doty about royalty deeds.[103]

The delegation spent the morning of January 11 conferring with officials from the BIA and Interior "mostly about the matters of delays in the handling of lease matters." Curry met with others about the income tax issues. That afternoon, another meeting was held with Doty and a group of officials on royalty deeds. The point of contention was that individuals without capital wanted to be able to sell up to 50 percent of any royalties from an oil lease. The BIA was concerned that they would be blamed for not fulfilling their role as trustee in cases where the sale of royalties generated no income.[104]

The following Monday, January 14, Curry first met with Reddoor, Knorr, and Ironring, and then the delegates went to Capitol Hill to confer with the Montana congressional delegation. The afternoon was spent at the Interior Department with Doty and other officials discussing royalty deeds.[105]

The Fort Peck delegation made quite an impression in Washington. The delegates and bureau and Interior Department officials made many statements that foreshadowed termination. Ideally, the idea of termination was the ending of a trust relationship between a group of Indians and the federal government; the Indian group would proceed toward self-determination without help from or supervision by the federal government. Whether this was entirely clear to the Fort Peck delegation when they used the language of self-determination and home rule was not clearly discernable.

Myer wrote John W. Johnson, the Acting Superintendent, Fort Peck Agency, on January 30, 1951 that the lawyer for the Black Hills claim, Ralph Case, and the lawyer for the Assiniboine claims, Delmar W. Holloman of Davies, Richberg, Tydings, Beebe & Landa, were not concerning themselves with the Fort Peck community claims. Thus Myer said that "the objection in the penultimate paragraph of our August 29, 1950, letter is withdrawn." However, the claims contract still languished unapproved.[106]

Curry reported to Bayuk on February 8, 1951 that he had just returned from meeting with D'Ewart. It was unclear how well Curry knew the congressman prior to the visit of the delegation from Fort Peck. More land for Poplar and the new airport lands were discussed. Concerns were expressed about where poor Indians had to live, and the problem of "Indian towns" developing on the edge of predominantly white towns, encouraging segregation. The congressman had tried to find more resources for the Frazer-Wolf Point Irrigation Project, first from the Bureau of Reclamation and then from the Department of Agriculture, and then felt that maybe private sources of revenue might have to be identified. Consolidation efforts for improved land usage rounded out the discussion. Curry hoped that Bayuk could talk with Indian leaders about these matters and then communicate their sentiments. Curry concluded, "I already have excellent rela-

tions with Murray's office, thru [sic] his son Charley. I would like to strengthen our relations with D'Ewart."[107]

David Buckles, once again chairman, wrote to Chapman on February 9 about Curry's claims contract for Fort Peck, declaring that further delay in the approval was threatening the tribes' submission of their claims briefs by the August 13 deadline.[108] The appeals were being handled by a special committee chaired by W.H. Flanery.[109] Curry wrote the executive board on March 8, 1951 to report that the SI had finally overruled the action of the CIA on his claims contract. He was still waiting on final approval of the general counsel contract. Convinced that the delegation's lobbying for the contracts was the reason they were finally being approved, Curry wrote, "I appreciate your help and will try to do my work for you in such a way as to show you how grateful I am."[110] Curry wrote to Congressman D'Ewart on March 14, 1951 to explain that while he had four of fourteen contacts approved, the Fort Peck general counsel contract was unresolved.[111]

Doty had led Curry to believe that he would have an answer about the contracts by the middle of March. Extremely discouraged, Curry wrote to Ickes on March 20, 1951, threatening to abandon the Fort Peck contracts altogether. Curry had begun to doubt Chapman's and Doty's intentions.[112] In a sense, Curry's tangle with Myer had only just begun. In a letter presumably sent to his clients on March 26, 1951, Curry charged that Myer was seeking statements from Indians questioning Curry's performance. Apparently on March 20, Myer had circulated statements to the press and to field offices of the bureau that certain of Curry's tribal attorney contracts would be cancelled because of statements by "Indians themselves that I have been negligent in my work." Curry charged that such a "scandalous statement is part of the campaign by Myer to run me out of business." Because Curry was able to marshal "Indian groups," which through him had opposed some of the CIA's policies, he was trying "to do by defamation what he has failed to do by administrative action because Secretary of Interior Oscar L. Chapman has stopped him." The committee set up by Chapman had cleared Curry of any negligence, but Myer's actions had been reversed.[113] Bayuk reported on March 28 that the necessary language for the contracts was ready for an executive board meeting to be held on April 2, 1951.[114] Curry responded, fine-tuning the language for the resolutions in correspondence dated March 30, 1951.[115] Bayuk made the changes and the resolution was passed and put into the mail on the same day, April 2, 1951.[116]

Tribal member Jim Archdale wrote Curry on April 3, 1951 that many of the leaders at Fort Peck were feeling anxious about claims and the narrowing time frame for filing. Archdale, while outraged that Curry was being treated unfairly on the contract approval issue, was also ready to advise Curry to "put your personal animosities and hates outside and get down to business and get our business agoing [sic] so we can do something."[117] Two days later, Buckles wrote Curry that the resolutions were enclosed, and copies were also sent to the area office, but most alarming, Buckles reported that Superintendent Crawford had refused to sign the general counsel contract. Crawford thought Bayuk should be the local attorney, irrespective of the relationship Bayuk already had with Curry.[118] In a letter of the same date, Buckles wrote to SI Chapman explaining that the resolutions for the Curry contacts were forwarded, but were not signed by Crawford "for the reason that he had not been authorized to do so by his superiors."[119]

On May 17, Curry was notified by the SI that his contract, dated February 12, 1950 for the prosecution of tribal claims against the United States, was approved. The second contract was still under appeal.[120]

Tax liability was extending more comprehensively into all corners of life on the reservation. Frances L. Horn answered a question posed by William R. Smith of Oswego, about the taxability of "repayment cattle." She indicated that legislation was signed into law on May 24, 1950, which provided for "repayment cattle" to be paid for in cash or in-kind. Under this new legislation, repayment cattle were not considered "trust property," and therefore were subject to taxation when the cattle were paid for. Any additional cattle borrowed under the program would also be taxable.[121]

Eva Mae Smith, former tribal clerk, wrote her boarding school classmate Ruth Muskrat Bronson, then the Executive Director of NCAI, on June 15, 1951. Active in the NCAI, Smith reported on the individuals hoping to join in the activities of the organization. However, she also reflected on the local political situation:

Our bitter opponent and chief criticizer in everything worthwhile, Dolly Akers got herself elected on the Executive Board of our Tribal Council, and she and her partner in crime, William Knorr will attend the Governors Council. I do hope that they won't listen to her while she is there.

She uses everybody who can help her in her selfish schemes for profiteering from the Indian people, and I am very much afraid that she has great plans to use Mr. Curry. I hope that he will go very cautiously. I am not acquainted with Mr. Curry personally and do not know anything about him outside his working activities, but he certainly is being criticized here because of his drinking with members of the tribe. I am not interested in this, but because I believe that he can do very good work for the Indian people everywhere and fight the Indian Bureau, so that we can get our problems presented to the proper channels of our Govt. I hope that Mr.

Curry will not give people an opportunity to criticize him for anything.

This reservation is divided into several factions and it seems that all of our activities are so closely watched, most of us have to walk the straight and narrow every day. Maybe this doesn't make sense to you living in a big city as Washington, D.C., but out here in the sticks where our communities are very small and the people all live closely together, we know what everybody is doing most of the time.

We certainly got ourselves beat at the last Tribal election. We had been working on a reservation program which we thought would be good for our Indian people and had big plans of revising our constitution and by-laws, and they were all smashed in the head by people who were led by Dolly and Bill Knorr. It is indeed very discouraging and sometimes I feel like "what's the use," but after thinking it over, I just can not imagine our people being ruled by people who do not have interests of anybody but themselves at heart.

My husband tells me not to spend so much time with people who are easily led by such leaders as Mrs. A. and who can't think for themselves but always feel so sorry for them so I keep right on going.

Bronson probably sent a copy of this letter to Curry so he would aware of Smith's observations and opinions, especially about Curry's personal behavior, but also about the political divisions on the reservation.[122]

As the claims submission deadline approached, Curry wrote Chapman, on July 9, 1951, to request a report on behalf of the Fort Peck tribes, "a complete accounting [to] be rendered to them with respect to all the lands, funds, and other property of these Indians over which your Office has exercised the powers of a guardian or trustees [sic] in possession." Curry then became very specific:

In particular, but not by way of limitation, an account is requested with respect to the following trust funds:

(a) The funds belonging to the said Indians as result of the Act of May 1, 1888, 25 Stat. 113, and the appropriations pursuant to said Act.

(b) Funds received in payment for the lands of said Indians which were sold or otherwise disposed of pursuant to the Act of May 30, 1908, 35 Stat. 558 and subsequent Acts.

(c) Funds received in compensation for rights of way through the lands of said Indians pursuant to the Act of May 1, 1888.

(d) Compensation received for leases and permits for the use of and the removal of resources from the lands of said Indians.

(e) All debts and charges to and payments from trust funds of said Indians.[123]

Curry closed the letter with the statements that he was authorized to receive such an accounting on behalf of the Fort Peck tribes, and that since the filing deadline for claims, August 13, 1951, was fast approaching, "it is respectfully requested that the accounting be forwarded as soon as possible."[124] This obviously was an impossible request, but it raised the question of what such an accounting would entail, and whether the department and bureau were prepared to produce such a report. There was no realistic way the department or bureau could do this work in such a short time. This would provide the justification for the accounting claim submitted to the ICC.

Tribal Executive Board member Dolly Akers wrote Senator Murray on July 19, 1951, expressing impatience over the time being taken to approve the oil leases of the C.H. Murphy Oil Company that had been made in April 1950. She stated, "The Fort Peck people are anxious for the Murphy Oil Company [MOC] to begin drilling operations." She explained that she had written before, trying to get the lease approval expedited:

The Tribal Council has passed resolutions in April and June of this year wherein it was their desire to have the Tribal oil monies paid to its members on a per capital basis. The economic conditions of the Fort Peck Tribe is such that these funds are urgently needed.[125]

The same day, Akers and William Knorr sent copies of Akers' letter to Murray to Curry, urging Curry "to find out why we have been given the run around on this matter for almost two years." They noted that a well drilled directly south of Wolf Point by the Shell Oil Company had been brought into production on July 13, and "here we set [sic] like bumps on a log doing not one thing for our Indian people."[126]

Jim Archdale, in a letter to Curry dated July 23, 1951, expressed his exasperation at the legal representation for the Assiniboine claims and the seeming indifference of the attorneys: "I can't for the life of me can [sic] understand anybody can defend so raw deals, swindler, steals even by the Government."

It is really a queer state of affairs, when the Government plays in the role of robber, a thief and then lays down conditions under which we can take them into court, and we Indian tribes of the United States are forced to accept those conditions in order, and perhaps led into a belief that the Government might settle these honest debts. Here in America the political atmosphere is liberty and freedom, but the machinations of those in power is dictatorial, over bearing, and absolutely heartless, I suppose this oil will be lost by the Assiniboines and our basic rights trampled. Jim, don't feel I am attacking our government, I am only telling you a story often told on every reservation in these United States, and oh, how I'd love to be with you and tell the con-

gress [NCAI] about many more. We also have forty one thousand acres of tribal land, which was to be sold by the government 40 years ago, and is not solid title is in the Fort Peck Indians. Today Indian Bureau attorneys and the Indian Bureau contends we ceded that land, and the question is raised, there may be oil on this land, and I understand contracts were signed by our Council to drill for oil by some oil company, but the Honorable Commissioner will not approve the contract. Under the Indian Reorganization Act we understand all such lands were to be restored to the tribes, and that authority of law didn't seem to be recognized by the Indian Bureau. In other words the Bureau does not protect, it takes away our property where ever it can, the interests of the U.S. government is paramount to that of the Indian tribes. You can read this letter to the Convention, Jim, and greetings from Fort Peck, and from one whose heart is with you all the way.[127]

Frances L. Horn wrote Knorr and Akers on July 24, 1951 that although Curry was at the National Congress of American Indians annual meeting in St. Paul, she had contacted Senator Murray's office to pressure for approval of the oil leases. She also reported that she was able to reach Harry Critchfield of the Lands Division of the BIA, who explained that 450 individual leases were involved, and verification of ownership had taken considerable time. Only four or five leases remained to be verified and sixteen acres of tribal land also still needed verification.[128]

Archdale wrote Curry on July 28 that the most recent resolutions about claims might be imprecise due to the haste of their preparation. The need for an attorney as general counsel was paramount with the first oil well having been brought in near Vida. Archdale appreciated that Bayuk was available to the executive board because legal advice was needed, and a "watch-dog on the

Indian bureau and the oil companies."[129]

Curry received the first printed petitions for the two claims put before the ICC on July 27, 1947.[130] M. Rex Lee, Acting CIA, responded that same day to Curry's demand for an accounting, and especially his request for the accounting report prior to the filing deadline of the ICC:

Section 14 of the Indian Claims Commission Act gives tribal claims attorneys access to all relevant files in the various Government agencies needed to prosecute tribal claims under the Act. It is the duty of the attorney to make his own examination of the relevant information in those files, and the obligation he has undertaken by contract with the tribe cannot be avoided or shifted by demanding an accounting.[131]

Curry sent a formal report, dated April 3, 1951, to the executive board. Progress on the claims prepared for the ICC was evident with the printed petitions. The lobbying efforts continued for approval of the oil leases. The unsold surplus lands that the tribes wanted returned continued to be monitored, and a resolution was needed to act further on this. Most critical, however, was the need to get the general counsel contract approved. Just prior to this report, Standing Rock tribal leaders had gone to Washington, and their refusal to leave until Curry's contract for their representation was approved had proved successful. While the last Fort Peck General Council proposal for a delegation to Washington had been defeated, Curry suggested that the sooner the matter of his contract could be accomplished, the sooner many other delayed matters could be addressed.[132]

Knorr sent a telegram to the SI on August 9, 1951, demanding immediate approval for Curry's contract. The chairman also sent a telegram to Senator Murray pointing out that the contract had been pending for eighteen months.[133]

Both the Bureau of Indian Affairs and the Interior Department continued to deny Curry pertinent information. On August 12, Curry again requested access to bureau records.[134] On this same date, Curry drafted a memo to NCAI officers and committeemen on the matter of "disclosure of official documents." He contended that several officials of the bureau had constricted access to information and particularly to documents, referring to this as an "iron curtain."[135]

Curry wrote Knorr on August 17 about the delay in the approval of the oil leases. He named the individuals who made the decisions at several levels, and the assurance he had been given that only one lease was left to be verified. In this same letter, Curry gave him an update on approval of the general counsel contract. Curry expressed his outrage that part of the process appeared to take place in secrecy.[136]

Myer tersely replied to Curry's arguments for access to the two documents: "The letters of Assistant Secretary Doty that are quoted in your letters sustained, on the merits, our prior action in not making these documents available to you. I regard the Assistant Secretary's letters as disposing of the issue."[137]

The protection of mineral rights, including oil and gas, had become increasingly important to the executive board. Knorr wrote Curry on August 30, 1951 that the board had taken action in June to "protect the Fort Peck allottees interest in oil, gas, and minerals," which he had explained in a letter to Fickinger on August 25. Fickinger had written Crawford on August 20 that "the reservation should not be in perpetuity but for a life or for a number of years." This statement alarmed members of the board:

When a white man exchanges land with an Indian, if the white man wishes to reserve his mineral rights, he does not state for life or for a number of years, he merely reserves his oil, gas and mineral rights. We are of the opinion that the same procedure can and should apply to Fort Peck Indians.

Knorr pointed to the irony that the bureau had for many years resisted issuing patents in fee to Indians, while at the same time engaging systematically in the sale of thousands of acres of Fort Peck Reservation land by supervised sale. In such sales, the allottee or owner never was asked to sign a deed of any kind. Knorr declared, "[I]t has been contended, therefore, the Indian people can recover their oil, gas and mineral rights from lands which have been sold in this manner, as the Indian Bureau should have protected their wards from this loss."[138] Knorr concluded that "we would like to have you investigate the legal and recovery phase of this matter.[139]" The contract for this kind of work, however, still had not been approved. Bayuk wrote Curry on September 2, 1951 that authority for approval of land sales had been transferred from Washington to the area offices, which while "arbitrary and high-handed" could not be stopped or changed.[140] Curry wrote letters dated September 5 both to Knorr and Crawford, indicating his investigation of sales of lands without withholding mineral rights.[141]

The Fort Peck General Counsel contract crisis continued. In a remarkable letter marked "Personal and Confidential," Harold Ickes wrote Chapman on September 14, 1951 about his concern that the "departmental policy in Indian Affairs seems to be gathering accelerated speed in the wrong direction," and that he did not have time to lose. Approval of attorney contracts from all appearances was so straightforward. While Ickes concurred with the positions taken by Curry and the Fort Peck Indians, others were becoming aware of the department's actions. He mentioned that he had corresponded with Alexander Lesser, Executive Director of the Association on American Indian Affairs, who was planning to go to court if necessary "to test your right to sign and promulgate the shabby

proposals of your intra-departmental committee which would restrict rather than enlarge the rights of the Indians to employ their own counsel."

Ickes confessed his own temptation to make public his critique of the "maladministration of Indian Affairs by Commissioner Myer." He had even drafted letters to Chapman about Indians and other issues, "which I had no happiness in writing, and which you would have had no happiness in reading," but in the end had not sent them. Rather, Ickes wrote that he wanted to communicate with him "in friendly frankness," aware of all of the time they had worked together after "I asked President Roosevelt in 1933 to appoint you Assistant Secretary of the Interior." Only in the past weeks had Ickes finally stated that Chapman was responsible for the "damnable decisions of Myer and White," and "rulings that are made by the Bureau of Indian Affairs, especially if they go out over your name." Ickes declared, "I kept hoping that you and not Myer, would finally determine Indian policy and that, therefore, the decisions would be inline with what you said and did in Indian Affairs before you became Secretary."

Urged to go to President Truman on this issue, Ickes noted that he did not want to embarrass Chapman. Only on one occasion did Ickes mention to the President, in passing and which he promptly reported to Chapman, that "his administration might run into real trouble on account of Dillon Myer's misbehaviour towards the Indians." Ickes noted that he had never asked anything personally of the President. He urged Chapman to find the courage to reverse himself and "get back to the solid ground on Indian matters."[142] There was no evidence that this letter influenced Chapman in the contract matter.

Dolly Akers wrote to Curry on September 17, 1951 that "the biggest problem confronting Fort Peck at the present time is loss of oil, gas and mineral rights." She noted that there must be a viable claim against the government for loss of mineral rights through trust land sales, since thousands of acres had been sold by the Indian Bureau. If such sales were for the protection of Indian "wards," then "it most certainly was the responsibility of that Indian Bureau to go all the way and protect their incompetent wards against the loss of oil, gas and mineral rights." Fickinger wrote Knorr that the executive board did not have the authority to act on individual allottees' lands. If this was the case, then the responsibility must rest directly on the Indian Bureau for the loss of rights in the land. Akers asked Curry to examine the legal ramifications of this situation.[143] Curry responded on October 6, 1951 that the remedy might have to be special legislation of Congress, considering the scope of such an investigation and the difficulties with the access to records. Curry pointed out that this was an example of why the need for legal advice to be available to Indian tribes was so important.[144]

Curry reminded Akers of her promise that if his contract approval appeal had not been resolved by September, she would come to Washington. He asked if she and the other delegates might not come to Washington early in October and stay until the contract was approved. Curry also mentioned that other Indian delegations were expected to be in Washington at the same time.[145]

Other developments occurred in mid-October. A delegation of BIA officials visited Fort Peck and met with the executive board on October 20, 1951. The members of the delegation were Mr. Utz, Mr. Critchfield, Mr. Arnold, Mr. Carter, and Mr. Lee. Secretary Bernard Standing explained that it was discovered that the officials were visiting reservations along the Highline, and consequently, the board requested that the delegation visit Fort Peck Reservation. Assistant CIA Utz explained that the primary reason for

the visit was to secure firsthand information of the problems confronting Indian people of the various reservations. Utz revealed that there was a reorganization occurring within the bureau that meant cutting staff positions "which is due to the simple reason that the Indian Bureau works in conjunction to the appropriations which is given the Bureau by Congress." Utz explained that "various questions confront the Indian Bureau when the Bureau goes to Congress for an appropriation," but that the bureau would not seek as part of its appropriation any loan program except money that was being paid back into revolving credit programs, unless Congress passed a rehabilitation program. Such a program would assist people on the reservations "who have a goal they are working toward [which] will be assisted in every manner possible to help themselves more on the road to competency due to the fact that the Bureau does not wish to go indefinitely." It was more the wish of the bureau "to see anyway possible for individual Indians to acquire loans outside the Bureau thus relieving the Bureau of [extending] credit."[146]

Board members had many questions. Securing loans with trust lands was virtually impossible. The collapse of responsibilities among bureau divisions was also a concern. The requirements for performance bonds to protect the lessor were also discussed. With so much land still in individual hands, restrictions upon the way it might be made profitable were substantive. Issues of consolidating heirship lands for the benefit of all heirs were discussed. Fickinger explained that a survey of reservations in the Billings area was underway because many people were feeling deprived or unprotected. Rather, he said "an economical and social society [was] being taken of the reservation in connection with the development of the Missouri Souris project" for forward planning. The ongoing problem of Indian children born off-reservation and how they could be properly enrolled was also addressed. Critchfield suggested that it was up to the tribes to decide what constituted the criteria for enrollment, subject to the approval of the Secretary of Interior. The meeting concluded with discussion about sending a delegation to Washington, but Utz advised that warning was needed if information was to be required of the CIA.[147] The minutes of this meeting failed to convey whether board members really comprehended what they were being told or the consequences that might result from the bureau's reorganization.

Akers wrote Curry on October 26, 1951 that he seemed more concerned with his contract approval than with the loss of oil rights. She asserted that the loss of oil rights "is a case which should be handled under your claims contract." She further speculated:

If all of these Fort Peck people who have lost their mineral rights through the negligence of the Indian Bureau, banded together and filed a suit against the government in the court of claims, the recovery would be an average of $20,000 each for approximately four or five hundred people.

She said that the Tribal Executive Board had been criticized for employing an attorney but not yet receiving legal advice, especially when some of this work could be justified as claims work. On the issue of coming to Washington on a delegation, Akers noted that she had been diagnosed with a heart condition, which made it impossible to come on a delegation that year.[148]

Myer, writing through the area office to Knorr, attempted to clarify the situation about the sale of royalty interest. After citing the applicable statutes, Myer stated,

The consistent policy of this Office and the Department has been to discourage the sale of royalty interest in restricted Indian lands, except where there is urgent need for funds or there are other special circumstances which justify an exception. Most of the requests for the sale of royalty interests originate in areas where the values are highly speculative and the market for the leases is not stabilized. It is generally difficult if not impossible to make a determination of actual values. As an exception to this policy, the Department has authorized the sales of not to exceed one-half of the Indian-owned royalty interests where the facts warranted such action.[149]

Could it be that the bureau did not want to employ enough employees to keep track of such details?

The executive board at its meeting on November 8, 1951 called on the "bureaucracy" in a series of supposedly coordinated agencies to cease "the run-around" and "expedite Indian business." The resolution charged the superintendent with gaining this efficiency. If he failed to do so, they called for his replacement.[150] Frustrations were clearly rising.

Archdale wrote Curry a long letter on November 26, 1951 to point out rising concerns among Fort Peck tribal members about oil and gas discoveries. Doubts were materializing about the effectiveness of the agency office to handle the new details. The loss of mineral rights on land sales since the beginning of allotment must be almost "incalculable." The failure of the "guardian government" could only be imagined. Archdale had only heard recently about the success of individual Indians filing suits in local courts in Oklahoma in recovering their oil and gas interests. He speculated whether this could be replicated, but he also recognized that it took money to sue, and it was clear that most tribal members could not go to court. He noted that Congressman D'Ewart was coming to the reservation on November 29. Archdale suggested that there was an Indian Office letter replying to a delegation to Washington of which he had been a member, dated February 25, 1918, which would give Curry more context about disposition of lands. He said it contained a hearing before Assistant CIA Edgar B. Meritt, and one of the letters had been signed by CIA Cato Sells.[151]

Knorr informed Fickinger on December 10, 1951 that in response to the secretary's invitation, the Fort Peck tribes would bring a delegation to Washington shortly after Christmas. He stated: "We do not want any technical or any other objections from Indian Bureau officials to prevent us from using tribal funds for this purpose." The chairman stated that a General Council was scheduled on December 15 to elect delegates, and a draft resolution stated the agenda of the delegation: first, the approval of the general counsel attorney contract that had been appealed, and to seek final approval; and second, "the delegation shall proceed . . . to obtain a solution of the various tribal legal and administrative problems that have been neglected because the Commissioner has prevented us from using our own money to retain the attorneys of our own choice."[152]

The General Council meeting on December 22, 1951 selected Santee Iron Ring, Chairman William C. Knorr, Dolly Akers, and Edwin Reddoor as the delegation.[153] A resolution was prepared "requesting and demanding the approval of the General Representative Contract of James E. Curry, Washington, D.C. with the Indians of the Fort Peck Reservation (Assiniboine-Sioux Tribes)."[154] Within a day or two of arriving in Washington, the delegation appeared at a hearing with Chapman. They also appeared before Doty on January 7. The delegation did not have to wait long to see the effectiveness of their presentation. Doty finally approved the Curry contract for general counsel on January 9, 1952.[155]

On January 7, the delegation met with H. Rex Lee to discuss the Fort Peck resolutions about income tax, the investigation of the agency, and the request for a special team of clerks to handle the extra business caused by the oil boom. On Tuesday, January 8, the delegation met with the Montana congressional delegation, and met further with Doty and his staff. The evening was spent with Curry preparing for the congressional hearing the next day. The morning of January 9, the delegation testified before the Indian Subcommittee of the House Committee on Interior and Insular Affairs, and the rest of the day was spent in one-on-one conferences with Senator Murray and other members of Congress.[156]

The Fort Peck delegation met with CIA Myer, Associate CIA H. Rex Lee, Lewis Sigler, Chief Counsel for BIA, and Harry Critchfield, Land Division of the BIA, on the morning of January 10, 1952. Avery Winnemucca sat in as a guest. In a long discussion about sale of royalty rights, Myer insisted upon either total trusteeship or patent in fee being issued so that the BIA had no responsibility for any consequences of what people did with their land or rights in the land. For the commissioner, it was one or the other. Myer insisted that before he would change policy, all angles would have to be well thought out. He cited a number of specific cases where the BIA had acted in individual cases, and then were taken by tribes to court or in front of the Indian Claims Commission. He declared that he wanted to act in the interest of all Indians, not just a few.

The delegation tried to convince the CIA that petitioners seeking to sell 50 percent of their royalty interests needed the money and the opportunity to sell was at hand. Myer was reluctant to approve sales when values were in such flux, and he stated over and over again that, as a trustee, he did not want to be blamed if expectations were not met. At the end of the meeting, Myer's associates admitted that the BIA was hard-pressed to fulfill one of its major and basic responsibilities in realty matters because of declining appropriations. In other words, complicated sales were more difficult to monitor, and the personnel crisis meant further delays and more paperwork. Lee summarized the meeting in these terms: first, the policy about mineral rights had been made by the Secretary of Interior many years ago and was still in effect, so any applications for sale of interests would be considered under the current policy; second, a protest against the policy could be registered by asking the CIA to review it with the SI; and third, the overall pattern of the regulations on this matter should be examined and considered in light of possible changes.[157] Several members of the delegation, particularly Akers and Knorr, joined Curry in being quite skeptical of the officials' statements. Doty and his staff spent the rest of the day with the delegation. On January 11, the delegation discussed with many bureaucrats the delays in handling lease matters. On Monday, January 14, the delegation, conferred again with the congressional delegation and the rest of the day was spent discussing royalty deeds with Doty, Flanery, and Critchfield. The delegation left for home the next day.[158]

While the delegation was still in Washington, Vice-Chairman David Buckles wrote Curry that tribal members generally had some reservations about Bayuk being Curry's local fieldman. Buckles pointed out that Bayuk had often represented non-Indian parties in court against Indians, so some felt he was playing both sides of the legal street. Buckles simply wanted Curry to understand the situation.[159]

On January 15, Myer sent a memo to Hale Power, Legislative Counsel, in the Division of Land Utilization, in the Office of Assistant SI Doty, about a telegram Myer had received from the Fort Peck delegation. Myer rejected the procedure offered in the telegram, seeing it "completely contrary to the Secretary's oil policy

as stated in his memorandum of 1942." Ironically, this was the policy declaration made by Harold Ickes when he was SI, mostly in response to the oil exploration efforts directed to Indian lands because of the energy needs of World War II. Myer declared that the conditions that influenced the policy in the first place were being replicated, and changing the policy would be for a minority of Indians:

It must be remembered that if this policy is changed it will involve a complete reversal of policy in the Dakotas, the rest of Montana, Oklahoma, and any other areas where oil has been discovered on allotted lands. Such a change of policy would throw an administrative burden on this office and on the Geological Survey as well as the Secretary's Office which I think would be impossible to administer under the present setup.

Therefore I suggest that before any change is made in this policy serious consideration be given to all the problems that may be involved and it may be desirable to review the policy with the responsible committees of Congress.[160]

Doty's reply, dated January 18, 1952, reiterated that the ten-year-old policy had proved a wise one. He stated from his perspective the Fort Peck delegation position:

Your delegation insists that because of the special circumstances of this case the policy should be waived. They believe that failure to relax the policy provisions may result in irreparable damage to the tribal members, that they are capable of negotiating their own sales, and are willing and anxious to "hedge" their losses or gains and personally abide by and be responsible for the consequences.

However, Doty contended that "the existing policy" applied to Indian lands throughout the country, and went on to say changing the policy was not possible with the trusteeship needed to keep Indians from being "victimized . . . in the hysteria of an incipient oil boom." Doty then outlined two approaches to prepare for a sale of 50 percent of royalty interests allowed by the policy—either by supervised sale, or application for patent in fee, so that the owner of land could arrange their own sale.[161]

Authorized by Chairman Knorr, Akers responded to Doty's letter. She told Doty that this letter was similar to one Knorr had received that blamed the Indians for not having a lawyer when it was "your Department" who would not approve the contract: "it is about as arrogant a letter as we have ever received from a public official." The statements about doubting the support of tribal members for the delegation's representations were baseless and disrespectful. The avenues offered by the policy were impractical and sales already applied for awaited approval. Why would buyers want their money tied up while waiting on the bureau's "red tape"? But the final insult was that any Indian who "wants to take himself off the hook" was reduced to applying for a patent in fee against his wishes. Akers concluded: "In other words, you are again putting into effect the 'forced patent' policy that disgraced the administration of Indian Affairs the early part of the century. I think you should be ashamed of yourself."[162] The result was a standoff. Fair Dealers had made their impression, for better or worse. To complicate matters, John Akers had an application pending to sell 50 percent of his royalty interest in a parcel in the Murphy Oil lease area. For his wife, this was a test of much of the discourse that had passed between Doty and the Fort Peck delegation.[163]

Rufus Ricker and George Washington visited Bayuk on January 25 to discuss the state of claims of the Sisseton and Wahpeton bands of Sioux Indians against the U.S. government, based on the treaty of July 23, 1851. They presented Bayuk

with proceedings of hearings before committees of Congress from the Serial Set. The Sioux had received twelve payments prior to the Uprising of 1862 and the subsequent suspension of payments. The Sisseton Tribe, Sisseton Agency, Sisseton, South Dakota, Fort Totten Sioux, Fort Totten Agency, Fort Totten, North Dakota, and the Sisseton-Wahpeton of Fort Peck Agency were seeking this claim. Ricker and Washington reported that all three tribes received a per capita payment in 1908 in the amount of $157.40, but that was the only payment made. They wanted to know the status of the claim. The matter had been addressed by the Supreme Court at one point and was referenced in 277 U.S.S.C. 424, and the matter was last before Congress for any consideration in 1939. The gentlemen asked for a report on this claim and whether the matter was before the ICC.[164]

Edwin J. Reddoor, one of the delegates to Washington, wrote Curry on January 31, 1952, asking him to attend a General Council meeting on February 9, to report on the accomplishments of the recent delegations. One of the delegates had returned and reportedly was saying the delegation had been a failure. Reddoor asked for minutes and any proceedings of their meeting with Myer.[165] Attending this meeting on such short notice proved problematic for Curry.

Dolly Akers had stayed behind in D.C. to engage in further representations to Congress. Curry included a note to his Fort Peck file, dated February 1, 1952, that recorded a conversation between Dolly Akers and Dillon S. Myer in the hall outside his office. Akers had tried to see him about a telegram she had sent the commissioner the previous day about the duties of a Mr. Taylor presently on the Fort Peck Reservation. Myer responded that he was not accustomed to providing details of an ongoing investigation on a reservation. Akers asked if the tribal officers should not be allowed to participate in the investigation, and said that the chairman wanted to know its purpose. Myer said the chairman should ask for the information himself. Akers explained that as an official delegate, she was empowered by the chairman to ask for this information. Myer told Akers that she was sure she was an official delegate, but maybe he was investigating that point, too, and he walked away.[166] On February 4, Akers had appeared before the Subcommittee on Appropriations to argue for the elimination of the area offices of the BIA. In a letter to Congressman B. Jensen, chair of the subcommittee, she outlined nine points as to why the area office deserved elimination. She observed in closing a sentiment in Congress:

I believe it is the honest desire of Congress to close out the Indian Bureau as soon as possible, to end Indian wardship, to cut down the amount of Federal spending for Indians. However, if Congress can be convinced this goal would be more quickly reached by spending part of the money (now allocated to area offices) on the reservation agencies, it seem to me as though Congress might direct such a change.[167]

A special meeting of the Tribal Executive Board was held on February 5, 1952 with Taylor, identified as a representative of the commissioner's office. He came to have a "frank discussion of problems" facing the Fort Peck Indians. The reports of an "oil boom" needed verification. Taylor left Washington the same day he received his assignment, and no notice of his arrival was given to the superintendent or the chairman. In connection with oil, Taylor sought answers to four questions:

1. What should be the policy on the sale of ½ interest in oil royalties, and how many Indians want to sell them? As you know, the U.S. Geological Survey states that accurate land and mineral values cannot be estimated at this time for Fort Peck. Not enough is known about the amount of oil available.

2. What should be done about the sale of an undivided half of mineral rights?

3. What are the advantages and disadvantages of negotiated sales vs. sales through the advertising and bidding procedure?

4. What is the relationship of the above questions to obtaining a patent-in-fee?[168]

Another question that Taylor wanted to explore was "an unofficial reaction" to "home rule." The chairman's comments in Washington were quoted to the executive board, especially those made before the Subcommittee on Indian Affairs about the progressive characteristics of the Fort Peck families. Knorr appeared to have suggested that tribal members could handle their own affairs and needed less supervision. Congressman Morris had asked the chairman if he was "ready to state that the Fort Peck people would like to be entirely out from under the jurisdiction of the Bureau of Indian Affairs." Knorr had refused to be put on the spot. Akers also spoke to this question, saying that more authority needed to be delegated to the agency level, and complaining about the uselessness of the area offices. If more authority were delegated locally, "then we could get some of our tribal business completed." She also said that there was no "reason for the Indian Bureau to be continued for another 150 years," and "I think the time has come when we are going to have to stand on our own feet and be citizens just like anybody else." Taylor commented, "My impression is that the Fort Peck Indians are pretty well advanced and compare favourably with any similar cross-section of the United States populations," and "If I have the wrong impression, I hope you will correct it."[169] Taylor stated that Commissioner Myer was "willing to sit down from your tribal representatives at any time and work out a problem for terminating the Bureau's activities at Fort Peck," and "he will take the necessary legislation to the Congress with you any time it can be worked out." Taylor went on:

... if the tribe does not want all restrictions removed, he is willing to sit down and work out a problem for gradually transferring increasing responsibilities to the tribe. This will require specific written agreements as to what is the tribe's responsibility and what is the Bureau's responsibility. In some instances it may require legislation relieving the Bureau of part of the responsibility it now has by law.[170]

Taylor then asked if there had been sharp dealings over land between Indians and Indians, and Indians and whites. This query was based more on rumor than on specific complaints, Taylor said.[171]

Considerable discussion ensued. Knorr and Reddoor both spoke to the problem many people had in raising capital. There being a shortage of loan money, the sale of royalty interest opened another avenue for raising capital. Yet once a patent in fee was issued, the land became liable for taxes, and the counties on the reservation were aggressive in pressing this. The Reddoor petition was still under consideration and was among the five awaiting approval. George Washington, clearly aware that Reddoor, John Akers, and others were involved in petitions and that some members of the executive board also had interests in the matter, stated that he had stood for election to represent the "Tribe," but as far as he was concerned, this was an individual matter, and must remain so, including estate lands where there were undivided interests. Knorr responded, "We are trying to bring about relief for the Indians. The Government holds onto the land till it becomes so complicated." Taylor asked board members for more opinions about the "oil questions." Bernard Standing said that old or young should be allowed to go ahead and sell out, via a patent-in-fee arrangement. Knorr said that the two avenues were all that were available, and the bureau and Interior Department were not willing to change the policy. What was being sidestepped was that "income taxes [have to be paid] from everything you derive from your allotment." While 85 percent of tribal members were educated and competent to take care of their own business, many Indians had a genuine fear of taxes: "What he [Mr. Taylor] wants to know is whether the people as a whole would rather hang onto their oil royalties but if you want to sell, do you want a supervised sale or a patent-in-fee?"[172]

After Knorr read from the letter of Doty restating the policy on oil royalties, Taylor read the portion of the policy from 1942 written by Harold L. Ickes, without explaining when it was written or the context in which the policy was made.[173] Others spoke, including Henry Archdale, asking that all options be left open, wishing there was a category for Fort Peck Indians based upon their capabilities. Taylor asked for a poll by a show of hands "as to how many want the sale of ½ oil royalties on a bid basis-restricted sale through the [BIA] office." Apparently, the board was reluctant to do this. Knorr stated, "We're coming to taxes and we can't get away from it." Taylor again asked who "would like to sell ½ of their oil royalties right now?" Nellie MacDonald suggested they go to Congress for other rules and regulations. Taylor begrudgingly acknowledged this option, but pressed again: "How many feel that there should be a negotiated sale after this discussion?" Joe Reddoor jumped in:

I think Mr. Taylor is pushing the question too fast. We're only a handful of the reservation and we can't decide. It isn't up to a small group. We are victims of some international set-up. On the other hand, we have a big potential income on the reservation.[174]

Henry Archdale moved to leave it up to the individual to sell by patent in fee or by supervised sale, George Washington seconded it, and the vote was five for and two opposed. Taylor said, "That finishes oil."

Taylor moved on to the home rule question, and stated that the Indians at Fort Peck, by all appearances, were "well advanced." Nimrod Davis gave his assessment:

There are about 3000 Indians, more or less, on this reservation. The adults are not all competent to look after the welfare of their own affairs. They can not look after the business on their own. There are a few that are able to. They have homes, cattle, farms. They can take care of themselves. They can be turned loose. Out of 3000 Indians they are not all competent to look after their own business. I talked about it to people and they don't like to be turned loose.[175]

Knorr asked Davis, "How many Indians is the State taking care of today?" Davis replied:

150 of them from Tribal funds. I am getting Old Age Assistance because I am an old man. There is no charity in receiving money from the State. Last month I got $41.00 from the State but if I die now, out of my land someone is going to pay the State back what they allowed me. I know it. All the old people when they pass away, the estate has to pay back what is owed. So I am not in favour of Mr. Knorr's saying that something like 90 [percent] more or less are educated men. Not all of them can transact business of their own.[176]

Taylor asked, "Would it also be your understanding that in the general population that same exists? Does Fort Peck have more in proportion to other States?" Archdale replied, "I think there

are more Indians on welfare than white people [in Roosevelt County]." Suggestions were made that lessees might make checks directly to landowners to lessen the work in the grazing department, but Taylor dismissed this, knowing that the control of grazing permits would not be complete without controlling the flow of money. The meeting ended.[177] Obviously, there was a diversity of opinion and a more complicated demographic pattern to the reservation than Knorr and his supporters had tried to present. Whether Taylor got what he was looking for was indeterminate.

Curry, in correspondence to Bayuk dated February 9, 1952, said he was convinced that the Taylor investigation was the investigation that the delegation had asked for in their presentations in Washington. The delegation had intended to turn up the complaints of Indians against the agency and put this on the record. When they failed to get any response from the bureau, the delegation had declared that they would conduct their own investigation. To preempt this, Taylor was sent to the reservation, but he was there to whitewash the agency and do whatever he could to discredit the delegation. Taylor refused to discuss his authority to act, and Myer refused to reveal anything about what was being done. Curry advised Knorr to make a stenographic record of the meeting with Taylor on February 5, and to send a copy to him. He observed:

I don't think Myer is going to do himself any good with this kind of tactics. I am reasonably sure that the Indians will stand behind their officers. However, I want to know as fully as possible just what Taylor is up to so that we can take any counter steps here that may be necessary.

Curry ended with a long paragraph about how the executive board could conduct its own investigation.[178]

Curry finally wrote Vice-Chairman David

Buckles on February 11 about Buckles' advice that tribal members were divided by some of the clients Bayuk had represented in the past. The sorting out of interests always was a challenge to a lawyer, and Curry quoted from the Canon of Professional Ethics of the American Bar Association to demonstrate that lawyers often were confronted with representing conflicting interests. Bayuk had acted for the City of Poplar in many matters, and Curry knew that when he engaged him to work as his local associate. While Curry believed these were not sufficient to limit Bayuk's effectiveness on the tribes' behalf, he declared he would not put Bayuk in situations of conflict. Curry said he would ask Bayuk to declare his interests and what he would do to mitigate these in relationship to his representation of the tribes, and Curry would present this to the board. Curry also noted that he knew of Buckles' previous disagreements with Bayuk, and said that he hoped common sense would prevail because in a few months time Bayuk had demonstrated his value.[179] On this same date, Curry wrote Bayuk outlining the terms for his compensation.[180] Bayuk, upon reviewing the letters Buckles had sent Curry claiming bias in representing white people against Indians, said that he thought it better for Curry to find another associate counsel for the tribe.[181] Curry wrote Bayuk on February 21 asking him to reconsider, since if it had not been Buckles' complaint, it might have been another. Asking Bayuk to make his declaration was really demonstrating his compliance with the ethics of the profession, and in a sense, was the best protection in case anyone else would want to "raise hell with us."[182]

The board's Enrollment Committee prepared changes to the tribes' enrollment procedures and criterion, and announced that the recommendations were on the agenda for the next General Council scheduled for February 23, 1952. The major point was that one-eighth degree of blood

was being required for enrollment.[183]

Consequences of the Theodore Taylor foray to the reservation were only just beginning. Dolly Akers wrote Curry on February 21 to remind him of the phone conversation they had with Knorr prior to Akers' departure, when the chairman was "quite upset" about the action removing all tribal monies from the Fort Peck Agency. He had only found out from talking with Mr. Johnson, the Agency Chief Clerk. The tribes had been operating from a Tribal IIM Account system and tribal monies were being paid out at the agency, but this was done with the supervision of F.M. Haverland of the Billings Area Office, who was the Assistant Area Director as well as a Special Disbursing Agent. The stipulation in the Land Enterprise Program had been for all funds received to place money in a special land project account in the Traders State Bank in Poplar. However, all funds had been removed from Fort Peck and placed in a Helena bank, and "we must operate back and forth to Billings and then the money will be paid from the Helena Bank by Mr. Haverlord." Akers countered: "[I]t is my opinion that the Tribe can elect or appoint someone as Treasurer [and] get him bonded and have complete control." She asked for Curry to study this matter. She was still hoping he would be able to come out to Fort Peck on the first of March.[184] She closed saying, "the relief situation is acute and up to date there is no solution in sight."

Following up on a conversation about the report of the Taylor visit to Fort Peck and the oil leases that still had not been approved, Curry wrote Associate CIA H. Rex Lee on February 23, 1952, at Knorr's request. Curry reminded the associate commissioner that he had said the report was "purely administrative," that as to those parts which request administrative action affecting the tribe, the tribe would eventually be advised, but because Lee had yet to review the report, he could not furnish a copy. Curry pointed out that Knorr had complained that "certain administrative policies had been set up at Fort Peck by Mr. Taylor without consulting the tribal officials." He was most concerned that, despite the most urgent request of the tribes for oil leases to be paid, Taylor had placed these third in priority. Even after a meeting with Crawford in December, when it was agreed that oil leases needed to be given priority, a significant backlog remained. Could Crawford be instructed by wire to give them immediate priority? Knorr was also very concerned about how Taylor might be representing the state of affairs at Fort Peck.[185]

As a sign of the pressures being brought upon Tribal Executive Board members, Knorr and Akers wrote Curry on February 29, 1952 to protest the practice of "Indian Service officials to expend tribal funds for the Indian relief load on the Fort Peck Reservation." Clearly bothered by having no control over their tribal monies, Knorr and Akers felt some action was needed. They considered expenditures from tribal funds for relief purposes illegal. Curry was requested to try and recover the money, and was authorized to make a claim based on a violation of the treaty rights of the Fort Peck tribes. This was based on the previous history of Congress appropriating gratuities when tribal funds were not available. No specific treaty was cited as the basis of this request.[186]

The General Council, held on March 1, 1952, primarily discussed proposed changes in tribal enrollment criteria, but Akers spoke briefly about the struggle for sale of royalties. She tried to explain how the 1942 Ickes policy was increasingly unrealistic because Indians needed more freedom in exercising personal affairs. She explained that when she had been pressed for examples of individuals who were being constrained by the policy, she invited her husband to come to Washington so he could speak to Interior Department officials about his attempt

to sell 50 percent of his mineral rights. Dolly Akers as a board member and recent delegate to Washington was attempting to legitimize the time given to changing the current policy. Both Knorr and Akers were aware that many tribal members did not have oil leases, and were not sympathetic to advantages being allowed the small class of individuals who had them.[187]

The enrollment resolution was thoroughly discussed. Bernard Standing, chair of the enrollment committee, presented five principles, explaining that for future per capita payments, an up-to-date tribal roll was needed. The five articles were read to the assembly:

1. All children of Indians, Sioux or Assiniboine, whose parents are enrolled on the official Fort Peck Agency rolls, who have 1/8 degree or more of Indian blood are eligible for enrollment and eligible to participate in all tribal benefits regardless of the place of birth and the residence of the parents.

2. Children born out of wedlock, when the mother refuses to name the father or the father denies paternity, eligibility is to be determined by using ½ of the degree of blood of the mother.

3. All children of adopted individuals shall not be eligible for enrollment and shall not be eligible to participate in any tribal benefits.

4. When the date of a per capita payment or other payments are determined, all those who were on the rolls for one year prior to that date will be eligible to receive their payment. Payments for those who died during that one year period would be made to the estate.

5. The enrollment shall be left open for a period of one year after the date of approval by the Secretary of the Interior. Upon the expiration of that one year period the rolls of the Fort Peck Sioux and Assiniboine Tribes will be forever closed.[188]

Knorr explained that it was up to the tribes

to decide who was eligible for enrollment. The discussion focused on the implications of these principles, and for some the implications of increased membership in the face of future distributions were discouraging because it meant decreased per capita payments. Sentiment was expressed that no one should be stricken from the rolls. With the current roll, Standing reported that most recently 1,680 children were added and 248 were rejected. Akers rose and asked to amend the first principle: "All children of Indians, Sioux or Assiniboine whose parents or grandparents are enrolled on the official Fort Peck Agency rolls are eligible for enrollment and eligible to participate in all Tribal benefits regardless of the place of birth and the residence of the parents." The vote resulted in 103 for, and 100 opposed.[189]

The discussion of the other principles ensued. There was sentiment that if adoptees had no Sioux or Assiniboine blood, their children should not be enrolled. This motion was unanimously passed. Sentiment was expressed that the roll should be periodically reviewed rather than closed, which would keep the wardship relationship intact. Again a motion was made and passed.[190] The council adjourned with the notice that another General Counsel would be scheduled when Curry could be present.[191]

An article in the *Poplar Progressive*, dated March 6, 1952, had the headline, "Murphy Expects to Complete Well This Week; Work on Other Wells Progresses." Production from the wells was not far in the future.[192]

Dolly Akers wrote Senator Murray a long letter, dated March 10, 1952, to explain what had been learned from Taylor's inspection. The massive backlog of land management paperwork would take 1.3 man years to process. He pointed out "that this backlog of work accrued on account of the reduction in force in the land section staff from three to one civil service employee in 1947, at the time when the Congress made severe appropriation cuts for salaries of employees." He did acknowledge there had been tangible assistance from tribal clerks. Akers referred to Taylor as a "per diem specialist" who had not been present long enough to recommend tangible changes. She then turned to recommending the removal of Superintendent Crawford, making four specific charges.[193] She wrote a similar letter to Senator Zales N. Ecton, blaming "confusion" at the Fort Peck Agency on Crawford, whom she urged be removed.[194]

A special meeting of the executive board convened on March 20, 1952 to discuss irregularities in the administration of grazing leases. In one case, new leases were delayed and confusion arose over who actually held leases. This was being held up by several of the board members as an administration problem with the agency.[195]

SI Chapman wrote Curry on March 21, 1952 to allow access to documents that Curry had requested in October 1951, but of course, Curry would have to pay for copying, or else examine the documents in the department.[196]

At a hearing, the Senate Committee on Interior and Insular Affairs on March 24, 1952, convened by Senator Clinton B. Anderson, heard from Carl Whitman. From the Blackfeet Reservation, Whitman was asked to comment on an affidavit taken from the chief of police in Poplar about a meeting of representatives from the Blackfeet, Fort Berthold, and Fort Peck Reservations with their tribal attorney, James E. Curry. While the hearing focused on the matter of tribal attorneys and their approvals, the meeting in question was examined because the chief of police reported that Curry had sponsored a drinking party among the attendees. No one was arrested, but the police chief had made sure individuals were safe and not driving while intoxicated.[197]

Dolly Akers was beside herself and wrote Senator Murray that Crawford must be removed.

She explained that a petition was being circulated among the Fort Peck tribal members. Despite a recent snowstorm, over 200 signatures had been collected. A good number of non-Indians were complaining about the "laxity and maladministration of Fort Peck Agency." She noted that Santee Iron Ring and Knorr had been "beating the drum for the Republicans." While she said she was the Republican precinct committeewoman of Roosevelt County, she could get letters from her Democratic counterparts if this was needed. She forwarded a previously passed resolution about getting rid of Crawford.[198]

Among a series of General Council Resolutions, dated March 29, 1952, was one based on the findings of Taylor's inspection, requesting the Indian Bureau prepare and submit to the executive board an amended plan of operations for the Land Services Project, so that sufficient personnel could be put immediately to the "log jam on land transactions."[199] A Tribal Executive Board resolution, dated March 31, 1952, expressed confidence in the tribal attorneys. The board urged Montana's U.S. senators to insist that Curry testify at Senator Anderson's hearings, and that no report be ordered until he did so. The resolution also asked that the delegation introduce a statement into the *Congressional Record* condemning the Interior Department's efforts to deprive Indians of their right to choose attorneys.[200] Curry spent the next days lobbying the Montana congressional delegation, writing them each letters to counter the personal attacks on his reputation, and especially the SI's opinion that possibly all of Curry's contracts needed to be reconsidered.[201] Curry reviewed a draft statement that Senator Ecton read to the Senate subcommittee on the attorney contract issue.[202]

Curry apparently ended up working with Congressman Wesley D'Ewart on a number of Fort Peck initiatives. The languishing surplus lands matter that had been bothering the Fort Peck leaders was a perennial problem. Curry wrote to the executive board to report that D'Ewart had suggested introducing an omnibus land bill to facilitate land transfers of the former surplus lands, the submarginal lands, the town site lands, and the airport lands.[203] Curry outlined the procedures in the proposed legislation to facilitate the administrative practice jointly of the general council of the Fort Peck tribes, the Department of the Interior, and a local board representing all affected interests. Submarginal and surplus lands needed to be transferred to the tribes in exchange for concessions for lands to be transferred to several of the reservation towns, lands for airport development, and certain submarginal lands for non-Indian interests. Ideally, this bill would authorize the Secretary of the Interior to make the necessary transfers and execute the required legal documents to make the settlement final, "but such authority should be conditioned upon his obtaining the consent of the local board above mentioned and the General Councils of the Tribes." The delegation of decisions to the local level was a pragmatic, practical application of the discourse calling for "homerule" in Indian affairs. Curry did say that if the Department of Interior preferred, the agreement could be submitted to Congress for final approval.[204] Curry sent a copy of the letter to the congressman to CIA Myer and solicited his comments.[205] The bureau and the Interior Department were noncommittal.

During the next six months, many issues simply became further developed. Oil development was moving forward. The Murphy Oil Company's first test well proved successful.[206] An oil lease sale was announced for April 30, 1952, and among the bidders, the Murphy Oil Company was the high bid on parcels it sought.[207] Dolly Akers wrote to Curry on May 3, 1952, asking him to come for a one-day conference with a Murphy Oil Company representative, stating "we have numerous oil problems." She explained that Murphy had drilled three wells: No. 1 was a dual producer, No. 2 was too slow to be a commercial producer, and No. 3 was reported to be almost as good as No. 1. Consequently, a meeting was scheduled where the Tribal Executive Board, Geological Survey representatives, and the Murphy Oil Company representatives would "designate the lands that participate in the oil wells." Akers was already suspicious of the motives of the companies bidding, and was particularly concerned that more than 100 tracts had no bids against them. The board did not want to give its approval without legal advice.[208]

After all the hard work by Curry and E'Ewart, Congressman Mike Mansfield was pressured by constituents to introduce H.R. 6535, a bill meant to restore to former submarginal lands owners' mineral rights in said lands in exchange for 25 percent of the value paid by the United States to secure the lands. Other similar bills had also been introduced, and of course were adamantly opposed by the Fort Peck tribes.[209]

The post-war economy had improved due to a drop in government defense spending, but the police actions in Korea, beginning in June 1950, were contributing to the rise of the "military industrial complex" that Eisenhower identified at the end of the 1950s. Political control of Congress had shifted back and forth since 1946, when the GOP had taken both houses. In 1948, the Democrats had retaken control, but the influence of conservative forces was growing, particularly during the Cold War, when the negative rants and witch hunt investigations of Senator Joseph McCarthy led to the national elections in 1952.[210] War debt and a range of new and old obligations led the House Appropriations Committee in the spring of 1952 to cut the Indian Service's appropriation estimate for the fiscal year 1952 from $71,425,000 to $65,000,000, with the admonition

that the bureau would be expected to do more with less.[211]

Between 1945 and 1955, the attitude prevailed that Indians did not need the U.S. government as a protective trustee, but rather needed to be treated equally and acculturated into the mainstream of American society, in the spirit of the "melting pot" metaphor, which was being promoted for all other minorities. The opportunity to bring suits before the Indian Claims Commission would serve as a severance package for the tribes, as they were expected to become individual citizens without any advantages of collective traditions. The overall implications of citizenship in this period were being transformed into an acculturated ideal of being just like whites and becoming taxpayers and full participants in the larger society. But this ignored the racinated character of American society, especially the compositional factors of the reservation rural economy and on- and off-reservation towns.[212]

Adding oil discovery and exploration to the mix of interests contributed to the struggle among various factions of tribal members and non-Indians living on the reservation. For several reasons, the April 30 lease sale was important to everyone interested in this new phase of economic development. Outside of the two units constituting larger parcels, other checkerboarded lands had also been offered. The Tribal Executive Board was more interested in larger and adjacent parcels being leased in units, whereas the oilmen wanted to pick and choose, leasing tracts that were more likely to contain oil. The board wanted more landowners to benefit.[213] Confusion soon arose, however, about whether the companies would be required to drill on each lease parcel secured in the April 30 sale. Curry believed that they were, and the Fort Peck tribes quickly adopted this position.

A special meeting of the executive board

on July 21, 1952 focused on the Murphy Oil Company's protest of the requirement to drill a test well on each of the nine parcels it had leased.[214] Interior and bureau officials were reluctant to enforce what was clearly stated in the terms of the sale, and delayed final approval of the leases. This was further compounded by the statements made by the area director against "certain Indian attorneys," blaming these attorneys for "deceiving Indians." The Murphy Oil Company had attempted to limit its drilling commitment by suggesting language for a rider to the leases, which it submitted to the Fort Peck Agency and the U.S. Geological Survey regional office. The leaders of the Fort Peck tribes, long on the record for opposing the creation and expenditures of the area offices, were determined that this layer of the bureaucracy was preoccupied with promoting "government by gossip in Indian Affairs."[215] Curry wrote to Myer on July 30, 1952 with questions about the enforcement of the literal language of the leases, asking the bureau to assist the Murphy Oil Company to fulfill the commitment to drill nine test wells in the lease lands it had secured.[216] Another sale was offered on July 31, 1952 and another was due on August 19, 1952.[217]

Under the somewhat misleading headline "Sioux Need Self-Rule Analyst Says," a *Great Falls Tribune* piece with a dateline of Billings stated that Ben Reifel, a Rosebud Sioux tribal member who worked for the bureau, declared a more "effective" governing body was needed. After a two-week study of the Fort Peck Reservation, he noted that many members of the tribe thought a "stronger self-governing unit" was needed to decide ". . . better use of lands . . . obtained, educational loans for younger members of the tribe, better use could be made of existing reservations schools, and tribal members would be more inclined to get together and solve mutual difficulties. . . ."[218] This was part of the bureau's

public criticism of the General Council.

Curry attempted to negotiate a solution. While technically the bureau was responsible for protecting the property rights of tribal members who had leases with the oil company, Curry simply did not trust the bureau and Interior Department attorneys.[219] He went to Denver to meet with representatives of the Murphy Oil Company on August 6, 1952, and discovered that the company's excuse for the delays was that the requirement was vague and a matter of interpretation. Curry warned the executive board that Murphy Oil Company was considering withdrawing entirely, based on the delays caused by the tribes and the government, but mostly the latter.[220]

Meanwhile, the approval of assignments by Curry of the Fort Peck claims contract was again delayed. Myer took it upon himself to write a very inflammatory letter to the chairman of the Fort Peck tribes criticizing the assignment of interest in the claims contract. The CIA declared that he felt that Curry was not doing the work but taking half the contract, and because Curry was doing so with the ten other groups named in the letter, he was not representing the full interests of the Fort Peck tribes. Myer also referred to the disapproval of the general counsel contract, which was overturned in appeal, and he held the same opinion about that.[221]

Crawford, on August 12, 1952, wrote to Murphy Oil Company approving a sixty-day extension on the April 30 leases because the executive board had tabled all the proposed leases that had been presented for approval on July 24, 1952.[222]

The national columnist Drew Pearson published an editorial in the *Washington Post* on August 1952, exposing what he thought were the issues of attorneys representing Indian tribes, and in this piece he used James E. Curry as his negative example.[223] In response, Curry sent a letter to the editor, dated August 18, 1952, to several western newspapers, defending the right of Indian tribes to independent legal representation in the face of Myer's personal incriminations. Myer, who was on a tour of western reservations, was scheduled to visit the Fort Peck Reservation, and Curry wrote that he also would attend.[224] Curry also wrote the Tribal Executive Board on August 18 to ask if there was any dissatisfaction, because if there was, he was willing to step aside and let the board choose another attorney.[225]

Commissioner Myer intended to visit all areas and every agency in the Indian Service, and on August 21, 1952, he arrived in Poplar and met with the Tribal Executive Board. This was the first visit by a CIA to the Fort Peck Reservation. First, the commissioner was invited to address the board and asked to limit his remarks to fifteen minutes. He described the current problems as "our problems" in presenting programs to legislative committees and especially appropriation committees. The overall cost of operating schools and hospitals was escalating, as was criticism of the bureau. Briefly, Myer presented his opinions about what he called "emancipation":

Our position, I think, has been quite clear. We're not interested in hanging onto the responsibility of trusteeship any longer than the Indian folks feel that we should carry it. We're ready, if it is generally agreed by the Indians that we should get out of business, to discuss it with the Secretary and with Congress and try to get legislation to complete that job.

On the other hand, we're not interested in staying in business and assuming the responsibility for and taking the blame and letting somebody else have the authority and carry off the gravy for somebody else. I say the gravy—I mean taking the gravy from other Indians. And we feel if there is anything that is intended in the trusteeship responsibility that we have it is intended that we should protect the Indian interests whether it is tribal or individual interest. If we're not doing it properly they ought to get somebody else to do it, now.

We have also said that we are ready to sit down and try to work out a program to be relieved of part of our responsibilities by legislation if we can come to an agreement, that we should be relieved without interfering with other work. We are working with a number of tribes where they are assuming additional responsibilities, with a complete understanding on our part. We have a pretty thorogoing [sic] understanding and written agreements and some of them are saying that we are pushing them too fast.[226]

Myer was then asked about the rejection of Curry's claims contract. The executive board had re-endorsed their attorney the previous day. The commissioner had tried to stay above the fray, but Curry had made a point of being present, and took advantage of the opportunity to question the artificial manner in which Myer and the SI were harassing attorneys like Curry and Felix Cohen, who were also the most pointed and competent of critics. Myer tried to sidestep the issue. Curry pressed for the precise wrongdoing as the basis for the claims contract rejection, suggesting that if he had done anything wrong, he also should be dismissed as general counsel. Myer finally admitted that because Cobb and Weissbrodt were, in his opinion, doing the actual work of the claims research, he could not understand what Curry was doing to advance the claim. Curry had to insist that the responsibility for the claim was between the "Tribe" and him, and to have it said that he had "abandoned that responsibility" was "a gross misrepresentation of fact." Curry declared that whether others were hired to perform work to fulfill a contract was really not the business of the CIA, making the analogy to the Attorney General not personally trying every government legal action.[227]

Chairman William N. Knorr appealed to the CIA to approve more expense money for Curry, stating that it was required for a series of visits needed for legal advice on oil development. Even with the necessary resolutions placed before him, Myer refused to accept them, saying that they would have to be processed. This gave Knorr the opportunity to complain that the time it took the bureau to act often significantly inconvenienced the tribes, and at times, delays were detrimental to the tribes' interests.[228]

Myer tried to change the subject, suggesting that Knorr's stand on self-rule implied that the tribes wanted to be "released from trusteeship," and if that was the prevailing sentiment, the commissioner was ready "to take the procedures to do so." Knorr was quick to point out that "the [Fort Peck] Indians should be turned loose, it's in the record that I said I couldn't speak for the balance of my people." Councilmen Norman Hollow, Edwin Reddoor, and George Washington commented on the representation of progressive disposition of tribal members that Knorr had made, but they also did not advocate the end of trusteeship. Councilwoman Dolly Akers spoke next to explain why Knorr felt it so important to make his clarifications to the CIA. Fort Peck tribal members were being compared to the majority of Navajo in the rural areas of that reservation, who had only about 10 percent of members with any education and facility with English. She noted, "At all times, Congressmen and the Indian Bureau are prone to put us all in one pot and to deal with us as if we didn't have any more education than those people." But many statements that had been made in these hearings had been "misconstrued," in her opinion, which had prompted the Taylor investigation of the delegates and the veracity of their constituencies. Rather than investigating the

conditions at Fort Peck, the effort was directed at the delegates. Myer denied this, saying that Taylor was sent to report on a range of issues. Akers quoted statements about his not being interested in problems or having any authority to discuss them. Myer again tried to emphasize that the discussions with the delegates were about the "question of programming" and whether or not the Fort Peck "Tribe" was ready to negotiate self-rule. The end of one program did not mean the resources were to remain for another use directed by the tribes. The next topic of discussion concerned the newly assumed authority of the area office to administer the agency finances, especially those appropriated to support tribal government. It came out that the transition between tribal secretaries had resulted in delayed production of copies of resolutions and minutes, some by as much as three months. Knorr said that with the recent appointment of Alvin Warrior in the position, the backlog was being addressed. Further discussion addressed the administration of leases and access of tribal members to lease money placed in their accounts, especially new regulations on sales of lands between Indians that would have to be reviewed in Washington and the area office.[229]

Next, Chairman Knorr pressed the commissioner about oil rights in trust lands and the restriction on their sale. Knorr publicly asked for the commissioner's support for legislation that would restore mineral rights to all allottees from 1927 forward. Knorr and Akers went on, at length, questioning why tribal members had to forfeit their mineral rights after their lifetime, leaving nothing to their heirs, or had to apply for a fee patent to be able to make decisions about their mineral rights. Myer admitted that policies of the bureau and Interior Department were influenced by the Oklahoma experience with oil development, coupled with the demands of administering trust responsibilities concerning oil leases and associated rights.[230] Myer was only willing to consider negotiation of alternate arrangements with "competent" tribes that were willing to allow individualism to dominate their affairs rather than collective interests, so non-IRA tribes such as the ones on Fort Peck would require agreements that had legislative approval. Just as he did before the Fort Peck Tribal Executive Board, Myer continued to deny that the bureau was forcing individual tribal members to secure patents in fee. Curry suggested that the position taken by the CIA about this matter was politically motivated, was due to his personal disagreements with Curry, and that the policy in practice was the equivalent of the era of forced patents. On the issue of competency, Norman Hollow asked why Myer would not let "the Indian people retain their mineral rights forever." Myer actually replied that record keeping was too complicated for lands and their fractionated parcels, suggesting it was easier for the bureau to be rid of the trust responsibilities in such cases. Curry asked the commissioner if he would support an omnibus bill to address a range of land matters, and after Myer said he had supported every bill over the years introduced on the submarginal lands, he was noncommittal on a comprehensive regime to the land matters on the Fort Peck Reservation.[231]

Myer announced that he needed to leave to remain on schedule. Board members tried to ask him other questions, but the commissioner could not be swayed. Dinner and further discussion time, and even a tour, had been planned, but Myer would not yield. He deferred several questions to the experts and other bureaucrats in the department, and he urged the precise use of the administrative processes of the department, refusing to make any further clarifications on the spot. The closing exchange between Knorr and Myer consisted of the commissioner saying to "Billy" Knorr that he had come to the conclu-

sion "that regardless of what he did he was not right, sorry that this was his impression of the sentiment of the meeting." Knorr responded that he did not feel that way, "but it is only once in a lifetime that a Commissioner comes out and pays us a visit." Myer responded that if he stayed in the job, he would try to get back.[232]

The Murphy Oil Company sponsored an Oil Discovery celebration in the last days of August in Poplar. As part of the festivities, C.H. Murphy, Jr. was given an Indian name by Chief Santee Iron Ring, and then the CEO announced the company's intention to drill nine new wells in the Poplar area. Even though there was heavy rain one of the days, many people attended the event. Murphy and all the top staff from the oil company were present.[233]

Soon, however, relations between the Murphy Oil Company and the Fort Peck tribes became more complicated. C.H. Murphy, Jr., by August 28 had resigned his role as "unit operator" of the East Poplar Unit and claimed the right to name a successor.[234] Upon the recommendation of the CIA, new leases for the East Poplar unit were to be executed, but Fred Kirgis, the lawyer for the company and a former Interior Department solicitor, submitted unsigned leases to the Fort Peck Tribal Executive Board. Curry, in a letter dated September 17, 1952 to Fred Taylor, the District Landsman for the company, expressed his outrage:

However, the most distasteful thing is the seemingly very tricky way in which you submitted the leases to the Board. As I understand it, the leases were not signed by you. If the Board had signed them, or any of them, there is no certainty that the Company would ever sign. To the contrary, you seem to reserve the right to sign them or not as you please.

Curry realized that the MOC was reserving their right to withdraw.[235] In a letter of the same date, Curry wrote to Myer for copies of communications to Superintendent Crawford about the Murphy leases of April 30 and interpretations of the drilling commitments, and also sought his advice on the matter of the Skelly and Tidewater leases.[236] Curry reported to the executive board on September 18, 1952 that he thought the board should insist the company stand by their drilling commitment. Of course, Curry pointed out that the company attorney, being a former assistant solicitor of the department, was probably in cahoots with Myer and Chapman in trying to remove him from tribal contracts. Curry's solution was another delegation to Washington to press the fight there.[237] Curry was also outraged that Crawford, in a letter dated August 6, 1952, had granted all of the companies holding oil leases sixty-day extensions on fulfilling their drilling commitments.[238]

Myer reversed his original opinion about Murphy Oil Company's compliance to drill nine wells based on leases awarded on April 30, 1952, justifying his action with several arguments. First, even if they were legally in the right, the Fort Peck Indians might lose a lawsuit. Second, there was a significant threat that the company might just walk out on the deal. Curry responded that the officials were siding with the Murphy Oil Company and not acting in the best interests of the Fort Peck tribes. When he was asked what he wanted the government to do, Curry suggested the government sue the company to force them to comply with the nine drilling commitments, and that the government bring other forms of pressure to bear upon Murphy Oil as well. Since the extended time of the lease expired at midnight, October 11, 1952, the tribes had to act either to approve the leases or to make the company a counterproposal.[239] Curry sent Wolfsohn copies of all his communications with the executive board so that the Assistant SI would know the precise nature of Curry's representation of the

discussions on September 18.[240] Curry further summarized what he characterized as important facts respecting the Murphy Oil Company leases in a report that could support legal action.[241]

On September 25, Curry wrote SI Chapman, within days of the end of the MOC lease option period, that the tribes wanted the Interior Department to "assume full responsibility for the final disposition of the [Murphy Oil Company] matter." The Tribal Executive Board sent the text of Resolution 3-52 to Curry by telegram, which Curry included in his letter, asking for action from the SI within twenty-four hours of receipt.[242] On October 16, however, Curry was still in the dark as to what Murphy Oil had done about its April 30 leases.[243]

The summer and fall of 1952 were dominated by the national presidential election campaign, and much of what was debated was the "police action" by the United Nations in Korea, with domestic issues taking a backseat. The Republican candidate Dwight D. Eisenhower voiced the terminationist sentiment urging "full justice for all American Indians." This was the same summer and fall that Myer was making his tour to promote termination in the guise of self-rule among Indian reservations. Eisenhower spoke of his admiration for the Indian soldiers he had commanded who had fought so gallantly in World War II. Eisenhower emphasized that Indians were citizens and should not be denied their constitutional rights. But he also "wanted to eliminate the wasteful dollars and energy expended by the BIA, which he claimed obstructed responsibility for improving the conditions of Native Americans." Ike promised programs that would give Indians "equal opportunities for education, health protection, and economic development," and that Indians would have a say in selecting the next CIA.[244]

During the campaign, many of Myer's opponents spoke about the need for a new CIA. Adlai

Stevenson was caught up in speaking about the Korean conflict, and meanwhile, Myer was busy campaigning for "federal withdrawal," and clearly had aspirations of continuing as CIA. Yet Indians who were supporting Eisenhower "did not anticipate any repercussions that might occur from his plan to free them of second-class citizenship." Unfortunately, Stevenson was not able to gain support from many Indians, which simply aided Eisenhower's candidacy, and the Democratic candidate passed up a number of opportunities to present his ideas to Indians.[245]

President Truman, campaigning for the Democratic ticket, came through Montana on a whistle-stop tour on the last day of September 1952:

President Harry Truman, a non-smoker, puffed away on an Indian Peace pipe for a few minutes here on Tuesday before giving his second whistle-stop talk in Montana.

A group of Assiniboine Indians in war-bonnets gathered on the rear platform of Truman's train and offered an Indian peace prayer. Chief First To Fly then lit the peace pipe and passed it to the President.

After the Chief Executive took a few puffs, Rep. Mike Mansfield, who was also on the platform said, "The President doesn't smoke. What he did here was for the first time."[246]

Conservatism was rising among the electorate. Eisenhower won the election and the Republican Party gained control of Congress. Dolly Akers, the day after the election, sent a telegram to Curry, saying that she had heard that the National Republican Committee was forming an Indian Advisory Committee, and she hoped she could be a member. She commented on the outcome of the campaign: "We worked hard and are pleased with Eisenhower Victory. This will rid the Indians of the Chapman plague."[247]

Meanwhile, the relations with the Murphy Oil Company had not yet been sorted out. The additional sale of leases, in which the Murphy Oil Company also bid for parcels on August 19, simply provoked further opposition. Myer rejected these lease bids, but the company protested.

The executive board authorized Curry to reply about Murphy Oil's position of November 24.[248] Curry warned the executive board that it could not legitimately reject the company's bids without there being "firm commitments from another bidder on better terms." Curry asked to evaluate any such offers before decisions were made about them.[249] Curry sent a telegram to William Knorr and Alvin Warrior, dated December 22, 1952, stating that if the executive board wanted additional time to reconsider the Murphy leases on tracts 62, 63, 69, and 70, they must request more time of Superintendent Crawford. In Curry's opinion, the superintendent could withhold repayment of the company's deposit.[250]

In the post-election period, many Indian organizations and reservation political leaders stood ready to advise on the selection of a replacement for Dillon S. Myer. Unfortunately, as the Eisenhower administration sorted out its new appointees, SI Douglas McKay was in no hurry to name a new CIA. Myer's crusade for termination had become the locus of power among congressional committee members on Indian Affairs, sponsoring statutes that were actually determining federal Indian policy, without any concern for the "negative repercussions affecting Indians," so he justified his own demise. Eisenhower's philosophy, endorsed by the electoral mandate, presented an "undaunted devotion to conforming all segments of society into a unified nation verified the federal advocation [sic] of a revitalized, patriotic America." With a vision of a "conservative, nationalistic, and strong American," it was natural to assume that "American Indians were [expected] to become simply Americans."[251] Of course, this coincided with the rise of McCarthyism, which attacked movements or efforts for diversity and alternative means as "Un-American," suspicious, and "disloyal to the United States." As historian Donald Fixico observed, "Simultaneously, public indifference swept Native Americans toward the Eisenhower melting pot in which everyone would be just an American."[252]

In December 1952, the BIA submitted a list to Congress enumerating specific American Indian nations it felt were "ready to undergo . . . complete termination of all federal services" and "an end to the exercise of federal trust responsibility over their affairs." Promoted as a measure to "liberate American Indians tribes from federal domination," the concept of termination was really intended to "do away with tribes [and their] reservation," at least those that had not been amenable to conversion into resource and profit generators for the U.S. economy. Designated by the BIA as being ripe for immediate dissolution were the Nez Percé and Coeur d'Alene, the Osage in Oklahoma, the Menominee in Wisconsin, the Salish and Kootenai (Flathead) in Montana, the Turtle Mountain Anishinabé (Chippewa) in North Dakota, the Six Nations and others in New York, the Potawatomi and other nations in Iowa, the Klamath and other nations in Oregon, and all the nations located within western Washington, Texas, Michigan, Kansas, Nebraska, and Louisiana.

The culmination of this process occurred with the approval of House Concurrent Resolution 108, otherwise known as the "Termination Act," on August 1, 1953. H.C.R. 108 did not itself bring about termination, but called for enactment of specific statutes that would terminate selected Indian nations:

Major [termination] legislation affecting particular [nations] came out of the second session of the Eighty-third Congress in 1954. Among the [nations] involved were the comparatively large and wealth Menominee of Wisconsin and the Klamath of Oregon—both owners of extensive timber resources. Also passed were acts to terminate . . . the Indians of western Oregon, small Paiute bands in Utah, and the mixed bloods of the Uintah and Ouray Reservations. Approved, too, was legislation to transfer administrative responsibility for the Alabama and Coushatta Indians to the state of Texas. . . . Early in the first session of the Eighty-fourth Congress, bills were submitted to [terminate the] Wyandotte, Ottawa, and Peoria [nations] of Oklahoma. These were finally enacted early in August of 1956, a month after passage of legislation directing the Colville Confederated Tribes of Washington to come up with a termination plan of their own. . . . During the second administration of President Dwight D. Eisenhower, Congress enacted only three termination bills relating to specific [nations] or groups. Affected by this legislation were the Choctaw of Oklahoma, for whom the termination process was never completed, the Catawba of South Carolina, and the Indians of the southern California *Rancherias*.

All told, 109 indigenous nations or portions of nations were unilaterally dissolved by congressional action between 1953 and 1958. Concomitantly, Congress passed the earlier-mentioned Public Law 280 in 1954, increasingly placing unterminated reservations under state jurisdictional authority, and, in 1956, Public Law 959, known as the "Relocation Act." The latter corresponded closely to a steadily diminishing congressional allocation of funds for federal obligations to unterminated Indians, which resulted in deterioration of such things as educational and health services (already very poor) on the reservations, spiraling unemployment among reservation Indians (already the highest of any population group), and a net decline in reservation per capita income (already the lowest in North America).

P.L. 959 provided funding to underwrite moving expenses, establishment of a new residence, and a brief period of job training to any Native American willing to relocate "voluntarily" to one or a number of federally approved urban centers. The law led to a sudden mass exodus of Indians from their reserved territories, with some 35,000 being relocated to such places as Los Angeles, San Francisco, Denver, Phoenix, Minneapolis, Seattle, Boston, and Chicago during the years 1957-1959 alone. Despite early (and ongoing) indications that relocation was a disaster, both for the individuals involved and for their respective nations, by 1980 ongoing federal pressure had resulted in the "migration" to cities of slightly over half of all American Indians— about 880,000 of the approximately 1.6 million reflected in the 1980 census. As Oglala Lakota activist Gerald One Feather put it,

The relocation program had an impact on our . . . government at Pine Ridge. Many people who could have provided [our] leadership were lost because they had motivation to go off the reservation to find employment or obtain an education. Relocation drained off a lot of our potential leadership.

It is not that no resistance was mounted to termination and relocation. To the contrary, it was considerable and sustained. The Blackfeet of Montana, for example, acting in consultation with attorney Felix S. Cohen—whom they'd naturalized as a citizen of their nation and who had been a key member of John Collier's Indian Bureau during the formative phases of the IRA— physically occupied their tribal buildings against BIA impoundment and successfully argued on the basis of prior litigation to prevent Myer's policies from being implemented against them. Similarly, the Oglala Lakotas of Pine Ridge—in

a confrontational strategy described by Myers as "Communist inspired"—employed Cohen's advice to bar implementation of BIA termination efforts on their reservation. Despite the fact that Myer came within a hair's breadth of having "A Bill to Authorize the Indian Bureau to Make Arrests without Warrant for Violation of Indian Bureau Regulations" passed in collaboration with reactionary Senator Pat McCarran, these sorts of standoffs continued throughout the 1950s.

More broadly, the Association of American Indian Affairs (AAIA), spearheaded by articulate and determined spokespersons such as Avery Winnemucca (Pyramid Lake Paiute), Popavi Da (San Ildefonso Pueblo), Manual Halcomb (Santa Clara Pueblo), Rufus Wallowing and John Wooden Legs (Northern Cheyenne), William V. Creager (Laguna Pueblo), Thomas Main (Gros Ventre), Norman Hollow (Fort Peck), Servino Martinez and Paul Bernal (Taos Pueblo), and Ben Chief (Oglala Lakota), also in consultation with Cohen, put up a fierce fight centering on concentrated public relations and lobbying efforts. As a defense against further terminations, AAIA avidly enforced IRA colonialism. It was joined in this posture by the National Congress of American Indians (NCAI), headed by Earl Old Person (Blackfeet) and assisted by Cohen's associate and fellow IRA liberal, attorney James E. Curry. This response was effective, at least insofar as by 1958, Interior Secretary Fred Seaton was willing to assert publicly that the Eisenhower administration would no longer support legislation "to terminate tribes without their consent."

The IRA liberals had won, garnering a visible base of support in Indian Country that had been absent during the period of reorganization itself. This was accomplished even while they assisted their more reactionary counterparts in "clearing away much of the dead wood" represented by native nations that had earlier rejected colonial status and engineered reservation demography to allow increased utilization of the native land base by U.S. corporations. In the context of Indian activism that emerged during the 1960s and '70s, some of the worst results of the Eisenhower-era onslaught were rolled back. For instance, after protracted struggles, federal recognition of certain terminated nations, such as the Siletz of Oregon and the Menominee's, was "restored." Still, incalculable damage had been done, not only to those nations actually terminated, but to the willingness of most remaining native governments to challenge federal authority. To reinforce the latter circumstance, H.C.R. 108 was left dangling like a Damoclean sword over Indian national decision-making for another decade, until it was negated, at least in part, by the Indian Civil Rights Act of 1968. Relocation, meanwhile, continued full-force until "the BIA in 1980 finally shut down its urban employment centers."

By the time Eisenhower had appointed Earl Warren Chief Justice of the Supreme Court in 1953, assimilation and integration had come to the fore, as did "an indirect attempt to assimilate Indians into the mainstream by extending civil rights to all minorities." Already the rising movement for civil rights was snowballing to cover the idiosyncratic experience of Indians "to live in coexistence with non-Indians." Fixico observed,

Meanwhile, the Congress and BIA pursued efforts to de-humanize Native Americans and to immerse them in the mainstream society. Such leadership in the federal bureaucracy, in the name of the civil rights issues and assimilation, strove to strip Native American people of their heritage and prepare them for mainstream conversion under the guise of termination. The Eisenhower dream of creating an American of one people enhanced the federal policy to assimilate American Indians, but the reality was a non-receptive mainstream that harboured prejudices against Native Americans and other minorities. Fortunately for Native Americans, Eisenhower took little time to select a replacement for Dillon Myer. Myer was controversial and had perhaps acted too hastily in pushing termination. Now, the newly elected president wanted a man whom Indians could trust—Glenn L. Emmons.[253]

In the end, Eisenhower broke his campaign promise about Indian input in the selection of his CIA. ✪

1 Francis Paul Prucha, *The Great Father: The United States Government and the American Indians*, abr. ed. (Lincoln: University of Nebraska Press, 1986), 340.

2 Ibid.

3 Ibid., 341.

4 Ibid.

5 The class of claims were three-fold and broadly identified: 1) "claim in law or equity under the Constitution, laws, treaties of the United States, and Executive Orders of the President" 2) "between the claimant and the United States were revised on the grounds of fraud, duress, unconscionable consideration, mutual or unilateral mistake"; and a final claim were those "based upon a fair and honorable dealings that are not recognized by any existing rule of law or equity" (quoted by Prucha, *The Great Father*, 341-342).

6 *Indian Land Cessions in the United States*, 18th Annual Report of the Bureau of American Ethnology, 1896-96, Part 2, Charles C. Royce, compiler (Washington, D.C.: Government Printing Office, 1899), 521-997.

7 Prucha, *The Great Father*, 342.

8 Ibid., 343.

9 See Helen Hornbeck Tanner, "Ermine Wheeler-Voegelin (1903-1988), Founder of the American Society for Ethnohistory," *Ethnohistory* 38 (Winter 1991):58-72; and Helen Hornbeck Tanner, University of Detroit Mercy Law Review 76 (1999): 693.

10 Prucha, *The Great Father*, 242-243.

11 George Brown Tindall and David E. Shi, *America: A Narrative History*, 4th. ed. (New York: W.W. Norton & Company, 1996), 1292-1293.

12 Quoted in Prucha, *The Great Father*, 343.

13 Ibid.

14 Ibid.

15 Quoted in Prucha, *The Great Father*, 344.

16 Ibid.

17 Prucha, *The Great Father*, 344.

18 See the lists in Table 1, John Collier's Withdrawal Recommendations, and Table 2, William Zimmerman's Withdrawal Recommendation, Kenneth R. Philp, *Termination Revisited: American Indians on the Trail to Self-Determination, 1933-1953* (Lincoln: University of Nebraska Press, 1999), 72-75.

19 Quoted in Prucha, *The Great Father*, 344; see Richard Drinnon, *Keeper of Concentration Camps: Dillon S. Myer and American Racism* (Berkeley: University of California Press, 1987), 163-172, for more details of the program Myer was expected to implement.

20 Prucha, *The Great Father*, 344-345.

21 Ibid., 345.

22 Ibid.

23 Ibid.

24 Compilation of Materials Relating to the Indians of the United States and the Territory of Alaska, Including Certain Laws and Treaties Affecting Such Indians, Subcommittee on Indian Affairs of the Committee on Public Lands, U.S. House of Representatives, Toby Morris, Subcommittee Chair, Making Study of Problems in Connection with the Public Lands of the United States Pursuant to H. Res. 66 (81st Congress, 2nd Session), 13 June 1950, 742-743, Chrono File, General History 1939-1959, Docket 184 Collection, Fort Peck Tribal Archives, Poplar, Montana.

25 Ibid., 742-743.

26 Ibid., 742.

27 Ibid., 743.

28 Arnold H. Olsen, Attorney General of Montana, "Taxation-Automobiles-Indians-Crow Indian Reservation-Leases-Trust Patented Lands," May 10, 1949, Volume 23, Opinion No. 302, copy in Curry Papers, Folder 1A-1949, Box 89, Archives—National Museum of the American Indian, Smithsonian Institution, Suitland, Maryland [hereinafter "Curry Papers"].

29 Minutes, General Council, September 17, 1949, Curry Papers, Folder #1, File 1949, Box 89.

30 Curry, Washington, D.C., to James Archdale, Poplar, Montana, September 30, 1949, and sample contracts, Curry Papers, Folder #1, File 1949, Box 89.

31 Archdale, Poplar, Montana, to Curry, Washington, D.C., October 31, 1949, Curry Papers, Folder #1, File 1949, Box 89.

32 Superintendent Diehl, Fort Peck Agency, Poplar, Montana (hereinafter cited as "FPA"), to Curry, Washington, D.C., 2 November 1949, Curry Papers, Folder #1, File 1949, Box 89.

33 Curry, Washington, D.C., to Archdale, Poplar, Montana, 4 November 1949, Curry Papers, Folder #1, File 1949, Box 89.

34 William Zimmerman, Jr., Asstistant CIA, Bureau of Indian Affairs (hereinafter cited as "BIA"), Washington, D.C., to Diehl, FPA, November 15, 1949, Curry Papers, Folder #1, File 1949, Box 89.

35 Diehl, FPA, to Curry, Washington, D.C., December 5, 1949, Curry Papers, Folder #1, File 1949, Box 89.

36 Curry, Washington, D.C., to Diehl, FPA, December 6, 1949, Curry Papers, Folder #1, File 1949, Box 89.

37 Curry, Washington, D.C., to Diehl, FPA, December 6, 1949, Curry Papers, Folder #1, File 1949, Box 89.

38 Newspaper announcement of the sale, December 10, 1949, Curry Papers, Folder #1, File 1949, Box 89.

39 Resolution, Fort Peck Tribes Executive Board, December 10, 1949, Curry Papers, Folder #1, File 1949, Box 89.

40 Diehl, FPA, to Curry, Washington, D.C., December 29, 1949, and "Statement of Services Rendered to the Fort Peck Tribe, September, 1949 to Date of Appeal," 17 September 1949 to 28 September 1950, Curry Papers, Folder #1, File 1949, Box 89.

41 Curry, Washington, D.C., to Archdale, Poplar, Montana, December 26, 1949, Curry Papers, Folder #1, File 1949, Box 89.

42 I.S. Weissbrodt to Curry, "Claims of Indians of the Fort Peck Indian Reservation," February 1, 1950, Curry Papers, Folder #2, File 1950 January-Feb, Box 89.

43 Diehl, FPA, to CIA, Washington, D.C., February 13, 1950, Curry Papers, Folder #2, File 1950 January-Feb, Box 89.

44 "Statement of Services, Sept. 1949 to Date of Appeal," Curry Papers, Folder #1, File 1949, Box 89.

45 Ted Haas, Interior Solicitor, BIA, Washington, D.C., to Howard Trinder, Tribal Executive Board and President, American Indians of Montana, Poplar, Montana, January 26, 1950, Curry Papers, Folder #2, File 1950 Jan.-Feb., Box 89.

46 Francis L. Horn, memorandum to Curry, "Taxability of Personal Property on Indian Reservations," not dated, Curry Papers, Folder #2, File 1950 Jan.-Feb., Box 89.

47 Grog Schoman, Commissioner of Internal Revenue, Washington, D.C., to Congressman Mike Mansfield, Washington, D.C., January 25, 1950, Curry Papers, Folder #2, File 1950 Jan.-Feb., Box 89.

48 Paul L. Fickinger, Area Director, Billings Area Office, Billings, Montana, to Curry, Washington, D.C., February 27, 1950, Curry Papers, Folder #2, File 1950 Jan.-Feb., Box 89.

49 Ibid.

50 Fickinger to Zimmerman, Washington, D.C., February 21, 1950, Curry Papers, Folder #2, File 1950 Jan.-Feb., Box 89.

51 Diehl, FPA, to Curry, Washington, D.C., March 6, 1950, Curry Papers, Folder #2, File 1950 Jan.-Feb., Box 89.

52 Curry, Washington, D.C., to Diehl, FPA, March 30, 1950, Curry Papers, Folder #2, File 1950 Jan.-Feb., Box 89.

53 Horn, Curry Office, Washington, D.C., to Chairman David Buckles, Fort Peck Tribal Executive Board, Poplar, Montana, March 7, 1950, Curry Papers, Folder #2, File 1950 Jan.-Feb., Box 89.

54 See the Curry-Bayuk correspondence in the Curry Papers, Fort Peck Folders.

55 Curry, Washington, D.C., to Buckles, Fort Peck Tribal Executive Board, Poplar, Montana, March 24, 1950, Curry Papers, Folder #2, File 1950 Jan.-Feb., Box 89.

56 Minutes, Executive Board, Special Meeting, March 23, 1950, Curry Papers, Box 89, Folder #3 Mar-April 1950; the collection of minutes in the Curry Papers is incomplete for this period.

57 Minutes, Executive Board, April 13, 1950, Curry Papers, Box 89, Folder #3, Mar.-Apr. 1950.

58 Oscar Chapman, IS, Washington, D.C., to Speaker of the House of Representatives, Washington, D.C., April 21, 1950, Curry Papers, Box 89, Folder #3, Mar-April 1950.

59 Fort Peck Executive Resolution 10-50, April 10, 1950, Curry Papers, Box 89, File #3, Mar.-Apr. 1950.

60 Buckles, Tribal Council, Poplar, Montana, to Senator Carl Hayden, Washington, D.C., May 18, 1950, Curry Papers, Box 89, File #4, May-July 1950.

61 "Joint Meeting of Indian Delegates and their Senators and Representatives From the States of Montana, Nebraska, North Dakota, and South Dakota," with signature lines for Edwin Red Door and Rufus Ricker, May 10, 1950, Curry Papers, Box 89, File #4, May-July 1950.

62 Curry, Washington, D.C., to Buckles, Poplar, Montana, May 13, 1950, Curry Papers, Box 89, Folder #4, May-July 1950.

63 Buckles, Poplar, Montana, to Curry, Washington, D.C., May 18, 1950, Curry Papers, Box 89, Folder #4, May-July 1950.

64 Curry, Washington, D.C., to Buckles, Poplar, Montana, May 20, 1950, Curry Papers, Box 89, Folder #4, May-July 1950.

65 Minutes, Executive Board, May 11, 1950, Curry Papers, Box 89, Folder #4, May-July 1950.

66 Curry, Washington, D.C., to Diehl, FPA, May 27, 1950, Curry Papers, Box 89, Folder #4, May-July 1950.

67 Curry, Washington, D.C., to Bayuk, Wolf Point, Montana, May 27, 1950, Curry Papers, Box 89, Folder #4, May-July 1950.

68 Minutes, Special Meeting, Executive Board, May 31, 1950, Curry Papers, Box 89, Folder #4, May-July 1950.

69 Dillon Myer, CIA, Washington, D.C., to Edwin Reddoor and Rufus Ricker, Poplar, Montana, through Superintendent, FPA, June 7, 1950, Curry Papers, Box 89, Folder #4, May-July 1950.

70 Minutes, Executive Board, June 8, 1950, Curry Papers, Box 89, Folder #4, May-July 1950.

71 Ibid.

72 See folders "Attorneys' Contracts: Indians Rights to Counsel, 1950-1954," National Congress of American Indians (NCAI) Papers, Archives NMAI-SI, Suitland, Maryland

73 Bayuk, Poplar, Montana, to Curry, Washington, D.C., June 6, 1950, Curry Papers, Box 89, Folder #4, May-July 1950.

74 Curry, Washington, D.C., to Myer, Washington, D.C., June 8, 1950, Curry Papers, Box 89, Folder #4, May-July 1950.

75 Curry, Washington, D.C., to Bayuk, Wolf Point, Montana, June 11, 1950, Curry Papers, Box 89, Folder #4, May-July 1950.

76 Ibid.

77 Summary of Activities of the Tribal Executive Board, January 1, 1950 to June 30, 1950, prepared by Alvin Warrior, Secretary, Curry Papers, Box 89, Folder #4, May-July 1950.

78 Ibid.

79 Ibid.

80 Ibid.

81 Ibid.

82 Myer, Memo to BIA Officials and Tribal Councils, Order No. 556, August 8, 1950, Curry Papers, Box 89, Folder #5, Aug-Oct 1950.

83 Curry, Washington, D.C., to Buckles, Poplar, Montana, September 9, 1950, Curry Papers, Box 89, Folder #5, Aug-Oct 1950.

84 Ibid.

85 Ibid.

86 Buckles, Poplar, Montana, to Curry, Washington, D.C., September 15, 1950, Curry Papers, Box 89, Folder #5, Aug-Oct 1950.

87 Curry, Washington, D.C., to Harold L. Ickes, Washington, D.C., and attached draft brief and list of exhibits, October 16, 1950, Curry Papers, Box 89, folder #5, Aug-Oct 1950.

88 "Statement of Services Rendered to the Fort Peck Tribe, September, 1949 to Date of Appeal," September 17, 1949 to September 26, 1950, included in the appeal exhibits, Curry Papers, Box 90, Folder #1, Nov-Dec 1950.

89 Draft Appeal Brief, 29, attached to correspondence, Curry to Ickes, 16 October 1950, Curry Papers, Box 89, Folder #5, Aug-Oct 1950.

90 "Before the Secretary of the Interior of the United States, Appeal, In the Matter of Two Contracts for Legal Services Between James E. Curry and the Fort Peck Indians (Abridged copy without exhibits)," November 17, 1950, Curry Papers, Box 90, Folder #1, Nov-Dec 1950.

91 Statement of Chairman William C. Knorr, January 4, 1951 [before a hearing before the SI, Washington, D.C.], Report of Delegation of Fort Peck Indians, January 2 to January 15, 1951, 35-38, Curry Papers, Box 90, Folder #4, January-February 1951.

92 Statement of Mrs. Dolly Akers, January 4, 1951 [before a hearing before the SI, Washington, D.C.], Report of Delegation of Fort Peck Indians, January 2 to January 15, 1951, 39, Curry Papers, Box 90, Folder #4, January-February 1951.

93 Report of Delegation of Fort Peck Indians, January 2 to January 15, 1951, 35-38, Curry Papers, Box 90, Folder #4, January-February 1951.

94 T.H. Watkins, Righteous Pilgrim: The Life and Times of Harold L. Ickes, 1874-1952 (New York: Henry Holt, 1990), 854.

95 Statement of Ickes, January 4, 1951 [before a hearing before the SI, Washington, D.C.], Report of Delegation of Fort Peck Indians, January 2 to January 15, 1951, 35-38, Curry Papers, Box 90, Folder #4, January-February 1951.

96 The record of the other groups that also testified and the gist of their sentiments appears in the Report of Delegation of Fort Peck Indians, January 2 to January 15, 1951, 4, Curry Papers, Box 90, Folder #4, January-February 1951; Ickes' statement is on pp. 35-38.

97 Report of Delegation of Fort Peck Indians, January 2 to January 15, 1951, Curry Papers, Box 90, folder #2, January-March 1951.

98 "The Assiniboine and Sioux Tribes of the Fort Peck Indian Reservation, Montana," press release for the afternoon papers, January 9, 1951, Curry Papers, Box 90, Folder 2, January-March 1951.

99 Report of Delegation of Fort Peck Indians, January 2 to January 15, 1951, 2, 12, 14-16, Curry Papers, Box 90, folder #2, January-March 1951.

100 Ibid., 16-17.

101 Ibid., 17.

102 Ibid., 19.

103 Ibid.

104 Ibid., 6-11.

105 Ibid.

106 Myer, Washington, D.C., to John W. Johnson, Acting Superient, FPA, January 30, 1951, Curry Papers, Box 90, Folder #2, January-March 1951.

107 Curry, Washington, D.C., to Bayuk, Poplar, Montana, February 8, 1951, Curry Papers, Box 90, Folder #2, January-March 1951.

108 Buckles, Fort Peck Tribal Executive Board, Poplar, Montana, to Chapman, Washington, D.C., February 9, 1951, Curry Papers, Box 90, Folder #2, January-March 1951.

109 W.H. Flanery, Office of the Solicitor, Department of Interior, Washington, D.C., to Curry, Washington, D.C., February 13, 1951, Curry Papers, Box 90, Folder #2, January-March 1951.

110 Curry, Washington, D.C., to Fort Peck Tribal Executive Board, Poplar, Montana, March 8, 1951, Curry Papers, Box 90, Folder #2, January-March 1951.

111 Curry, Washington, D.C., to Congressman Wesley A. D'Ewart, Washington, D.C., March 14, 1951, Curry Papers, Box 90, Folder #2, January-March 1951.

112 Curry, Washington, D.C., to Ickes, Washington, D.C., March 20, 1951, Curry Papers, Box 90, Folder #2, January-March 1951.

113 Curry, Washington, D.C., to "Dear Friend," March 26, 1951, Curry Papers, Box 90, Folder #2, January-March 1951.

114 Bayuk, Poplar, Montana, to Curry, Washington, D.C., March 28, 1951, Curry Papers, Box 90, Folder #2, January-March 1951.

115 Curry, Washington, D.C., to Bayuk, Poplar, Montana, March 30, 1951, Curry Papers, Box 90, Folder #2, January-March 1951.

116 Bayuk, Poplar, Montana, to James E. Curry, Washington, D.C., April 2, 1951, and Resolution, Fort Peck Tribal Executive Board, 2 April 1951, Curry Papers, Box 90, Folder #3, Apr-May 1951.

117 Archdale, Poplar, Montana, to Curry, Washington, D.C., April 3, 1951, Curry Papers, Box 90, Folder #3, Apr-May 1951.

118 Buckles, Poplar, Montana, to Curry, Washington, D.C., April 5, 1951, Curry Papers, Box 90, Folder #3, Apr-May 1951.

119 Buckles, Poplar, Montana, to Chapman, Washington, D.C., April 5, 1951, Curry Papers, Box 90, Folder #3, Apr-May 1951.

120 Mastin G. White, Acting Assistant SI, Washington, D.C., to Curry, Washington, D.C., May 17, 1951, Curry Papers, Box 90, Folder #4, Apr-May 1951.

121 Horn, Washington, D.C., to William R. Smith, Oswego, Montana, June 8, 1951, Curry Papers, Box 90, Folder #5, June-July 1951.

122 Eva May Smith, Wolf Point, Montana, to Mrs. Bronson, Washington, D.C., 15 June 1951, Curry Papers, Box 90, Folder #5, June-July 1951.

123 Curry, Washington, D.C., to Chapman, Washington, D.C., July 9, 1951, Curry Papers, Box 90, Folder #5, June-July 1951.

124 Ibid.

125 Dolly C. Akers, Wolf Point, Montana, to Senator James E. Murray, Washington, D.C., July 19, 1951, Curry Papers, Box 90, Folder #5, June-July 1951.

126 Ackers and William Knorr, Chairman, Tribal Executive Board, Wolf Point, Montana, to Curry, Washington, D.C., July 19, 1951, Curry Papers, Box 90, Folder #5, June-July 1951.

127 Archdale, Poplar, Montana, to Curry, St. Paul, Minnesota, July 23, 1951, Curry Papers, Box 90, Folder #5, June-July 1951.

128 Horn, Washington, D.C., to Knorr and Akers, Wolf Point, Montana, July 24, 1951, Curry Papers, Box 90, Folder #5, June-July 1951.

129 Archdale, Poplar, Montana, to Curry, Washington, D.C., July 28, 1951, Curry Papers, Box 90, Folder #5, June-July 1951.

130 "Accounting Petition," Fort Peck Indians of the Fort Peck Reservation Montana, Petitioner, v. The United States of America, Respondent, and "Petition" [Disposal of Surplus Lands], Fort Peck Indians of the Fort Peck Reservation, Montana, Petitioner, v. The United States of America, Respondent, Curry Papers, Box 90, Folder #5, June-July 1951.

131 M. Rex Lee, Acting CIA, Washington, D.C., to Curry, Washington, D.C., July 27, 1951, Curry Papers, Box 90, Folder #5, June-July 1951.

132 Fort Peck Tribal Executive Board, memo from Curry, Washington, D.C., August 3, 1951, Curry Papers, Box 90, Folder #6, Aug-Sept 1951.

133 W.C. Knorr, telegram to Chapman, and Knorr, telegram to Senator James E. Murray, both dated August 9, 1951, Curry Papers, Box 90, Folder #6, Aug-Sept 1951.

134 Curry, Washington, D.C., to Myer, Washington, D.C., 12 August 1951, Curry Papers, Box 90, Folder #6, Aug-Sept 1951.

135 Curry, Washington, D.C., memo to NCAI Officers and Committeemen, "Disclosure of Official Documents," August 12, 1951, Curry Papers, Box 90, Folder #6, Aug-Sept 1951.

136 Curry, Washington, D.C., to Knorr, Wolf Point, Montana, August 17, 1951, Curry Papers, Box 90, Folder #6, Aug-Sept 1951.

137 Myer, Washington, D.C., to Curry, Washington, D.C., August 20, 1951, Curry Papers, Box 90, Folder #6, Aug-Sept 1951.

138 Knorr, Poplar, Montana, to Curry, Washington, D.C., August 30, 1951, Curry Papers, Box 90, Folder #6, Aug-Sept 1951.

139 Ibid.

140 Bayuk, Poplar, Montana, to Curry, Washington, D.C., September 2, 1951,

Curry Papers, Box 90, Folder #6, Aug-Sept 1951.

141 Curry, Washington, D.C., to Knorr, Wolf Point, Montana, and Curry, Washington, D.C., to Superintendent James C. Crawford, FPA, Poplar, Montana, both dated September 5, 1951, Curry Papers, Box 90, Folder #6, Aug-Sept 1951.

142 Ickes, Southwest Harbor, Maine, to Chapman, Washington, D.C., September 14, 1951, Curry Papers, Box 90, Folder #6, Aug-Sept 1951.

143 Akers, Wolf Point, Montana, to Curry, Washington, D.C., September 17, 1951, Curry Papers, Box 90, Folder #6, Aug-Sept 1951.

144 Curry, Washington, D.C., to Akers, Wolf Point, Montana, October 6, 1951, Curry Papers, Box 90, Folder #6, Aug-Sept 1951.

145 Ibid.

146 Minutes, Special meeting of the Executive Board, October 20, 1951, Curry Papers, Box 90, Folder #7, Oct-Dec 1951.

147 Ibid.

148 Akers, Wolf Point, Montana, to Curry, Washington, D.C., October 26, 1951, Curry Papers, Box 90, Folder #7, Oct-Dec 1951.

149 Myer, CIA, Washington, D.C., to Knorr, Wolf Point, Montana, November 2, 1951, Curry Papers, Box 90, Folder #7, Oct-Dec 1951.

150 Resolution No. 8, Fort Peck Executive Board, November 8, 1951, Curry Papers, Box 90, Folder #7.

151 Archdale, Poplar, Montana, to Curry, Washington, D.C., November 26, 1951, Curry Papers, Box 90, Folder #7, Oct-Dec 1951.

152 Knorr, Helena, MT, to Fickinger, Area Director, Billings, Montana, December 10 1951, Curry Papers, Box 90, Folder #7, Oct-Dec 1951.

153 Minutes, General Council, December 22, 1951, Curry Papers, Box 90, Folder #7, Oct-Dec 1951.

154 Resolution, General Council, 23 December 1951, Curry Papers, Box 90, Folder #7, Oct-Dec 1951.

155 Doty, Washington, D.C., to Knorr, Poplar, Montana, January 9, 1952, Curry Papers, Box 91, Folder #1, January 1-11, 1952.

156 Report of the Delegation of Fort Peck Indians, January 2 to January 15, 1952, Curry Papers, Box 91, Folder #2, January 12-31, 1952.

157 "Conference between the CIA and a Delegation of Indians from the Fort Peck Reservation," Interior Department, transcript, January 10, 1952, Curry Papers, Box 91, Folder #1, January 1-11, 1952.

158 Report of Delegation of the Fort Peck Indians, January 2 to January 15, 1952, Curry Papers, Box 91, Folder #2, January 12-31, 1952.

159 Buckles, Poplar, Montana, to Curry, Washington, D.C., January 12, 1952, Curry Papers, Box 91, Folder #2, January 12-31, 1952.

160 Myer, Washington, D.C., to Hale Power, Legislative Counsel, Division of Land Utilization, Office of Assistant SI Doty, Washington, D.C., January 15, 1952, Curry Papers, Box 91, Folder #2, January 12-31, 1952.

161 Doty, Washington, D.C., to Knorr, Poplar, Montana, January 18, 1951, Curry Papers, Box 91, Folder #2, January 12-31 1952.

162 Akers, Roger Smith Hotel, Washington, D.C., to Doty, Washington, D.C., January 20, 1952, Curry Papers, Box 91, Folder #2, January 12-31 1952.

163 Akers, Washington, D.C., telegram to Knorr, Wolf Point, Montana, January 19, 1952, Curry Papers, Box 91, Folder #2, January 12-31 1952.

164 Bayuk, Poplar, Montana, to Curry, Washington, D.C., January 25, 1952, Curry Papers, Box 91, Folder #2, January 12-31 1952.

165 Edwin J. Reddoor, Poplar, Montana, to Curry, Washington, D.C., January 31, 1952, Curry Papers, Box 91, Folder #2, January 12-31 1952.

166 Untitled note, February 1, 1952, Curry Papers, Box 91, Folder #3, 1-16 February 1952.

167 Akers, Washington, D.C., to Congressman B. Jensen, Washington, D.C., February 5, 1952, Curry Papers, Box 91, Folder #3, Feb. 1-16 1952.

168 Minutes, Special Meeting Executive Board, February 5, 1952, Curry Papers, Box 91, Folder #3, 1-16 Feb. 1952.

169 Ibid.

170 Ibid.

171 Ibid.

172 Ibid.

173 Ibid.

174 Ibid.

175 Ibid.

176 Ibid.

177 Ibid.

178 Curry, Washington, D.C., to Bayuk, Poplar, Montana, February 9, 1952, Curry Papers, Box 91, Folder #3, 1-16 February 1952.

179 Curry, Washington, D.C., to Buckles, Vice Chair, Tribal Executive Board, Poplar, Montana, February 11, 1952, Curry Papers, Box 91, Folder #3, 1-16 February 1952.

180 Curry, Washington, D.C., to Bayuk, Poplar, Montana, February 11, 1952, Curry Papers, Box 91, Folder #3, 1-16 February 1952.

181 Bayuk, Poplar, Montana, to Curry, Washington, D.C., February 15, 1952, Curry Papers, Box 91, Folder #3, 1-16 February 1952.

182 Curry, Washington, D.C., to Bayuk, Poplar, Montana, February 21, 1952, Curry Papers, Box 91, Folder #4, 17-29 February 1952.

183 Fort Peck Tribal Members, announcement by Fort Peck Tribal Council, February 15, 1952, Curry Papers, Box 91, Folder #3, 1-16 February 1952.

184 Akers, Wolf Point, Montana, to Curry, Washington, D.C., February 21, 1952, Curry Papers, Box 91, Folder #4, 17-29 February 1952.

185 Curry, Washington, D.C., to Rex Lee, Asso. CIA, Washington, D.C., February 23, 1952, Curry Papers, Box 91, Folder #4, 17-29 February 1952.

186 Knorr and Akers, Wolf Point, Montana, to Curry, Washington, D.C., February 29, 1952, Curry Papers, Box 91, Folder #4, 17-29 February 1952.

187 Minutes, General Council, March 1, 1952, Curry Papers, Box 91, Folder #5, 1-12 March 1952.

188 Ibid., 2.

189 Ibid., 4.

190 Ibid., 4-5.

191 Ibid., 5.

192 "Murphy Expects to Complete Well This Week . . . ," *Poplar Progressive*, March 6, 1952, Curry Papers, Box 91, Folder #5, 1-12 March 1952.

193 Akers, Wolf Point, Montana, to Murray, Washington, D.C., March 10, 1952, Curry Papers, Box 91, Folder #5, 1-12 March 1952.

194 Akers, Wolf Point, Montana, to Senator Zales N. Ecton, Washington, D.C., March 14, 1952, Curry Papers, Box 91, Folder #6, 13-20 March 1952.

195 Minutes, Special Meeting Executive Board, March 20, 1952, Curry Papers, Box 91, Folder #6, 13-20 March 1952.

196 Chapman, SI, Washington, D.C., to Curry, Washington, D.C., March 21, 1952, Curry Papers, Box 91, Folder #7, 21-31 March 1952.

197 Excerpt from Testimony of Carl Whitman, Hearing, Senate Committee on Interior and Insular Affairs, March 24, 1952, Curry Papers, Box 91, Folder #7, 21-31 March 1952.

198 Akers, Wolf Point, Montana, to Murray, Washington, D.C., March 24, 1952, Curry Papers, Box 91, Folder #7, 21-31 March 1952.

199 Resolution of Fort Peck General Council, March 29, 1952, Curry Papers, Box 91, Folder #7, 21-31 March 1952.

200 Resolution of the Fort Peck Tribal Executive Board, March 31, 1952, Curry Papers, Box 91, Folder #7, 21-31 March 1952.

201 Curry letters to Senators Murray and Ecton, and Congressman Wesley D'Ewart, April 2, 1952, Curry Papers, Box 91, Folder #8, 1-13 April 1952.

202 "Statement by Senator Zales Ecton on Attorney Contracts," April 4, 1952, Curry Papers, Box 91, Folder #8, 1-13 April 1952.

203 Curry, memo to Fort Peck Executive Board, April 15, 1952, Curry Papers, Box 91, Folder #9, 14-30 April 1952.

204 Curry, Washington, D.C., to D'Ewart, Washington, D.C., April 15, 1952, Curry Papers, Box 91, Folder #9, 14-30 April 1952.

205 Curry, Washington, D.C., to CIA, Washington, D.C., April 15, 1952, Curry Papers, Box 91, Folder #9, 14-30 April 1952.

206 "Oil Interest in Montana Section of Williston Basin is Given Added Stimulation by Discovery, Helena Independent-Record, April 18, 1952, Curry Papers, Box 91, 14-30 April 1952.

207 See Bid Sale Summaries, dated April 30, 1952, Curry Papers, Box 91, Folder #9, 14-30 April 1952.

208 Akers, Wolf Point, Montana, to Curry, Washington, D.C., May 3, 1952, Curry Papers, Box 92, Folder #1, 1-19 May 1952.

209 Curry, Washington, D.C., memorandum to Fort Peck Tribal Executive Board, Poplar, Montana, May 4, 1952, Curry Papers, Box 92, Folder #1, 1-19 May 1952.

210 Tindall and Shi, America: A Narrative History.

211 Fickinger, Billings Area Director, Billings, Montana, memorandum to Superintendents and Tribal Councils, Billings Area, May 9, 1951, Curry Papers, Box 92, Folder #1, 1-19 May April 1952.

212 See Paula Wagner's recent study, "They Treated Us Just Like Indians": The Worlds of Bennett County, South Dakota (Lincoln: University of Nebraska Press, 2002).

213 "Fort Peck Indians Oil Tracts Joined to Larger Acreages," June 3, 1952, Curry Papers, Box 92, Folder #3, June 1952.

214 Minutes, Special Meeting Executive Board, July 21, 1952, Curry Papers, Box 92, Folder #4, July 1952.

215 "Statement of William Knorr, Chairman of the Executive Board of the Fort Peck Indians," 23 July 1952, Curry Papers, Box 92, Folder #4, July 1952..

216 Curry, Washington, D.C., to Myer, Washington, D.C., July 30, 1952, Curry Papers, Box 92, Folder #4, July 1952.

217 "Notice of Sale, No. 9," filed under date July 31, 1952, Curry Papers, Box 92, Folder #4, July 1952; "Notice No. 12, Sale of Oil and Gas Mining Leases, Tribal and Allotted Indian Lands," August 19, 1952, Curry Papers, Box 93, Folder #1, 1-20 August 1952.

218 "Sioux need Self-Rule, Analyst Says," July 3, 1932, Curry Papers, Box 92, Folder #4, July 1952.

219 Curry, Washington, D.C., to Fred L. Kirgis, Attorney for Murphy Oil Company, Denver, Coloradolorado, August 1, 1952, Curry Papers, Box 93, Folder #1, 1-20 August 1952; Crawford, Poplar, Montana, to Curry, Washington, D.C., August 1, 1952, with attachment, language of drilling commitments in previous bid tenders, Curry Papers, Box 93, Folder #1, 1-20 August 1952; and Curry, Washington, D.C., to Myer, Washington, D.C., August 6, 1952, detailed case with attachments for enforcement of the drilling commitments of lessees, Curry Papers, Box 93, Folder #1, 1-20 August 1952.

220 Curry, Denver, Coloradolorado, memorandum to Special Oil Lease Committee and the Tribal Executive Board, August 6, 1952, Curry Papers, Box 93, Folder #1, 1-20 August 1952,

221 Myer, Washington, D.C., to Chairman, Fort Peck Tribal Council, through Superintendent, FPA, August 12, 1952, Curry Papers, Box 93, Folder #1, 1-20 August 1952.

222 Crawford, Poplar, Montana, to Murphy Corporation, Denver, Colorado, August 12, 1952, Curry Papers, Box 93, Folder #1, 1-20 August 1952.

223 "'Justice' for Indians Comes High," Washington Merry-Go-Round, Drew Pearson, Washington Post, August 14, 1952, Curry Papers, Box 93, 17-31 September 1952.

224 Curry, Washington, D.C., form-letter— "To the Editor," August 18, 1952, Curry Papers, Box 93, Folder #1, 1-20 August 1952.

225 Curry, Washington, D.C., memorandum to Tribal Executive Board, August 18, 1952, Curry Papers, Box 93, Folder #1, 1-20 August 1952.

226 Minutes, Fort Peck Tribal Executive Board, August 21, 1952, Curry Papers, Box 93, 21-31 August 1952.

227 Ibid.

228 Ibid.

229 Kenneth R. Philp, John Collier's Crusade for Indian Reform, 1920-1954 (Tucson: University of Arizona Press, 1971), 153-154; 158.

230 Ibid.), 154.

231 Minutes, Fort Peck Tribal Executive Board, 21 August 1952, Curry Papers, Box 93, 21-31 August 1952.

232 Ibid.

233 "Murphy to Drill Nine New Wells in Area; Celebration Brings Disclosure Poplar Oil Field Enlargement Plains . . . ," The News Herald [Wolf Point, Montana], September 4, 1952, v. 39, n. 34, 1, Curry Papers, Box 93, 1-16 September 1952; Akers, Wolf Point, Montana, to Curry, Washington, D.C., September 1, 1952, Curry Papers, Box 93, 1-16 September 1952.

234 Indenture, "Resignation of Unit Operator . . . ," August 7, 1952, Curry Papers, Box 93, 1-16 September 1952.

235 Curry, Washington, D.C., to Fred Taylor, District Landsman, Murphy Oil Company, Denver, Colorado, 17 September 1952, Curry Papers, Box 93, 17-31 September 1952.

236 Curry, Washington, D.C., to Myer, CIA, Washington, D.C., September 17, 1952, Curry Papers, Box 93, 17-31 September 1952.

237 Curry, Washington, D.C., to Fort Peck Tribal Executive Board, Poplar, Montana, September 18, 1952, Box 93, 17-31 September 1952, Curry Papers, Box 93, 17-31 September 1952.

238 Curry, Washington, D.C., to Crawford, Poplar, Montana, September 18, 1952, Curry Papers, Box 93, 17-31 September 1952.

239 Curry, Washington, D.C., to Fort Peck Tribal Executive Board and the Special Oil Lease Committee of the Board, Poplar, Montana, September 20, 1952, Curry Papers, Box 93, 17-31 September 1952.

240 Curry, Washington, D.C., to Joel Wolfsohn, Assistant SI, Washington, D.C., September 20, 1952, Curry Papers, Box 93, 17-31 September 1952.

241 Curry, Washington, D.C., to Special Oil Lease Committee, Fort Peck Tribal Executive Board, Poplar, Montana, September 21, 1952, Curry Papers, Box 93, 17-31 September 1952.

242 Curry, Washington, D.C., to Chapman, Washington, D.C., September 25, 1952, Curry Papers, Box 93, 17-31 September 1952.

243 Curry, Washington, D.C., to Knorr, Wolf Point, Montana, telegram, October 16, 1952, Curry Papers, Box 94, 16-31 October 1952.

244 Donald L. Fixico, Termination and Relocation: Federal Indian Policy, 1945-1960 (Albuquerque: University of New Mexico Press, 1986), 69-71.

245 Ibid.

246 "Indians Give President 'First Smoke,'" Great Falls Tribune, Vol. 66, No. 139, October 1, 1952, 1, 4; Curry Papers, Box 94, 1-15 October 1952.

247 Akers, Wolf Point, Montana, to Curry, Washington, D.C., telegram, November 5, 1952, Curry Papers, Box 94, November 1952.

248 Knorr, Wolf Point, Montana, to Washington, D.C., telegram, December 5, 1952, Curry Papers, Box 94, December 1952.

249 Curry, Washington, D.C., to Knorr, Wolf Point, Montana, December 17, 1952, Curry Papers, Box 94, December 1952.

250 Curry, Washington, D.C., to Knorr or Alvin Warrior, Poplar, Montana, telegram, December 22, 1952, Curry Papers, Box 94, December 1952.

251 Fixico, Termination and Relocation, 75-77.

252 Ibid., 77.

253 Ibid.

~

CHAPTER 13

Indian Policy during the Eisenhower Administration and the Crises of Authority Leading to the New Fort Peck Constitution, 1953-1960

David R. Miller, Ph.D.

Aconstitutional crisis had been building on Fort Peck for some time. The ease by which small factions could seize control of General Council meetings had led to many detrimental developments. The political culture of the tribes needed renewal, revitalization, and restabilization. The Interior Department and BIA had grown weary of complaints from so many quarters within the Fort Peck tribes, and frustrated by what appeared to be significant waste of resources. While the march to constitutional reform was imprecise, a new constitution was ratified in time for a period of new programs and new funding in the 1960s. Stability in legal representation remained an issue throughout this period.

A General Council convened at Fort Peck on January 3, 1953, and a resolution was adopted to allow voting by secret ballot rather than by asking voters to stand and be counted in an assembly. The purpose of the council was to select delegates to go to Washington.[1] However, resolutions that should have been prepared in advance of the General Council were incomplete, and the assembled council balked at choosing a delegation until the resolutions were ready.[2]

James E. Curry's ability to advise the Tribal Executive Board was increasingly hamstrung by the CIA's refusal to approve his general counsel contract. Consequently, Curry could not visit Fort Peck during the fall of 1952. Confusions arising from miscommunications were evident in Norman Hollow's questions to Curry about why he had turned the conflict about the Murphy Oil Company over to the CIA prior to its October 11 expiration. What would be the consequences if the CIA made decisions unfavorable to the will of the Fort Peck leaders?

Curry wrote the Tribal Executive Board on January 29, 1953, explaining the difficulties he was experiencing because the "old" CIA and "old" SI had embargoed his legal contracts, including his representation of the Fort Peck tribes. This prevented him from hiring other lawyers to assist with his work, and suspended his collection of fees and expenses. It also prevented him from "holding the Government responsible for the mishandling of the April oil leases at Fort Peck and from exposing the scandalous conduct of Indian Bureau officials on Fort Peck matters." To complicate matters, a subcommittee chaired by Senator Clinton B. Anderson had recommended that Curry be prosecuted for "unethical practices." Curry saw this as a political attack on his efforts to vigorously represent his clients' interests. He also noted that on his last day in office, Chapman had advised Curry that the committee investigating the possibility of debarring Curry from representing Indians could not complete its task, but Chapman left the "embargo" in place. Curry hoped that the new administration would make sure that reason prevailed about his contracts and expenses.[3]

The Fort Peck and Blackfeet delegation, including Dolly Akers, William Buffalo Hide, Brian Connelly, George Panhiem, Carl A. Grant, and William J. Spanish, the only representative from Fort Peck, arrived in Washington on February 1. The joint delegation sent a telegram to President Eisenhower, dated February 21, 1953, asking that Dillon Myer be immediately removed as CIA.[4]

Taking advantage of Congressman D'Ewart's interest, in mid-February, Curry drafted a bill on the reconveyance to individual Indians of mineral rights beneath the post-1927 allotments. In a letter dated February 23, 1953, Curry described to Councilman William R. Smith the work the delegation could perform to support this legislation.[5] D'Ewart introduced H.R. 3413 on February 24, 1953, "A Bill to grant oil and gas in lands on the Fort Peck Reservation, Montana, to individual Indians in certain cases."[6] The delegation also lobbied to have the embargo lifted on Curry's contract with all the tribes he represented, including Fort Peck.

Within days of her return home, Dolly Akers was charged with the assault of a federal officer pertaining to an incident on March 13, 1952 involving Superintendent Crawford. She received a summons to appear before the U.S. District Court for the District of Montana, Havre Division, in Glasgow, on April 8, 1953.[8] In a letter on the front page of *The Herald News* on March 26, 1953, Akers contended that the charges were trumped up to silence her and get her removed from the executive board.[9] Akers wrote Curry a long letter, dated April 13, 1953, describing the events and the subsequent trial. Since she had not been arrested, she was only served a summons, and did not receive a copy of the indictment until she arrived at the federal district court. The witnesses for the prosecution were Superintendent Crawford, former Agency Clerk Johnson, and an FBI agent named Mason Melvin. Akers was the only witness in her defense.[10] She was convicted and sentenced to a sixty-day suspended sentence with one year of probation, and the judge took into consideration the fact that because of "my leadership and prominence among the Indian people that many innocent people would suffer along with me." He stated that this particular incident would not have occurred "if I had not violated the dignity of the Indian."

As this incident exemplified, the confrontational nature of the factionalism on Fort Peck Reservation was intensifying. This new effort to derail Dolly Smith Cusker Ackers' rising influence was not the first or the last. Originally a Democrat when she served a term beginning in 1932 as the first Indian, as well as the first Indian woman, elected to the Montana legislature, she wanted to be a part of the larger movement that included the Indian "New Deal." After failing to become a supervisor of Indian relief in Montana, she was hired in May 1937 with Senator Murray's help as an assistant to one of the Fort Peck Agency

The History of the Assiniboine and Sioux Tribes of the Fort Peck Indian Reservation: 1600 - 2010

social workers. Although she worked hard, she did not have formal training, and eventually her position was eliminated. Because of her political activism, she was encouraged to seek a position in the Indian Service in another state. She was eventually transferred within the Indian Service to Pine Ridge Agency in South Dakota.[11] Beginning on December 10, 1939, she worked there for almost two years, during which time she married her second husband, John Akers. Again, she felt she was being passed over for promotion.[12] In response to a group of Oglala Sioux "leaders" who were concerned about being excluded from the Indian Reorganization Act, Dolly wrote Senator Murray a detailed letter advocating for people who had asked for her help. In so doing she was stepping out of bounds as a government employee by communicating directly with politicians, which eventually led to her dismissal.[13] She was already beginning her political migration from Democrat to Republican. By the mid-1940s, she was elected to the Fort Peck Tribal Executive Board.[14]

However, on June 1, 1946 in a General Council called for the purpose, she was impeached of her position on the TEB. Assistant CIA Zimmerman in a letter dated July 24, 1946 recognized the impeachment.[15] Although that same month she was nominated as Democratic Committeewoman for Roosevelt County, this was the end of the road for her with the New Dealers, and she soon became a Republican.[16] The next years were characterized by many tribal members lining up with one of the two mainstream political parties. Among her supporters, William Knorr and Santee Ironring also were Republicans. In a sense, Dolly fostered a form of populism, working hard to help individuals who had called on her for assistance, mostly with getting things done with various jurisdictions of government. There was little middle ground; her supporters were for her, and her detractors were against her.

Many on the other side saw themselves participating in a New Deal version of self-determination, even though the Fort Peck Tribes had rejected the Indian Reorganization Act. Some had taken additional education courses, others had directly benefited from government programs, and many had been administrators of programs. In a sense, these people were "organization" men and women who believed in due process, administrative fairness, democratic principles of equity for all, and addressing needs systematically. Austin Buckles, Jim Archdale, and Norman Hollow had been active as TEB members for years, and were subscribers to the goals fostered by the New Deal Democrats.[17] As the groundswell toward termination was rising, those who fought against the elimination of trust status knew what had happened historically when fee patents were issued to individuals and many who were unable to pay taxes lost their lands. Ironically, BIA Realty was in favor of increasing the number of fee patents, a method that decreased expenditures because it required less paperwork. While both factions used the rhetoric of self-determination, each was driven ideologically and politically by vastly different goals, interpretations, and motivations.

Preparations were made to use the secret ballot in the upcoming tribal election. Crawford provided lists of district voters, and nominating petitions were due on March 16, 1953.[18] An attempt was made at a special meeting of the executive board on March 30 to void the decision for the secret ballot, but this was thwarted by the BIA chief clerk, who opined that the will of the General Council could not be reversed without another General Council meeting.[19] Eva Mae Smith, former tribal secretary, told Curry that Chairman Knorr was particularly opposed to the secret ballot, and because he had not been nominated for any office, he was "looking for any technical reason to throw it out."[20] However, work on election regulations took much longer than anticipated, so the election was set for April 15, 1953.[21] Curry visited Poplar from April 9 to 13, 1953, to deal with the fact that two very different elections had been called for April 15: one by the executive board based on a voice vote at a General Council meeting, and the other by the superintendent that would implement the secret ballot. Curry, in a paper dated April 11, 1953, discussed both elections and the problems inherent in each. The decision by the General Council of December 13 altered the Tribes' constitution, and therefore had to be carried out. Moreover, even if it implemented the secret ballot, the superintendent's authority to call an election was doubtful. A set of election regulations would have to be drafted and then accepted by a General Council, or the CIA's acceptance of the election results also might be problematic.[22]

Curry wrote the Tribal Executive Board on April 14, 1953, presenting a thirty-five-page draft of election regulations.[23] In a memorandum for the General Council dated April 15, 1953, he presented three options to ensure that the election was properly conducted. The general council adopted a resolution for the secret ballot on April 15, and moved the election to April 18, utilizing the implementation election format planned by Superintendent Crawford.[24]

Seven hundred forty-eight votes were cast in the election, the largest recorded vote to date. The new chairman was Austin Buckles, with Pauline Buckles serving as acting secretary. Returning board members were Norman Hollow, Carl Walking Eagle, and Bernard Standing. New board members were Alice Collins, James Sweeney, John Earl Wetsit, Kermit Smith, Minnie Olson, William Boyd, William Youpee, Thomas Buckles, and John Half Red.[25]

Meanwhile, the SI's embargo on Curry's contracts was finally lifted, and contracts for the claims and general counsel representations were also approved.[26] Orme Lewis, Assistant SI, wrote Curry on March 12, 1953, to lift the embargo with the caveat that the department had noted the conclusions about Curry in the January 3, 1953 report of the subcommittee of the Committee on Interior and Insular Affairs. Curry was given a set of warnings.[27]

Oil development on Fort Peck was expanding, fueled by lease tenders approved in the summer and fall of 1952 and the first months of 1953. The number of wells being drilled by Murphy Oil exceeded twenty by April 1953. The differences with the company had faded once the tribes recommended that the agency not return a deposit made for the August leases.[28] After its first well, the next several wells drilled had come up dry, and when the Tribal Executive Board insisted on fulfilling drilling commitments with all leases taken, the company felt it was in a bind. As Murphy Oil Company drilled more wells, however, the number that produced steadily increased, making the East Poplar Unit an extremely productive investment, and eventually an income generator for the Fort Peck Tribes.[29]

A major problem facing Austin Buckles' administration in its first weeks was how to meet its basic expenses, because there was no evidence of what accounts had existed for the previous executive board. First, the board sought access to a $6,000 contingency fund, and also asked the area office for a five-year audit of expenses and revenues.[30]

Curry wrote Norman Hollow on May 9, 1953 that Congressman D'Ewart's office would schedule hearings on the mineral rights restoration bill when a Fort Peck delegation could be present. Curry was getting impatient because the board had not decided about sending a delegation. However, Curry said he understood if the delay on the delegation was directly connected to the funding crisis.[31]

The executive board approved leases on tribal

lands with six oil companies on May 21, and also selected a delegation to meet with USGS officials in Casper, Wyoming. The board approved the leases of all bids in which a drilling commitment was included, and tabled a four-way joint bid by four companies on an 880-acre block because it lacked a drilling commitment.[32] Although oil development was increasing, there was no immediate income for salaries and programs. Buckles wrote the SI on May 26, 1953, emphasizing the importance of releasing the contingency fund and stating that the $10,000 limit on immediate administrative expenses was inadequate.[33] Clarence A. Davis, the Solicitor for Interior, finally explained to Curry that the issue was more about general appropriation than the proper justification for an increase of the limit. He pointed out that the Klamath were trying to get a $15,000 limitation lifted or raised, and again, the issues were administrative restraint and accountability.[34] By early July, Curry persuaded D'Ewart to introduce legislation to address the tribes' financial bind.[35]

On May 26, Curry reported on the pre-trial Conference on the Revaluation Claim before the Indian Claims Commission (ICC) that had been held the previous day. David Cobb and Abraham Weissbrodt for Fort Peck contended that enough evidence had been presented to justify a final decision in favor of the Fort Peck Indians. The reassessment of homesteads allowed in the 1920s had undermined the purpose and intent of the 1908 allotment agreement. However, the government contended "(a) that the Indians had no legal interest in this land, (b) that the government had no obligation to abide by the original appraisals, and (c) that the claims should have been filed in the Assiniboine or Sioux cases." The Fort Peck attorneys asserted that the courts have already "overruled these contentions as a matter of law," and therefore, the only proper proof needed were the facts "that the lands were

actually sold at less than the appraised value," and "that the Indians thereby lost a certain amount of money to which they were entitled." Nevertheless, the government attorneys would not budge, contending they would "try to show that the Fort Peck Indians were a group of vagabonds who obtained refuge at the Fort; and that it was never intended that they should have title to the property." Consequently, they would "try to show the parties were in agreement in 1908 and thereafter that the United States would not be bound by the original appraisal." This would allow "the government to be able to sell the whole area for a thin dime, turn the dime over to the Indians, and walk out of the situation scot-free of liability." None of the government's positions were supported by evidence.[36]

Vice-Chairman James Archdale and Delegate Joshua Wetsit accompanied Curry to the hearing before the Subcommittee on Indian Affairs of the House Committee on Interior and Insular Affairs, where testimony was presented about H.R. 3413. Curry spoke first:

Prior to 1927, allotments were made of tribal land under which the allottees received the trust title not only to the surface of the land but also to the underground rights. In 1927, a law was passed which provided as to allotments subsequently made, that the oil and gas rights should be retained in the Tribe. The purpose of the D'Ewart Bill is to transfer to the post-1927 allottees the mineral rights under their lands which under the 1927 Act have, up to now, been retained by the Tribe [sic]. Where the allottees are deceased, then the transfer is to be made to the heirs of the original allottees.

Curry added that "certain Indians" had transferred land to the tribe in fee simple and received back only their surface rights. The D'Ewart bill allowed the transfer to all Indians of their oil and gas rights that they then retained. Joshua Wetsit felt that the Tribes should retain the 80,000 unallotted acres, but that the 7,000 allottees who had not received their mineral rights should have these restored. Jim Archdale reported that approximately 1,500 newly born Indian children possessed no land at all. Several GOP congressmen asked about whether whites might be disadvantaged by the proposed legislation, demonstrating how little they understood about rights in the trust lands.[37]

At the June 15 meeting of the executive board, a resolution was passed to remove the $10,000 limit on the board's budget. The resolution asked D'Ewart to introduce a bill seeking an appropriation to pay salaries and expenses for the executive board, patterned after H.R. 3406, which provided for salaries and expenses of the Klamath Indian Tribe.[38] No one seemed to foresee what this might mean.

Meanwhile, the effort to finalize H.R. 3413 so it could be voted out of committee was delayed by the executive board's questions. One change was that authority for the tribe should come from the executive board and not the General Council.[39] The bill was scheduled to be discussed June 29 in the subcommittee, and the department's report was expected by this date. Jim Archdale recommended that the bill not refer to the executive board or the General Council, but rather that Congress directly transfer the rights to individuals who were eligible. Curry recognized that this would require a General Council resolution.[40] The estimated appropriation was $87,551.61. Buckles was very concerned that Archdale's suggested amendments had not been approved by the executive board, stating that neither Archdale nor Joshua Wetsit was authorized to do tribal business. The chairman opined that he was not aware of the necessity to refer all land issues to the General Council, but acknowledged that the General Council and executive board tended to duplicate or even do things three times, or to change their positions.[41]

On July 15, the White House nominated New Mexico businessman Glenn L. Emmons for CIA.[42]

On July 30, 1953, Orme Lewis, Assistant SI, recommended to Congressman A.L. Miller, Chairman of the Committee on Interior and Insular Affairs, passage of H.R. 3413, "To grant oil and gas in lands on the Fort Peck Indian Reservation, Montana, to individual Indians in certain cases." The restoration of oil and gas rights to post-1927 allottees would affect some 700 allotments. Based on the request by the General Council of the Fort Peck Tribes, the initial language restored rights to the last owner of the allotment. However, the department favored the original allottee or heirs, irrespective of the fact that many 1927 allottees had disposed of their lands. Lewis raised the matter of encouraging patent-in-fee applications to competent Indians. Clearly, Lewis was not aware of how conflicted many tribal members felt about this. Lewis suggested that a referendum might be needed with at least 30 percent of the membership voting to implement the restorations. Lewis also discussed funding for restoring or compensating heirs. The precise nature of the Tribes' resources was unclear, and estimates of unobligated tribal balances appeared to fall short of the amount needed to implement the legislation. No offer was made to appropriate the funds, but rather, the Tribes would pay this cost.[43]

On July 30, Chairman Austin Buckles appeared before the Subcommittee on Indian Affairs, Committee on Interior and Insular Affairs, asking for action on H.R. 3413. He presented a resolution supporting the bill's passage and recommended changing references in the text from "General Council" to "Tribal Executive Board."[44]

Acting Executive Officer Fred H. Massey reported to Billings Area Office Director Paul L. Fickinger, on July 30, 1953, that Buckles called on him to discuss reimbursing the executive board for expenses incurred for tribal business prior to July 1, 1953. The money for the 1953 fiscal year had been expended by the previous executive board, and a report on expenditures and authorizations was requested.[45]

The year 1953 was dramatic for Indian Affairs. The GOP-controlled 83rd Congress was responsible for many changes. While there was considerable discourse about removing barriers for "minorities," the goal of many initiatives was the quick assimilation of Indians into American society. Indian cultures were considered irrelevant. Reservations were considered the product of separate and unequal treatment, with little understanding of what treaties or negotiated executive agreements meant to Indian people. Conservative Republicans in charge of congressional committees favored termination for competent Indian tribes. By June 1953, a preoccupied Congress entertained a resolution that threatened all tribes with termination. House Resolution 108 was sponsored by Wyoming Representative William Harrison, and was sponsored in the Senate by Washington Senator Henry Jackson.[46]

Within weeks, the resolution was voted out of committee and sent to the floor of the House, where it was quickly approved without serious debate on July 27, 1953. "Korea, racial desegregation issues, and McCarthyism obscured the resolution, giving it minimal attention at best."[47] Most significantly, the resolution identified the first five groups to be terminated: the Menominee of Wisconsin, the Flatheads in Montana, the Klamath in Oregon, the Potawatomie of Kansas, and the Turtle Mountain Chippewa in North Dakota.[48]

A parallel development was passage of Public Law 280, signed into law on August 15, 1953, that allowed five named states to assume jurisdiction for law enforcement on named reservations within their respective boundaries. This signaled the beginning of transfers of authority from the federal government to states, which further facilitated termination.[49] While Montana was not one of the named states, the impact of this legislation was still felt there.

Particularly frustrated about the lack of funds for his administration, Buckles wrote the SI on August 1, 1953, about a recent decision of the Solicitor of the Interior Department not to apply the 1948 limitation level to the Fort Peck Tribes. As a result, all the work of the Tribes halted. Buckles was reluctant to have people work without pay, knowing that Congress might not authorize retroactive pay. However, the chairman was particularly critical of advice given by BIA personnel on several matters, since the advice sometimes resulted in "gross and unfair injury to individuals." Buckles appealed to the SI and CIA as businessmen, stating how important it was to "operate on sound business lines." He also asked to see the new CIA.[50]

H. Barton Greenwood, Acting CIA, responded on August 7, 1953, expressing concern that in the midst of their financial contingency, the Tribes were attempting to increase the expense limits of their tribal attorney. Greenwood was particularly taken aback by Curry's statement that the problems of individuals with leases were hard to distinguish from the "business problems of the Tribe." Greenwood had written Curry on April 8 requesting more detail about the services Curry was providing the Tribes, but he had not to date been answered. Greenwood then turned to the chairman's August 3 letter. Although the previous executive board had exhausted all funds for salaries and wages, the solicitor stated that no additional funds could lawfully be spent until the beginning of the next fiscal year.[51] New monies were made available on July 1, 1953, already placed at the discretion of the Superintendent. In response to criticism of agency personnel, Greenwood quoted from Curry's general counsel contract about his responsibility to advise the

Tribes. Emphasizing that Curry was not to represent individual tribal members in his role as tribal attorney, Greenwood reported that the solicitor had asked for particular scrutiny of Curry's expense claims. Greenwood expressed disappointment that on the chairman's recent visit to Washington, no meeting was sought to discuss these matters.[52] Curry was outraged at Greenwood's letter, considering it an attempt to foment dissatisfaction about Buckles' and Curry's work. Curry urged Buckles to fight back.[53]

Federal legislation was passed and signed into law in the summer of 1953, repealing the Indian liquor laws on all patent-in-fee lands within reservations. Again, the aim was to eliminate certain discriminatory laws against Indians.[54] This was controversial even among tribal members at Fort Peck. Historically, all liquor sales were prohibited in Indian country. In 1948, Congress clarified that this term included all Indian reservations. Shortly afterwards, Congress exempted fee lands in "non-Indian communities" from the Indian liquor prohibition. Thus, liquor sales in Wolf Point and Poplar are permitted under federal law.

After passing this statute, Congress in 1953 gave tribes a "local option" to allow and regulate liquor sales on reservations. To date, the Fort Peck Tribes have not enacted an ordinance that permits sales on the Fort Peck Reservation, but the state has licensed sellers everywhere on the reservation, ignoring federal law. The state's position is that it simply licenses sellers of liquor under state law, and does not warrant that the licenses it issues are valid under federal law. Thus, sales of liquor outside of Poplar and Wolf Point likely violate federal law. In the 1990s, a tribal referendum on whether liquor sales should be banned failed. Thus, sales of liquor continue to occur outside of Wolf Point and Poplar.

Since 1953, access to alcohol has had a profound impact. Endemic alcoholism has destroyed many families, and has left generational damage and undermined many aspects of Assiniboine and Sioux cultures and societies. Children have been abandoned and record numbers are in foster care or adopted out. The transfer of knowledge between generations has been subverted and in many cases, abandoned. Ethical and moral order has been disregarded, resulting in criminal activities that run the gamut. Costs have gone through the ceiling in law and order, and its responses, and also in the health consequences where expenses have been astronomical and consumptive, causing many fiscal year demands to have months of shortfall. While fertility since outstrips morbidity in the overall population of the reservation, alcohol takes a high toll in auto accidents, liver and kidney diseases, and overall self-destructive behavior. Alcohol has been no friend to the Fort Peck peoples.[55]

In his column "Jim Says . . ." for August 24, James Archdale reported that the Fort Peck Tribes had decided to continue the Oil Discovery Celebration, setting the dates for early September in American Legion Park. The events to celebrate were the discovery of oil and twenty-seven current wells pumping, with more to be drilled, the greatest crop year in the "short history of wheat farming," "equal privileges to all races and discriminatory laws removed from United States Statutes," and "the stopping of a shooting war in Korea, where many of our Indian and white teenagers are in the front lines, and many in the prisoner-of-war camps."[56]

Curry had favorable impressions of the new CIA. The CIA was leaving for a western tour, but was not coming to Montana, but Curry suggested that he be invited to visit Fort Peck Reservation.[57]

Chairman Buckles wrote Greenwood on September 15, 1953, that he had not been able to convene a meeting of the executive board to discuss Greenwood's letter. Buckles pointed out that he had used the "deep freeze" metaphor because no one in tribal government had been paid to date, and the agency had told him that funds were still not available. While tribal expenditures were paid through the agency by voucher, the board wanted a different arrangement for salaries and expenses. The chairman said that it was "beginning to look as though we are being pushed out of business."[58]

Newly appointed CIA Glenn Emmons arrived in Poplar in mid-October. A public meeting in the Poplar Armory was attended by 150 people, and in the course of the two-hour meeting, thirteen "spokesmen" asked questions or commented about the problems and expectations of tribal members. Emmons commented on how well the meeting was conducted and that he had learned more at Fort Peck than on any other reservation he had visited. The commissioner had lunch with fifty-eight BIA employees, toured the East Poplar Unit oil fields, and visited the Riverside and Fort Kipp districts.[59]

The chairman on November 13, 1953 invited twenty key individuals to a meeting aimed at "establishing a method of procedure to handle our tribal business in a more efficient and businesslike manner. . . . the thought in mind is to reorganize and plan policies of our own nature to replace those of the BIA even to the extent, that at some near future date, we will be able to administer our own affairs." He proposed a series of meetings beginning on November 17, and then on the second Tuesday of each month, which was two days prior to the regularly scheduled TEB meeting. The names of those invited appeared on the invitation, representing the full range of views: Charles A. Brocksmith, Glasgow; Willard Sweeney, Frazer; William Smith and Leonard Smith, Oswego; Joseph Day, Kermit Smith, Dolly Akers, Eva Mae Smith, and Freda Beazley, Ray Track, and Alex Sansaver, all from Wolf

Point; Jesse Kirn, James Long, James Archdale, James Helmer, and Hope MacDonald, all from Poplar; Norman Hollow, Brockton; James Boyd, Brockton; Willard Manning, Culbertson; and Thomas Murray, Homestead. Buckles then offered sample questions that might prompt discussions. "Should we allow land exchanges so that those who are going to operate and maintain farming and livestock enterprises can consolidate their holdings equivalent to an economic unit?" "Should land purchases between individual Indians be continued for the purpose of consolidation?" "Should we protest the present Indian Office policy which now restricts the above, and sets a precedent that if you want a fee patent it will be obtained on all or none basis? This in effect is a forced patent." He then listed additional topics for discussion: the shrinking of the reservation due to patent-in-fee lands, enrollment, a per capita payment, restoration of mineral rights to allottees, taxation, separation of the tribes and liquidation of tribal assets, and the tribe's need for a business manager. The chairman asked for every one's "whole hearted cooperation."[60]

At the next regular executive board meeting on November 24, a discussion was held with Superintendent Crawford about Resolution 108, which declared that Congress wanted to make all Indians within the boundaries of the United States, as rapidly as possible, subject to the same laws and entitled to the same rights, privileges, and responsibilities as other citizens of the United States, ending their status as wards of the United States. Kermit Smith joined Chairman Austin Buckles, James Archdale, Minnie Olson, and the tribal secretary on an ad hoc committee intended to develop a program that would lead to the goal of the resolution was broached. The committee was expected to report at the December 10 meeting.[61]

On December 4, 1953, Buckles called for another meeting of the advisory board on

December 8, declaring that attendees should "prepare your minds with some definitive procedure we should follow in order to formulate some type of tribal government and policies." The impact of this rhetoric can only be imagined. Buckles reported that "our discussions, suggestions and ideas will be centered on a Constitution and bylaws, whether it will be to amend the one we are now operating under or to draft a new one entirely" and if there was time, "we should start the formulation of a land policy."[62] The chairman then noted that he had "received some criticism for establishing this board," but because participation had to be voluntary (an indirect reference to the financial situation), he totally understood choices about participation, and nothing would be held against anyone.[63] The degree to which his initiative was understood as an open discussion to enable this dialogue, or was perceived as a move beyond the mechanisms of the 1927 Constitution and thus provided political ammunition to his detractors, was unclear. Chairman Buckles knew the Tribes needed to prepare for the impact of the shift in policy.

Curry attended the Special Executive Board meeting on January 4, 1954, which was considering whether to continue his contract. Curry said that whatever happened about the general counsel contract, he would probably continue the claims contract. While the board had agreed to increase his fee from $3,000 to $10,000 a year, Curry had not even collected the full $3,000, and also he had unpaid expense accounts from several years back. Curry understood the dynamics that had produced the current situation, but he was very concerned about developments that could be "very, very injurious to the tribe." Curry stayed in Poplar for two weeks, mainly discussing the framework for a series of bills to be introduced to Congress. He returned to Washington with Chairman Austin Buckles and Councilmen Tom Buckles and William Youpee.[64]

The first new bill was Home-Rule Bill H.R. 7650, introduced by D'Ewart on February 2, 1954, authorizing a referendum to establish a system of tribal government under which the Fort Peck Tribes would have full control of all tribal affairs and property, "provided only that the land held in trust for the tribes by the United States shall not be leased for long terms without the approval of the SI, and that said lands shall not be sold without the consent of Congress." Nothing in the act gave the tribal government control over the private affairs or property of individual Indians.[65] Senator Murray introduced the Senate version, S. 2898, which was read twice and referred to the Senate Committee on Interior and Insular Affairs on January 22, 1954.[66]

Curry help draft an Omnibus Indian Lands Bill that created a Fort Peck Indian Lands Commission that could dispose of all outstanding land matters, which was the substance of H.R. 7649.[67] Senator Murray introduced the Senate version, S. 2899, which was read twice and referred to the Senate Committee on Interior and Insular Affairs.[68] Throughout this time, the agency was offering patent-in-fee lands for sale almost monthly. A notice dated February 2, 1954, offered 227 parcels, with portions of mineral rights retained or available for purchase.[69]

The oil boom was also continuing. The Murphy Oil Company's application for a new participation Area "C" in the East Poplar Unit was approved as of January 19, 1954, and the company notified Crawford of this.[70]

Austin Buckles was well aware that disseminating information about his accomplishments was important for both tribal members and non-Indians. He also knew that engaging in a concerted effort in Washington to use the legislative processes was controversial. The chairman sent a lengthy telegram, dated February 10, 1954, to Hope McDonald, the tribal reporter at *The Poplar Standard*, reporting on the hard work by

the other Fort Peck delegates and the cooperation of the Montana congressional delegation.
He also noted that the same kinds of runarounds
from the Dillon Myer era at the BIA were still the
norm. Buckles planned to attend the hearing on
February 12, 1954 for the bill to restore mineral
rights for the post-1927 allotments. The hearing
resulted in the report accompanying the bill
being edited, sent to the floor on February 24,
and referred back to committee. Hearings were
expected on the Fort Peck Home-Rule Bill and
the Lands Commission Bill in mid-March.

Buckles had argued before Assistant Solicitor
William Kassler for the release of tribal funds
to allow the executive board to function on a
basic level. The funds had been frozen by the
area office, so they had been unable to obtain a
reversal of the decision at that time. While having
a delegation testify in the hearings in March
would be optimal, sending a delegation required
finances. Meetings about paying Curry were
also held with the chief attorney for the BIA,
the Executive Office of the Bureau, the CIA, and
Assistant SI Orme Lewis. Lewis promised them a
decision in a week.[71]

Buckles concluded,

President Eisenhower promised the Indians that
they would find him and his associates fighting
against the sort of discrimination that was practiced by former Commissioner Dillon Myer. But it
seems that none of the "fighting advocates" have
been appointed to the Indian Bureau. We get the
impression that the organization is still being
run by the same Bureaucrats that ran it before
Eisenhower was elected and that the three new
men appointed by him are captives of the hundreds who [were] held over from the old administration. . . . The Government has tied up our
tribal funds to prevent us from paying necessary
Executive Board expenses and also to prevent our
paying reasonable legal fees. . . . This is especially

outrageous since we have millions of dollars
worth of tribal property that needs protection.
We are prevented from using our own money,
of which we have enough, to defend that property. We do not want to continue in the degraded
position of stooges for the Indian Bureau. We do
not want to assume any longer the responsibility
for protecting Tribal property without power
and authority to spend the Tribal money for the
expenses of doing so.

If our present efforts to force the Government
to unfreeze our Tribal funds do not succeed, I
will recommend that all the Tribal officers and
the entire Executive Board should resign and
refuse to serve any longer in a position where
they cannot operate effectively in behalf of their
people.[72]

Other board members questioned the effectiveness of mass resignation.[73]

Working with Curry, the delegation prepared
the text for Bill S. 2931, introduced by Senator
Murray on February 8, 1954, proposing paying
salaries and expenses of officials of the Fort
Peck Tribes from unobligated tribal funds.[74] The
delegation continued to press the Bureau and
Interior Department for a full accounting of
their funds in the U.S. Treasury.

The delegation also acquired a list of 435 allottees or their estates whose land was scheduled to
go out of trust on December 31, 1953. They tried
to find out if fee patents were being issued for
these lands, and if there was any way to extend
the trust period, since all these lands would then
become subject to taxation.[75]

Edwin Reddoor was a member of the delegation led by Chairman Buckles, but he also was
chairman of the Fort Peck Sioux Tribal Council,
so he met with the lawyer for the Sioux claims,
Ralph Case. Santee Iron Ring, Iron Bear, and
William Youpee were also in two meetings
in which enrollment matters were discussed.

Speaking about claims that affected eight reservations, Case was calling for a careful study of each reservation's enrollment criteria and the state of the rolls, preparing for when claims might be dispersed. However, he noted that Fort Peck was unique, since the Sioux of Fort Peck were "under a common Tribal Council" with Assiniboines. The Sioux delegates expressed a desire to be incorporated under the IRA, even though all Fort Peck tribal members had voted against it. Case advised the Sioux that this might be possible, but they did not act on his advice.[76]

In Poplar, a special meeting of the executive board was held on February 19, 1954. A letter from the CIA to the chairman dated February 18, 1954, rejected the proposed increase in the Curry contract because "its approval [was] not the best interests of the Indians."[77] The possibility of the board members resigning en masse in protest was discussed, but most members opposed this tactic. Buckles called from Washington during the meeting and talked with Norman Hollow and Kermit Smith. A telegram was sent to the President and the Montana congressional delegation over Acting Chairman James Archdale's signature asking for payment of the attorney's contract and delegation expenses. Other resolutions on oil and gas matters were passed.[78] Archdale wrote Curry on February 22, 1954 that the board sought a more complete report from Buckles before acting on the proposal to resign en masse, and that the board felt officials in the Interior Department had not explained their rejection adequately, so a General Council had been called for February 27 to discuss approval of Curry's "tribal contract and the increase in your salary."[79]

In a special meeting of the executive board on February 25, a resolution was passed approving an insurance policy, that indemnified Chairman Austin Buckles and delegates Bill Youpee and William Boyd, protecting the tribes against any

mishandling of affairs without legal advice. Should any of the three no longer continue on the board, replacements would be chosen.[80] In the meeting the next day, Buckles reported on the progress of tribal bills before Congress, and how discouraged he was. Buckles read part of the "Report of the Survey Team of Bureau Reorganization" regarding the "Withdrawal Program," and this was discussed at length. The board voted to oppose the Flathead Termination Bill before Congress. Curry was retained pending developments in his contract matter.[81]

At the General Council on February 27, Buckles expressed how very discouraged he was with the attitude in Washington, especially concerning twenty-six bills for orders of withdrawal that had been introduced for various tribes, many without their consent. The runarounds from the BIA had not diminished with the advent of a new administration, and the words Commissioner Emmons had spoken when he was in Poplar about consultation were simply not true. Buckles stated that the Tribes could not let others determine their futures. With its limited access to tribal funds and the solicitor's legal opinions limiting access to the funds in the U.S. Treasury, Fort Peck's situation was dire. The bill the delegation had put before Congress was meant to force this matter. Sending another delegation to Washington would result in another big fight with the powers that be, and possibly with tribal members, especially since criticism of the chairman's most recent trip had hardly subsided. Buckles explained that he wanted to send a delegation to Washington, but the limitations on spending tribal funds undermined this plan. Another delegation would have to fight for the same things as previous delegations had for the past forty years, simply asserting Fort Peck's right to self-determination. The fight was for real control over the tribes' money. Executive board members had worked four months without pay

President Gerald Ford with Fort Peck Tribal Councilman Caleb Shields at the White House, at the end of the Trail of Self Determination Caravan to Washington, D.C., July 16, 1976. The President later sent Mr. Shields a copy of the picture with a letter.

Some members of the Fort Peck Reservation Tribal Executive Board, 1977. Front row, from left to right: Stanley Yellow Robe, Joseph Red Thunder, Norman Hollow, Myrna Greufe (secretary), Pearl Hopkins, June Stafne. Back row; James Black Dog, Caleb Shields, Lida Menz, Orville Grainger, Alpheus Big Horn, Ray White Tail Feather, Josse Kirn, Dean Blount.

Some members of the Tribal Executive Board and some staff members, 1975–1977.

Fort Peck Tribal Councilman Caleb Shields and Fort Peck Community College President Mike Tellup, 1980.

Tribal Chairman Norman Hollow (left) accepts the Small Business Administration award from Montana Governor Ted Schwinden in recognition of Hollow's leadership capabilities, 1982.

Fort Peck Tribal Executive Board, 1985–1987.

Minerals Director Lawrence "Larry" Wetsit, Vice Chairman, Joe Red Thunder, Senator John Melcher, Chairman Norman Hollow.

Dr. James Shanley and Jerome 'Buster' Fourstar, 1991.

Tribal Centennial Parade, July 1986. Five living tribal chairmen were present. Left to right, Kenneth Ryan, Norman Hollow, Joe Red Thunder, William "Bill" Youpee, and Pete Eagle.

Some members of the Tribal Executive Board and staff members, 1978. Front row, left to right: Ray K. Eder, staff member; Harold Dean Blount; Lida Menz; Myrna Greufe, secretary; Catherine Spotted Bird, staff member. Back row, left to right: Jim Black Dog; Stanley Yellow Robe; Senator John Melcher; Chairman Norman Hollow; Vice Chairman Joe Red Thunder.

Fort Peck Tribal Chairman Caleb Shields with President Bill Clinton and Carol Juneau in Billings, Montana, 1996–1997.

Montana Indian leaders meeting with President Bill Clinton in Billings, Montana, 1996–1997.

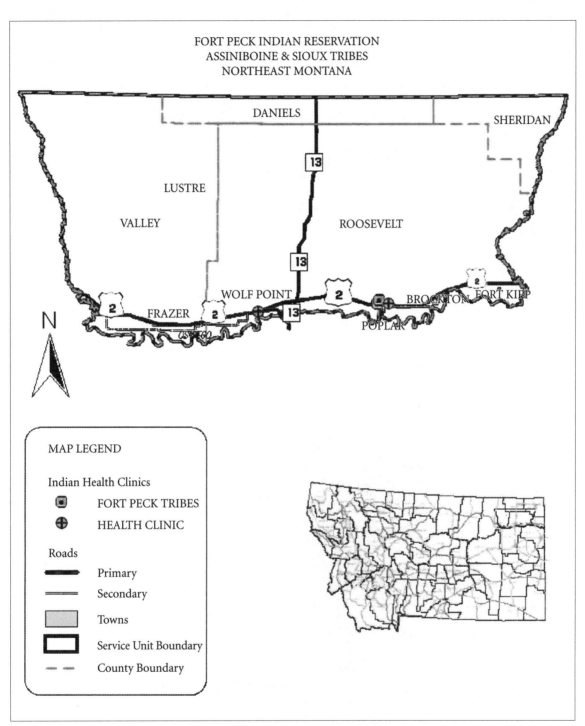

FORT PECK INDIAN RESERVATION
ASSINIBOINE & SIOUX TRIBES
NORTHEAST MONTANA

DANIELS

SHERIDAN

13

LUSTRE

VALLEY

ROOSEVELT

13

13

2

WOLF POINT

2

N

FRAZER

2

OSWEGO

13

BROCKTON FORT KIPP

2

POPLAR

MAP LEGEND

Indian Health Clinics

FORT PECK TRIBES

HEALTH CLINIC

Roads

Primary

Secondary

Towns

Service Unit Boundary

County Boundary

Fort Peck Indian Reservation with counties and major highways delineated, 2007.

Fort Peck Tribal History Book Committee, December 6, 2007. First row, seated, left to right: Victor Perry, Leland Spotted Bird, Lois Red Elk, Sharon Red Thunder, Gladys Jackson, Robert Fourstar, Dr. James Shanley, George Redstone. Second row, standing, left to right: Del Wayne First, Dr. Robert McAnally, Joseph Miller, Garrett Big Leggins, Caleb Shields, Dr. Joseph McGeshick. Not present: Dr. Margaret Campbell, Lawrence Wetsit, Kenneth Shields, Wayne Boyd, Paul Finnicum, Darrell Youpee.

Dr. James Shanley, President of Fort Peck Community College, 2007.

Helen Youpee (Mrs. Brush Horn) at thirty years of age, date unknown.

A gathering of tribal members in the mid-1950s.

Charles Phillip Red Boy, holding daughter, Mrs. Red Boy, two unidentified men, date unknown.

Lucille Bets His Medicine with a girl and young man, date unknown.

Demonstration in Washington, D.C., 1994.

Chairman Floyd Azure. Honored by FPCC students and staff at the 2012 spring round dance. Poplar High School, Poplar, MT. L-R Jackie Christian, Michelle Tibbits (taking picture) Chairman Azure, Daniel Shauer, Adrianne Ricker, Jessie Murray.

FPCC spring round dance, 2012. Frazer, MT. FPCC Vice President of Community Services Larry Wetsit and wife, Edna Wetsit.

Sean Bighorn, Sioux singer. FPCC spring round dance, 2012. Poplar High School, Poplar, MT.

Fort Peck Community College. Robert V. Dumont Building, classrooms, community center, computer lab, instructor offices. Wolf Point, MT. Named for the late Robert V. Dumont, Fort Peck Assiniboine educator.

Fort Peck Community College. Greet The Dawn Building, administration, business office, financial aid and student services. Poplar, MT

Medicine Bear Complex. Fort Peck Tribes Headquarters and BIA Offices. Poplar, MT

The History of the Assiniboine and Sioux Tribes of the Fort Peck Indian Reservation: 1600 - 2012

Yellowstone buffalo at Fort Peck.

Tribal Buffalo Ranch Ceremony. North Poplar, MT. L-R Tribal Councilman Tommy Christian, Montana Governor Brain Schwietzer, Fort Peck Tribal Chairman Floyd Azure, Fort Belknap Tribal President Tracy King.

last year, and the tribal election officials from the recent election were only just being paid.

The other continuing struggle concerned the attorney contract. Four weeks had been wasted in runarounds on it in Washington, all because the BIA and Interior Department did not want more confrontations with Indians, but without them, little or no action would result. Buckles read Curry's letter of February 19, 1954, in which he stated that the government's unwillingness to see Indians represented with legal counsel, especially about disputes with the government itself, was disconcerting. Curry stated: "I feel that the [Fort Peck] Indians would be better off with no lawyer than with a lawyer who is working under the limitations that the Indian Bureau imposes on me." Curry then gave sixty days notice of termination of his contract unless conditions changed, and thanked the council for its many efforts to fight for approval of his services, stating that this was a fight for Indian rights and not for his personal gain. "I hope that Indians will sometime gain the right to spend their own funds to protect their own rights."[82]

Buckles also read from his letter of February 29 to SI Douglas McKay appealing the decision about the Curry contract, but also indicating that Curry had resigned effective in sixty days.[83] Buckles explained that he had gone to Washington at the executive board's direction to prepare and introduce bills in Congress, including one removing limitations on tribal funds, one restoring oil and gas rights, a home-rule bill asking Congress "to give us control and the management of our own Tribal business, our Tribal lands and Tribal assets," and another bill setting up the Lands Commission to address land issues within the reservation. If necessary, Buckles promised to call for a referendum on the bills.[84]

Buckles then turned to the proposed reorganization of the Bureau of Indian Affairs. There was no indication of whether the survey team

had ever visited Fort Peck. However, education and extension had already been turned over to the county and the state. The next transfers were to be law and order, health, roads, and everything but land management. There was no real sense of how local entities felt about such a wholesale transfer. Buckles observed:

It is very definite that the withdrawal of Federal responsibility on trust property is coming. . . . I met three of the delegates from Flathead who were fighting this withdrawal as they didn't want it. Then three women came from Flathead who wanted this withdrawal—they are for it. That is just what dissension creates—fighting one another instead of fighting together. . . .

The withdrawal on this reservation is already here. The Bureau in effect is forcing patents on Indians. Our reservation is diminishing so rapidly that before long we won't have any lands left. I have records showing 70 per cent of our reservation gone into fee patent status. I don't know if this will be our last stand. When I say destruction—that is what it means.[85]

The chairman noted that non-Indians were recognizing that termination was going to cost local jurisdictions considerably, and the source of these revenues was not obvious. This predicament simply posed another potential threat to tribal assets. He suggested that sending a delegation be considered, even though it would mean that the Tribal Executive Board would have to forgo pay during this struggle. He again asked if the General Council wanted to authorize a delegation. Finally, it was decided that six delegates should be sent. Nominations were made and fourteen names were put forward to be considered by secret ballot, with each voter voting for six names. Buckles asked the council to pay expenses and authorize the delegation. Delegates were allowed $10 per day for lodging and $8 per diem. While it was hoped the delegation could obtain official recognition, lack of official recognition should not discourage the delegates, since "we are fighting for our lives and I don't believe we should heed to some of the dictatorial regulations." It was so moved and passed.[86]

The House passed the mineral rights restoration bill on March 1, 1954, and referred it to the Senate and the U.S. Senate Committee on Interior and Insular Affairs.[87]

In a special meeting of the Tribal Executive Board, on March 3, 1954, the Billings area office proposed closing the Indian hospital in Poplar in favor of community hospitals in other "cities" on the reservation. This was another manifestation of the larger bureau's and Interior Department's plan for "withdrawal," which the executive board formally opposed. Meanwhile, the election of another delegation to Washington was set for March 20, the Assiniboines in one column on the ballot and the Sioux in another.[88] The Tribal Executive Board identified twelve points for the delegates to pursue. They were expected to depart on March 22, 1954, for an anticipated stay of twenty days.[89]

Superintendent Crawford advertised ninety-three parcels of "submarginal" land available for farm and grazing leases, to be open on March 30, 1954. Dolly Akers sent a statement dated March 25, 1954, to the delegation in Washington, objecting to the lands being leased without consulting the tribes.[90] The executive board passed a resolution and dispatched it to Washington in an effort to stop the sale.[91]

In Washington, the delegation wrote SI Douglas McKay on March 30, thanking him for the appointment to see him, but stating that Harry Sellery, Indian Bureau Counsel General, had asked for a statement in writing about what they wanted to discuss. Hollow explained that the tribes were committed to fulfilling the contract with Curry, stating "we Indians are fully responsible for this policy of insisting that we

be permitted to have the services of Mr. Curry." Hollow hoped the SI "will not force us to accept legal representation from someone chosen by Government officials."[92]

McKay refused to allow an increase in Curry's compensation. The delegation filed out of the secretary's office and held a news conference, distributing a prepared statement about all of the matters confronting the Fort Peck tribes that required legal consultation. Particularly cited was the amount of individually owned trust lands being put on the tax rolls, a practice the tribes hoped to halt. It was reported that the delegation was trying to get a meeting with President Eisenhower.[93]

On April 2, 1954, the Fort Peck delegation appeared before the House Interior and Insular Affairs Subcommittee on Indian Affairs. Speaking to the initiative for home rule, the spokesman stated that the tribes were wary of being granted more "power to handle their own affairs" if they could not have competent legal representation and pay the tariff for such advice. The subcommittee promptly tabled the bills, but then reversed its action and held the bills for further study while "tribal sentiment" about them was investigated. Hollow told the subcommittee the tribes did not want the bills approved unless the matter of their attorney's salary increase was settled.[94]

At a special meeting of the board on April 19, 1954, the delegates to Washington—Norman Hollow, Hope McDonald, Kermit Smith, Willard Sweeney, and William Youpee—reported about the issues taken up with bureau officials. Curry's contract was discussed. A motion was passed to ask that Curry work at least another month.[95]

The Interior Department's report on S. 2932, written by Assistant SI Fred G. Aandahl, was sent to Senator Butler, Chair, Committee on Interior and Insular Affairs, on April 16, 1954, discussing authorization of salaries and expenses of officials of the Fort Peck Tribes. Unfortunately, Aandahl stated that the legislation was consistent with other withdrawal legislation, rather than taking Fort Peck's position of trying to establish access and control of its tribal assets without a wholesale rejection of trusteeship.[96] The GOP began to describe this legislation as "emancipation" bills, exemplifying the one-track mind of termination proponents in Congress, the Indian Bureau, and the Interior Department.[97]

In a special meeting of the board on May 3, 1954, Norman Hollow advised that in the future, Montana-wide Indian delegations should go to Washington and work in concert. Hollow reported statements made by a Mr. Shipman in Washington concerning the living conditions of Indians at Hill 57 near Great Falls. Shipman stated that conditions there were not good, nor were the conditions on many Montana reservations. Congressman D'Ewart tried to challenge this statement, but Hollow declared "that if Congressman D'Ewart ever comes to Fort Peck Reservation this summer, I, personally, will take him over the reservation and show him that 'Hill 57' conditions actually exist here. . . ." With the support of the board, Buckles called Murray's office to check various bills, especially the funds limitation bill. Buckles advocated changing the constitution to better protect the tribes' rights. A committee to work on a new constitution, comprised of Minnie Olson, Norman Hollow, Alice Collins, William Youpee, and James Archdale, agreed to meet on May 5.[98]

The tribes were faced with finding a new local attorney. An initial interview with V.G. Koch of Sidney, Montana, was to be conducted by Austin Buckles, Norman Hollow, and Kermit Smith.[99] CIA Glenn L. Emmons wrote Curry on May 28, 1954, declaring that the Fort Peck Tribes' general counsel contract was terminated, since sixty days had lapsed from the date Curry had conditionally resigned.[100] On July 16, 1954, I.S. Weissbrodt

wrote Curry on behalf of the legal firm Cobb and Weissbrodt declaring that Curry had resigned from the Fort Peck claims contract and had assigned all interest to Cobb and Weissbrodt.[101]

Buckles also reported on the progress of the legislation restoring mineral rights. With its passage, a referendum on it would be held. More disconcerting for the chairman was the rate that tribal members were taking fee patents. The "frightful picture" was that 80 percent of allotted lands were deeded. Buckles was convinced that the reasons for reforming the constitution and bylaws had become self-evident, and the matter was soon expected to be the subject of a General Council. Finding a new lawyer would be difficult. Many were interested, but such decisions needed to be made by the board, which would require constitutional provision. The chairman then described a range of interference: denial of tribal salaries and expenses, denial of a hearing on handling of oil and gas advertisements and leases, and federal approval of a budget paid for with tribal funds without tribal consent.[102]

On June 29, 1954, Public Law 449 authorized payment of salaries and expenses of officials of the Fort Peck tribes from unobligated tribal funds, subject to the approval of the Secretary of the Interior.[103]

The Buckles administration prepared to adopt what was called the 1954 constitution, but this became quite contentious. The draft constitution and bylaws relegated General Councils to meetings of either the Assiniboine or Sioux Tribes, and positioned the TEB as the main institution of governance. Membership was defined with minimum blood quantum, and the TEB's administrative responsibilities and powers were clearly defined. Procedures for referendum and referral gave the tribal General Councils a finite role.[104] The draft was taken to district meetings for discussion. On October 16, 1954, a General Council was convened to adopt a new constitution. Before it was established that the meeting was a representative body, Wilbur Loves Him and Peter Eagle stated that more time was needed to consider the document, but a motion passed to continue the meeting. Chairman Buckles declared that the meeting was the General Council for everyone, and encouraged discussion. Superintendent Clinton Talley declared:

There has to be legal entity with anything in order to get proper recognition from Congress and the Department—we need the Constitution and bylaws. . . . Congress is never sure when they are dealing with a group of people who are representing tribes whether or not they are honored legally by the tribe to transact their business before the Congress. Likewise, the Department finds itself sometimes hard-put to know whether they are actually dealing with a legal body representing a large number of people. . . . I believe the Indian Tribes of this country are facing about the most important period in their history.[105]

The specification of the TEB as a delineated organization was intended to provide stability as a governmental entity, which was not often the situation with the unpredictable consequences arising from General Councils. Norman Hollow noted that as part of several delegations to Washington, DC, he was told by several members of Congress and the Interior Department that Fort Peck did not have a constitution and bylaws; he stated that an essential document was needed. Others asked for more time; still others spoke of needing to protect the Tribes from the "withdrawal" that appeared inevitable, so the sooner the constitution was adopted, the sooner the Tribes could defend themselves. Eventually William Smith's motion for adoption was brought to a vote; 123 voted for adoption, while forty-one opposed it.[106]

Two other contentious issues are in the document. The requirements for candidacy for offi-

cers and executive board members also described cause for removal, including the "conviction in any court of a misdemeanor or felony and/or involving dishonesty."[107] This level of moral turpitude became debatable. The other delineated the precise blood quantum of either one-fourth or one-eighth degree Assiniboine or Sioux blood for children born to any tribal member to attain tribal membership.[108] This also put the tribes on the political spot, since Congress had made several attempts to legislate minimum requirements for federal recognition and tribal membership.[108]

Due to Fort Peck's status as an "unorganized tribe" (because it had not accepted the Indian Reorganization Act), final approval rested with the BIA, so legislative actions had to be channeled through the Reservation Superintendent, then the Area Director, then the CIA, and finally to the SI. The constitution and by-laws were sent to the department for review and approval before the TEB referred them to a reservation-wide referendum by secret ballot. Buckles felt that securing department approval first would avoid local disappointment, even if it meant making changes first; however, the process moved more slowly than he anticipated. Meanwhile, Buckles and the TEB used the new constitution as the instrument for governance, assuming approval was forthcoming.[110]

The faction in favor of home-rule was motivated by the prospect finally to profit from oil development. They reasoned that termination would eliminate the BIA's paternalistic oversight, including oversight of tribal funds accumulating in the U.S. Treasury that should be put at the discretion of the tribes. Of course, they felt that any other tribal funds should still be available for local decisions. Sentiments were becoming increasingly diverse about how to realize the promise of energy development, which had yet to be even minimally fulfilled. Home rule advocates preferred the General Council mechanism, in which supporters were marshaled to secure the public will, but this often meant organizing to dominate a given meeting. This faction also held in suspicion decisions made by voters utilizing the "secret ballot," a process they felt could be easily open to fraud. On the other hand, public voting by division of the house in a General Council let it be known who stood where, literally, on any given issue.[111]

Based partly on the election procedures in the new constitution and bylaws, Austin Buckles was re-elected Chairman and James Archdale, Vice-chairman, as were most of the members of the executive board in the election of April 15, 1955.[112]

On May 6, John J. Akers, husband of Dolly C. Akers, filed suit in the district court of the First Judicial District of the state of Montana for Lewis and Clark County, challenging the electoral procedures by which the chairman and executive board were elected. The action finally ended up in federal court. The federal judge considered the case from May 17, 1955 until February 27, 1956, when it was remanded back to state district court. However, Judge Louck, the Circuit Judge for Roosevelt County, recused himself.[113]

The new executive board took up the work on constitutional amendments begun by the previous board, and also addressed enrollment matters and the choice of a new general counsel. Thomas Dignan of Glasgow was chosen, but the paperwork on the selection never left the agency, even though the executive board assumed the application was proceeding through the necessary channels. However, many matters had been delayed for several months because of the Akers suit. For example, on February 7, 1956, the executive board was told by the BIA in Washington to do no further work on an enrollment ordinance "pending determination of the Akers suit."[114] The area office authorized the hiring of T.H. Burke of Burke & Hibbs, Billings, MT, to represent the defendants in the Akers case.[115] The budget

for the tribes for fiscal year 1956 was $203,023, and the chairman's salary was set at $3,410 per annum, equivalent to GS-5. Other councilmen were paid $10 per day, $3 per diem, and $.07 per mile within the Fort Peck Reservation, and $9 per day per diem outside the reservation. Per diem for trips to Washington were $12 for transportation and $10 for services.[116]

Austin Buckles said that from May 1955 to January 1956, the members of the TEB "were hounded and pressured into calling a General Council by the Akers faction. This resulted in factionalism among and between members of the tribes." Consequently, the calling of a General Council rested completely with the Executive Board.[117]

On June 11, 1955, an unofficial "general council" was finally convened by the Akers faction, with Henry Begs His Own serving as acting chairman because members of the TEB were absent. The agenda focused on the 1954 constitution and by-laws, the state of law and order, and the "wasteful spending of our tribal funds." The acting chairman opened the meeting by stating that Mr. Akers in his legal action was not suing the Tribes, but rather was seeking to void the April election because "our tribal money is being wasted." Forty-nine voted for a motion to rescind the October 16, 1954 approval of the new constitution and bylaws, and none opposed it. Other motions to remove Superintendent Talley and to stop all spending of tribal money until the Akers suit was settled were also approved.[118]

The general impression on the reservation was that considerable amounts of money were accumulating in the U.S. Treasury from the energy boom that should be available for a per capita payment, but several delegations to DC had been told that a defined membership ordinance was needed first. This would require an updated reservation-wide roll of qualified members. This issue was particularly contentious; so much had to be resolved before a referendum on a membership ordinance could be held, and this could not be accomplished in a General Council.[119] However, the Akers faction disregarded this detail. In Buckles' words, "throughout the factionalism there is continuous mud-slinging, propaganda and agitation among the [tribal] members. During these months when the TEB was hamstrung from making decisions on so many matters, the Buckles-Archdale administration was accused of 'stealing thousands of dollars from Tribal funds.'" The Akers faction alleged that the 1955 administration had spent over $200,000 of tribal funds and that $2,000,000 was unaccounted for.[120] Ironically, because Fort Peck was an unorganized tribe, there were no bonded officers or board members, and therefore the Superintendent and the Chief Clerk had to issue all checks. Dolly C. Akers and George Thompson, Jr., launched a campaign to remove the chairman and vice chairman, but also advocated removal of Talley.[121]

Chairman Buckles pressed ahead to secure the legal services of Thomas Dignan and Francis Gallagher of Glasgow, MT, in a contract dated November 22, 1955. The TEB approved the contract and forwarded it to the BIA and Interior Department.[122] The Akers faction also disputed this action. Buckles stated that the "continued insistence of the Akers faction" on a General Council was wearing him and TEB members down.[123]

Convening in Poplar on January 7, 1956, forty-seven Sioux tribal members and Mrs. Akers, the sole Assiniboine member present, purported to hold a General Council. Chairman Buckles declared that from what he observed, this meeting could not be considered a reservation-wide general council because Assiniboines were inadequately represented. Both the chairman and vice chairman refused to preside and left the assembly. The meeting continued with their

so-called tribal business, but soon recessed with the intention of reconvening on January 28. Chairman Buckles, Vice Chairman Archdale, and Tribal Secretary Eder were not notified. Seventy-four tribal members, the vast majority of whom were Sioux with a few more Assiniboines present, attended the meeting. After elaborate discussion, resolutions were passed removing the chairman and vice-chairman in absentia, and in their place, Dolly C. Akers was elected chairman and George W. Thompson, Jr., vice chairman. The council then chose delegates for an immediate trip to Washington—William Knorr, Dolly Akers, William Youpee, and Henry Begs His Own. However, the delegation could not get approval of the superintendent or the area office, so expenses remained temporarily contested. Believing she could lobby for the necessary recognition, Akers set off for Washington without delay.[124]

Initially, the TEB, in Austin Buckles' words, "were not concerned or figured the rump council actions very serious." The meetings on January 7 and January 28 "were assumed a continuation of a Sioux council, but the group declared it otherwise."[125] Once in Washington, Former Montana Congressman and Acting Assistant SI Wesley A. D'Ewart helped Akers get her General Council actions confirmed, and pulled strings to get her delegation recognized and their expenses paid with tribal funds. Delegates Youpee and Begs His Own joined her there.[126]

The Billings Area Office Field Solicitor issued an opinion on February 21 at the request of BIA in Washington about the legal status of the January 1956 General Councils and their actions. The minutes for the two councils had been sent to DC, and presumably the solicitor saw them. Based on the information the Akers delegation had provided, he declared the meetings legally called.[127] The 1954 constitution made General Councils venues only of tribal claims matters, but much to Austin Buckles' chagrin, he learned that the solicitor's office in Billings was "unaware" of the 1954 constitution and by-laws, even though the document had presumably been forwarded up the organizational structure. Therefore, the field solicitor was applying the 1927 constitution to the circumstances.[128] Austin Buckles and James Archdale were unofficially informed on March 16 that they had been removed from office.[129]

On this same day, Dolly Akers, Begs His Own, and Youpee met with CIA Glenn L. Emmons, with Superintendent Talley and Assistant CIA Greenwood also in attendance. The main issue discussed was the official constitution and bylaws. Akers argued for the 1927 constitution while disparaging the 1954 document. Emmons and Greenwood agreed with her, and she asked for written confirmation to that effect.[130]

Besides the Akers delegation, another led by Norman Hollow as acting chair of the TEB also was in DC to protest the takeover; and a third delegation was there on Assiniboine claims business.[131] The Hollow delegation, which was already in Washington by March 13, 1956, could only stay until March 23, so its members sought an extension.[132] Meanwhile, Austin Buckles and James Archdale had also gone to Washington to protest their removal and had asked the Assistant SI that expenses arising from their trip be approved "until such reasonable time as is required to bring about a settlement of the questions confronting our Tribes' Executive Board with respect to the official conduct of the Tribes' business."[133]

In a press release dated March 24, 1956, the Interior Department and the Indian Bureau denied responsibility for the political situation at Fort Peck. The Deputy Solicitor, Edmond T. Fritz, had ruled on March 23, 1956 that expenses could only be paid for delegates chosen at the General Council meetings of January 7 and 28. Fritz declared that CIA had "too broadly con-

strued" his memorandum dated March 13; in his interpretation, the General Councils of January 7 and 28 were legally binding and Chairman Austin Buckles and Vice-Chairman James Archdale had been legally and "effectively removed." Austin Buckles declared:

We have never recognized the delegation to Washington headed by Dolly Akers as officially representing the Fort Peck Indian Tribes and it seems to us who are officers and members of the Executive Board of the Fort Peck Indian Tribes that this memorandum opinion from the Deputy Solicitor to the Commissioner of Indian Affairs puts the whole matter of whom is running our tribes right back in the Commissioner's lap.

Buckles said he had been promised but never received confirmation that he and Archdale had been removed from their offices. The field solicitor at the Billings area office ruled on February 21 that the Akers delegation would not be paid from tribal funds. However, the BIA also refused to pay Buckles' travel expenses on March 21, so he appealed to D'Ewart on March 22. Senator Murray brokered a conference in his office on March 20, and Deputy Solicitor Fritz stated that he had never ruled that Buckles and Archdale had been removed from their positions. Fritz also stated that "he was sure that the Secretary of Interior had no desire to interfere in tribal elections, and, in his opinion, the Secretary had no power to do so." Buckles and Archdale were determined to press the CIA for a "clear ruling" on their status. An impending oil lease sale on April 4, 1956 required clarification of the Tribes' leadership.[134]

In an opinion of the Interior Department's solicitor, a subsequent General Council on April 7 was not official because it did not adhere to the 1927 constitution. An opinion dated April 23, 1956 stated that although temporary officers could be appointed, a new election was needed to end the factionalism "now existing on the reservation." Because the 1954 constitution had not been approved in Washington or ratified by "the qualified voters of the tribe as required by regulation," the April 7 meeting was not properly authorized.[135]

Thomas Dignan, the tribes' new attorney, on March 27 wrote on behalf of Acting Chairman Norman Hollow to Deputy Solicitor Edmond T. Fritz, attempting to clarify the leadership situation. Dignan pointed to issues in the June 1 and June 7, 1956, meetings of the General Council, and stated that Dolly Akers should not sit as chairperson because she was not working for the best interests of the Tribes. The prevailing issue was the bylaw that required the use of a secret ballot, which, of course, was not performed in the meetings of June 7 and 28.[136]

Buckles and Archdale along with Councilmen Leslie Four Star, Henry Archdale, Edwin Reddoor, William R. Smith, and Norman Hollow met in Washington with SI Douglas McKay and CIA Glenn L. Emmons on March 28, 1956. They stated that the Fort Peck Tribal Executive Board delegation and the Fort Peck Assiniboine delegation were returning to Fort Peck Reservation "in disgust and contempt for what has happened in the issue at hand."[137] D'Ewart replied that the matter had been referred to the legal staff.[138]

A General Council was called for April 7, 1956 in Poplar, and the notice was signed by seven district committeemen or chairmen and paid for by the Poplar district of the Assiniboine and Sioux tribes. Freda Beazley, Eva Mae Smith, and W.R. Smith reported via telegram to Senator Murray on April 8, 1956 on the work of the general council the previous day. Copies were also sent to Congressman Lee Metcalf and to Emmons. Dolly Akers and her followers refused to acknowledge a telegram from Emmons stating that the General Council called for April 7 was not "a legal

meeting." Superintendent Talley was not allowed to make the announcement to the assembly. After all executive board members chosen in the previous election were voted out, an election was held for a new executive board. Akers was elected chairman and George Thompson, vice-chairman. Beasley and the Smiths protested and asked that the solicitor render his long-deferred decision on the Fort Peck political crisis. The text of the telegram concluded: "Take what other action is necessary for our protection against such communistic strategy."[139]

Emmons wrote Buckles on April 13, 1956 about the competing delegations in Washington and attempted to explain why the Akers delegation was allowed to draw expenses for reimbursement. The CIA refused to freeze funding for tribal programs, but rather offered platitudes.[140]

Having served four terms (1946-1954), Wesley A. D'Ewart ran for U.S. Senate in 1954 against Senator James Murray, and at the height of McCarthyism tried to red-bait Murray. Murray defeated D'Ewart, 50.4% to 49.6%. Both President Eisenhower and Vice President Nixon campaigned for D'Ewart in the state, and after D'Ewart's defeat, he accepted a temporary appointment as Assistant to the Secretary of Agriculture from January to September 1955. He then was appointed Assistant Secretary of Interior. However, this position required Senate approval, so D'Ewart served in an acting capacity until his confirmation was defeated in July 1956.[141]

Buckles wrote D'Ewart that he had not received any payment for per diem and transportation expenses of his return trip from Washington. He disagreed with paying the Akers delegation's expenses, since she had proceeded to Washington without permission from either the CIA or the executive board. While the April 7 actions had been declared illegal, the lack of recognition of the amended 1927 constitution also was problematic. Buckles asserted that D'Ewart might want to reflect upon his past associations with Akers, who had "initiated this rumpus which has resulted in anarchy," and "she and her followers repeatedly mentioned your name and that of Hon. Representative Fjare as being very cooperative in their gains."[142] D'Ewart wrote Senator Murray on April 23, 1956 that the solicitor had decided that the amended 1927 constitution was the constitutional document governing the combined Tribes on the Fort Peck Reservation, but also stating that the removal of the chairman and vice-chairman was "effective."[143]

Buckles wrote the CIA on April 26, 1956 that the CIA had addressed him as chairman in the letter of April 13, which he appreciated. However, based on the misinformation of his subordinates and other delegates, the previous determination of March 13 had been "too broadly construed," leaving the validity of his chairmanship and the authority of the constitution in limbo. John Akers' protest of how the election was conducted had only complicated matters. Buckles again explained that the TEB had conducted tribal business and the election of 1955 on the basis of the 1954 constitution, which had been adopted in a General Council on October 16, 1954. He reiterated that TEB was awaiting suggestions for changes to that document from the CIA and SI, before referring it to a referendum. Buckles, with legal advice, claimed that Public Law 449 had been violated by the purported executive board, and Fort Peck funds were disbursed through the bonded officers of the bureau and Interior Department. He also contended that variable information available to solicitors, whether in Washington or in area offices, had resulted in injustice and duplicated services to Indians. Buckles then turned personal, stating that "the Assiniboine and Sioux Tribes are in a state of anarchy brought about by a woman petty-fogger

who has influenced someone officially." Buckles astutely pointed to a ten-year grudge Akers had borne since her impeachment, which had never been officially rescinded.[144]

A telegram from the Montana congressional delegation to Buckles on May 1, 1956 reported that the Interior Department had ruled that even though the meeting of April 7 had been illegal and none of the actions and elections stood, the removal of the chairman and vice-chairman had still been effective, and the only solution was to call a new election under the 1927 amended constitution. The TEB as constituted prior to the meeting of April 7 had authority to act, according to the solicitor.[145]

Senator James Murray, Chair of the Senate Committee on Interior and Insular Affairs, arranged an informal hearing on May 20, 1956 to discuss the Fort Peck political situation. Charles Murray, administrative assistant to the senator, chaired the meeting until the senator was available. Senator Mike Mansfield, Congressman Lee Metcalf, William E. Coburn (Senate Interior and Insular Affairs Committee Counsel), Wesley A. D'Ewart (Assistant SI-Public Land Management), Edmund T. Fritz (Assistant Solicitor-Interior), E. Rex Lee (Associate CIA-BIA), Clinton Talley (Superintendent, Fort Peck Agency), Thomas Dignan (Attorney for the Fort Peck Executive Board, Fort Peck Reservation), and Austin Buckles attended. The discussion began by outlining the limitations of the 1927 Constitution and Bylaws and the amendment to use a secret ballot in all decision-making, adopted April 15, 1953. Affirmation of the Constitution and Bylaws adopted on October 16, 1954 was described, intimating that the document had been reviewed at the Area Office with the suggested changes incorporated, and it was assumed that the vetting by the BIA and Interior was underway. The election of 1955 was conducted following the 1954 Constitution, which prompted the complaint in *Akers vs. Fort Peck Indians*. Solicitor Fritz was asked about his opinion validating the Akers delegation elected at the General Councils of January 7 and 28, 1956. Fritz denied that this was his intention, and also denied that he was effectively validating one constitution over another. Austin Buckles emphasized the department had never officially informed him of his removal, causing a "disruption and disorganized the Fort Peck Tribal Government." He noted that he had not seen minutes for these two meetings until he arrived in Washington. The solicitor agreed to review the entire situation in light of the Constitution of 1954, but the question about who was responsible for the recognition question, much to Buckles' chagrin, went unanswered. It was agreed that the TEB had authority to act until the next election.[146]

Superintendent Talley asked that Buckles explain the solicitor's decision of May 1 and his suggestions for "stabilizing Tribal organization" to a meeting of tribal members at the superintendent's office on May 22, 1956.[147]

Compromise did not satisfy Buckles. He wrote Curry on July 3, 1956, asking Curry to represent him in his struggle to remain in power and to counter the attacks on him. Buckles sent Curry documents asking for an assessment as to whether a suit was tenable.[148] Curry's file did not include his response.

The TEB convened in a special meeting on May 17, 1956 and elected Norman Hollow Acting Chairman with the understanding that he would serve until the next election. The meeting had been convened at the written request of councilmen Edwin J. Reddoor, Leon Spotted Bull, and James Sweeney. Superintendent Talley asked that Catherine Eder be confirmed as secretary of the TEB to cover financial responsibilities in particular, and this was done. Two appointed members to the board, James Earl Wetsit and Leslie Fourstar, were disqualified from serving due to

potential violation of the 1952 amendment to the constitution requiring secret balloting at the district level.[149] In a special meeting of the TEB on May 24, 1956, a request for a General Council for June 16 was approved, but in another special TEB meeting on June 1, it was pointed out that the requirement for thirty days notice had not been met. What was really needed was soliciting sentiment at the district level and confirming that elections at any level needed to be by secret ballot. Rumors about a per capita payment were circulating, but the obstacle of creating an up-to-date roll still remained. Austin Buckles spoke to the need for the TEB to "set up" an enrollment ordinance, but he pointed out that a General Council could not make any final decisions when there needed to be a referendum. A motion was made to rescind the action on May 28 for a General Council on June 16, because people on the west end of the reservation wanted to wait on the outcome of the Akers suit.[150] A General Council in Poplar on August 4 re-affirmed the contract with attorneys Dignan and Gallagher.[151] Dolly Akers and George Thompson were elected in the special election two days later.

Those who had opposed the Akers-Thompson faction, particularly re-elected councilmen, requested a meeting with the Billings area office staff on October 2, 1956. The Akers group had apparently had a similar meeting with the area office staff "last week." Councilmen Edwin J. Reddoor, Lester Youpee, Charles Track, James Sweeney, Leslie Four Star, and Henry Archdale were joined by James Archdale, attorney Thomas Dignan, and Tribal Secretary Catherine Eder. Reinholt Brust, Assistant Area Director for Administration, represented the area staff, with Bielefeld and Pease of the Field Solicitor's office also present. While the TEB meetings had been called by the chairman, Catherine Eder explained that the chairman took her rough draft minutes and rewrote them, but she as secretary would not sign the certification until minutes were approved by the whole board. The group discussed the chairman's authority and various trends in expanding or contracting responsibilities, especially relative to signing authority. The membership ordinance would have to define how membership was determined, or it would fall to the SI. Membership criteria also had to be incorporated into any new effort for constitutional reform. The group discussed the issue of due notice for all meetings of the TEB, including the chairman's claim that she could call a meeting whenever she felt one was needed, claiming it was "tradition" and asking all board members to sign a waiver of notice. The politics of protesting were made explicit, demonstrating the ways in which the tribal secretary or individual councilmen would be compromised. The chairman had no vote except to break a tie, but acting chairmen still retained their right to vote in matters before the board. Norman Hollow had been authorized to sign documents by resolution when he was acting chairman of the TEB. The question was raised about oil leases in particular, which originally all board members had signed. The SI determined, however, that the chairman and secretary should sign leases. James Archdale spoke against the chairman's ability to influence by "maneuvering the Indians, purchasing and bribing Indian people." The chairman was called an influence seeker, and she used General Councils in which her supporters could be organized and the TEB diminished. The area office people confirmed that if the chairman presented a motion to the council, whatever was proposed (short of violations of law) and approved by a vote could stand as a substantive action. For example, motions to remove individuals from office, even if they were elected by districts, could be so enacted. The meeting ended on this alarmist note.[152]

Having had almost two months to reflect upon the outcome of the special election, Austin

Buckles wrote Sister Providencia on November 30, 1956 that Fort Peck tribal business was virtually at a "standstill" and "turmoil" had produced significant "confusion." He noted that he had lost by fourteen votes and Jim Archdale by twelve, and both had been denied recounts. He also noted that two different lists of registered voters had appeared at all polls, meaning that some voters were denied the right to vote. Buckles related how Chairman Akers was creating intolerable working conditions for Catherine Eder, the tribal secretary, putting her desk in a cold hallway, foisting receptionist duties upon her, and hiring other clerks to do what were normally her duties. TEB meetings had become free-for-alls: Actions and motions were brought to the board but never voted upon or received Akers' approval unless she saw fit to certify them. Tribal files were commandeered and disrupted, the vice chairman had taken over the tribal car, and long-distance phone calls were out of control. "The wording of some documents and minutes of the files have been changed to serve their purposes." Austin reported the Superintendent and Area Director had told him to avoid forcing the hand of the Akers-Thompson group. The officials wanted to give the faction enough rope to hang themselves, and the BIA did not want to become involved. Buckles described the problems with attorney contracts, and how the current group had disputed the availability of legal advice. He finished by saying, "I wish that I was a good writer or historian because our predicament would make quite a story and I contend certain Department and Bureau Officials are fully responsible."[153]

On December 17, 1956, Chairman Akers notified the TEB that for all future meetings, they must submit a notice of a prepared resolution and give it to the chairman "for study" and "after acceptance and consideration of resolution by Chairman, the resolution will be referred to the proper committee."[154]

Chairperson Akers believed that Fort Peck Tribal government prior to her election had been "conducted improperly and [at] times illegally." She perceived that the six board members lead by Norman Hollow were resisting her efforts to conduct the TEB meetings according to the 1927 constitution and bylaws, and she claimed that the "attitude of six Board members placed Fort Peck Tribal government in confusion."[155]

The relationship between the parties further disintegrated. Chairman Akers refused to preside over another special meeting called by three sitting TEB members on December 21, 1956, so Edwin J. Reddoor was elected the chair of the meeting. Leslie Four Star presented a resolution adopted at the Assiniboine Council on December 15 in Wolf Point calling for Akers' removal as chairman, declaring her unfit to represent the Tribes and stating that she had failed to work for their best interests because of "her undesirable character." The TEB adopted motion by a vote of eight in the affirmative for removal of Dolly Akers.[156]

The Akers group's main promise was that they would secure a per capita payment from funds presumably accruing from the energy boom. In her newsletter dated December 31, 1956, Akers presented her interpretation of what she contended were a minority controlling the spending of tribal funds.[157] Austin Buckles felt that Akers and Thompson were sidestepping the real issues with such actions as demanding Superintendent Talley's removal, claiming he was to blame for preventing the release of $3 million of tribal money. Buckles claimed, "Talley has no authority to release this money on deposit with the Treasurer of the United States."[158]

Akers continued her attack upon Talley, describing as interference various expenses that had been paid with his approval. She sent a detailed "appeal" to the CIA dated January

24, 1957, blaming Talley for violating the tribal constitution, not following department rules, regulations, and directives, and accusing him of "refusing to cooperate with the duly elected, qualified and acting officers of the Executive Board of the Fort Peck Tribal Council." She contended that her opponents' efforts, aided by Talley, undermined the 1927 constitution.[159] The reconstituted TEB had sent a telegram to Senator Murray on January 7 demanding Talley's removal: "His removal will end quisling type of tribal government on Fort Peck which is comparable to communistic actions prevailing in foreign countries."[160]

The special TEB meeting scheduled for January 4, 1957 was delayed because the Council Chamber was locked, and after waiting for an hour outside, the meeting was moved to the Poplar Armory, further emphasizing the refusal of the chairman and vice chairman to preside.[161] A regular meeting scheduled for February 14, 1957 was also delayed because four locks had been placed on the Tribal Office Chamber; the meeting was moved to the Tribal Law and Order Office building.[162]

In a TEB meeting on February 26, 1957, Chairman Akers declared there was no need to meet because she was waiting on a legal opinion. She stated that the TEB had been "operating illegally" for some time. She called on Melvin Buckles to report a conversation with Acting Superintendent Burke, who commented that the Akers suit had nothing to do with a proposed per capita payment, but rather was a case against the Oil and Gas Committee. Word of mouth had circulated that the new members of the TEB were not to be recognized, and she felt she could not preside at the meeting. Tribal Secretary James J. Eder reminded her that he had an opinion from A.E. Bielefeld, the field solicitor of the Billings Area Office, that confirmed Mrs. Akers as chairman but also declared the "old" TEB members were duly elected members. Norman Hollow insisted a new opinion was forthcoming. The minutes reported that "considerable arguments erupted" among those present; "Mrs. Akers, pounding wildly with her gavel, announced, 'I am Chairman, and there will be no meeting conducted here.'"[163]

Arguments at the next meetings (March 14 and 22) turned on who should be tribal secretary. Chairman Akers did not have confidence in James J. Eder, because she could not control him. The chairman sought to appoint her supporter, Frances Linner. Akers argued that the tribal secretary should do his or her work in the tribal chambers. Norman Hollow said that then the chairman should return files and tribal office equipment to the tribal chambers and not lock anyone out. Another point was that when typed minutes were available, the documents were going missing, supporting Eder's challenges. The chairman and her supporting TEB members maintained that minutes from past meetings were also missing. Certifications by the chair of individual meetings required a signature, complicating the matter, as did the fact that the councilmen's mailboxes, where minutes were to be placed once prepared, were also in the chambers. After wrangling about this, Norman Hollow asked Chairman Akers why she protested every action of the TEB. The chairman declared that Eder should not be secretary when "there are a lot of more deserving tribal members who should have Mr. Eder's job." The arguing continued, but then eight members of the TEB moved to get on with important business.[164] Newly appointed Superintendent David Weston made a formal statement to the March 22 meeting, promising "a fair and impartial administration at the Agency," expecting honest dealings and accepting elected officials as representatives for the Tribes. Weston was very straightforward about countering what he had been informed was "a great deal of misunderstanding among the members of the tribe [sic] concerning proper procedures under which the forthcoming election is to be held." He reminded the TEB that no one could be elected to the board in a General Council, such as the one scheduled for April 15. Anything emanating from such a meeting would not be recognized.[165]

At a special meeting held on March 30, Chairman Akers protested and refused to certify minutes for the March 22 meeting, not wanting her actions or the statement by Superintendent Weston on the record. A majority of TEB members sought to have Vice Chairman Thompson take the chair. An attempt to have minutes of previous meetings read delayed other actions. Tribal secretary Eder declared that times sheets could not be submitted for processing if TEB minutes were not certified. The text of Public Law 449 was read in full to the meeting to emphasize accountability.[166]

The special meeting on April 6, 1957 was another standoff. The meeting was called to address a number of unauthorized bills for unapproved expenditures. The TEB had arrived prior to the scheduled time, but finally at 11 a.m., the tribal secretary called the meeting to order and an acting chair was selected because the chairman and vice chairman were not present. Several bills were read (most had been paid under protest), and meanwhile Chairman Akers arrived and took a seat. After the noon recess, the TEB waited for the chairman to come to the chambers to preside. When she did not appear, the acting chairman presided over the rest of the meeting.[167] The chairman dominated the regular meeting on April 11, 1957 with another filibuster, disappointing even her supporter former chairman William Knorr, who told her to stop her obstructionism.[168]

Several district councilmen races in the Fort Peck General Election held on April 15 were fiercely contested. A special meeting of the TEB was scheduled for April 29, but several seats were still undecided, and therefore quorum was at issue. A tie between Maurice Big Horn and Leon Spotted Bull was settled when Big Horn withdrew. Earl Jones' election as representative for Riverside was challenged when it was reported he had voted in Poplar and therefore disqualified himself. Lester A. Youpee, the next highest vote getter, was declared elected. James J. Eder was re-appointed tribal secretary with the authority to hire additional help and to keep all time records. Standing committees were named for the coming term.[169] The chairman blocked attempts to proceed in several ways. Councilman William Youpee told the chairman to cooperate or else be replaced by a temporary chairman so the meeting could proceed. Akers stated that the TEB was not going to legislate her removal if she could help it. When the chairman refused to preside, Leslie Four Star was elected acting chair. The chairman's brother, William R. Smith, an Oswego councilman, asked Superintendent Weston what was to be done about seating the disputed members of the TEB, and Weston stated that the TEB had the authority to settle the dispute. Problems of proper notification and failure to declare a clear agenda wasted more time for all present.[170]

On May 9, the supporters and detractors of the chairman sought to move their opposing agendas forward. Area Office people and the field solicitor were invited in hopes that the latter might act as a moderator and "give unbiased interpretations of the Fort Peck Tribes' Constitution and By-Laws," meaning the 1927 document. Council supporters of the chairman—Kermit Smith, Alfred Manning, Melvin Buckles, and Carl Walking Eagle—submitted a "minority report" about the meeting to

SI Fred Seaton, dated May 20, 1957, describing the other faction as seven board members voting as a block. Eleven resolutions were passed, but were not presented to the chairman for notice or referred to the standing committees. Among these were the membership ordinance and the plan for a referendum vote. The writers contended that issues for membership had to be dealt with by General Council, not the TEB.[171] The resolution passed on May 9 by the TEB to draft an enrollment ordinance was necessary to securing a per capita payment. A Tribal Enrollment Committee would be created, consisting of one member from each district and a seventh to serve as well, with the committee choosing its chair and secretary. The draft ordinance included specific criteria:

(a) All persons of Indian blood whose name appears on the roll of the Assiniboine and Sioux Tribes of the Fort Peck Indian Reservation, Montana, as used for the purpose of making a per capita payment in 1932 to the members of the Tribes, and their descendants of at least one-fourth (1/4) degree of Assiniboine and/or Sioux blood of the Assiniboine and/or Sioux Tribes of the Assiniboine and Sioux Tribes of the Fort Peck Indian Reservation, Montana, excluding those who are now or hereafter enrolled with any other Indian tribe or band.

(b) Reservation residence of the parents at the time of birth of such descendents is not an enrolment [sic] requirement.

(c) Persons hereafter enrolled must be citizens of the United States.

(d) A Tribal Enrollment Committee consisting of seven (7) members shall be established for the purpose of preparing a membership roll of the Tribes and to pass on and approve all future applications for enrollment. Said roll, together with a certificate of the Executive Board as to its correctness, shall be submitted to the CIA for his approval, and when so approved shall constitute the membership of the Tribes as of the date of certificate of the Executive Board.

(e) Each District on the reservation shall choose one member. . . .[172]

Chairman Akers in a communication with Percy E. Melis, director of the Billings area office, on May 10, 1957 declared that she had stood alone to defend the "original" constitution of the Tribes. She quoted a communication from the CIA to the TEB, dated April 10, 1953, that the General Council, not the TEB, held authority over membership matters. The chairman criticized Melis and the field solicitors for suggesting publicly that a referendum be held to decide the matter: "The membership question is the Fort Peck Tribal members' greatest issue at the present time."[173]

Chairman Akers and TEB members Alfred Manning, Melvin Buckles, and Carl Walking Eagle presented a minority report, dated May 22, 1957, to Superintendent Weston, protesting actions at a TEB meeting held May 17. She claimed that her minority faction was being "steamrollered" by the majority.[174]

Chairman Akers' June 1957 newsletter addressed what she was doing to secure a per capita payment, and declared that the "only road block preventing a per capita payment" was "the question of membership." She suggested that the question could be settled at a General Council on June 16. She quoted the CIA communication of April 10, 1953, and indicated that the authority of the General Council in membership matters was affirmed in another communication of that date. In May, at Thomas Dignan's recommendation, a General Council had been called for June 16, but the TEB rescinded this approval on June 1, not wanting to create a forum to the chairman and her supporters. The chairman cited minutes from the fall and winter of 1956, in which Norman Hollow and seven other board members consistently voted against calling a General Council. She suggested that this group was not interested in doing what was necessary to secure a per capita payment.[175]

On June 6, Acting Area Director M.A. Johnson responded to Chairman Akers' protest by quoting the field solicitor that an amendment to the bylaws was needed so a referendum could be authorized.[176] Chairman Akers sent Solicitor Fritz the June 6 communication on June 11, commenting that the area director was apparently issuing legal opinions, reinforcing her argument that the various BIA and Interior Department officials were undermining the 1927 Constitution.[177]

The Office of the Field Solicitor communicated on June 7 with the Director of the Area Office, commenting upon the Fort Peck TEB resolution that provided an interpretative summary of the powers, authorities, and processes of committees in relationship to the TEB and the chairman. The office expressed concern about the redefined committees having been given powers outside the authority of the TEB. It made a series of suggestions about how the TEB could continue to control committee actions while retaining its authority.[178]

Acting CIA W. Barton Greenwood wrote Area Director Percy E. Melis on July 29, 1957 to discuss in detail the proposed attorney contract for general counsel services with the firm Skedd, Harris, and Massman. The two-year contract was to cost $10,000 annually. Greenwood noted that seven TEB councilmen urged approval, while one member protested the contract. Chairman Akers also filed a petition with 180 names of those opposing approval of the contract. The contract was referred to the solicitor for recommended action, and had been returned without concurrence. The tribal constitution required action on the contract by a general council. Greenwood observed:

We fully realize the administrative difficulties and ramifications which will result from this matter. The turmoil, however, which exists at Fort Peck will continue so long as the tribal government is pulled in various directions by the advocates of the General Council and by the advocates of the TEB.

The present Tribal Constitution and By-Laws of the Fort Peck Tribes is so loosely drawn that it is of little use in dealing with the difficulties and the many issues which constantly develop among the factions within the tribal membership as related to the tribal government. The long history of dissension and strife between the Assiniboine and the Sioux of the Fort Peck Reservation, as you know, has now resulted in certain members of both tribes advocating as the only solution to the growing impasse, the separation of the two tribes governmentally and a separate governing body for each tribe. Since reservation resources and financial assets are owned jointly by both tribes, any division of resources would, of course, require appropriate legislation by the Congress. Thus far, neither group has offered a feasible plan which would result in an equitable division of the reservation resources and the financial assets of the tribes.

Urging the Area Office and the agency superintendent to pay particular attention to Fort Peck tribal membership, the CIA stressed the need to encourage cooperation, or "to tolerate their differences and to resolve such differences in accordance with the present tribal governmental framework." Greenwood also asserted, "The modification, amendment, or complete replacement of the present tribal constitution would accomplish much toward an orderly tribal government."

According to Greenwood, to move forward with this contract, compensation needed to be calculated differently, and the succession of services needed to rest with the law firm rather than an individual lawyer.[179] Frustration with the situation at Fort Peck was growing.

Edmund T. Fritz, the Deputy Solicitor for the Department of the Interior, wrote the CIA on July 9, 1957 about the minority report submitted on May 20 about the proposed membership ordinance. TEB's majority decision to submit the ordinance to a referendum vote rather than a General Council was an attempt to get wider participation of tribal members in the decision about membership. The area director had examined the participation rates in seven General Councils held since 1951, and concluded that 10 percent or less of the tribal members participated in such meetings. Non-resident tribal members were particularly disadvantaged. One example was a meeting on June 11, 1955 when only twenty-eight persons constituted the majority of the fifty-five persons present, demonstrating how a small group of people could control any decisions made at such meetings. Fritz asserted:

It is my opinion that the Executive Board of the Fort Peck Tribes lacks authority, without approval of the general council, assembled, to submit a membership ordinance to a referendum vote. This does not suggest that a referendum is not the most democratic and desirable means of obtaining an expression from all of the members of the Fort Peck Tribes.

The 1927 Constitution had constraints on electing delegates or adopting other Indians into the tribes, which had to be accomplished by a General Council rather than the TEB. Was a General Council a specific meeting of tribal members, or was it in fact the collective membership of the Fort Peck Tribes? Fritz suggested the latter interpretation in case of administrative action.[180]

However, the battle between the factions was becoming increasingly protracted. In a special meeting on July 30, 1957, Superintendent Weston asked to speak once the business of the day was concluded. His statement was paternalistic in tone and demonstrated the frustration that he and other levels of the bureaucracy in the BIA and Department of Interior and the Montana congressional delegation were feeling. Weston stated that time had been wasted on matters that should have taken minutes instead of hours. He pointed to serious issues needing deliberations and decisions that were never considered. "In a recent closed-door session, I reminded you that if you did not transact business properly, that it would be necessary for me to refuse to make payment to you as officers of the tribe and members of the Board." He mentioned a meeting on July 29, at which the only thing accomplished was the reading of the minutes of the previous meeting. Weston emphasized that the failure of the TEB to act was "hampering the operations of the Agency Office," and therefore, because of a failure to act, Weston outlined a set of procedures "for guidance in future operations":

1. I must insist that in the future all Resolutions passed in regular or special meeting of the Board be delivered to me, properly authenticated, within 24 hours after action by the Board. This can be accomplished by securing the signatures of your Secretary and Chairman during the Board meeting when action is taken.

2. I must insist that I be given a draft copy of the minutes of your meeting within 72 hours immediately following the meeting of the Board.

3. I must insist that you get down to business and take action by acceptance or rejection of major issues presented with a reasonable length of time.

The superintendent then declared: "Failure to comply with these instructions will result in my refusal to approve claims for compensation by the Officers and members of the Board."

Meetings called for 10:30 a.m. that did not begin until at 1 p.m. were also problematic for him. He declared that if anyone received pay and compensation for "services rendered to the Tribe," he expected persons to "perform service commensurate with the pay" to be received. Asked if people wanted to do their business outside the agency, he replied "that as long as the land of individual Indians remain in trust, it will be his position to control this land," and if anyone "wants to do his or her own business, they should apply for a patent in fee."[181]

It is unclear whether Akers' protest was written before or after the TEB meeting on July 20, 1957. She complained that most TEB members were spending tribal funds for excessive office supplies and the salaries of four clerks, all for work that should be done by the tribal secretary. She complained most that she did not have basic secretarial support for her work.[182]

Councilmen Alfred Manning and Kermit Smith, supporters of Chairman Akers, complained to Superintendent Weston on August 2, 1957 that actions "taken to upset or disturb the duties and salary of the Fort Peck Tribal Chairman" were occurring. They claimed that the voters who had put the chairman in office were being unfairly disadvantaged in the budget item for July 29 that called for reassignment of the chairman's salary. The councilmen cited a solicitor's decision in the fall of 1956 requiring a two-thirds vote to void previous resolutions affecting the duties and pay of the chairman.[183]

Acting CIA W. Barton Greenwood wrote Area Office Director Melis on August 5, 1957 that a solicitor's opinion did not agree with Interior Department's and BIA's positions, resulting in the conclusion that a General Council would be needed after all for approval of a membership ordinance.[184]

True to his warning of July 30, Superintendent Weston issued a list of claims on August 13, 1957, that he had refused to pay to TEB officers and members, giving specific reasons for his position. The chairman was docked for failing to sign documents that had been properly passed by the TEB. Members of the Budget Committee were docked for failure to report back to the TEB as required. The Oil and Gas Committee members, the Lands and Lots Committee members, and the Law and Order Committee members were docked for failure to make proper reports to the TEB. Once the "deficiencies" were corrected, the superintendent would issue the necessary checks.[185]

In a special meeting of the TEB on August 29, 1957, a resolution was adopted appealing to the SI and CIA to recognize the 1954 Constitution and Bylaws as the operating documents for the Tribes' government. With a quorum of ten present, a vote of six constituted the majority.[186] Although the chairman signed the resolution as the presiding officer, she and Councilmen Kermit Smith, Alfred Manning, and Melvin Buckles submitted a minority report dated September 6, 1957. The objectors asked whether the version brought to the General Council was final or simply a draft. Akers noted that at a later date, modifications were being made, incorporating eleven objections or recommendations. The objectors then asserted that the 1954 Constitution did not exist because it had not been approved by the SI. They pointed out that the discussion between Austin Buckles and Senate Interior and Insular Affairs Committee Counsel Coburn during the March 20, 1956 informal hearing had stressed that a referendum had not yet been held on the 1954 Constitution and Bylaws. Consequently, the subsequent changes also needed to go back to General Council for final approval. "[W]e are convinced," the objectors wrote, "that this document was prepared by some of the holdovers from the John Collier regime who believe in and are advocating a communistic form

of Government for the Indians." They argued that the TEB's most recent vote was made to retard further the attention to the tribes' business. Referring to Weston's admonitions, they blamed the six member majority of the TEB. Government officials were calling the situation at Fort Peck a "national scandal." The unsettled controversy from the last election in the Riverside District was not being resolved by special election because that would give an advantage to the majority faction. Expenditures and "unauthorized power and authority" given to the tribal secretary were serious problems. The writers called on the SI to call a General Council to settle the matter.[187] Akers wrote a long letter to CIA Glenn L. Emmons, dated September 10, 1957, explaining in great detail the obstructionism her group was experiencing from the majority.[188]

Tribal Secretary James J. Eder sent members of the TEB a memorandum dated September 19, 1958 documenting an exchange he had with Chairman Akers about what Eder characterized as an "unauthorized seizing of minutes." On the early afternoon of September 19, the chairman entered the tribal secretary's office and requested twelve copies of the TEB meeting minutes for September 3, 1957. Eder explained that he had been instructed by the Programming and Resolution Committee that each member of the TEB be given only one copy of meeting minutes. Attempting to pull rank, the chairman said that she was entitled to ask for as many copies of the minutes as she wanted. Eder explained that he was following the wishes of the TEB members on the committee. Akers declared that only the TEB in a meeting of the whole could make such a rule. He gave the chairman her copy of the minutes. On his desk were the rest of copies, labeled with the intended recipients' names and ready to be distributed. The chairman seized the copies and dared the secretary to stop her. He made no such attempt, and she left his office.[189]

At the request of the Billings Area Office Director, Field Solicitor A. E. Bielefeld opined on September 23, 1957, about the validity of the resolution on the authority of the TEB to regulate the chairman's pay. While the authority of the overall resolution was sustained, the appointed committees and approvals at that level were improper. All aspects of the approval were found in order.[190]

In a special TEB meeting on October 15, 1957, Chairman Akers declared that "due to the fact that there isn't a full membership quorum, the Board can't act. . . . ." Superintendant Weston countered that if there was a quorum to meet, then there was a quorum to act. Accepting the chairman's interpretation would protest all actions done by the TEB since April 1957. Chairman Akers sarcastically said "that this just might be done." The chairman then asserted that all resolutions must come to her desk in advance of introduction and consideration. Weston countered by charging the committee on programming and resolutions to make sure the resolutions were prepared for introduction and decision.[191]

While continuing a recessed special TEB meeting on October 21, Chairman Akers said that she was opposed to the TEB "spending too much money." She again declared that all business for the TEB should come via the chairman's desk. She said that even sending people to NCAI meetings was opposed in some quarters. Youpee noted that whenever he went to Washington, he had proper authorization, suggesting that the chairman sometimes did not. The chairman said that she was not paid when she went without authorization, but Superintendent Weston stated that she did receive her regular salary.[192]

On October 29, 1957, Superintendent Weston acknowledged a letter from Akers protesting actions by the TEB on a new land policy on September 19. The superintendent informed the chairman and the TEB that he was "not honoring any actions taken by the Board after the agenda of the special meeting was completed."[193]

The chairman wrote on November 9, 1957 to Deputy Solicitor Edmund Fritz to report on the recent regular visit of the Billings area director. Late in the afternoon of October 28, Area Director Melis and Superintendent Weston met the chairman in her office. Akers stated that the BIA was allowing six "obstructionist Board members to control and expend excessive amount of Tribal funds." She reminded the area director that one seat had remained vacant since May 9, 1957. Melis indicated that he had informed the TEB on May 9 that they should call a special election for the Riverside District. The chairman showed Melis copies of the numerous letters she had written on this issue.[194]

In a regular meeting of the TEB on December 16, 1957, the chairman asked why both factions could not be present at an upcoming Inter-Tribal Policy Board meeting. One of her supporters on the TEB, Melvin Buckles, was excused to see someone at the hospital. The question was called, but the chairman balked, saying that she could not put the question to a vote when there were only six TEB members present. William R. Smith stated that Weston had said six board members were a quorum for meeting or conducting business. Akers said she was waiting on a legal opinion on this point. William Youpee pointed out that she asked the board to do what Weston wanted or to ignore his advice depending on whether it worked to her advantage.[195] Squabbles over secretarial services and costs for temporary showed the pettiness of debates in the TEB.[196] In many cases, interaction was reduced to various interpretations of parliamentary procedure. In one case when the chairman refused to call a question and bring a matter to a vote, the majority of the TEB demanded the vice-chairman preside so the meeting could move forward.[197] This led to another situation on February 20, 1958, when the chairman refused to preside until at least seven members were present, but once that number was reached, she was prepared to preside. A debate ensued about what effect this would have on documents from the meeting and the signatures required. Some wondered whether pay would be held up because of the confusion. The chairman cited the practice that when she came into the room, whoever was presiding would give up the chair to her. The vice chairman, who was acting as presiding officer, was confirmed in this role for the rest of the meeting. Chairman Akers' attempts to lecture the board were declared out of order, and all business conducted at the beginning of the meeting was reaffirmed in a second vote.[198]

On March 11, 1958, Field Solicitor A.E. Bielefeld issued his opinion about that six of ten members did constitute a proper quorum for meeting and business. All present and participating should be paid.[199]

Reflecting upon the perspective of her supporters, Dolly was perceived as a champion for the powerless and an effective advocate and interpreter for individuals needing to ameliorate the intrusions of various levels of government into their lives. Because she was effective in the eyes of her supporters, she did sincerely want to help her people, especially and exclusively her supporters. She placed a high premium upon loyalty; she did for others, and then they did for her. However, she was politically adversarial, which her opponents experienced to the extreme—political bossism reservation-style.

On April 3, 1958, the chairman supported a resolution designed to help individual tribal members seek modifications of loans. The resolution, which was approved on November 30, 1945, provided for emergency short-term loans. The procedures were discussed with the superintendent and then put in place.[200] On April 25, 1958, a resolution approved individuals

and amounts for the short-term credit program, which was a response to drought conditions on the reservation.[201]

The burden on reservation farmers and ranchers in particular, and on land owners in general, meant that financial pressures to sell lands, including trust lands, out of desperation were growing. By the end of May, Senator Murray, chairman of the Senate Committee on Interior and Insular Affairs, secured a delay for Indian land sales for the balance of the current congressional session, because many tribal governments, including that of Fort Peck, were concerned about the rate that lands were being taken out of trust to be sold.[202]

In her June newsletter, Chairman Akers asked for publication of a financial report so all tribal members could have information about the expenditures from tribal funds. She contended that a financial report of May 30 was misleading and failed to give the grand total spent by the board, especially for travel. Chairman Akers went on:

It is the earnest desire and duty of your chairman to secure the greatest good for all tribal members—this can only be accomplished by conducting tribal affairs in accordance with the Tribes' Constitution and By-Laws. The Indian Bureau has constantly reminded the board members certain matters can only and must be settled in General Council.[203]

Superintendent Weston sent a memo to Akers disapproving of the resolution dated June 24, 1958, for a delegation from the Assiniboine Council. Weston said that the TEB initiative for a delegation would also need action by a General Council. The Interior Department's approval of the attorney contract with the Assiniboine Council did not appear to necessitate a delegation to Washington.[204]

From April to June 1958, a land use policy was drafted. The policy was partially prompted by the need to renew the revocable permit for submarginal lands totaling 85,377.77 acres currently in use at Fort Peck, which would expire on December 31, 1958. The policy was sent for review to the area office, with responses due April 10, 1958. The next version of the land use policy, which included a renewal of the revocable permit, was ready to be forwarded to the Central Office for final action.[205]

On June 29, 1958, Glenn L. Emmons, CIA, responded to five complaints about Fort Peck tribal financial matters that Akers had sent him on March 21. The CIA declared that the accusations were untenable. Examination of procedure and outcomes did not reveal problems in financial practice. The CIA found nothing to prompt concern about the administration of the Billings Area Office or the Fort Peck Agency.[206]

Considerable opinions fraught with frustration about what was happening with the TEB and the role of the chairman were playing into this, setting the stage for a confrontation. A critical General Council was convened in Frazer, on September 6, 1958, by Chairperson Akers. At the beginning of the meeting, William Knorr stated that some people had been waiting for four-and-a-half years for such a meeting. He had been disappointed by the administration of tribal affairs over the last three years, feeling that the board had been acting like "dictators," and "that this was just like Russia now." Contentious debate broke out between Norman Hollow and Austin Buckles, on one side, who asked that the board resolution calling the General Council be followed, and Knorr, who asked that past practice be followed. Akers ruled that the council would decide about the number of sergeants-at-arms, and already members of the audience were shouting "no." Austin Buckles then urged compliance with the resolution. Akers stated that support for the resolution was "unnecessary," because "this was a peoples' council, and that the

people will decide who is to be the Sergeants-at-arms." Akers then said she wanted the assembled council to vote from the floor about how to proceed, and she asked all in favor to rise. Again, sentiment in the house was very mixed, since people did not know what they were being asked to vote upon. Akers said the vote from the floor would pick the sergeants-at-arms and tallymen.[207]

More "nos" were heard, and "stopped the procedure of Tribal business for a few minutes, and there was quite a bit of confusion." James Archdale was recognized by the chair, and he called for order and for following the resolution authorizing the council, which included hiring the people who were to act as sergeants-at-arms and tallymen and tallywomen. Akers declared that a sergeant-at-arms was elected, Vearl H. Denny, and that a vote on the Knorr motion was next. She asked that the selection of tallymen from the floor be put to a vote. Denny asked three men to help with the vote on the Knorr motion, and reported 154 votes for the motion. Declaring a mix-up, Akers asked for a re-vote. After a conference among the officers, Akers said the mix-up had been resolved. The vote for opposition to the Knorr motion was called, and 185 votes were reported. However, Akers reported that the tallymen would be chosen from the floor, reporting the vote as 154 for and 113 opposed. Cries of protest went up from the crowd. The tribal secretary took the microphone and reported that the vote was 154 for, 185 opposed, so the motion was lost. Clamor went up for the Hollow motion. Put to a vote, the executive board resolution appointing individuals to serve as officers of the General Council was sustained, with a vote of 206 for and none opposed. A count of the house was taken, and 464 voters were present.[208]

William Youpee then presented General Council Resolution #1 to remove Dolly Akers from her office as chairman "for not working for the best interests of the two tribes, and forever barred from holding office or representing the Assiniboine and Sioux Tribes." Several tried to second the motion. Melvin Buckles secured the microphone and seconded the motion, and wanted the entire executive board to be included. "More shouting and confusion reigned for a few seconds."[209] Akers stated that a motion was before the house with the amendment to remove the entire executive board, and "more bedlam broke loose with this announcement." Attempting a delay, Akers asked that the minutes of the last general council be read, but none were available. A disagreement ensued between several members of the council and Akers over the Youpee motion and who precisely had seconded it. Tribal Secretary Eder was directed by the chair to read the Youpee resolution and motion. Buckles explained that while he seconded the motion, he did so on behalf of the entire executive board. Confusion continued about whether the proposal for removing the chair included the executive board. Leslie Four Star stated that removal of board members should be left to the districts, and for the General Council to act, amendments to the constitution would also need to be rescinded. Melvin Buckles stated that vacancies on the board would require another election, but the board had not acted on this. Akers stated that the motion requesting the chair and board be removed was before the house, and asked for all in favor to rise. Again confusion resulted among the assembly. George W. Thompson, Jr., asked that the vote on the motion be declared out of order, without acting on the amendment.

The General Council was at a standstill. People were walking around by the chair shouting for an opinion, and Field Solicitor A.E. Bielefeld, who was in attendance, requested an opinion on this point of order from Tribal Secretary James J. Eder.[210] Eder declared that the council was to vote on the amendment, followed by a vote on the motion. William Knorr secured the microphone and began ranting about the powers of the General Council, but was drowned out by the "jeers" of those assembled. Pete M. Eagle then secured the floor and spoke in Dakota, saying he was going to interpret Knorr's statements for those who did not understand English. However, he went on to say "that the Executive Board has been spending the Tribes' money extravagantly for the last few years," and he declared "that the Executive Board should be removed." Leslie Fourstar, an Assiniboine speaker, stated that Eagle's translation was not correct. Speaking in Assiniboine, he explained the procedure for taking a vote on the first motion before the house and the Buckles amendment. Akers called for a vote on dismissing the current executive board, but again, so many members of the General Council protested that she called instead for a vote on the Buckles amendment. Those in favor were asked to stand, and the result was 198 for. Then those against were asked to stand, and the total was 217 against, so the motion failed.

Akers then stated that "this council is getting out of hand." She demanded that the main motion be acted upon. More confusion ensued, and more requests were made for the vote on the main motion. "Tempers were beginning to rise, and the Sergeants-in-arms were having quite a time to control the members of the Council." Field Solicitor A.E. Bielefeld was asked to give his opinion on how to proceed with parliamentary procedure, and he stated that dispensing with the amendment usually meant moving on to a vote on the main motion. Knorr again took the microphone and tried to address the council, but he was shouted down. Akers continued to stall, but the mood of the council grew more hostile. Bielefeld again addressed the council, repeating that a vote on the main motion was in order. A short debate ensued between Bielefeld and Akers, while the assembly continued to demand a vote.

Melvin Buckles took the microphone and moved that a division of the assembly was needed for an accurate count. Others shouted that this was out of order. Again, order had to be restored by the sergeants-in-arms.

Buckles and Akers declared there would be a division of the assembly, but further protests arose. Akers declared that there was a motion before the house to remove the tribal chairman, asking all in favor to rise and be counted. Those in favor were asked to go to the north side of the hall and those opposed to the south side. The votes were counted with 279 for removal, and 189 opposed. Edwin Reddoor asked to be recognized, but was shouted down, because the chair no longer had authority to recognize anyone. Akers was physically driven from the room and chased out the door. The tribal secretary temporarily presided, noting that the vice-chairmanship was also in contention. The General Council was called upon to elect a temporary chairman to preside over the remainder of the meeting. George Thompson, Jr., and Louis Youngman, Sr., were nominated. George Thompson, Jr., was elected and assumed the chair. James Archdale presented a second resolution stating that no one found guilty of a felony or misdemeanor, or of not working for the best interests of the Indians of the Fort Peck Reservation, could stand for office. During the discussion, the category "misdemeanor" was dropped, making parking tickets or public intoxication allowable. The vote taken was 260 for and sixteen opposed. Finally, Freda Beazley moved from the floor that the Tribal Executive Board be empowered to draft a constitution and bylaws and appoint an advisory committee to assist with this task. Once drafted, the new constitution and bylaws were to be put to a referendum. The vote was unanimous. One final motion was passed to endorse James Archdale in his candidacy for president of the National Congress of American Indians.[211]

The fallout of the General Council action removing the chairman was immediate and significant. Louis Youngman, chairman of the Poplar District; Ted Manning, vice chairman of the Poplar District; Melvin Buckles, TEB member from the Poplar District; Andrew Red Thunder, Poplar; Edwin Reddoor, Poplar; and W.C. Knorr, Wolf Point, all supporters of Chairman Akers, sent a petition dated September 16, 1958 to SI Fred Seaton. They protested how the meeting was conducted and how alleged violations were committed against the constitution and bylaws, even though Akers had presided for much of the meeting. The first point was that hiring additional tallymen and tallywomen in numbers exceeded the TEB resolution facilitating the General Council, even though the chairman had insisted upon this in defiance of the TEB's authority. The second point was that the sergeant-at-arms and tallymen had contributed to preventing

. . . the duly elected, qualified and acting Chairman of the Fort Peck Council from presiding at the aforesaid General Council meeting and forcibly ousted said Chairman, to-wit: Dolly C. Akers, as presiding officer, by the use of physical force and violence, so that the said Chairman was prevented from performing her duties under the Constitution and By-Laws of the Fort Peck Tribal Council; and that in so removing said Chairman, assault and battery was committed upon her person, so that she was bruised about the arms and body[.]

The petitioners contended that the conflict about removal of the chairman caused many of Akers' supporters to leave before votes were held. The issues of determining blood quantum for enrollment, employment conditions for attorneys hired by the Tribes, tribal land transfer to a non-Indian, adoption of a Canadian national, and elimination of the misdemeanor clause preventing persons from being candidates for election were acted upon under the succeeding chairman, and consequently were affected by Chairman Akers' removal. Many of these points were open to debate, but the fact that they were being made meant that Chairman Akers did not accept the vote taken in the General Council in Frazer.[212] It was if the public confrontation and subsequent humiliation made her more determined to fight for her political survival.

Superintendent Weston, having witnessed the General Council on September 6, recognized Akers' ouster, while acknowledging that various appeals would probably occur. Akers responded that she felt the superintendent was acting prematurely. In a news article dated September 25, 1958, Akers contended the signed resolution had not yet been presented to the superintendent. She asserted her right to continue in office until a full review was completed by "proper officials."[213]

Based on reports in the press, the majority group of the TEB asked Thomas Dignan to write Field Solicitor A.E. Bielefeld to express their views. The TEB had called the General Council held on September 6 at Frazer. Notices were published in newspapers serving the reservation and posted in all districts. The resolutions for enabling the General Council were sustained by majority vote. Each resolution before the council was discussed by Dignan. Resolution No. 1, the removal of the chairman, followed the precedent that a member of the TEB who was "found guilty and not working for the best interest of the Indians of the Fort Peck Reservation shall be automatically dropped." This had been used against Austin Buckles and Jim Archdale as chair and vice-chair, so the right of the General Council to remove persons from positions was established. Vice Chairman Thompson's right to assume the role of presiding officer of the meeting was clearly delineated, and was affirmed by the council in a vote of 278-171. Resolution

No. 2 eliminated conviction of a misdemeanor as an obstacle to candidates, to apply retroactively. Resolution No. 4 approved Dignan's general counsel contract, so it could be forwarded to the SI for approval. With 479 voting members present, the TEB felt the decisions and resolutions of this General Council were legal and binding.[214]

Responding to the petition dated September 16 by six tribal members, A.E. Bielefeld on October 3 prepared a detailed discussion of the ten points protested and what was known or needed to make any necessary determinations at the area level.[215]

On October 10, 1958, Dolly Akers, "Chairman, of the General Council and Executive Board of the Fort Peck Tribes" and seven others entered a notice of appeal to the SI. Relative to the "Fort Peck General Council, Frazer, Montana, Sept. 6, 1958." The document began with the words, "Notice of Appeal from the Decision of the Superintendent of the Fort Peck Indian Agency, the Decision of the Field Solicitor and Area Director, Indian Affairs, Billings, Montana, and Answer to the Brief filed by Thomas Dignan, Esq., Attorney at Law, Glasgow, Montana." Six points outlined what was to be discussed in detail in the full appeal, all asserting that the proceedings and alleged business transactions from the meeting of the September 6 General Council should be considered null and void.[216]

The full appeal, dated October 20, was directed to the CIA, and was meant to appeal the decision of the superintendent, area director, and field solicitor, the brief by Dignan (October 1), and the minutes of the General Council of September 6. The superintendent's and the area office's acceptance of Chairman Akers' removal was the central issue. Considering Dolly C. Akers' disagreements with James J. Eder, the appeal began with comments on the meeting minutes, which Akers contended was "a biased expression of prejudiced sentiments." She really was against Dignan, and she sidestepped his October 3 arguments, stating that Bielefeld's interpretation arose from his being taken in by Dignan. The opposing TEB members and those who had been removed in the wrangle over the TEB membership had printed copies of the Bielefeld and Dignan briefs to distribute to members. She asked where the money came from for "such reckless expenditure of moneys to be paid out of our tribal funds for this purpose?" She complained about how the majority members of the TEB had dominated business. They had thwarted efforts for over a year to have a General Council, but when told they must have a General Council to make certain decisions, they called for one. The two vacancies from Riverside, in Akers' opinion, meant that without calling a special election, the TEB had been operating illegally for some time. The additional sergeants-at-arms and recording secretaries were all friends and "in league with this remnant group." She also contended:

The General Council meeting was scheduled to be held at Frazer, Montana, because of the convenience of those members living in the western part of the reservation, and off Reservation, and in and around Glasgow, Montana, where a large portion of the friends and followers of the remnant group resides. So it can be seen that this meeting was well planned, and rigged to suit their purposes . . . .[217]

The appeal document turned to the resolution removing Chairman Akers from office "for not working for the best interests of the two tribes, and forever barred from holding office or representing the Assiniboine and Sioux Tribes." An amendment was offered that would remove the entire TEB, but the appeal document suggested that the vote on the motion was confused. The appeal also suggested that Akers could not be deprived of her vested constitutional rights

by being prevented from seeking public office in the future. A second resolution eliminated commission of misdemeanors as obstacles to elected office that had been enacted in 1952. The appeal criticized the assumption that the General Council also could reinstate persons forced out of office by this criterion.[246]

The appeal accused George W. Thompson, Jr., elected vice chairman, of selling out because of his financial circumstances and readily accepting the chair of the General Council of September 6 when Chairman Akers was removed. It also attacked James J. Eder, said to be a "Negro" with Indian blood, who was adopted as a tribal member on February 19, 1946 again; Dolly Akers denigrated his political career.[219]

The appeal criticized Thomas Dignan's proposed attorney contract, which was the subject of the fourth resolution. The Dignan contract had been unapproved since 1956, and while a series of reasons was catalogued, the fact that he was the attorney for the opposition to Chairman Akers and her supporters made him the object of criticism. The appeal concluded with how the actions and the disorder of the meeting were mediated, reiterating how the SI had a role in the establishment of a government for all the Fort Peck Indian people.[220]

Dolly Akers, on October 28, 1958, complained to Franklin C. Salisbury, the assistant solicitor in Washington, DC, that he had accepted an account of the proceedings from the General Council that appeared in the *Wolf Point Herald News* on September 11, 1958 uncritically. No *Herald News* reporter had attended the General Council. Akers contended the version in the minutes written by James J. Eder "cannot be accepted as a true and corrected report." She was outraged that Salisbury was being so susceptible. She drew a series of distinctions between the removal of Austin Buckles and the attempt to remove her as chairman. She especially stressed that the attempt to remove her was illegal, and therefore null and void.[221]

Dolly C. Akers was particularly adamant wrote against Thomas Dignan's contract that was approved at the September 6 General Council. Already in Washington, DC, to lobby for her political survival, in the first of a series of letters, Akers (still calling herself chairman) wrote Glenn L. Emmons, CIA, on November 3, 1958. Part of what she objected to was that members of the TEB whom she opposed had sought Dignan as the Tribes' attorney, and she had refused to utilize his services while she was chairman. In this first missive, she went on at great length about how the September 6 General Council had not been called with the necessary thirty days notice, nor was the full agenda announced in advance. She partially blamed Dignan for not giving proper advice on this matter, and therefore, the council and all that emanated from it should be considered null and void. Of course, that would also include the action taken for her removal.[222] Writing Emmons again on November 12, Chairman Akers corrected her November 3 communication, stating that her claim that Area Director Percy Melis had been at the General Council was incorrect. She again declared at great length that the basic requirements for the September 6 General Council had not been met. She demanded that the General Council and all its actions be considered null and void.[223] Two days later Akers wrote again, this time quoting at length from *Robert's Rules of Order* on the issue of notice and an advance agenda.[224]

Growing impatient, Dolly Akers and her supporters wrote the CIA on November 24, 1958, seeking the status of their request to have "all the proceedings and alleged business interactions" of the General Council of September 6 declared null and void. They reported that the Fort Peck TEB was operating with the apparent approval of all levels of the BIA.[225]

In response to a request from the CIA, the assistant solicitor of the Indian Legal Activities section, a memo dated December 3, 1958, examining in detail the General Council on September 6, 1958. The assistant solicitor found that the meeting was "legally convened and conducted." The attempt to bar the chairman from holding future office must be rejected, but the removal of the chairman, "though procedurally indefensible from the point of view of common law standards," was within the authority of the General Council, and attempts retroactively to amend the constitution to place individuals back in positions from which they had been removed without an election by secret ballot could not be recognized. The removal dynamic required some kind of finding of guilt for certain offenses, but there were no explicit procedures for doing so. The CIA was advised to "reject the purported removal of the Chairman until such a finding is entered to support the conclusion."[226]

On December 28, Dolly Akers wrote Elmer Bennett, deputy SI, that the "considerable delay and procrastination on the part of the Indian Bureau to render a decision" about the meeting of September 6 "was placing the rank and file Indians in dire need." She asked for immediate action upon her appeal brief and many letters.[227]

The delineation she was waiting for came in a letter from the CIA dated January 5, 1959. Emmons indicated that after careful review of her appeal, he had concluded that the meeting was legally convened and conducted. The assistant solicitor's opinion was discussed. The 1927 constitution provided the basis for the authority to drop "automatically" any TEB member "found guilty in not working for the best interest of the Indians of the Fort Peck Reservation." Yet there were no removal proceedings, nor was there a factual written finding; rather, in the words of the CIA, "in the present case, in contrast, there was no finding, only a bald conclusion." The sentiment for removal was palpable. Emmons noted that he was not entirely in agreement with the solicitor's opinion, but he was "constrained to abide by his legal advice and reject General Council Resolution No. 1 as having not been properly enacted under the present amended constitution." In his mind, certainly another General Council could be called and the proposition of removing the chairman reconsidered. He followed the legal opinion about the other business acted upon in the September 6 council. However, he again advised that "the present amended constitution has not provided the basis for sound and effective tribal government." Emmons concluded:

We consider it unfortunate when actions of a General Council, which are decisively made by a group whose intent is clear, must be rejected on legal or technical grounds simply because constitutional provisions were unintentionally breached. Notwithstanding, the views of this Bureau are being submitted to the Area Director, the Superintendent, and Executive Board for their guidance.[228]

Although Akers had been temporarily saved by a technicality, this was hardly a ringing endorsement of her overall position, and in fact supplied more ammunition to her opponents.

Akers the next day sent Emmons a telegram, seizing on his point that the Dignan contract approval was to be considered on its own merits. She urged him to reread her letter of November 3 in which she discussed the attorney's proposed contract, which she viewed as legal advice to the majority group dominating the TEB.[229]

The embattled chairman had spent much of the fall and early winter in Washington, DC, pressing her fight. Press coverage began suggesting that she had been "reinstated," but constitutional struggles were again at hand. The majority faction of the TEB realized that

the struggle was far from over. The CIA in his action to deny Akers' appeal did strike down the first two resolutions made in the September 6 meeting—the removal of the chairman and the retroactive re-seating of four individuals removed because of a 1952 constitutional amendment that was repealed in the second motion. These individuals who had served since September 6 were out again because of the CIA's unwillingness to sanction a retroactive application of the constitutional change.[230]

In the regular scheduled TEB meetings on January 8 and 9, 1959, Superintendent Weston was asked to "present pertinent correspondence" to the second meeting. Emmons' January 5 letter, a second Emmons communication about the James J. Eder allotment, and a letter from Roger Ernst, Assistant SI, to the superintendent about changes to the proposed Fort Peck Constitution and Bylaws were read. Attendees openly speculated on whether the business accomplished at all meetings since the September 6 General Council was valid, especially those held when Chairman Akers was in Washington. Weston thought this was not problematic, but Austin Buckles suggested that perhaps the opinion should be requested in writing. A resolution called a General Council for January 24, 1959 to review the various recent BIA opinions, but the vote ended in a tie, with one not voting. Weston praised the TEB for attending to the implications arising from the September 6 General Council.[231] The TEB requested an urgent meeting with Area Office officials in Billings to discuss proposed revisions to the constitution.[232]

In a special TEB meeting on January 16, 1959, several resolutions were passed. One authorized a delegation of non-tribal TEB members to travel to Washington, DC, at their own expense, "to counteract any proposals detrimental to the tribes." Another called for a General Council at Frazer High School on January 31, 1959. Another called for a formal appeal of the CIA's January 5 opinion. Another called for district meetings to study the proposed constitution and bylaws, and allocated money for lunches; another authorized announcements in the local papers about the dates of the district meetings. An extensive discussion of changes to be made to the Land Use Policy resulted in a resolution adopting an amended policy. Another resolution authorized wages to William Youpee, Carl Walking Eagle, and George W. Thompson, Jr., for their services since the General Council of September 6.[233]

In a special TEB meeting on January 20 called for the specific purpose of selecting a delegation to go to Washington, Norman Hollow, Austin Buckles, Howard Trinder, and George Thompson, Jr., were chosen to represent the views of tribal members on the CIA's January 5 opinion.[234]

On January 20, 1959, Chairman Akers and her nine supporters sent another detailed communication to Commissioner Emmons protesting approval of attorney Thomas Dignan's contract as tribal general counsel. Making a series of arguments and citing case law, Chairman Akers offered the kind of presentation that might have been persuasive at the beginning of the decade, when the Interior Department tried to restrict legal representation to a simpler level, but her argument was really overkill. She demonstrated how she controlled the General Council dynamic, and how she used this to undermine approval of Dignan's contract.[235]

In a memo dated January 21, 1959, TEB members W.R. Smith, James Sweeney, Henry Archdale, Roy Sansaver, Leslie Four Star, Maurice Big Horn, Kermit Smith, Melvin Buckles, and Alfred Manning, identified as "The Assiniboine and Sioux Indians of the Fort Peck Reservation, Montana," appealed to SI Fred A. Seaton. They particularly objected to the striking down of the resolution of the September 6 General Council

that removed Dolly C. Akers as chairman. They attached the resolution, formally placing the appeal before the SI.[236]

The Montana congressional delegation weighed in with a communication to the SI dated January 23, 1959. They expressed their collective concern that the Central Office had overruled the agency superintendent and area solicitor, thus reinstating the chairman, when there was common knowledge among the larger reservation community that one of the purposes of the meeting was to remove her. While there had been no recital of charges, the assumption was rampant, and Mrs. Akers's supporters did not ask for a rationale; rather, the purpose was authorized in the Tribes' constitution. The issues emergent in the business of the Fort Peck Tribes made the issue of counsel obvious. The delegation asked for immediate approval of the attorney contract and affirmation of the area solicitor's position, and asked for a full secretarial review of the legality of the chairman's removal.[237]

Chairman Akers, writing on January 23, 1959, notified Superintendent Weston that she protested all actions taken at all TEB meetings held after January 5, 1959.[238] Because of such political pressure, the Dignan general counsel contract was subjected to a new level of scrutiny.[239]

Incensed by the progress of developments, Chairman Akers and TEB members Alfred Manning, Fort Kipp District; Melvin Buckles, Poplar District; and Kermit Smith, Wolf Point District; on January 27, 1959, wrote the SI with their objections to matters transacted in the TEB meeting of January 16, 1959, including the setting of a date for a General Council for January 31, 1959. The chairman objected that she and the three councilmen had not received notice of the meeting on January 16, and therefore, it was an illegal act without an announced agenda, as was the General Council. Finally, they noted the meeting of January 16 did not have a quorum, and according to Robert's Rules of Order, without a bylaw allowing a smaller number, the majority of the membership of eleven councilmen would be seven. Since it did not meet this requirement, the Chairman declared the meeting and its actions "to have been taken to be null and void and of no effect."[240] The chairman was informed that the letter was sent to Superintendent Weston for a report.[241]

In a telegram dated February 2, 1959, Councilmen Manny (Kermit) Smith and Melvin Buckles wrote Chairman Akers in DC, saying Superintendent Weston asked her to have Assistant Secretary Bennett request a meeting of a delegation of both factions to make presentations to him. They asked her to order the superintendent to have mileage per diem paid out locally per the tribal secretary's authority. The councilmen reported that "opposing faction now have four delegates there and four more coming." As supporters of the chairman, they declared, "We want to be heard too."[242]

Kermit Smith, TEB member, Louis Youngman, Jr., District Chairman, Melvin Buckles, TEB member, Andrew Red Thunder, Edwin Reddoor, Sioux Council Chairman, and Theodore Manning, District Vice Chairman, wrote a letter dated February 3, 1959, to Elmer T. Bennett, assistant SI, Washington, DC, to report on the multiple resolutions voted in the "alleged General Council Meeting of the Fort Peck Tribes" held on Saturday, January 31, 1959. The correspondents contended the General Council was not properly called, and then pronounced all its actions invalid. They called for Superintendent Weston's removal for interfering in tribal governance.[243]

Akers and her regular nine supporters, in a brief dated February 3, 1959, appealed the CIA's ruling about the business enacted at the General Council of September 6, 1958. She pressed again her objections to the Dignan contract, and declared that the CIA's approval of the contract

on January 27, 1959, was "wrongfully, unjustly, and detrimental to the best interests of the Fort Peck Tribes. . . ."[244]

Delegates Austin Buckles, George W. Thompson, Jr., Norman Hollow, and Howard Trinder announced their presence in Washington on February 11, 1959, in a memo to Roger Ernst, assistant SI. Specifically, they appealed the commissioner's decision of January 5, 1959 and other matters covered in the General Council resolutions of January 31, 1959. They elaborated on the evidence they had filed two weeks previously to demonstrate how the department had usurped the powers of the Tribes. They re-summarized the actions arising from the September General Council and response to the CIA's decision and reasserted that 1) the Fort Peck Tribes refused to acknowledge Dolly Akers' reinstatement as Chairman of the Tribes; 2) the constitutional amendment passed in September reinstated officers and TEB members suspended by action of the Fort Peck Agency Superintendent on the misdemeanor issue; and 3) official approval was sought for the General Council action of January 31, 1959. The delegation asked for an investigation of the "economic and welfare status" of the Tribes and correction of "maladministration of the federal trusteeship responsibility."[245]

The reservation's Indian farmers and ranchers had discovered a means of sub-leasing submarginal land, and thus were seeking to keep their operations solvent by continuing the practice. They had been hard hit by drought that growing season. Part of the larger delegation to Washington called itself the Advisory Committee for the Fort Peck Indian Farmers and Ranchers. The group sought a meeting with the CIA to discuss renewal of the submarginal lands permit that was about to expire. Between 1933 and 1943, the competition for use of Indian lands had escalated between non-Indian and Indian leasees, so the BIA devised a way for tribal councils to lease submarginal lands for the equivalent of two cents an acre, which they were permitted to re-lease to actual users for a profit of ten cents an acre. However, a group of western U.S. Senators thought non-Indian land users were being exploited. They tried to obstruct continuation of this practice, and went so far as to state that it was cheating the United States out of important revenue. Consequently, the policy was changed to charge the Tribes one-half of the rental "commensurate with the rental earned by comparable neighboring lands," an arrangement said to be more equitable to the government and the Tribes. Since 1954, nine other tribes had their permits expire and had to move to the fixed rental to gain a renewal. In the meeting with Assistant CIA E. J. Utz, the Advisory Council (Norman Hollow, Austin Buckles, Howard Trinder, Claude R. Trinder, and George W. Thompson, Jr.) stated that while in principle it was accepted that the Tribes would be charging half of the appraised rental, this was economically problematic when in the past three years the average yield from harvested lands had been seven bushels per acre. Ironically, these lands and the farmers on them were not eligible for U.S.D.A. crop support programs, which they thought was discriminatory. The advisory council wanted justification of their exception to growing support crops and of the proposed rental rate under a new use permit for submarginal lands. The business of the TEB was to serve the interests of the Tribes, and while there had already by 1959 been numerous attempts to legislate a return of these lands within reservation boundaries to the Tribes, interest in the lands and the resources within them was simply increasing.[246]

The Fort Peck delegation had expanded with the arrival of more individuals. Austin Buckles and Norman Hollow, joined by "J and H Archdale, Sweeney, Fourstar, Youpee, Walking Eagle, Bighorn, Spotted Elk, McClammy-Boyd,

Yellowrobe," sent a telegram on February 13, 1959 to Roy Sansaver and Eva Mae and Bill Smith to report the progress being made. They had been informed that CIA Glenn L. Emmons on February 13, 1959 mailed letters to Dolly C. Akers and Area Director Percy Melis ruling that the January 31 General Council was "properly conducted." The CIA also approved the three resolutions "ousting Akers" as chairman, recognized all delegates currently in Washington, and called for a referendum on changes being drafted for the constitution. The delegation indicated that the resolutions renewing the submarginal lands rental agreement and program and requesting removal of the current superintendent were being considered.[247]

The CIA's letters to Akers and Melis contained the same details but were very different in tone and approach. In the communication to Akers, the CIA explained that he was replying to her wire to him from Chicago on February 8, 1959, challenging the general council held on January 31, as being contrary to the CIA directive of January 5. Emmons went on to delineate what he had written on January 5 compared with approval of the General Council of January 31:

My letter of January 5 was in response to a challenge of the constitutionality of certain actions taken by the General Council held September 6, 1958, at Frazer, Montana. In the case of those resolutions, which the Solicitor's Office advised were in contravention with the Tribes' constitution, I could not and did not approve.

The commissioner explained that in the solicitor's opinion, standards had been put forward for General Councils, but the department considered these procedures advisory, not mandatory. In the examination of the General Council held January 31, 1959, all was found in order, and therefore, "find that the General Council was in proper session and was properly conducted."

This pertained to Resolutions No. 1, No. 2, and No. 5; No. 3 was not adopted, and No. 4 and No. 6 were being reviewed. The CIA's letter of the same date to Melis repeated this information, but then stressed the CIA's need to be kept advised on the progress of the proposed constitution. The CIA declared, ". . . a new constitution would be a great advantage to the tribes and serve to eliminate some of the unproductive issues which have been so consistently present."[248]

The deposed chairman and her immediate supporters wrote on February 14 to Elmer T. Bennett, Deputy SI, unaware that a letter was in the mail informing her of her removal as chair. The letter discussed a meeting on February 11 with Superintendent Weston and Akers' repeated objections to the meetings and actions of January 1959.[249]

Mrs. Akers and her supporting TEB members Melvin Buckles, Kermit Smith, Alfred Manning, Louis Youngman, Edwin Reddoor, and Ted Manning wrote on February 16, 1959, to SI Fred A. Seaton, saying she understood there was a letter addressed to her from CIA Emmons approving the General Council held January 31, 1959 in Frazer. Whether she had actually received her letter was moot. She accused the CIA of violating "all ethics, rules, and regulations established by usage for 50 years." She cited a 1953 telegram from the SI saying that all appeals must follow the chain of order beginning with the superintendent, then Area Office, then CIA, and finally the SI. In her opinion, the CIA was not in compliance. She reported that she had met with Field Solicitor Bielefeld in Billings on February 13, when he told her he had not yet rendered a decision on the January 31 meeting. She further declared: "We charge Emmons with disregard and contempt of the Fort Peck Tribes Constitution. Fort Peck Tribes Constitution must be upheld by Interior Officials if tribal government is to continue in existence." The com-munication concluded with the statement: "We request proper, legal consideration of the January 31, 1959 meeting, and Commissioner Emmons' February 13 letter."[250]

An article titled "Fort Peck Tribal Board Orders General Election" in the *Great Falls Tribune* on February 17, 1959, quoted Acting Chairman Roy Sansaver's announcement that the next tribal election would be held on April 15. Sansaver had been elected acting chairman until the election, when all tribal offices would be open for the next two-year term. A referendum on the proposed constitution was also on the ballot. The second half of the article discussed the crisis around Dolly Akers' removal, and the challenges to the General Council held at the end of January. Most revealing was the final para-graph, in which causes for Akers' removal were delineated:

The resolution asking for the removal of Chairman Akers from office was based on four charges. These being that (1) she had disrupted the tribal government for the past two years to such an extent that the tribes are unable to properly continue business or progress in their affairs while she is such tribal chairman; (2) the said Dolly C. Akers has unduly influenced Indian Bureau employees in the central office in reversing the decision of the Area Solicitor and Superintendent; (3) the said Dolly C. Akers has consistently endeavored to have the sub-marginal lands turned over to Roosevelt County, Montana or to persons not members of the tribes; (4) the said Dolly C. Akers, by her actions, has caused the loss to the tribes of minerals located in and under the Arthur L. Nordwick lands. The vote to remove Akers was 140 for her removal and 0 against. Thirty-three voters obtained [sic]."[251]

Roger Ernst, assistant SI, in a telegram February 19 to Dolly Akers acknowledged hers of

February 17, promising to "review the situation," and that she would be given a final reply at a later date.[252]

Two articles appeared in the February 20, 1959 *Poplar Standard*, publishing correspondence about Akers' fate as chairman. "Commissioner Issues Ruling on Akers' Removal" reprinted the CIA's letters of February 13 to Area Director Percy Melis and Dolly Akers verbatim. Another article titled "Akers Challenges Ruling Made by Bureau Official" included the two February 16 protest letters to the SI.[253]

Running out of straws, Akers cowrote with TEB members Melvin Buckles, Kermit Smith, Alfred Manning, and Louis Youngman, chair, Poplar District; Edwin Reddoor, secretary of the Sioux Nations Council; and Ted Manning, vice chairman, Poplar District, to other GOP politicians. In a letter dated February 28, 1959, they asked Senator Barry Goldwater for assistance "to restore to the Fort Peck Indian people a legal Tribal Government." They blamed the six-member faction of holding "the controlling vote, having two years frivolously dissipated Fort Peck Tribal money." They represented themselves as continuously presenting to the CIA "good proper legal briefs" about the "disgraceful Fort Peck situation." They declared: "we are now forced to believe that the BIA must be consorting with certain Fort Peck Indians and protecting illegal, improper actions of the said Fort Peck Indians." They were formally protesting the actions of CIA Emmons, trustee of "our property and tribal money," and called on the Senator to investigate the commissioner.[254]

Superintendent Weston wrote Akers and Melvin Buckleson on March 30, 1959, that he found he had not written a confirmation of discussions concerning "your letter of protest dated February 11, 1959." Of course, the letter was protesting the actions of a January 30 meeting. The CIA by letter of February 13 "notified you of

his acceptance of the validity of the meeting of January 30 and the subsequent General Council of January 31, 1959." Dismissively, the superintendent said there was no further necessity to consider the validity of the meeting of January 30.[255]

In the tribal general election on April 15 1959, Austin Buckles was elected chairman, Edwin Reddoor vice chairman, and Theodore Manning sergeant-at-arms. TEB members elected were Norman Hollow, Melvin Buckles, Henry Archdale, Sr., Enright Jackson, James Black Dog, William Youpee, Pearl Redstone, Kermit Smith, Alfred Manning, Roy Sansaver, and Leslie Fourstar. The final seat on the board rotated between Mark Eder, Sr., Harry Johnson, Alfred Manning, Earl Jones, and James Helmer.[256]

The crisis in the political processes of the Tribes continued to revolve around several fundamental constitutional issues. The democratic nature of the General Council could also produce tyranny, depriving members who could not be present of the ability to express their will. While the General Council acted as a check on the work of elected leaders, many issues needed more thorough examination and deliberation than was possible in what was often a single-day General Council meeting.

Based on the work of the executive board and its constitutional advisory committee, a revised constitution and bylaws were presented at the General Council convened on January 31, 1959. Under the authority of the 1927 Constitution, the proposed constitution was submitted to tribal members in the tribal election of April 15, 1959, but it was defeated. At a meeting of the General Council on June 6, 1959, a resolution proposing resubmitting the new constitution to a second referendum was defeated.[257] According to a newspaper account, the entire June 6 meeting was a contentious struggle between subgroups. One subgroup sought to have the meeting closed down, but failed. Those seeking a per capita payment very much wanted the General Council to proceed. Another group wanted a per capita payment without defining membership criteria, and this was defeated. One attempted to have the TEB draft an enrollment ordinance to be presented to the membership for enactment. A substitute motion by Dolly Akers recommended that the ordinance specify the degree of blood quantum for membership, and be subject to a referendum vote, and this passed. A poll of the various degrees of blood quantum was put to the assembly, and the greatest number of people present favored one-eighth degree as the minimum for enrollment and membership.[258]

Rex Lee, Associate CIA, wrote the TEB chairman on September 14, 1959, stating that review of two versions of a proposed membership ordinance led to the discovery in the central office of census rolls from 1940 and 1943. He hoped the basis would be the most current rolls. However, using a census roll would require a provision permitting removal of persons not entitled to enrollment or addition of eligible persons. Preventing injustices was paramount. This provision could be enlarged to "permit the correction of degree of blood and place a time limit within which corrections may be made." Lee pointed out that many constitutions permitted a five-year period for corrections. The other proposal included a one-quarter minimum of Assiniboine or Sioux blood, and included the provision for accepting blood quantum retroactively. Lee asserted that the department would not support retroactively disenrolling eligible people. Only once the current membership roll had been compiled and approved would the department cease to object to "an enrollment limitation by blood quantum."[259]

The TEB in a special meeting on September 17, 1959, adopted a motion by William Youpee that a constitution and bylaws committee be created within the board with each district represented.

The committee was composed of Norman Hollow, Carl Walking Eagle, William Youpee, Roy Sansaver, Pearl Redstone, and Leslie Fourstar. Committee meetings were to include the tribal attorney when possible. Leslie Fourstar's motion that the enrollment ordinance be gotten out immediately and put to a referendum vote was adopted.260

In a controversial move, the executive board voted to hold a constitutional referendum on October 1, 1960. The board met on September 17, 1960, without notice as stipulated by the Tribal Election Ordinance, appointing an election supervisor and election judges three days prior to the announced referendum. Based on this development, a complaint was filed with the superintendent. At a regular meeting of the executive board on September 29, 1960, the board decided to postpone the referendum, and suggested setting a new date at the next regular meeting. The tribal secretary was to arrange for announcing the postponement over the local radio station, KVCK Wolf Point, which he did the next day. However, Austin Buckles called the radio station asking that the announcements be discontinued. Some confusion resulted. Posted announcements stated that the referendum was to take place on October 1, 1960, which it did. The overall election turnout was low, with 355 votes cast from a total of 1,008 eligible voters. However, 542 absentee ballots had been cast, making this the largest number of absentee ballots ever cast in a Fort Peck referendum or election.[261] The final vote was 756 for and 141 against.[262]

Questions were raised about the validity of several absentee ballots. On October 4, 1960, the chairman of the Wolf Point district protested to the Area Office director, stating that unauthorized people had voted in the referendum. Opponents of the new constitution appealed on November 14, 1960, to the SI, arguing that the recent referendum violated the 1927 Constitution.[263]

Assistant Secretary of Interior George W. Abbott approved the revised constitution and bylaws of October 1, 1960 and set aside the 1927 Constitution in a letter dated November 30, 1960.[264]

The tempestuous decade had left aspects of Fort Peck tribal government in tatters, exhausted and divisive. The new constitution and bylaws marked the beginning of a new era of political life. Changes were a-coming. ✸

1 "Fort Peck Tribes To Demand Vote By Secret Ballot," *The Poplar Standard*, v. 44, no. 12, p. 1, Curry Papers, Box 93, January 1953.

2 Minutes, General Council, January 3, 1953, James E. Curry Papers, Box 95, January 1953, Archives of the National Museum of the American Indian, Smithsonian Institution, Suitland, Maryland (hereinafter cited as "Curry Papers"), Box 93, January 1953.

3 Curry, Washington, DC, to Fort Peck Tribal Executive Board, Poplar, MT, January 29, 1953, Curry Papers, Box 95, January 1953.

4 Akers et al., Washington, DC, to President Dwight D. Eisenhower, The White House, Washington, DC, February 21, 1953, Curry Papers, Box 95, February 1953.

5 Curry, Washington, DC, to William R. Smith, Oswego, MT, February 23, 1953, Curry Papers, Box 95, February 1953. 1953, Curry Papers, Box 95, March 1953.

9 "Dolly Akers Gives Explanation Background, Circumstances Following Charge of Assault," *The Herald News*, v. 40, no. 11 (March 26, 1953), p. 1, Curry Papers, Box 95, March 1953.

10 "Assault Case Opens Federal Court's Term: Mrs. Akers, Official of Fort Peck Tribe, Charged with Slapping Indian Official." *The Glasgow Courier*, v. 48 (April 9, 1953), p. 1, Curry Papers, Box 95, April 1-16, 1953.

11 Dolly Cusker affidavit before U.S. Commissioner, 15 August 1938, Dolly C. Akers (DCA) Papers, Montana Historical Society (hereinafter "MHS") Box1, f13 "Tribal Materials"; Akers, (Wolf Point, MT) to Senator Burton K. Wheeler, Washington, DC. Austin Buckles Family Papers, Fort Peck Tribal Archives, folder "Evidence Envelop"; Senator Elect James E. Murray, Washington, DC, to John Collier, CIA, Washington, November 14, 1934, and Senator James E. Murray, Washington, DC, to Dolly Cusker, Poplar, MT, June 7, 1935. DCA Papers, MHS Bx1, folder "Personal-Historical."

12 Akers, Asst. Social Worker, Pine Ridge Agency, through W.O. Roberts, Supt. Pine Ridge Agency, to CIA, Washington, DC. DCA Papers MHS Bx1, folder 1-4 "Personal-Historical."

13 Dolly Cusker, Pine Ridge, SD, to Senator James E. Murray, Washington, DC, January 27, 1940. DCA Papers, MHS Box 1, folder "Personal-Historical"; Senator James E. Murray, Washington, DC, to Dolly

Cusker, Pine Ridge, SD, April 10, 1941. DCA Papers, MHS, Bx1, folder "Personal-Historical."

14 Dolly C. Akers was first elected to the TEB in 1945-46 but was impeached June 1, 1946 (see references to the impeachment in Thomas Dignan, Glasgow, MT, to A.E. Bielefeld, Field Solicitor, BIA, Billings, MT, October 1, 1958. DCA Papers, MHS, Box 1, folder "Dolly Akers 1942-1959") and was again elected to TEB in the 1947-49 administration of Chairman William Knorr.

15 Ibid.

16 Certificates of Nomination, July 20 and July 26, 1946, Akers Papers-MHS, Box 1, Akers-Personal, file 1-4.

17 Austin Buckles refers to the perception of him as a paper-pusher in an office, and therefore, a "new dealer"; see his campaign statement "MI TAKU YE," April 13, 1953. Austin Buckles Family Papers, Fort Peck Tribal Archives, Poplar, MT, folder "Tribal Affairs."

18 Eva Mae Smith, Wolf Point, MT, to Curry, Washington, DC, March 30, 1953, Box 95, April 1-16, 1953.

19 Minutes, special meeting, Executive Board, March 30, 1953, Curry Papers, Box 95, March 1953.

20 Smith, Wolf Point, MT, to Curry, Washington, DC, March 30, 1953, Curry Papers, Box 95, April 1-16, 1953.

21 "Notice of Tribal Election," April 10, 1953, Curry Papers, Box 95, April 16, 1953.

22 Curry to Fort Peck Tribal Executive Board, April 11, 1953, Curry Papers, Box 95, April 1-16, 1953.

23 Curry, Memorandum for the Tribal Executive Board re: Tribal Elections, April 14, 1953, and "Election Regulations of the Sioux and Assiniboine Tribes of the Fort Peck Reservation, MT," Curry Papers, Box 95, April 1-16, 1953.

24 Resolution No. 46-52, April 15, 1953, Curry Papers, Box 95, April 1-16, 1953.

25 Minutes, special meeting, Tribal Executive Board, April 21, 1953, Curry Papers, Box 95, April 17-31, 1953.

26 W. Barton Greenwood, Acting CIA, Washington, DC, to Curry, Washington, DC, April 30, 1953, Curry Papers, Box 95, April 17-31, 1953; Curry, Washington, DC, to J Bayuk, Poplar, MT, May 11, 1953, Curry Papers, Box 96, May 1-14, 1953.

27 Orme Lewis, Assistant SI, Washington, DC, to Curry, Washington, DC, March

12, 1953, Curry Papers, Box 95, April 17-31, 1953.

28 Statement of Services Fort Peck Tribes, for the period December 12, 1952 through March 11, 1953, submitted May 2, 1953, p. 1, Curry Papers, Box 96, May 1-14, 1953.

29 Curry, Washington, DC, to Fort Peck Tribal Executive Board, May 3, 1953, Curry Papers, Box 96, May 1-14, 1953.

30 Curry, Washington, DC, to Austin Buckles, Chairman, Fort Peck Tribal Executive Board, Poplar, MT, "Clearance of Funds for Tribal Council Expenses," May 4, 1953, Curry Papers, Box 96, May 1-14, 1953.

31 Curry, Washington, DC, to Norman Hollow, Brockton, MT, May 9, 1953, Curry Papers, Box 96, May 1-14, 1953.

32 "Fort Peck Tribal Board Acts on Leases," *Great Falls Tribune*, May 23, 1953, Curry Papers, Box 96, May 15-31, 1953.

33 Buckles, Poplar, MT, to SI, Washington, DC, May 26, 1953, Curry Papers, Box 96, May 15-31, 1953.

34 Clarence A. Davis, Solicitor, Interior, Washington, DC, to Curry, Washington, DC, July 3, 1953, Curry Papers, Box 96, July 1-28, 1953.

35 Curry, Washington, DC, to Chairman and Tribal Executive Board, July 9, 1953, Curry Papers, Box 96, July 1-28, 1953.

36 Curry, Washington, DC, to Fort Peck Tribal Executive Board, May 26, 1953, Curry Papers, Box 96, May 15-31, 1953.

37 Curry, Washington, DC, to Fort Peck Tribal Executive Board, June 15, 1953, Curry Papers, Box 96, June 1953.

38 "Group (Tribal Executive Board) Passes Resolutions on 4 Subjects," *The Poplar Standard*, v. 44, no. 35 (June 19, 1953), p. 1, Curry Papers, Box 96, June 1953.

39 Curry, Washington, DC, to Congressman E.Y. Berry, Chairman, Subcommittee on Indian Affairs, Committee on Interior and Insular Affairs, Washington, DC, June 24, 1953, Curry Papers, Box 96, June 1953.

40 Curry, Washington, DC, to Fort Peck Tribal Executive Board, June 24, 1953, Curry Papers, Box 96, June 1953.

41 Buckles, Poplar, MT, to Curry, Poplar, MT, July 1, 1953, Curry Papers, Box 96, June 1953.

42 *The Poplar Standard*, "Emmons is named Commissioner of Indian Affairs," v. 44, no. 40 (July 24, 1953),

p. 1, Curry Papers, Box 96, July 1-28, 1953; Larry W. Burt, *Tribalism in Crisis: Federal Indian Policy, 1953-1961* (Albuquerque: University of New Mexico Press, 1982), 15-16.

43 Orme Lewis, Assistant SI, Washington, DC, to Congressman A.L. Miller, Chairman, Committee on Interior and Insular Affairs, House of Representations, Washington, DC, July 30, 1953, Curry Papers, Box 96, July 29-31, 1953.

44 "Statement of Austin Buckles, Chairman of the General Council and of the Executive Board of the Assiniboine and Sioux Tribes of the Fort Peck Reservation, MT," before the Subcommittee on Indians Affairs, Committee on Interior and Insular Affairs, House of Representatives, July 30, 1953, Curry Papers, Box 96, July 29-31, 1953, and supporting documents.

45 Act of April 28, 1948 (62 Stat. 237), Fred H. Massey, Acting Executive Office, BIA, Washington, DC, to Paul L. Fickinger, Billings Area Office Director, Billings, MT, July 30, 1953, Curry Papers, Box 96, July 29-31, 1953.

46 Quoted in Donald L. Fixico, *Termination and Relocation: Federal Indian Policy, 1945-1960* (Albuquerque, NM: University of New Mexico Press, 1986), 93-94.

47 Ibid., 94.

48 "House Okays Bill to Free Indians," *The Poplar Standard*, p. 1, Curry Papers, Box 96, July 29-31, 1953.

49 See context in Fixico, *Termination and Relocation*, 111-133.

50 Buckles, Washington, DC, to SI, Washington, DC, August 1, 1953, Curry Papers, Box 97, August 1-12, 1953.

51 Despite the fact that Public Law 502, 80th Congress, 2nd Session (62 Stat. 203) provided that such funds were available only on a fiscal-year basis.

52 H. Barton Greenwood, Acting CIA, Washington, DC, to Buckles, Poplar, MT, August 7, 1953, Curry Papers, Box 97, August 1-12, 1953.

53 Curry, Washington, DC, to Buckles, Poplar, MT, August 10, 1953, Curry Papers, Box 97, August 1-12, 1953.

54 James E. Curry, Washington, DC, to Buckles, August 11, 1953, Curry Papers, Box 97, August 1-12, 1953

55 "Jim Says . . . ," *The Poplar Standard* (August 11, 1953), Curry Papers, Box 97, August 1-12, 1953.

56 "Jim Says . . . ," *The Poplar Standard* (August 24, 1953), Curry Papers, Box 97, September 13-31, 1953.

57 Curry, Washington, DC, to Fort Peck Tribal Executive Board, September 7, 1953, Curry Papers, Box 97, September 1953.

58 Buckles, Poplar, MT, to Greenwood, Washington, DC, September 15, 1953, Curry Papers, Box 97, September 1953.

59 "Fort Peck Indians Given Opportunity to Voice Problems; Most Indians Well Pleased with Emmons," unidentified and undated newspaper article (ca. October 23, 1953), Curry Papers, Box 97, October 1953.

60 Chairman Austin Buckles, Poplar, MT, to Dolly Akers, Wolf Point, MT, November 13, 1953. DCA Papers, MHS, Bx1, folder "Personal-Historical."

61 Minutes, Executive Board, November 24, 1953, Curry Papers, Box 97, November-December 1953.

62 Memo/call for meeting, Advisory or Planning Board members, 4 December 4, 1953. DCA Papers, MHS, Bx1, folder "Personal-Historical."

63 Ibid.

64 "Poplar and Vicinity Local and Social News," *The Poplar Standard*, v. 45, no. 14 (January 22, 1954), p. 8, Curry Papers, Box 98, January 7-31, 1954.

65 Copy of H.R. 7650, February 2, 1954, Curry Papers, Box 98, February 1954.

66 S. 2839, 83rd Cong. 2nd Sess., introduced by Murray, January 22, 1954, Curry Papers, Box 98, January 7-31, 1954.

67 H.R. 7649, February 2, 1954, Curry Papers, Box 98, February 1954.

68 S. 2899, 83rd Cong. 2nd Sess., introduced by Murray, January 22, 1954, Curry Papers, Box 98, February 1954.

69 Notice of Sale of Indian Land, Fort Peck Indian Reservation, Fort Peck Agency, Poplar, MT, February 2, 1954, with attached Schedule of Lands to be Sold, Description, Curry Papers, Box 98, February 1954.

70 William J. Wynne, Supervisor of Contracts and Division Orders, Murphy Corporation, El Dorado, AR, to Crawford, Poplar, MT, February 4, 1954, Curry Papers, Box 98, February 1954.

71 Buckles, Washington, DC, to Hope McDonald, the tribal reporter at *The Poplar Standard*, February 10, 1954, Curry Papers, Box 98, February 1954.

72 Ibid.

73 Minutes, Special Meeting, Executive Board, February 19, 1954, Curry Papers, Box 98, February 1954.

74 S. 2931, 83rd Cong., 2nd Sess., introduced by Murray, February 8, 1954, Curry Papers, Box 98, February 1954.

75 Untitled list, February 11, 1954, Curry Papers, Box 98, February 1954.

76 Ralph H. Case, Washington, DC, to Edwin Reddoor, Poplar, MT, February 15, 1954, Curry Papers, Box 98, February 1954.

77 Glenn L. Emmons, CIA, Washington, DC, to Buckles, Poplar, MT, February 18, 1954, Curry Papers, Box 98, February 1954.

78 Minutes, Special Meeting Tribal Executive Board, February 19, 1956, Curry Papers, Box 98, February 1954.

79 J. Archdale, Acting Chairman, Tribal Executive Board, Poplar, MT, to Curry, Washington, DC, February 22, 1954, Curry Papers, Box 98, February 1954.

80 Resolution 48-54-1, Fort Peck Tribal Executive Board, February 25, 1954, Curry Papers, Box 98, February 1954.

81 Minutes, Special Meetings, February 25 and 26, 1954, Curry Papers, Box 98, February 1954.

82 Curry letter in the minutes of General Council, February 27, 1954, Curry Papers, Box 98, February 1954.

83 McKay letter in the minutes of General Council, February 27, 1954, Curry Papers, Box 98, February 1954.

84 Minutes of General Council, February 27, 1954, Curry Papers, Box 98, February 1954.

85 Ibid.

86 Ibid.

87 H.R. 3413 in the Senate, March 2, 1954, Curry Papers, Box 99, March 1954.

88 The agenda included: 1) Funds Limitation Bill, 2) Home Rule Bill, 3) Submarginal Land Bill, 4) Oil and Gas Restoration Bill, 5) Attorneyship, 6) Status of Agency Hospital (Health), 7) Taxation, 8) Education, 9) General Land Policy, 10) Law and Order, 11) The following claims: (a) Fort Peck Tribes, (b) Assiniboine Claims, (c) Black Hills Claim, and 12) Emergency Tribal matters pertinent to the Tribe. Minutes, Special Meeting, March 3, 1954, Curry Papers, Box 99, March 1954.

89 Resolution 53-54-1, Fort Peck Tribal Executive Board, March 15, 1954, Curry Papers, Box 99, March 1954.

90 Akers, Wolf Point, MT, to Fort Peck delegates in Washington, DC, March 25, 1954, Curry Papers, Box 99, March 1954.

91 Resolution 57-54-1, Special Meeting, Tribal Executive Board, March 30, 1954, Curry Papers, Box 99, March 1954.

92 Hollow, Chairman of the Delegation, Washington, DC, to Douglas McKay, SI, Washington, DC, March 30, 1954, Curry Papers, Box 99, March 1954.

93 "State Indians Fight McKay Over Pay Boost for Lawyer," *Great Falls Tribune*, v. 67, No. 323, April 3, 1954, Curry Papers, Box 99, April 1954.

94 Ibid.

95 Minutes, Special Meeting, Tribal Executive Board, April 19, 1954, Curry Papers, Box 99, April 1954.

96 Fred G. Anndahl, Assistant SI, Washington, DC, to Senator Hugh Butler, Chairman, U.S. Senate Committee on Interior and Insular Affairs, Washington, DC, April 16, 1954, Curry Papers, Box 99, April 1954.

97 Dolly C. Akers, Wolf Point, MT, to Committee on Interior and Insular Affairs, U.S. House of Representative, Washington, DC, through Senator James E. Murray, February 28, 1954. DCA Papers, MHS, bx9, folder "Termination"; Curry, Washington, DC, to Edwin J. Reddoor, Poplar, MT, May 20, 1950, Summary of a meeting with Senators and Congressmen from North and South Dakota, MT and Nebraska attended by Delegates from Cheyenne River, Standing Rock, Fort Peck, and Santee, May 20, 1950, James E. Curry papers collection, in Fort Peck Tribal Archives, Poplar, MT; Laurence Hauptman discussed the impact of this legislative ideology upon the Iroquois in this same period, see *The Iroquois Struggle for Survival: World War II to Red Power* (Syracuse: Syracuse University Press, 1986), 14, 38-39, 40, 42, 49.

98 Minutes, Special Meeting, Tribal Executive Board, May 3, 1954, Curry Papers, Box 99, May-June 1954; the reference to Hill 57 was to the squalid conditions that the community of landless Cree and Métis people were living in outside Great Falls, MT.

99 Minutes, Special Meeting, Tribal Executive Board, May 25, 1954, Curry Papers, Box 99, May-June 1954.

100 Emmons, Washington, DC, to Curry, Washington, DC, May 28, 1954, Curry Papers, Box 99, March 1954.

101 Weissbrodt, Washington, DC, to Curry, Washington, DC, July 16, 1954, Curry Papers, Box 99, July-November 1954.

102 Buckles, Poplar, MT, to Curry, Washington, DC, July 21, 1954, Curry Papers, Box 99, March 1954.

103 Public Law 449, 68 Stat. 329, Curry Papers, Box 99, March 1954.

104 Minutes, General Council, October 16, 1954, Fort Peck Chairmen's collection-Austin Buckles, folder "Tribal Governance Matters," Fort Peck Tribal Archives, Poplar, MT; "Constitution and By-Laws of the Assiniboine and Sioux Tribes of the Fort Peck Indian Reservation, MT," n.d. (circa 1954), Exhibit A, *John J. Akers, Plaintiff, vs. Assiniboine and Sioux Tribes of the Fort Peck Indian Reservation, MT, and association, John Cooper, Area Director, Clinton Talley, Superintendent, Fort Peck Indian Reservation, and Austin Buckles, Chairman, James Archdale, Vice Chairman, William Youpee, Edwin Red Door, Carl Walking Eagle, Lester A. Youpee, Leon Spotted Bull, Norman Hollow, Charles H. Track, Kermit Smith, Fred Buckles, Henry Archdale, James Sweeney, and Alice Collins, William Boyd, Thomas Buckles, John Half Red, Minnie Olson, John E. Wetsit, and Bernard Standing, Defendants*, In the District Court of the First Judicial District of the State of Montana, In and For the County of Lewis and Clark, No. 24995. Austin Buckles Family Papers, "Evidence" Envelope, Fort Peck Tribal Archives, Poplar, MT.

105 Ibid.

106 Ibid.

107 1954 Constitution and By-Laws, 4.

108 Ibid., 1.

109 Minutes, General Council October 16, 1954, 10.

110 Austin Buckles, "Fort Peck Crisis" document, n.d. (post-February 7, 1956, most recent date mentioned within the document), Austin Buckles Family Papers, Fort Peck Archives, Poplar, MT.

111 The TEB had passed Resolution No. 46-52 on December 13, 1952, which addressed the political process concerns of the Department of Interior and the BIA, and mandated "secret ballot elections similar to County and State" (elections), ibid.

112 Ibid.

113 *John Akers, Plaintiff, vs. Assiniboine and Sioux Tribes et al., Defendants*, In the District Court of the First Judicial District of the State of Montana, In and For the County of Lewis and Clark, No. 24995, Austin Buckles Family Papers, "Evidence" Envelope, Fort Peck Tribal Archives, Poplar, MT.; Buckles, "A Brief Resume and Statement of Facts Leading to the Present Crisis on the Fort Peck Reservation," prepared for Montana Congressional Delegation and CIA, April 9, 1956, Curry Papers, Box 99, 1956.

114 Ibid.

115 Ibid.

116 Resolution No. 2-55-1, Fort Peck Tribal Executive Board, May 19, 1955, Curry Papers, Box 99, March 1954.

117 Austin Buckles, "Fort Peck Crisis."

118 Minutes, General Council, June 11, 1955, "Evidence" Envelope, Austin Buckles Family Collection, Fort Peck Tribal Archives, Poplar, MT.

119 Austin Buckles, "Fort Peck Crisis."

120 Ibid.

121 Ibid.

122 Chairman Austin Buckles to Tribal Executive Board (hereinafter TEB), Memorandum forwarding contract with Dignan and Gallagher, Glasgow, MT, November 22, 1955, DCA Papers, MHS, Box 1, f16, "Tribal materials unfoldered 4."

123 Austin Buckles, "Fort Peck Crisis." "Attorney Contract," Dignan and Gallagher, Attorneys, Glasgow, MT, with Fort Peck Tribes, November 22, 1955. DCA Papers, MHS, Box 1, f16 "Tribal Materials unfoldered 4."

124 Austin Buckles, "Fort Peck Crisis."

125 Ibid.

126 Ibid.

127 Ibid.

128 Ibid.

129 Ibid.; reference to point 5, the annotation by Austin Buckles to Telegram, March 16, 1956 (A.E. Bielefeld, Acting Field Solicitor, Billings, MT, to John P. Burke, Acting Supt. Fort Peck Agency, Poplar, MT) and reference point 6, a summary of the telephone conversation, March 16, 1956, in which removal was indicated by saying Buckles and Archdale were no longer officials of the tribes, in log of copies of correspondence attached to letter July 3, 1956. Austin Buckles, Poplar, MT, to James E. Curry, Washington, DC, Curry Papers, Box 99, folder "1956."

130 Memorandum, Dolly Akers, Official Delegate, Fort Peck Reservation, to CIA Glenn L. Emmons, March 16, 1956, "Subject: Mal administration Fort Peck Agency under Supt. Talley and Buckles," DCA Papers, MHS, Box 6, folder "Loan Program (Short Term), 6/3."

131 Reference is made to the three delegations by an administrative assistant, Branch of Tribal Affairs, BIA, DC, in the attempt to schedule various meetings with officials. Austin Buckles, even though relegated to unofficial status, accompanied the Hollow delegation (Norman Hollow, Henry Archdale, Edwin Reddoor, and Leslie Fourstar, who was also a delegate with the Assiniboine Council delegations). Superintendent Talley and Attorney Thomas Dignan also attended all conferences. Memo, Louise G. Perkins, Administrative Assistant, Branch of Tribal Affairs, BIA, Washington, DC, to Fort Peck Tribal Delegations, March 20, 1956, attachment to Glenn L. Emmons, CIA, Washington, DC, to Chair, Fort Peck TEB, through Acting Area Director, M.A. Johnson, dated March 28, 1956, Austin Buckles Family Collection, Fort Peck Tribal Archives, Poplar, MT.

132 Emmons, Washington, DC, to Area Director, Billings, MT, telegram March 13, 1956, Curry Papers, Box 99, 1956.

133 Buckles, Washington, DC, to D'Ewart, Washington, DC, March 22, 1956, Curry Papers, Box 99, 1956.

134 Press Release, March 24, 1956, Curry Papers, Box 99, 1956.

135 Edmund T. Fritz, Deputy Solicitor, Interior, Washington, DC, to CIA, Washington, DC, May 1, 1956, M-36344/ Fort Peck Tribal Affairs, Curry Papers, Box 99, 1956.

136 Thomas Dignan, Glasgow, MT, to Edmond T. Fritz, Deputy Solicitor, Interior Department, Washington, DC, March 27, 1956, Curry Papers, Box 99, 1956.

137 Buckles et al., to McKay and Emmons, Washington, DC, March 28, 1956, Curry Papers, Box 99, 1956.

138 D'Ewart, Washington, DC, to Buckles et al., Poplar, MT, April 3, 1956, Curry Papers, Box 99, 1956.

139 Freda Beazley et al., Poplar, MT, to Murray, Washington, DC, telegram, April 8, 1956, Curry Papers, Box 99, 1956.

140 Emmons, CIA, Washington, DC, to Buckles, Poplar, MT, April 13, 1956, Curry Papers, Box 99, 1956.

141 Jon Bennion, *Big Sky Politics: Campaigns and Elections in Modern Montana* (Missoula: Five Valleys Publishing, 2004), 35-37.

142 Buckles, Poplar, MT, to D'Ewart, Washington, DC, April 17, 1956, Curry Papers, Box 99, 1956.

143 D'Ewart, Washington, DC, to Murray, Washington, DC, April 23, 1956, Curry Papers, Box 99, 1956.

144 Buckles, Poplar, MT, to Emmons, CIA, Washington, DC, April 26, 1956, Curry Papers, Box 99, 1956.

145 Murray et al., Washington, DC, to Buckles, Poplar, MT, May 1, 1956, Curry Papers, Box 99, 1956. Interior Solicitor Edmund T. Fritz wrote to Commissioner Emmons on May 1, 1956 with his opinion (M-36-344) addressing matters that had accumulated since his previous opinion dated April 23, 1956 (M-36342), that had addressed the minimal requirements for calling and operating a general council. The calling of the meeting of April 7 had not met the standards outlined for conducting general councils. The recommended solution was a special election initiated by the TEB as constituted and elected prior to the April 7 meeting. Memorandum, Edmund T. Fritz, Solicitor, Interior, Washington, DC, to CIA, Washington, DC, May 1, 1956, "Fort Peck Tribal Affairs, M-36-344," Austin Buckles Family Collection, "Unlabeled Envelop #1," Fort Peck Tribal Archives, Poplar, MT.

146 Stenographic Transcript of Informal Conference before the Montana Congressional Delegation and Committee Staff of the U.S. Senate Committee on Interior and Insular Affairs, Washington, DC, March 20, 1956, DCA Papers, MHS, Box 1, Folder "Tribal Materials (unfoldered)#2 (folder 1/14)."

147 Superintendent Clinton O. Talley, Fort Peck Agency (hereinafter cited as "FPA"), Poplar, to Buckles, Poplar, MT, May 18, 1956, Curry Papers, Box 99, 1956.

148 Buckles, Poplar, MT, to Curry, Washington, DC, July 3, 1956, Curry Papers, Box 99, 1956.

149 Minutes, Fort Peck TEB, Special Meeting, May 17, 1956, DCA Papers, MHS, Box 6, folder "Tribal Membership 1956-1959." This meeting

was recessed until May 24, 1956, and another meeting was held on May 28, but minutes for these meeting were not in the file.

150 Minutes, Fort Peck TEB, Special Meeting, June 1, 1956, DCA Papers, MHS, Box 6, folder "Tribal Membership 1956-1959." The budget for Fiscal Year 1957 was also approved at this meeting.

151 Minutes, Fort Peck TEB, Special Meeting, June 4, 1956, DCA Papers, MHS, Box 6, folder "Tribal Membership 1956-1959."

152 Minutes of a Meeting, Billings Area Office, with six TEB members and others," October 2, 1956, Austin Buckles Family Papers, folder "Unlabeled Envelop #1," Fort Peck Tribal Archives, Poplar, MT.

153 Austin Buckles, Poplar, MT to Sister Providencia, College of Great Falls, Great Falls, MT, Austin Buckles Family Papers, folder "Unlabeled Envelop #2," Fort Peck Tribal Archives, Poplar, MT.

154 Memorandum, Chairman Dolly C. Akers, to TEB members, December 17, 1956, Austin Buckles Family Papers, folder "Unlabeled Envelop #1," Fort Peck Tribal Archives, Poplar, MT.

155 Dolly Akers, Chair, to Superintendent, FPA, Poplar, MT, March 17, 1958, "Subject: Resolution 182-58-1," DCA Papers, MHS, Box 1, folder "Tribal Materials, Unfoldered #3."

156 Minutes, TEB Special Meeting, December 21, 1956, Extracts from Minutes Collection, Austin Buckles Family Papers, folder "Unlabeled Envelop #1," Fort Peck Tribal Archives, Poplar, MT.; Resolution No. 61-56-2. Fort Peck TEB, December 21, 1956, Austin Buckles Family Papers, folder "Unlabeled Envelop #1," Fort Peck Tribal Archives, Poplar, MT.

157 Dolly Akers, Chairman, Fort Peck Tribes, Newsletter to Tribal Members, December 31, 1956, DCA Papers, MHS, Box 1, folder "Personal-Historical."

158 Newsclipping, "Fort Peck Reservation . . . Former Tribal Chairman says Issues Camouflaged," unidentified newspaper (January 17, 1957), DCA papers, MHS, Box 1, folder "Personal-Historical."

159 Dolly Akers, Chair et al., to CIA, Washington, DC, January 24, 1957, DCA Papers, MHS, Box 1, folder "Tribal materials, unfoldered Number 1."

160 George Thompson, Vice Chairman, Fort Peck Tribes, with Melvin Buckles,

Poplar District Committeeman, Louis Youngman, Poplar District Committeeman, Earl Jones, Riverside District Committeeman, Carl Walking Eagle, Riverside District Committeeman, Reuben Counter, Fort Kipp District Committeeman, Elmer Red Eagle, Fort Kipp District Committeeman, Henry Begs His Own, Poplar District Chairman, Britton Fast Horse, Riverside District Chairman, Patrick Necklace, Fort Kipp District Committeeman (sic, "Chairman"), to Senator James E. Murray, Washington, DC, telegram, January 7, 1957, DCA Papers, MHS, Box 1, folder "Tribal Materials, Unfoldered, Number 2."

161 Minutes, TEB Special Meeting, January 4, 1957, Extracts from Minutes Collection, Austin Buckles Family Papers, folder "Unlabeled Envelop #1," Fort Peck Tribal Archives, Poplar, MT.

162 Minutes, TEB Regular Meeting, February 14, 1957, Extracts from Minutes Collection, Austin Buckles Family Papers, folder "Unlabeled Envelop #1," Fort Peck Tribal Archives, Poplar, MT.

163 Minutes, TEB Special Meeting, February 26, 1957, Extracts from Minutes Collection, Austin Buckles Family Papers, folder "Unlabeled Envelop #1," Fort Peck Tribal Archives, Poplar, MT.

164 Minutes, TEB Special Meeting, March 14, 1957, and Regular Meeting, March 22, 1957, Abstracts from Minutes Collection, Austin Buckles Family Papers, folder "Unlabeled Envelop #1," Fort Peck Tribal Archives, Poplar, MT.

165 Statement of Superintendent David Weston, FPA, to TEB, March 22, 1957, Austin Buckles Family Papers, folder "Unlabeled Envelop #1," Fort Peck Tribal Archives, Poplar, MT.

166 Minutes, TEB Special Meeting, March 30, 1957, Extracts from Minutes Collection, Austin Buckles Family Papers, folder "Unlabeled Envelop #1," Fort Peck Tribal Archives, Poplar, MT.

167 Minutes, TEB Special Meeting, April 6, 1957, Extracts from Minutes Collection, Austin Buckles Family Papers, folder "Unlabeled Envelop #1," Fort Peck Tribal Archives, Poplar, MT.

168 Minutes, TEB Regular Meeting, April 11, 1957, Extracts from Minutes Collection, Austin Buckles Family Papers, folder "Unlabeled Envelop #1," Fort Peck Tribal Archives, Poplar, MT.

169 "Tribal Affairs Face Unity Test in New Factional Flare-Up," *The Poplar Standard,* v. 48, No. 26 (May 3, 1957), 1, 6, copy in DCA Papers, MHS, Box 6, folder "Minority Reports, Attorney, etc. 1957."

170 Minutes, TEB Special Meeting, April 29, 1957, Extracts from Minutes Collection, Austin Buckles Family Papers, folder "Unlabeled Envelop #1," Fort Peck Tribal Archives, Poplar, MT.

171 Memorandum, TEB members—Kermit Smith, Alfred Manning, Melvin Buckles, Carl Walking Eagle, and Sergeant-at-Arms Clarence Long Tree, to Fred Seaton, SI, Washington, DC, May 20, 1957, DCA Papers, MHS, Box 6, folder "Minority Reports, Attorney, etc. 1957."

172 "Tribal Enrollment Ordinance Drafted by Committee," unidentified newspaper (May 30, 1957), DCA Papers, MHS, Bx1, folder "Tribal Materials Unfoldered Number 2." The TEB had kept in mind the advice provided in the communication, Glenn L. Emmons, CIA, Washington, DC, through the Area Director, to the Chairman, Fort Peck Tribes, April 10, 1956, DCA Papers, MHS, Bx1, folder "Tribal Materials Unfoldered Number 2."

173 Dolly C. Akers, Chairman, to Percy E. Melis, Billings Area Office Director, Billings, MT, May 10, 1957, DCA Papers, MHS Box 6, folder "Minority Reports, Attorney, etc. 1957."

174 Chairman Dolly C. Akers, and TEB members Alfred Manning, Melvin Buckles, Carl Walking Eagle, to David P. Weston, Superintendent, FPA, Poplar, MT, May 22, 1957, DCA Papers, MHS, Box 6, folder "Minority Reports, Attorney, etc. 1957." Also see Dolly C. Akers, Chairman, TEB, Poplar, MT, to Senator James E. Murray, Washington, DC, June 13, 1957, which includes a discussion about how she and her supporters were being "steamrollered" by area office and local BIA and the field solicitor's offices to accept the contract with Hubert J. Massman; the chairman cited the CFR 25, section 15.8 about employment of attorneys. She suggested this whole maneuver was probably at "the suggestion and invitation of Austin Buckles and his group." She asserted again the role of the general council being essential in this task. DCA Papers, MHS, Box 6, folder "Minority Report, Attorneys, etc. 1957." On June 27, Edmund T. Fritz, Deputy Solicitor, wrote the CIA had discussed whether the TEB had authority to decide matters between the meetings of the general council,

that the TEB had authority to acted, including approval of attorney contracts, and in the past the department had approved actions TEB as well as the general council. Edmund T. Fritz, Deputy Solicitor, Interior, Washington, DC, to CIA, Washington, DC, June 27, 1957, DCA Papers, MHS, Box 6, folder "Minority Reports, Attorney, etc. 1957."

175 Newsletter, Chairman Dolly C. Akers, to Members of the Fort Peck Tribes, n.d. (approximately mid-July 1956), DCA Papers, MHS, Box 6, folder "Tribal Membership, 1956-1959."

176 M. A. Johnson, Acting Director, Billings Area Office, Billings, MT, to Dolly C. Akers, Chairman, FP TEB, Poplar, MT, June 6, 1957, DCA Papers, MHS Box 6, folder "Minority Reports, Attorney, etc. 1957."

177 Chairman Dolly C. Akers, TEB, Poplar, MT, to Mr. Fritz (Interior, Washington, DC), June 11, 1957, DCA Papers, MHS Box 6, folder "Minority Reports, Attorney, etc. 1957."

178 Field solicitor to the Billings Area Office Director, June 7, 1957, DCA Papers, MHS, Box 6, folder "Resolution 1-53, Signing Documents by Chairman."

179 W. Barton Greenwood, Acting CIA, Washington, DC, to Percy E. Melis, Area Director-BIA, Billings, MT, July 29, 1957, DCA Papers, MHS Box 6, folder "Minority Reports, Attorney, etc. 1957." Also see "Akers States Council Must Be Consulted," *The Herald News,* v. 44, No. 27, DCA Papers, MHS, Box 1, folder "Dolly Akers, 1942-1959."

180 Edmund T. Fritz, Deputy Solicitor, Interior, Washington, DC, to CIA, Washington, DC, July 9, 1957, DCA Papers, MHS Box 6, folder "Minority Reports, Attorney, etc. 1957."

181 Minutes, TEB Special Meeting, July 30, 1957, Excerpts from Minutes Collection, Austin Buckles Family Papers, folder "Unlabeled Envelop #1," Fort Peck Tribal Archives, Poplar, MT, DCA Papers, MHS, Box 6, folder "Minority Reports, Attorney, etc. 1957."

182 Dolly C. Akers, Chairman, TEB, Poplar, MT, to David P. Weston, Superintendent, FPA, Poplar, MT, July 30, 1957, DCA Papers, MHS, Box 6, folder "Minority Reports, Attorney, etc. 1957."

183 Alfred Manning, Executive Board Member, Fort Kipp, and Kermit Smith, Executive Board Member, Wolf Point, to David P. Weston, Superintendent,

FPA, Poplar, MT, August 2, 1957, DCA Papers, MHS, Box 6, folder "Minority Reports, Attorney, etc. 1957."

184 W. Barton Greenwood, Acting CIA, Washington, DC, to Percy E. Melis, Billings Area Director, BIA, Billings, MT, August 5, 1957, DCA Papers, MHS, Box 1, folder "Tribal Materials (Unfoldered) 4."

185 David P. Weston, Superintendent, FPA, Poplar, MT, to the TEB, Poplar, MT, August 13, 1957, DCA Papers, MHS, Box 1, folder "Tribal Materials (Unfoldered) 4."

186 Resolution #99-57-8, August 29, 1957, DCA Papers, MHS, Box 1, folder "Tribal Materials (Unfoldered) 4."

187 Dolly C. Akers, Chairman, TEB, and TEB members—Kermit Smith, Alfred Manning, and Melvin Buckles, September 6, 1957, DCA Papers, MHS, Box 6, folder "Minority Reports Attorney, etc. 1957."

188 Dolly C. Akers, Chairman, TEB, Poplar, MT, to Glenn L. Emmons, CIA, BIA, Washington, DC, September 10, 1957, DCA Papers, MHS, Box 6, folder "Resolution I-53, Signing Documents by Chairman."

189 Memorandum, James J. Eder, Tribal Secretary, Fort Peck TEB, to the members of the TEB, September 19, 1957, Austin Buckles Family Collection, Fort Peck Tribal Archives, Poplar, MT, folder "Unlabeled Envelop #1."

190 A.E. Bielefeld, Field Solicitor, Billings, MT, to Director, Billings Area Office, Billings, MT, September 23, 1957, DCA Papers, MHS, Box 1, folder 1/15, "Tribal Materials (Unfoldered) 2."

191 Minutes, TEB Special Meeting, October 15, 1957, Excerpts from Minutes Collection, Austin Buckles Family Papers, folder "Unlabeled Envelop #1," Fort Peck Tribal Archives, Poplar, MT.

192 Minutes, TEB Special Meeting, October 21, 1957, Excerpts from Minutes Collection, Austin Buckles Family Papers, folder "Unlabeled Envelop #1," Fort Peck Tribal Archives, Poplar, MT.

193 Minutes, TEB Special Meeting, October 29, 1957, Excerpts from Minutes Collection, Austin Buckles Family Papers, folder "Unlabeled Envelop #1," Fort Peck Tribal Archives, Poplar, MT.

194 Dolly C. Akers, Chairman, Poplar, MT, to Edmund Fritz. Deputy Solicitor, Interior, Washington, DC, November

9, 1957, DCA Papers, MHS, Box 6, folder "Minority Reports Attorney, etc. 1957."

195 Minutes, TEB Special Meeting, December 16, 1957, Excerpts from Minutes Collection, Austin Buckles Family Papers, folder "Unlabeled Envelop #1," Fort Peck Tribal Archives, Poplar, MT.

196 Minutes, TEB Special Meeting, January 10, 1958, Excerpts from Minutes Collection, Austin Buckles Family Papers, folder "Unlabeled Envelop #1," Fort Peck Tribal Archives, Poplar, MT.

197 Minutes, TEB Special Meeting, February 7, 1958, Excerpts from Minutes Collection, Austin Buckles Family Papers, folder "Unlabeled Envelop #1," Fort Peck Tribal Archives, Poplar, MT.

198 Minutes, TEB Special Meeting, February 20, 1958, Excerpts from Minutes Collection, Austin Buckles Family Papers, folder "Unlabeled Envelop #1," Fort Peck Tribal Archives, Poplar, MT.

199 A. E. Bielefeld, Field Solicitor, Billings, MT, to Area Director, BIA, Billings, MT, March 11, 1958, DCA papers, MHS, Box 1, folder "Dolly Akers 1942-1959."

200 Resolution No. 230-58-4, with draft document, "Modification of Agreement The Fort Peck Tribes Declaration of Policies and Plan of Operations Tribal Credit Short Term Emergency Loan Program," April 3, 1958, DCA Papers, MHS, Box 6, folder "Loan Program (Short Term)" ("1958-1959 Fort Peck Credit"), 6/3.

201 Resolution No. 234-58-4, April 25, 1958, DCA Papers, MHS, Box 6, folder "Loan Program (Short Term)" ("1958-1959 Fort Peck Credit"), 6/3.

202 BIA Press Release, "Dept. Agrees to Delay Indian Land Sales for Balance of Congressional Session at request of Senator Murray," May 28, 1958, DCA Papers, MHS, Box 1, folder "Tribal Materials (unfoldered) 3," 1/15.

203 "Akers Asks Publication (of) Expenditures," Poplar Standard (June 6, 1958), DCA Papers, MHS, Box 1, folder "Personal-Historical."

204 Memo, David Weston, Superintendent, FPA, Poplar, MT, to Dolly C. Akers, Chairman, FP TEB, Poplar, MT, June 24, 1958, DCA Papers, MHS, Box 1, folder "Personal-Historical."

205 "Land Use Policy" (Draft) n.d. (ca. April/June 1958), DCA Papers, MHS, Box 1, folder "Tribal Materials

(Unfoldered) 2." Also see Memo, Percy E. Melis, Area Director, BIA, Billings, MT, to Superintendent, FPA, Poplar, MT, "Review of Land Use Policy enacted by the FP TEB and Resolution No. 188-58-2," April 10, 1958, DCA Papers, MHS, Box 1, folder "Tribal Materials (unfoldered) 2." Also see Percy E. Melis, Area Director, Billings, MT, to Superintendent, FPA, Poplar, MT, "Submarginal Lands, Revocable Permit Expiring December 31, 1958." April 10, 1958, DCA Papers, MHS, Box 1, folder "Tribal Materials (Unfoldered) 2." Also see David P. Weston, Superintendent, FPA, Poplar, MT, to Chairman, FP Tribes, Poplar, MT, "Proposed Tribal Land Use Policy contained in Resolution No. 293-58-6," June 25, 1958, DCA Papers, MHS, Box 1, folder "Tribal Materials (Unfoldered) 2" (folder 1/14)

206 Glenn L. Emmons, CIA, Washington, DC (through the Area Director) to Dolly C. Akers, Chairman, Fort Peck TEB, Poplar, MT, June 29, 1958, Austin Buckles Family Collection, Fort Peck Tribal Archives, Poplar, MT, folder "Unlabeled Envelop #1."

207 Minutes, General Council, September 6, 1958, Billings Area Office Fort Peck Documents Collection, National Archives and Records Administration (hereinafter cited as "NARA"), Central Plains Regional Archives, Lenexa, Kansas.

208 Ibid.

209 Ibid.

210 Ibid.

211 Ibid.

212 Petition, Louis Youngman, Chairman, Poplar District; Ted Manning, Vice Chairman, Poplar District; Melvin Buckles, TEB member, Poplar District; Andrew Red Thunder, Poplar, MT; Edwin Reddoor, Poplar, MT; and W.C. Knorr, Wolf Point District; to Fred A. Seaton, SI, Washington, DC, September 16, 1958, DCA Papers, MHS, Box 1, folder "Dolly Akers, 1942-1959."

213 Newsclipping "Declares Ouster Recognition Not Proper—Akers Says, Chairmanship right is Valid," Wolf Point Herald (September 25, 1958), DCA Papers, MHS, Box 1, folder "Personal-Historical."

214 Thomas Dignan, Dignan and Gallagher, Glasgow, MT, to A.E. Bielefeld, Field Solicitor, Interior, Billings, MT, October 1, 1958. DCA Papers, MHS, Bx1, folder "Dolly Akers, 1942-1959."

215 A.E. Bielefeld, Field Solicitor, Billings Area Office, Billings, MT, to Area Director, BIA, Billings, MT, October 3, 1958, DCA Papers, MHS, Box 1, Folder "Dolly Akers, 1942-1959."

216 Dolly C. Akers was joined by TEB members Melvin Buckles, Kermit Smith, and Alfred Manning, and Louis Youngman, Chairman of the Poplar District, Ted Manning, Vice-Chairman of the Poplar District, Andrew Red Thunder, member of Poplar District, Edwin Reddoor, of Poplar District, and W.C. Knorr, of Wolf Point District, and "for and behalf of numerous other duly quali-fied members of the Fort Peck Tribes." Notice of Appeal (to the SI), Fort Peck General Council, Frazer, Montana, Sept. 6, 1958," "Notice of Appeal from the Decision of the Superintendent of the Fort Peck Indian Agency, the Decision of the Field Solicitor and Area Director, Indian Affairs, Billings, Montana, and Answer to the Brief filed by Thomas Dignan, Esq., Attorney at Law, Glasgow, Montana," October 10, 1958, DCA Papers, MHS, Box 1, folder "Dolly Akers, 1942-1959."

217 Charles Hall, Wolf Point District, was added to the others on the full appeal document, listed in the Notice of Appeal. Dolly C. Akers, Chairman, Fort Peck Tribes et al., to CIA, Washington, DC, October 20, 1958. An appeal to decision of the superinten-dent, area director, and field solicitor, brief by Dignan (October 1) and minutes of GC of September 6, DCA Papers, MHS, Box 1, folder "Dolly Akers, 1942-1959."

218 Ibid.

219 Ibid.

220 Ibid.

221 Dolly C. Akers, Chairman, Fort Peck Tribes, Poplar, MT, to Franklin C. Salisbury, Assistant Solicitor, Interior, Washington, DC, October 28, 1958, DCA Papers, MHS, Box 1, folder "Dolly Akers, 1942-1959."

222 Dolly C. Akers, Chairman, Fort Peck Tribes, Washington, DC, to Glenn, CIA, Washington, DC, November 3, 1958, DCA Papers, MHS, Box 1, folder "Dolly Akers, 1942-1959."

223 Dolly C. Akers, Chairman, Fort Peck Tribes, Washington, DC, to Glenn L. Emmons, CIA, Washington, DC, November 12, 1958, DCA Papers, MHS, Bx1, folder "Dolly Akers, 1942-1959."

224 Dolly C. Akers, Chairman, Fort Peck Tribes, Washington, DC, to Glenn L. Emmons, CIA, Washington, DC, November 14, 1958, DCA Papers, MHS, Bx1, folder "Dolly Akers, 1942-1959."

225 Dolly C. Akers, Chairman, Fort Peck Tribes, Washington, DC, to Glenn L. Emmons, CIA, Washington, DC, November 24, 1958, DCA Papers, MHS, Box 1, folder "Dolly Akers, 1942-1959."

226 Memorandum, Assistant Solicitor, Indian Legal Activities, Interior, Washington, DC, to CIA, Washington, DC, December 3, 1958, Austin Buckles Family Papers, Fort Peck Tribal Archives, Poplar, MT, folder "Unlabeled Envelop #1."

227 Dolly C. Akers, Chairman, Fort Peck Tribes, Washington, DC, to Elmer Bennett, Deputy SI, Washington, DC, December 28, 1958, DCA Papers, MHS, Box 1, folder "Dolly Akers, 1942-1959."

228 Glenn L. Emmons, CIA, Washington, DC, to Chairman, TEB, Poplar, MT (through the Area Director, Billings, MT), January 5, 1959, Austin Buckles Family Papers, Fort Peck Tribal Archives, Poplar, MT, folder "Unlabeled Envelop #1."

229 Telegram, Dolly Akers, Chairman, Fort Peck Tribes, Washington, DC, to Glenn L. Emmons, CIA, Washington, DC, January 6, 1959, DCA Papers, MHS, Box 1, folder "Dolly Akers, 1942-1959."

230 "Dolly Akers Reinstated by Indian Bureau Ruling." *Great Falls Tribune*, v. 72, no. 242 (January 11, 1959), 1, Austin Buckles Family Papers, Fort Peck Tribal Archives, Poplar, MT, folder "Unlabeled Envelop #1."

231 Minutes, Recessed TEB Regular Meeting, "Rough Draft," January 9, 1959, Austin Buckles Family Papers, Fort Peck Tribal Archives, Poplar, MT, folder "Unlabeled Envelop #1."

232 "Tribe May Vote on Constitution: Department Okays Proposed Changes," *Billings Gazette*, (January 14, 1959), 1, Austin Buckles Family Papers, Fort Peck Tribal Archives, Poplar, MT, folder "Unlabeled Envelop #1."

233 Minutes, TEB Special Meeting, "Rough Draft," January 16, 1959, Austin Buckles Family Papers, Fort Peck Tribal Archives, Poplar, MT, folder "Unlabeled Envelop #1."

234 Resolution #458-59-1, January 20, 1959. Also see Minutes, TEB Special Meeting, "Rough Draft," January 20, 1959, both in Austin Buckles Family Papers, Fort Peck Tribal Archives, Poplar, MT, folder "Unlabeled Envelop #1."

235 Dolly C. Akers, Chairman, Fort Peck Tribes, Poplar, MT et al., to Glenn L. Emmons, CIA, Washington, DC, January 20, 1959, DCA Papers, MHS, Box 1, folder "Dolly Akers, 1942-1959."

236 Memorandum, W.R. Smith, James Sweeney, Henry Archdale, Roy Sansaver, Leslie Four Star, and Maurice Big Horn, and unsigned names of Kermit Smith, Melvin Buckles, and Alfred Manning, identified as "The Assiniboine and Sioux Indians of the Fort Peck Reservation, Montana," to Fred A. Seaton, SI, Washington, DC, January 21, 1959. Also see Resolution No. 446-59-1, January 16, 1959. Both in Austin Buckles Family Papers, Fort Peck Tribal Archives, Poplar, MT, folder "Unlabeled Envelop #1."

237 Montana Congressional Delegation: Senator Mike Mansfield, Senator James E. Murray, and Congressman Lee Metcalf, and Congressman LeRoy Anderson, to Fred A. Seaton, SI, Washington, DC, January 23, 1959, Austin Buckles Family Papers, Fort Peck Tribal Archives, Poplar, MT, folder "Unlabeled Envelop #1."

238 Dolly C. Akers, Chairman, Fort Peck Tribes, 2837-29th Street NW, Washington, DC, to David P. Weston, Superintendent, FPA, Poplar, MT, January 23, 1959, DCA Papers, MHS, Box 1, folder "Dolly Akers-Personal."

239 W. Barton Greenwood, Acting CIA, Washington, DC, to Percy E. Melis, Area Director, BIA, Billings, MT, January 27, 1959, DCA Papers, MHS, Box 1, folder "Dolly Akers, 1942-1959."

240 Dolly C. Akers, Chairman, with TEB members, Alfred Manning, Fort Kipp District, Melvin Buckles, Poplar District, and Kermit Smith, Wolf Point District, to Fred A. Seaton, SI, Washington, DC, January 27, 1959, DCA Papers, MHS, Box 1, folder "Personal."

241 Roger Ernst, Assistant SI, Washington, DC (through the Billings Area Director) to Mrs. Dolly Akers, Chairman, Fort Peck Tribes, Poplar, MT, February 2, 1959, DCA Papers, MHS, Box 1, folder "Personal."

242 Telegram, Manny Smith and Melvin Buckles, Wolf Point, MT, to Mrs. Dolly Akers, 2837 29th Street NW, Washington, DC, February 2, 1959, DCA Papers, MHS, Box 1, folder "Personal."

243 Kermit Smith, TEB member, Louis Youngman, Jr., District Chairman, Melvin Buckles, TEB member, Andrew Red Thunder, Edwin Reddoor, Sioux Council Chairman, and Theodore Manning, District Vice Chairman, to Elmer T. Bennett, Assistant SI, Washington, DC, February 3, 1959, DCA Papers, MHS, Box 1, folder "Personal."

244 Dolly C. Akers, Chairman, Fort Peck Tribes, "for herself and for and on behalf of: Louis Youngman, Chairman, Poplar District; Ted Manning, Vice Chairman, Poplar District; Andrew Red Thunder, Poplar District; Edwin Red Door, Poplar District; Charles Hall, Wolf Point; Alfred Manning, Fort Kipp District; Melvin Buckles, Poplar District; Kermit Smith, Wolf Point District; and William Knorr, Wolf Point District;" to Fred A. Seaton, SI, Washington, DC, February 3, 1959, DCA Papers, MHS, folder "Dolly Akers, 1942-1959."

245 Austin Buckles, George W. Thompson, Jr., Norman Hollow, and Howard Trinder, Everett Hotel, Washington, DC, to Roger Ernst, Assistant SI, Washington, DC, February 11, 1959, Austin Buckles Family Papers, Fort Peck Tribal Archives, Poplar, MT, folder "Unlabeled Envelop #1."

246 E.J. Utz, Asst. CIA, Washington, DC, to Percy Melis, Director, Area Office, Billings, MT, February 11, 1959, DCA Papers, MHS, Box 1, folder, "Tribal Materials (unfoldered) #3."

247 Telegram. Austin Buckles and Norman Hollow, (J and H Archdale, Sweeney, Fourstar, Youpee, Walking Eagle, Bighorn, Spotted Elk, McClammy-Boyd, Yellowrobe), to Roy Sansaver, Eva Mae and Bill Smith, February 13, 1959, Austin Buckles Family Papers, Fort Peck Tribal Archives, Poplar, MT, folder "Unlabeled Envelop #1."

248 Glenn L. Emmons, CIA, Washington, DC, to Dolly C. Akers, Poplar, MT, February 13, 1959, DCA Papers, MHS, Box 1, Folder "Personal." Glenn L. Emmons, CIA, Washington, DC, to Percy Melis, Director, Area Office, BIA, Billings, MT, February 13, 1959, DCA Papers, MHS, Bx1, folder "Tribal materials (Unfoldered) #3."

249 Dolly C. Akers, "Chairman," Fort Peck Tribes, with Melvin Buckles, TEB member; Louis Youngman, District Chairman; Edwin Reddoor, Member, and Ted Manning, Vice Chairman, Poplar District; February 14, 1959, DCA Papers, MHS, Box 1, folder "Personal."

250 Dolly C. Akers, with TEB members Melvin Buckles, Kermit Smith, and Alfred Manning, with Louis Youngman, Edwin Reddoor, and Ted Manning, to Fred A. Seaton, SI, Washington, DC, February 16, 1959, Austin Buckles Family Papers, Fort Peck Tribal Archives, Poplar, MT, folder "Unlabeled Envelop #1."

251 "Fort Peck Tribal Board Orders General Election," Great Falls Tribune (February 17, 1959), DCA Papers, MHS, Bx1, folder "Personal-Historical."

252 Telegram, Roger Ernst, Asst. SI, Washington, DC, to Mrs. Dolly Akers, February 19, 1959, DCA Papers, MHS, Bx1, folder "Personal," 1/1.

253 "Commissioner Issues Ruling on Akers' Removal," and "Akers Challenges Ruling Made by Bureau Official," Poplar Standard, v. 48, no. 14, (February 20, 1959), 1-2, DCA Papers, MHS, Bx1, folder "Personal."

254 Dolly C. Akers, Chairman, TEB members Melvin Buckles, Kermit Smith, Alfred Manning, and Louis Youngman, Chair, Poplar District; Edwin Reddoor, Secretary Sioux Nations Council; Ted Manning, Vice Chairman, Poplar District, to Senator Barry Goldwater, Washington, DC, February 28, 1959, DCA Papers, MHS, Bx1, folder "Personal."

255 David P. Weston, Superintendent, FPA, Poplar, MT, to Mrs. Dolly C. Akers, Wolf Point, MT, and Melvin Buckles, Poplar, MT, March 30, 1959, DCA Papers, MHS, Bx1, folder "Personal."

256 See the appendix in this volume listing persons elected to serve in the administration for 1959-1961.

257 Joseph W. Culbertson, Tribal Secretary, "Appeal and Protest of the Executive Board of the Fort Peck Reservation," December 5, 1960, Billings Area Office Fort Peck Documents Collection, NARA-Lenexa, Kansas.

258 "General Council Meets in Verbal Flurry—Membership, Blood Quantum Go to the Tribes in Referendum; Tribes Kill Per Capita Payment Try." Poplar Standard (June 12, 1959), DCA Papers, MHS, bx1, folder "Personal."

259 Rex Lee, Associate CIA, Washington, DC, to Chair, TEB, Poplar, MT, September 14, 1959, DCA Papers, MHS, Box 6, folder "Minority Report, Attorney, etc. 1957."

260 Minutes, TEB special meeting, September 17, 1959, DCA Papers, MHS, Box 6, folder "Minority Report, Attorney, etc. 1957."

261 Joseph W. Culbertson, Tribal Secretary, "Appeal and Protest of the Executive Board of the Fort Peck Reservation," December 5, 1960, Billings Area Office Fort Peck Documents Collection, NARA-Lenexa, Kansas.

262 Certificate of Adoption, Constitution and Bylaws with Amendments Incorporated, Fort Peck Tribes, October 1, 1960.

263 Culbertson, "Appeal and Protest of the Executive Board of the Fort Peck Reservation."

264 George W. Abbott, Assistant SI, Washington, DC, to Superintendent Dale Baldwin, FPA, Poplar, MT, November 30, 1960, Billings Area Office Fort Peck Documents Collection, NARA-Lenexa, Kansas.

CHAPTER 14

~

A Renewed Tribal Government and Economic and Social Development: Discovering Potential, 1960-1980

James Shanley, Ed.D, Caleb Shields, D.H.L., and Joseph R. McGeshick, Ph.D., with David R. Miller, Ph.D.

WHEN the country elected President Kennedy in late 1960, the impetus toward termination, relocation, Public Law 280, and the barefaced assault on tribal sovereignty of the 1950s seemed to be waning. The next decade, especially the years under Democratic President Johnson, echoed with self-determination and a national war on poverty in every part of the country, including Indian country. The overall rhetoric, backed up by tangible implementation of new federal government programs on reservations, gave the Assiniboine and Sioux Tribes new hope. Although civil rights, the Vietnam War, and the assassinations of the Kennedy brothers and Martin Luther King, Jr., created intense conflicts between liberals and conservatives throughout the nation, the 1960s actually brought some prosperity to many Indian communities, Fort Peck included.

In 1959, the year before Kennedy was elected, Austin Buckles was again elected chairman of the Fort Peck tribes, and Dale Baldwin was superintendent of the BIA. One month before the general election in 1960, they confronted changes in tribal politics when tribal members at Fort Peck voted for a new tribal constitution and bylaws that replaced the 1927 Constitution and differed from it in many explicit ways. First and foremost, the new document called for a Tribal Executive Board (TEB) consisting of a chairman, vice-chairman, secretary-accountant, a sergeant-at-arms, and twelve board members, all elected from the outlying reservation districts and each serving a two-year term. According to the constitution, the TEB's powers are subject only to the powers of the General Council. Besides the duties enumerated in the constitution, tribal government also dealt with referendum and amendment matters and tribal enrollment. One key aspect of the constitution was the enrollment issue. Prior to 1960, members of the

Assiniboine and Sioux Tribes needed only to prove they were lineal descendants of those on the Fort Peck tribal rolls. After the new Fort Peck Tribal Constitution was adopted, a tribal member needed to be one-fourth Assiniboine and/or Sioux.[1]

From the adoption of the 1960 Constitution through the next twenty years, a series of new federal government programs allowed communities at Fort Peck to enjoy improved health care, new schools and learning opportunities, modern housing projects, industrial employment, innovative entrepreneurial avenues, and numerous social programs. When Kennedy officially took office in January 1961, agriculture remained the mainstay of the local economy. For most Indian families living on the reservation, however, income was increasingly insufficient to maintain a decent standard of living. Unemployment was rampant.[2]

According to the 1960 U.S. Census, more than half the Indian families in Roosevelt County received less than $3,000 in 1959, while a survey conducted in 1962 by the Fort Peck Agency showed that about two-thirds of the Indian families on the reservation received less than that.[3] Unemployment remained chronic, and economic development was almost nonexistent. Armed with a new constitution and bylaws, the Assiniboine and Sioux settled into the last four decades of the twentieth century ready to encounter postmodern economic and political forces.

As tribal government focused on the new mandates of political process, social welfare, member enrollment, jurisprudence, allotted and tribal land, resource management, and many other issues, reservation communities looked forward to a more efficient representative government that would respond to their needs. However, tribal politics often added to, if not directly created, some of the problems within the reservation.

In late fall of 1961, William "Bill" Youpee was elected chairman of the tribes. In the next ten years, he became one of the strongest political leaders, bringing much-needed social and economic programs to the reservation. However, problems continued due to the three spheres, or "worlds," that existed at Fort Peck. After four years of supervising the Bureau of Indian Affairs, Superintendent Stanley Lyman (1961-67) observed, " . . . our society often speak[s] of two worlds, the Indian and the non-Indian. A third world is apparent at Fort Peck—the world of the BIA. These three worlds exist side by side with little lateral communication."[4] He continued,

There is agreement among local whites, the local Indians and many BIA employees that in order to get along with Indians you have to "understand" them. "Understand" in this case does not mean to understand the reasons for Indian behavior or points of view, but rather to accept the fiction that Indians are, by their very nature, different from white men and that a white man, in order to get along with Indians, must know how to "handle" them.

Superintendent Lyman elaborated further:

Unspoken by either, but accepted by both, is the underlying belief that the Indian is generally and by nature lazy, dirty, unreliable, and immoral and that he lives the way he does because he likes to. This was originally a strictly white view that grew out of an even older white belief that the Indian was, in fact, little better than an animal. Deeply offended and angered at this white view of himself, the Indian, over the years has nevertheless accepted it to an alarming and soul-deadening degree. Loudly and even belligerently he will deny this view is true, but in his heart is the awful fear that the white man is right.[5]

He ended:

By agreeing to accept this view of himself the Indian pays a heavy toll in self respect, but he relieves himself of responsibilities and demands that would otherwise be placed on him. He need not be reliable because after all he is "just an Indian" and you can't expect anything else from an Indian. The local white man, by agreeing to accept this view, absolves himself of any blame for treating Indians in a less than fully human manner, and the BIA employee uses this device to salve his conscience for his failure to improve the lot of the Indian.[6]

In an in-depth examination of the BIA in 1965, Lyman wrote that BIA employees were of two types: the professional and technical people who were for the most part products of Midwestern Euro-American culture and training, and the clerical employees who were mostly local tribal members whose background was usually the same as those they served. He said that many of the non-Indian employees lacked the capacity or desire to understand why Indian behavior and points of view differed from their own. They worked with Indians during the day, but on their own time, they associated with the BIA fraternity or, to a far lesser degree, with members of the local white community. At the same time, the local Indian employees got caught up in a parallel web of problems that was only heightened by family and community factionalism.[7]

In 1962, tribal members called the first General Council under the 1960 Fort Peck Tribal Constitution. The impetus was to address the most pressing issues—tribal government and elections. Article IV, Section 1 of the Tribal Constitution states, "Upon petition of at least ten percent of the eligible voters of the Tribes, a General Council shall be called by the Chairman . . . [and] a quorum shall consist of one hundred eligible voters of the Tribes." On several occasions, tribal members or tribal council members

called for a General Council, but they either failed to reach a quorum or did not follow constitutional requirements. Chairman Youpee received the petition from several reservation districts to address 1) a referendum for a constitutional amendment to reduce the Tribal Executive Board (TEB) to a chair, vice-chair, sergeant-at-arms, six board members, and secretary/accountant; 2) modifying investments; 3) forming a delegations committee; 4) establishing a constitution and bylaws committee from members outside the TEB; 5) prohibiting any board member from selling land to the tribes or securing any new leases on tribal and submarginal land during their tenure of office; 6) notifying the superintendent of the BIA that in the event that the recommendations of the General Council were not carried out by the TEB, the General Council would reconvene in ninety days to rescind all the TEB's actions and enactments; and 7) limiting the working committee to one working day per week. The General Council also requested a financial report from the tribes.[8] The petition for a General Council was declared invalid, so a General Council was not held. Instead, Youpee called for a community meeting to address the people's issues and concerns.

The request for the General Council demonstrated the level of political contention at Fort Peck. During that time, however, there was one entity to help ease those troubles. In 1958, the tribes began their long relationship with Washington, D.C., attorney Marvin Sonosky. He assisted in writing the 1960 Tribal Constitution and later served as general legal counsel for the Fort Peck tribes. Sonosky's firm helped the tribes establish and operate a complete and functioning tribal government. Sonosky assisted the tribes in exercising their powers of sovereignty, in resisting intrusions on their authority by both federal and state governments, and in protecting and expanding the land base, water rights, natural resources, and environment, as well as maximizing tribal of control oil and mineral revenues.[9]

After adoption of the 1960 Constitution, many thought that tribal politics would reflect a progressive government. Sonosky's firm gave much-needed guidance, but problems persisted. BIA Superintendent Stanley Lyman wrote in 1965, "The Fort Peck Tribes operate under the 1960 Constitution which was designed to relieve tribal government from the domination of the unwieldy general council. The circumstances of its formulation led to many compromises in this document and much improvement is needed."[10] He commented that representation on the TEB was "grossly unequal" and surmised that with only about 35 percent of the available votes, a tribal member could easily get elected to the TEB. Lyman said that too many tribal members ran for political office for the "spoils they can obtain or the vengeance they can wreak on an enemy." Each election was usually followed by "witch hunt[s]" by the victors, while the losers "called for a general council to embarrass or overthrow the elected officials."[11]

President Lyndon B. Johnson in his State of the Union address on January 8, 1964, pointed out that nineteen percent of Americans lived below the poverty line; consequently, he chose to unleash a war on poverty. Congress responded, sending the Economic Opportunity Act of 1964 to the President to sign into law on August 20, 1964. The act authorized a new entity, the Office of Economic Opportunity (OEO), to oversee new programs, one of the first being the Neighborhood Youth Corp (NYC). Project Head Start launched its first summer program in 1965.

The first programs began operating on the Fort Peck Reservation in the 1965-66 fiscal year. Senators Lee Metcalf and Mike Mansfield announced on January 28, 1966 that the Economic Development Administration (EDA) had declared the reservation and the four north-east Montana counties eligible to participate in programs established by the Public Works and Economic Development Act of 1965.[12] In mid-February, OEO reported that Fort Peck Reservation had received $100,000 to begin the war on poverty effort locally. These funds were used for Neighborhood Youth Corp (NYC), for 33 in-school students ($11,890) and 100 in-school student work incentive programs ($60,330); Project Head Start for 18 children at Brockton ($4,368) and 15 at Poplar ($3,950); and for six volunteers for Volunteers in Service to America (VISTA) ($20,100).[13]

The NYC programs were designed to counter the increased drop-out/stop-out rates among young people over 16 and under 27. Within the nation's reservations, underage or just barely legal young people committed more than 3,000 offenses annually. The NYC programs provided work situations and counseling to encourage participants to stay in school, or to pass the GED. Programs were offered in both the summers and during the regular school year.[14] Supported by Department of Labor resources, the NYC programs were administered locally.[15]

Three hundred of the first 2,500 VISTA volunteers were sent to reservations, and by the June 1966, nine were in service on the Fort Peck Reservation. The model was to become a "domestic peace corps," not imposing solutions but encouraging people to work together and create solutions from partnerships large and small.[16] While VISTA tried specifically to recruit American Indians as volunteers, the program did not have many takers.[17]

By June 1966, federal OEO grants were beginning to flow to the Fort Peck Tribes. The tribes established a Community Action Agency in late June to receive the diverse program monies. Community Action Programs (CAP) were described as "resources for self-help to those who live on Federal Indian reservations."[18]

Twenty-nine individuals from the five communities (Poplar, Wolf Point, Brockton, Oswego, and Frazer) were recruited for an Economic Opportunity Advisory Committee on June 23. Gordon Wilson was elected chairman and Frances Bemer secretary; Harold Boyd served as Acting Director. Initially, a request for Health and Home Management Aides was submitted, mostly because the need for such workers was so great, and seven other components were identified: program administration, Head Start (full-year programs), neighborhood service centers, and work experience programs, quite possibly in conservation and beautification roles, child daycare centers, and a small business development center.[19]

Before the major funding for full-year Head Start operations had begun to flow, several VISTA volunteers in September 1966 organized a pre-school program in the Wolf Point First Presbyterian Church. Through community-wide donations, a group of low income children were accommodated for several months. This volunteer and community effort in Wolf Point confirmed the demand for Head Start programs across the reservation.[20] Head Start was initially funded by OEO up to 90 percent, based on the demands arising from widespread community support of low income populations. The two community actions programs, the Four County CAP and the Fort Peck CAP, submitted proposals for full-year programs for the 1966-67 fiscal year.[21]

Another offshoot support program was legal aid to those who could not afford a lawyer. A practicum program, the Montana Defender Project, begun at the University of Montana Law School with private money, provided law students to do the legwork on cases in which court-appointed attorneys were serving indigent individuals.[22]

Another accomplishment that summer was that a dozen Fort Peck students were sent to the initial Upward Bound program at Eastern Montana College—Billings: Katherine Bauer, Howard Bemer, Daveetta Big Leggins, Warren Buck Elk, Karen Growing Thunder, Geraldine Hollowhorn, James Iron Leggins, Donovan Red Boy, Myrna Red boy, Theodora Ricker, Jackie Weeks, and Jo Ann Youpee. The main objectives of program were "to develop motivation, academic skills, social and cultural understandings, and self confidence necessary to develop and succeed in college."[23]

In early summer 1967, the Fort Peck Community Agency formed an "alcoholism team" to promote sobriety and to work to solve the problems of recovering alcoholics. This included establishing Alcoholic Anonymous chapters and working on ways to extend Indian Public Health Services to alcoholic tribal members.[24] Eventually, a treatment center was established.

One necessity that overshadowed politics and touched every family and extended family on the reservation was housing. Prior to the late 1960s, families on Fort Peck, as on many other reservations across the country, lived in substandard housing on the edges of towns like Poplar and Wolf Point. Families from other reservation communities like Frazer, Oswego, Brockton, and Fort Kipp also often existed in one-room dwellings with limited plumbing and electrical necessities, and some even lived in rudimentary log homes with dirt floors.

During President Johnson's administration, the Department of Housing and Urban Development (HUD) was created in 1965 to improve housing standards and conditions and to offer avenues to home financing. A product of FDR's National Housing Act of 1934, which had created the Federal Housing Administration (FHA), HUD extended its help to Fort Peck and other reservations by the late 1960s. Although the Fort Peck Tribal Housing Authority (FPHA) was created in 1962 to manage construction and maintenance of low-rent and mutual help tribal housing projects, federal monies were the source of those activities. The first two housing projects were at Poplar and Wolf Point, consisting of two dozen duplexes. Families enjoyed new bedrooms, spacious living areas and dining rooms, and kitchens with modern appliances. The Poplar units were finished in 1963, and those in Wolf Point were completed in 1964. A year after HUD was created, the Fort Peck Housing Authority (FHPA) approved construction of fifty Mutual Help houses, twenty in Poplar, twenty in Wolf Point, and ten in Brockton. Indian housing projects on Fort Peck have been managed from floor plans to construction, and, in some cases, with the exception of Mutual Help units, continued maintenance has been provided under the support of HUD.

By 1970, many families in the reservation communities of Poplar, Wolf Point, Brockton, Fort Kipp, Frazer, and Oswego were living in new modern homes. In Poplar and Wolf Point, the FPHA clustered the residences either very near or just outside the city limits, but they were connected to municipal water and sewer systems. In those cases, the FPHA added the cost of connecting to city services to the general cost, and users paid monthly fees. In the other areas, towns like Brockton, Fort Kipp, Frazer, and Oswego were not yet incorporated and lacked the tax base to construct and maintain municipal water, sewer, and garbage services. In those areas, the FPHA, with much of the funding and assistance coming from the Indian Health Service (IHS), undertook joint responsibility of water and sewer services.

The beginning of the last three decades of the twentieth century created new interests among the membership on the Fort Peck Reservation. In November 1968, a HUD grant of $129,197 helped build community halls in Wolf Point, Poplar,

Fort Kipp, Frazer, and Brockton. These structures provided venues for community events and also for wakes and funerals. Later, the tribes, with funds from the EDA, oversaw construction of three new cultural centers in Oswego, Poplar, and Brockton. Those structures housed museums, cultural activities like powwows, wakes and funerals, and recreational activities.

Another major issue confronting the Assiniboine and Sioux tribes was health care. Since 1955, health care at Fort Peck fell by default under the responsibility of the Public Health Service (PHS). Prior to that, the BIA functioned as the sole health caregiver for the Fort Peck Assiniboine and Sioux. In the Sweet Grass Hill Treaty of 1888, which for all practical purposes initiated the specific Assiniboine and Sioux-federal government relationship, government negotiators and head tribal signatories included health care for the future of the tribes.[25] From 1911 to 1917, Congress directly appropriated monies for Indian health care, and as early as 1919, congressional leaders recommended transferring Indian health care services to the PHS. However, the BIA opposed the transfer, arguing that health care should not be separated from educational and societal efforts.

Much like housing improvement, the IHS focused on the reservation's two major population centers, Wolf Point and Poplar, establishing two small clinics in those towns. Although local community hospitals had operated in both places since the 1950s, most of their patients were non-Indians. By 1960, reservation medical personnel offered limited care, and a few years into the decade, Wolf Point and Poplar constructed new hospitals that cared for tribal members in emergencies and then invoiced the IHS for those services. But the vast majority of clients at these facilities were non-Indians. In March 1960 in Poplar, community officials broke ground for a $650,000 hospital; nine months later, construction started on Wolf Point's new hospital on the north side of town. After 1962, tribal members, as well as non-enrolled spouses and some non-enrolled adults from other reservations living on Fort Peck, used these IHS clinics as well as local hospitals. IHS doctors and nurses in Wolf Point worked out of a remodeled and relocated house purchased from the old Glasgow Air Force Base north of Glasgow, and provided patients with regular general health care. The clinic in Poplar, a larger facility with more staff, worked in the same manner, though it also employed a full-time dentist.

The IHS recruited medical students who, after graduation, traded a certain number of years of service for tuition, fees, and other financial aid, while local doctors occasionally contracted with the IHS. The IHS service unit director functioned as the chief administrator.

Since World War I, Indians' participation in U.S. wars had been proportionately higher than that of any other racial or ethnic group in Montana. As the Vietnam War escalated in the mid-1960s, Fort Peck tribal members joined in record numbers. One veteran, Francis "Mackie" Two Bulls, was one of the most decorated Vietnam veterans. A Marine and Army Special Forces member, Two Bulls won three Silver Stars, two Bronze Stars, eight Purple Hearts, and many other medals and citations.[26] Many of the missions he participated in are still classified as secret. Another veteran, Franklin D. Chopper of Brockton, for whom American Legion Post #61 in Brockton was named, was one of the first American Indians killed in action in June 1967.[27] Poplar's American Legion Post #54 is named for veteran Nathan Crazy Bull. Merle Lucas of Wolf Point was awarded the U.S. Army's Bronze Star for his service in Vietnam, 1966-68.[28] Many veterans from Fort Peck served with the highest of honors, and Veteran's Day remains one of the most honored days among the Assiniboine

and Sioux. Like many American Indian groups across the nation, the people at Fort Peck have always respected their veterans, including those who served in Vietnam. Fortunately, when they returned, they were welcomed with dignity and honor, unlike many non-Indians who returned home to resentment and hostility.

Once federal agencies began to address problems of substandard housing and limited health care, the U.S. Department of Agriculture (USDA) began distributing supplemental food under the Commodity Supplement Food Program to Fort Peck tribal members who qualified. The roots of supplementary food distribution on the reservation also date back to the treaty days. From the late-nineteenth and well into the twentieth century, the federal government issued monthly rations of beef, flour, coffee, and other staples at the agency headquarters. The USDA first administered several programs that distributed commodity foods, which the federal government purchases to support farm prices. The first commodity distribution program began during the Great Depression, when it was known as the Needy Family Program. This was the main form of food assistance for low-income people in the United States, including Indian reservations, until the Food Stamp Program was expanded in the early 1970s.

Chairman Bill Youpee led an important defense of tribal control of programs in January 1970. The Tribes had successfully been awarded a major sum from HUD for land planning on the reservation and for the towns of Poplar and Wolf Point, and although these required matching funds, the largest amount was to come from the Tribes. The chairman and tribal attorney Marvin J. Sonosky appeared in Helena before the state Board of Planning and Economic Development to refuse non-Indian demands for representation and voting power on a planning body. Chairman Youpee insisted that the planning would be done by the Tribes, and while non-voting non-Indian representation would be welcome, decisions would be made by the TEB.[29] In March, the Tribes again informed the Seattle Regional Office of HUD and the Montana Board of Planning and Economic Development that if control of the funds was not granted to the Tribes, the Tribes would refuse the grant. Chairman Youpee said the Tribes submitted their grant through the state of Montana because that was HUD's preference, but the experience of trying to organize a joint board was soured when non-Indians outvoted Indians. This was unacceptable for a planning process meant to benefit the reservation.[30] Again in May, Chairman Youpee outlined the obstacles to the control of planning he had asserted was the Tribes' responsibility. The Montana planning board countered that because jurisdictions like Wolf Point were incorporated, they could not legally give the "Indians" complete control. The chairman wanted the Tribes to be completely in control and perhaps to "subcontract work to the State Planning Department and let them work through the other government agencies [and jurisdictions]."[31] This assertion of sovereignty symbolized a change in how the Tribes were seeing their role in their own affairs, but also signaled to non-Indians a fuller participation of the Tribes in their self-determination. The "stalemate" was discussed in the media again in December, HUD having gotten cooperation on two other reservations. The media asked why it was such a big deal for Fort Peck.[32]

Almost as foreshadowing, Nixon announced on July 8, 1970 his administration's commitment to self-determination, attempting to "build upon the capacities and insights of the Indian people." This rejection of termination was overt and deliberate and anticipated the Indian Self-Determination and Education Act of 1975. Contracting directly with Tribal governments was looming on the horizon. District

Secretary Dolly C. Akers read a letter from CIA Louis Bruce, dated August 14, 1970, to all reservation superintendents to the Wolf Point District meeting. The BIA planned to roll out by FY1973 its full implementation of self-determination with increased dependence on tribal governments and employees for delivery of many programs and services. Several council persons were unsure what the implications of this development were, and warned that this possible federal intrusion into tribal government should be viewed with caution.[33]

In 1967, the BIA appointed Anson Baker, a tribal member of the Fort Berthold tribes, as the first Indian superintendent at the Fort Peck Agency. Baker served until 1971, when William Benjamin replaced him and served until 1973. By the early 1970s, the Fort Peck tribes had worked out some of their governmental problems, especially regarding tribal elections and government. In August 1970, the tribes approved a constitutional amendment calling for at-large elections, departing from the district method. They also voted to accept absentee voting in all tribal elections. The district method was abandoned due to a Supreme Court ruling on equal representation. In 1971, the Fort Peck tribes elected Joseph Red Thunder as Chairman, and he served one term, but he later became Vice-Chairman from 1973-1975, and then served a remarkable eight terms as Vice-Chairman (1977-1993). By 1975, Indian preference in the BIA and IHS became federal law and seemed to be a step toward finally allowing Indians to develop their own futures, but this BIA mandate backfired in many instances. Some Indian personnel embraced their bureaucratic identities instead of their tribal identities, and in some areas, the BIA became more rigid under Indian supervision. These employees often were caught up in the same web of factionalism, social pressure, suspicion, deception, and uncertainty as many of the local Indian population.

Policing the reservation presented many problems from the start of the reservation. From the early Indian police of old reservation days to contemporary cross-deputized officers, curbing crime on Fort Peck has been challenging. Jurisdiction problems always created obstacles for both Indian and non-Indian police. In August 1960, the Fort Peck tribes took control of the old Poplar city jail, now a museum on the Fort Peck Community College (FPCC) Poplar campus, and by 1980, a modern, safe facility was constructed east of the Poplar city hospital. The BIA took over policing the Fort Peck Reservation on a limited and tentative basis in July 1966 because the TEB did not budget for the 1967 operations. Concerned that jurisdiction might pass to the state, the tribes worked with the BIA to maintain an Indian police force. Before the 1960s, Congress severely cut appropriations for the BIA, at which time the BIA asked the tribes to temporarily assume the cost of law and order until appropriations were restored. In the interim, the TEB asked the city councils of Poplar and Wolf Point to support the Tribes' position, which they did. However, misunderstandings about jurisdiction and questions of whether a non-Indian police officer could arrest tribal members and vice versa continued to arise. As late as July 1966, according to then-BIA Superintendent Stanley Lyman, the arrest of Indians by city or county police was lawful. He stated that the sheriff and his deputies and the city police had the right to detain tribal members who committed offenses on the reservation for the BIA police.[34]

After passing the Civil Rights Act of 1965, Congress passed the Indian Civil Rights Act (ICRA) of 1968 to impose upon tribal governments certain restrictions and protections afforded by the U.S. Constitution. Before 1968, Indian governments were not bound by Fifth Amendment guarantees. Since 1896, *Talton v. Meyers* and subsequent Supreme Court cases

had affirmed that tribal governments were not arms of the federal government, and were exempt from many of the constitutional protections governing their actions in punishing individual tribal members for criminal acts. After a number of congressional hearings about abuses tribal members endured at the hands of corrupt, incompetent, or tyrannical tribal officials, Congress enacted the ICRA. After 1968, Fort Peck tribal members enjoyed limited protection under tribal law until the Tribes adopted the Law and Justice Code in 1985. The ICRA had nine major provisions: the right to free speech, press, and assembly; protection from unreasonable search and seizure; the right to a speedy trial, to be advised of charges, and to confront any adverse witnesses; the right to hire an attorney and protection against self-incrimination; protection against cruel and unusual punishment; protection from double jeopardy or ex post facto laws; the right to jury trial; and equal protection and due process under the law.[35]

The enactment of the Indian Civil Rights Act on April 11, 1969 brought American Indians under the protections of the Bill of Rights of the U.S. Constitution for the first time. State intrusions into tribal affairs were limited by tribal consent in ways they had not been before. Indians could bring a *habeas corpus* action in federal courts against their own tribal courts if necessary.[36] In a community meeting on April 26, sponsored by the Fort Peck Legal Services of the Montana Legal Services Association, what was actually in the law was clarified, and then the discussion turned to the inequality of many Indians compared to the larger society.[37] Discussion continued at another meeting on May 10.[38] The following October, over seventy people gathered at the Wolf Point Community Hall and formed a new civil rights organization, adopting the name "Okiwajina," meaning "all for one and one for all" or "unity." Attendees recounted stories of inequality, and emphasized the need for a group through which they could organize and implement actions for change. June Stafne was elected chair, Janet Youngman was chosen as Secretary-Treasurer, and people were tapped to organize meetings in all the communities on the reservation, with Larry Juelfs, "circuit rider" attorney of Wolf Point, named the group's legal advisor.[39] Over the next weeks, the association had to defend its claims of injustices to non-Indians. The group refined its articulation to foster understanding and to work against injustices.[40] Carson Boyd, one of the founders of Okiwajina, urged the school boards to decrease discrimination in the area schools, perhaps by Indians being elected to school boards.[41] In the spring of 1969, Walter Buckles and Daniel Roberts, identified as Okiwajina members, ran for seats on the District 45 Elementary School Board.[42]

As the 1960s ended, the nation looked back on ten years of unforeseen change and development. For American Indians, change and an awakening of self-awareness characterized that decade. Throughout the country, both reservation and urban tribes were taking back their identities and making decisions for themselves. Residual populations that had remained in urban areas since the 1950s relocation program recognized the power of exercising not only their civil rights, but also their treaty rights. One movement that surpassed all other Pan-Indian organizations was the American Indian Movement (AIM). AIM's inception stemmed from the conclusion that the federal government and the BIA's supervision were destroying tribal populations, and Indians needed to deal with their own problems to survive in postmodern America. AIM was initiated in the Minnesota State Prison when two Ojibwas (Chippewa), Clyde Bellecourt and Edward Benton-Banai, organized Indian prisoners. After being paroled, Bellecourt organized Minneapolis' large Indian population, mainly Ojibwa, to

defend themselves against police stereotyping and brutality.[43]

Originally, AIM attached itself to the civil rights movement of the 1960s, but its leaders soon realized they needed a different approach. In July 1968, Bellecourt, Benton-Banai, George Mitchell, and Dennis Banks officially founded the American Indian Movement. AIM's underpinnings rested on Indian fishing rights, land protests, treaty rights, and civil rights activism, but the movement owed its most direct cause to the federal relocation program that had dumped tens of thousands of reservation Indians in cities like Minneapolis, San Francisco, Los Angeles, Chicago, Seattle, Phoenix, and Denver. AIM fought for jobs, education, housing, and equal protection under the law. It attracted hundreds of members and thousands of supporters from those populations.

Russell Means, born on the Pine Ridge Reservation in South Dakota, began his fight for Indian rights with AIM in the late '60s. He became the first national director of AIM and has remained active in the movement to this day. AIM brought worldwide attention to the injustices and privation faced by American Indians, both past and present.[44]

AIM soon spread to reservation populations. All over Indian country, elders and religious leaders such as Frank Fools Crow and Leonard Crow Dog called for reforms of the BIA and tribal governments and asked AIM leaders for assistance. On the national level, many urban Indian populations responded to AIM's message. One group of urban Indians in California, supported by tribal members from many reservations across the United States and Canada, organized the takeover and occupation of Alcatraz, an abandoned federal prison on a island in San Francisco Bay. Those Indians and their supporters held the prison from November 1969 until June 1971. They wanted to make the island an educational and cultural center, and demonstrated the cultural diversity and resolve of American Indians. From the end of the 1960s through the 1970s, the Fort Peck Tribes and many federally recognized tribal groups voiced their shared demands for improved social programs. This was due to the national movement of tribal governments and private organizations calling for the federal government to live up to past agreements.

AIM laid much of the groundwork for increased tribal self-government and treaty rights. Longtime chairman and TEB member Caleb Shields was one among many Fort Peck tribal members, including George "Fish" Redstone, Myrna Boyd and her family, Darrell "Curley" Youpee, Traci Ackerman, Vaughn Dix Baker, Lois Red Elk, Colleen Clark, the Theresa McKay family, Hank Adams, Larry Connor, David Campbell, Pearl Nation, Shirley Shields Redstone, Jonny Lee Bearcub, and the Karen Olson family, who fought for Indian rights on a national level. They witnessed the Alcatraz occupation in 1969; the successful Trail of Broken Treaties takeover of the Department of the Interior building in Washington, D.C., in 1972; the siege at Wounded Knee in 1973 where AIM and the Lakota Nation made a stand for native rights; the Trail of Self Determination of 1976 to attempt another takeover of the South Interior Department building during the nation's Bicentennial Celebration; and the Longest Walk in 1978, which helped defeat several Indian termination bills being considered in the U.S. Congress that year.[45]

In reaction to AIM's progressive ideas and incessant activities on and off the reservations, the BIA helped organize the National Tribal Chairman's Association (NTCA) in 1971. NTCA used federal funding and support and was often charged with being influenced by BIA administrators and executive policies. After his defeat as Tribal Chairman, Bill Youpee became a leading proponent of the NTCA, serving in various capacities in the organization. The NTCA positioned itself as an alternative to AIM, opposing most of AIM's policies and actions. BIA officials always regarded AIM with suspicion, and some reservation leaders and tribal members at Fort Peck thought AIM was a negative force that could undermine many of the advances tribal people had made since World War II. After the 1972 AIM takeover and weeklong occupation in Washington, D.C., the Fort Peck development director feared the Tribes could suffer, and that property damages that occurred could be parceled out among the tribes and might even lead to de facto termination. Despite the differences in vision between AIM and its opponents, Fort Peck members found themselves supporting both sides. AIM's influence soon waned, but its lasting contributions of raised consciousness endured.[46]

During the late 1960s and early 1970s, Indians all over the country began renewing their traditional forms of spirituality and attempting to bring back their languages and practice their religions. Although families and communities at Fort Peck had always maintained their traditional spirituality in ceremonies, rituals, and prayers (usually through song), a renewed awareness surfaced in both Assiniboine and Sioux cultures. By the late 1970s and early 1980s, both tribes were holding Medicine Lodge Ceremonies (Sun Dances), Sweat Lodges, Pipe Ceremonies, Naming Ceremonies, and Adoption Ceremonies. Medicine Lodges are held annually by the Assiniboine and Sioux, and relatives and friends from other areas gather for those ceremonies. The Native American Church, a religion that uses the peyote cactus as a sacrament, advocates abstinence from alcohol, and incorporates some parts of Christianity along with other practices, also had a small following among the Sioux.

Even though powwows harbor many elements of tribal spirituality and tradition, their overall aim has always been to bring together extended families, communities, and tribes, mainly for social ends. Indians dance, sing, give gifts in honor of family members, have naming and adoption ceremonies, compete for prize money, show off personal regalia, and experience genuine bonding at these annual summer gatherings. At Fort Peck, as at all Montana reservations, each community has held its own powwow since the 1950s. Originally called "Celebrations," these weekend events are planned throughout the year. The Fort Peck powwow season begins in Frazer with the Red Bottom Celebration in June. It is followed by Brockton's Badlands Celebration and Fort Kipp's Celebration at the end of June. In mid-July, Poplar celebrates the Wahcinca Oyate Celebration, and on the first of August, Wolf Point holds the Wadopana Celebration. The Poplar Indian Days event during the Labor Day weekend ends the season. From the 1950s through the 1980s, Poplar hosted one of the largest powwows in the country, the Oil Celebration.

The tribal election of 1973 brought Norman Hollow to the chairman's position. Hollow led the tribal government in new directions. The successes of the Fort Peck Tribes during the 1970s and early 1980s can be credited to his leadership. Hollow, a Sioux from Fort Kipp, worked closely with TEB members, local and state leaders, agencies, and the BIA on tribal business from 1973 to 1985. Born in 1919 on a farm in the eastern part of the reservation, Hollow was the longest serving tribal chairman, and in June 1991 was granted an honorary doctorate from Montana State University, Bozeman. In 1974, the BIA appointed James O. Jackson acting superintendent. He served until 1975, when the BIA gave the job to Burton Ryder, the second Indian to hold that post since Superintendent Anson Baker.

While the federal government assisted in the added vigor and continuity on the reservation during this period, tribal leaders pursued economic development. Agriculture had always been the most important renewable resource since the early reservation days and continues as the most sustainable enterprise. Even up until the early 1960s, families relied on community gardens throughout the reservations for fundamental food supplements. On a much larger scale, however, mostly non-Indians farmed and ranched within the boundaries of the reservation. Although a number of Indian families also engaged in agriculture, most tribal members did not, even though they owned land or a divided interest in it. The trust status of those tribal lands encumbered their holdings, and land fractionalization also created problems for Indians who wanted to farm their own acreages. Local banks and lending institutions refused to loan capital to those whose land was held in trust by the federal government and administered by the BIA.

Consequently, leasing was really the only viable option for tribal landowners, leaving them at the mercy of BIA bureaucracy and control. The BIA sent out bids to lease mainly fractionalized trust land to non-Indians. Those non-Indians paid the leases, and the money then went into Individual Indian Money (IIM) accounts and was paid to tribal landowners in federal government checks each year or month, depending on the size of the acreage and number of landowners who held an interest in the parcel. A mere handful of Indian farmers were able to establish successful agricultural operations, and a few more farmed and ranched on a small scale with very limited success. Since returns in agriculture were so unevenly distributed, it is not useful to average out gross income from agriculture on the reservation across the population. Many non-Indians had quite large incomes and extensive holdings in land and equipment, and many others struggled to make land payments and mortgages. Some made it, and some did not. More typically, tribal members who inherited an interest, almost always an undivided interest, in trust land received a small amount of lease money from time to time through their IIM accounts. By the mid-1980s, approximately 82 percent of the total land on the reservation was being used by the non-Indian population, either through ownership or leasing.[47]

For the Assiniboine and Sioux Tribes, economic development stood as the frontrunner of the future. Endeavors small and larger characterized these developments. Under Chairman Buckles, the TEB created an Indian Development Committee and pledged on February 9, 1961 to cooperate with the BIA and the Roosevelt County Industrial Development Committee.[48] Led by Chairman William Youpee, the TEB reorganized the Economic Opportunity Advisory Committee, into the "Fort Peck Reservation and Roosevelt County Planning and Improvement Council."[49] In 1968, when the rest of America was reaching its peak in social and political unrest, the Fort Peck tribes made steady economic progress. The Sioux Maid Cooperative, Wolf Point, and Owinja (meaning blanket or quilt) Cooperative, Poplar, quilting cooperatives, were formed with the help of CAP personnel who facilitated OEO long-term loans for groups of women to make quilts, pillows, and potholders for sale.[50] The U.S. Department of Labor announced in February 1968 that Fort Peck was among the sixteen largest reservations "to be areas of concentrated unemployment or underemployment making them eligible for special preferences in the award of certain governmental contracts."[51]

The role of the federal government's Economic Development Administration in the Tribes' economic development initiatives cannot be overstated. The Native American economic development strategy of EDA pivoted on the principle that economic development should be predicated on the participation of the Indian community in solving problems. As Rodney R. Miller wrote in his NAES paper about the strategy:

Experience had revealed that for any Native American endeavor to be successful, the Indian must assume a leadership role in its development and implementation. Secondly, a comprehensive and coordinated effort should be mobilized from the various agencies and departments within the federal infrastructure which provides support to the various Indian programs. Emphasis should be placed on the need for integrated planning directed toward altering conditions in the home, school, community and the relevant area as a whole.[52]

EDA treated and engaged with individual reservations specific to their circumstances and situation, a major change since "historically, Federal/Indian program efforts were not coordinated."[53] Working with the Indian Desk at EDA, the TEB moved forward with plans both short- and long-term. A joint meeting of the Tribes with the government development offices of OEO, EDA, and HUD was held in Poplar on August 13, 1968, to discuss a plan for economic development for the Fort Peck Reservation. Four major "areas of concern" were discussed: unemployment and underemployment; decline of tribal income; general living conditions; and loss of trust lands by individual sales.[54] Eleven goals were identified to "offset the financial decline and promote better living conditions on the reservation": 1) develop an industrial park to encourage industry to move into the area; 2) obtain defense contracts for Fort Peck Tribal Industries, of which the Fort Peck Tribes would own 51 percent; 3) construct new community buildings in Fort Kipp, Brockton, Wolf Point, Oswego, and Frazer; 4) investigate possibilities of tourism on the reservation and surrounding area; 5) build a motel, restaurant, and museum center; 6) investigate mineral resources of the area; 7) explore increased processing of locally produced agricultural products; 8) obtain funds to hire a management trainee for the Fort Peck Housing Authority; 9) obtain funds to hire a tribal newspaper editor who could act as tribal publicity-tourism specialist; 10) establish a program for training participants in the housing programs; and 11) begin to develop an overall land use plan for the reservation in cooperation with the towns within the reservation.[55]

This list represented many of the initiatives that the Tribes either explored or attempted in the next decade. The meeting ended with the compliment that the Fort Peck Reservation had never been better positioned to receive appropriations for its projects.[56]

As early as 1966, the Tribes applied for EDA money for development of an industrial park, but were unsuccessful in this initial effort. After a consultant's report was completed, the Poplar site was chosen, mostly because of proximity to an extant railroad spur to the site. Two TEB members, William McClammey and Joseph Culbertson, and BIA Planning Officer Joan Broomfield met with EDA officials in Seattle to get the project underway.[57] The park was meant to be a developed sub-division where streets were paved, lots laid out, transportation facilities provided, and water mains, sewer lines, electricity, and gas lines were ready for immediate use. The facility was to provide a developed site so negotiations with prospective companies could be expedited.[58] In February 1969, the Tribes received an EDA grant of $283,200 for constructing the industrial park.[59]

Even before the industrial park was built, the Tribes ventured into an enterprise with the Department of Defense (DOD). The "Rifle Factory," as it was first affectionately called, was

established in 1968 and was the first tribally owned industry on Fort Peck. The contract with the Air Force was to repair and rebuild 44,400 M-1 rifles (World War II and Korean Conflict era) with a Small Business Administration (SBA) loan amounting to $706,804. CAP and OEO granted $107,789 to train workers, and the BIA provided $40,000 for on-the-job training. The original intention was to employ 118 individuals. Dynalectron, a major aerospace corporation from Fort Worth, TX, and an experienced military contractor, was awarded a management contract of $168,720 by Fort Peck Industries, and supervised the actual rifle repairs.[60] Since no building existed for this kind of enterprise within the new industrial park, the Rifle Factory was located in the old National Guard Armory in Poplar. In April 1969, the industries were dedicated with a special honoring of Senator Lee Metcalf, thanking him for his assistance in securing the DOD contract. Dignitaries from the Pentagon also attended, and CIA Robert Bennett made his first visit to Fort Peck Reservation.[61] Chairman Bill Youpee was able to be magnanimous about taking credit for his leadership of the TEB at the beginning of an era of major economic development. With the first contract heading for on-time completion at the end of 1969, Fort Peck Industries won a second rifle-repair contract for $736,000 to repair and overhaul 37,000 M-14 rifles for the U.S Air Force. The plant was reported to employ 123 Tribal members, 75 percent of whom used to be on welfare and were reported not to have had full-time jobs previously. Dynalectron remained in the management role until completion of this contract in October 1972.[62]

While partisan in nature, Chairman Youpee summarized his administration's successes in economic development and promised what he would do if re-elected in the October 1969 tribal election. Youpee stated in his campaign advertisement that he had brought over $3 million in new federal programs and industry to the Fort Peck Reservation and created over 600 new jobs. He noted that projects completed included a $200,000 sewer and water project at Frazer; $354,000 for the industrial park in Poplar; and $818,000 for housing in Brockton, Wolf Point, and Poplar. He stated that he had brought in the initial contract with C&M Construction Company, employing 25 with the $800,000 project, and Fort Peck Tribal Industries, employing 123 with over $759,000 awarded to the reservation. The chairman took credit for aiding the reservation's young and old through Head Start, housing programs, emergency foods programs, the Neighborhood Youth Corps, and economic and community development. He noted that he had won a $164,000 planning grant for a land study, and $232,000 for building community buildings for Frazer, Oswego, Wolf Point, Brockton, and Fort Kipp. The advertisement ended with the chairman's promise to bring an additional $7 million in new federal programs that would create 900 new jobs.[63]

The Rifle Factory won a third contract for $35,000 in rifle repairs in October 1971, which allowed 80 people to continue working.[64] Fort Peck Tribal Industries secured a contract for $262,518.15 to cover production of 18,432 general purpose cleated wooden boxes in assorted sizes; the order was placed by the General Services Administration (GSA) through provisions in the Small Business Act to negotiate with a minority-owned company on a non-competitive basis.[65]

As the Rifle Factory phased out, the Tribes initiated a wider search for more business development opportunities. The SBA hired Cambridge Marketing Services of Cambridge, MA, to suggest new products for production by Fort Peck Tribal Industries. The recommended categories included "electrical products/office equipment rebuilding, vending machine rebuilding, mechanical calculator assembly, automotive parts rebuilding, baby gate assembly, and [finally] miscellaneous."[66] The closure of Fort Peck Tribal Industries in May 1973 led to a concerted effort over the next months by Chairman Norman Hollow, the TEB, the Montana congressional delegation, the Department of Defense, and the Defense Products Division of Brunswick Corporation to secure a manufacturing and production contract to produce camouflage net modules for the U.S. Army. In the interim, the TEB loaned Fort Peck Tribal Industries money to keep a general manager on salary.[67]

The initial experience with DOD contracts had been lucrative and made training and hiring of tribal members who normally were not brought into any reliable labor force a success. Could this be continued? By January 1974, the TEB entered into a management agreement with Brunswick Corporation for the operation of Fort Peck Tribal Industries. TEB also authorized Brunswick to use the newly constructed industrial storage facility in the industrial park. In March, Fort Peck Tribal Industries and Brunswick crafted a five-year plan. With this defined, Fort Peck Tribal Industries was situated to approach SBA for a loan to operate a plant to produce camouflage netting products for the U.S. Army. By joining with another Brunswick-operated plant at Fort Totten Indian Reservation (Devil's Lake, ND) in the summer of 1974, Fort Peck Tribal Industries was successful in obtaining the $9 million contract. This new effort was a direct descendant of the Rifle Factory, and also owed its existence to DOD minority contracts. To produce 40,000 modules (nets) on an annual basis over three years, Fort Peck Tribal Industries was reincorporated as "A&S Tribal Industries" with a new management agreement with Brunswick. Recently trained Indian managers with Fort Peck Tribal Industries were hired into various middle management positions. By January 1975, under the newly formed Assiniboine and Sioux Tribal Industries (ASTI), production of camouflage net modules was launched. After months of seeking another business to get a plant working at the Industrial Park, ASTI turned to the Brunswick Corporation. An agreement between these entities gave new economic life to the reservation and by the mid-1980s made ASTI the largest employer in eastern Montana. The Brunswick Corporation handled management, engineering, accounting, and marketing of the netting operation for three years for roughly 10 percent of the profit. At the same time, Brunswick Corporation executives, whose salaries were deducted before the profits were computed, were to select and train the Indian workers, almost always tribal members, who would eventually manage the plant. Reservation unemployment went from about 80 percent to about 40 percent over a six-year period. ASTI's factory set up operations in a four-acre complex within the industrial park. The production operations employed 160 employees.[68]

The process started at the Indianhead Corporation of Alabama, which manufactured the netting and shipped it to Poplar. The workers at ASTI manufactured the nets and then shipped them to Devils Lake, North Dakota, where employees of the Sioux Manufacturing Corporation on the Fort Totten Indian Reservation attached plastic camouflage to the nets and then turned them over to the U.S. Army. These nets were used to cover military equipment and also minimized electronic surveillance. Through December 1981, 223,290 modules were produced, resulting in sales of $27,874,000.[69]

Between the end of the rifle factory and the initial effort by ASTI to begin manufacturing nets, a large manufacturing building was constructed in the industrial park with federal funds from the EDA. The Poplar Industrial Park was used to facilitate construction of portable-housing components for the FPHA and other consumers. C&M Construction, the first leasee in the park, initially wanted to build modular homes at the new industrial site, and received the contract to build fifty low-rent dwellings in October 1968.[70] Committed to using local Indian labor, the company poured footings and had under construction a $50,000 building in the industrial park intended to be completed by spring.[71] The first home was built in two sections and then bolted together before being moved to the foundation. Once in place, minor finishing work was accomplished. A damp summer caused a number of delays.[72] By August 1972, C&M's plant was described as having "the capacity to construct four 3-bedroom sectional units simultaneously, and can turn out 1.5 to 2 houses per week." These units were fabricated in complete sections inside the plant. Using special trailers, the units were transported and placed on the foundations. C&M's methods were said to boost the local economy through employment of thirty skilled and semi-skilled workers on a full-time basis. Besides supplying the housing needs of the FPHA, opportunities for producing houses for other markets in eastern Montana and western North Dakota remained an option.[73]

Also during this period, the FPHA was planning construction of several hundred homes under HUD and Turnkey III programs for Indian families, but unfortunately, no Indian ownership or management materialized in the operation of C&M Construction and the tribes remained reluctant to buy into the venture. This was partly because of the unpredictability of HUD funding from project to project. The company went bankrupt in 1973. In June 1976, ASTI needed additional manufacturing space and convinced the Tribes to lease the remaining 14,000 square feet in the eastern section of the storage facility. This was made possible by the completed housing manufacturing contract with FPHA by the Dan J. Brutger Construction Company of Billings.[74]

Again, Chairman Norman Hollow had led the way to the success of ASTI. The Tribes made history and debunked the common stereotypes that American Indians are unreliable, do not stick to schedules, and generally have a bad work ethic, and also that Indian politics make it near impossible to get any stable economic venture started. That all changed as ASTI filled orders and met deadlines under federal government inspection. Three full-time Defense Contract Administration Services (DCAS) inspectors, David Boyd, Alan Longtree, and Joyce McGeshick (all tribal members), were on hand to give the government's approval to ASTI products destined for the U.S. Army. At this time, those on the ASTI Board of Directors were President Norman Hollow, Vice-President Dana McGowan, Secretary Joe Day, Treasurer Raymond White Tail Feathers, and Company Directors Stanley Yellowrobe, Stanley Nees, and Leonard Boxer. On-site managers were Alpheus Bighorn, Ben Greyhawk, Robert Fourstar, Patrick Bushman, Ron Smith, and Harold Dean Blount.[75]

In September 1975, alongside ASTI, the tribes formed the Fort Peck Manufacturing Company, owned jointly with the ESCO (Electric Steel Company) Corporation of Portland, OR. By 1976, the new venture manufactured earth-moving equipment, specifically grinding the slag off cast cutting teeth and heat tempering for large earth-moving equipment. It employed between twenty-five and forty people during its tenure at the Poplar Industrial Park. The company was able to move into the empty warehouse that had previously produced prefabricated homes for FPHA, and the Tribes' planning group applied for and received a $546,000 "Industrial Park Improvements and Supports Facility Project" grant to renovate to ESCO's specifications and to build a railroad spur directly into the park; this

work was completed on November 1, 1975. ESCO supplied all the specialty equipment. Similarly to other plants, they had a non-Indian general manager. Shipments were made on the Burlington Northern Railroad either to Portland or Danville, IL. The total investment by both parties was approximately $2 million in "capital, machinery, equipment and real estate." The private commercial enterprise had a maximum manufacturing capacity of 240 tons of castings per month. This well-run quality operation was productive until 1980, when a worldwide recession began and demand for finished products for the mining and excavation industries collapsed. By July 1982, the plant had ceased operations.[76]

Multiplex West (eventually called West Electronics), another Fort Peck Tribes' business venture, started operations in 1970 and to date is the longest-lived tribal enterprise. It was initially described as "an electronics company which builds and repairs teletype and other communications equipment."[77] It eventually also produced electronic subassemblies of various sorts, including alarm systems. The company also filled special private contracts. The Tribes created the Assiniboine and Sioux Development Cooperation (ASDC) in July 1970, and moved to create a jointly owned corporation (51 percent owned by the Tribes and 49 percent by Multiplex Communications, Inc.) under the name Multiplex West. The eligibility of the Tribal business to secure loans and grants allowed the prospering firm to grow without making large capital outlays. The availability of labor, which could be trained with the help of specific grants, also was attractive to the Delaware-based company. Special fees were granted to Multiplex Communication, Inc., in exchange for administrative services. Charles Candela was the first manager in 1970 and was still in charge in 1983. The SBA offered Multiplex in March 1971 a loan for $173,700 for essential plant renovations and equipment purchases, and ASDC provided a 10 percent match ($19,300). However, there were many fits and starts, and the first attempts to secure contracts were unsuccessful. In the company's second year, it secured a small commercial contract from Western Electric ($50,000) on the condition that Multiplex Communication guarantee the work. The first government contract was secured eighteen months after Multiplex West became operational for producing tube checkers for the U.S. Army. To capitalize on the future, in June 1973, the Tribes purchased 1,000 shares of preferred stock, at the cost of $40,000, that funded an expansion to produce "a low priced CRT (video) terminal for editing." However, by August 1974, the government contract was rejected. Multiplex Communications shared with Multiplex West the manufacture of its latest product, the TE100 circuit switch, which kept the operation viable. In 1974, RCA Global Communications placed an order and was impressed with the quality of the product, and with this endorsement, U.S. Army and Navy contracts materialized.[78] Using grants from OEO and the Manpower Assistance Training Act, and several years of BIA on-the-job training funds, and in cooperation with several of the high schools, a core work force was identified and trained.[79] Since it is not dependent upon local raw materials or markets, the operation has sustained longevity. It began with about thirty employees and at times dwindled to less than ten, but has continued to be viable. First located in the old Armory building, it soon moved to a large building near the industrial park. It remained a small but fairly stable operation. The Tribes moved to become the sole owner in July 1975, when Multiplex Communications, Inc. transferred its 49 percent share, and the company was renamed West Electronics, Inc. The next six years saw steady growth.[80]

By March 1979, ASTI needed expanded facili-

ties. The Fort Peck Tribes applied to the EDA for an "A&S Tribal Industries Manufacturing Process, Remodeling and Joint Shipping Project." Once approved, 13,500 square feet were added to the facility for manufacturing, shipping, and receiving areas. The expansion was ready to use by May 1989 at a cost of $475,000 (80 percent funded by EDA and the rest provided by the Tribes from ASTI profits). In April 1979, diversification efforts meant that skill transfers from the netting operations were turned to manufacturing and marketing small camouflage nets for commercial hunting, bird-watching, photographic concealment, and outboard motor covers, bow covers, face masks, and game carriers for waterfowl hunters. These products were marketed in 1980, and by the end of 1981, sales of $263,000 were realized. With the addition of a sales force in North America and Europe, sales for 1982 were in excess of $500,000. Efforts continued to find other opportunities to manufacture leisure products that utilized camouflage.[81]

The Tribes received support from EDA for a planning office in the spring of 1969.[82] Another EDA-sponsored venture was encouraging tourism.[83]

Uniquely, the Nixon administration's commitment to self-determination engendered a political environment that allowed Congress to create new programs and policies for advancing reservations' economies. As Rodney J. Miller noted, from 1970 to 1975 a window opened that allowed the Comprehensive Employment and Training Act of 1973 to be enacted. This gave rise to Indian Manpower Programs that established CETA programs on reservations, which later were replaced by programs of the jobs partnership training bill. While Nixon's policy directive about self-determination was eventually thwarted by "bureaucratic inertia, poor administration and controversy," efforts were made to turn over administration and decision-making to

Indian people. For example, the Indian Financing Act of 1974 established a revolving loan fund for reservation development, but also enabled interest subsidies and development grants for up to 40 percent of required capital and authorized SBA and other agencies to respond to economic and circumstantial needs. The Housing and Community Development Act of 1974 allowed for a "specific set-aside funding component to be utilized in the provision of Community Development Block Grants Discretionary funds to eligible Indian tribes." These funds could be "utilized for a variety of social and economic development programs, projects and activities," all locally determined. Between 1975 and 1981, the Fort Peck Tribes received funds annually. President Ford signed into law the Indian Self-Determination and Education Assistance Act of 1975 "to promote the full participation in the government and education of Indian people, to provide for the full participation of Indian tribes in programs and services conducted by the Federal government for Indians."[84] The Fort Peck Tribes attempted to utilize every program for which they were eligible.

Along with the issues of housing, health care, economic development, and education, the Tribes looked at developing their law and order system. Before the 1960s, tribal police operated under the authority of the BIA, and local, county, and municipal law enforcement also policed the reservation. During that time, tribal courts operated on a limited basis. The 1960 Constitution authorized the Fort Peck Tribal Court System, which operated under the Tribal Comprehensive Code System and since 1981 had been partially funded under the Indian Self-Determination Act.[85] Judges who heard cases after 1960 included David B. Johnson, Harriet Kirn, and William "Tully" McClammy, who in the 1980s gave way to Judges A.T. "Rusty" Stafne, Robert Welch, Bryce Wildcat, and Richard "Dude" Jackson. The tribal

court system strove to provide all persons within its jurisdiction judicial protection and due process. The Fort Peck Tribal Court System operated a multi-court system, civil and criminal, with fully staffed courtrooms, mainly in Poplar. In the early 1980s, it expanded to Wolf Point, but due to budget cuts had to hold the court only in Poplar.

The BIA had been active on the Fort Peck Indian Reservation for generations. Although some were unenthusiastic about the agency's paternalistic nature, the BIA provided necessary services to tribal members. Eventually, the majority of BIA employees were tribal members, especially in the superintendent's office. Dennis Whiteman served out the decade as BIA superintendent of the Fort Peck Agency from 1979 to 1980 and 1983 to 1988.[86] Whiteman later served again as superintendent in 1996 to 2002.[87]

The 1970s also witnessed opportunities for federal health programs that eventually led to the creation of the Tribal Health Department (THD). The THD was established in 1973 by a $20,000 grant from the IHS under the directorship of Robert Dumont, who later helped establish the Native American Education Services (NAES) College at Fort Peck. Larry Burshia took over as director from 1978 to 1988. He was followed by Gary James Melbourne, who continues to serve as director. The Tribal Health Director, with direct supervision from the TEB, was responsible for project compliance to P.L. 93-638 contracts from the IHS. One of its jewel programs is the Fort Peck dialysis program, which began in 1988 and now serves over thirty Indian and non-Indian patients. In 1978, the THD and IHS moved into a new health-care facility, the Verne E. Gibbs Health Center. Twelve years later, Wolf Point opened the Chief Redstone Health Clinic. Both offer a range of services, including family health, a full-time dentist, mental health, and diabetes clinics.

Developing alongside the Tribal Health

Department was the Spotted Bull Treatment Center (SBTC). The SBTC started out in 1972 as the Fort Peck Alcoholism Program, a detoxification center and halfway house directed by Jack Pipe. The center was in the old BIA building and operated under the Office of Native American Programs (ONAP). Melvin Eagleman assisted in those early years by obtaining funding through the National Institute of Alcohol Abuse and Alcoholism (NIAAA). In 1970, President Richard M. Nixon signed the Comprehensive Alcohol Abuse and Alcoholism Prevention, Treatment, and Rehabilitation Act (Public Law [P.L]. 91-616), called the "Hughes Act" for the pivotal role Senator Harold E. Hughes played in its passage. This law recognized alcohol abuse and alcoholism as major public health problems and created the NIAAA to combat them. However, the IHS felt the center and halfway house were not successful and wanted to include adolescents. Under the direction of Melvin and Larry Eagleman in 1974, the SBTC became a stand-alone agency of the tribes. The ONAP Director at the time, George "Fish" Redstone, wrote the Community Food and Nutritional Program grant that allowed the SBTC to start feeding its clients. By 2000, it offered pre- and post-service treatment with monies from contracts with the IHS. The SBTC has its own large center just off Highway 2 in Poplar that was built with tribal money and constructed by FPCC's building trades department.

The first attempt at a tribal news bulletin was the *Eyapi Oyaye*, published intermittently from December 1962 through 1966. In 1970, the *Wotanin* began as a bi-monthly newsletter, published by VISTA in cooperation with the TEB. In January 1975, the *Wotanin* became *Wotanin Wowapi* and was sanctioned as the official weekly newspaper of the Fort Peck Reservation and the Assiniboine and Sioux Tribes. Terry Boyd was the first editor of the *Wotanin* and eventually the *Wotanin Wowapi*, fol-

lowed by Bonnie Clincher in 1976. The newspaper is partially funded by the TEB and reports all Indian and non-Indian news. Its reporters cover the area from Frazer to Fort Kipp, and inform the public about TEB meetings, powwows, politics, social news, crime, and sports. The *Wotanin Wowapi* had an earlier beginning when Ed Broaddus, a Vista worker, started printing reservation news on legal-size mimeograph paper.[88]

As early as 1970, the federal government, along with the BIA, began giving much of its authority back to the Fort Peck tribes. By November of that year, Lewis Bruce, the BIA commissioner, declared the bureau's intention to return control of tribal matters to the tribes and phase out the administrative functions of the BIA by 1973.[89] Tribal governments would administer programs that up until then had been handled by the BIA, such as social services, road construction and repairs, and economic planning. Like other municipalities, many tribal programs became eligible for funding under the 1975 Indian Self-Determination and Education Assistance Act, which allowed tribes to negotiate directly with the BIA. Programs like law and order, maintenance of roads, and housing now had potential funding, although they had to compete on a national level. The Indian Self-Determination Act opened up economic and social avenues never before available to the Fort Peck tribes. Increased self-governance defined the government-to-government relationship between federally recognized tribes and the federal government. In principle, the act gave the Fort Peck tribes authority to assume responsibility for various government services.

Reacting to national Indian activism and the Fort Peck Tribes' actions in economic development, awareness of civil rights, treaty rights, and social improvement, the non-Indian population within and surrounding the reservation moved to counter what they viewed as encroachment into their areas of control. Much of the feeling was racially motivated. On July 29, 1976, a non-Indian group that feared a jurisdictional takeover of the entire reservation by the Fort Peck Tribes met in a local motel banquet room to voice their fears. The group, about seventy people in all, consisted of farmers, ranchers, bankers, business- and landowners, and teachers. They called themselves Concerned Citizens for Equal Rights, and were closely connected to Montanans Opposing Discrimination (MOD), a state group set on fighting the rising political and economic power of Indian tribes.[90] In September 1976, MOD drew over 200 people at the Wolf Point Elks Club using the same rhetoric. The meeting was also attended by some local Indians who left with feelings of chaos, turmoil, and violence. The Fort Peck MOD started out as the old Fort Peck Grazing Association, which in the 1940s and '50s joined together to deal with jurisdictional issues, water, mineral and timber rights, and grazing rights. That fall, a group of local tribal members led by William "Bill" Whitehead, Caleb Shields, and Wayne Martell protested outside the Elks Club.[91] In October, tribal council members responded with calm indignation. Chairman Hollow felt that MOD and its supporters should have approached the tribal council instead of going public. One gesture that attempted to bridge the gap between the races, however, was introduced in March 1981 by Tribal Executive Board member Caleb Shields, who suggested a measure to the Wolf Point and Poplar city councils for cross-deputizing Indian and non-Indian police officers. The measure also allowed non-Indian officers to testify in tribal court.[92]

The Supreme Court decisions on the principle of "one man, one vote" were accumulating in case law[93] and provoked a return to the elections ordinance at the time of the 1971 election.[94] The tribal election format, involving district representation adopted in an amendment in

1953, did not conform to the equal protection clause of the Fourteenth Amendment of the U.S. Constitution or to the Indian Civil Rights Act. The population numbers were far from the same in each district, provoking complaints. Federal Court Judge James Franklin Battin ordered that the election comply with the one-man, one-vote principle. Consequently, in the 1971 election, the districts were considered precincts for purposes of at-large voting.[95] However, due to many tribal members' strong sentiments about district constituency, the newly elected TEB, dominated by ten newly elected councilmen and women and a new chairman and vice-chairman, promised a referendum on the issue, and within days of their election appointed a thirteen-person committee to study the issue for six months and produce a report.[96]

The committee was required to consult closely with Tribal Attorney Marvin J. Sonosky. Part of the dynamic was to show that election units, in this case "districts," needed to include roughly equivalent numbers of voters. This would require a detailed census, and all Indians members and non-members residing on the reservation were to be enumerated. This of course also provoked a discussion about the status of non-resident tribal members who were granted voting rights under the 1960 Constitution. Prior to a series of meetings in each of the districts, the committee met with Sonosky on April 9, 1980 and reviewed the central issues. The original six districts were a geographical creation and not demographically equal, but to maintain a scenario of districts, two, four, or six would require regular censuses, reapportionment, and redrawing of district boundaries to maintain equal population with a 10 percent deviation. The committee did ask Sonosky to prepare a series of draft ordinances to put to the referendum vote, and these included "staggered terms for board members; elimination of the vice-chairman and sergeant-at-arms; tribal chairman to serve only two consecutive terms; having a tribal primary election and elimination of absentee voting."[97] The final report of the Referendum Committee was submitted in mid-October 1980 to the TEB.[98] No action was taken nor was a referendum vote scheduled. The costs of censuses and of mounting a referendum vote were included in the report.[99]

Former Chairman Dolly C. Akers was involved in an important series of legal actions that continue to be cited because Indian women have had to fight for dower rights when they are excluded from their deceased husbands' wills. John J. Akers died in February 1959, and had executed three wills within less than two years. He had become a chronic alcoholic and in his third will had disinherited his wife by granting her $1 and then assigning rights to his trust lands and mineral rights to his sisters. A disputed claim with the Internal Revenue Service assigned responsibility both to the estate of John J. Akers and his surviving wife. Mrs. Akers pursued a full range of legal and procedural recourse, including two cases that went to federal court and three times to the Interior Board of Indian Appeals. In the end, her appeal to the U.S. Supreme Court in the October term 1974 was denied.[100] Approximately five thousand cases a year are submitted to the Supreme Court for review, and fewer than five percent are granted. Some felt sympathy for Mrs. Akers' position, but she had no recourse once probate had been established by examiners. Her husband's competency was not considered a critical factor, even though Mrs. Akers tried to contend the contrary.

The Fort Peck Tribes also developed their educational system during the 1960s and 1970s. They knew that without sound and accessible education, the Assiniboine and Sioux would suffer in the future. Looking back to the days of boarding schools of the early reservation makes contemporary educational possibilities look like

a scholar's paradise. Fort Peck Indian students always attended public school in the reservation communities, but most attended the tribal day and boarding schools in Poplar and Wolf Point. Since public education was, and still is, for the most part, financed through local property taxes, and since Indian lands were tax-exempt, most local schools such as Poplar, Wolf Point, Brockton, and Frazer needed additional funds to operate efficiently. Consequently, there is still seldom any person on Fort Peck whose parents or siblings did not attend some off-reservation government or Christian boarding school. For many years before the 1960s, Assiniboine and Sioux parents sent their children to places like Chemawa Indian School in Oregon, Pierre and Flandreau, SD, Riverside and Anadarko, OK, Stephan, a Catholic school also in South Dakota, the Mormon Placement Program, and Haskell Junior College in Lawrence, KS. In response to local tax issues and public schools on Indian reservations, on April 16, 1934, Congress passed the Johnson-O'Malley (JOM) Act, which provided minimal funding to schools that qualified due to their Indian student population. For years, JOM funds went directly to the state and then to the local school districts' general funds.[101]

JOM provided a narrow avenue that allowed more tribal students to attend local public schools. In 1950, Congress passed what was to become known as Impact Aid, federal assistance to local public schools. That year, Congress approved public laws to assist local school districts with construction and costs of public educational activities impacted by federal defense efforts. The so-called "impact aid" laws were an extension of a 1941 federal emergency measure, the Lanham Act.[102] The precedence of the Lanham Act, the rising educational burden placed on local school districts near military bases, and the advent of the Korean War (1950-1953) contributed to the subsequent passage of the Impact Aid laws. But it was not until 1965 that Impact Aid monies directly offset most of the costs of educating the large influx of Indian students in local reservation schools. Nationally, education at Fort Peck benefitted from liberal leaders like Senator Ted Kennedy, who led a subcommittee on education, and the 1971 education booklet *An Even Chance* that outlined the nation's need for educational reform.[103] At the state level, Fort Peck tribal member Dorrance Steele acted as the assistant Indian education coordinator for the state of Montana, and Earl Barlow, a Blackfeet, also helped local Indian education committees on Fort Peck and other Montana Indian reservations.

In early 1971, Wolf Point became the first school in Montana to form a local Indian Education Committee to administer and plan educational programs under JOM. JOM committees soon emerged in Poplar, Frazer, and Brockton. By the late 1970s, they were investigating dropout rates, teacher retention, and incorporating Assiniboine and Sioux language and culture into the classroom. Although state lawmakers passed Indian Education for All (IEFA) legislation at their constitutional convention in 1972, they failed to put up the money for its implementation. The law lay dormant for the next thirty years, when lawmakers finally appropriated funds for IEFA to schools throughout the state. Like Impact Aid monies, however, IEFA funds went directly into the local district coffers with the possibility of being diverted to offset non-IEFA educational costs. By the turn of the century, Indian student populations in Poplar, Frazer, and Brockton made up 90 percent of the student bodies. Wolf Point struggled to keep many of its Indian students in school until they graduated, which remains a problem to this day.[104]

If there ever were a program that worked directly with the future of the Assiniboine and Sioux people, it is the Head Start Program that was established in 1965. Head Start operated on federal funds, JOM funds, and others, and supplied comprehensive preschool services to tribal children three to five years old who met established income guidelines. Head Start offered medical examinations, including vision and hearing screenings, dental exams, immunizations, nutrition, educational opportunities, parental involvement, and social services. They graduate hundreds of students every year in preschools at Fort Kipp, Poplar, Wolf Point, Frazer, and Brockton. The program is one of the longest running federal programs that contribute to stopping the cycle of poverty in the United States. Initially, Head Start was part of President Johnson's War on Poverty when Congress passed the Economic Opportunity Act of 1964 that helped disadvantaged children.[105] One person who provided the leadership within the Fort Peck Head Start Program was Viola Bearcub Wood, who has worked in the program for over thirty-five years.

One of the brightest aspects of Indian education was the establishment of Fort Peck Community College (FPCC). FPCC's beginnings go back to 1969, when Dawson Community College, located 100 miles south of the reservation in the eastern Montana town of Glendive, offered the first extension courses to Fort Peck college students. Those services continued through the spring of 1978. Meanwhile, a cooperative agreement for offering on-reservation college courses was formed with Miles Community College in Miles City when that institution received a Title III grant for developing institutions. That relationship also ended in 1978. Meanwhile, the Assiniboine and Sioux tribes established the Fort Peck Education Department in 1977, which laid the foundation for the development of FPCC. The Fort Peck tribes officially chartered FPCC in 1978. The original charter established a six-member board of directors, which governed FPCC until the fall of 1987, when it was expanded to nine members. The first classes in 1977 had a $30 tuition rate for a three-credit course, with $3 for books.[106]

The major goal of FPCC was to provide an educational base for the preservation of the Assiniboine and Sioux cultures and for the advancement of the people on the reservation. One individual who worked on getting FPCC started in 1977 was Dr. Robert McAnally. Initially working with staff members Robert Dumont, Robert Smith, Mickey McAnally, Kay Bauer, Ann Lambert, Wilber Red Tomahawk, Eugene Boyd, Terri Clark, and Helen Christian, McAnally was instrumental in the early success of FPCC. After working with NAES College, graduating from the University of Montana's law school, and acting as in-house counsel for the Fort Peck tribes, he drifted back to FPCC in the 1990s and became Vice President of Student Affairs. After a stint as Vice President of Academic Affairs, he returned to teaching full-time at the college.

Another institution of higher learning at which over seventy tribal members earned four-year degrees in community services was the Native American Education System (NAES). NAES's central administration was located in Chicago, and at one time it had three other study sites besides Fort Peck. Robert Dumont and William "Sonny" Whitehead were instrumental in developing the Fort Peck NAES site. FPCC and NAES shared an old IHS building on Wolf Point's south side near the old IHS clinic, and also used another building in Poplar. Unfortunately, in the spring of 2000, the central campus, in consultation with NAES alumni at Fort Peck, discontinued classes at the Fort Peck site. In the late 1970s and throughout the 1980s, NAES-Fort Peck was on the rise, and a number of tribal members sought community-based degrees via this route.

These two decades were a productive time for the Tribes and for many tribal members. The many benefits and challenges were balanced with many social problems that still consumed the lives of so many, in that much of modernity cut both ways. Leaders and followers were adjusting their agendas, taking these into the next decades. ✵

1   Fort Peck Tribes Constitution and By-Laws, Enrollment Ordinance, Sec. 1(b).

2   Stanley Lyman, Superintendent, Bureau of Indian Affairs, Fort Peck Agency [hereinafter cited as "FPA"] Report 1965, p. 61; copy in Dolly C. Akers Papers, Montana Historical Society (MHS), Helena, Montana, 1960 unemployment rates on Fort Peck Reservation and/or Roosevelt Co.

3   Ibid., p. 3, 1960 income levels on Fort Peck Reservation.

4   Ibid., p. 5. Stanley Lyman, Superintendent, Bureau of Indian Affairs, Fort Peck Agency Report 1965, 5.

5   Ibid., 9, 10.

6   Ibid.

7   Ibid., 10-18.

8   *Herald News*, v. 49, no. 28, July 12, 1962, 1.

9   Letter from Sonosky, Chambers & Miller to Caleb Shields, August, 2007, Caleb Shields Papers.

10 Lyman, FPA Report 1965, 36-37, Akers Papers, MHS.

11 Ibid.

12 "Fort Peck is Eligible for E.D.A. Funds." *Poplar Standard*, v. 55, no. 16, January 28, 1966.

13 "Over $100,000 Invested in Area in War on Poverty," *Poplar Standard*, v. 55, no. 19, February 18, 1966, 8.

14 "Narrative Report by NYC Staff." *Poplar Standard*, v. 55, no. 28, April 22, 1966, 2.

15 "Neighborhood Youth Corp Explained," *Poplar Standard*, v. 55, no. 40, July 15, 1966, 1.

16 "Worker Writes of VISTA: Solving Problems Its Job," *Poplar Standard*, v. 55, no. 34, June 3, 1966, 6.

17 "VISTA Seeks Indian Volunteers," *Poplar Standard*, v.55, no. 34, June 3, 1966, 8.

18 "Community Action Agency Forming on Reservation," *Poplar Standard*, v. 55, no. 37, June 24, 1966, 2.

19 "Officers Elected for Economic Opportunity Advisory Committee," *Poplar Standard*, v. 55, no. 38, July 1, 1966, 3.

20 "VISTA kindergarten Depends upon Community Support," *Poplar Standard*, v. 55, no. 49, September 16, 1966, 6).

21 Ibid.

22 "Program Provides Legal Aid to Indians," *Poplar Standard*, v. 55, no. 37, June 24, 1966, 2.

23 "Twelve Students Complete Upward Bound," *Poplar Standard*, v. 55, no. 44, August 12, 1966, 4.

24 "Team Created to Meet Problems of Alcoholism on Ft. Peck Reservation," *Poplar Standard*, v. 56, no. 34, June 2, 1967, 1.

25 William L. Bryan, Jr., *Montana's Indians: Yesterday and Today* (Helena, Montana: American & World Publishing, 1996), 46.

26 Interview, Wayne Two Bulls, August 15, 2007.

27 Ibid.

28 "Merle Lucas Honored by Two Awards," *Poplar Standard*, v. 58, no. 52, October 24, 1969, 1.

29 "Tribes Insist on Free Hand in Planning for Reservation, *Poplar Standard*, v. 59, no. 13, June 23, 1970, 1.

30 "Board Withdraws if HUD Funds Not Directed to Tribes; Insist Indian Control of Planning," *Poplar Standard*, v. 59, no. 20, March 13, 1970, 1.

31 "Tribes Remain Firm on HUD Fund Stand," *Poplar Standard*, v. 59, no. 29, May 15, 1970, 1.

32 "HEW [Committee] Reviews Tribal Planning Stalemate," *Poplar Standard*, v. 60, no. 6, December 4, 1970, 1.

33 "Eventual Control Tribal Matters byTribes Is Goal," *Poplar Standard*, v. 60, no. 3, November 13, 1970, 1.

34 Lyman, FPA Report 1965, 51.

35 David E. Wilkins, *American Indian Politics and the American Political System* (New York: Rowman & Littlefield Publishing, 2002), 115-16, 138-39, 146, 149.

36 "Signing of Civil Rights Bill Will Give Nation's Indians Protections of Constitution," *Poplar Standard*, v. 57, no. 27, April 19, 1968, 4.

37 "Poplar Meet Discusses Civil Rights," *Poplar Standard*, v. 57, no. 29, May 3, 1968, 1.

38 "Indian Legal Benefits Will Be Explained," *Poplar Standard*, v. 57, no. 30, May 10, 1968, 2.

39 "Discrimination Charges Met with Formation 'Okiwajina': Boycotts Suggested; Indian Citizen Air Grevances at Meeting," *Poplar Standard*, v. 57, no. 51, October 18, 1968, 2.

40 "Stafne Sees WP 'Common' Goal." *Poplar Standard*, v. 58, no. 7, December 13, 1968, p.1.

41 "School Board Letters Bring Comment from Okiwajina Leader." *Poplar Standard*, v. 58, no. 22, March 28, 1969, p. 1.

42 "Okiwajina Candidates to Speak." *Poplar Standard*, v. 58, no. 23, April 4, 1969, p. 1.

43 Wilkins, *American Indian Politics . . .*, 42, 115, 201, 206-11.

44 Russell Means, with Martin J. Wolf, *Where White Men Fear to Tread: The Autobiography of Russell Means* (New York: St. Martins Press, 1995).

45 The caravan receives attention in Paul Chaat Smith and Robert Allen Warrior, *Like a Hurricane: The Indian Movement from Alcatraz to Wounded Knee* (New York: New Press, 1996); reports were filed and published in the local papers: "Area Students March on 'Trail of Broken Treaties,'" *Poplar Standard*, v. 61, no. 51, October 20, 1972, 1; "WP, Poplar Students Sit It Out in BIA Building," *Poplar Standard*, v. 62, no. 2, November 10, 1972, 1; "Broken Treaties Caravan Destined for Wash. D.C.," *Wotanin*, v. 3, no. 18, October 25, 1972, 1; "Trail of Broken Treaties" (Map) *Wotanin*, v. 3, no. 8, October 25, 1972, 4. A number of individuals from Fort Peck participated in the Longest Walk in 1978.

46 Wilkins, *American Indian Politics*," 204-206.

47 "Overall Economic Development Plan: Fort Peck Reservation and Roosevelt County Redevelopment Area," Fort Peck Tribal Executive Board and the Roosevelt County Planning and Improvement Council, ca. 1970, 22; also see the reversal of the pattern due to the TEB's use of FHA loans and land repurchases, Bryan, *Montana's Indians*, 50-51.

48 Resolution No. 466-61-2, February 9, 1961, Fort Peck TEB; Rodney R. Miller, "Economic and Industrial Development on the Fort Peck Reservation of Montana," NAES College-Fort Peck and Antioch University, 1983, 38-39.

49 Resolution No. 555-67-3, March 27, 1966, Fort Peck TEB; Rodney R. Miller, "Economic and Industrial Development . . . ," 39.

50 "Poplar Gets New Industry," by Joan Broomfield, *Poplar Standard*, v. 57, no. 17, February 9, 1968, 1.

51 "Reservation Given Gov't Preference," *Poplar Standard*, v. 58, no. 18, February 16, 1968, 1.

52 Rodney R. Miller, "Economic and Industrial Development . . .", 41.

53 Ibid.

54 "Fort Peck Tribes Discuss Reservation Improvement," *Poplar Standard*, v. 57, no. 44, August 16, 1968, 1.

55 Ibid.

56 Ibid.

57 "Poplar Picked for Industrial Park" *Poplar Standard*, v. 57, No. 20, March 1, 1968, 1.

58 Ibid.

59 "$283,200 Granted Tribes' Industrial Park," *Poplar Standard*, v. 58, no. 15, February 7, 1969, 1.

60 "Rifle Repair Project to Employ 118 on Reservation," *Poplar Standard*, v. 58, no. 9, December 27, 1968, 1.

61 "Industries Dedication Ceremonies Start MondaySecretaries of Defense, Air Force, and Interior Department," *Poplar Standard*, v.58, no. 23, April 4, 1969, 1.

62 "Poplar Gets Big Contract—to Repair, Overhaul 37,000 Rifles," *Poplar Standard*, v. 58, no. 52, October 24, 1969, 1; Rodney R. Miller, "Economic and Industrial Development", 45-46.

63 "Vote Bill Youpee for Tribal Chairman" (election advertisement), *Poplar Standard*, v. 58, No. 52, October 24, 1969.

64 "Tribes Get Third Army Contract," *Poplar Standard*, v. 60, no. 51, October 15, 1971, 1.

65 "Fort Peck Industries Get Contract," *Poplar Standard*, v. 60, No. 26, April 23, 1971, 1.

66 Rodney R. Miller, "Economic and Industrial Development", 46-47.

67 Ibid., 47.

68 Ibid., 50; Charles Nolley, "An Ethnographic Study of Industry on the Ft. Peck Reservation" (master's thesis, University of Montana, 1982); and Scott Daniel Warren, "Landscape and Place-Identity in a Great Plains Reservation Community: A Historical Geography of Poplar, Montana" (master's thesis, Montana State University, 2008).

69 Rodney R. Miller, "Economic and Industrial Development," 50.

70 "Let to Build 50 Homes," *Poplar Standard*, v. 58, no. 1, November 1, 1968, 1.

71 "$283,200 granted Tribes' Industrial Park," *Poplar Standard*, v. 58, No. 15, February 7, 1969, 1.

72 "Factory Completes First Home in 50-House Project," *Poplar Standard*, v. 58, No. 40, August 1, 1969, 1.

73 "Low Cost Housing Program Loan Okayed for Fort Peck Reservation," *Poplar Standard*, v. 61, no. 42, August 18, 1972, 1.

74 Rodney J. Miller, "Economic and Industrial Development," 51.

75 A&S Industries Newsletter, March 1983.

76 Rodney J. Miller, "Economic and Industrial Development," 69-74.

77 "Multiplex Seeks 80 New Trainees," *Poplar Standard*, v. 60, no. 35, June 25, 1971, 1.

78 Rodney J. Miller, "Economic and Industrial Development," 59-63.

79 Ibid.

80 Ibid., 64.

81 Ibid., 52.

82 "Reservation Gets $35,480 Grant for Planning Staff," *Poplar Standard*, v. 57, no. 21, March 8, 1968, 1.

83 "$38,807 to Tribe for Industry," *Poplar Standard*, v. 58, no. 2, November 8, 1968, 2.

84 Rodney J. Miller, "Economic and Industrial Development," 65-66.

85 Fort Peck Tribes 1991 Annual Report, 16.

86 See list "Fort Peck Indian Agency Superintendents" in this volume.

87 Ibid.

88 Personal Communication, Ed Broaddus, January 2011.

89 *Herald News*, vol. 57, no. 46, November 12, 1970, 1, 6.

90 *Herald News*, vol. 63, no. 39, September 23, 1976, 1, 6.

91 Ibid.

92 *Wotanin Wowapi*, March 1981.

93 *Reynolds v. Sims, 377 U.S. 533* (1964); *Avery v. Midland County, 390 U.S. 474* (1968); *Salyer Land Co. v. Tulare Lake Basin Water Storage District, 410 U.S. 719* (1973).

94 Resolution #4-53, FP TEB.

95 "Red Thunder Wins Head Tribal Post," *Poplar Standard*, v.61, no. 2, November 5, 1971, 1.

96 "Referendum Committee Studies Re-districting," *Wotanin Wowapi*, April 24, 1980, copy in folder "Referendum Committee," Box 8, Dolly C. Akers Papers, Montana Historical Society.

97 Ibid., 12.

98 "Referendum Committee Submits Final Report," *Wotanin Wowapi*, v. 11, no. 16, October 24, 1980, 4.

99 "Draft final report." "Referendum Committee" folder, Box 8, Dolly C. Akers Papers, Montana Historical Society.

100 Copy of the Petition to for a Writ of Certiorari the U.S. Supreme Court, folder "Personal" folder 1, Box 1, Dolly C. Akers Papers, Montana Historical Society.

101 Wilkins, *American Indian Politics and the American Political System*, xxiv, 132.

102 Ibid.

103 NAACP Legal Defense and Education Fund, with the cooperation of the Center for Law and Education, Harvard University, *An Even Chance*. (New York, 1971).

104 Denise Juneau and Mandy Smoker Broaddus, "And Still the Waters Flow: The Legacy of Indian Education in Montana," *Phi Delta Kappan*, November, 2006, 193-197.

105 Wilkins, *American Indian Politics and the American Political System*, 136, 222.

106 *Herald News*, vol. 63, no. 37, September 3, 1976. 1, 6b.

CHAPTER 15

The Search for Prosperity in a Time of Building: Preparing for the Twenty-first Century, 1980-2000

James Shanley, Ed.D, Caleb Shields, D.H.L., and
Joseph R. McGeshick, Ph.D., with David R. Miller, Ph.D.

WHILE many on the reservation were experiencing reasonable beginnings of increased prosperity, the Tribes' priorities were inter-related. Economic development that would lead to employment opportunities was certainly on the list. Resource development continued to accelerate. Utility taxes and severance taxes were devised that increased tribal revenue, but these met legal challenges that threatened them. In this period, a mix of self-reliance and self-determination directed many initiatives.

In 1980, the BIA appointed Dorrance Steele superintendent of the Fort Peck Agency. Steele, a Sioux from Poplar, became the first enrolled member of the Assiniboine and Sioux Tribes to hold that position. He supervised the BIA at Fort Peck until 1982, and was replaced by acting superintendent David Allison (1982) and then Daniel T. Hardwood (1983). They were followed by two more Indian superintendents, Thomas Whitford (1983) and Dennis Whiteman (1983-1988). Whiteman managed the BIA agency for five years and developed a genuine rapport with tribal government. He was known for his fairness and understanding. The Tribes and the BIA remained among the largest employers of tribal members.

The Fort Peck tribes had entered the last twenty years of the century with optimism and increased self-confidence. From 1983 to 1993, the Fort Peck Tribes enjoyed a rather stable existence. ASTI was the largest employer on the reservation, and in the midst of national welfare reform, the Tribes encouraged more accountability in how tribal resources were utilized. Tribal members settled into the next decade assisted by new and existing programs like the Tribal Employment Rights Office (TERO), which administered areas of Indian preference in contracting, subcontracting, and employment in both the private and federal sectors

Established in July 1980 by a TEB resolution, TERO also functioned as a tribal agency that initiated job referrals, employment counseling, compliance checks, training sessions, and other employment assistance.

A related program, the Job Training Partnership Act (JTPA) began around the same time. Congress passed JTPA in 1983, and the Fort Peck Tribes used this program to serve members who were classified as displaced workers, homeless, economically disadvantaged, or youth or older workers. JTPA offered such members training, education, and other support, and has provided a vital service for nearly thirty years.

ASTI in 1981 secured a sole-service contract to manufacture phenolic terminal strips for Western Electric. By 1983, ASTI had produced 5,000 pieces to the necessary specifications. Western Electric anticipated a purchase of 100,000 pieces annually, and $125,000 in sales. This initiative coupled with the production of camouflage products for commercial sales (see Chapter 14) provided predictable employment for a number of individuals. Reorganization of space in the plant created greater efficiencies. In the search for new products, as early as 1979, the company explored the possibility of producing various sheet-metal deep-draw items for the U.S. government, particularly deep-draw aluminum medical chests and insulated food containers. In the summer of 1980, the U.S. Army Defense Procurement Center awarded two contracts to ASTI, one for production of 15,613 medical supply chests in the amount of $2,200,000 and a second for $1,100,000 for 10,000 food chests. However, the plant had to be expanded to take on these contracts. During the summer of 1980, a $1,600,000 construction effort added another 39,500 square feet to the facility, financed by a SBA loan and ASTI earnings. Later in 1980, the U.S. Army Defense General Supply Center awarded ASTI a facilities contract to provide

industrial plant equipment and tools. These were taken from "idle government-owned machinery and equipment inventories at an acquisition cost of $466,000. Construction of the new area of the plant began the summer of 1981 and was completed in June 1982. Deep-draw production commenced in July 1982.[1]

The new addition accommodated a modern machine shop, chemical cleaning and paint lines, heat-treating ovens for annealing processes, and twenty-five mechanical and hydraulic presses varying in size from ten to 900 tons in capacity. The manufacturing process transforms metal from a flat sheet into three-dimensional objects.

The accomplishments of ASTI and its partnership with Brunswick Corporation were celebrated on August 12, 1982, when 300 workers and more than one thousand residents of Poplar and Wolf Point joined military and government dignitaries to dedicate the newly expanded facility. At this event, Chairman Norman Hollow, who also served as chairman of the ASTI Board, declared that "the Tribes are proof that industrialization of Indian people is possible." He also asserted that this kind of economic development countered the stereotype that American Indians can accomplish results only through give-away programs.[2]

By 1981, ASTI had annual sales of $5,200,000, earnings of $754,000, and equity valued at $4.8 million. The next year, annual sales were projected to $8 million, generating about $1 million in profit, and resulting in $6 million in equity.[3]

In 1983, Rodney J. Miller wrote an NAES degree paper assessing the economic developments at Fort Peck to date, reporting the Tribes' "excellent position." He noted that in 1982, ASTI had received an additional contract financed by another SBA loan for $5,800,000 for producing 60,000 more camouflage nets. A follow-up contract for $6,400,000 guaranteed production of another 60,000 nets from April 1983 through

June 1984.[4] The work shift was a full day in May 1982, with a partial second shift. However, in July 1983, the plan was for twenty-four hour operation, with three shifts running six days a week, providing employment opportunities for 450 area residents, 75 percent Indians and 25 percent non-Indians. At that pace, the projected income was expected to rise to $14 million by 1986.[5]

The other major tribally owned company, West Electronics, Inc., yielded gross sales in 1982 in excess of $1 million, with similar sales predicted for 1983. By that year, twenty-two workers were completing production contracts for the U.S. Army in St. Louis, MO, and Monmouth, NJ. The company had another commercial contract with Digital Products of Long Island, NJ, and was negotiating with the U.S. Postal Service for additional production. The products manufactured included "shipboard communications equipment, cable harnesses, chassis wiring, printed circuit card assembly and money change making equipment."[6]

West Electronics Incorporated (WEI) was re-incorporated under a new charter in 1986, completely owned and operated by the Fort Peck Tribes. The original and primary function of the company had been electronic manufacturing for both government agencies and commercial customers. In the late 1980s and early 1990s, the company mainly manufactured materials for the U.S. government and "was very successful in the execution and delivery of these contracts and resulting products." Nevertheless, the company was vulnerable both to government downsizing and procurement cutbacks. Renewing itself, the company in 1995 was certified and admitted into the U.S. SBA Disadvantaged Business 8(a) Program. With this status, the company entered the information technology services industry. In August 1996, West entered into "a major information technology (IT) procurement services management contract for the U.S. Department

of Justice and continued this work for the U.S. Treasury Department through 2005." Profits from these ventures have allowed West Electronics to develop other opportunities. Joining with DRS Technologies (formerly ESSI), WEI has become a specialist in U.S. Army "Fuel System Supply Points" (FSSP). Having graduated from the 8(a) program in 2005, WEI continues to fulfill FSSP contracts at its plant in the Industrial Park in Poplar, employing over fifty tribal members.[7]

However, as national priorities in foreign policy and national defense shifted, DOD contracts decreased during the 1990s, and consequently ASTI, which was dependent on military contracts, went into serious decline.

Economic resources have always contrasted with other kinds of resources. Elders have always been an important resource to the Assiniboine and Sioux people. Traditionally, they were the keepers of knowledge and functioned as the communal educational system. They had the experience and patience to pass on knowledge to future generations. Who was considered an elder shifted from context to context. In 1976, a federal grant allowed the Fort Peck Tribes to develop the Senior Citizens Feeding Program, and by 1978, it provided noon meals to elderly Assiniboine and Sioux in the four major reservation communities. Funding now comes mainly from the tribal budget, supplemented by a federal Title VI grant and a state Title III grant. The program serves 55,000 meals a year.[8]

In the early 1980s, the Fort Peck Tribes paid for burials of deceased members. The Tribes worked out a deal with the local mortuary so that no matter whether a Fort Peck tribal member died on or off the reservation, tribal resources up to $1,300 were available to meet the costs of burial. By the end of the twentieth century, the amount had climbed to $4,000.

Many other programs helped the Tribes serve the Assiniboine and Sioux people and allowed families and communities to share in the success of the last forty-seven years. One in particular that literally reaches all parts of the reservation is the Fort Peck Transportation System, established in September 1977, and managed to this day by Leta Atkinson. Its routes run from Frazer to Fort Kipp and all communities in between. Anyone on the reservation, whether Indian or non-Indian, can use the buses. Since its inception, rates have gone from two cents per mile, with single and round-trip rates and weekly special rates, to fifty cents per mile. Another program managed by Philip Granboise started serving the Fort Peck Tribes in the early 1970s, the Fort Peck Tribal Enterprise. The program provides many services to the reservation communities, such as building and repairing reservation roads, snow removal, and sewer and water installation. Originally a service to level irrigation land on the reservation in the early 1960s, it developed into a crucial tribal department.[9]

Individual Indian oil leases operated under much the same management as Indian land leases for agribusiness. Oil was first discovered on the Fort Peck Indian Reservation in the late 1940s, and later, both trust and fee lands were explored in the early 1980s. Two major oil fields, the Lustre field twenty-five miles north of Wolf Point and the Poplar field just north of that town, were part of the larger Williston Basin Oil Field and produced the major portion of Fort Peck tribal oil revenues. The average royalties from those wells amounted to 12 percent, and major oil companies such as ARCO, Sun Oil, and Exxon, and local companies like Murphy Oil operated within the boundaries of the reservation.[10] Starting in the late 1970s, the TEB began an aggressive move into the oil business. By 1984, the Tribes had drilled their own well, the Wenona (sic) (meaning "First Girl"). This was the first American Indian oil well in northern plains history, and marked a greater role for the Fort Peck

Tribes in the oil industry. Soon royalties topped 16 percent and later soared to 25 percent. Some like the Wenona Well reached 55 percent.[11] This activity compelled the TEB to establish the Tribal Minerals Office that regulated drilling by oil companies on tribal land. It also monitored oil activity on non-Indian land. Lawrence "Larry" Wetsit, who later served as TEB chairman from 1989-1991, was the first director of that office.

After the success of the Wenona Well, the Fort Peck Tribes realized that enormous potential losses could result if they hit a dry hole. Due to their tax-exempt status, they did not enjoy the tax write-offs that their private counterparts in the oil business did. Consequently, in the late 1980s, they contracted with U.S. Energy for 25 percent royalties during the payout period, which was after drilling costs were recovered, and 55 percent while the well produced. The beginning of the 1990s witnessed a lull in oil activity on trust lands, but the vast majority of capital from the oil industry that was directly connected to tribal members was money paid for oil leases. Those dollars passed directly into the non-Indian-owned businesses of the local economy.[12] Beginning in 1980, the Tribes began negotiating a pipeline lease through the reservation with the Northern Border Pipeline Company (NBPL). The reservation pipeline formed a small but significant part of NBPL's overall 1,249-mile interstate pipeline system that transported natural gas from the Montana-Saskatchewan border to interconnecting pipelines in the upper midwestern United States. On June 13, 1980, the Fort Peck Tribes leased tribal land to NBPL for a fifty-three-foot-wide right-of-way for fifteen years with a right of renewal without further change for another fifteen years. This was a major economic development for the Tribes that arose from the proposal to construct the Northern Border gas pipeline across the reservation. This proposal was negotiated with the assistance of Reid Chambers of the Sonosky law firm. Northern Border was obligated to provide at least forty jobs to tribal members during the construction of the pipeline, and to observe Indian preference in its hiring on the reservation. The original construction of the Northern Border gas pipeline provided millions of dollars of contracts for A&S Construction, a tribally owned company, and a large number of construction jobs for tribal members. Construction on the reservation portion began in 1982 and ended a year later. In the first part of the new century, the Sonosky firm also worked with the Tribes to renew the Northern Border right-of-way, which continues to provide substantial compensation to the Tribes.

The Tribal Executive Board, with the assistance of the Sonosky firm, began to develop and enforce severance and utilities taxes. In the late 1980s, the Tribes and law firm persuaded the federal court of appeals for the Ninth Circuit that the tribes had the authority to impose a utility tax on the Burlington railroad that crossed the reservation. A decade later, the Ninth Circuit invalidated a Crow tribal tax that bore some similarity to the Fort Peck utilities tax. As a result, Burlington stopped paying the tax. Consequently, the Sonosky firm represented the Fort Peck Tribes against Burlington in federal and tribal court suits concerning the validity of the tax. Ultimately, these cases were settled by compromise under which Burlington pays the Tribes sums representing a substantial portion of the tax.

Taxation was a misunderstood issue in terms of whose, what, and when taxes applied to the Fort Peck Tribes and their members. Initially, the Tribes and their members were exempt from state and local taxes. Even federal taxes did not apply to Indians when income was derived from trust land. As governments encroached on tribal sovereignty, however, tribal members were increasingly scrutinized and resented by local whites and their governments. In the 1970s, the Fort Peck Tribes began to exert their opposition to state and local taxation. One of the first tax issues for the tribes arose in 1976, when then-TEB member Caleb Shields paid his car property tax to the county in protest. He claimed the county had no authority to tax his property because he was a tribal member living on the reservation. Five years later in 1981, Shields and the Fort Peck Tribes won their case. Initially, the ruling applied to all Indians on the reservation, but after a cigarette tax case involving the Colville Tribe of Washington was resolved, it only applied to enrolled Fort Peck tribal members. Other taxes, especially on cigarettes, alcohol, and gasoline, came into question. By 1992, the Fort Peck Tribes had negotiated several tax agreements with the state of Montana and received annual shares of those taxes.[13] Tribal members also exercised their exemption to state income taxes. Tribal legal counsel Marvin Sonosky was instrumental in all of the Fort Peck tribes' tax cases and negotiated agreements during those years.[14]

By 1983, when Docket-184 monies (the fruits of an accounting claim pursued for several decades and finally settled out of court) were available to each reservation community, the WPCO and PCO and the towns of Frazer, Oswego, Brockton, and Fort Kipp started to look toward further developing their communities. Community organizations resulted from the people's fear of losing representation on the Tribal Executive Board because of the voting-at-large issue. In 1979, Wayne Martell proposed community meetings as a means of getting the people's voice into tribal government. The first community organization was the Frazer Town Council, formed in 1975 by Elliott Todd, Larry Hamilton, Thelma Blount, and others. The Frazer Town Council developed a small youth center, a volunteer fire and ambulance service, and other community projects and events. Docket-184, a $16-million accounting claim awarded to the Fort Peck Tribes in 1983, set aside 30 percent of the money for community development and paid out 70 percent in a per capita payment.[15] Each reservation community had to determine community boundaries and take a head count of community members. Each community developed different projects with its share of the set-aside money. Wolf Point developed its project in phases. Phase I was construction of a 20,000-square-foot building on the east side of town. Originally, Phase II just called for a casino, but after meeting with ASTI managers, the company agreed to make space for a 7,700-square-foot manufacturing venture. Unfortunately, ASTI backed out, and WPCO was left with a large empty area in its building. In the interim, WPCO opened the Silver Wolf Casino on July 4, 1987, with a 400-seat bingo hall, cafe, and video poker area.[16]

Initially, PCO used its Docket-184 money for two construction projects. The first was the arbor at the Iron Ring Pow Wow grounds north of Poplar. The second was the Poplar Community Center building. PCO then bought the old Poplar bowling alley and converted it into a roller rink. Later, PCO constructed a building that became the Poplar Post Office that was leased to the U.S. Postal Service. Oswego and Frazer used their money to buy satellite dishes for their community members. Oswego retained $69,000 of its Docket-184 money and planned to build a fire station, but that project did not see fruition.[17]

In the early 1990s, Frazer used its additional funds to buy the old Cliff Quam store and developed A&S Plastics, a venture with the Blackfeet Pencil Company of Browning, MT, that manufactures plastic pen components. After only a few months, however, the building burned to the ground. The Tribes collected the insurance money, over $100,000, and gave it back to the

Frazer community. Fort Kipp used its share of Docket-184 money to build the Jim Black Dog Hall, and Brockton still has most of its funds, occasionally using interest for holiday parties and gifts for its community.[18]

In the fall of 1985, the Assiniboine and Sioux elected Kenneth E. Ryan as tribal chairman. Joseph Red Thunder served as vice-chairman. Although Norman Hollow ended his twelve-year tenure as tribal chairman, he still ran for a seat on the TEB and won. He serves another five terms as TEB councilman, giving him forty-five years of service, more than any other political leader. Ryan served one term. During his leadership, a small faction of tribal members contacted the Department of Interior's Office of Inspector General (OIG) in Washington and accused the tribal government of corruption and graft. The OIG came into the tribal offices and seized all tribal records. After six months, its investigation revealed that the charges were groundless, that political jealousy was the impetus for the investigation, and that the OIG had overstepped its authority by examining records involving tribal money and assets.

Concerns about elders, political accountability, reservation communities, and taxation persisted into the 1980s. However, elders, politicians, communities, and families could not ignore one issue that remained taboo until a group came together in the early 1980s to address it. Under the administration of Chairman Ken Ryan, concerned tribal members met to shape how the Fort Peck Tribes were going to deal with domestic and family abuse. Leading the way were Chairman Ryan, Patty McGeshick, a former tribal prosecutor who successfully tried the first case of child sexual abuse in Fort Peck Tribal Court, Dr. James Shanley, Fort Peck Community College president, future chairman Lawrence "Larry" Wetsit, and Jackie Weeks, tribal administrator.[19] After Ryan testified before Congress in 1985, the Fort Peck Tribes received special funding, and in 1987 established the Sexual Assault Victims Treatment Program (SAVTP), later renamed the Family Violence Resource Center. The SAVTP first concentrated on sexual assault but expanded to other support services for families. It remains a crucial department on the reservation, working with police, the courts, and social services. It also mitigates the impact of victim trauma and operates a twenty-four-hour-a-day hotline.[20]

Ray White Tail Feather, who followed Chairman Ryan, was elected for the 1987-1989 term. He established an Economic Development Commission to encourage various sectors of the communities to assess and plan for economic improvement.

During the mid-1980s, another issue arose that divided Indians and non-Indians—water rights. The mighty Missouri River serves as the southern boundary of the reservation and is fed by numerous streams within the reservation. In May 1985, the state of Montana and the Fort Peck tribes signed a historic compact that led to the delineation of water rights for the reservation. The first of its kind in the nation, the Fort Peck Water Rights Compact allowed the Assiniboine and Sioux Tribes to divert over one million acre-feet of water each year from the Missouri River and other arteries, or to consume just over half that amount of water annually.[21] Despite often bitter negotiations, the compact moved forward through the efforts of chairman Hollow and TEB members Caleb Shields and Walter Clark and attorney Reid Chambers. Initially, the Winter's Doctrine, a 1908 federal Indian law canon that stemmed from a Montana water rights case, implicitly reserved Indian water rights. Unfortunately, during the conservatism of the 1950s, Congress attached the McCarren Amendment to pending legislation in 1952. The amendment waived sovereign immunity for the

United States in state water rights litigation. In 1983, the Supreme Court ruled that Indian water rights were also included under the McCarren Amendment. By the mid-1980s, the Fort Peck tribes and the state of Montana had two options—litigation or negotiation. Fortunately, they chose the latter. The Tribes established a Water Rights Office in February 1986, and the Department of the Interior approved the Tribal Water Code in October 1986.[22] Twenty years later, the Water Rights Compact was the main underpinning of the Missouri River initiative (Fort Peck-Dry Prairie Regional Water Authority), a $275 million federal water pipeline project for the reservation and most of northeastern Montana, that began in 1992 through the initiative of Chairman Shields and a Native American attorney with the Sonosky firm, Mary Pavel. This project addressed the need for quality water throughout the region, a partial response to energy development contamination of subsurface water resources.[23]

As the Assiniboine, Sioux, and other tribes around the country worked out their social and economic difficulties, a "new buffalo" emerged in a manner no one could have predicted. During the Reagan and Bush administrations of the 1980s, the federal government fell into a backlash of conservatism. Programs were cut, and competition for funds became increasingly severe. In the late 1970s, in an effort to expand economic development, the Penobscot Tribe of Maine and the Seminole Tribe of Florida opened the country's first American Indian gaming operations by offering big bucks bingo. State officials quickly tried to claim jurisdiction, both criminal and civil, over the tribes. The Seminole won a Supreme Court decision that found a state could prohibit gambling within its boundaries only if that form of gambling was against the laws of the state for all of its citizens. In addition, since *California v. Cabazon Band of Indians* (1987),

Indian tribes are guaranteed the right to operate any form of gaming already permitted within the states in which they reside.[24]

Consequently, tribal governments throughout the country initiated gaming operations. Those that had the demographic base, especially of non-Indian populations, harbored the golden goose. Due to what the states characterized as a vested interest, since most of the big-spending gamblers were non-Indian, the federal government was pressured to pass the Indian Gaming Regulatory Act (IGRA) of 1988 that outlined three types of Indian gaming: Class I, traditional games (i.e., stick and hand games); Class II, low-stakes gaming; and Class III, high-stakes casino-type gaming. IGRA also mandated that tribes could not exceed the type of gaming that their particular state prohibited and called for tribes and states to enter into gaming compacts outlining gaming activities.[25] Since Fort Peck lacked the demographic base, coupled with the state of Montana's attitude toward Indian gaming and traditional opposition to Indian tribes in general, the Assiniboine and Sioux operated only diminutive bingo halls and video poker casinos. In the late 1990s, in an effort to help the economically depressed mining town of Butte, MT, the state legislature considered allowing Butte to operate Class III gaming. That idea died because if it had been successful, the measure would also have allowed the state's Indian tribes to operate that class of gaming. Since Indian gaming benefits are not distributed evenly among tribes, and because of the mainstream stereotype of rich Indians, gaming remains one of the most misunderstood American Indian issues.[26]

Another measure the Fort Peck Tribes addressed was a central accounting system. In 1985, during the administration of Chairman Ryan, who received an honorary doctorate from University of Montana, Missoula, in 1995, the Fort Peck Tribes instituted a central finance system that controlled all tribal budgets. This was in response to the Paperwork Reduction Act of 1980, by which Congress intended to improve the usefulness and effectiveness of single-audit reporting. Before 1985, most tribal programs had administered their own budgets, leading to a number of incidences that resulted in a few convictions of directors or personnel of tribal programs who had misappropriated funds. During 1989-91, Chairman Larry Wetsit worked extensively with program directors, emphasizing program efficiencies, stressing increased delivery of services to tribal members, and economizing to create reserve funds. Five years later, the Fort Peck Tribes again restructured the auditing system under the Single Audit Act Amendments of 1996. Prior to that, some tribal programs and their directors ran into financial trouble. Fortunately, the central finance system greatly reduced misuse of tribal funds. Currently, the Fort Peck Tribes employ a full-time comptroller who examines tribal accounts and spending and whose work is audited annually.[27]

On January 28, 1987, the tribes continued exercising their civil authority when Richard Whitesell of the Billings BIA Area Office gave final approval of the Fort Peck Tribal Utility Tax. The tax placed a 3 percent tax on utility company property that crossed trust land. Utility companies like Northern Border Pipeline, Burlington Northern Railroad (BN) (as of December 31, 1996, Burlington Northern & Santa Fe Railroad (BNSF)), and others were subject to the tax. In March of that year, BN sued in federal district court in Great Falls and won a temporary injunction. However, in late 1988, the tax was upheld. The Fort Peck Tribes' budget gained about $2 million a year from the utilities tax. BN at the time was running an average of twenty-six freight trains a day on its main line, which by 2000 meant that more than 619,000 cars passed through the reservation on the 1887 congressionally authorized right-of-way. Consequently, from 1987 to 1999, the Tribes imposed an annual ad volorem tax of 4 percent on the railroad. BN also contested the imposition of a similar tax by the Blackfeet on the right-of-way in its reservation in 1991. The initial case involving the Fort Peck Tribes "held that the congressionally-conferred right-of-way used by BN was on trust land and that the ad valorem tax was therefore valid."[28] In a Supreme Court case in 1997, *Strate v. A-1 Contractors*, the court held that "a right-of-way granted by the federal government and crossing through Indian trust land is the equivalent of non-Indian fee land."[29] Building on *Strate* and another case involving BNSF, *Burlington N.R.R. v. Red Wolf*, which treated a BN right-of-way over a different Indian reservation as non-Indian fee land, the Crow tribe asserted its right to tax. Again the Ninth Circuit Court of Appeals, in *Big Horn County Electric Cooperative v. Adams*, overruled *Strate*, and upheld an ad valorem tax on property located on a congressionally granted right-of-way. Challenges by BNSF to changes in case law were turned back, because the Tribes argued that their tax was justified under *Montana v. United States*, based on uncertainties of cargos and abilities to respond to exceptional circumstances. The Court of Appeals vacated the case, and left the Tribes and the railroad to seek an accommodation. In a negotiated arrangement, the BNSF makes an annual donation to the Fort Peck Tribes for use of the right of way through the reservation.[30]

Politics on Fort Peck are often a microcosm of national politics. The scale is only overshadowed by intensity. The political foundations of the Fort Peck Tribes experienced changes in the last twenty years of the twentieth century. Some well-known tribal leaders during those two decades were Caleb Shields, who served for twenty-four consecutive years on the board, Chairman Ray K. Eder, who served as a TEB member for six

terms and as vice-chairman for four terms, and Walter Clark, an Assiniboine from Frazer who served as a council member for thirteen terms starting in 1979. Many other tribal leaders helped the Assiniboine and Sioux gain prominence, including Pearl Hopkins, Stanley Yellowrobe, Eugene Culbertson, Raymond White Tail Feather, June Stafne, Jesse Kirn, Merle Lucas, Arlyn Headdress, and Spike Bighorn.

Lawrence "Larry" Wetsit was elected tribal chairman in 1989 and served until 1991. He demonstrated that with diligent administration and an emphasis upon frugality, a reserve fund could be created for the long-term viability of the Tribes. Wetsit led the Fort Peck Tribes into the last decade of the twentieth century. He was followed by TEB member Caleb Shields, who served as chairman for three terms (1991-1997). He was first elected in 1975 to the TEB, where he served twelve consecutive terms until his retirement in October 1999.

Tribal politics were not the only venue in which Assiniboine and Sioux members functioned. Fort Peck is noted for its string of state legislators. Dolly Akers was elected to the Montana state legislature in the 1930s, and William "Bill" Whitehead was next elected from the reservation in 1996. Both fought for Indian rights. The government appointed Wyman Babby BIA superintendent. He held that post for seven years, from 1989-1996.

As tribal communities grew in the 1980s and 1990s, the need for more housing and new housing programs emerged at Fort Peck. Under the 1996 Native American Housing Assistance and Self-Determination Act, HUD restructured the tribal housing program. The Fort Peck Tribes now apply for housing under the block grant system. The FPHA administers 531 units under the Rental Housing Program and 241 units under the Homeownership Program (Mutual Help). Since the early 1960s, the FPHA has constructed

1,149 homes, both on scattered sites around the reservation and in community projects, for Assiniboine and Sioux families. Of those, 377 have been paid off and turned over to tribal homeowners. Adding to all of that reservation construction was the new Medicine Bear Tribal and BIA building complex in 1996, which offered spacious and comfortable offices and a TEB chambers.[31]

The Silver Wolf Casino in Wolf Point remained the only community-operated (WPCO) casino on the Fort Peck Reservation. Again, due to the demographic character of the area, its operations are limited. In 1990, with a $105,000 loan from Citizen's First National Bank in Wolf Point, WPCO purchased Great Divide Manufacturing, a Helena-based company that contracted with the DOD. WPCO relocated its new company to the manufacturing space it had reserved for the ASTI venture back in 1983, and changed the name to Looking Eagle Manufacturing, the Indian name of Assiniboine member and former TEB member Merle Lucas. It became 8-A certified, and manufactured military targets and ammunition pouches.

By 1990, FPCC was one of the most successful reservation tribal colleges. Dr. James Shanley, an Assiniboine who was the former president of Standing Rock Community College in Fort Yates, ND (now Sitting Bull Community College), provided the leadership. From 1984 to the present, Shanley shaped FPCC into one of the leading American Indian institutions of higher learning. Under Shanley's tutelage, FPCC grew from a small reservation-based community college to an institution that serves over 400 students and offers numerous two-year degrees and certificates. From 1990 on, FPCC cooperated with four-year institutions like Rocky Mountain College in Billings, Montana State University-Northern in Havre, and Montana State University-Bozeman to offer four-year degrees to reservation stu-

dents. Shanley remains one of the most highly respected national Indian education leaders. He served as President of the American Indian Higher Education Consortium (AIHEC) in 1978, when the Tribal Controlled College Act was passed, and for three terms starting in early 2000. FPCC continues to provide higher education to reservation populations. In 2003, the college expanded to a new Wolf Point site with construction of a 12,000-square-foot building with classrooms, instructor offices, a spacious community meeting room, information technology center, and a distance learning center that connects to other colleges around the country. The building was named after longtime Fort Peck activist and educator Robert V. Dumont, who led the Native American Educational Services (NAES)-Fort Peck college program for fifteen years, and who died in May 1997. NAES managed the tribal archives program for almost two decades, but with the demise of NAES, the college assumed the archives mandate. FPCC had always offered classes in Wolf Point, mostly at the old NAES site, but with the new building, its presence has enabled Wolf Point, like Poplar, to enter the world of higher education.

The second Clinton administration sought to address the fiscal health of the U.S. government, and after a substantial showdown with a Republican Congress, included in its FY97 Budget Reconciliation bills a number of proposals for welfare reform. The individual bill was titled "Personal Responsibility and Work Opportunity Reconciliation Act of 1996," with the combined purposes of fixing the "welfare system," and ending "welfare as a way of life." The main elements were the concepts of "workfare," lifetime time limits, and personal responsibility. While it gave a nod to the idea of personal responsibility, the Clinton welfare reform plan focused on putting people back to work, increasing job programs, and supplementing child-care programs for persons on welfare and the working poor. However, the Republicans pressed to downsize the budget by "reducing those who would be eligible for welfare (legal immigrants, children born to families already on welfare, children born to unmarried women), eliminating the entitlement status of programs . . . , and eliminating many programs and rolling the remaining programs into block grants to the states."[32]

These changes affected many low income and more destitute tribal members, especially the provision that welfare was restricted to only so many months in the life of a given individual. Many longtime recipients of welfare were cut off. This left the dilemma of how to respond. The Tribes had the option to administer their own program, but the implications for tribal resources were obvious. Instead, other means were pursued. One was that FPCC, following its mandate as a community college, wrote grants and secured funding for people who might pursue training.[33]

The 1990s brought increased scrutiny of the BIA. During the first months of the Reagan administration, budgets were being cut across government. In an effort to minimize its cut, the BIA told Congress that it had a $20 million in discretionary funds, "discretionary" meaning that the SI had the authority to spend this money for the benefit of tribes without going through the normal appropriation process. However, the appropriations committees questioned the sources of this money. By 1982, the BIA revealed that the fund included interest earned on trust money. The next question was how much of this was trust money, and the BIA estimated that half was trust and half was "federal." Congress was shocked at the trusteeship of the BIA taking $10 million for itself, and subsequently abolished the discretionary designation and assigned the money to an escrow account. All of this was

done, however, without a detailed accounting. The Tribes brought an accounting suit in December 1987, stating, "we pleaded a national class action for all tribes and Indians in the United States in the same position as Fort Peck with respect to an accounting." The suit arose

. . . from the BIA's practice of investing trust money at interest, and keeping the trust money for itself, . . . [and] kept this practice secret from the Tribes and individual Indians. The Tribes did not know what was going on and certainly the individual Indians did not know. The BIA made no reports to the Tribes, or to individual Indians, that disclosed that the BIA was investing the trust money and not turning the interest over to the beneficial owners of the principal.[34]

The Tribes' general counsel explained that trying to locate early oil production figures in consultation with the BIA went nowhere because of gaps in the record. Consequently, the claim was made for the period August 1946 to 1983. The process was prone to abuses:

For each oil and gas sale the BIA placed the bidders' 25% deposits in a special deposit account awaiting the outcome of the sale. The BIA invested that money at interest. When the sale was completed with a lag time of up to two years, the BIA returned principal of the 25% deposit to the bidder and kept the interest for itself. During the period there were multiple bidders at each sale.[35]

Beyond lists of bids from sales late in 1962, earlier records were not found, and in some cases, records were reconstructed, some using newspaper sources. The court ordered the government to account and declared it liable. First, the government attempted to stall, but then moved to attempt reconstruction of the record. At one point, the government wanted access to tribal records, but the court denied this. The court issued an order on April 11, 1995, that the government must account:

(1) For all money kept by the Government, mainly interest, earned by the Government's investment of trust money, including bid deposits in Special Deposit accounts; and (2) for all interest lost by reason of the Government's failure to invest or timely to invest trust money. This will require the collection and review of the accounting records that show what was done with the money.[36]

By January 1997, Sonosky reported that the government's attorney and accountants had begun negotiation of an out-of-court settlement. Arthur Anderson, the accountants, advised Sonosky that their costs would amount to approximately $2 million and that the entire case might be worth in excess of $3 million. However, this was radically underestimated based on the search for records and analysis, which was accurately $5.7 million.[37] In attempt to placate the court, the BIA distributed checks to various individuals at Fort Peck, but it turned out to have returned too much, and then it demanded repayment or engaged in recovery activities, none of which enhanced its credibility. The final settlement still hinged on whether the BIA and Interior Department could document their financial dealings with the Fort Peck Tribes.

It is important to realize that this effort by the Tribes overlapped with the beginnings of the class-action initiative begun by Eloise Cobell. On June 10, 1996, Cobell and a group of Blackfeet Indians from Montana filed a class-action lawsuit against the federal government, naming then-Interior Department Secretary Bruce Babbit as one of the defendants. Originally titled *Cobell v. Babbit*, the case has changed to *Cobell v. Norton*, *Cobell v. Kemphorne*, and finally *Cobell v. Salazar*, but it is generally called the Cobell case.[38] Cobell and her co-plaintiffs represent between 250,000 and 500,000 members of Indian tribes across the nation who claim that the U.S. government has incorrectly accounted for Indian trust assets. Although those assets belong to individual Fort Peck tribal members and members of other tribes, they have been managed by the Department of Interior as the fiduciary trustee since the establishment of the reservations. Cobell and the other plaintiffs claim that the amount totals $176 billion. As was the case in the Fort Peck Tribes' action on accounting for oil production proceeds, no single fiduciary institution has ever managed so many trust accounts as the Department of Interior has over the last 125 years.

At the BIA, 1996 saw the return of Superintendent Dennis Whiteman, who served until 2002. Meanwhile, the Fort Peck Tribes ended the century by electing Spike Bighorn (1997-1999) and Arlyn Headdress (1999-2001) as chairmen. Headdress also had served previously as a five-term TEB member. In 1997, during the last year of Chairman Caleb Shields' tenure, a General Council was called. Initially, the petition was declared invalid due to the signature process, but Shields worked with petitioner Liza Blackhoop, and finally the petition was approved. The main issue of the General Council was the amount of the upcoming December per capita payment. At the meeting, which took place at the Poplar Cultural Center, someone called for replacing Chairman Shields and also for suspending the use of Robert's Rules of Order. Shields ruled the motion out of order because the tribal chairman is required to chair the meeting of the General Council, and suspending Robert's Rules of Order was unconstitutional under the 1960 Fort Peck Tribal Constitution and Bylaws. That ruling ended the motion, which was not challenged. After discussion, the General Council agreed to initiate and recommend a resolution to the TEB for a $200 per capita payment. Since the TEB enacts laws for the Fort Peck Tribes, Chairman Shields presented the General Council's resolution to the TEB, which referred it to the tribal Finance Committee. It died there because the tribal budget could not afford a per capita payment of that size.[39]

As the Assiniboine and Sioux Tribes look back through the decades of the twentieth century, reservation families can take confidence from the building of their communities and their accomplishments, especially in the area of sports and academic achievements. High schools like Frazer, Brockton, Poplar, and Wolf Point have produced some of the best athletes in the state. Whether they run cross-country or compete at basketball, the athletes from the Fort Peck Reservation remain representative in their athletic prowess. Between Poplar and Wolf Point, they hold twelve state basketball championships. Frazer, Brockton, and Poplar are renowned for their state cross-country champions and their impressive runners. Completion rates of students who are tribal members from secondary and post-secondary education have increased.

The Fort Peck Tribes have been among the most progressive of Montana's Indian tribes. The future holds many new challenges, but with competent and intelligent leadership and sufficient resources, the leaders at Fort Peck continue to work for the future of their members. Federal Indian policy of the 1990s was based on a model of continuing pluralism and a recognition that tribes were here to stay. Federal policy has ceased to discriminate against individual Indians and sought to strengthen tribes. However, nothing in the history of federal Indian policy justified confidence in the continuation of the current federal Indian policy of self-determination. Certain groups and individuals opposed tribal assertion of rights and were aggressively seeking to abolish those rights. However, the growing sophistication of tribal governments and their increasing

assertion of treaty and statutory rights, coupled with growing support for tribal sovereignty from non-Indians, made changes to the Indian self-determination policy difficult.

The events and actions of the first 150 years reveal the hardships the Tribes have endured on the reservation. The last fifty years show how the Tribes have developed not only their natural and human resources, but also their emergent political authorities within tribal government. Vast monies have been expended to provide for the needs of tribal members, not only through spending tribal funds, but also through acquisition of federal funds provided to the tribes in compliance of the treaties and statutes. Management of natural resources, especially oil revenues, has brought substantial sums into the Tribes' annual budgets, along with lease income from their lands and monies from tax agreements with the state of Montana.

While other governments, national and state, were assessing their economic situations, tribal government was faced with its own reality checks. The downturn of federal funds to tribes nationwide was rationalized due to the cost of war efforts and the growing federal deficit. The Fort Peck Tribes and other tribes nationwide can only overcome this situation by rebuilding their internal infrastructures, carefully managing their tribal assets, and providing leadership to maintain the strong ties the tribes have developed with federal and state governments in the last half century.

The Fort Peck Tribes, as non-1934 IRA tribes, operated under their 1927 Constitution until the adoption of the present constitution in 1960. Since that time, the constitution was amended by referendum seven times, first in 1971 and last in 1991. These amendments were needed for specific purposes, but none were intended to spur economic growth and social well-being. In many reservation Indian communities, including those on Fort Peck, neocolonial IRA constitutional governments or non-IRA constitutions have operated for more than sixty years, and are often accepted by tribal members as the given government. This provides another source of resistance to change. Many tribal communities and governments and their constituencies may not believe they have the resources to meet the challenge of change. Consequently, the actions of many tribal communities and governments do not suggest immediate change or response to an increasingly competitive global, national, and local environment for economic and social development and advancement. If the general community is not well disposed toward changing its constitution or creating a new one, then little can be done. Circumstances may be deferred to when a more local crisis develops that points to an immediate need for change regardless of the weight of traditions and interpretations of the past.

The U.S. government's policy since 1975 has meant enhancing American Indian nations' opportunities for self-governance, and this has led numerous Indian tribes to amend their constitutions for nation-building purposes. Like emerging democracies worldwide, American Indian nations created new constitutions to foster greater governmental stability and accountability, to increase tribal members' support of government, and to provide a firmer foundation for economic and political development. In short, constitutional reform initiatives like those of the past have been one of the most important examples of the exercise of tribal self-governance and sovereignty by American Indian nations. ✪

1 Rodney R. Miller, "Economic and Industrial Development on the Fort Peck Reservation of Montana," NAES College-Fort Peck and Antioch University, 1983, 53-54.

2 Ibid., 55.

3 Ibid., 56.

4 Ibid.

5 Ibid., 56-57.

6 Ibid., 57.

7 See http://westelectronics.com/profile.php, consulted October 15, 2011.

8 Fort Peck Tribes 1991 Annual Report, 21.

9 Ibid.

10 William L. Bryan, Jr., *Montana's Indians: Yesterday and Today* (2nd ed.). Helena: American and World Geographical Publishing, Inc., 1996, 50.

11 Ibid., 51.

12 Ibid.

13 Sonosky, Chambers, Sachse, et. al, Memorandums 1992-1999, Fort Peck Tribal Operations Records, Fort Peck Tribes, Poplar, Montana.

14 Ibid.

15 Interview with George Redstone, 8-20-07; also see folder, "Dockets 184, 279A, and 10-81L," Caleb Shields Papers.

16 Redstone Interview.

17 Ibid.

18 Ibid.

19 Interview with Patty McGeshick, 8-12-07.

20 Ibid.

21 Bryan, *Montana Indians*, 53; see discussion about the negotiation in Mary McNally, Developing American Indian Water Rights in Montana: Law and Local Context. Ph.D. dissertation, Geography, University of Chicago, August 1991, see Chapter 5, "Fort Peck Negotiations," 113-152.

22 McNally, "Indian Water Rights in Montana," 157.

23 http://dnrc.mt.gov/cardd/ResourceDevelopment/regionalwater/dryprairieoverview.asp, viewed October 31, 2011.

24 David E. Wilkins, *American Indian Politics and the American Political System*. (Lanham: Rowman and Littlefield Publishers, Inc., 2002), 164-172.

25 Ibid., 166.

26 Bryan, Montana Indians, 47; Federal Indian Gaming Regulatory Act, P.L. 100-497, 25 U.S.C. 1988.

27 Personal communication with Larry Wetsit, November 15, 2011.

28 *Burlington Northern Railroad Company, v. The Blackfeet Tribe of the Blackfeet Indian Reservation*, Blackfeet Tribal Business Council, Earl Old Person, Chairman; Archie St. Goddard, Vice-Chairman; Marvin Weatherwax, Secretary; Eloise C. Cobell, Treasurer; and *Burlington Northern Railroad Company, v. Fort Peck Tribal Executive Board*; Fort Peck Tribal Tax Commission; Assiniboine and Sioux Tribes of the Fort Peck Indian Reservation; Kenneth E. Ryan, Tribal Chairman; Paula Brien, Tribal Secretary/Account, U.S. Court of Appeals for the Ninth Circuit, Nos. 88-4428, 88-4429, 924 F.2nd 899 (March 18, 1991); and *Burlington Northern Santa Fe Railroad Company, a Delaware Corporation v. The Assiniboine and Sioux Tribes of the Fort Peck Reservation, Montana; Arlyn Headdress, Chairman of the Fort Peck Tribal Executive Board; Mervyn Shields, Director, Tax Department of the Assiniboine and Sioux Tribes*, U.S. Court of Appeals for the Ninth Circuit, No. 01-35681, D.C. No. CV-01-00034-JDS, Opinion (March 17,2003), 3812, 323 F.3d 767.

29 Ibid., 2003, 3812, see footnote 1.

30 Ibid.,

31 Fort Peck Tribal Housing Authority Records, Poplar, Montana.

32 12 August, 1996, Legislative Update, George Waters and Tim Seward, to "All Tribal Clients," RE: "Welfare Reform/Budget Reconciliation—P.L 104-193, Caleb Shields Papers, Notebook No. 12, file F.

A definition of an entitlement program "means if a person qualifies for benefits the federal government guarantees that they will receive those benefits"(Waters and Seward, 2).

33 James Shanley, "Welfare Reform and the Tribal Colleges: Who's Left Holding the Bag? *Tribal College Journal.* Spring 1997: 27-28; American Indian Higher Education Consortium, and the Institute for Higher Education Policy. *Tribal College Contributions to Local Economic Development, February 2000: Tribal College Research and Database Inititative Report* 2 (Alexandria, VA: American Indian Higher Education Consortium, 2000), see segment, "Tribal Colleges and Welfare Reform,"18.

34 April 22, 1994, Marvin J. Sonosky, Sonosky, Chambers, Sachse, et. al., Washington, DC, to Chairman Caleb Shields, Fort Peck Tribes, Poplar, MT, "RE: Indian Money Proceeds of Labor (IMPL) case in the Federal Court of Claims (163.24), 1; Caleb Shields Papers, Notebook No. 9, file B.

35 18 April 1996, Marvin J. Sonosky, Sonosky, Chambers, Sachse, et. al., Washington, DC, to Lawrence M. Munson, Fort Peck Minerals Resource Office, Poplar, MT, "Re: *Assiniboine and Sioux v. United States, Court of Federal Claims, No. 773-87-L (163.24),*" 1; Caleb Shields Papers, Notebook No.9, file B.

36 14 April 1995, Marvin J. Sonosky, Sonosky, et. al., Washington, DC, to Fort Peck Tribal Executive Board, Poplar, MT, Memorandum No. 72-95. "Subject: IMPL Case, *Assiniboine and Sioux Tribes, et al., v. United States, No. 773-87-L*—Court of Claims holds Government Liable (163.24), 1; Caleb Shields Papers, Notebook No. 9, File B.

37 16 January 1997, Marvin J. Sonosky, Sonosky, et. al., Report on meetings with the Government Attorney and Accounts. Caleb Shields Papers, Notebook No. 9, File B.

38 *Cobell, et al. v. Salazar, et. al.*, Case No. 1:96CV01285 (D.D.C.).

39 Folder "General Council, 1997," Caleb Shields Papers.

~

CHAPTER 16

The New Millennium 2000-2012
James Shanley, Ed.D.

THE dawn of the twenty-first century found the Fort Peck Tribes trying to hold their own in a changing world. Arlyn Headdress, who had previously been elected a tribal council member, became Chairman in 1999. Dennis Whiteman was still BIA Superintendent, an office that he held until 2002, when he retired and was replaced by Spike Big Horn. The economic outlook in northeastern Montana was turning bleak, as it was in most small rural communities throughout the West. The tribal industries were struggling. The majority of U.S. manufacturing was going overseas, government contracting policies were very erratic, and agriculture was a break even or bust operation for most farmers and ranchers.

On September 11, 2001, the World Trade Centers in New York were destroyed by hijacked airplanes. The United States invaded Afghanistan and overthrew the Taliban government, but Osama Bin Laden eluded capture. In 2003, the United States and coalition forces invaded Iraq, eventually overthrowing the government and capturing Saddam Hussein, who was executed by his own people.

The tribal people at Fort Peck responded to the national emergency as they had since World War I. Dozens of young men and women joined the service and eventually served in the Middle East. Fortunately, although service members from Fort Peck were wounded during this decade, no one was killed. The war waxed and waned in Iraq and found focus in Afghanistan by 2010.

The Fort Peck Reservation started the decade with relative calm and stability. During the coming years, however, major incidents took place that had significant impacts on the Fort Peck Tribes. The Bureau of Indian Affairs reorganized into three separate branches. Tribal politics flared during mid-decade, bringing much turmoil and the specter of General Councils that had not been seen since the 1950s. The tribes moved to attempt modernization of the constitution. Economic development fell and rose in uncontrollable waves.

In November 2001, Arlyn Headdress was re-elected chairman for a third time, narrowly defeating former tribal councilman John Morales by fifty-three votes. Ray Eder was elected vice-chairman, and George Ricker Sr. became sergeant-at-arms. Tommy Christian, Leonard Crow Belt, John Pipe, Ray Whitetail Feather, Eugene Culbertson, Pearl Hopkins, Leland Spotted Bird, Rick Kirn, Walter Clark, Robert Welch, A. T. Stafne, and Barbara Birdsbill were elected to the council.

In 1999 the Fort Peck Tribes established their first bison ranch on land twenty-five miles north of Poplar. Although individual farmers and ranchers had owned bison over the years, this marked the first time the Tribes had reestablished the animal that had supported the people in the distant past. The name adopted by the TEB for the ranch was Turtle Mound Buffalo Ranch because of the many badland mounds that dot the region. One large predominant mound resembled a turtle. The ranch averages between 240-250 head of bulls, cows, and calves. They donate fifteen to twenty buffalo each year to various groups such as elders, pow wow committees, schools, FPCC, and many other cultural functions. In addition to running a cultural herd, the Assiniboine and Sioux Turtle Mound Buffalo Ranch also manages a small business herd that allows tribal and non-tribal individuals and groups to purchase selected animals. For a two- to three-year-old bull or cow, the cost averages about $650 but can run as high as $1,500 for a trophy bull. The two herds run on three pastures totaling over 7,000 acres.[1]

Nationally, Indian Affairs were also reaching a 911 of their own. In 1996, Elouise Cobell, a Blackfeet banker, filed a class-action lawsuit against the Secretary of the Interior, demanding an accounting of the Individual Indian and tribal trust accounts since 1887.[2] The premise of the suit was that the Bureau of Indian Affairs as trustee for the federal government had mismanaged these accounts and the property from which that income had been derived. The lack of credibility of the BIA's management had been building for decades. Many records were missing, and some of those that existed were incomprehensible, disintegrating, or damaged.

Congress had responded by passing the American Indian Trust Reform Act in 1994. The BIA made little progress, however, which prompted Cobell to file her suit in 1996. In 1999, a federal judge cited Bruce Babbitt and Robert Ruben (Secretary of Interior) for contempt because the Bureau of Indian Affairs had been unable to produce key documents for the lawsuit.

Federal District Judge Royce Lamberth presided over the case. It was soon evident that the judge was appalled by the position taken by the Department of Interior. Initially, the Cobell estimate for the missing Individual Indian account funds amounted to $176 billion. The government said the amount was much less. In a memorandum opinion dated December 12, 1999, Lamberth said:

The United States mismanagement of the IIM trust is far more inexcusable than garden-variety trust mismanagement of a typical donative trust. For the beneficiaries of this trust did not voluntarily choose to have their lands taken from them; they did not willingly relinquish pervasive control of their money to the United States. The United States imposed this trust on the Indian people. As the government concedes, the purpose of the IIM trust was to deprive plaintiffs' ancestors of their native lands and rid the nations of their tribal identity. Defendants' cry of "trust us" is offensive to the court and insulting to plaintiffs, who have heard that same message for over one hundred years.[3]

By 2002, the Bureau of Indian Affairs implemented reforms by reorganizing to meet the increasingly negative publicity generated by the Cobell lawsuit. Consequently, the Bureau of Indian Affairs split into three distinct agencies: the Bureau of Indian Affairs, the Bureau of Indian Education, and the Office of American Indian Trust, all remaining under the direction of the Department of Interior Assistant Secretary for Indian Affairs.

Gale Norton, Secretary of the Interior under President George W. Bush, proposed creating a new agency called the Office of Trust Assets Management. The new agency was to assume all functions related to the management of trust funds earned by tribes and individual Indians. The Bureau of Indian Affairs retained management of other Indian programs that served tribes such as law enforcement, general assistance, roads and transportation, and child and family services.

In 2006, the Bureau of Indian Affairs Education Agency was created to deal with all education services from schools to colleges formerly managed by the BIA. The Fort Peck Tribes and most other tribes strongly opposed the reorganization of the Bureau of Indian Affairs and testified many times to that effect. Most tribes felt that the federal government plans were a "defensive measure" against the Cobell lawsuit even though the DOI created a task force to consult tribes to propose alternatives. Government officials met with tribal representatives, mostly throughout the west in Bismarck, Phoenix, Rapid City, and Minneapolis, but little if anything was accomplished in terms of local tribal input about reorganizing the BIA. Fort Peck wanted the Office of the Special Trustee for American Indians (OST) and Office of Trust Fund Management (OTFM) abolished and the Regional Offices downsized. In January 2002, the TEB authorized their law firm, Sonosky, et

al., to file suit against Gale Norton, Secretary of Interior, and U.S. Treasury Secretary Paul O'Neill for an accounting of Fort Peck trust funds and related relief.[4] "The bottom line is that we do not support a plan that is designed to address the Department's litigation needs and not the needs of the Tribes," Arlyn Headdress testified on October 23, 2002. The Tribes' opposition had little effect on the reorganization, which became fully operational by 2006.[5]

Individual Indian trust accounts were not the only victims of mismanagement. The BIA also mishandled numerous tribal trust funds and non-monetary trust assets and resources. In January of 2002 the Fort Peck Tribes filed suit seeking an accounting of the Tribes' trust funds, assets and resources that the BIA had mismanaged for over decades. The Tribes sought an accurate accounting of their past and present funds and resources in their litigation against the government. No monetary amount was established at that time.[6] Other tribes throughout the country also filed their own individual suits seeking compensation for the government's mismanagement of their money and resources.

During the 1980s and early 1990s, the Fort Peck Tribes had created a reserve fund from the substantial oil revenue that accrued over those years. Eventually, oil revenue dropped off. The tribal government worked under a system that stipulated that the tribal budget could only be based upon the estimated revenue for the coming year and that at least that amount was to be maintained in the reserve fund. Over the years, the Tribes, through per capita payments and other program efforts, began to exhaust the reserved funds. In August 2002, budget deficits began to loom, as was reported by the tribal newspaper, the *Wotanin Wowapi*. Although the system had worked well for decades, the continual demand on tribal programs and funds was beginning to take a toll that would eventually lead to both a funding and a political crisis over the next two years.

In February 2001, members of the Sisseton-Wahpeton Sioux Council (SWSC) voted on and accepted a constitution and by-laws by a vote of 19-0. They elected Calvin First as the Chairman and Melissa Buckles as the Vice Chairman. Other officers included Del First, Secretary; Judy Fourstar, Treasurer; and Barbara Fast Horse, Mike Fast Horse, Pat Klotz, Iris Grey Bull, Agnes Ward, and Priscilla Chopper as District Representatives. This group established itself as descendants of the Sisseton-Wahpeton Dakotas. In the early 1860s, Dakota bands, including the Sisseton and Wahpeton bands living in Minnesota, were deprived of approximately 27 million acres of their land without adequate consideration. [See Chapter 3.] They eventually filed claims against the United States with the Indian Claims Commission. Soon a settlement was reached, and by congressional act in June 1968, funds to fulfill their obligations were appropriated.[7] By that time, many members of the Dakota bands that were affected had relocated to North and South Dakota, as well as to the Fort Peck Reservation in northeastern Montana. When the first settlement funds were dispersed in the early 1980s, the Tribal Executive Board of the Assiniboine and Sioux Tribes administered the funds, and per capita payments were made to thousands of Sisseton-Wahpeton enrolled at Fort Peck. Unfortunately, some of the per capita payments went to tribal members who were not Sisseton-Wahpeton or their lineal descendants. Due to that error, in 1998, Congress passed the Mississippi Sioux Tribes Judgment Fund Distribution Act that authorized a payment of $5 million, of which $740,000 (13 percent) went to the Sisseton-Wahpeton Sioux at Fort Peck.[8]

On April 12, 2004, the TEB passed a resolution 12-0 recognizing "the Sisseton-Wahpeton Sioux Council as the body authorized to con-duct formal business on behalf of the Sisseton-Wahpeton Sioux of [the] Fort Peck Reservation."[9] Also on that date at their own meeting, the SWSC passed a resolution to allow officers to set up an account in accordance with the BIA 1034 form that is required for dispersing federal monies. They also voted to look for the best interest-bearing account.[10]

Throughout 2004 and well into 2005, the SWSC went through a number of officer changes. In August 2005, the SWSC approved, by a vote of 14-6, purchasing Nemont Water Conditioning in Wolf Point for $300,000. A month later in their September 12, 2005 meeting, a motion was made by Donna Buckles-Whitmer to have appraisals done for Nemont and an additional building in Wolf Point that some Sisseton-Wahpeton members thought would be more feasible and a better investment. Four days later, various members of the SWSC filed a temporary restraining order in Tribal Court to prevent officers from purchasing Nemont Water until the appraisal was complete. The next day, the SWSC officers filed a motion to dismiss.[11] The SWSC had a meeting in October 2005, at which they selected a new secretary and treasurer. Helen Ricker was selected as secretary and Myrna First was voted in as treasurer, while Calvin "Bear" First was still Chairman. Also at the meeting, then-BIA Superintendant Spike Bighorn, who was a former Assiniboine and Sioux Tribal Chairman (1997-1999), told the SWSC that in early October 2004, the Office of Special Trustee (OST) in Albuquerque contacted him about obtaining an account to deposit Sisseton-Wahpeton judgment funds in. During the meeting, the SWSC also voted to request in writing a letter from OST indicating that all claims money would go directly to the SWSC and not the Fort Peck Tribes.[12]

Meanwhile, the TEB put a freeze on SWSC funds deposited in the 1st Community Bank in Wolf Point and went on record recognizing

Melissa Buckles as Chairman, Vermae Taylor as Vice Chair, Midge Clancy as Secretary, and Delphine Lamae as Treasurer of SWSC. Calvin "Bear" First, Jr. and Linda Comes Last, former SWSC officers, were respondents in a tribal court case in which a temporary restraining order was petitioned by Donna Buckles-Whitmer, Iris Grey Bull, Vermae Taylor, Midge Clancy, Vivian Jones, and Laverne Jones. The court dismissed the order and newly elected officers. Calvin "Bear" First, Myrna First, and Linda Comes Last were reaffirmed in their positions.[13]

On Saturday, December 9, 2006, the Nemont Water business that the SWSC officers had purchased burned to the ground; arson was suspected. The tribal authorities eventually charged a Wolf Point man, Karsen Wayne Bushman, who pled guilty and was sentenced to five years in prison.[14] It seemed that since its inception and the acquiring of the $740,000 in settlement funds, the SWSC sailed in troubled waters, mostly brought on by the original SWSC officers and their handling of the SWS people's money. The problems with the SWSC grew so dire that the TEB met in early 2007 to discuss them. Also present at that meeting was then-BIA Superintendant Toni Greybull. She told the TEB that the only tribal resolution the BIA recognized was from April 2004 (TEB Resolution #481-2002-04), which recognized as SWSC Chair Calvin "Bear" First (Myrna First is his mother) and Vice Chair Melissa Buckles, Del First as secretary, and Judy Fourstar as treasurer. In confusion, then-SWSC Chair Agnes Ward and Treasurer Linda Comes Last stated that Spike Bighorn, BIA Superintendant in 2005, had recognized them. In the interim, Vice Chair Buckles was removed and Agnes Ward was appointed to his seat. Also, Calvin "Bear" First resigned after SWSC officers awarded him $25,000 for his work in researching the SWS claim. Delwayne First accepted that position, but also resigned, which was how Agnes

Ward moved into the chair position.[15] What emerged from the tribal court proceedings and the inner quarrelling and dissention among the members of the SWSC was two factions: The Firsts, Ward, Comes Last, and others fought against Buckles-Whitmer, David Boyd, Clancy, and others for control of the SWSC. That spring, new SWSC officers were elected (Sunday, March 4, 2007) by eighty members present at a meeting in the Poplar Cultural Center (a total of 3,800 SWS members are enrolled members of the Fort Peck Tribes). In that election, David Boyd was elected Chairman. The new Treasurer was Jewel Hannah and Midge Clancy was elected as Secretary, while Donna Buckles-Whitmer won the Vice Chair position.[16]

Again the Firsts, Ward, and Comes Last faction fought that election. On March 8, 2007, they filed suit in Judge Sam Haddon's Federal District Court in Great Falls against TEB Chairman John Morales and Acting BIA Superintendent Toni Greybull to show cause why they sanctioned and recognized a new election for the SWSC. Billings attorney Tom Towe was retained and paid with SWSC funds. The court lacked jurisdiction, and the case was sent back to tribal court.[17]

After the tribal court received the remand, the TEB voted 9-2 that new elections were to be held in thirty days and the current SWSC officers as of 2/12/07 were not legal: Agnes Ward, Myrna First, and Linda Comes Last.[18] In a move to stop the four current SWSC officers from conducting business on behalf of the SWSC and Nemont Water Company, Tribal Chief Judge Richard Jackson granted a temporary restraining order. More than $687,000 in Mississippi Sioux (SWS) judgment money was released, Nemont Water Company was purchased, and over $380,000 was invested in LPL Financial Services in Glasgow Gary Wageman. Later, Judge Jackson had SWSC officers Agnes Ward and Linda Comes Last arrested for violation of the temporary restraining order because of seven withdrawals totaling $178,691.42 from an account at First Community Bank in Wolf Point.[19]

Again in April 2007, the SWSC held a meeting, and again, new board members were elected. They also voted to put SWSC under a steering committee of the Sioux General Council. Meanwhile, Nemont Water received an insurance check for $202,000, and nobody seemed to know who was in control of the SWS finances. On April 13, the SWSC voted to shut down Nemont Water and fire the manager. Soon after that action, the ousted SWSC officers(Ward, First, and Comes Last) filed federal racketeering charges against the current SWSC officers (Boyd, Buckles-Whitmer, Clancy, et. al.), the board of directors of Nemont Water, and a majority of the TEB.[20] The SWSC officers who had been removed still claimed they were the legal officers of the SWSC. As a result, they gave a local Indian construction company from Poplar the bid to rebuild Nemont Water in Wolf Point. Despite the election and temporary restraining order, they were still conducting business on behalf of the SWSC.

By the beginning of 2008, the TEB and the Tribal Court System started to mediate with the two factions of the SWSC and eventually let the matter play out in Tribal Court. The case finally found itself in the Fort Peck Court of Appeals in which the Appellate Judges reversed a 2007 lower court decision that gave authority to the TEB to call for a new election of the SWSC. The Fort Peck Appellate Court declared the March 2007 officers invalid and gave the SWSC the authority to call for new elections, not the TEB. They reversed Judge Jackson's earlier ruling and allowed for the return of the former officers, Myrna First, Linda Comes Last, Agnes Ward, and Gina Bearfighter.[21] The court ruled that the SWSC has "powers beyond that of a claims council and that the SWSC is authorized to determine election matters."[22] That ruling seemed to take the steam out of those SWSC members who had been fighting for a more transparent process for the financial and business dealing of the SWSC officers. So far, the Tribal Appellate Court ruling stands, leaving the SWC people with no money, a building in Wolf Point that cannot be appraised because it is not up to current building standards, outstanding tax and attorney bills, and a future that looks rather ominous.

Although the first few years of the new millennium seemed daunting for the Fort Peck Tribes, the region looked to the oil industry as one of the brightest economic paths for future. However, there remained another side of the oil industry that proved less helpful. Since the early 1950s, oil exploration and drilling, coupled with increased use of pesticides and herbicides by reservation farmers, continually contaminated local groundwater, springs, streams, and the water table. In 1992, the TEB passed a resolution to support efforts to get good drinking water to each reservation community. Headed by then-TEB member Caleb Shields, what was to become the Assiniboine and Sioux Rural Water Supply System (ASRWSS) began lobbying Congress for a water pipeline project that would bring fresh drinking water to the Fort Peck Reservation. The project eventually joined efforts with the Dry Prairie Rural Water System, a similar water pipeline system created to serve off-reservation communities that had drinking water problems. Together, these two systems comprised a regional project called the Fort Peck Reservation Rural Water System and eventually shared common facilities, including the intake plant (located southwest of Wolf Point near where the Lewis & Clark Bridge crosses the Missouri River) and water treatment plant (located six miles east of Wolf Point just north of U.S. Highway 2). The Fort Peck Tribes operate the tribal system, and the DOI will hold the system in trust for the tribes. Eventually, the system will treat 13 million gallons of water per day and pump that water through 3,200 miles of pipeline by twenty mainline pump stations for over 30,000 people on and off the reservation.[23] That water usage by both reservation and non-reservation communities is part of the Fort Peck Tribes' allocation of one million acre feet of water per year under the 1985 Water Compact signed with the state of Montana.[24]

In March 2002, Congress approved $175 million for the A&S Rural Water Supply System and $51 million for the Dry Prairie Water System. In 2003, the tribe broke ground for the system. The intake plant was the first phase and was finished in 2005. The next phase was the water treatment plant and lagoon, started in 2005 and scheduled to be finished sometime in 2012. Funds from the American Recovery and Reinvestment Act of 2009 were used to complete the first phase of the water treatment plant, and they are also being used for the second phase as well as for the water pipeline between Wolf Point and Poplar.[25]

In the fall of 2003, four candidates filed for the office of Tribal Chairman: Arlyn Headdress, the incumbent; John Morales, who had nearly beaten Headdress in 2001; Leland Spotted Bird, a sitting Tribal Council member; and Thomas (Stoney) Anketell, an oil and gas specialist for the BIA and a former council member. In the late October election, John Morales won the election with 862 votes, beating his closest rival, incumbent Arlyn Headdress, by 272 votes. In addition to Morales, Ray Eder won Vice Chair; George Ricker, Sr. became Sergeant-at-arms; and council members elected were Bill Whitehead, Frank Smith, Eric Bruguier, Leonard Crowbelt, Walter Clark, Robert Welch, Tom Christian, Merle Peterson, A. T. Stafne, Rick Kirn, Sharon Red Thunder, and Abe Chopper, who was elected in a special election on December 1, 2003. The election brought

five new members to the council, representing a massive shift from previous elections that had almost invariably re-elected incumbents.[26]

The new Tribal Chairman was an affable young man of thirty-five who had previously sat on the council from 1995-1999. He had run for chair two previous times, in 1999 and 2001. He had been a popular athlete in basketball and boxing, and he represented new young leadership that promised to represent the people.

Chairman Morales' first term started out with a major disagreement between the chair and the council. On November 21, 2003, the chairman suspended three tribal employees "pending an investigation." The employees were Raymond (Abby) Ogle, economic development officer; Henry Headdress, transportation planner; and Denver Atkinson, who was the director of the Tribal Employment Rights Office (TERO). The council at the next regular board meeting objected, saying that the personnel policies had not been followed. The meeting degenerated because the chair refused to recognize motions to stop the suspensions. It was clear to the council that the chairman had the constitutional authority to suspend employees. However, since the council had by resolution adopted personnel policies and procedures, clearly the chairman was required to follow policy. Even more confusing was his refusal to recognize motions on the floor. The constitution required that the Executive Board Meetings be conducted using Roberts Rules of Order. The board had never, however, established a parliamentarian to adjudicate issues and had only loosely followed the rules. This meeting set the tone for many meetings to come, with the chairman in opposition to the council.[27]

On March 2, 2003, Chairman Morales terminated the three employees who had been suspended in November after an investigative report was completed with the assistance of the Dorsey and Whitney law firm.[28]

In the meantime, the Fort Peck Tribes continued to operate under severe budget restraints. The tribes had been in negotiations with the Northern Border Pipeline Company for some time to renew the lease/easement agreement that the tribes had signed initially in 1980 for thirty-three miles of pipeline access on the Fort Peck Reservation. The tribal council had passed a resolution on February 23, 2004, that would have given the tribes $7.4 million dollars for an agreement with Northern Border Pipeline.

At a special Tribal Executive Board Meeting on April 5, 2004, Chairman Morales publicly stated that he refused to sign the agreement. He qualified his refusal by saying that this issue needed wider exposure to the tribal members and should perhaps be considered at a General Council.

The Tribal Council as a whole disagreed. The financial strain on the tribes had started to be felt throughout the programs, and there was a substantial need to raise additional revenue. In addition, Tribal Council members felt that the chairman was constitutionally bound to follow their directives. In the April 5 meeting, Councilman Rick Kirn, who had been on the Northern Border Negotiation team during the last term, said, "we shouldn't allow the Chairman to do this, when this body speaks and writes resolutions, you [Chairman Morales] have a duty to follow through. We gave you direction and you refused. Once we speak, it should be adhered to."[29]

On April 14, Chairman Morales announce that he was preparing for a General Council to make the decision on whether he should sign the agreement with Northern Border Pipeline. "If I have to personally walk across the reservation carrying the agreement to show its flaws, I will," Morales told the tribal newspaper, the *Wotanin Wowapi*.[30] Again, the underlying concern for the Tribal Council was a shortfall in revenue for the tribal budget. Tribal councilman Eric Brugier

stated that "the tribes may not be able to meet a $7.9 million budget for next year on just the reoccurring income, which means that jobs will have to be cut." It was felt that from a practical standpoint, there was not enough time or money to renegotiate a new agreement with Northern Border Pipelines.[31]

General Councils were viewed by most Tribal members as an anathema in the period prior to the passage of the 1960 constitution. When opposing sides lost a political fight, they would call for a General Council in a venue other than a regular election to overturn their political enemies. Often there would be verbally dueling General Councils with more than one group "officially" representing the Fort Peck Tribes. The new constitution in 1960 dealt specifically with the problem of General Councils. Article IV-Governing Body, Section 1 states,

The governing body of the Tribes shall be known as the Tribal Executive Board subject to the powers of the General council. A General Council may initiate ordinances or reject with ninety (90) days any enactment of the Executive Board. Upon petition of at least ten (10%) of the eligible voters of the Tribes, a General Council shall be called by the chairman at a place within the Fort Peck Reservation designated in the petition; a quorum shall consist of one hundred (100) eligible voters of the Tribes. A stenographic transcript shall be kept of all proceedings of the General Council.[32]

This provision spelled out clearly the manner in which the General Council could be called and limited the powers of such a council to initiation of ordinances or the rejection of Tribal Executive Board action. The requirement for a petition signed by 10 percent of the eligible voters that spelled out the specific action to be taken was a formidable hurdle. Many petitions were initiated between 1960 and 2004. In most cases, the petitions were denied because of the number of signatures, invalid signatures, or the petition did not clearly spell out the ordinance to be initiated or the Tribal Executive Board action to be rejected. There was only one instance in which a legitimate General Council was petitioned for and held. This occurred in 1990 when then-Chairman Caleb Shields received a petition for a General Council.

The General Council was held on January 8, 1990. The only item on the petition was an additional $127 per capita payment. Of the people attending, 285 voted for a per capita payment and twenty-seven voted against it. The petition had been initiated because people were upset that the tribal council had voted to raise their salaries.[33]

Chairman Shield officially reported the results of the General Council to the Tribal Executive Board on January 24. The Tribal Executive Board rejected the recommendation of the General Council, stating that the financial condition of the Tribes made a per capita payment unfeasible.

On May 10, 2004, Chairman Morales again refused to recognize motions brought to the floor by Rick Kirn, the chair of the Minerals Committee. The motions involved Larry Monson, the Tribal Geologist who had been furloughed. Chairman Morales had taken action against Munson without following procedures. Kirn stated, "I'm ready to write up charges to see you [Chairman Morales] removed." The discussion continued for some time about the powers of the chair, the Tribal Executive Board, and the General Council.[34]

On Monday, May 24, Rick Kirn presented a written statement of charges against Chairman Morales, who was then suspended from office by the Tribal Executive Board by a vote of 10-1. The charges were that the chairman had failed to carry out three duly authorized resolutions, which was a violation of his constitutional duties. The TEB barred Morales from the Tribal Office,

locked his office, and set a hearing date (which was the second step of the removal process) for Monday, June 14, 2008.[35]

Morales, speaking at a meeting of supporters on Tuesday night, declared that he was still the tribal chairman and called for a General Council. The chairman detailed his actions to the audience that had led him to his removal. He said that the actions needed to be settled in a General Council, which would truly show the wishes of the people.

On Sunday, June 13, a meeting that was called a General Council was held at the Poplar Legion Park Arbor. However, a petition establishing the legality of the General Council had not presented to the acting tribal chairman, Ray K. Eder. Suspended Chairman Morales stated the he was still chairman and he had accepted the petition.

Nearly 600 people attended the meeting at the Poplar Arbor. The tribal newspaper articles from June 10, 2004, stated that the "General Council was not legal, and so many of those attending were people who had supported the Chairman during the election."[36] Morales presented several motions: to remove the ten council members who had suspended him; to not sign the Northern Border Pipeline agreement; to uphold personnel actions and terminate the legal contract with the Sonosky and Chambers law firm in Washington, D.C. Of the 600 people, 484 registered to vote. All agenda items passed unanimously. For a majority of tribal members, the "General Council" was considered more or less a political rally outside the correct legal context.

On June 14, the hearing on the suspension and removal of Chairman Morales was held at the tribal building in Poplar. Due to limited seating, the audience was seated by invitation only. Rumors of a possible riot at the meeting prompted a tense security check. Police officers screened people coming into the meeting, and loudspeakers were set up outside the building for those who could not be seated inside. Chairman Morales arrived with legal counsel Leighton Reum and an associate, Lanny Diserly.

After the meeting was called to order by Vice Chairman Ray K. Eder, a prayer was said and the Council recited the Pledge of Allegiance. According to the minutes, Morales and his legal counsel requested the meeting be considered a TEB committee meeting rather than a full TEB meeting. Vice Chairman Eder denied the request and Reid Chambers of the Sonosky law firm was recognized to present the factual evidence that was relevant to the charges against Morales. Three charges were brought against the Chairman and presented to the TEB on May 24th by Councilman Rick Kirn. They all centered around Morales' refusal to carry out duly authorized resolutions passed by the TEB: 1) refusal to sign the Northern Border Pipeline Agreement; 2) refusal to follow personnel policies and procedures by a duly authorized TEB resolution , which provide for a fair and equitable supervision of tribal employees; and 3) the Chairman's use of unauthorized legal counsel [that] resulted in release of personal confidential information relating to the employees and tribes. As Chambers outlined each charge, he was interrupted several times by Morales and his legal counsel, who after a number of attempts to ask questions expressed that they would not participate any longer in the proceedings. Morales and his legal counsel then left the meeting. Chambers eventually completed his presentation and the TEB call for a vote. A vote to remove the Chairman was then held. Eleven members voted yes, with Marvin Youpee being the lone dissenter.[37]

John Morales did not accept his removal. He immediately wrote letters to Bureau of Indian Affairs officials at the local, regional, and central office levels. He also wrote to the tribal secretary-accountant demanding that the council members removed by the "General Council" be notified. There were no affirmative responses to Morales' challenge.

On June 17, 2004, after Ray Eder automatically replaced John Morales as Chairman, Roxanne Gourneau as the person who had won the second number of highest votes was sworn in as Tribal Vice-Chairperson. Gourneau was the first female vice-chairperson in the Tribes' history.

During the week of July 15, another "General Council" was held at the arbor in the Poplar Legion Park. About 300 people attended, and 212 voted unanimously to reverse the actions of the tribal council. Morales insisted that the power of legality of General Councils was being misinterpreted by the Executive Board.[38]

In early August, the Executive Board signed the Northern Border Pipeline agreement. The agreement granted NBP the option to lease easement for its pipeline from 2011-2061. The tribes obtained a rental rate of $1,500,000 per year. NBP also agreed to pay the tribal utility tax and increase rates if the pipeline was expanded. Obviously, this agreement, because of a signing bonus, bailed the tribes out of their extremely tight fiscal position.

In late August, the three employees suspended and then terminated by John Morales were reinstated with back pay.

The November general election saw an unprecedented number of Montana Tribal members elected to the Montana State legislature. Locally, Margaret Campbell was elected to the House of Representatives, and Frank Smith was elected as a senator. Jonathan Windy Boy, a tribal member from Rock Boy, was elected to represent House District 32, which covers Valley County and part of the Fort Peck Reservation. In total, eight tribal members statewide were elected to the legislature.

Throughout the spring of 2005, the Tribal Executive Board held six hearings across the reservation on constitutional amendments the board was proposing. The amendments sought to create primary elections and extend terms of office to four-year, staggered terms. The hearings were lightly attended with minimal comments from the tribal electorate. On June 4, a special election to consider the amendments was held. Again, voter turnout was low, with only 23% of eligible voters going to the polls, and the constitutional changes were soundly defeated. Many people thought that the measures were self-serving ways of benefiting incumbents to the Tribal Executive Board.[39]

At the end of October 2005, John Morales was again elected as tribal chairman, defeating three-term councilman Tom Christian. Roxanne Gourneau was elected Vice Chairperson. Roxann Bighorn, Floyd Azure, Marvin Youpee, Arlyn Headdress, A.T. Stafne, Leonard Crow Belt, Abe Chopper, Thomas (Stoney) Anketell, Ray Eder, Frank Smith, Walter Clark, and Darryl Red Eagle were elected to the council, and George Ricker, Sr. was re-elected as Sergeant of Arms.[40]

The week after the election, on November 4, Chairman Morales fired, for the second time, Denver Atkinson, the director of the Tribal Employment Rights Office. Reactions to the dismissal were muted compared to the first suspension and termination. This was due in part because Atkinson was a non-tribal member married to a tribal member. The recent election had also signaled support for Chairman Morales and his previous actions.

On November 17, 2006, the *Wotanin Wowapi* reported the resignation of Leonard Smith, the CEO of A&S Tribal Industries.[41] The industries had been struggling for over a year. Successful government contracting had kept the company profitable during the first five years of the new millennium. However, government purchasing policies were increasingly erratic. The government would offer initial contracts to minority firms but then fail to sustain them over the

years. A&S Tribal Industries had suffered from a similar scenario after Operation Desert Storm, the first Gulf War. Efforts to manufacture for the private sector had little success. CEO Smith had tried approaching the problem with a multi-pronged effort by creating small 8-A eligible businesses. However, eventually cash flows dried up, and A&S became more or less defunct for the remainder of the decade.

West Electronics and its sister company, Fort Peck Technologies, were able to maintain much more stability throughout the decade. Although these companies did not require as large a workforce as A&S Tribal Industries had during its heyday, they were able to provide relatively stable employment for between fifty and 100 employees.[42]

During July 2006, Chairman Morales began to prepare a petition to hold a General Council. The petition called for action to three topics. The first was adoption of a Code of Ethics ordinance for the Tribal Executive Board. A second ordinance was to adopt certain amendments to the land-use policy. The third and most controversial action involved the seating of Richard Kirn on the Tribal Executive Board. Kirn had not been elected in the 2005 election but had received the thirteenth highest number of votes for the twelve executive board positions. Earlier in that year, A.T. Stafne had resigned from the executive board due to illness. Approved constitutional amendment #7(e) states: If any other seat becomes vacant it shall be automatically filled by the person receiving the next highest number of cumulative legal votes from all districts in the previous election.[43]

Rick Kirn should have been automatically seated after the Stafne resignation. However, Kirn had made the motions to suspend and ultimately remove Chairman Morales from office. The chairman and his supports did not want to see Kirn on the Executive Board and so chose to take the matter to a "General Council."

On August 27, 2006, an assembly was convened by the Tribal Chairman, John Morales, at the arbor in the Poplar Legion Park. Although it was described as a duly called council, documentation that the petition was legal was never submitted. Approximately 750 tribal members attended, of which 631 were registered to vote. Most of those attending the "General Councils" held previously by Chairman Morales were his political supporters. At this General Council, a much wider variety of people representing different points of view from across the reservation attended. All three motions presented to the people were defeated. Chairman Morales graciously accepted the results and congratulated Kirn on his coming appointment to the Executive board.[44]

Rick Kirn was seated on the Tribal Executive Board, and tribal government continued to be a constant struggle between the chairman and members of the board until the next election in 2007. The situation, however, did not deteriorate as it had in 2004.

The political turmoil that plagued the mid-decade overshadowed a severe but almost silent health crisis. Since the creation of the Indian reservations and written treaties, agreements, and executive orders, the health care of Indians has continually been in decline in terms of money and adequate personnel and facilities. In May 2003, the Department of Health and Human Services took over the Indian Health Service (IHS), which was established in 1955 after the BIA discontinued its direct support of health services. During the last three decades, health care on the Fort Peck Indian Reservation witnessed some improvements with the construction of two new health clinics. (See Chapter 14.) However, the Assiniboine and Sioux, as well as tribal members from other tribes who were residing on the reservation for one reason or another, experienced a system of health care

delivered by IHS, a division of PHS. Patients had been plagued by long waits, were seen by doctors who knew little of their health histories or the patients themselves, and experienced lack of access to medicine and treatment. There were many horror stories that involved misdiagnosis of illness and even non-treatment. Of course, many of those problems stemmed from the Fort Peck Reservation not having enough contract money to service tribal needs. Throughout the first decade of the new century, the IHS service at Fort Peck remained at a Level 12, which gave only the highest priority cases referrals for specialized treatment elsewhere.[45] This "life or limb" policy created a major rift between administrators, doctors, and staff employed by the IHS and tribal patients. Those patients in turn approached their tribal elected officials, sent protest letters to the Area Office, and voiced their concerns in public forums. The situation became so dreadful that the Fort Peck Tribal Executive Board declared a health crisis and contracted Dr. Kermit Smith, an enrolled Assiniboine from Wolf Point, to compile a report on the state of health care on the Fort Peck Indian Reservation. Smith reported that it would take ten to fifteen years to recuperate from the shortage of health-care providers and improve services.[46] By mid-decade, Congress was providing $3,800 to $3,900 per Indian for health-care services nationally. The Fort Peck clinics were only funded at 62 percent of their actual need. Regional IHS Director Pete Conway met with the TEB and in a heated question and answer session, five critical areas of health care were addressed: the placing of patients at higher risk due to the lack of doctors; the failure of IHS to fill vacant doctor positions; the need for patient transportation; the lack of facility renovations; and the need for efficient evaluation of the service to unite as a whole.[47] The IHS continued to be plagued by multiple problems. Budgets continued to be cut, personnel problems remained the primary concern, and facilities were not upgraded, leaving the tribal people in a continual health crisis.

In 1970, a Vista worker named Ed Broadus and local volunteers started a small news flyer. It was mimeographed and given away free throughout the communities. In 1972, it officially became the *Wotanin Wowapi* and soon served as the official newspaper of the Fort Peck Assiniboine and Sioux Tribes. The payroll was funded by the tribal government and advertising. The matters of open journalistic standards and freedom of the press were never really accepted by the Tribal Executive Board. When articles critical of the TEB or tribal initiatives were published, the TEB would periodically call the editors into the council and read them the riot act. Eventually, Terry Boyd, the first editor of the paper, moved on and Bonnie Clincher, who had worked in advertising, became the editor. Although political interference with news reporting continued throughout the years, it was mostly on a verbal grumbling level, and the *Wotanin Wowapi* operated as a free newspaper that was financially supported by the Fort Peck Tribes. This changed dramatically on March 28, 2006, when Chairman John Morales fired Clincher and had the office of the newspaper locked.[48]

Chairman Morales appointed Iris Allrunner and Lois Red Elk interim editors of the paper. The chairman cited several violations of policies for the firing. However, Clincher asserted that the chairman had warned her when she questioned the legitimacy of his travel to Florida, which was where his family lived.

The firing did not deter Clincher. Within a week, she, with the help of Richard Peterson, had started an independent newspaper, *The Fort Peck Journal*. The newspaper was successful from the publication of the first issue and continues to this day as an independent newspaper. In July 2007, Clincher received the Native American Journalism Association's highest honor, the Wassaja Award, which recognizes Indian journalists "who stand firm in their beliefs that tribal governments and leaders should not influence tribal newspapers."[49]

The original tribal newspaper, the *Wotanin Wowapi*, did not fare as well. Readership declined over the next several months due to its lack of independence, and the paper went out of circulation in January 2008 due to its inability to become self-sufficient.

In October 2007, A.T. (Rusty) Stafne was elected chairman of the Fort Peck Tribal Executive board, defeating incumbent John Morales by 301 votes. Garrett Big Leggins was elected Vice-Chair and John Weeks, Sergeant-at-arms. Council members elected were Rick Kirn, Arlyn Headdress, Bill Whitehead, Abe Chopper, Gene Culbertson, Tom Christian, Donna Buckles-Whitmer, Floyd Azure, Darryl Red Eagle, Louis Peterson, Ingrid Firemoon, and Peter Dupree.[50]

On December 10, 2007, the Tribal Executive Board voted to have a constitutional convention to examine the Tribes' constitution. Draft rules for the constitution were developed by Fort Peck Community College. The convention was set for July 8-10, 2008, with seventy-four members selected at large from each community, the Assiniboine and Sioux councils, and members of the TEB, who were allowed to appoint one additional member.[51]

This constitutional convention was organized in three sections: executive, legislative, and judicial. Chairman Stafne appointed Dr. James Shanley to lead the executive section; Charles Trinder to lead the legislative section; and Robert McAnally to lead the judicial section. Proposed changes were submitted to the convention by the community prior to the actual meeting.

Chairman A.T. Stafne selected as delegate John Pipe, former councilman; Vice-Chair Garrett

Big Leggins named Reese Reddoor; Sergeant-at-arms John Weeks named Coy Weeks, his nephew, with Ashley Dupree as alternate. Among the council members, Gene Culbertson named Ray Jean Belgarde; Donna Buckles Whitmer named Gary Braine; Floyd Azure named former chairman John Morales; Pete Dupree named Robert Daniels; Darryl Red Eagle named former councilman Marvin Youpee with Howard Azure as alternates; Louse Peterson named Keith Red Elk; Abe Chopper named Herman Red Elk, with Marlon Red Elk as alternate; Ingrid Firemoon named Melissa Buckles; Rick Kirn named Kim Murray with Davetta Marchant, his mother; Bill Whitehead named attorney Pat Smith and Caleb Shields, former councilman and chairman, respectively, as alternates; Tom Christian named Robert McAnally; and Arlyn Headdress named Mickey McAnally.

Delegates from the community organizations in Brockton included Russell Kirn, Brockton Community Organization chairman, and Kermit Boyd, community member. In Wolf Point, Darlene Archdale and George Redstone, Indian Landowners Association; Larry Wetsit, Nemont Telephone; court administrator Rita Weeks; and Colleen Clark were chosen. In Oswego, Edward G. Bauer, Russell White, with alternates Patti Stump and James MacDonald were selected. In Frazer, the delegates were Dori Talks Different, Jewel Ackerman, and Dean Blount. In Poplar, David Mathison, Delton Brown, Conrad Scott, Sharon Red Thunder (all PCO officers), and Bonnie Red Elk, with Marvin Youpee as alternate, were chosen.

From the Sioux council, delegates were Helen Youpee Ricker, Debbie Johnson, Kim Johnson, Benjamin Wise Spirit, Ann Bushman, Iris Grey Bull, Dave F. Boyd Sr., Helen Belcher, Catherine Spotted Bird, Midge Clancy, Melvin Scott, III, June Clark, Hazel Cantrell, Tara Longtree, and Coleen Birdsbill. Delegates from the Assiniboine Council were Perry Lilley, Ron Moccasin, Dana Runs Above, Donna Anheman, Lyle Denny, Nadine Adams, Ron Jackson, Dr. Jim Shanley, Joan Blount, Phillip Smoker, Horace Pipe Sr., Cleo Hamilton, Chuck Trinder, Ron Dumont, and Lynette Clark, with alternates Patty Pipe, John Doney Jr., Sydney Campbell, and Florence Buck.[52]

The convention produced many proposed changes ranging from changing the name of the Fort Peck Assiniboine and Sioux Tribes to Nakota and Dakota Nations to establishing a nonrenewable resource trust fund. The convention met again on July 22 to sort out the proposals and actually produce amendments. After the session on July 22, there still remained work to complete and a legal review.

The Tribes hired the Sonosky law firm to conduct a legal review, which revealed several flaws in the proposed amendments. In general, the attorneys did not favor sweeping changes of the constitution. It was felt that the 1960s document, although unclear in some areas, had served the tribes well. They suggested that before many portions were presented to the public, there should be an extensive rewriting effort.

The general constitutional amendments that ended up being submitted to the voters at the tribal election in October, 2009 included establishing primary elections, adding a bill of rights, establishing a judicial branch of government, creating an open meeting and information provision, establishing budget restraints and a trust fund, and many minor language revisions.

The amendments were forwarded to the Tribal Executive Board and were placed on the fall ballot in 2009 in their entirety. The proposed constitutional amendments failed during the fall election by a vote of 683 for and 926 against. The comments of many voters indicated that they supported some of the amendments, but not all. The entire package was complicated because people were having to make choices at the ballot box.[53]

In November 2008, Barack Obama was elected the President of the United States. Obama had been supported by the Fort Peck Tribal Executive Board and, as a man of color, was widely supported by tribal members. Obama had campaigned on a strong platform to help American Indians. However, the new president came into office facing the worst financial problems that the United States had faced since the Great Depression. In addition, the U.S. was still engaged in wars in both Iraq and Afghanistan.

During the Montana 2009 biennial legislative session, third-term representative Margaret Campbell became the house majority leader. She had served as the minority whip during the 2007 session. Campbell, a Fort Peck tribal member, was the first American Indian to serve as the majority leader in the house for the Montana legislature.

In the October 2009 tribal election, incumbent chairman A.T. (Rusty) Stafne narrowly beat Councilman Floyd Azure by a vote of 730 to 695 votes. Along with Stafne, the following won election: Roxann Bighorn, Vice Chairperson; John Weeks, Sergeant-at-Arms, Tom Christian, Councilman; Darryl Red Eagle, Councilman; Stoney Anketell, Councilman; Donna Buckles-Whitmer, Councilwoman; Eugene Culbertson, Councilman; Peter Dupree, Councilman; Leonard (Bighorn) Crowbelt, Councilman; Charles Headdress, Councilman; Robert Welch, Councilman; Dale DeCoteau, Councilman; Tony Shields, Councilman; and Frank Smith, Councilman.[54]

The last year of the first decade of the new millennium saw a generally improving picture on the Fort Peck reservation. Stimulus money from the Obama administration began to flow to various tribal programs, particularly tribal roads. A new $13 million jail had been approved, and groundbreaking had taken place. Work continued on expanding the Fort Peck Water System, and Fort Peck Community College began work on a Tribal library and technology center. State road construction and other projects also began in the area.

In July 2009, six employees were fired by the Bureau of Indian Affairs, Fort Peck Agency, after a local review and an inspector general auditor found that more than $1.6 million had been embezzled from the Tribal Credit Program. As the investigations continued, a total of twelve people were eventually indicted, including Florence White Eagle, the superintendent of the Fort Peck Agency. The scheme was implemented by the BIA's administrative officer, Tony Greybull, who passed away prior to the audit.[55]

This theft was ironic because it came right on the heels of settlement of the Cobell lawsuit, which had criticized the Bureau of Indian Affairs' management of Tribal monies. Although those charged with theft were Bureau of Indian Affairs employees, they were all Fort Peck tribal members.[56]

By 2010, Fort Peck Community College had grown significantly in enrollment and infrastructure. In its first official semester, FPCC enrolled sixty-five students, compared with 2010's current enrollment average of 450 students per semester, a growth of 592% in thirty-three years. Also, the number of programs offered at FPCC has increased substantially.

In 1981, FPCC offered four Associate of Arts Degrees, five Associate of Applied Science Degrees, and five certificate programs. Currently, FPCC offers six Associate of Arts Degrees, five Associate of Science Degrees, four Associate of Applied Science Degrees, and ten certificate programs. FPCC has grown from offering courses in borrowed space only in Poplar to a full-fledged campus offering courses in Poplar, Wolf Point, and Glasgow, in over twenty new and renovated buildings that include a certified daycare center, library, bookstore, dormitories, and faculty housing.

Other notable successes are FPCC's dedication to the promotion and support of distance education programs that allow FPCC graduates to attain bachelor's and master's degrees in business and education onsite without encountering the barriers they would otherwise have to overcome if they had to relocate. Since the first articulation agreement with MSU-Northern and Rocky Mountain College and through current articulation agreements with MSU-Billings and the University of Mary, FPCC has provided the means for sixty-two students to complete a bachelor's degree in business administration, applied management, and business technology, and twenty-two students have attained master's degrees in business administration. In addition, FPCC has proudly provided the means for ninety-four students to attain a degree in elementary education as well as sixteen master's degrees in education and special education endorsements via distance learning. Most of those graduates are currently teaching in schools on the Fort Peck Assiniboine and Sioux Reservation. As is the true nature of community colleges, most FPCC graduates, including those with bachelor's and master's degrees, are highly sought after and currently employed by the local tribe, Indian Health Service, Bureau of Indian Affairs, FPCC, and other local businesses.

In the 1950s, an oil formation was identified in the Williston Basin and named the Bakken Formation. The formation extends over northwestern North Dakota, northeastern Montana, and into Saskatchewan, Canada. Oil was actually struck in 2000 at the Elm Coulee Oil Field, which was located south of the Fort Peck Reservation across the Missouri River. Discoveries in North Dakota coupled with an oil drilling tax break moved most activity to North Dakota. The estimates for the Bakken Field at the time were over 200 billion barrels of oil with recoverable oil now estimated at 24 billion barrels. In addition,

the United States Geological Survey (USGS) estimates that there could be 1.85 trillion cubic feet of natural gas as well as 148 million barrels of natural gas liquids in the Bakken.

This oil field continues to generate higher and higher production estimates. The drilling for oil involves new technologies called diagonal drilling that couples with hydro rock fracturing techniques.

Obviously, the latest boom creeping closer and closer to the Fort Peck reservation has tremendous future implications. The eastern area of Roosevelt County has already experienced a large influx of people working in the Bakken.

After almost twenty years of litigation on the Cobell case, President Obama signed legislation approving the settlement and authorizing $3.4 billion in funds on December 8, 2010, stating that the historic settlement "marks another important step forward in the relationship between the federal government and Indian country."[57] A few weeks later, the United States District Court for the District of Columbia granted preliminary approval to the final settlement. This will be the largest government pay-out in this type of class action suit. The settlement approves $1.5 billion to be divided among some 300,000-plus Indians who have an Individual Indian Money (IIM) Accounts with the BIA. The BIA will get $1.9 billion to start a new program of buying back and consolidating tribal land that is encumbered by the fractionation phenomenon that exists within millions of tribal acres. Lastly, a $60 million scholarship fund will be set up for Indian students. One of the main problems in the settlement was the amount of money the Indian plaintiffs' lawyers would receive. The lawyers wanted more that $233 million, while the Obama administration claimed they should get no more than $50 million. U.S. District Judge Thomas Hogan awarded them $99 million, while most Indian plaintiffs will receive $1,500.[58]

Back in 2002, in reaction to the Cobell case, the Fort Peck Tribes had initiated a lawsuit against the government for the mismanagement of tribal trust assets, funds, and resources. Their litigation alleged that the BIA, as the agent of the government, failed to provide an accurate accounting of Fort Peck Tribes' trust funds and non-monetary trust assets and resources. Consequently, the Tribes' suit did not designate a specific dollar amount. They wanted an accounting to determine how much money and what resources were mismanaged. As the decade came to an end and a new one began, the Tribes and the government eventually negotiated a settlement in January 2012. Initially the government offered a settlement of $53 million, which the Tribes rejected. The government came back with a counter of $64 million. Eventually, the Tribes countered with an amount totaling $89 million, to which the government offered $75 million. Every Tribal Executive Board member traveled to Washington, DC, in late February to meet with BIA and U.S. Attorney officials, as well as their attorneys, to settle the ten-year-old lawsuit. The $75 million settlement is the largest settlement in Fort Peck tribal history. The money will allow the tribes to develop and expand their economy in terms of health care, construction, roads, elder and youth programs, courts, traditional culture, and many other areas. Social programs will also benefit. Tribal Chairman Floyd Azure stated, "Basically, this is just another treaty. Signing the agreement gives new respect for each other. It's two nations coming together."[59]

As the decade wound down, the tribes looked back on significant changes. The Bureau of Indian Affairs was reorganized. The Sisseton Wahpeton Sioux Council revealed the murky status of a tribe within a government framework of two existing tribes. Despite numerous trips to both tribal and federal court, the status and authority of the groups remained in a blurred and incomplete legal position.

The services of the Indian Health Service were severely depleted. However, by the end of the decade, that had been somewhat remedied by Congress. Construction of the water pipeline was well underway, and generally the job outlook on the reservation was brighter than it had been for the past decade. ✲

1 Robbie Magnan, Head Tribal Game Warden, Ft. Peck Tribes, Poplar, MT, August 15, 2011.

2 *Cobell, et. al. v. Salazar, et. al.*, Case no. 1:96-ev-01285 (D.D.C.), 2011.

3 http://www.indiantrust.com/docs/99.12.21-memorandum_opinion.pdf, 5.

4 *Wotonin Wowapi*, v. 33, no. 42, October 23, 2002, 1.

5 *Wotonin Wowapi*, v. 35, no. 42, October 24, 2004, 1.

6 Fort Peck Tribes Press Release, February 27, 2012, http://fortpecktribes.org/press_release.

7 P.L. 90-352, 82 Stat. 239.

8 P.L. 105-387.

9 Fort Peck Tribes Resolution #481-2004-04.

10 Midge Clancy, Chairwoman, Sisseton-Wahpeton Sioux Council (SWSC), Wolf Point, MT, June 24, 2011.

11 *Wotonin Wowapi*, v. 36, no. 32, August 15, 2005, 1.

12 Meeting Minutes, SWSC, October 15, 2005.

13 *Wotonin Wowapi*, v. 37, no. 29, July 20, 2006, 1.

14 *Wotonin Wowapi*, v. 37, no. 49, December 14, 2006, 1.

15 *Wotonin Wowapi*, v. 38, no. 7, February 15, 2007, 1-3.

16 *Wotonin Wowapi*, v. 38, no. 10, March 8, 2007, 1.

17 *Ft. Peck Sisseton and Wahpeton Sioux Executive Council, et. al. v. Ft. Peck Executive Board;U.S. Department of the Interior, et. al.*, Case no. CV-07-29-GF-SEH (D.C. G.F), 2008.

18 *Fort Peck Journal*, v. 7, no. 7, February 15, 2007, 1.

19 *Fort Peck Journal*, v. 7, no. 13, March 29, 2007, 1.

20 *Wotonin Wowapi*, v. 38, no. 14, April 15, 2007, 1; v. 7, no. 25, June 21, 2007, 8.

21 *Fort Peck Journal*, v. 17, no. 30, August 26, 2007, 6; Midge Clancy, Chairwoman, SWSC, Wolf Point, MT, June 24, 2011.

22 *Fort Peck Journal*, v. 8, no. 47, November 20, 2008, 1.

23 DryPrairieWaterAuthority2006.com.

24 Tom Escarsega, Director, Assiniboine and Sioux Rural Water Supply System, Poplar, MT, July 20, 2011.

25 *AssiniboineandSiouxRualWaterSupply Systems.com.*

26 Tribal Election Results, 2003, Ft. Peck Tribal Secretary/Account Office, Poplar,MT.

27 Meeting Minutes, TEB, November 25, 2003.

28 *Wotonin Wowapi*, v. 35, no. 9, February 26, 2004, 7a.

29 Meeting Minutes, TEB, April 5, 2004.

30 *Wotonin Wowapi*, v. 35, no. 16, April 15, 2004, 1, 10a.

31 Ibid.

32 Ft. Peck Tribes Constitution and By-Laws, Article IV, Sec. 1., Amendment no. 2, Approved May 5, 1972.

33 Meeting Minutes, GC, January 8, 1970.

34 *Wotonin Wowapi*, v. 35, no. 20, May 13, 2004, 9a.

35 Meeting Minutes, TEB, May 24, 2008.

36 *Wotonin Wowapi*, v. 35, no. 24, June 10, 2004, 1, 9a.

37 Meeting Minutes, TEB, June 14, 2004.

38 *Wotonin Wowapi*, v. 35, no. 29, July 10, 2004, 1, 9a.

39 Special Tribal Election Results, 2005, Ft. Peck Tribal Secretary/Account Office, Poplar, MT.

40 Tribal Election Results, 2005, Ft. Peck Tribal Secretary/Account Office, Poplar, MT.

41 *Wotonin Wowapi*, v. 36, no. 46, November 17, 2005, 1.

42 ftpecktribes.com.

44 Ft. Peck Tribes Constitution and By-Laws, Amendment no. 7(e), approved May 5, 1972.

44 *Wotonin Wowapi*, v. 37, no. 35, August 31, 2006, 1.

45 *Wotonin Wowapi*, v. 34, no. 37, September 11, 2003, 1.

46 *Wotonin Wowapi*, v. 35, no. 23, May 12, 2004, 1.

47 *Wotonin Wowapi*, v. 36, no. 36, August 25, 2005, 1.

48 Meeting Minutes, TEB, March 28, 2006.

49 *Fort Peck Journal*, v. 7, no. 29, July 19, 2007, 2.

50 Tribal Election Results, 2007, Ft. Peck Tribal Secretary/Account Office, Poplar, MT.

51 Meeting Minutes, TEB, December 10, 2007.

52 2007 Constitutional Convention Appointments, Ft. Peck Tribal Secretary/Account Office, Poplar, MT.

53 Constitutional Convention Election Results, 2007, Ft. Peck Tribal Secretary/Account Office, Poplar, MT.

54 Tribal Election Results, 2009,8Ft. Peck Tribal Secretary/Account Office, Poplar, MT.

55 *Fort Peck Journal*, v. 9, no. 29, July 16, 2000, 1, 13.

56 USGS.gov.

57 indiancountrytodaymediannetwork.com.

58 indiancountrytodaymediannetwork.com.

59 Floyd Azure, Chairman, Fort Peck Tribes, Poplar, MT, February, 9, 2012.

Epilogue
James Shanley, Ed.D.

The dawn of the twenty-first century found the Fort Peck Tribes trying to hold their own in a changing world. Arlyn Headdress, who had previously been elected as a tribal council member, became Chairman in 1999. Dennis Whitman was still BIA Superintendent, an office that he held until 2002, when he retired. He was replaced by Spike Big Horn. The economic outlook in northeastern Montana was turning bleak, as it was in most small rural communities throughout the West. The tribal industries were struggling because the majority of United States manufacturing was going overseas, government contracting policies were very erratic, and agriculture was a break-even or bust operation for most farmers and ranchers.

On September 11, 2001, the World Trade Centers in New York were destroyed by hijacked airplanes. The United States began gearing up for a world-wide war on terror. The United States first invaded Afghanistan and overthrew the Taliban government, but Osama Bin Laden eluded capture. In 2003, the United States and coalition forces invaded Iraq, eventually overthrowing the government and capturing Saddam Hussein, who was executed by his own people.

The tribal people at Fort Peck responded to the national emergency as they had since World War I. Dozens of young men and women joined the service and eventually served in the Middle East.

Nationally, Indian affairs were also reaching a 9-11 of their own. In 1996, Eloise Cobell, a Blackfeet banker, filed a class-action lawsuit against the Secretary of the Interior, demanding an accounting of the handling of individual Indian and tribal trust accounts since 1887. The premise of the suit was that the Bureau of Indian Affairs as trustee for the federal government had mismanaged these accounts and the property from which that income had been derived. The lack of credibility in the BIA's management had been building for decades. Many records were missing; some were incomprehensible, disintegrating, or damaged.

Congress had responded by passing the American Indian Trust Reform Act in 1994. The BIA made little progress, however, which prompted Cobell to file her suit in 1996. In 1999, a federal judge cited Bruce Babbitt and Robert Ruben (Secretary of Interior) for contempt because the Bureau of Indian Affairs had been unable to produce key documents for the lawsuit. In 2002, Judge Roy Lamberth found Gale Norton, then Secretary of Interior, in contempt for her failure to comply with earlier court orders. Lamberth authorized a court consultant to hack into the trust account system to test the security system. The hacker was able to enter the accounts and change data. The judges then ordered the BIA to shut down the system and improve the security. As a response, the BIA withheld thousands of Individual Indian Money Accounts to punish the tribes and raise a political backlash to the Cobell case.

In May 2003, the bureau introduced a new reorganization plan that was approved by Secretary Norton. The plan split the bureau into three divisions: an Office of Special Trustee, the Bureau of Indian Affairs, and a Bureau of Indian Education.

Although the Cobell lawsuit has yet to be resolved, the overall impact has permanently changed the Bureau of Indian Affairs. Despite its remaining obligations in such areas as law and order, roads, education, and environmental protection, the bureau is focusing primarily on the trust responsibilities for tribal and individual Indian land, minerals and other resources.

Locally, Arlyn Headdress was defeated by John Morales in the 2003 elections. Chairman Morales, a former Tribal Executive Board member, was critical of an agreement that the previous executive board had negotiated with the Northern Border Pipe Line for a future lease. The disagreement escalated during the early months of 2004, and the board removed Morales as chairman in May 2004. Vice-Chairman Ray K. Eder served out the remainder of the term, which ended June 14, 2004. Despite having been removed, John Morales still retained significant popular support among the people of Fort Peck and ran again for chairman in 2005. Morales beat Tom Christian using a platform of "For the Common

People." During that period, several large public gatherings were held that were called general councils, but these meetings were never shown to comply with the constitutional requirements of a general council.

In the fall of 2004, Frank Smith, a Tribal Executive Board Member, was elected to the Montana State Senate. Dr. Margie Campbell was elected as a representative to the State House. Dr. Campbell, a Fort Peck tribal member, also served as Vice-President for Community Services at Fort Peck Community College. Both were re-elected in 2006, and Campbell served as the Democratic Minority Whip in the House.

The years 2000–2007 were filled with many fascinating situations and events. These remain to be detailed in later volumes. The Fort Peck Assiniboines and Sioux continue to persist in an ever-changing world. This history has been written to shed some light on the endurance of these peoples, their struggles and their triumphs.

Just before this history book went to press, the Fort Peck Reservation held their tribal elections on October 27, 2007, and the voters replaced Chairman John Morales with A.T. "Rusty" Stafne, a previous three-term Tribal Executive Board member and longtime Chief Tribal Judge of the tribal courts. In addition, a new Vice-Chairman, Garrett I. Big Leggins, and a new Sergeant-at-Arms, John W. Weeks, were elected, along with six of the twelve voting members of the Tribal Executive Board. The board members were Rick Kirn, Louis Peterson, William "Sonny" Whitehead, Eugene "Gene" Culbertson, Abraham B. "Abe" Chopper, Sr., Peter "Tonto" Dupree, Floyd Azure, Thomas "Tommy" Christian, Arlyn Headdress, Donna Buckles Whitmer, Darryl Red Eagle, and Ingrid Fawn Firemoon. ✸

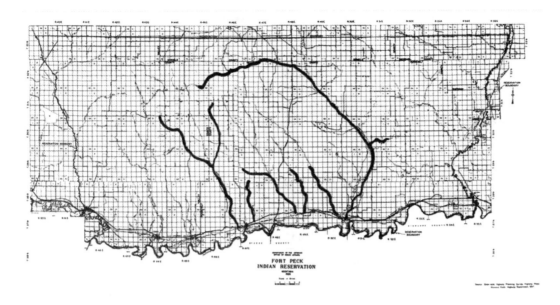

Map of the Fort Peck Reservation with principal waterways outlined on it, produced by Bureau of Indian Affairs employee Donald "Ducky" LaVay, 1983. The outline of the waterways resembles a buffalo.

The Tribal Flag, designed by Roscoe White Eagle in 1975, depicts the two Indian tribes of which the Fort Peck Tribes are comprised. The Assiniboine and Sioux Tribes are united to form the membershp of the reservation.

List of Fort Peck Tribal Chairmen

NAME:	TERM:
Floyd Azure	2011-2013
A.T. "Rusty" Stafne	2009-2011
A.T. "Rusty" Stafne	2007-2009
John Morales	2005-2007
Ray K. Eder	2004-2005 Replaced John Morales June 14, 2004
John Morales	2003-2004 Removed from office June 14, 2004 by TEB
Arlyn Headdress	1999-2001
Ray K. Eder	1999-Finished Term
Spike Bighorn	1997-1999 Resigned Aug. 1, 1999
Caleb Shields	1991-1997
Lawrence "Larry" Wetsit	1989-1991
Kenneth Ryan	1987-1989
Norman Hollow	1973-1985
Joseph Red Thunder	1971-1973
William Youpee	1961-1971
Austin Buckles	1959-1961
Roy L. Sansaver	Acting Chairman 1/31/1959 to 4/15/1959
George Thompson, Jr.	Elected Acting Chairman @ General Council Mtg. 9/6/1958
Dolly Akers	1957-1958 Removed @ General Council Mtg. 9/6/1958
Austin Buckles	1953-1957
William Knorr	1951-1953
David Buckles	1949-1951
Pete Eagle	1947-1949
Carl Walking Eagle	1945-1947
George Washington	1941-1945

Rocky Mountain Regional Office
Billings, MT

NAME:	TERM:
Keith Bear Tusk	1994-2006
Richard C. Whitesell	1983-1994
Anson A. Baker	1979-1982
James F. Canan	1962-1978
Percy E. Melis	1956-1962
John M. Cooper	1954-1956
Paul L. Fickinger	1946-1954
Edward Parisian	2006-2012

The History of the Assiniboine and Sioux Tribes of the Fort Peck Indian Reservation: 1600 - 2012

Past Tribal Leadership

1999-2001
Chairman: Arlyn Headdress
Vice-Chairman: Ray K. Eder
Sgt. at Arms: Russell White

Board Members
Eugene Culbertson
Barbara Birdsbill
Raymond White Tail Feather
Leonard Crow Belt
Richard Kirn
John Pipe
Tom Christian
Pearl Hopkins
Roxanne Gourneau
Patt Iron Cloud Eder
Dale Headdress
Leland Spotted Bird

1997-1999
Chairman: Spike Bighorn*
Vice-Chairman: Nathaniel Long Hair**
    Ray K. Eder***
    Alfred "Togo" Lizotte****
Sgt. at Arms: George Ricker, Sr.

Board Members
Eugene Culbertson
John Pipe
Walter Clark
John Morales
Robert Welch
Vermae Taylor
Pearl Hopkins
Patricia Crawford
Raymond White Tail Feather
Leland Spotted Bird
Caleb Shields
Barbara Birdsbill*

Resigned August 1999; Ray K. Eder
    assumed Chairmanship
**died in office September 4, 1998;
    replaced by Ray K. Eder
***assumed Vice-Chairmanship when
    Nathaniel Long Hair died in office
****assumed Vice-Chairmanship when
    Ray K. Eder assumed Chairmanship

1995-1997
Chairman: Caleb Shields
Vice-Chairman: Nathaniel Long Hair
Sgt. at Arms: Adrian "Sweet Pea" Fourstar,
    Sr.

Board Members
John Morales
Walter Clark
Pearl Hopkins
James Granbois
Norman Hollow*
Thomas Anketell III
June Stafne
Barbara Birdsbill
Eugene Culbertson
Spike Bighorn
Raymond White Tail Feather
Robert Welch
*Roxanne Gourneau replaced Norman
    Hollow by R#1579-96-9

1993-1995
Chairman: Caleb Shields
Vice-Chairman: Ray K. Eder
Sgt. at Arms: Adrian "Sweet Pea" Fourstar,
    Sr.

Board Members
Gene Culbertson

John Pipe
Merle Lucas*
Norman Hollow
Spike Bighorn
Barbara Birdsbill
Larry Burshia
Walter Clark
Dennis Blount
Pearl Hopkins
Leighton Reum
Raymond White Tail Feather
*Suzanne Jones replaced Merle Lucas
    June 27, 1994

1991-1993
Chairman: Caleb Shields
Vice-Chairman: Joseph Red Thunder*
Sgt. at Arms: Adrian "Sweet Pea" Fourstar,
    Sr.

Board Members
Eugene Culbertson
John Pipe
Arlyn Headdress
Norman Hollow
Spike Bighorn
Merle Lucas
Stephen Clincher
Walter Clark
Raymond White Tail Feather
Pearl Hopkins
Ray K. Eder
Dennis Blount
*Died in office and not replaced. Position
    remained vacant, as Mickie McAnally
    declined to be seated; info from Caleb
    Shields, FPCC researcher.

1989-1991

Chairman: Lawrence Wetsit
Vice-Chairman: Joseph Red Thunder
Sgt. at Arms: William "Buck" Smith

Board Members
Norman Hollow
Stephen Clincher
Eugene Culbertson
Merle Lucas
Pearl Hopkins
Walter Clark
Spike Bighorn
Caleb Shields
Ray K. Eder
Dennis Blount
Kenneth Smoker, Jr.*
Peter "Tonto" Dupree
*Resigned January 12, 1990 and replaced
    by Arlyn Headdress, February 1990

1987-1989

Chairman: Raymond White Tail Feather
Vice-Chairman: Joseph Red Thunder
Sgt. at Arms: William "Buck" Smith

Board Members
Arlyn Headdress
Levi Olson
Norman Hollow
Kenneth Smoker, Jr.
Jim Pipe
Leonard Bear
Walter Clark
Peter Dupree
Gene Culbertson
Caleb Shields
Ray K. Eder
Pearl Hopkins

1985-1987

Chairman: Kenneth Ryan
Vice-Chairman: Joseph Red Thunder
Sgt. at Arms: William "Buck" Smith

Board Members
Ray K. Eder
Eugene Culbertson
Kenneth Smoker, Jr.

Dean Blount
Arlyn Headdress
Walter Clark
Pearl Hopkins
Jonny Stiffarm
Norman Hollow
Willie Weeks
Levi Olson
Caleb Shields

1983-1985

Chairman: Norman Hollow
Vice-Chairman: Joseph Red Thunder
Sgt. at Arms: William "Buck" Smith

Board Members
Lyle Firemoon
Arlyn Headdress
Walter Clark
Barney Lambert
Howard Bemer
Nathaniel Longhair
Harold Dean Blount
Ray K. Eder
Orval Grainger
Caleb Shields
Tom Escarcega
Kenny Smoker, Jr.

1981-1983

Chairman: Norman Hollow
Vice-Chairman: Joseph Red Thunder
Sgt. at Arms: Henry Buck Elk

Board Members
Harold D. Blount
Eugene Culbertson
Lyle Firemoon
Kenneth Smoker, Jr.
Walter E. Clark
Orval Grainger
Pearl Hopkins
Nathaniel Long Hair
Wayne Martell
Bernard Lambert, Sr.
Raymond White Tail Feather
Caleb Shields

1979-1981

Chairman: Norman Hollow
Vice-Chairman: Joseph Red Thunder
Sgt. at Arms: Henry Buck Elk

Board Members
Nathanial Long Hair
Orval Grainger
Caleb Shields
Wayne Martell
Bernard Lambert, Sr.
Jesse Kirn, Sr.
William Youpee
Walter E. Clark
Gerald Red Elk
Pearl Hopkins
June Stafne
Harold D. Blount

1977-1979

Chairman: Norman Hollow
Vice-Chairman: Joseph Red Thunder
Sgt. at Arms: Henry Buck Elk

Board Members
Lida Menz
Orval Grainger
Caleb Shields
Stanley Yellowrobe
Alpheus Big Horn, Sr.
Jesse Kirn, Sr.
Raymond White Tail Feather
William Youpee
James Black Dog
Pearl Hopkins
June Stafne
Harold Dean Blount

1975-1977

Chairman: Norman Hollow
Vice-Chairman: Verne Gibbs
Sgt. at Arms: Nathaniel Long Hair

Board Members
Lida Menz
Leonard Boxer
Caleb Shields
Stanley Yellowrobe
Alpheus Big Horn, Sr.

1959-1961..

Chairman: Austin Buckles
Vice-Chairman: Edwin Reddoor
Sgt. at Arms: Theodore Manning

Board Members
Norman Hollow
Melvin Buckles
Henry Archdale, Sr.
Enright Jackson
James Black Dog
William Youpee
Pearl Redstone
Kermit Smith
Alfred Manning
Roy Sansaver
Leslie Fourstar
Mark Eder, Sr.*
Harry Johnson*
Alfred Manning*
Earl Jones*
James Helmer*
*Paid as Board Members

1957-1959

Chairman: Dolly Akers*
    George Thompson, Jr.**
    Roy L. Sansaver***
Vice-Chairman: George W. Thompson, Jr.
Sgt. at Arms: Vearl Denny

Board Members
Maurice Big Horn, Sr.
William Youpee
Leslie Fourstar
Roy Sansaver
Carl Walking Eagle
Kermit Smith
James Sweeney
Lester A. Youpee
Melvin Buckles
Henry Archdale
Alfred Manning
William "Buck" Smith
* removed at General Council Meeting of
    September 6, 1958
** replaced Dolly Akers at General
    Council Meeting of September 6,
    1958.

*** acting Chairman on January 31, 1959
    until April 14, 1959 (tribal resolution
    #469-59-2)

1955-1957

Chairman: Austin Buckles
Vice-Chairman: James Archdale
Sgt. at Arms: Peter Dupree

Board Members
Henry Archdale
James Sweeney
William Youpee
Kermit Smith
Edwin J. Reddoor, Sr.
Charles H. Track
Carl Walking Eagle
Alice Collins
Leon Spotted Bull
Lester A. Youpee
Norman Hollow
Fred Buckles

1953-1955

Chairman: Austin Buckles
Vice-Chairman: James Archdale
Sgt. at Arms: Peter Dupree

Board Members
John Half Red
Alice Collins
Bernard Standing
Minnie Olson
Norman Hollow
Carl Walking Eagle
William Ogle
William Youpee
James Sweeney
Tom Buckles
John Earl
William Boyd

1951-1953

Chairman: William Knorr
Vice-Chairman: David Buckles
Sgt. at Arms: William Boyd

Board Members
Henry Archdale

Bernard Standing
Joseph Day
Joseph Red Thunder
Dolly Akers
Nimrod Davis
Jacob Big Horn
Edwin J. Reddoor
Norman Hollow
George Washington
Theodore Four Eagle Boy
Carl Walking Eagle

1949-1951

Chairman: David Buckles
Vice-Chairman: Howard Trinder
Sgt. at Arms: Kirkwood Smith

Board Members
Leslie Fourstar
Charles Track
Edwin Reddoor
Carl Walking Eagle
Alvin Warrior
Henry Buck Elk
Austin Buckles
George Boyd
Fred Buckles
William Knorr
Jacob Big Horn
Norman Hollow

1947-1949

No Records Available

1945-1947

Chairman: Carl Walking Eagle
Vice-Chairman: Peter Eagle
Sgt. at Arms: Santee Iron Ring

Board Members
George Boyd, Sr.
Charles Thompson
Joseph Hamilton
Bernard Standing
Maurice Big Horn
Harry Hollow
Henry Archdale
Rueben Feather Earring
Rufus Ricker, Sr.

Charles Hall, Sr.
Alvin Warrior
James Archdale

1943-1945
Chairman: George Washington
Vice-Chairman: Peter Eagle
Sgt. at Arms: unknown

Board Members
Grover Cleveland
Rufus Ricker, Sr.
Charles Thompson
James Archdale
Herman Red Elk, Sr.

1941-1943
Chairman: George Washington
Vice-Chairman: Peter Eagle
Sgt. at Arms: George Boyd & Peter
   Dupree

Board Members
James Archdale
Herman Red Elk
John Half Red
Carl Walking Eagle
Joshua Wetsit
Charles Thompson
James Crazy Bull
Roy Sansaver
Harvey Hamilton
Grover Cleveland
Nimrod Davis
George Boyd, Jr.

FORT PECK INDIAN AGENCY SUPERINTENDENTS

	LOCATION	YEAR	FROM	TO	NAME
1	Milk River	1	1870	1870	Lieutenant G. E. Ford
2	Milk River	1	1870	1870	A.S. Reed
3	Fort Peck	3	1871	1873	Andrew J. Simmons
4	Fort Peck	3	1873	1875	W. W. Alderson
5	Fort Peck	2	1876	1877	Thomas J. Mitchell
6	Fort Peck-Poplar	3	1877	1879	Wellington Bird
7	Poplar	5	1879	1883	Major Nathan S. Porter
8	Poplar	3	1883	1885	Samuel E. Snider
9	Poplar	1	1885	1885	Burton G. Parker
10	Poplar	2	1885	1886	Henry R. West
11	Poplar	1	1886	1886	Henry Heth (Special Indian Agent)
12	Poplar	4	1886	1889	Dale C. Cowen
13	Poplar	5	1889	1893	C.R.A. Scobey
14	Poplar	6	1893	1898	Captain Henry W. Sprole
15	Poplar	7	1898	1904	C.R.A. Scobey
16	Poplar	13	1905	1917	Major C. B. Lohmiller
17	Poplar	5	1917	1921	E.D. Mossman
18	Poplar	3	1921	1923	James B. Kitch
19	Poplar	5	1923	1927	P.H. Moller
20	Poplar	4	1927	1930	Charles Eggers
21	Poplar	4	1930	1933	H.D. McCullough
22	Poplar	2	1933	1934	C.L. Walker
23	Poplar	6	1934	1939	John G. Hunter
24	Poplar	4	1939	1942	O.C. Gray
25	Poplar	2	1942	1943	E.R. Hall (Acting Supt.)
26	Poplar	6	1943	1948	F.A. Asbury
27	Poplar	3	1948	1950	E.J. Diehl
28	Poplar	4	1951	1954	James D. Crawford
29	Poplar	3	1954	1956	Clinton O. Talley
30	Poplar	2	1956	1957	Harvey W. Starling (Acting Supt.)
31	Poplar	3	1957	1959	David P. Weston
32	Poplar	3	1959	1961	Dale M. Baldwin
33	Poplar	6	1962	1967	Stanley D. Lyman
34	Poplar	5	1967	1971	Anson A. Baker
35	Poplar	3	1971	1973	William L. Benjamin
36	Poplar	2	1974	1975	James O. Jackson (Acting Supt.)
37	Poplar	5	1975	1979	Burton A. Ryder
38	Poplar	2	1979	1980	Dennis T. Whiteman (Acting Supt.)
39	Poplar	1	1980	1980	Davind Pennington (Acting Supt.)
40	Poplar	3	1980	1982	Dorrance Steele
41	Poplar	2	1982	1983	David Allison (Acting Supt.)
42	Poplar	2	1982	1983	Daniel T. Harwood (Acting Supt.)
43	Poplar	1	1983	1983	Thomas Whitford
44	Poplar	6	1983	1988	Dennis T. Whiteman
45	Poplar	1	1988	1989	Helen Pawlowski (Acting Supt.)
46	Poplar	7	1989	1996	Wyman D. Babby
47	Poplar	1	1996	1996	David Pennington (Acting Supt.)
48	Poplar	1	1996	1996	John Graves (Acting Supt.)
49	Poplar	7	1996	2002	Dennis T. Whiteman
50	Poplar	1	2002	2002	Edward Lone Fight (Acting Supt.)
51	Poplar	1	2002	2002	Toni Greybull (Acting Supt.)
52	Poplar	3	2003	2006	Spike Bighorn
53	Poplar	1	2006	2006	Florence White Eagle (Acting Supt.)
54	Poplar	5	2007	2011	Florence White Eagle
55	Poplar	2	2011	2012	Rhonda Knudsen (Acting Supt.)

Indians on the Fort Peck Reservation who served in the United States Military

Male Veterans

A

Abbott, Earl G.
Abbott, Donald
Abbott, Kenneth F.
Abbott, Lawrence D.
Ackerman, Charles
Ackerman, Michael
Ackerman, Ray
Ackerman, Wesley III
Ackerman, Wesley George
Ackerman, Wilbert
Akers, Mark
Adams, Charles
Adams, Harold "Buddy"
Adams, Henry L.
Adams, Irey James
Adams, Lance W.
Adams, William L.
Adams, Lewis S.
Adams, Matt
Adams, Michael D.
Adams, Tommy
Adams, Todd
Agosto,, Joey
Allvarez, Joe
Allvarez, Robert
All Runner, Fred
Anderson, Aaron Wayne
Anderson, Earl J.
Anderson, Fred
Anderson, John David
Archdale, Anthony D.
Archdale, Antoine M.
Archdale, Douglas
Archdale, Frank
Archdale, Frederick W.
Archdale, Ivan

Archdale, Leslie
Archdale, John A.
Archdale, Melvin "Sonny"
Archdale, Percy
Atkinson, Denver, Jr.
Atkinson, Jack D.
Atkinson, Wyatt
Ayers, Jack
Azure, Alfred
Azure, Joseph S.
Azure, Matthew
Azure, Marvin L.
Azure IV, Roy
Azure, Roy

B

Bad Hawk, Del
Bad Hawk, Jacob, Sr.
Baker, Royce
Baker, Vaughn
Ball, John
Barnett, Dennis
Bauer, Bryon
Bauer, Byron
Bauer, Chris
Bauer, Fred, Jr.
Bauer, Joseph G.
Bauer, Joseph L.
Bauer, Justin Wayne
Bauer, Sam
Bauer, Tom
Bell, Michael
Bear, Earlwin
Bear, Gerald C., Sr.
Bear, Joe
Bear, Leonard A., Jr.
Bear, Leonard, Sr.
Bear, Nathan
Bear, Percy

Bear, Wilfred "Max"
Bearcub, Adam, Jr.
Bearcub, Adam, Sr.
Bearcub, Archie, Jr.
Bearcub, Archie, Sr.
Bearcub, John, Jr.
Bearcub, Herschel Wayne
Bearskin, George R.
Beauchamp, Albert R.
Beauchman, Louis J.
Beauchman, Patrick L.
Beauchman, Raymond D.
Beauchman, Robert L.
Beaudry, Victor
Bell, Mike
Belcher, Walter
Belgarde, Kermit A.
Belgard, Burton
Belgard, Leo J.
Belgard, Maurice
Berger, Jeffrey M., Sr.
Bergie, Joseph
Bergie, Ronald
Bergie, Thomas B.
Beston, Darrell
Beston, Jaimie
Beston, Joseph
Beston, Joe
Beston, Ryan
Beston, Yancy
Bets His Medicine, Carlus
Bets His Medicine, Doyle
Bigby, Kevin (Welch)
Bighorn, Barry
Bighorn, Dennis D.
Bighorn, Fredrick M.
Bighorn, Gregory
Bighorn, Jacob
Bighorn, Jason R.

Bighorn, James
Bighorn,, Leonard
Big Leggings, Kurt
Bird, Harry Sidney
Bird, Reede
Bird, Victor
Birdsbill, Darrell
Birdsbill, Verdell
Birthmark, Darrell "Chubby"
Blackdog, Brian
Blackdog, James
Blackdog, Matthew Earl
Blackdog, Robert
Blackdog, Robert
Blackdog, Vincent R.
Black Tail, Wallace
Black Thunder, Russell
Blackwell, Charles J.
Blount, Dennis B.
Blount, George W. III
Blount Harold D.
Blount, Waylon
Blue Earth, George E.
Blue Earth, Richard
Boise, George
Bokas, Thomas G., Jr.
Bokas, William L.
Booth, Everett E.
Bow, Henry
Bow, Percy
Bow, Randolph H.
Boyd, Brian
Boyd, Carl M.
Boyd, Carson H.
Boyd, Darly "Jackie"
Boyd, David
Boyd, David
Boyd, Dewayne J.
Boyd Eugene

Boyd, James A.
Boyd, James W.
Boyd, Sr, Jonathon E.
Boyd, John
Boyd, Harold J.
Boyd, Lewis
Boyd, Llewellyn J
Boyd, Lowell J.
Boyd, Lowell J.
Boyd, Michael
Boyd, Robert A.
Boyd, Sam
Boyd, Sam
Boyd, Vernon D.
Boyd, Vernon L.
Boyd, William J.
Boxer, Louie
Boxer, Lawrence
Boxer Leonard
Boxer, Louie J.
Boxer, Miles
Boxer, Tony
Broken Leg, George L.
Brown, Abraham
Brown, Arthur
Brown, Arthur
Brown, Delmar
Brown, Hubert
Brown, Leslie L.
Brown, Melvin
Brown, Michael T.
Brown, Morris D.
Brown, Richard
Brown, Robert
Brown, Roy
Brown, Robert G.
Brown, Robert
Brown, Ronald
Brown, Thomas D. "Pud"
Browning, Everett, Jr.
Browning, Roger
Bruguier, John A.
Brunelle, Allen D.
Brunelle, Allen W.
Brunelle, Roger
Buck Elk, Bernard
Buck Elk, Darryl K.
Buck Elk, Erick J.
Buck Elk, Gideon

Buck Elk, Harvey
Buck Elk, Robert.
Buckles, Allen W
Buckles, Arthur
Buckles, Barry
Buckles B.T.
Buckles, Benjamin
Buckles, David W.
Buckles, Donald J.
Buckles, Duane L.
Buckles, Earl D.
Buckles, Fred
Buckles, Fred
Buckles, James L.
Buckles Kevin
Buckles, Louie V.
Buckles, Melvin
Buckles, Melvin M.
Buckles, Patrick M.
Buckles, Ralph E.
Buckles, Robert D.
Buckles, Ronald
Buckles, Ronald W.
Buckles, Ronald W.
Buckles, Ryan Wade
Buckles, Thomas D.
Buckles, Walter
Buckles, Wesley C.
Buckles, Wesley M.
Budak, Zack
Bull Chief, Nathan
Burger, Archie
Burger, Frederick
Burshia, Aloysius
Burshia, Lawrence D.
Burshia, Michael
Burshia, Patrick
Burshia, Raymond
Burshia, Ronald M.
Bushman, Robert

C
Cain, Wallace
Campbell, Clarence
Campbell, Harvey
Campbell, Malcolm
Campbell, Robert
Campbell, Robert T.
Campbell, Stephen C.

Campbell, Thomas L.
Cantrell, Courtney L.
Cantrell, Courtney
Cantrell, John
Cantrell, Leonard D.
Cantrell, Llewellyn, J.
Cantrell, Michael P.
Cantrell, Newton J.
Cantrell, Orin
Cantrell, Richard, Jr.
Cantrell, Otto, Jr.
Carl, Warren, Jr.
Carmichael, John
Carnicom, Gene
Carrillo, Romeo
Carter, Gregory L.
Centennial, Colon J.
Chase, Joseph
Chaser, Jackson C.
Christian, Darrell
Christian, John
Christian, Thomas
Chopper, Abraham
Chopper, Franklin D.
Chopper, Vernon
Clancy, Charles E., Jr.
Clancy, Edison
Clancy, Joseph
Clancy, Ralph
Clancy, Wilfred J.
Clark, Bernard
Clark, Darrell
Clark, Donald
Clark, Earl
Clark, Earl
Clark, Elmer J.
Clark, Kristopher D.
Clark, James
Clark, John B.
Clark, Mabel
Clark, Michael "Mickey"
Clark, Mitchell
Clark, Patrick
Clark, Richard A.
Clark Walter E.
Claymore, Terrence
Clincher, Silas
Cloke, Raymond
Cloud, Orville

Cloud Boy, Joe
Colter, John
Collins, Gerald J.
Collins, Lawrence D.
Collins, Peter J.
Collins, Steven P.
Conner, Fred M
Conner, George
Conner, James
Conner, Larry H.
Conner, Raymond B.
Coughlin, Jerome
Coulter, John
Courchene, Charles L.
Courchene, Curtis
Courchene, David
Courchene, Jerry
Courchene, Kevin R.
Courchene, Richard M.
Courchene, Phillip
Courchene, Shane M.
Cox, Alvin
Cox, Donald
Cox, Julius
Cox, Melvin
Cox, Nelson
Craft, James A.
Crawford, Freedom
Crawford, John
Crazy Bull, Matt
Crazy Bull, Murphy
Crazy Bull, Nathan
Crowe, Michael
Crowe, Sherman
Crowe, Sherwin
Crowe, Stanley
Crowe, Theodore
Culbertson Dale
Culbertson, Eugene M.
Culbertson, Harold
Culbertson, Howard
Culbertson, Joe
Culbertson, Joseph P.
Culbertson, Pierre
Culbertson, Sam
Culbertson, William
Cummins, Jeffrey S.

D

Damon, Bruce
Damon, Celestice
Damon, Frank
Damon, John F.
Damon, Ronald
Daniels, Alan M.
Daniels, Jonathan
Daniels, John Daniels,
Robert A.
Daniels, Roy W.
Darnell, Ira
Darnell, Theodore "Teddy"
Dauphine, Edward J.
Davis, Charles Ed
Davis, Gene
Davis, Melvin J.
Dawson, Delmar L.
Dawson II, John
Day, Joe
Day, Stuart
Decker, Robert J.
DeCoteau, Carroll J.
DeCoteau, Charles L.
DeCoteau, Elmer D.
DeCoteau, Emerson A.
DeCoteau, Lester D.
DeLong, Louis
DeLorme, Amable
DeMarrias, Abe
DeMarrias, George, Jr.
DeMarrias, George, Sr.
DeMarrias, James
DeMarrias, Martin D.
DeMarrias, McGeorge, Sr.
Denny, Lyle
Denny, Marcus J.
Denny, Orrian
Desjarlais, Francis R.
Desjarlais, Harold
Desjarlais, Ronnie G.
Desjarlais, Ronald
Desjarlais, Orville
Dimas, Cory
Dimas, Troy
Diserly, Arlie
Diserly, Cornelius
Diserly, Frank
Doney, James

Doney, Jonny Dale
Doney, Micheal
Douglas, Arnold
Douglas, John
Drum, Allen
Drum, Gary
Drum, Neil
Drum, Silas M.
Dumaree, Alexander R.
Dumont, Ronald
Dumont, Vernon
Dupree, George
Dupree, John K.
Dupree, John W.
Dupree, Jestin
Dupree, Leonard E., Jr.
Dupree, Leonard, Sr.
Dupree, Raymond, Sr.
Dupree, Colma
Dupree, Duncan V.

E

Eagle, Elmer R.
Eagle, Frank
Eagle, Francis
Eagle, Joseph
Eagle, Kenneth D.
Eagle, Kenneth
Eagle, Luther
Ealy, Joseph
Eagle Boy, Arnold C.
Eagle Boy, Louis W.
Eagle Boy, Melvin
Eagle Boy, Nelson
Eagle Boy, Terry
Eagleman, Charles
Eagleman, Chester
Eagleman, Chuck
Eagleman, John I,
    Tribal Scout, Indian Wars
Eagleman, John J. II
Eagleman, Lawrence I., Sr.
Eagleman,Melvin, Sr.
Eagleman, Catlin
Eagleman, Quincy John
Eagleman, Vernon
Eder, Bert
Eder, Cary
Eder, Charles J.

Eder, Curtis
Eder, Earl
Eder, George J.
Eder, Jack
Eder, James L., Sr.
Eder Lloyd
Eder, Mark, Jr.
Eder, Martin Dale
Eder, Phillip
Eder, Ray K.
Eder, Robert A.
Eder, Robert
Eder, Roland John
Eder, William H., Sr.
Edeline, Robert
Emerson, Roy
Escarcega, Bob
Escarcega, Charles
Escarcega, Joe, Sr.
Escarcega, Joel
Escarcega, Joseph, Sr.
Escarcega, Thomas, Sr.
Escarcega, Thomas
Escarcega, Vernon

F

Failing, Chad
Failing, Mervin W.
Failing, Michael
Falcon, Alex J.
Falcon, Edwin C.
Farnsworth, Gary
Farrelly, Francis J.
Fast Horse, Alan
Fast Horse, John
Fast Horse, Michael J.
Ferguson, Joseph "Shep"
Ferguson, William
Figueroa, Jose
Firemoon, Dawson
Firemoon, Delwayne S.
Firemoon, Leroy
Firemoon, Lyle
Firemon, Thomas E.
Firemoon, Vincent R.
Firemoon, Wesley
First, Frederick Dean
First, Jerome V.
Fischer, Doratello

Fisher, Harold
Fisher, Raymond E.
Fisher, Roger E.
Fisher, Russell J.
Flynn, Ernie
Flynn, Jay Edwin
Flynn, Melvin
Flynn, Lionel
Flynn, Thomas C.
Flynn, Thomas J.,
    Marines, Navy, WWII
Flynn, Melvin C.
Follett, Abel, Marines
Follett, Dennis V.
Follette, Herman
Follette, Verle
Forrest, Leroy Foster,
Russell Fourbear, Ervin
Fourbear, Dennis
Fourbear, Joray
Fourbear, Virgil
Fourstar, Adrian J., Jr.
Fourstar, Carl, Sr.
Fourstar, Leslie, Jr.
Fourstar, Phillip
Fourstar, Robert P.
Fourstar, Wallace C.

G

Garcia, Robert
Garfield, Archie
Garfield, Benjamin
Garfield, Daniel A.
Garfield, Lawrence J., Jr.
Garfield, Leon B
Garfield, Robert
Gibbs, Richard V.
Gibbs, Vern E.
Gomez, Richard
Gone, Thomas L
Good Bird, Gerald
Goodbird, Raymond, Jr.
Good Boy White, Andrew
Good Soldier, Ambrose
Good Soldier, Joseph
Goodwill, Clinton E.
Gourneau, Frank
Gourneau, Terrance P.
Grainger, Daniel

Grainger, John Daniel
Grainger, Howard "Sol"
Grainger, Ronnie
Granbois, Dennis Army
Granbois, Ernest (Buzz)
Granbois, Phillip III
Granbois, Rick
Grandchamp, Alfred
Grandchamp, Dusette
Grandchamp, Nelson
Grandchamp, Phillip
Grandchamp, Robert
Grant, Paul "Paulie"
Gray Hawk, Benjamin
Gray Hawk, Llewellyn
Gray Hawk, Lakota
Gray Hawk, Stephen
Green, Duane
Green, Thomas
Gregg, Clark L.
Gregg, Lewis
Grey Bear, Abraham E.
Grey Bear, Galen
Grey Bear, Oral
Grey Bull, Arthur, Jr.
Grey Bull, Harold M.
Grey Bull, Milo
Grey Bull, Matthew
Grey Bull, Raymond "Ole"
Grey Bull, Richard
Grey Bull, Tom
Grimes, John C.
Growing Thunder, Adrian

H
Hale, Aldred
Hale, Justin
Hale, Mervin
Half Red, Loyal Lloyd
Hamilton, Anthony D.
Hamilton, Aaron V
Hamilton, Dale W.
Hamilton, David B.
Hamilton, Joe
Hamilton,, Harry
Hamilton, Harry
Hamilton, Harold P.
Hamilton, Harvey W., Jr.
Hamilton, Joe

Harrison, Tim
Hawk, Maynard
Hawk, William R.
Hayes, August H.
Hazen, Gerald
Headdress, Anthony M.
Headdress, Charles
Headdress, Christopher R.
Headdress, Dale
Headdress, Mitchell D.
Headdress, Owl
Headdress, Sheldon
Headdress, Wesley
Healy, Brian
Helmer, James
Helmer, Robert V.
Helmer, Warren
Henderson, Stanley
Hendrickson, Greg
Hendrickson, Kevin
Hendrickson, Lionel "Buddy"
Henschel, Lonnie W. Army
Hernandez, Archdale
  Francisco
High Eagle, Alfred
Hoenck, Robert
Hollow Horn, Emerson L.
Hollow Horn, Stanley
Hollow Horn, Stanley, Jr.
Hollow Horn, Vernon G.
Hopkins, Robert, Jr.
Hopkins, Robert, Sr.
Hotomanie, Larron K.
Howard, Joseph W.
Hughes, Richard B.

I
Iron Bear, Alfred, Sr.
Iron Bear, Alfred, Jr.
Iron Bear, Harry, Sr.
Iron Bear, Harry, Jr.
Iron Bear, Joseph
Iron Cloud, Irvin
Iron Cloud, Thomas Ira
Iron Leggins, Joseph
Iron Ring, Cyril
Iron Shield, Thomas J.

J
Jackson, Clinton
Jackson, Darrell
Jackson, Enright W.
Jackson, George
Jackson, Gerald
Jackson, Germaine
Jackson, Joseph A.
Jackson, Ryan
Jackson, Maynard
Jackson, Melvin E.
Jackson, Theodore
Jackson, Wilbert F.
Jackson, William E.
James, Matthew Army
Jaruzel, John
Jaruzel, Thomas
Johnson, Isadore B.
Johnson, Lionel
Johnson, Rueben
Johnston, Harold
Johnston, Marion
Johnston, Raymond
Jones, Edgar
Jones, Edgar
Jones, Frank
Jones, Manford W.
Jones, Matthew
Jones, Marcell Eder
Jones, Ralph N., Jr.
Jones, Ralph N., Sr.

K
Keiser, George
Keiser, Raymond G.
Keiser, Wilbert
Keiser, Wilbert
Kennedy, Kenneth K.
Kirn, Douglas
Kirn, Jesse J.
Kirn, Leslie C.
Keother, Steven
Knorr II, William
Knowlton, Richard L.

L
LaBlanc, George
Lemay, Edward
Lamb, James

Lamb, Raymond R.
Lambert, Bernard
Lambert, Dennis "Sonny"
Lambert, Edward
Lambert, Gerald "Geish"
Lambert, James
Lambert, John
Lambert, Joseph
Lambert, Mervin
Lambert, Norman
Lambert, Robert
Lambert, Wilfred WWII
LaRoque, George M.
LaRoque, Robert
Left Hand Thunder, Willard
Leggett, Thomas
Lester, Allen
Lester, Asa W.
Lester, Chester
Lester, Clayton R.
Lester, Stanley
Lethridge, Duke
Levay, Frank "Butch"
Levay, Patrick
Levay, Peter
Lindsay, Edward
Lindsey, Robert
Lingle, Timothy
Little Head, Arnold S.
Little Head, Benjamin, Jr.
Lizotte, Alfred P., Jr.
Lizotte, Alfred P., Sr.
Loans Arrow, Albert F.
Lone Bear, Gary
Lone Bear, Reede
Longee, Alfred
Longee, Jeremiah Robert
Longee, Jim
Longee, Louis
Longee, Richard
Longee, Robert L.
Longee, Samuel, Jr.
Longtree, Clarence, Jr.
Longtree, Clarence, Sr.
Longtree, Harry
Longtree, Harry C.
Longtree, Mark Moses
Longtree, Robert, Jr.
Longtree, Robert, Sr.

Longtree, Roy
Longtree, Stanley
Loves Him, Orville
Loudermilk, James W.
Low Dog, Joseph, Sr.
Low Dog, Norman
Lowry, Fred F.
Lucas, Merle
Luchau, Ronald
Lussier, Lamont

M
Magnan, Lewis
Magnan, Robert
MacDonald, Clarence, Jr.
MacDonald, Colonel
MacDonald, Donald "Sandy"
MacDonald, George "Bud"
MacDonald, James R.
MacDonald, John R.
MacDonald, Frank, Jr.
MacDonald, Malcolm J., Jr.
MacDonald, Malcolm L., Sr.
Madison, Guy
Magnan, Edmond A.
Magnan, David
Magnan, Gene
*Mail, Gordon
Mail, John
Mail, Russell
Maloney, Daniel
Manning, Dale
Manning, John
Manning, Malcolm D.
Martell, Anthony M.
Martell, Brandon T.
Martell, Cale
Martell, Charles, Jr.
Martell, Charles, Sr.
Martell, Floyd, Jr.
Martell, Frank
Martell, Gary
Martell, George
Martell, George
Martell, Lloyd, Jr.
Martell, Martin M.
Martell, Max
Martell, Maxim W., Sr.
Martell, Rudy

Martell, Wayne
Martin, David R.
Martin, Dewayne
Martin, Kenneth R.
Martin, Larry
Martin, Leo J.
Martin, Leroy
Martin, Kenneth R.
Martin, Mason C.
Martin, Robert Wayne
Martin, Richard D.
Martin, Thomas D.
Marottek, Lance R.
Mason, Leslie L.
Mason, Gilbert
Mason, Jesse, Jr.
Mason, Leslie L.
Mason, Monte
Mason, Victor H.
Mason, Wesley S.
Masters, Alva
Masters, Richard
Matthews, Michael E.
McAnally, Harry
McAnally, Robert
McAnally, Thomas
McClammy, Daniel A., Jr.
McClammy, Daniel A.
McClammy, George, Sr.
McClammy, James H.
McClammy, John Q.
McClammy, Jubal
McClammy, Loren
McClammy, William "Tolly"
McClammy, Willis H., Jr.
McClammy, Willis H., Sr.
McClammy, Willis E.
McConnell, Richard
McConnell, Brian
McConnell, Loren
McGeshick, Albert
McGeshick, Fred A.
McGowan, Dana Easton
Medicine Horse, David D., Jr.
Meinert, Gary V.
Melbourne, James III
Melbourne, James M.
Melbourne, Manuel P.
Melzer, Ernest L.

Menz, David R.
Menz, Emery W.
Menz, Fred
Menz, John
Midthun, David E.
Miller, Frank S.
Miller, Gerald
Miller, Isaac W.
Miller, Joseph, Jr.
Miller, Joe, Sr.
Miller, Laverne A. Reddog
Miller, Richard
Miller, Willard
Mitchell, Fred
Mitchell, Henry
Mitchell, Robert D.
Mitchell, Theodore R.
Mitchell, Col. Theodore L.
Mitchell, Warren
Mitchell, William R.
Moccasin, Ronald D., Sr.
Montclair, Clayton R., Sr.
Montclair, Robert, Sr.
Moran, Bernard E.
Moran, Charles V.
Moran, Donald L.
Moran, Gabriel
Moran, P.S.
Moran, Ruben H.
Moran, Stanley, Jr.
Moran, Steven M.
Moran, Sylvester R., Sr.
Morin, Robert
Morsette, John H.
Mudgett, Jerrid
Murdock, Albert George
Murdock, Douglas
Murdock, Dugal
Muskrat, Halle D.
Muskrat, Malcolm
Murray, James E.
Murray, John H.
Murray, Isaac
Murray, Robert
Murray, Robert D.
Murray, Thomas C.
Murray, William B.
Myrick, Angus, Jr.
Myrick, Christopher A.

Myrick, Emery
Myrick, Paul W.
N
Nakkan Smith, Jack E.
Nation, Frank L.
Necklace, Felix
Necklace, Philmore J
Necklace, William
Necklace, William J.
Nelson, Robert
Neutgens, Joseph
Norgaard, William

O
Obershaw, Henry
Ogle, Raymond L.
Ogle, William
Olson, Kenneth
Olson, William John
Ostwald, Bruno
Owens, Calvin
Owens, Cleveland
Owens, Henry L.
Owens, Lewis C.
Owens, Levo Cleveland, Jr.
Owens, Merlin E.
Owens, Reginald P.

P
Packineau, Willis
Parker, David W.
Parker, Ryan
Patino, Roberto
Perry, Frank
Peterson, Cpl. Gary
Pickett, Thomas
Pipe, Harrace
Pipe, Herman, Sr.
Pipe, Horace
Pipe, Jack
Pipe, Jared
Pipe, Myron B.
Pipe, Richard A.
Poitra, Julius
Poitra, Packin
Proctor, Arnold M.
Proctor, Frank E.
Proctor, Herben
Proctor, James J.

Proctor, James L.
Proctor, Joe WWI
Proctor, Richard
Proctor, Robert Renz
Proctor, Russell W.
Proctor, Steven C.
Proctor, Steven

R
Raffaell, Lee Anthony
Raining Bird, Doyle
Raining Bird, Joe
Raining Bird, Theron
Rasor, Gene Navy
Rasor, Gregg V.
Rasor, Kevin K.
Rasor, Jean Francis
Rattling Thunder, Francis E.
Rattling Thunder, Terry
Red Boy I, Archie Army
Red Boy II, Archie WWI
Red Boy, Darren
Red Boy, Donovan
Red Boy, Dwight Korea
Red Boy, George E. Navy
Red Boy, Leland
Red Boy, Reno
Red Boy, Shirley Q.
Red Boy, William J.
Redd, Adam
Redd, Mark
Reed, William J.
Reese, Curtiss R.
Reinlasoder, Karl
Red Dog, Lawrence
Red Dog, Leland
Red Dog, Leslie Charles
Reddog, Lyle
Reddoor, Charles Bearfighter
Red Door, David
Red Door, Edwin
Red Door, Joe
Red Eagle, Darryl
Red Eagle, Gary
Red Eagle, Keith
Red Eagle, Elmer Sterling
Red Eagle, Sterling
Red Eagle, Sterling
Red Eagle, Tolly

Red Eagle, Vernon, Sr.
Red Elk, Archie
Red Elk, Bobbie
Red Elk, Gerald, Jr.
Red Elk, Gerald
Red Elk, Greg II
Red Elk, Herman III
Red Elk, Herman, Jr.
Red Elk, Keith
Red Elk, Kenneth
Red Elk, Robert
Red Fox, David F.
Red Fox, Jim
Red Lightning, Keeler Henry
Redstone, Everett Allen,
Redstone, George M.
Redstone, Justin
Redstone, Chance
Redstone, Raymond
Redstone, Trexler
Red Thunder, Calvin, Jr.
Red Thunder, Darrell
Red Thunder, Joseph
Renz, Charles "Sonny Boy"
Reum, Clayton
Reum, Donald
Reum, George Marines
Reum, James P.
Reum, Jim
Reum, John S.
Reum, Leighton
Reum, Martel "Marty"
Reum, Sam
Ricker, Charles E.
Ricker, Darryl
Ricker, Donald
Ricker, Eugene
Ricker,, Francis
Ricker, George
Ricker, Harry
Ricker, Ira R.
Ricker, Ivan
Ricker, Joseph
Ricker, William "Willie"
Ricker, Orville
Ricker, Richard
Ricker, Ronald
Ricker, Sr, Rufus F.
Ricker, Theodore

Ricker, Tom
Ricker, Virgil
Rider, William T.
Roberts, Burton A.
Roberts, Daniel
Roberts, Dean
Roberts, Ivan
Robertson,, Richard
Robbins, Ronald
Robbins, Charles
Robinson, Frank
Rowe, Andrew J.
Rowe, Clarence D.
Rowe, Charles A.
Rowe, Daniel, L.
Rowe, Frances D.
Rowe, Herbert E.
Rowe, Justin
Rowe, Lester D.
Rowe, Michael
Rowe, Richard, B.
Runs Through, Willis. T.
Runs Through, Douglas
Runs Through, Marion, Sr.
Runs Through, Marion, Jr.
Runs Through, Mason, Sr.
Runs Through, Mason
Runs Through, Matthew
Russell, Wallace
Russell-Eagleman, Dan
Russell, Demirree
Russell, Joe
Ryan, Richard
Ryder, Kenneth, E., Jr.

S
Saala, Charles, S.
Samuel, Michael Paul
Sanders, Paul
Savior, George, Sr.
Savior, Alvin
Savior, Earlwin, S.
Savior, Earlwin, L.
Savior, Sam
Sayers, Warren
Sayers, Kenneth
Schauers, Martin
Schauers, Alexander
Schauers, Daniel "Boone"

Schauers, Gary
Schauers, Jerry
Scott, Vernon
Scott, Art
Scott, Conrad
Scott, Gerald
Scott, Melvin
Scott, Raymond
Sears, Thomas Edward
Sears, Andrew
Sears, Benjamin
Sears, Billy
Sears, Francis, A.
Sears, Gale
Sears, Gordy
Sears, Wayne
Sepudveda, Verner
Shanley, James
Shanley, Richard
Shawl, James
Sherman, David J.
Sherill, Andrew James
Shields, William, H., Jr.
Shields, Anthony, Sr.
Shields, Anthony
Shields, Caleb, P.
Shields, Darrell S., Jr.
Shields, Edward L.
Shields, Frances A.
Shields, Joseph, Sr.
Shields, Julian, Sr.
Shields, Kenneth, Sr.
Shields, Kenneth, Sr.
Shields, Leslie
Shields, Lester W.
Shields, Lonnie W.
Shields, Mervyn
Shields, Mikkel, D.
Shipto, Vernon
Shooting Bear, James
Sibley, Stanley
Sifuentes, Zane T.J.
Sly, Anthony
Small, Melvin, Allen
Small, Austin, A.
Small, Curtis,
Small, Ed H.
Small, Gerald
Small, Robert D.

Small, Sylvester J.
Smith, Adam
Smith, Jerome
Smith, Charles Lynn
Smith, Dale E.
Smith, Dale N.
Smith, Duane T.
Smith, Ed
Smith, Everett W.
Smith, Frank
Smith, James A
Smith, Jerry
Smith, John W., Jr.
Smith, Leonard, Sr.
Smith, Leonard
Smith, Matt
Smith, Michael C.
Smith, Michael L.
Smith, Raymond E.
Smith, Richard A.
Smith, Robert
Smith, Ronald V.
Smith Walter M.
Smoker, William R.
Smoker,, Allyn H., Sr.
Smoker, Kenneth
Smoker, Llewellyn
Snell, Loren, Jr.
Snell, Roy E.
Spendler, Roy E.
Spotted Bird, Frank
Spotted Bird, John A.
Spotted Wolf, Llewellyn
Spotted Wolf, August
Spotted Wolf, Austin
Spotted Wolf, Clarence G.
Spotted Wolf, John
Squires, Denzel
Squires, Marvin G.
Stafne, Arnt T.
Standing, Curtis
Standing, Gifford
Standing Bear, Clyde
Standing Bear,
Steele, Donald
Steele, Dorrance "Curly"
Steele, Fred
Steele, Meade
Steward, Sifroy Seth

St. Germaine, Andrew D.
St. Germaine, Art, Jr.
St. Germaine, Art, Sr.
St. Germaine, Christopher N.
St. Germaine, Dave
St. Germaine, Francis
St. Germaine, Joseph
St. Germaine, Roger
St. Germaine, Timothy
Stibbits, Harry W.
Stiles, Douglas
Stiffarm, Kipp
Stormy, Clarence
Stormy, Johnny
Strauser, Roger Byron
Stump, Pete L.
Sugg, Jeffrey D.
Sugg, Ernest L.
Sugg, William H.
Summers, Ernest
Summers, Fred
Summers, James H.
Summers, Ralph, Sr.
Summers, Robert I., Sr.
Summers, Rusty
Summers, Stormy
Sweeney, Wm J.
Squires, Denzel
Swift Eagle, Sherwin
Szymanski, John

T
Talbert, Elston
Tapaha, Dusan
Tapaha, Edison E.
Tattoo, Morris, Jr.
Taylor, Dennis
Thomas, Richard
Thompson, Dean
Thompson,Edward
Thompson, George, Jr.
Thompson, George, Sr.
Thompson, James E.
Thompson, James S., Jr.
Thompson, Kyle
Thompson, Richard
Thompson,Russell D.
Three Star, Harry, Sr.
Toaves, Marvin, Jr.

Todd, Benedict, Jr.
Todd,Douglas
Todd,Elliott
Todd, Kermit C.
Todd, Lawrence D.
Todd, Palmer
Todd, Rodney
Track, Kenton
Track, Raymond
Trinder, Charles C.
Trinder, Charles H.
Trinder, Charles R.
Trinder, Col. Claude R.
Trinder, Jason R.
Trinder, Thomas R.
Trottier, Kenneth Trudell,
Turning Bear, Charles
Two Bulls, James
Two Bulls, Charles "Bud Bud"
Two Bulls, John
Two Bulls, Francis "Macky"
Two Bulls, Warren G.
Two Bulls, Wayne
Tyler, Jimmie

V
Vandall, Lyle
Vondall, David
Vollertson, John

W
Wakan, George
Wakan, Julius
Walker, Clarence
Walking Eagle, Donald, Jr.
Walking Eagle, Donald, Sr.
Walking Eagle, Eddy
Walking Eagle, Victor
Walla, Michael
War Club, Charles E.
War Club, Charles
Ward, Dallas
Warrior, Leslie E.
Webster, Wayne
Weeks, David S.
Weeks, Gary James
Weeks, George B.
Weeks, George S.
Weeks, John G.

Weeks, Lonnie P. III
Weeks, Owen F., Sr.
Weeks,, Owen F., Jr.
Weeks, Robert J.
Weeks, Warren
Weeks, William "Chub"
Weinberger, Arrow
Weinberger, Donald
Weinberger, Donald R.
Weinberger, Floyd
Weinberger, Frank
Weinberger, George
Welch, Allison W.
Welch, Francis
Welch, Robert
Wettlin, Joshua
Wetsit, Donald F.
Wetsit, Hans
Wettlin, Leonard Dale
Whipkey, Raymond Alfred
White, Andrew "Good Boy"
White, Conrad M.
White, Glenn P.
White Bear, Cody
White Bear, Donald
White Bear, Fred Conner
White Bear, Maynard
White Bull, Jacob, III
White Cloud, A.J.
White Eagle, Darrell
White Eagle, Joe R.
White Eagle, Ken
White Eagle, Roscoe
White Eagle Thurman
White Hawk, Daniel
White Head, Donovan, Sr.
White Head, Joe R., Sr.
White Head, Kenneth
White Head, Moses
White Horse, William
White Horse, Burton K.
White Horse, Moses
White Tail Feather, Raymond
Whitright, Chauncey F.
Whitright, James
Whitright, Hubert
Williams, Henry
Williams, Pete
Williams, Rod

Williams, Ronald D.
Williams, Ronald H.
Wilkins, Russell Brent
Wilson, Paris C.
Wilson, Richard "Shorty"
Wise Spirit, John
Wright, Huber
Wright, James
Wolf Guts, Robert

Y

Yellow Hammer, Brad
Yellow Hammer, Joseph
Yellow Hammer, Ronald, Jr.
Yellow Hawk, Elmer
Yellow Hawk, Willie
Yellow Owl, James
Yellow Owl, Myron L.
Yellow Owl, Raymond
Yellow Owl, Matthew
Yellow Owl, Wallace
Yellow Owl, William
Yellow Robe, Alvin J.
Yellow Robe, Calvin
Yellow Robe, John
Yellow Robe, Leo N.
Yellow Robe, Leo S.
Yellow Robe, Roy
Yellow Robe, Matt
Yellow Robe, Stanley, Sr.
Yoder, Wallace F.
Young, Clifford
Young, Emerson
Young Bear, Donald
Young Bear, Rudolph
Youngman, Clifford
Youngman, Arnold, Jr.
Youngman, Douglas
Youngman, DeWayne
Youngman, Gabriel
Youngman, Howard
Youngman, John
Youngman, Julius
Youngman, Lawrence
Youngman, Louis A.
Youngman, Lewis D., Sr.
Youngman, Michael W.
Youngman, Monte
Youngman, Paul

Youngman, Warren C.
Youpee, William C.
Youpee, Allen
Youpee, Bernard
Youpee, Cary
Youpee, Dwight
Youpee, Gary
Youpee, Jim
Youpee, John Russell
Youpee, Joseph
Youpee, Leroy, Jr.
Youpee, Lester
Youpee, Lloyd, Sr.
Youpee, Louie
Youpee, Pierre
Youpee, Waylon

Z

Zamora, Carlos

Female Veterans

A

Archdale, Arlys

B

Bad Hawk, Joy Lynn
Bauer, Brenda
Bear, Debra Hillard
Bearcub, Laura
Bearcub, Patricia Ryerson
Beston, Vangie
Bigby, Carol Welch
Big Leggings, Rhonda Lynn
Blacktail, Beverly Ackerman
Blair, Louise
Blue Earth, Hope
Boxer, Pauline R.
Boyd, Loetta
Boyd, Sirena Jaruzel
Buckles, Marissa Kay
Burger, Myrtle O. Lacy

C

Cain, Karen Lone Bear
Cantrell, Betty Marie
Carabello, Evelyn Day
Catudio, Sandra Ferguson
Catches, Cassie

Clancy, Adria J.
Clark, Kystal
Clark, Mable
Clark, Michelene
Claymore, Gwendalyn J.
Corpron, Ashley
Coulter, Anna Diserly
Country, Leslie Follete

D

Daniels, Terry Enlow
Darnell, Sharon
DeMarrias, Abrienne
Dupias, Georgia

E

Eder, Macella Eder
Estrada, Mary Margaret

F

Ferguson, Jordis Sandau
Firemoon, Crystal
Firemoon, Ingrid
First, Wilma
First, Lois Greybull
Fourstar, Sasha

G

Gallego, Lena Legget
Garcia, Gloria Red Eagle
Garfield, Mildred Archdale
Goodman, Kathy
Greybear, Ava Martin
Grey Bull, Marcella
Grey Bull Winifred
Grey Hawk, Judy
Growing Thunder, Vera

H

Hamilton, Barbara
Hamilton, Evelyn E.
Hanna, Jewel
Harada, Michelle Feather
  Earing
Herald, Alex
Hertz, Lillian
Hollowhorn, Crystal Barber
Hopkins, Shannon

I

Ironbear, Lisa

J

Jackson, Melissa
Jackson, Melanie Cole
Jaruzel, Sirena
Jem, Natalie Longee
Johnson, Janice

K

Kao, Fannie Smith
Kennedy, Marilyn
Knowles, Marie

L

LaRoche, Belva
Law, Lyla Firemoon
Lone Dog, Mercy Clincher
Longtree, Traci
Lone Bear, Janet L.
Lone Bear, Lacey

M

MacDonald, Jennifer
MacDonald, Mercy
Mail, Gwendolyn Johnson
Marchant, Danielle
Martin, Juanita Redstone
Mason, Rhonda
Mason, Christine Jackson
Martinez, Rynette Melbourne
McNeil, Audrey
Menz, Dore
Miller, Lavern
Morales, Arden
Moran, Philline
Murray, Barbara
Moore, Edith Proctor

O

Overland, Esther

P

Purdy, Linda Old Horn

R

Red Elk, Viola
Red Boy, Judy
Red Boy, Sharon

Red Boy, Evanda Weeks
Red Dog, Sarayh
Red Door, Irma
Red Thunder, Evelyn
Red Thunder, Julia
Ricker, Angela
Rising Sun, Lonnelle
Roeddler, Danielle Windchief
Runs Through, Allison

S
Scott, Angel
Scott, Shelia
Sears, Barbara

Shanley, Erin
Shields, Cindy
Shields, Viola
Shipto, Evangeline
Simmons, Andrea
Sloan, Andrea
Smith, Sunni
Smoker, Jeri
Spotted Bird, Ida
Stadel, Barbara
Steen Patricia
Stewart, Velda Firemoon
Stuart, Charlene
Stump, Patricia

T
Tapaha, Wilberta
Tatoosis, Joyce
Track, Edith
Track, Lorraine
Thompson, Kacie

W
Walking Eagle, Ida
Walking Eagle, Mercy
Warrior, Nellie
Weeks, Caressa
Weinberger, Adrienne
 Fourstar

Wettlin, Raylynn
White Bear, Donnetta
Whitehead, Barbara
Wounded Face, Josie

Yellow Hammer, Ashley
Yellow Robe Lea N.
Yellow Robe, Mattie
Youngman, Muriel
Youpee, Bernice

1775 Standing Buffalo and his band of Teton Sioux reach the BlackHills.

1771 The first major small pox outbreak.

1787 Congress passes Northwest Ordinance declaring that the "land and property [of Indian tribes] shall never be taken from them without their consent."

1803 Tribes of the Louisiana Purchase Territory officially came under U.S. jurisdiction.

1826 Treaty of 1826-Assiniboine

1837 Second major smallpox outbreak

1842 First wagons cross Sioux country on Oregon Trail.

1851 Fort Laramie Treaty between the United States and plains tribes recognizes Sioux ownership of 60 million acres of land, but allocates Powder River and Big Horn country to other tribes.

1851 Treaty with Assiniboines, Blackfeet, Gros Ventres and Crows for a hunting area—Rocky Mountains east to the mouth of the Yellowstone.

1852 May 24, Treaty of Fort Laramie Amended.

1854 & 1861 Nebraska Territory defined.

1855 October 17, Treaty with Blackfeet Nation. (Defines and restricts the hunting grounds of the Assiniboine. Refinement upon the 1851 Fort Laramie Treaty.)

1855 Fort Stewart: Built on the Missouri River near present Blair, MT built by Frost, Todd & Co.

1857 Sitting Bull kills "Hohe" family by Poplar River

1860 Fort Kipp built on the Misouri River above the mouth of the Big Muddy, built by Jim Kipp.

1860 Mining Boom-first large non-Indian population for Montana.

1861 Fort Poplar-Built on the Missouri River near the Poplar River, built with help of Chas. Larpenture.

1861 & 1864 Dakota Territory defined.

1862 Sioux wars begin with Santee uprising in Minnesota. Minnesota Massacre: Begin movement of Sioux toward Montana.

1862 Homestead Act passes Congress.

1865 End of Civil War.

1865 United States negotiates treaty with "friendly" Sioux bands.

1866 United States enters negotiations with hostile Sioux over travel routes to Montana. Red Cloud declares war when United States moves to fortify Bozeman Trail. Sioux annihilate Colonel William Fetterman and his troops.

1867 & 1868 Indian Peace Commission negotiates final treaties with Indians (last of 370 Indian Treaties on August 13, 1868.)

1868 Fort Buford military reserve established from the Assiniboine land.

1868 &1869 Addendum: Gros Ventre, Assiniboine, And River Crow assigned to Upper Milk River Agency.

1868 Treaty of 1868 establishes Great Sioux Reservation as permanent home of the Sioux Nation and preserves Powder River and Big Horn country as "unceded Indian territory."

Fort Laramie Treaty

Lakota Declaration

1868 End of Treaty Making Period

1869 January 2, Sitting Bull captured mail carrier between Fort Hall and Fort Peck

1868-1869 Sub-Agency built to furnish rations to the lower Assiniboine, Sioux, Gros Ventre and River Crows; located south of the Milk River and called Fort Browning.

1870 Baker Massacre.

1870 Grant's Peace Policy-Fort Peck awarded to Methodist.

1870 Montana census (non-Indians) : 20,595

1871 Fort Peck Agency established at old Fort Peck to serve lower Assiniboine and Sioux.

1871 Indians attach themselves to the Agency.

1871 August 18 Executive Order—Fort Buford

1871 The U.S. no longer recognizes Sioux or any other tribes as an autonomous group.

1872 United States aids Fort Peck Agency.

1872 August 26, Grand Peace Council at Fort Peck.

1873 Boundaries of Blackfoot Reservation began to change.

1873 Fort Peck Agency opened at the confluence of the Milk River and the Missouri Rivers.

1874 Established north of the Marias River and Missouri River extending from the summit of the Rockies to the Dakota line set aside as an undivided reservation for Blackfeet,

Assiniboine, Gros Ventre and Sioux.

1874 April 15—Act of Congress.

1875 L.A. Fitch goes to Fort Peck to teach Indians to toil the land and some of the rudiments of education.

1875 December 3, order for Indians to go back to the reservation.

1875 April 13—Executive Order

1875 December 3, order for Indians to go back to the reservations.

1876-1877 Sioux Campaign with Sitting Bull.

1876 January 31—Date set for Sioux to return to reservation from hunting expedition or be considered as hostiles.

1876 June 25—Battle of the Little Big Horn.

1877 Started moving the Fort Peck Agency to Poplar River and General Miles stationed at Fort Peck to maintain order.

1877 The Fort Peck Agency was moved to a site on which a portion of the town of Poplar now Stands

1877 Sitting Bull fled into Canada.

1879 Presbyterians secured permission from the Methodists for a mission on the reservation.

1880 Indians compelled to settle on reservation.

1880 11th Infantry established at Poplar Creek.

1880 Establishment of a military post at a point just north of Poplar, and known as Camp Poplar River. It was abandoned about 1893.

1880 Presbyterian Mission established at Fort Peck.

1880 July, Executive Order: much of the region south of the Misouri River had been opened to white settlement.

1881 Chief Gall surrenders.

1881 First Indian Tribe Allowed to Sue the Gov't.

1881 When Sitting Bull surrendered at Fort Buford in 1881, his warriors came to Fort Peck and Camped on the site of the town of Poplar.

1883 Rev. George Wood moves from Poplar Creek to Wolf Point to establish church.

1883 April 10—Sun Dance and other Sioux customs and religious practices are forbidden by Secretary of the Interior.

1883 Winter—Buffalo Exterminated in Northeastern Montana.

1883 Starvation on the Fort Peck Indian Reservation.

1885 February 28, Proposal to divide the reservation.

1885 Northwest Rebellion in Sask., Canada.

1885 February 28 proposal to divide reservation in to smaller sections. (Greater Blackfeet)

1886 Order prohibiting Sundances.

1886 May 15, Secretary of the Interior authorized new contract for reservation

1886 December 28, Fort Peck agreement signed at Fort Peck. A treaty, establishing the confines of the Fort Peck reservation, was entered into between the Indians and the government

1887 February 8, Congress passed the Dawes General Allotment Act which granted 160 acres to each Indian family head and 80 acres to each other single person over eighteen.

1887 February 11, Treaty signed by adult Indians giving the United States 17,500,000 acres of land and the division of the remaining 6,000,000 into three separate reservations.

1887 Railroads through Reservation in Northern Montana

1887 Teacher moves into Wolf Point.

1888 May 1, Congress passed the act of fixing the boundaries of the three reservations.

1888 May 1, Act of Congress — Agreement which established the Fort Peck Reservation

1889 Cut the rations of beef to Indians on reservation.

1889 March 2, Sioux Act reduces reservations to present size.

1889 Statehood for Montana.

1889 Ghost Dance Religion

1889 Wounded Knee

1893 Army abandoned Camp Poplar River.

1895 Capt. 8th Cav. Acting Agent Wm. Sprole suggests to the Commissioner of Indian Affairs;"a canal to be taken out of the Missouri river, running the entire length of the Reservation,…"

1896 Government aid to Indian Missions discontinued.

1897 Catholics establish mission at Fort Peck.

1902 July, Makaicu Presbyterian church established southwest of Brockton.

1904 December, Manisda Presbyterian church established at Chelsea.

1905 Canipa Presbyterian church organized in Wolf Point in connection with the Mission School.

1908 May 30—Allotment Act for land on Fort Peck.

1908 May 30—Act of Congress Five irrigation projects for Fort Peck Reservation were contemplated in an act of Congress. These projects were never completed.

1909 Yankton and Assiniboine Council elects Business Committee and considers certain applications for enrollment.

1912 November 11-Good Voice Hawk's Winter Count interpreted by Ben Harrison.

1913 July 25—The surplus lands on reservation were opened for homestead entry.

1924 June 2—Indians Granted U.S. Citizenship.

1926 January 1100 Indians received checks for $100 each. The estimatd numbers of Indians on the reservation on government rolls is about 2400.

1927 March 2—Act of Congress

1927 Fort Peck Tribes Constitution

1927 There is a large encampment of Indians at Chicken Hill for their 5-day July Fourth Celebration.

1928 January 30—Docket J-31 in U.S. Court of Claims

1930 June 9—Senate Joint Resolution No. 167

1930 July 23—Docket J-31 Amended

1931 Irrigation Activities: The Little Porcupine unit has 2400 acres under constructed canels with a storage of 3800 acre feet depending upon the spring runoff.

1933 April 10—Docket J-31 Dismissed U.S.C.C.

1933 Submarginal Lands Act

1934 May 7—U.S. Supreme Court Refusal

1934 June 18—Indian Reorganization Act authorizes self government for all tribes.

1946 August 13—Indian Claims Commission Established.

1948 United Nations Convention on the Punishment of the Crime of Genocide.

1950 April 26—Docket 62 in Indian Claims Commission

1952 December 12—Docket 62 Dismissed I.C.C.

1954 June 8—Appeal Docket I-53 Dismissed U.S.C.C.

1954 October 25—U.S. Supreme Court Refusal

1960 Fort Peck Tribes Constitution & By-laws Revised

1967 Indian Policy Statement on Policy and Legislation.

1968 Poplar Gun Factory established, eventually became Assiniboine & Sioux Tribal Industries (ASTI)

1972 Congress passes the Indian Education Act.

1972 *Wotanin Wowapi*, first tribal newspaper, founded.

1974 ASTI officially launched by TEB to work toward 8-A status.

1978 Indian Claims Commission dissolved

1979 March 31—Assiniboine Claims Council reformed

1979 December—Hearnings on S. 1796

1980 October 10—Act of Congress

1981 January 12—Docket 10-81-L Filed U.S.C.C.

1981 August 13—U.S.C.C. judgment

1983 Fort Peck Tribes win $16 million in docket-184 (30% for community developments and 70% for per capita payments)

1984 TEB recognizes Community Organizations (Frazer, Wolf Point, Oswego, Brockton, and Ft. Kipp).

1984 Single Audit Act for Tribal Government

1985 TEB and state of Montana signed first tribal-state Water Compact.

1988 TEB recognizes Associate Members (1/8 blood degree minimum).

1990 General Council held to vote on per capita payment.

1991 Fort Peck Community College (FPCC) granted accreditation by NW Commission on Colleges and Universities.

1992 First Class III Gaming Compact signed with the state of Montana.

1992 Assiniboine & Sioux Rural Water Supply System (ASRWSS) established.

1994 FPCC given Land Grant Institution status, enabled FPCC to apply for USDA grants

1994 Congress passes the American Indian Trust Reform Act.

1996 Eloise Cobell files class action suit against U.S. government over mismanagement of Federal Indian trust monies and property.

1999 TEB established the Fort Peck Buffalo Ranch twenty miles north of Poplar.

2001 Sisseton-Wahpeton Sioux Council established and recognized by TEB (Fort Peck members to receive $740,000 of a $5 million award).

2002 Congress approved $175 million for ASRWSS for new water treatment plant and water pipeline.

2003 Department of Health and Human Services took over the Indian Health Service (IHS) Fort Peck IHS operated at a Level 12 (Life or Limb Policy).

2006 *Wotanin Wowapi* shut down by Chairman John Morales. *The Fort Peck Journal,* independent newspaper founded by Bonnie Clincher, former editor/publisher of the *Wotanin Wowapi.*

2006 FPCC accreditation reaffirmed.

2008 *Wotanin Wowapi* officially closed.

2008 Fort Peck Tribes Constitutional Convention held amendments proposed.

2009 Voters reject proposed amendments.

2009 Cobell Case settled for $3.4 billion. Settlement held up by several individual tribal member appeals.

2012 Fort Peck Energy drills two wells on east side of the reservation.

2012 Fort Peck Tribes settle with U. S. for $75 million for mismanagement of tribal trust money and resources.

2012 Yellowstone buffalo brought to the Fort Peck Reservation.

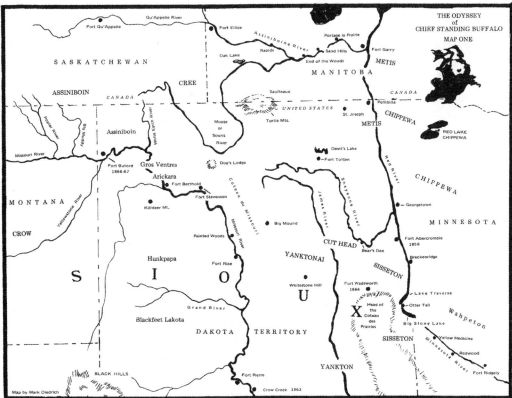

The Odyssey of Chief Standing Buffalo. The two maps show river and state boundries of the greater plains areas including portions of Saskatchewan, Canada. Source: Mark Diedrich, *The Odyssey of Chief Standing Buffalo* (Minneapolis: Coyote Books).

The Authors

Joseph R. McGeshick, Ph.D., was born in north-eastern Montana on the Fort Peck Indian Reservation. He grew up in the small Hi-Line town of Wolf Point on the Missouri River. He is an enrolled Sokaogon Chippewa (Mole Lake, Wisconsin) on his father's side and is also Assiniboine/Sioux (Fort Peck, Montana) on his mother's side. He has worked in Indian education for the past thirty years as a teacher, administrator, and writer. McGeshick has taught at the high school, community college and university levels. His first book, a collection of poetry titled *The Indian in the Liquor Cabinet and Other Poems*, was published in 2006, and his second, *Never Get Mad at Your Sweetgrass*, a collection of short stories, was published in 2007. In 2008, he co-authored the first edition of *The History of the Assiniboine and Sioux Tribes of the Fort Peck Indian Reservation, Montana: 1800-2000*. His next work is a novel titled *Sister Girl* due out in the summer of 2012. McGeshick lives and writes in eastern Montana.

David R. Miller, Ph.D., is emeritus professor of Indigenous Studies at the University of Regina. He received his B.A. from Dakota Wesleyan University, an M.A. in history from the University of North Dakota, and an M.A. and Ph.D. in anthropology from Indiana University-Bloomington. He was the Associate Director of the D'Arcy McNickle Center for the History of the American Indian, The Newberry Library, Chicago, from 1981-1985, and then served three years as the Dean of Instruction at Fort Peck Community College during the time when the institution received its first full accreditation. After a year as a post-doctoral fellow in the Anthropology Department of the National Museum of Natural History of the Smithsonian Institution, Washington, DC, Dr. Miller became the Department Head of Indian Studies at Saskatchewan Indian Federated College-University of Regina, which later became First Nations University of Canada. In 1995, he returned to full-time teaching and taught for a total of 21 years. He has pursued scholarship about the cultural history of the Assiniboine people in Montana and Canada, the other groups in the transborder region, Métis and Dakota/Lakota diasporas in British North America, and the Cree peoples who eventually became a founding population on the Rocky Boy Reservation. The history of the study of Indians is also a longstanding interest. This critical gap in the literature spurred him to pursue historical data about the peoples of the Fort Peck Reservation during research for his dissertation, continuing periodically over twenty years and consequently enabling him to contribute to the Fort Peck history book projects. He continues to reside in Regina, SK.

James E. Shanley, Ed.D, was born and raised on the Fort Peck Assiniboine-Sioux Reservation in northeastern Montana. He is an enrolled member of the Assiniboine tribe. Shanley attended public schools in Poplar, MT, and graduated from Poplar High School in 1964. He attended Eastern Montana College in Billings, MT, graduating with a B.S. in Education in 1968. He served in the U.S. Army from October 1968 to October 1970, including one year in Vietnam in the infantry. He then moved to North Dakota as an adult education teacher for United Tribes Educational Technical Center. He has worked in a variety of educational administrative positions since that time.

In 1974, Shanley was appointed president of Fort Peck Community College in Poplar, MT, a position he held until his retirement in 2011. He completed a Ph.D. in educational administration at the Center for Teaching and Learning, University of North Dakota, Grand Forks, ND, in 1980. He is a member and past president of both the American Indian Higher Education Consortium, and the American Indian College Fund.

Caleb Shields has had a long and active life in tribal affairs, not only locally but also at the national level. He was first elected to the Fort Peck Tribal Executive Board in 1975 and served twenty-four consecutive years, surviving twelve elections before retiring from politics in late 1999. He

served as tribal chairman for his last three terms.

Prior to returning home to Fort Peck in 1973, he served in the Navy for six years and worked in the electronics field for Vanguard Electronics, an aerospace firm in Los Angeles.

Most of Shields' early life was spent in Indian boarding schools at Pawnee, Oklahoma, and Pierre and Flandreau, South Dakota, but he finished high school at Poplar in 1956. He completed three years of higher education at the Western States College of Engineering in Los Angeles.

It has always been Shield's dream to write a history book of the Fort Peck tribes, after realizing none had ever been done before. Shields had gathered archival material over the years to start a book after his retirement. His dream was fulfilled when Fort Peck Community College hired him to coordinate the writings of this book. He considers it a labor of love on behalf of the Assiniboine and Sioux people of Fort Peck.

Shields is a enrolled Sioux of the Fort Peck Tribes and is the grandson of the last chief of the Fort Kipp Community, Chief Andrew Red Boy Shields.

Dennis J. Smith began Native American instruction as Fort Peck Community College Dean of Instruction from 1983 to 1985. From 1989 to 2001 he served as Director and Assistant Professor of American Indian Studies at Morningside College (Sioux City, Iowa). He is Associate Professor of History and Native American Studies at the University of Nebraska at Omaha (2002-present).

Smith's instruction and research focus on Native Americans, especially Fort Peck Reservation history. He earned an M.A. in History from the University of Montana in 1983, and his graduate professional paper examined James J. Hill's Manitoba Railroad (later the Great Northern Railroad) right-of-way easement across the Fort Berthold and Fort Peck Reservations, 1886-1888. He received a Ph.D. in History from the

University of Nebraska-Lincoln in 2001. His dissertation focused on Fort Peck Assiniboine and Sioux history to 1888.

Smith is an enrolled Fort Peck Reservation Assiniboine, a member of the Hudeshabe (Red Bottom) Band, and a descendent of Chief Red Dog.

INDEX

Illustrations and photos are indicated with *f*.

McConnell, William J., 166, 167–169, 170
McCrary, George, 99, 106
McCullough, Halle D., 298, 299–304, 552
McDonald, Hope, 416–417, 436
McGee, Walter, 345
McGeshick, Albert, 557
McGeshick, Fred A., 557
McGeshick, Joseph, 426f
McGeshick, Joyce, 495
McGeshick, Patty, 512–513
McGowan, Dana, 495
McGowan, Dana Easton, 557
McGregor, James H., 256
McIntyre, Charles, 169
McKay, Douglas, 436, 442
McKay, Theresa, 489
McKeel, H. Scudder, 323
McLaughlin, James, 127, 195–197
McLeod River area, 20
McNeil, Audrey, 560
McNeil, John, 118, 124
M Company, Montana National Guard, 334
McPhaul, John, 211
Mdewakanton Sioux
    attacks/battles, 52
    homeland areas, 30
    intertribal relationships, 30–31
    name origins, 28
    in tribe divisions, 35–36
    See also Dakota Sioux
Means, Russell, 488
measles, 43
medical chests, production, 508
Medicine Bear Complex, 432f, 516
Medicine Bear (father)
    appointment as chief, 47
    attacks/battles, 52, 53, 60, 61–62
    farming request meeting, 106–107
    gun trade proposal, 98
    intertribal relationships, 58, 62
    peace talks, 53, 67, 76, 77
    reservation demand, 60
    Sitting Bull talks, 95–96
    treaties/agreements, 54, 61
    tribe size, 58
    See also Cuthead Sioux entries
Medicine Bear (son), 150
Medicine Cloud, 92
Medicine Cow, 49
Medicine Horse, David D., Jr., 557
Medicine Knoll Creek area, 44, 49
Medicine Lake Game Refuge, 339
Medicine Lake school, 326
Medicine Lodge Ceremonies, 24, 489
medicine men, 24, 39, 160
Medicine Walk, Belle, 148
Meinert, Gary V., 557
Melbourne, Gary James, 497
Melbourne, J., Jr., 286f
Melbourne, James III, 557
Melbourne, James M., 557
Melbourne, Manuel P., 557
Melbourne, Susan, 549
Melcher, John, 422f, 423f
Melis, Percy E., 449, 453, 460, 464, 546
Melvin, Mason, 408
Melzer, Ernest L., 557
membership, tribal. See enroll-
    ment policies
Menominee Tribe, 396, 398, 413
Menz, David R., 557
Menz, Dove, 560
Menz, Emery W., 557
Menz, Fred, 557
Menz, John, 557
Menz, Lida, 419f, 423f, 548–549
Meriam Report, 163
Meritt, E. B., 220, 242, 245, 254
Metcalf, Lee, 287f, 442, 443–444, 492
Methodist Episcopal Church, 125, 128, 149
Métis communities, 45, 57, 115, 119–121, 128, 129, 178, 437, 471n98
Métis Rebellion, 178
Meyers, Talton v., 487
Michael, L. F., 215–216, 217, 219–220, 221–222, 227
Midewiwin Ceremony, 179
Midthun, David E., 557
Milburn, George R., 149
Miles, Nelson, 93, 94, 95, 119
Miles Community College, 501
military conflicts. See attacks/
    battles; veterans
military contracts, 492, 493–494, 495, 508–509, 516, 533
military service. See veterans
Milk River Agency
    deterioration/neglect, 59, 100, 101
    establishment, 56–57
    farming efforts, 100
    intertribal relationships, 57–59, 78
    name change, 85
    population statistics, 62, 69
    relocation, 77–78, 79–80, 100–101
    Sioux arrival, 59–62, 67–68
    smallpox epidemic, 59
    See also food entries
Milk River area
    Assiniboines, 43, 58
    Gros Ventres, 56
    Hunkpapa Sioux, 115
    hunting ground assignments, 57
    irrigation systems, 169
    Métis, 119, 120, 178
Milk River community, 193, 200, 211
Milk River Pumping Division, 211
Miller, A. L., 412
Miller, Frank S., 557
Miller, Gerald, 557
Miller, Isaac W., 557
Miller, Joe, Sr., 557
Miller, Joseph, 426f
Miller, Joseph, Jr., 557
Miller, Lavern, 560
Miller, Laverne A. Reddog, 557
Miller, Richard, 557
Miller, Rodney, 289f
Miller, Rodney J., 496, 508–509
Miller, Rodney R., 491
Miller, Willard, 557
millet crops, 258
Millie Lacs area, 28, 29, 35
mineral rights
    Chippewas, 184
    during the 1920s, 256, 269, 293, 297, 313n12
    during the 1950s, 378–379, 417, 436, 437
    See also oil rights and develop-
        ment
Minneconjou Sioux
    attacks/battles, 52, 82, 94
    homeland areas, 33, 46, 71
    name origins, 32
    during Sitting Bull's escape, 96
Minnesota River area, 30, 35, 45
misconduct allegations
    during the 1870s, 59, 117–118
    during the 1880s, 149
    during the 1890s, 170
    in 1916, 216–223
    during the 1920s, 269–270, 296–297
    during the 1930s, 304, 324
    after the 1930s, 337, 537
    See also Akers, Dolly; claims
        actions; Morales, John
missionaries, 15–16, 70, 134f
    See also churches entries
Mississippi Sioux Tribes Judg-
    ment Fund Distribution
    Act, 526
Missouri River Division, 211
Missouri River Initiative, 513
Missouri-Souris Project, 339
Mitchell, Dan, 190, 198, 220
Mitchell, Fred, 557
Mitchell, George, 488
Mitchell, Henry, 557
Mitchell, Jack, 117
Mitchell, Martin, 121–122, 147–148, 248, 255, 261, 267
Mitchell, Mr. (at adoption cer-
    emony), 288f
Mitchell, Robert D., 557
Mitchell, Sarah, 137f
Mitchell, Theodore L., 557
Mitchell, Theodore R., 557
Mitchell, Thomas J., 89–93, 94–96, 97–98, 99–100, 103–104, 552
Mitchell, Warren, 557
Mitchell, William R., 557
Mnisida Presbyterian Church, 284f
Moccasin, Ron, 536
Moccasin, Ronald D., Sr., 557
MOD (Montanans Opposing
    Discrimination), 499
Mohr, A. L., 285f
Moller, Peter H., 260, 264–273, 278f, 296, 552
Montana Board of Planning and
    Economic Development, 485–486
Montana Defender Project, 483
Montana legislature, Indian
    heritage education, 12–13
Montana National Guard, 285f, 332–334
Montanans Opposing Discrimi-
    nation (MOD), 499
Montana Resources and Opportu-
    nities, 263
Montana v. United States, 515
Montclair, Clayton R., Sr., 557
Montclair, Robert, Sr., 557
Moore, Edith Proctor, 560
moose hunting, 17, 18
Morales, Arden, 560
Morales, John, 527, 529, 530, 531–532, 533–534, 535, 536, 544, 546–547
Moran, Bernard, E., 557
Moran, Charles V., 557
Moran, Donald L., 557
Moran, Gabriel, 557
Moran, Philline, 560
Moran, P.S., 557
Moran, Ruben H., 557
Moran, Stanley, Jr., 557
Moran, Steven M., 557
Moran, Sylvester R., Sr., 557
Morgan, Fred C., 254–255
Morin, Robert, 557
Morin, W. D., 285f
Mormon Church, 243, 257
Mormon-run school, 237, 239, 271
Morris, Congressman, 382
Morrow, Henry A., 60, 68
Morsette, John H., 557
Mossman, E. D.
    Business Committee relation-
        ships, 238, 240, 244
    correspondence statistics, 240–241
    grazing management, 236, 239, 240, 242, 244
    inspector reports, 240–241, 245, 273
    staffing inadequacies, 236, 239, 241, 242
    in superintendents list, 552
    Tribal Council request, 245–246, 254
Mossman, E. D. (writing on)
    alcohol consumption, 236, 237, 241, 243, 248–249
    cultural practices, 236, 239, 242–243, 247, 248
    farming, 237, 240, 243, 245, 249
    finances, 237, 238, 240, 241, 244, 245
    health care, 239, 241, 243
    housing, 237, 239, 241, 243, 249
    judicial system, 236, 237, 241, 242, 243, 248–249
    land allotment system, 237–238, 244, 249
    schools, 237, 239, 241, 243
    Washington, D.C. delegation, 246–248
Mountain Crows, 56, 57
Mountain Stoney bands, 21
MSU-Billings, 516, 538
MSU-Northern, 516, 538